Advances in Government Enterprise Architecture

Pallab Saha
National University of Singapore, Singapore

Information Science REFERENCE

INFORMATION SCIENCE REFERENCE

Hershey · New York

Director of Editorial Content:	Kristin Klinger
Director of Production:	Jennifer Neidig
Managing Editor:	Jamie Snavely
Assistant Managing Editor:	Carole Coulson
Typesetter:	Chris Hrobak
Cover Design:	Lisa Tosheff
Printed at:	Yurchak Printing Inc.

Published in the United States of America by
Information Science Reference (an imprint of IGI Global)
701 E. Chocolate Avenue, Suite 200
Hershey PA 17033
Tel: 717-533-8845
Fax: 717-533-8661
E-mail: cust@igi-global.com
Web site: http://www.igi-global.com

and in the United Kingdom by
Information Science Reference (an imprint of IGI Global)
3 Henrietta Street
Covent Garden
London WC2E 8LU
Tel: 44 20 7240 0856
Fax: 44 20 7379 0609
Web site: http://www.eurospanbookstore.com

Library of Congress Cataloging-in-Publication Data

Advances in government enterprise architecture / Pallab Saha, editor.

    p. cm.

  Includes bibliographical references and index.

  Summary: "This book is a compilation of chapters on government Enterprise architecture with the intention of informing professionals with different levels of enterprise architecture knowledge"--Provided by publisher.

  ISBN 978-1-60566-068-4 (hardcover) -- ISBN 978-1-60566-069-1 (ebook)

  1. Internet in public administration. 2. Public administration. 3. Management. 4. Information technology. I. Saha, Pallab, 1970-

  JF1525.A8A383 2008

  351--dc22

                          2008013117

British Cataloguing in Publication Data
A Cataloguing in Publication record for this book is available from the British Library.

All work contributed to this book set is original material. The views expressed in this book are those of the authors, but not necessarily of the publisher.

List of Reviewers

Santonu Sarkar
Accenture Technology Labs, India

Haiping Luo
Government Printing Office, USA

Jorge Marx Gomez
University of Oldenburg, Germany

Stephen H. Kaisler
George Washington University, USA

Frank J. Armour
George Mason University, USA

Steven Ring
The MITRE Corporation, USA

John Mo
RMIT University, Australia

Chris Aitken
Queensland Health, Australia

Marc M. Lankhorst
Telematica Instituut, The Netherlands

Dwight V. Toavs
National Defense University, USA

William S. Boddie
National Defense University, USA

Scott A. Bernard
Carnegie Mellon University, USA

Klaus D. Niemann
ACT! Consulting, Germany

Leonidas G. Anthopoulos
Hellenic Ministry of Foreign Affairs, Greece

Nigel Martin
Australian National University, Australia

Vassilios Peristeras
National University of Ireland, Ireland

Marijn Janssen
*Delft University of Technology,
The Netherlands*

Jay Ramanathan
Ohio State University, USA

Pallab Saha
National University of Singapore, Singapore

Table of Contents

Foreword xv

Preface xviii

Acknowledgment xxv

Section I
Frameworks and Methodologies

Chapter I
A Methodology for Government Transformation with Enterprise Architecture 1
Pallab Saha, National University of Singapore, Singapore

Chapter II
A Service-Oriented Reference Architecture for E-Government 30
Marc M. Lankhorst, Telematica Instituut, The Netherlands
Guido I.H.M. Bayens, Novius, The Netherlands

Chapter III
Role of Beacon Architecture in Mitigating Enterprise Architecture Challenges of the Public
Sector 56
Amit Bhagwat, Independent Consultant, UK

Chapter IV
Maturity Model Based on Quality Concept of Enterprise Information Architecture (EIA) 82
Hong Sik Kim, Korea Polytechnique University, Korea
Sungwook Moon, ComponentBasis, Co., Ltd., Korea

Chapter V
Measuring the Benefits of Enterprise Architecture: Knowledge Management Maturity 106
Alan Dyer, EWA, Australia

Section II
Leadership, Governance, and Management

Chapter VI
The Criticality of Transformational Leadership to Advancing United States Government
Enterprise Architecture Adoption 130
    William S. Boddie, National Defense University, USA

Chapter VII
Adaptive IT Architecture as a Catalyst for Network Capability in Government............................. 149
    Jay Ramanathan, The Ohio State University, USA
    Rajiv Ramnath, The Ohio State University, USA
    Anand Desai, The Ohio State University, USA

Chapter VIII
Design Integrity and Enterprise Architecture Governance... 173
    Chris Aitken, Queensland Health, Australia

Chapter IX
Policy Mapping: Relating Enterprise Architecture to Policy Goals 191
    Dwight V. Toavs, National Defense University, USA

Chapter X
Enterprise Architecture Management and its Role in IT Governance and IT Investment
Planning 208
    Klaus D. Niemann, act! Consulting GmbH, Germany

Chapter XI
The GEA: Governance Enterprise Architecture-Framework and Models........................... 229
    Vassilios Peristeras, National University of Ireland, Ireland
    Konstantinos Tarabanis, University of Macedonia, Greece

Chapter XII
Enterprise Architecture and Governance Challenges for Orchestrating Public-Private
Cooperation.. 263
    Bram Klievink, Delft University of Technology, The Netherlands
    Wijnand Derks, Telematica Instituut, The Netherlands
    Marijn Janssen, Delft University of Technology, The Netherlands

Section III
Realization and Deployment

Chapter XIII

People-Led Enterprise Architecture.. 285

    Neil Fairhead, Fujitsu Services, UK
    John Good, Serco Consulting, UK

Chapter XIV

Using Enterprise Architecture to Transform Service Delivery: The U.S. Federal Government's

Human Resources Line of Business 307

    Timothy Biggert, IBM Global Business Services, USA
    Kunal Suryavanshi, IBM Global Business Services, USA
    Ryan Kobb, IBM Global Business Services, USA

Chapter XV

Enterprise Architecture as Context and Method for Designing and Implementing

Information Security and Data Privacy Controls in Government Agencies..................................... 340

    Scott Bernard, Carnegie Mellon University, USA
    Shuyuan Mary Ho, Syracuse University, USA

Chapter XVI

Architecture Based Engineering of Enterprises with Government Involvement.............................. 371

    John Mo, RMIT University, Australia
    Laszlo Nemes, Nemes Consulting, Australia

Chapter XVII

Collaborative Enterprise Architecture for Municipal Environments.. 392

    Leonidas G. Anthopoulos, Hellenic Ministry of Foreign Affairs, Greece

Chapter XVIII

Government Enterprise Architectures: Enabling the Alignment of Business Processes

and Information Systems 409

    Nigel Martin, The Australian National University, Australia
    Shirley Gregor, The Australian National University, Australia
    Dennis Hart, The Australian National University, Australia

Compilation of References 438

About the Contributors 463

Index... 472

Detailed Table of Contents

Foreword xv

Preface xviii

Acknowledgment xxv

Section I
Frameworks and Methodologies

Chapter I

A Methodology for Government Transformation with Enterprise Architecture...................................... 1
    Pallab Saha, National University of Singapore, Singapore

Countries across the world are pushing their frontiers in Governance in the move to information economy, and governments play a pivotal role in this transformation. These governments employ modern information and communication technologies to serve the citizens and businesses better. Raising the effectiveness and quality of government services is not only a matter of leading edge technologies; it also involves visionary leadership, clear objectives and sound execution mechanism. The role of Enterprise Architecture in shaping E-Government programmes cannot be overstated. Within the context of Singapore's e-government initiative, this chapter describes the Methodology for AGency ENTerprise Architecture (MAGENTA), a rigorous, disciplined and structured methodology for development of agency enterprise architectures that enables agencies to align to and fully support the government's transformation objectives and outcomes. Mechanisms for agencies to align to the overall Government Enterprise Architecture are detailed. The chapter concludes with a set of recommendations for future enhancements and research.

Chapter II

A Service-Oriented Reference Architecture for E-Government... 30
    Marc M. Lankhorst, Telematica Instituut, The Netherlands
    Guido I.H.M. Bayens, Novius, The Netherlands

This chapter describes the development and future directions of service-oriented reference architecture for the Dutch government. The Dutch government has focussed on improving the service level of public agencies for several years. Electronic services play an important part in this, which requires a concerted effort across many organizations. A reference architecture has been created in order to guide the many different programmes and projects. This chapter describes the role of service orientation in e-government, and the creation, structure, and first results of this reference architecture for e-government. Furthermore, the chapter looks ahead at future developments in integrated, demand-driven service provisioning in e-government.

Chapter III

Role of Beacon Architecture in Mitigating Enterprise Architecture Challenges of the Public
Sector 56
Amit Bhagwat, Independent Consultant, UK

This chapter introduces the concept of Beacon Architecture as a formalized and ordered grouping of architectural elements, describing the constituents, their order, correlation and likely evolution of the grouping; and illustrating its specific value to the public sector. The first half of the chapter builds up to the concept, the reasons behind its specific nature, and its value to enterprises, especially in the public sector. For this, the chapter is split into a number of sections that may be studied separately and that also build up to introduce Beacon Architecture. The sections may be broadly divided as concepts, historical overview, illustrative case studies in public sector transformations along with a summary of peculiar architectural challenges they face, and a cyclical pattern to Architecture Development. After introducing and elucidating on concept and constituents of Beacon Architecture, the chapter delves into its correlation with architecture concepts in currency and its role in mitigating enterprise architecture challenges illustrated earlier in the chapter, before concluding on an assessment of future trends.

Chapter IV

Maturity Model Based on Quality Concept of Enterprise Information Architecture (EIA) 82
Hong Sik Kim, Korea Polytechnique University, Korea
Sungwook Moon, ComponentBasis, Co., Ltd., Korea

Quite a good amount of time has been spent seeking appropriate solutions to handle the giant information technology expenditure not only in government sectors but also in private sectors all over the world. Beginning with OMB, which substantially leads the U.S. governmental efforts in ITA/EA area, seems to be on the right path using process improvement concept in its ITA/EA maturity model (OMB, 2007-2). EA community still finds it difficult to introduce quality management concept into its business and practices. This chapter therefore suggests a practical ITA/EA maturity model based on the quality concept of enterprise information architecture (EIA), which is ROI–driven, practical and based on four-phased process improvement approach for the EA community. This approach could bring a substantial reduction in the costs and efforts in the entire ITA/EA area and provide sustainable development environment for the ITA/EA like the argument of the environmentalists.

Chapter V

Measuring the Benefits of Enterprise Architecture: Knowledge Management Maturity 106

Alan Dyer, EWA, Australia

Enterprise Architecture is the organising logic for business processes and Information Technology infrastructure, the purpose of which is to create a more effective organisation in the context of the business's strategy and goals. However, the ability to measure the effectiveness of any activities initiated under the guise of Enterprise Architecture is limited, even more so in those organisations, such as government agencies, that do not recognise financial return on investment. This chapter introduces the concept of Knowledge Management, linked to the strategic outcomes of Enterprise Architecture and proposes a maturity model framework for the measurement of Enterprise Architecture implementation. The chapter aims to provide a basis for discussion of a wider Capability Maturity Profile with architectural frameworks to help develop and measure the benefits of implementing frameworks and architectures.

Section II
Leadership, Governance, and Management

Chapter VI

The Criticality of Transformational Leadership to Advancing United States Government
Enterprise Architecture Adoption 130

William S. Boddie, National Defense University, USA

An effective enterprise architecture capability enables an organization to develop sound enterprise plans, make informed human, material, and technology resource investment and management decisions, and optimize key business processes. Despite U.S. Congressional legislation, U.S. Office of Management and Budget guidance, and U.S. Government Accountability Office reports and recommendations, many U.S. government leaders struggle in advancing EA adoption in their organizations. U.S. Government leaders must embrace transformational leadership to advance EA adoption. This chapter presents the Vision, Integrity, Communication, Inspiration, and Empowerment Transformational Leadership Model that describes competencies U.S. Government leaders need to advance EA adoption. The chapter also presents the Transformational Leadership and Enterprise Management Integration Framework that describes the relationship between transformational leadership and enterprise management functions.

Chapter VII

Adaptive IT Architecture as a Catalyst for Network Capability in Government................................ 149

Jay Ramanathan, The Ohio State University, USA
Rajiv Ramnath, The Ohio State University, USA
Anand Desai, The Ohio State University, USA

Public institutions that are organized in hierarchies find it difficult to address crisis or other unique requirements that demand networked solutions. This chapter first provides a prescriptive transaction-based method for achieving such networking organizations with information technologies (IT) and then discusses how the organization becomes more effective in non-routine responses to citizen requests. The chapter illustrates how the prescriptive transaction-based enterprise architecture framework was used for decision-making in a multi-year interdisciplinary industry-university collaboration resulting in a successful 311 system.

Chapter VIII

Design Integrity and Enterprise Architecture Governance 173
    Chris Aitken, Queensland Health, Australia

This chapter describes a design integrity framework for developing models of any entity of interest at various levels of abstraction. The design integrity framework presented describes and defines contextual, conceptual, logical and physical model types. The framework also defines a set of alignment attributes for each model type and explains how these are to be used to demonstrate alignment from initial concept and requirements through to actual physical implementation. These concepts are then applied in an organisational context to identify the roles necessary to support an EA governance framework and strong alignment from idea to implementation.

Chapter IX

Policy Mapping: Relating Enterprise Architecture to Policy Goals 191
    Dwight V. Toavs, National Defense University, USA

Few government executives can explain the enterprise architecture of his or her agency, and it is rare to find a political executive who is able to explain how their political objectives are furthered by government-wide enterprise architecture. This low level of awareness translates to enterprise architecture efforts that are often undervalued and under funded because the budget priorities of political and functional executives rarely include enterprise architecture. Not surprisingly, many points of tension exist as the CIOs and architects work to translate political goals into resources and architectural plans supporting the agency's programs. This tension, between the rational orientation of enterprise architecture advocated by the CIO and the political nature of policy goals sought by executives, often puts a CIO at odds with his or her organization's political and functional executives. This chapter discusses that tension, and advocates that CIOs and enterprise architects develop a "Policy Map" to bridge the gap between the political and the rational perspectives.

Chapter X

Enterprise Architecture Management and its Role in IT Governance and IT Investment
Planning 208
    Klaus D. Niemann, act! Consulting GmbH, Germany

A comprehensive enterprise architecture management has strategic and operative aspects. Strategic tasks cover the identification of appropriate fields of activity for information technology (IT) investments in accordance with business strategy and portfolio management. Enterprise architecture management is cross-linked with other IT management processes and delivers the necessary information for sustainable governance. The continuous analysis of the IT landscape, the deduction of measures for optimization and its controlling also belong to the tasks of architecture management. Standards for development and infrastructures are made, e.g. reference architectures and a "book of standards", whose implementation is overseen by solution architects throughout the operative architecture management.

Chapter XI

The GEA: Governance Enterprise Architecture-Framework and Models..229

Vassilios Peristeras, National University of Ireland, Ireland
Konstantinos Tarabanis, University of Macedonia, Greece

Departing from the lack of coherent and ready-to-use models and domain descriptions for public admin-istration, the chapter presents a set of generic models that serves as a top-level, generic and thus reus-able Enterprise Architecture for the overall public administration domain. This set of models is called Governance Enterprise Architecture (GEA). GEA has deliberately remained technology independent and following the Model Driven Architecture approach, GEA constitutes a computationally independent model for the domain. GEA has been derived from multi-disciplinary influences and insights and identifies two broad modeling areas, called governance mega-processes: Public Policy Formulation and Service Provision. These two, together with the object versus process perspective, form a four-cell matrix that defines four modeling areas for the GEA models. Until now, a large number of services have been mod-eled using GEA and more recently; an extended modeling effort has started with GEA being chosen for use by a national EU-country project. GEA can be also used as a knowledge infrastructure for applying semantic technologies. In this line, it has been used for creating a public administration specialization of a formal Semantic Web Service ontology, namely WSMO.

Chapter XII

Enterprise Architecture and Governance Challenges for Orchestrating Public-Private
Cooperation..263

Bram Klievink, Delft University of Technology, The Netherlands
Wijnand Derks, Telematica Instituut, The Netherlands
Marijn Janssen, Delft University of Technology, The Netherlands

This chapter presents an architecture aimed at supporting the coordination of public and private parties for creating a one stop shop and the main challenges therein. Public-private service network poses higher requirements on the architecture of a service network, whereas the variety in systems of the various organizations and different aims make it more difficult to develop such an architecture. Furthermore, it is difficult to isolate architectural challenges from governance aspects, as many architectural issues need to be complemented by governance mechanisms. Architecture and governance cannot be considered in isolation. Within this setting, a new architecture is created and presented for managing and orchestrating the interactions among governmental and private organizations.

Section III
Realization and Deployment

Chapter XIII

People-Led Enterprise Architecture...285

Neil Fairhead, Fujitsu Services, UK
John Good, Serco Consulting, UK

This chapter provides an approach to Enterprise Architecture that is people-led, as a contrast to being led by technology or modelling methodology. The chapter identifies the major stakeholders in Enterprise Architecture and suggests where in the organisation they may be found and how they may be connected with the Enterprise Architecture. It highlights the roles of stakeholders throughout the process of defining and implementing an Enterprise Architecture. The view of stakeholders managing the EA effort is described through the complete lifecycle, from setting the EA mission to sustaining the benefits after implementation. In proposing the adoption of such an approach, we aim to encourage a more direct link between Enterprise Architecture, the needs of the stakeholders it serves, and the pubic policy outcomes it enables.

Chapter XIV

Using Enterprise Architecture to Transform Service Delivery: The U.S. Federal Government's
Human Resources Line of Business 307

Timothy Biggert, IBM Global Business Services, USA
Kunal Suryavanshi, IBM Global Business Services, USA
Ryan Kobb, IBM Global Business Services, USA

This chapter provides a case study on how the U.S. Office of Personnel Management has led the establishment of the Human Resources Line of Business (HR LOB). It explains how the HR LOB program has used enterprise architecture to drive transformation to a new Human Resources service delivery model across the United States Federal government. The authors propose that the common view and vocabulary that EA artifacts provide, along with the collaborative governance that took place to create the artifacts, has produced a solid business foundation for this extensive business transformation effort.

Chapter XV

Enterprise Architecture as Context and Method for Designing and Implementing
Information Security and Data Privacy Controls in Government Agencies 340

Scott Bernard, Carnegie Mellon University, USA
Shuyuan Mary Ho, Syracuse University, USA

Government agencies are committing an increasing amount of resources to information security and data privacy solutions in order to meet legal and mission requirements for protecting agency information in the face of increasingly sophisticated global threats. Enterprise Architecture (EA) provides an agency-wide context and method that includes a security sub-architecture which can be used to design and implement effective controls. EA is scalable, which promotes consistency and alignment in controls at the enterprise, program, and system levels. EA also can help government agencies improve existing security and data privacy programs by enabling them to move beyond a system-level perspective and begin to promote an enterprise-wide view of security and privacy, as well as improve the agility and effectiveness of lifecycle activities for the development, implementation, and operation of related security and privacy controls that will assure the confidentiality, integrity, and availability of the agency's data and information. This chapter presents the EA3 "Cube" EA methodology and framework, including an integrated security architecture, that is suitable for use by government agencies for the development of risk-adjusted security and privacy controls that are designed into the agency's work processes, information flows, systems, applications, and network infrastructure.

Chapter XVI
Architecture Based Engineering of Enterprises with Government Involvement............................... 371
  John Mo, RMIT University, Australia
  Laszlo Nemes, Nemes Consulting, Australia

With a plethora of architectures, modeling techniques and methodologies on offer, it is difficult to decide how to begin building an enterprise and achieve seamless integration. This difficulty is most noticeable in consortia that need to deal with government participation. Various government projects have different objectives and agenda. In addition, changes in business environment as well as government policies impose extra conditions onto the project. Failure to comply with the project requirement can lead to loss of business and sometimes unexpected penalty. The chapter uses three case studies to show various ways of government involvements in projects. Based on the experiences of these cases, the chapter discusses how enterprise engineering can help creating and managing the enterprise that can engage government services successfully.

Chapter XVII
Collaborative Enterprise Architecture for Municipal Environments... 392
  Leonidas G. Anthopoulos, Hellenic Ministry of Foreign Affairs, Greece

E-Government evolves according to strategic plans with the coordination of central Governments. This top-down procedure succeeds in slow but sufficient transformation of public services into e-Government ones. However, public agencies adapt to e-Government with difficulty, requiring holistic guidance and a detailed legal framework provided by the Government. The setting up of common Enterprise Architecture for all public agencies requires careful analysis. Moreover, common Enterprise Architecture could fail to cover the special needs of small or municipal agencies. This chapter uses data from various major e-Government strategies, together with their enterprise architectures, in order to introduce a development model of municipal Enterprise Architecture. The model is based on the experience collected from the Digital City of Trikala, Greece, and results in "Collaborative Enterprise Architecture".

Chapter XVIII
Government Enterprise Architectures: Enabling the Alignment of Business Processes
and Information Systems 409
  Nigel Martin, The Australian National University, Australia
  Shirley Gregor, The Australian National University, Australia
  Dennis Hart, The Australian National University, Australia

This chapter describes the development and use of government enterprise architectures for the framing and alignment of the core business processes and enabling information systems at the Australian Bureau of Statistics (ABS) and the Centrelink Social Services agency. The chapter focuses on the construction and ongoing maintenance of public enterprise architectures that enable the alignment condition. An established research model has been used to guide the analysis and explication of the government business processes, enabling systems and architectures, and the resulting agency alignment. While the discussion acknowledges the existence of other formal and informal enablers of alignment, this chapter concentrates on the enterprise architecture enabler. The functionally integrated government business processes and information systems that are established within the instantiated enterprise architecture are examined.

Compilation of References 438

About the Contributors 463

Index 472

Foreword

The reasons one would "do" architecture for *anything* are two: a) complexity and b) change.

If the object you are trying to create is simple … that is, if, at a glance, you can see it in its entirety, at the level of definition that is required to create it … and if it is not likely to change appreciably over the period of its existence … then, you don't need architecture. You need a tool (a machete) … some material (some grass) … some time … and then … chop down grass … build a grass shack.

If, on the other hand, the object you are trying to create so complex that you cannot see it in its entirety at the level of definition required to create it … like an Airbus 380 … then forget the machete and grass … and it doesn't make any difference what tools you have, what material you have and how much time you have, you are not going to be able to create an Airbus 380. In this case, you NEED Architecture … that is, you have to be able to describe the object in order to create it.

If you can't describe the object you are trying to create at the level of definition required to create it, you can't create it … I don't really care how big or small, how simple or complex, what it's made of or what it is … a hundred story building, a locomotive, a super computer, an Airbus 380 … or an enterprise.

After you get the Airbus created and the price of oil goes up out of sight and the mobility of the population increases, and you want to change it to carry more passengers with greater fuel efficiency, how would you do that? You have to go back to the architectural descriptions that were produced in order to create it to begin with and that constitutes the baseline for changing it … that is, they are the baseline for changing the object IF they have been maintained to reflect any changes that have been made to the object instances.

If you want to change the object you have created and no architectural representations exist, then you have only three options: a) you can just make the changes required … like, change the jet turbines to nuclear engines, add a hundred seats, replace the aluminum surfaces with composites, etc. … and then try it and see if it will still work; or b) you can reverse engineer the architectural representations from the operating instance … like, disassemble the Airbus into its parts, with your micrometers measure every part to operating clearances, understand how the parts fit together, write it all down and then make the needed changes; or, c) scrap the existing instantiation and build a new one from scratch. These are the three possibilities for changing an object once it is created when the architectural representations have not been retained or maintained or if they were never produced in the first place.

In short, the reasons you do architecture have to do with complexity and change. Nothing magic is happening and nothing is happening by accident. The laws of nature are constant and there is no way to circumvent them.

I would submit that the modern Enterprise is the most complex object yet conceived of by human-kind. Enterprises are far more complex than Airbus 380's! And … an enterprise doesn't have to be all that big to be extremely complex.

I would observe that very many enterprises, and many of them very large enterprises, already exist. Where is all the enterprise architecture? I submit, the enterprises that are in existence today typically were never engineered. There is no enterprise architecture. The enterprises actually were never designed … they simply happened, one grass shack at a time. It is little wonder that enterprises, in general, don't work very well, are not very efficient and are very difficult to change. The problem comes after you have several square miles of grass shacks and the external environment changes to require a hundred story building. One more grass shack is not going to fix the problem.

I have been mixing the metaphor between enterprises and buildings but I hope the point is clear … the two reasons you need architecture for anything are complexity and change and there is not going to be a substitute for architecture.

I would also observe that public sector enterprises tend to be of the extreme complex variety. In the public sector, there is a wide variety of products and services. There also potentially is some common infrastructure to manage like finances, employment, land, administration. The public sector Enterprise typically decentralizes the products and services and centralizes the infrastructure management. The political issue tends to be who controls what which adds another dimension to the complexity.

When the environment becomes more demanding, that is the consumers demand more and better products and services and the suppliers have less available resources; and in the public sector, the consumers and the suppliers are basically, one in the same; it creates a very tenuous situation where something has to change. My opinion is, the issues of enterprise architecture are fundamental to ongoing stability of operation. How else are you going to dramatically improve the delivery of products and services and accomplish this with only the resources that are presently available? You only have to read the daily newspapers to find the public sector enterprises that are failing in this regard and not performing effectively.

In the private sector, the worst possible thing that can happen to an enterprise if it becomes dysfunctional, that is, if it can no longer produce marketable products or services with the available resources, is that it just goes out of business. In the public sector, when enterprises go dysfunctional, there are all kinds of problems: political problems, environmental problems, economic problems, emotional problems, sociological problems, in addition to going out of business!

Advances in Government Enterprise Architecture could not appear at a better time. We need the most advanced thinking humanly possible at this juncture in history. I have devoted nearly 40 years of my professional life to the subject of Enterprise Architecture. Tragically, the great preponderance of people in the world seem to still be searching for the holy grail, the quick fix, the "silver bullet", a technological panacea. My observation is, actual work is going to have to take place, engineering style of work, enterprise engineering work. Writing more code is NOT going to fix the problem and I don't care how much more code is written. The enterprise is going to have to be engineered and the "raw material" for doing engineering work is the set of descriptive representations that constitute the "architecture" for the object being engineered, in this case, the enterprise, in fact the public sector, government enterprise.

Enterprise architecture may well be the issue of the century. In fact, in 1999, I wrote an article by that name, "Enterprise Architecture: The Issue of the Century" in which I argued this case. In this short foreword, I hope I have convincingly established that enterprise architecture for public sector enterprises is especially critical.

It is comforting to know that there are some number of people giving the subject of enterprise architecture, particularly in its manifestation in the public sector, serious thought. As I mentioned above, we need all of the good thoughts and energy possible focused on this critical subject.

I appreciate Pallab Saha's effort to pull together this collection of material. I know the time and effort he has spent will benefit all of us immensely. I have encouraged Pallab before never to give up … to continue his good work. I hope this is only the beginning of a lot more advances in government enterprise architecture. And, in this simple foreword, I hope I have encouraged concentrated focus on the enterprise, not simply the systems or the technologies of the enterprise … but on THE ENTERPRISE, the government enterprise in particular.

John A. Zachman
Glendale, California
2008

John A. Zachman *is the originator of the Framework for Enterprise Architecture which has received broad acceptance around the world as an integrative framework, or "periodic table" of descriptive representations for enterprises. John is not only known for this work on enterprise architecture, but is also known for his early contributions to IBM's Information Strategy methodology (Business Systems Planning) as well as to their executive team planning techniques (Intensive Planning). He retired from IBM in 1990, having served them for 26 years. He presently is chairman of the board of Zachman Framework Associates, a worldwide consortium managing conformance to the Zachman Framework principles. He is chief executive officer of the Zachman Institute for Framework Advancement (ZIFA), an organization dedicated to advancing the conceptual and implementation states of the art in EA. He also operates his own education and consulting business, Zachman International (www.ZachmanInternational.com). John serves on the Executive Council for Information Management and Technology (ECIMT) of the United States Government Accountability Office (GAO). He is a fellow for the College of Business Administration of the University of North Texas. He serves on the advisory board for the Data Resource Management Program at the University of Washington and on the advisory board of the Data Administration Management Association International (DAMA-I) from whom he was awarded the 2002 Lifetime Achievement Award. He was awarded the 2004 Oakland University, Applied Technology in Business (ATIB), Award for IS Excellence and Innovation. John has been focusing on EA since 1970 and has written extensively on the subject. He is the author of the book, The Zachman Framework for Enterprise Architecture: A Primer on Enterprise Engineering and Manufacturing. He has facilitated innumerable executive team planning sessions. He travels nationally and internationally, teaching and consulting, and is a popular conference speaker, known for his motivating messages on Enterprise Architecture issues. He has spoken to many thousands of enterprise managers and information professionals on every continent. In addition to his professional activities, John Zachman serves on the Elder Council of the Church on the Way (First Foursquare Church of Van Nuys, California), the board of directors of Living Way Ministries, a radio and television ministry of the Church on the Way, the president's cabinet of the King's College and Seminary, the board of directors of the Los Angeles Citywide Children's Christian Choir and on the board of directors of Native Hope International, a Los Angeles-based ministry to the Native American people. Prior to joining IBM, John served as a line officer in the U.S. Navy and is a retired commander in the U.S. Naval Reserve. He chaired a panel on "Planning, Development and Maintenance Tools and Methods Integration" for the U.S. National Institute of Standards and Technology. He holds a degree in chemistry from Northwestern University, has taught at Tufts University, has served on the board of councilors for the School of Library and Information Management at the University of Southern California, as a special advisor to the School of Library and Information Management at Emporia State University, and on the advisory council to the School of Library and Information Management at Dominican University.*

Preface

The foundation of anything enduring is its architecture and design, enterprises included. Enterprise architecture (EA) is an important and evolving discipline that is becoming more discussed and talked about with every passing day. Nevertheless, to my knowledge, there exists very little guidance that rank high both on practical relevance and academic rigor. This book, along with my first book *Handbook of Enterprise Systems Architecture in Practice* has emerged out of my strong belief that 'well architected' enterprises consistently perform better. However this aspect has not been well explored and documented.

This is not a general book on EA. There are several books already covering the subject. But the caveat with current EA literature is that most available materials tend to overly focus on a specific framework or methodology thus limiting their utility. I have attempted to address some of these issues through my first book. That one, released in March 2007, has received several accolades and excellent feedback.

Over the past two decades, the largest implementations of EA have occurred in the government sector. This is natural as typically governments are the largest organizations in almost every country. It is further characterized by complex federated structures where individual government organizations work in their respective silos. Often this leads to and amplifies the fragmentation of business processes and duplication of systems and technologies, creating obstacles in cross agency interoperability. Government-wide architecture allows end-to-end business processes, standard technologies, rationalized data structure and modular e-services that can be assembled as required to deliver e-services. EA is a critical success factor for all types, scale and intensities of e-government programmes. The key goal of EA in government organizations is to make them citizen-centered, results-oriented and market-based. However at this point there are no books addressing this area. There is a very big gap in the current literature, and this book expects to address the current gap. This is a seminal book that will popularize the term GOVERNMENT ENTERPRISE ARCHITECTURE and trigger several other publications in the same subject area. This book, unlike any other available today, aims:

- To present and bring forth the current and future developments, issues and trends in EA for Government organizations.
- To integrate EA theory and concepts to field-tested methods, practical strategic issues and implementation challenges in the context of e-government.
- To illustrate development methods and the process cycle through case studies and detailed examples.
- To demonstrate the criticality of EA for e-government programmes.
- To provide insights into the impact of effective EA on IT governance, IT portfolio management, IT risks, IT outsourcing and service oriented architecture.

This book is a compilation of 18 chapters on government enterprise architecture written by practitioners and practicing academics from countries including Australia, Germany, Greece, Ireland, The Netherlands, Singapore, South Korea, United Kingdom, and United States of America. The chapters in the book have been selected with the intention to address professionals with a wide variety of interests and with different levels of EA knowledge. The book has a very strong practical orientation and is primarily targeted at:

- Government CIOs, IT/IS managers, architects, analysts and designers seeking better, quicker and easier approaches to respond to needs of their internal and external customers.
- Line-of-business managers concerned with maximizing business value of IT and business competitiveness.
- CTOs of business software companies interested in incorporating EA to differentiate their products and services and increasing the value proposition to their customers in the government sector.
- Consultants and practitioners desirous of new solutions and technologies to improve the productivity of their government clients.
- MIS and IT educators interested in imparting knowledge about this vital discipline.
- Researchers looking to uncover and characterize new research problems and programmes.
- IT professionals involved with organizational technology strategic planning, technology procurement, management of technology projects, consulting and advising on technology issues and management of total cost of IT ownership.

The book is structured logically into three sections.

- **Section I: Frameworks and Methodologies** focuses on approaches and mechanisms that organizations in the government use to develop their architecture blueprints. In the past two decades a lot of effort has been expended by several countries in developing their own frameworks, guidebooks, toolkits and methodologies. Section I intends to provide a glimpse of these activities.
- **Section II: Leadership, Governance and Management** shows how government agencies and organizations initiate and sustain their EA practices. Beyond frameworks, methodologies and artifacts, it takes good leadership, innovative governance and flexible management to sustain EA programme. Section II shows how these play a role and impact of these on the overall programme success.
- **Section III: Realization and Deployment** provides insights into how organizations employ EA to drive their transformation programmes, gain tighter business-IT alignment and realize business value out of their IT investments. This section consists of descriptions of the adoption of EA in large and small organizations with insights on key practical challenges they face and how the whole EA programmes are sustained.

SECTION I: FRAMEWORKS AND METHODOLOGIES

Section I is a collection of chapters describing approaches and methods used by organizations to plan and develop their EA blueprints.

Chapter I: Countries across the world are pushing their frontiers in governance in the move to information economy, and governments play a pivotal role in this transformation. These governments employ modern information and communication technologies to serve the citizens and businesses better. Raising the effectiveness and quality of government services is not only a matter of leading edge technologies; it also involves visionary leadership, clear objectives and sound execution mechanism. The role of Enterprise Architecture in shaping e-government programmes cannot be overstated. Within the context of Singapore's e-government initiative, this chapter, *A Methodology for Government Transformation with Enterprise Architecture* by **Pallab Saha** of the **National University of Singapore** describes the Methodology for **AG**ency **ENT**erprise Architecture (MAGENTA), a rigorous, disciplined and structured methodology for development of agency enterprise architectures that enables agencies to align to and fully support the government's transformation objectives and outcomes. Mechanisms for agencies to align to the overall government enterprise architecture are detailed. The chapter concludes with a set of recommendations for future enhancements and research.

Chapter II: *A Service-Oriented Reference Architecture for E-Government* by **Marc Lankhorst** of the **Telematica Instituut, Netherlands** and **Guido Bayens** of **Novius Business and Information Management, The Netherlands** describes the development and future directions of service-oriented reference architecture for the Dutch government. The Dutch government has focused on improving the service level of public agencies for several years. Electronic services play an important part in this, which requires a concerted effort across many organizations. A reference architecture has been created in order to guide the many different programmes and projects. This chapter describes the role of service orientation in e-government, and the creation, structure, and first results of this reference architecture for e-government. Furthermore, the chapter looks ahead at future developments in integrated, demand-driven service provisioning in e-government.

Chapter III: *Role of Beacon Architecture in Mitigating Enterprise Architecture Challenges of the Public Sector* by **Amit Bhagwat** introduces the concept of Beacon Architecture as a formalized and ordered grouping of architectural elements, describing the constituents, their order, correlation and likely evolution of the grouping; and illustrating its specific value to the public sector. The first half of the chapter builds up to the concept, the reasons behind its specific nature, and its value to enterprises, especially in the public sector. For this, the chapter is split into a number of sections that may be studied separately and that also build up to introduce Beacon Architecture. The sections may be broadly divided as concepts, historical overview, illustrative case studies in public sector transformations along with a summary of peculiar architectural challenges they face, and a cyclical pattern to architecture development. After introducing and elucidating on concept and constituents of Beacon Architecture, the chapter delves into its correlation with architecture concepts in currency and its role in mitigating enterprise architecture challenges with examples and illustrations from the British Government, before concluding on an assessment of future trends.

Chapter IV: Quite a good amount of time has been spent seeking appropriate solutions to handle the giant information technology expenditure not only in government sectors but also in private sectors all over the world. Beginning with OMB, which substantially leads the U.S. governmental efforts in ITA/EA area, seems to be on the right path using process improvement concept in its ITA/EA maturity model (OMB, 2007-2). EA community still finds it difficult to introduce quality management concept into its business and practices. This chapter, *Maturity Model Based on Quality Concept of Enterprise Information Architecture,* by **Hong Sik Kim** of the **Korea Polytechnique University** and **Sungwook Moon** of **Component Basis Inc., South Korea** therefore suggests a practical ITA/EA maturity model based on the quality concept of enterprise information architecture (EIA), which is ROI–driven, practical and based on four-phased process improvement approach for the EA community. This approach could bring a substantial reduction in the costs and efforts in the entire ITA/EA area and provide sustainable development environment for the ITA/EA like the argument of the environmentalists.

Chapter V: Enterprise architecture is the organising logic for business processes and Information Technology infrastructure, the purpose of which is to create a more effective organisation in the context of the business's strategy and goals. However, the ability to measure the effectiveness of any activities initiated under the guise of enterprise architecture is limited, even more so in those organisations, such as government agencies, that do not recognise financial return on investment. This chapter, *Measuring the Benefits of Enterprise Architecture: Knowledge Management Maturity* by **Alan Dyer** of the **Australian Defence Force Academy, University of New South Wales, Australia** introduces the concept of Knowledge Management, linked to the strategic outcomes of Enterprise Architecture and proposes a maturity model framework for the measurement of enterprise architecture implementation. The chapter aims to provide a basis for discussion of a wider capability maturity profile with architectural frameworks to help develop and measure the benefits of implementing frameworks and architectures.

SECTION II: LEADERSHIP, GOVERNANCE, AND MANAGEMENT

Section II of the book comprises of chapters that are useful in instituting and sustaining the EA practice within the government organizations.

Chapter VI: An effective enterprise architecture capability enables an organization to develop sound enterprise plans, make informed human, material, and technology resource investment and management decisions, and optimize key business processes. Despite U.S. Congressional legislation, U.S. Office of Management and Budget guidance, and U.S. Government Accountability Office reports and recommendations, many U.S. government leaders struggle in advancing EA adoption in their organizations. U.S. Government leaders must embrace transformational leadership to advance EA adoption. This chapter, *The Criticality of Transformational Leadership to Advancing the United States Government Enterprise Architecture Adoption* by William Boddie of the National Defense University, United States of America presents the Vision, Integrity, Communication, Inspiration, and Empowerment Transformational Leadership Model that describes competencies U.S. Government leaders need to advance EA adoption. The chapter also presents the Transformational Leadership and Enterprise Management Integration Framework that describes the relationship between transformational leadership and enterprise management functions.

Chapter VII: Public institutions that are organized in hierarchies find it difficult to address crisis or other unique requirements that demand networked solutions. This chapter, *Adaptive IT Architecture as a Catalyst for Network Capability in Government* by **Jay Ramanathan, Rajiv Ramnath** and **Anand Desai** of the **Ohio State University, United States of America** first provides a prescriptive transaction-based method for achieving such networking organizations with information technologies (IT) and then discusses how the organization becomes more effective in non-routine responses to citizen requests. The chapter illustrates how the prescriptive transaction-based enterprise architecture framework was used for decision-making in a multi-year interdisciplinary industry-university collaboration resulting in a successful 311 system.

Chapter VIII: *Design Integrity and Enterprise Architecture Governance* by **Chris Aitken** describes a design integrity framework for developing models of any entity of interest at various levels of abstraction. The design integrity framework presented describes and defines contextual, conceptual, logical and physical model types. The framework also defines a set of alignment attributes for each model type and explains how these are to be used to demonstrate alignment from initial concept and requirements through to actual physical implementation. These concepts are then applied in an organisational context to identify the roles necessary to support an EA governance framework and strong alignment from idea to implementation.

xxii

Chapter IX: Few government executives can explain the enterprise architecture of his or her agency, and it is rare to find a political executive who is able to explain how their political objectives are furthered by government-wide enterprise architecture. This low level of awareness translates to enterprise architecture efforts that are often undervalued and under funded because the budget priorities of political and functional executives rarely include enterprise architecture. Not surprisingly, many points of tension exist as the CIOs and architects work to translate political goals into resources and architectural plans supporting the agency's programs. This tension, between the rational orientation of enterprise architecture advocated by the CIO and the political nature of policy goals sought by executives, often puts a CIO at odds with his or her organization's political and functional executives. This chapter, *Policy Mapping: Relating Enterprise Architecture to Policy Goals* by **Dwight Toavs** of the **National Defense University, United States of America** discusses that tension, and advocates that CIOs and enterprise architects develop a "policy map" to bridge the gap between the political and the rational perspectives.

Chapter X: A comprehensive enterprise architecture management has strategic and operative aspects. Strategic tasks cover the identification of appropriate fields of activity for information technology (IT) investments in accordance with business strategy and portfolio management. This chapter, *Enterprise Architecture Management and its Role in IT Governance and IT Investment Planning* by **Klaus Niemann** of **ACT! Consulting, Germany** shows how enterprise architecture management is cross-linked with other IT management processes and delivers the necessary information for sustainable governance. The continuous analysis of the IT landscape, the deduction of measures for optimization and its controlling also belong to the tasks of architecture management. Standards for development and infrastructures are made, e.g. reference architectures and a "book of standards", whose implementation is overseen by solution architects throughout the operative architecture management.

Chapter XI: Departing from the lack of coherent and ready-to-use models and domain descriptions for public administration, this chapter, *The GEA: Governance Enterprise Architecture-Framework and Models* by **Vassilios Peristeras** of the **National University of Ireland, Ireland** and **Konstantinos Tarabanis** of the **University of Macedonia, Greece** presents a set of generic models that serves as a top-level, generic and thus reusable Enterprise Architecture for the overall public administration domain. This set of models is called *Governance Enterprise Architecture* (GEA). GEA has deliberately remained technology independent and following the model driven architecture approach, GEA constitutes a computationally independent model for the domain. GEA has been derived from multi-disciplinary influences and insights and identifies two broad modeling areas, called governance mega-processes: *Public Policy Formulation* and *Service Provision*. These two, together with the *object* versus *process* perspective, form a four-cell matrix that defines four modeling areas for the GEA models. Until now, a large number of services have been modeled using GEA and more recently; an extended modeling effort has started with GEA being chosen for use by a national EU-country project. GEA can be also used as a knowledge infrastructure for applying semantic technologies. In this line, it has been used for creating a public administration specialization of a formal Semantic Web Service ontology, namely WSMO.

Chapter XII: *Enterprise Architecture and Governance Challenges for Orchestrating Public-Private Cooperation* by **Bram Klievink, Wijnand Derks** and **Marijn Janssen** of the **Delft University of Technology, Netherlands** presents an architecture aimed at supporting the coordination of public and private parties for creating a one stop shop and the main challenges therein. Public-private service network poses higher requirements on the architecture of a service network, whereas the variety in systems of the various organizations and different aims make it more difficult to develop such an architecture. Furthermore, it is difficult to isolate architectural challenges from governance aspects, as many architectural issues need to be complemented by governance mechanisms. Architecture and governance cannot be considered in isolation. Within this setting, a new architecture is created and presented for managing and orchestrating the interactions among governmental and private organizations.

SECTION III: REALIZATION AND DEPLOYMENT

Section III provides insights into how organizations employ EA to drive their transformation programmes, gain tighter business-IT alignment and realize business value out of their IT investments.

Chapter XIII: *People-Led Enterprise Architecture* by **Neil Fairhead** of **Fujitsu Services** and **John Good** of **SERCO Consulting, United Kingdom** provides an approach to enterprise architecture that is people-led, as a contrast to being led by technology or modelling methodology. The chapter identifies the major stakeholders in enterprise architecture and suggests where in the organisation they may be found and how they may be connected with the enterprise architecture. It highlights the roles of stakeholders throughout the process of defining and implementing an enterprise architecture. The view of stakeholders managing the EA effort is described through the complete lifecycle, from setting the EA mission to sustaining the benefits after implementation. In proposing the adoption of such an approach, we aim to encourage a more direct link between enterprise architecture, the needs of the stakeholders it serves, and the pubic policy outcomes it enables.

Chapter XIV: *Using Enterprise Architecture to Transform Service Delivery: The U.S. Federal Government's Human Resource Line of Business* by **Timothy Biggert, Kunal Suryavanshi** and **Ryan Kobb** of **IBM Global Business Services, United States of America** provides a case study on how the U.S. Office of Personnel Management has led the establishment of the Human Resources Line of Business (HR LOB). It explains how the HR LOB program has used enterprise architecture to drive transformation to a new Human Resources service delivery model across the United States Federal government. The authors propose that the common view and vocabulary that EA artifacts provide, along with the collaborative governance that took place to create the artifacts, has produced a solid business foundation for this extensive business transformation effort.

Chapter XV: Government agencies are committing an increasing amount of resources to information security and data privacy solutions in order to meet legal and mission requirements for protecting agency information in the face of increasingly sophisticated global threats. Enterprise architecture (EA) provides an agency-wide context and method that includes a security sub-architecture which can be used to design and implement effective controls. EA is scalable, which promotes consistency and alignment in controls at the enterprise, program, and system levels. EA also can help government agencies improve existing security and data privacy programs by enabling them to move beyond a system-level perspective and begin to promote an enterprise-wide view of security and privacy, as well as improve the agility and effectiveness of lifecycle activities for the development, implementation, and operation of related security and privacy controls that will assure the confidentiality, integrity, and availability of the agency's data and information. This chapter, *Enterprise Architecture as Context and Method for Designing and Implementing Information Security and Data Privacy Controls in Government Agencies* by **Scott Bernard** of the **Carnegie Mellon University** and **Shuyuan Mary Ho** of **Syracuse University, United States of America** presents the EA[3] "Cube" EA methodology and framework, including an integrated security architecture, that is suitable for use by government agencies for the development of risk-adjusted security and privacy controls that are designed into the agency's work processes, information flows, systems, applications, and network infrastructure.

Chapter XVI: With a plethora of architectures, modeling techniques and methodologies on offer, it is difficult to decide how to begin building an enterprise and achieve seamless integration. This difficulty is most noticeable in consortia that need to deal with government participation. Various government projects have different objectives and agenda. In addition, changes in business environment as well as government policies impose extra conditions onto the project. Failure to comply with the project requirement can lead to loss of business and sometimes unexpected penalty. The chapter, *Architecture Based Engineering of Enterprises with Government Involvement* by **Laszlo Nemes** and **John Mo** of the **RMIT University, Australia** uses three case studies to show various ways of government involvements in projects. Based on the experiences of these cases, the chapter discusses how enterprise engineering can help creating and managing the enterprise that can engage government services successfully.

Chapter XVII: E-government evolves according to strategic plans with the coordination of central governments. This top-down procedure succeeds in slow but sufficient transformation of public services into e-government ones. However, public agencies adapt to e-government with difficulty, requiring holistic guidance and a detailed legal framework provided by the government. The setting up of common enterprise architecture for all public agencies requires careful analysis. Moreover, common enterprise architecture could fail to cover the special needs of small or municipal agencies. This chapter, *Collaborative Enterprise Architecture for Municipal Environments* by **Leonidas Anthopoulos** of the **Hellenic Ministry of Foreign Affairs, Greece** uses data from various major e-Government strategies, together with their enterprise architectures, in order to introduce a development model of municipal Enterprise Architecture. The model is based on the experience collected from the Digital City of Trikala, Greece, and results in "Collaborative Enterprise Architecture".

Chapter XVIII: *Government Enterprise Architectures: Enabling the Alignment of Business Processes and Information Systems* by **Nigel Martin, Shirley Gregor** and **Dennis Hart** of the **Australian National University, Australia** describes the development and use of government enterprise architectures for the framing and alignment of the core business processes and enabling information systems at the Australian Bureau of Statistics (ABS) and the Centrelink Social Services agency. The chapter focuses on the construction and ongoing maintenance of public enterprise architectures that enable the alignment condition. An established research model has been used to guide the analysis and explication of the government business processes, enabling systems and architectures, and the resulting agency alignment. While the discussion acknowledges the existence of other formal and informal enablers of alignment, this chapter concentrates on the enterprise architecture enabler. The functionally integrated government business processes and information systems that are established within the instantiated enterprise architecture are examined.

In conclusion, I hope that this book makes its contribution to the evolving discipline of EA, which is only going to gain importance in organizations. I would like to invite readers to share their comments about the book in addition to their success stories that may well spawn of future editions of this book.

Dr. Pallab Saha
National University of Singapore
2008

Acknowledgment

In 2006-07, as a result of a consultancy project for Infocomm Development Authority of Singapore, I was fortunate to lead the development of an Enterprise Architecture Methodology. The development of the methodology is complete and has now been designated as a best practice for Singapore Government agencies to adopt. After the publication of my first book *HANDBOOK OF ENTERPRISE SYSTEMS ARCHITECTURE IN PRACTICE*, I received several accolades and feedback that made me think about the great gap in literature that exists in the discipline of Enterprise Architecture.

The trigger for this book came as a result of my involvement in the development of the Enterprise Architecture Methodology for the Government of Singapore and the feedback I received after my first book. This book is a result of efforts and support of a lot of people. Without their advice, assistance and deep involvement, the book would not have achieved its current form. I would like to express my gratitude and thank all involved in the collation and review process of this reference book on Enterprise Architecture.

I would like to start with IGI Global who (again) gave me the opportunity to continue living my cherished dream. This book allowed me to make significant contributions to an emerging and timely discipline. A special word of thanks to **Julia Mosemann** of IGI Global who guided me with numerous e-mails and to **Dr. Mehdi Khosrow-Pour** who initially motivated me to think about writing a book.

I would like to specially acknowledge the contribution of the independent reviewers of the chapters, who readily agreed to review despite their own busy schedules, often working on very tight deadlines given by me. Herein goes my sincere thanks to:

- Frank Armour, George Mason University, USA
- Steven Ring, The MITRE Corporation, USA
- Dr. Santonu Sarkar, Accenture Technology Labs, India
- Dr. Haiping Luo, Government Printing Office, USA
- Prof. Jorge Marx Gomez, University of Oldenburg, Germany
- Dr. Stephen Kaisler, George Washington University, USA

Representing both industry and academia points of view, they provided excellent review comments that improved the overall submission quality. An important part of this book are the chapter authors. I appreciate their excellent contributions and want to thank them for assisting me in the review process.

This book would not have become a reality without the support of my mother **Shrimati Anima Saha**. I thank **Neeta**, my wife for her support, patience and love while this book was written. A special word of love goes to our adorable daughter **Anushka** (now a toddler and ready to go to the kindergarten). Above all, I would like to dedicate this book to my father **Late Shri Jagatbandhu Saha**.

Dr. Pallab Saha
National University of Singapore
2008

Section I
Frameworks and Methodologies

Chapter I
A Methodology for Government Transformation with Enterprise Architecture

Pallab Saha
National University of Singapore, Singapore

ABSTRACT

Countries across the world are pushing their frontiers in governance in the move to information economy, and governments play a pivotal role in this transformation. These governments employ modern information and communication technologies to serve the citizens and businesses better. Raising the effectiveness and quality of government services is not only a matter of leading edge technologies; it also involves visionary leadership, clear objectives and sound execution mechanism. The role of Enterprise Architecture in shaping E-Government programmes cannot be overstated. Within the context of Singapore's e-government initiative, this chapter describes the Methodology for AGency ENTerprise Architecture (MAGENTA), a rigorous, disciplined and structured methodology for development of agency enterprise architectures that enables agencies to align to and fully support the government's transformation objectives and outcomes. Mechanisms for agencies to align to the overall Government Enterprise Architecture are detailed. The chapter concludes with a set of recommendations for future enhancements and research.

INTRODUCTION

Since early 1990s, governments across the world have initiated movements to exploit and utilize information and communication technologies (ICT) to improve public sector service delivery. This is widely known as electronic government (e-government). According to the World Bank e-government refers to 'the use by government agencies of information technologies (IT) that have the ability to transform relations with the citizens, businesses and other arms of the government.' These technologies can facilitate better delivery of government services to citizens, improved interactions with business and industry, citizen empowerment through access to information and more efficient government management. The resulting benefits can be less corruption, increased transparency, greater convenience, revenue growth and cost reduction (The World Bank, 2003).

The adoption of e-government is usually anchored around government modernization programmes. The objectives of such modernization programmes are primarily to improve the way government services to citizens and businesses are delivered coupled with enhanced public sector efficiency. These can be summarized in three words – effectiveness, efficiency and agility (responsiveness). These are achieved through a combination of organizational and IT transformation mechanisms in which governance, management, division of labour, work processes and competencies are all impacted.

This chapter describes the development and implementation of government transformation programmes pertaining specifically to the role of Government Enterprise Architecture (GEA) and its role in e-government activities. The chapter starts with a discussion of benefits and challenges that countries around the world face in embracing e-government. The role of good e-government strategies in addressing key challenges and deriving maximum benefits are also briefly described.

The chapter then examines the current e-government maturity models (stage models). The purpose of this section is to provide a common frame of reference in assessing e-government programmes. This is important as the extent of benefits derived through e-government driven modernization programmes is directly correlated to their maturity levels (Government of Western Australia, 2004; Baum and Di Maio, 2000).

The chapter then identifies and elaborates the role of Enterprise Architecture (EA) in addressing e-government challenges. The manner in which EA supports the modernization programmes by facilitating the governments to move towards higher levels of e-government maturity is discussed (United States Federal Enterprise Architecture Programme Management Office, 2006; Government of British Columbia, 2004). A general mapping of e-government stage models and EA maturity is also presented to demonstrate the high degree of dependency between the two (Kreizman, Baum and Fraga, 2003).

Following the general discussion, the chapter continues to elaborate the aforementioned areas within the context of Singapore. This starts with a brief description of Singapore's e-government programmes and its evolution over the years (Tan and Gan, 2007). The evolution is mapped to earlier described e-government maturity models. The next section elaborates the EA methodology, called the **M**ethodology for **AG**ency **ENT**erprise **A**rchitecture (MAGENTA) that has been developed for the Singapore Government jointly by the National University of Singapore (NUS) and the Infocomm Development Authority of Singapore (IDA). The contribution of the EA methodology to support government transformation is discussed in detail. This is a first-hand description as the author led the development of MAGENTA (Saha, 2007a). However, any analysis presented in this chapter represents the author's own opinion.

Finally the chapter concludes with the identification of some plausible areas for future enhancements and research in line with emerging trends.

BACKGROUND

Overview of E-Government

E-Government involves use of ICT to facilitate the transformation of government services and operations aimed at providing an integrated government. The focus is to provide the right services (effectiveness) in an efficient and transparent manner that is agile and responsive to citizen and business needs. The importance and application of e-government can be summarized as:

- Citizen centric, not bureaucracy centric,
- Results oriented, and
- Market centric, actively promoting the knowledge economy.

According to the Organization for Economic Cooperation and Development (OECD) (2003), 'e-government enables the dual goals of efficiency and democracy to be met more cheaply and easily than previously envisaged but the new technologies go much further that this. They are starting to redefine the landscape of government by changing the relationships (power and responsibility) between players – between service providers and industry, between the public and private sectors and between government and citizens – by forging new organizational and economic structures, by introducing new processes at work and in the community and above all by opening new opportunities as well as posing new challenges, not least the threat of new digital divide.'

The four major areas of e-government span and scope include government-to-customer (G2C), government-to-business (G2B), government-to-government (G2G) and government-to-employee (G2E) interactions. Among the four areas, G2C and G2E involve interactions between government agencies and individuals, while G2G and G2B deal with government to organization interactions. In all four categories there is increasing tendency towards cross enterprise interactions

(Siau and Long, 2005). This approach in categorizing interactions challenges the traditional notion that e-government is simply more ICT projects / programmes in government agencies. E-Government, as we will see later, goes far beyond plain automation.

Every e-government programme starts with the development of e-government strategy, primarily a game-plan of how the government plans to achieve its e-government goals and objectives. Having an e-government strategy is fundamental to creating an execution plan. Typical components of e-government strategy include:

- The scope of e-government programme incorporating key areas to be addressed and identification of all stakeholders,
- A vision that is easily understood and succinctly expresses the government's concepts of and plans for e-government,
- Specific goals and objectives that can be monitored and measured to assess the programme,
- Identification of governance structures and mechanisms to support the programme,
- A methodology to determine organizational readiness,
- A process for identifying and prioritizing e-government initiatives, and
- A business model to sustain the e-government programme.

While the actual benefits of e-government programmes vary based on specific programme objectives, there are several underlying commonalities. The fundamental benefits of typical e-government programmes include:

- Integration and collaboration within and between agencies,
- Participation in government decision making,
- Access to government information and services,

- Delivery of government services in an effective and efficient manner, and
- Responsiveness (agility) in adapting to rapidly changing needs.

Overview of EA

Enterprise architecture is the organizing logic for an organization's core business processes and IT capabilities captured in a set of policies and technical choices, to achieve business standardization and integration requirements of the firm's operating model (Ross, Weill and Robertson, 2006). Metaphorically, an EA is to an organization's operations and systems as a set of blueprints is to a building. An organization's EA specifies business and technical governance platform on which the enterprise designs and builds its IT systems for business competitiveness. Typically, Government is the largest organization in almost every country and with size comes complexity.

EA effectively supports the business, enables information sharing across departments, divisions, agencies, enhances management's ability to deliver effective and timely services, and improves operational efficiencies in a disciplined manner through effective use of ICT. Committing to an on-going EA practice within an enterprise enables a business-aligned and technology-adaptive enterprise that is effective, efficient and agile. Business planners and IT planners can utilise EA to (Saha, 2007b; Ross, Weill and Robertson, 2006):

- Provide critical inputs to long term strategic planning processes,
- Define organization's business operating model and build a foundation for execution,
- Drive and justify business process improvement programmes,
- Coordinate and consolidate operations in the organisation,
- Take advantage of new enabling technologies,

- Reallocate resources, including organisation restructuring,
- Modernise legacy ICT systems and infrastructure,
- Protect critical ICT infrastructure from a business continuity point of view,
- Manage declining vendor support for ICT systems,
- Assess proposed technology solutions, and
- Manage and prioritise ICT system investments.

STAGES OF AND PROGRESS TOWARDS E-GOVERNMENT

Countries moving towards e-government tend to share a number of characteristics. The most visible commonality being their gradual progress towards increasing e-government maturity. Countries move through successive maturity levels by first building and then leveraging the execution foundation. Each stage typically involves learning about the application of IT and government process discipline as strategic capabilities. With the intent of incorporating the transition towards better e-government several e-government stage models have been proposed (Moon, 2002; Layne and Lee, 2001; Hiller and Belanger, 2001; United Nations and American Society for Public Administration, 2001; Deloitte and Touché, 2001; & Baum and Di Maio, 2000). A full discussion and analysis of each of these e-government stage models in beyond the scope of this chapter, nonetheless Table 1 shows a brief comparison of the currently available models (Siau and Yong, 2005).

For the purposes of this chapter Siau and Yong's five stage model (2005) will be used as this model represents a synthesis of all the other stage models. This synthesis makes it by far the most representative and comprehensive e-government stage model.

Table 1. Summary of e-government stage models

Model	Stages
Gartner's Four Stage Model (2000)	• Web presence • Interaction • Transaction • Transformation
UN's Five Stage Model (2001)	• Emerging • Enhanced • Interactive • Transactional • Integrated
Deloitte and Touché's Six Stage Model (2001)	• Information publishing / dissemination • Official two-way transaction • Multi-purpose portals • Portal personalization • Clustering of common services • Full integration and enterprise transaction
Layne and Lee's Four Stage Model (2001)	• Catalogue • Transaction • Vertical integration • Horizontal integration
Hiller and Belanger's (2001) and Moon's (2002) Five Stage Model	• Simple information dissemination (one-way communication) • Request and response (two-way communication) • Service and financial transaction • Vertical and horizontal integration • Political participation
Siau and Yong's Five Stage Synthesised Model (2005)	• Web presence • Interaction • Transaction • Transformation • E-democracy

All stage models represent e-government capability and maturity. Though not mandatory, countries usually traverse the stages in a gradual and phased manner leveraging on the points learned at each stage as they navigate. Stage models are an excellent way to design, implement and evaluate e-government programmes. For instance the Office of E-Government, Department of the Premier and Cabinet, Government of Western Australia uses the Gartner's four stage model and has linked its e-government goals to the stage model (Government of Western Australia, 2004). This is depicted in Figure 1.

There are several instances of successful e-government programmes where the countries have moved or are in the process of moving into the higher echelons of capability and maturity. Nonetheless, a survey of e-government literature reveals several challenges e-government programmes face. The primary challenges are grouped into: (1) information and data, (2) information technology, (3) organizational and managerial, (4) legal and regulatory, and (5) institutional and environmental challenges (Gil-Garcia and Pardo, 2005). While a full discussion on strategies needed to address these challenges is outside the scope of this chapter, the strong linkages between the challenges and key imperatives (discussed later) are clearly evident.

Figure 1. Achieving goals of e-government (Government of Western Australia, 2004) (reproduced with permission)

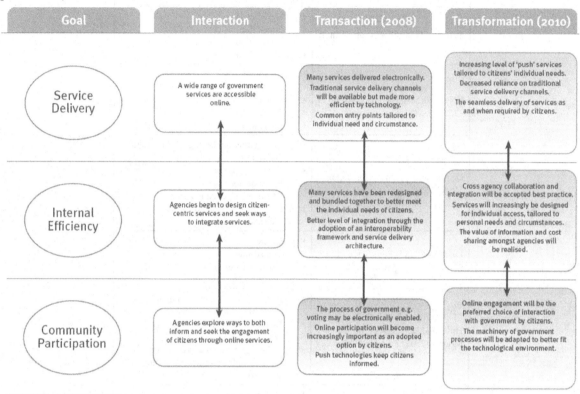

ROLE OF EA IN E-GOVERNMENT CAPABILITY AND MATURITY

As is evident from Figure 1, the time needed, system complexity and integration capabilities increase with the advancement of e-government stages (Siau and Yong, 2005, Kreizman, Baum, and Fraga, 2003). Concurrently, the benefits that countries derive out of their e-government programmes and the commensurate investments needed also increase. As a result there is always an element of trade-off and balance between e-government investments (time, money, human resources and technology) and benefits and achievements (effectiveness, efficiency and agility). In reality, countries face several significant challenges in advancing e-government capabilities and deriving its full benefits. In order to achieve the full

benefits of e-government significant investments are necessary but not sufficient. To ensure greatest value the delivery of information and services via the Internet requires a planned, coordinated and unified approach from all stakeholders. It requires a collaborated effort between agencies and ministries in order to be successful and advance e-government capability and maturity (Government of British Columbia, 2004). Some of the key imperatives to make this happen include:

- Leadership,
- Enterprise architecture and common standards,
- Improved accessibility and security,
- Protection of privacy and identity (authentication and authorization),
- Cultural change and business transformation,

Table 2. Summary of the role of EA in e-government programmes

Country	Brief Description of EA in E-Government Programme
Australia	The Australian Government Information Management Office (AGIMO) in the Department of Finance and Administration owns the e-government programme. It has developed the Australian Government Architecture (AGA), adapted from the Federal Enterprise Architecture (FEA). The AGA consists of five reference models (performance, business, data, application and technology), principles, patterns, standards, Service Oriented Architecture (SOA) repository and service catalogue. According to AGIMO 'the AGA aims to assist in the delivery of more consistent and cohesive service to citizens and support the more cost-effective delivery of ICT services by government.' Aimed at increasing cross-agency collaboration a set of eleven Cross-Agency Services Architecture Principles have also been defined. These principles, part of AGA, have been mapped to the e-government Strategy and Service Delivery Principles.
Canada	Canada's e-government programme has been rated as one of the most advanced in the world. It is characterized by broad-based services, high complexity and very high user acceptance. EA plays a critical role in its e-government programme. Owned by the Treasury Board of Canada (TBC) and driven by the Chief Information Office Branch (CIOB), Canada has a Federated Architecture Programme that started in 2000. The EA consists of a set of guidelines, common reference architectures, standards and policies. The strong business orientation of the e-government and EA initiatives is made explicit by having an integrated Business Transformation Enablement Programme (BTEP). Under the BTEP individual agencies are provided strategic design and planning methodology, handbook, templates, tools and service reference patterns. According to TBC 'BTEP's vision is to facilitate sustainable whole-of-government client or citizen-centred transformation and to provide the design and alignment tools that will enable rapid change. The Government of Canada Strategic Reference Model (GSRM) is the BTEP tool that enables the development of business architecture by providing a common language for generating models that map how a government enterprise, or programme or process actually works or could work better.'
Singapore	The relevant programmes here are the Integrated Government (iGOV 2010) and Singapore Government Enterprise Architecture (SGEA). This chapter does not describe in details the SGEA as this has been very well covered and described in **Chapter VII: Enterprise Architecture in the Singapore Government** by *Tan Eng Pheng* and *Gan Wei Boon* in the *Handbook of Enterprise Systems Architecture in Practice*.
Taiwan	Under the Executive Yuan, the Research, Development and Evaluation Commission (RDEC) is a ministerial agency responsible for e-Government development. The Department of Information Management under the RDEC is the administrative body for e-government related affairs, including overall planning, programme and budget review, and coordination among government agencies. The National Information and Communication Initiative Committee (NICI) plays the role of CIO in the e-government programme. Architecture initiatives here have focussed on planning, development of common platforms, systems integration and outsourcing. The key objectives include delivery of integrated services and cross-government collaboration.
UK	Under the management of the Office of the e-Envoy, UK has established its e-government programme UK Online. The Government Gateway is a centrally financed infrastructure solution connecting existing systems with different data structures. UK government has also developed and adopted an e-Government Interoperability Framework (e-GIF) that facilitates collaboration and cooperation amongst various agencies.
USA	The development of a Federal Enterprise Architecture (FEA) commenced the EA journey within the Federal Government. Led by the Office of Management and Budget (OMB), the purpose of this effort is to identify opportunities to simplify processes and unify work across the agencies and within the lines of business of the Federal government. As part of the FEA, the OMB has developed several reference models, practice guidance, transition framework, standards, maturity models and policies. The governance of the whole EA programme is guided by the Clinger-Cohen Act (1996). Additionally the E-Government Act (2002), Government Paperwork Elimination Act (1996) and Information Technology Management Reform Act (1996) also provide support to the programme. The FEA has been integrated to other management practices like IT Portfolio and Investment Management and Capital Planning developed by the US General Accountability Office (GAO). At the state level, the development of EA is spearheaded by National Association of State CIOs (NASCIO). NASCIO has developed a EA Toolkit for the benefit of all state level agencies.

- Governance, policy and legislative framework,
- Collation and collaboration.

A review of current literature reveals the criticality and centrality of EA to e-government programmes. Several countries across the world have anchored a significant portion of their e-government programme around a strong EA programme. Table 2 presents a summarised and representative list of countries and their e-government programmes along with the role EA plays in each. Table 3 shows how countries are using EA as a strategy to deal with and address e-government challenges. Several other e-government programmes and the role of EA are presented in the remaining chapters of this book.

It is amply evident from Table 2 and 3 that EA is critical to e-government and countries have recognised this. As discussed in the earlier section, countries usually traverse the stages of e-government capability and maturity in a gradual and phased manner leveraging on the points learned at each stage as they navigate. In

Table 3. Role of EA in addressing e-government challenges (Adapted and extended from Gil-Garcia & Pardo, 2005)

Category	Challenge	Role of EA in Addressing Challenge(s)
Information and Data	• Information and data quality • Dynamic information needs	Information Architecture (IA) within EA mandates development and compliance to common data standards. Usually such standards are captured as data principles / policies and data definition and usage requirements. Mapping to applications and business processes allows for complete visibility and control through the data lifecycle. Such practices take care of issues pertaining to inaccuracies, inconsistencies and incompleteness of data and derived information.
Technology	• Usability • Security • Technological incompatibility • Technology complexity • Technical skills and experience • Technology newness	Technology Architecture (TA) and Application Architecture (AA) require common technical and application standards. Architectural qualities are addressed through non-functional requirements. Issues pertaining to incompatibility, complexity and newness are addressed by a set of relevant principles and common standards. Agencies can use TA and AA to steer their technology acquisition initiatives.
Organizational and Managerial	• Project size and scope • Manager's attitude and behaviour • Stakeholder diversity • Lack of alignment • Multiple and conflicting goals • Resistance to change • Turf and conflicts	Most governments are known to have established a separate Programme Management Office (PMO) to manage the EA initiative (e.g. FEA PMO in the United States, AGIMO in Australia, IDA in Singapore). Challenges in this category are addressed by the PMO. Transition management is a core activity in EA Management and directly addresses some of the challenges. Some of the challenges are also addressed by governance practices. These include standard project management methodology, senior executive oversight, formal compliance process, business leadership in project teams, enterprise levels process owners among others (Ross, Weill and Robertson, 2006).
Legal and Regulatory	• Restrictive laws and regulations • Annual budget cycles • Intergovernmental relationships	Challenges pertaining to these categories are best addressed by good architecture governance and management. Every architecture framework (e.g. FEAF, DODAF, and TOGAF) places high importance to architecture governance. Designing architecture governance is a core activity in the development of EA. Useful governance practices include infrastructure renewal funding, IT steering committee, structures, centralized funding for enterprise applications and portfolio management (Ross, Weill and Robertson, 2006).
Institutional and Environmental	• Privacy concerns • Autonomy of agencies • Policy and political pressures • Environmental context	

much the same way organizations also graduate through the various stages of EA maturity (Ross, Weill and Robertson, 2006).

Architecture Maturity Model

In 2006, Ross, Weill and Robertson developed a four stage EA maturity model. These four stages are briefly described as follows and Table 4 discusses the meaning of the four stages within the context of government.

1. **Business silos architecture:** A stage where business units and functions within the organization operate to maximize their individual business unit and functional needs. IT systems and applications developed and deployed in this stage tend to be one-off localised solutions that cannot integrate with one another, thus creating fragmented business processes and all associated difficulties.

2. **Standardized technology architecture:** In this stage organizations convert some local applications into shared infrastructure. The key driving factor in this stage is technology standardization leading to reduction of technology diversity. It is typical in this stage for organizations to consolidate and standardize hardware. Organizations also initiate the reduction of software applications and systems performing similar functions. This stage is usually characterised by quick cost savings and ease of adoption.

3. **Optimized core architecture:** Organizations move from local view of data, applications and technology to an enterprise view in this stage. It involves elimination of data redundancies and more disciplined reduction of application and technology overlaps. By the end of this stage organizations tend to cleanly differentiate between enterprise level data, applications and technology that are shared versus localised data, applications

Table 4. Architecture maturity stages in the context of government

Architecture Maturity Stages	Relevance / Application in Government
1. Business Silos	In this stage the government agencies operate in their own respective silos. Almost all IT applications and systems are specific to the agency and have rarely any interoperability needs. There may be standards but only within the agencies, and complete lack of standards between them. Most IT investments are justified on the basis of efficiency (cost reductions). As a result government processes and services tend to be fragmented with no semblance of government process management. The key point to note here is that usually business functions or departments within such agencies also tend to operate in silo based models.
2. Standardized Technology	In this stage the government agencies are able to define and comply to certain technology standards pertaining to IT infrastructure. This allows them to reduce technology diversity and standardize on a few common platforms. Agencies in this stage usually increase access to shared data by introducing data warehouses, but transaction data is still embedded in individual applications. From the point of view of deriving direct economic benefits, this stage is by far the easiest to achieve and positions government entities to eventually move to standard data and business processes.
3. Optimised Core	Building on the foundations provided by common technology standards in the previous stage, agencies are now able to transition from a local view of data and applications to an enterprise view. This is made possible by having common data standards to support cross-agency business processes. Further, common data, applications and business processes allow government agencies to eliminate data and functional overlaps and redundancies.
4. Business Modularity	This stage takes benefit of the earlier two stages. By this time government agencies adhere to standardised technology, data, applications and business processes. The underlying common elements of the architecture are well-entrenched allowing the identification and packaging of reusable modules. The focus here is for agencies to be more flexible and adaptable to changing business needs by composing new solutions using available services or modules.

and technology that are suited to the needs of specific business units and functions.

4. **Business modularity architecture:** The last and final stage of architecture maturity is when organizations are adept at identifying their business processes (including their operating models). The core business processes are then used to identify reusable modules. The idea of reusability isn't limited to business processes alone, but extends into reusable data, application and technology capabilities. Often organizations in this stage offer such reusable elements as services that can be leveraged to build newer and customised solutions in tune with changing business needs. The key objective of this stage is to provide organizations with agility and flexibility.

Other notable EA maturity model has been defined and applied as part of the Federal Enterprise Architecture Framework (United States Federal Enterprise Architecture Programme Management Office, 2006). Table 5 maps the e-government maturity stages to EA maturity stages. The mapping identifies the most relevant architectural maturity needed in order to reach a specific e-government maturity level as a causal relationship.

SINGAPORE E-GOVERNMENT PROGRAMME

Introduction

Singapore is an island republic measuring about 700 sq. km. in area. It has a population of 4.7 million, resulting in a population density of 6700 persons per sq. km. About 75% of the households own personal computers and 65% of the households have access to the Internet. The household broadband penetration is more than 50% and mobile phone penetration close to 100%.

Evolution of E-Government Programme

E-government in Singapore is positioned and perceived as a means to reinvent the Government. Its core vision includes delighting customers and connecting citizens through the use of ICT. Over its 25 years of e-government journey, Singapore has put in place several plans (Tan and Gan, 2007). These successive plans have allowed Singapore to gradually build and enhance its e-government programme. As seen later, a series of consecutive plans is a key enabler for it to progressively move towards higher levels of e-government capability and maturity. Now it is widely acknowledged as having an advanced e-government (Infocomm Development Authority of Singapore, 2005). Table 6 describes the various e-government plans that have been in existence since 1980, their respective goals and objectives (Tan and Gan, 2007) and mapping to e-government stage model.

Besides the plans, another key factor contributing to the success of Singapore's e-government programme is its leadership. Called the iGOV Council, it represents the highest approving and decision making committee. The iGOV Council is chaired by the Permanent Secretary of Finance. Under the governance structure, the Ministry of Finance (MOF) is the custodian of nearly all ICT infrastructure, services and policies within the public sector (Infocomm Development Authority of Singapore, 2005).

OVERVIEW OF SINGAPORE GOVERNMENT ENTERPRISE ARCHITECTURE

EA has always been a core enabler in Singapore's e-government programme. The CSCP provided the government with the basic infrastructure needed for e-government in addition to some government systems. There was the realization of

Table 5. Mapping architecture maturity to e-government maturity stages

E-Government Maturity Stages	Architecture Maturity Stages				Explanation of the Mapping*
	Business Silos	Standardised Technology	Optimized Core	Business Modularity	
1. Web presence	+				In this stage agencies typically post simple, limited and static information through their websites. With information dissemination as the key focus area, the communication is primarily one-way. This is the point where almost all agencies still operate in their silos and the characteristics described in Figure 5 are evident.
2. Interaction	+	+			This stage provides for simple interaction between agencies and their users. The communication here is two-way and there are a few common technology standards and applications, though within the agency rather than at a cross-agency level.
3. Transaction		++	+		This phase allows users to conduct complete online transactions (including e-commerce and e-business transactions). This necessitates some level of data standardization to support cross-agency transactions. Nonetheless, the primary objective being common technology standards across the agencies, supported by some degree of common data and applications.
4. Transformation			+	++	Here the focus is to shift from mere process automation to integration across government agencies. Integration involves both vertical (governments in different levels) and horizontal (different departments and locations). Here citizens, businesses and governments are presented a single unified and harmonized face. This calls for high degree of collaboration and cooperation amongst the agencies.
5. E-democracy	**Not Applicable**				This stage requires more of a political transformation and does not directly map to any architecture maturity stage.

1.   *Mapping means the architectural maturity needed as enabler to achieve a specific e-government maturity level.*
2.   *"++" represents strong mapping and "+" represents weak mapping.*
3.   *Only the relevant stages are mapped. It is assumed that the earlier stages are already achieved.*

the need for well designed, reliable and scalable IT infrastructure. To take full benefit of eGAP I the Singapore public sector needed a coherent collection of policies, standards and guidelines to steer government agencies in the design, acquisition, deployment and management of ICT (Tan and Gan, 2007).

The first government-wide architecture programme was the service-wide technical architec-ture (SWTA). With individual agencies already having in place the basic IT infrastructure, SWTA was aimed to control technical diversity through the use of common systems and platforms for the deployment of e-services (Tan and Gan, 2007). The underlying premise was that common technology could propel interoperability among agencies and encourage collaboration. SWTA consists of nine technical domains for which policies, stan-

Table 6. Progression of Singapore's e-government journey

E-Government Plan	Brief Description
1. Civil Service Computerization Programme (CSCP) (1980 – 1999)	This represents the first formal plan in the e-government journey. It marked the initiation of computerization in the Singapore public sector. The focus was to build the basic IT infrastructure, improve internal operational efficiencies primarily through automation and elimination of paperwork. Over the two decades of its existence, the government evolved from using IT as a tool to improve productivity to leveraging the Internet to provide 24x7 services. Additionally, the government systems were also extended to the private sector for better synergies (e.g. TradeNet, MediNet and LawNet) (Infocomm Development Authority of Singapore, 2005). *CSCP maps to **Web Presence** and some degree of **Interaction** stages in the e-government maturity stage model.*
2. E-Government Action Plan I (eGAP I) (1999 – 2003)	In early 1990s, the need was felt to consolidate the computing resources in the form of shared data centre and a civil services network. This required a paradigm shift in the way government services were delivered and thus eGAP I was launched in June 2000. The vision – to be a leading e-government to better serve Singapore and Singaporeans in the new knowledge based economy (Infocomm Development Authority of Singapore, 2005). Aimed at moving citizens, businesses, public officers and the government towards the e-government vision, five strategic thrusts were defined (Tan and Gan, 2007). *eGAP I maps to **Interaction** stage in the e-government maturity stage model.*
3. E-Government Action Plan II (eGAP II) (2003 – 2006)	The focus of eGAP II was to achieve three distinct outcomes of delighted customers, connected citizens and a networked government by building on the efforts and outcomes of eGAP I. eGAP II was focussed to deliver accessible, integrated and value adding public services to customers (Infocomm Development Authority of Singapore, 2005). eGAP II delivered a networked government through common infrastructure, information management and technical standards, fostering inter-agency collaborations (Tan and Gan, 2007). *eGAP II maps to **Transaction** stage in the e-government maturity stage model.*
4. Integrated Government 2010 (iGOV 2010) (2006 – 2010)	iGOV 2010 is the currently active plan and is designed to guide agencies in reaping synergies and exploring new opportunities as an integrated government. This plan has four strategic thrusts – increasing the reach and richness of e-services, increasing citizens' mindshare in e-engagement, enhancing capacity and synergy in the government and enhancing national competitive advantage (Infocomm Development Authority of Singapore, 2005). *iGOV 2010 aims to target **Transformation** stage in the e-government maturity stage model.*

dards and guidelines have been defined (Tan and Gan, 2007).

Widespread adoption of SWTA allowed agencies transition to **Standardised Technology** level in the EA maturity stages (see Table 4). This was in line with the expectation as at that point eGAP I was the active plan and the key goal was to realize **Interaction** level in the e-government stages (see Tables 5 and 6).

The next obvious move was to realize the **Transaction** and **Transformation** levels. There was a recognition that such a move needed an expansion in the scope of the architecture to move beyond technology and to incorporate data, applications and most importantly business processes (Tan and Gan, 2007). This is when the development of the SGEA was initiated by the Government. Developed by the Ministry of Finance (MOF) and IDA, SGEA consists of four domain architectures, which are manifested in the form of structured reference models. These are the Business Reference Model (BRM), Data Reference Model (DRM), Technical Reference Model (TRM) and Solutions Reference Model (SRM). A detailed description of the SGEA is provided in **Chapter VII: Enterprise Architecture in the**

Singapore Government by *Tan Eng Pheng* and *Gan Wei Boon* in the *Handbook of Enterprise Systems Architecture in Practice.*

Within the current e-government plan, iGOV 2010, the SGEA is designed to directly support the **'enhancing capacity and synergy in the government'** strategic thrust. This kind of linkage between SGEA and iGOV 2010 clearly demonstrates the criticality of EA for the success of the ensuing e-government programme in Singapore. Figure 2 shows the chronological evolution and progress of Singapore's e-government and EA programmes.

METHODOLOGY FOR AGENCY ENTERPRISE ARCHITECTURE

Effective EA programmes are methodology based and process-driven. A methodology prescribes what must be done, when and how the steps link to one another (Bittler & Kreizman, 2005). EA is a process discipline. When institutionalised, EA leads to execution of an organisation's operating model and tighter alignment to business strategy. With the development of the SGEA reference

models there was a realization of the need to have a structured and well defined methodology for development of EA. MAGENTA is a multi-phase, iterative and non-linear EA methodology. It is intended to provide all agencies a holistic approach to EA development. It establishes a common mechanism to manifest an integrated architecture. The need for the development of MAGENTA stemmed from the following reasons:

- Integration to SGEA and iGOV 2010,
- EA as a discipline is an evolving field, resulting in the current body of knowledge being inconsistent (lack of consensus on EA definition, terminologies, goals, approaches, outputs, outcomes etc.) and incomplete, and
- Development in other countries, as briefly described in Table 2.

MAGENTA provides a rigorous, disciplined and structured approach that is tool and vendor agnostic. This methodology is intended to guide agencies develop their own EA. MAGENTA allows agencies to effectively transform the business, enable information sharing across departments,

Figure 2. Progress of Singapore's e-government and EA programmes

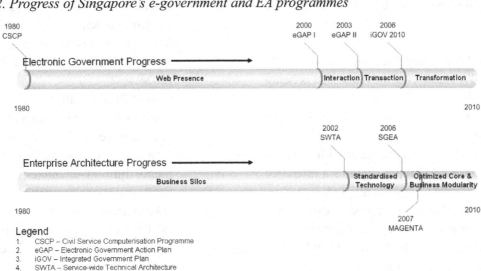

divisions and agencies, enhances management's ability to deliver effective and timely services and improve operational efficiencies in a disciplined manner through the effective use of Information and Communication Technologies (ICT). The methodology has the following objectives:

- To provide step-by-step guidance to develop and implement an agency-level EA.
- To focus agency efforts on the development and management of their EA, rather than on framework related issues.
- To create a common reference point for all architectural deliverables in terms of scope, and level of detail.
- A common unified approach to EA development and improve organisation EA maturity and capability

MAGENTA is a multi-phase methodology containing extensive figures, charts, tools, templates, examples, practitioner guidance and FAQs. The graphical view of MAGENTA is depicted in Figure 3. MAGENTA takes a practical approach by directing focus on core business processes of an agency. Business processes that are critical to the success of the agency by enabling strategic initiatives are identified as core business processes. Each phase of MAGENTA is structured in the following manner:

- **MAGENTA map:** Graphical view of MAGENTA identifying the phase that is being described.
- **Objective:** The key intent of executing the phase.
- **Inputs:** Items that are required to execute the phase. Each input contains a reference to the step(s) where it is utilised.
- **Outputs:** Items that are produced as a result of executing the phase. Each output contains reference to the step(s) that are utilised to produce the specific output.

- **Steps:** Activities performed in the phase shown both in graphical and detailed tabular form. Each step is numbered for easy reference. Each step makes reference to a Phase Tool and Phase Example as appropriate. Every step also identifies the role responsible for performing the step.
- **Phase tools:** Templates, guidelines and pointers that are useful in executing a specific step of the phase.
- **Phase examples:** Illustrations of outputs that are produced as a result of executing a specific step in the phase. The examples are intended to illustrate the outcome of executing specific step(s).

At the core of MAGENTA is government transformation and it is designed to address the key questions agencies typically face. These questions pertain to and include:

- **Business Performance**
  o What are our core business processes that are critical to the success of the strategy?
  o Where can we achieve dramatic improvements?
  o What are the key areas where we need to collaborate with other agencies in the Government?
  o What are the key information requirements to support the core business processes?
- **Investment Performance**
  o Which of the core business processes must receive our IT investments?
  o How do we categorise our IT investments into IT-enabled transformation?
- **IT Performance**
  o Which business processes have no IT support and where are we overspending?

o Where can we take benefit of common data, applications and technology?

o Where do we have redundancies and overlaps?

o What metrics do we need to assess the programme effectiveness?

As is evident from Figure 3, MAGENTA takes a two-dimensional approach to EA development. The vertical dimension captures the various groups of stakeholders separated as tracks. The focus of this dimension is to differentiate the concerns of different stakeholders and associate them to the relevant EA development activities. On the other hand the horizontal dimension depicts the developmental progress of EA, supporting both 'as-is' architectures and their analyses as well as 'to-be' architectures and their analyses to derive future architectural initiatives enabling the transition to

the 'to-be' architecture. A brief overview of the nine phases is provided as follows. The phases are numbered for identification purposes and do not represent strict adoption sequence.

- **Phase 1 → Establish Enterprise Architecture Programme:** This phase covers the activities that agencies must perform to prepare for an impending EA programme. Agencies that have just started out on their EA programmes may also find this phase useful as a checklist of items to be done and evaluate their progress.

- **Phase 2 → Scan and Analyze Current Business State:** This phase is targeted at the agency's core business processes from an end-to-end perspective. This phase understands the current business goals and initiatives with intent to clarify if the core

Figure 3. MAGENTA graphical view

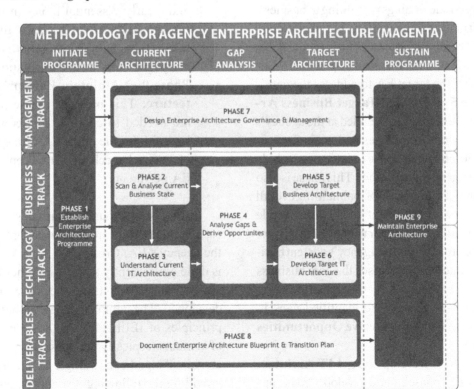

business processes are areas of focus for the agencies.

- **Phase 3 → Understand Current IT Architecture:** This phase envelops the agency's data, application and technology infrastructure. By understanding the overall business processes and governing business rules adopted by the agencies, the information architecture (IA) captures the information of the enterprise including data sharing and exchange. It also describes the specification, development and adoption of technologies to support the business requirements and agency goals. Finally, the phase also describes approaches and mechanisms for designing solution requirements, specifying architectural views and viewpoints, ascertaining system qualities and guiding the assembly of the solution elements that will meet end user needs.

- **Phase 4 → Analyze Gaps and Derive Opportunities:** This phase is a compilation of the gaps and findings pertaining to business, information, application and technology domains and the interdependencies between them. The objective of this phase is to articulate the target EA to address the gaps.

- **Phase 5 → Develop Target Business Architecture:** This is intended at the agency's core business processes and goals from an end-to-end perspective (which may include cross agency integration). This phase is also useful for the purpose of maintaining overall business-IT alignment of the EA. While **Scan and Analyse Current Business State** phase broadly sets the agency's current business state, this prioritises the core business processes from a target architecture point of view to address the identified gaps in **Analyse Gaps and Derive Opportunities** phase.

- **Phase 6 → Develop Target IT Architecture:** This phase aims to develop the data, application and technical architecture required

to support the target business architecture. The development of the target IT architecture also looks to address the gaps identified in **Analyse Gaps and Derive Opportunities** phase. While in structure this is similar to **Understand Current IT Architecture** phase, the focus here is the target point of view.

- **Phase 7 → Design Architecture Governance and Management:** This is to ensure that the architecture programme is successfully sustained within the agencies and meets overall IT governance expectations. As part of this phase, EA development is seamlessly integrated to investment management and system development lifecycle (Armour et. al., 2007).

- **Phase 8 → Document Enterprise Architecture Blueprint & Transition Plan:** This phase provides an outline of the documentation needed to capture the agency's EA with the intent of describing it thoroughly and clearly. Essential topics in this phase include guidance for good documentation, uses of the agency EA blueprint, structuring and organising the documentation.

- **Phase 9 → Maintain Enterprise Architecture:** This provides the activities that are needed to continue and complete the logical lifecycle of the EA through a series of feedback mechanisms to keep the agency EA pertinent.

In traversing through the various steps in phases, several artifacts are developed that constitute the agency's EA. Creation of the **EA Blueprint** is done concurrently along with other phases as the individual artifacts (i.e. the phase outputs) get developed. The complete blueprint based on the principles of IEEE 1471-2000, is a compilation of artifacts (typically the phase outputs) that are combined together as a single coherent blueprint providing the following distinct advantages:

- In the absence of a single unified blueprint, individual phase outputs may be viewed as isolated artifacts,
- The single unified blueprint provides a central anchor to appropriately reference the relevant phase outputs,
- It is easier to distribute and communicate the EA across the agency, fostering collaboration, and
- It is simpler to maintain the EA throughout its lifecycle.

MAGENTA does not assume a 'one-size-fits-all' approach to EA development. Though the methodology in itself is holistic and generic to encourage widespread adoption, agencies have the discretion to design and tailor their EA programmes to suit their business and technology objectives. This kind of flexibility to programme design encourages autonomy at the agency-level and supports the federated governance structure at the whole-of-government level, thereby enhancing the overall effectiveness of EA programmes. In adopting MAGENTA, agencies are encouraged to select the appropriate EA design model. Each design model represents the intersection of an agency's **EA Value Proposition** and **EA Emphasis**.

These two dimensions define four quadrants, each representing an EA design model: **Technology Standardisation Model, Business Standardisation Model, Technology Differentiation Model** and **Business Differentiation Model**. The design models, influenced by design priorities of the IT department (Ross, 2006), that typically apply to agencies (equally applicable to organisations at large) are shown in Figure 4. The typical distinguishing characteristics of each of the quadrants are shown in the figure. The choice of an EA design model is a critical decision for an

Figure 4. Enterprise architecture design models in MAGENTA

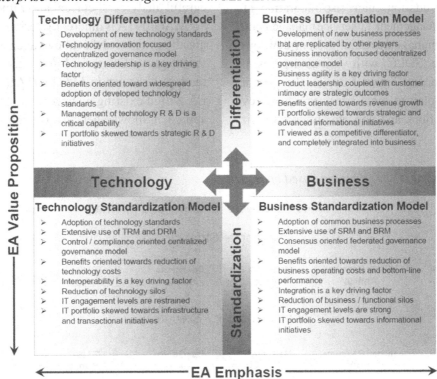

agency (organisation). The design model decision (or the lack of it) has a profound impact on the rest of the EA programme. Each model places different demands on the agency's EA programme with respect to its objectives, metrics, scope, intensity, resources, senior management involvement, outcomes and benefits – just to name a few. There have been instances, where agencies have included transitioning to a new design model as part of their overall EA programme migration plan. Such transitions are transformational as it entails new way of thinking and behaving, and are disruptive in nature.

Integrated Enterprise Lifecycle Approach with MAGENTA

EA in general provides significant business benefits to all organisations. As a result of years of sustained efforts in adopting IT, government agencies in developed countries demonstrate high degree of maturity in practices like strategic planning, IT strategic planning, technology standardization and data consolidation, enterprise integration, IT programme management, IT service management, IT portfolio management and system development lifecycle (SDLC) with various degrees of scope and intensity. Figure 5 depicts the current approach adopted in most agencies where key business functions and departments have their

respective strategies that set the overall direction. These strategies are then executed using formal annual and multi-year plans linked to the budget cycle. This often leads to 'silo' or 'stovepipe' functions within and between the agencies. It characterises the lowest level of architecture maturity. It is clearly evident that this approach is not suitable to take full benefit of common standards and seek collaboration opportunities with other government agencies (see Table 4). This is an important factor, as collaboration and sharing is a critical success factor in furthering Government transformation.

A plethora of practices and programmes often leads to confusion and resentment to anything new, EA included. Typical response in such scenarios includes furious efforts to measure and demonstrate the value of EA programmes. It is also typical for EA programmes not to be tightly coupled to other relevant management practices. The positioning of and linkages to and from EA vis-à-vis other relevant upstream and downstream management practices were finalized following careful analyses of current and future practices.

MAGENTA is inherently designed as a strategic alignment tool that allows agencies to realize the Integrated Enterprise Lifecycle. Figure 6 shows the approach taken by MAGENTA for positioning EA within existing management practices. This approach allows agencies to maintain linkages

Figure 5. Current IT / IS planning based approach

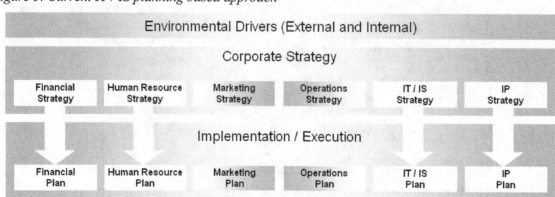

Figure 6. EA based approach with MAGENTA

between their respective functional strategies and plans (depicted as dotted line arrows in Figure 6). However as an enhancement, the EA layer between corporate strategy and implementation facilitates common standards, requirements, principles and effective governance and control. It is intended to allow agencies to move towards shallower 'silos' and seek greater collaboration opportunities both within and between agencies. This is further described later and portrayed in Figure 7.

Internally within an agency, linking EA to other management practices not only ensures its continuity and sustainability, but also tighter vertical and horizontal alignment (Armour et. al, 2007). Figure 7 is an expanded view of Figure 6, and shows the Integrated Enterprise Lifecycle approach realizable with MAGENTA. For the Government agencies it is critical to clarify the positioning of EA vis-à-vis other management practices like IT Planning, IT Portfolio Management because:

- Almost all EA programmes are primarily driven by the IT / IS department,
- EA is often equated to IT Architecture and hence relegated as 'yet another technology initiative',

- Integration leads to higher degree of management attention and as a consequence greater sustainability of the EA programme, and
- Facilitation of participation by individual agencies and contribution to overall GEA is critical to the success of Government transformation.

Adopting MAGENTA: A Generic EA Methodology

Moving forward MAGENTA continues to be referred by government agencies and adopted as needed. MAGENTA has been piloted in one of the government agencies. To provide a summarized view of the agency's EA, Figure 8 shows the template of a one-page schematic.

The template is meant for agencies' use to derive their respective agency EA schematic. The EA schematic is intended to portray the eventual target EA for an agency developing its EA using MAGENTA and is an effective management practice in high maturity organizations (Ross, Weill and Robertson, 2006). The template is organized to provide an easy-to-use tool that can be populated and usage scenarios built by answering a few simple questions. Table 7 pro-

Figure 7. Integrated enterprise lifecycle with MAGENTA

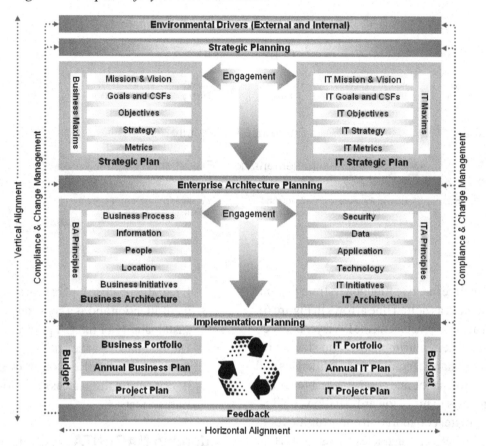

vides the explanation of the layers in the generic EA schematic (shown in Figure 8). Table 7 is also used to craft the usage scenarios.

The objectives of the agency specific EA schematic derived from the generic EA schematic (Figure 8) and the scenarios (Table 7) include:

- Portrayal of EA core view that can be linked to subsequent levels,
- Support for agency's target operating model and modular architecture maturity level,
- Depiction of relationships between domain architectures (business, information, solution and technology architectures) and different views as shown in Figure 9,
- Provision of clear line of sight for various usage scenarios as shown in Figure 10.

This is accomplished through building a few critical business scenarios, where such scenarios do not represent all potential paths and branches through the generic EA schematic, but simply a subset of LOBs, business functions, data entities, service components and enterprise systems and applications that get utilized to realize the scenario(s). The scenarios allow various stakeholders with varied responsibilities and organizational roles in the agency to 'find themselves' within the EA. This leads to better understanding of the influence and impact these stakeholders have on the EA and their role in it.

- Portrayal of architectural elements (business processes, data entities, application services,

Figure 8. Generic agency EA Schematic for developing target enterprise architecture

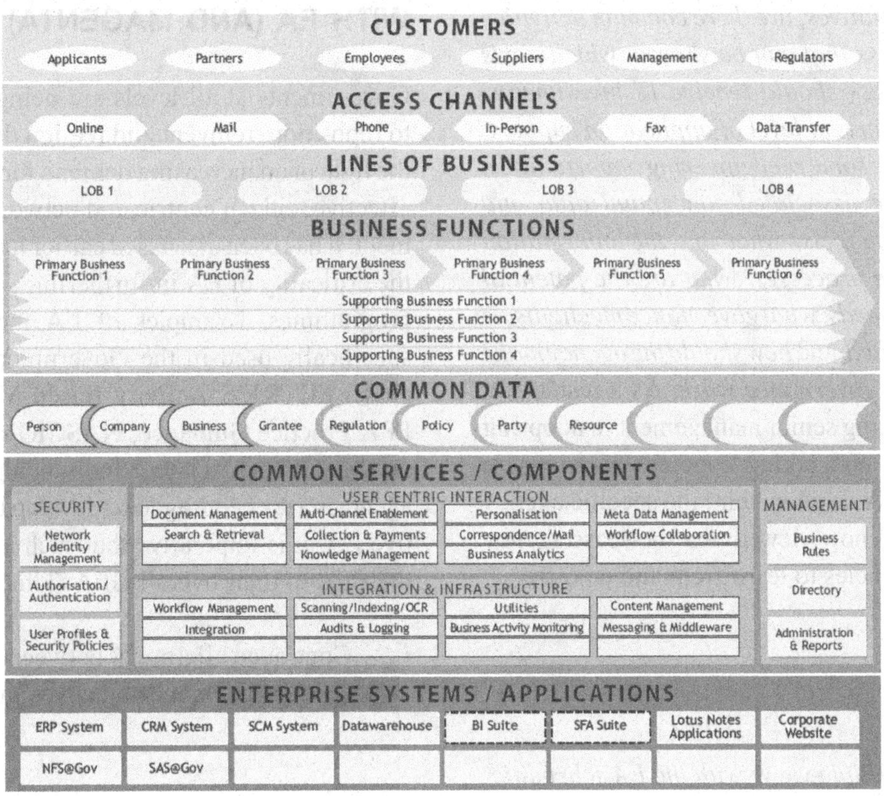

Table 7. Layers of the generic EA schematic / scenario summary template

	Brief Description
Customer	Identifies the requesting party desiring the agency service(s).
Access Channel	Identifies the access channel that the requesting party uses to request the service(s).
Line of Business (LOB)	Identifies which LOB the requested service belongs to or which LOB provides the service.
Business Function	Identifies the business function(s) that support the agency LOB which delivers the business service being requested.
Common Data	Identifies the data entities that the business functions (and the underlying business processes) utilize to support the fulfillment of the requested service.
Common Services / Applications	Identifies the service components required to provide the necessary functionalities and capabilities needed to deliver the requested business service.
Enterprise Systems	Identifies the systems / applications required to provide the necessary functionalities and capabilities needed to deliver the requested business service.

technical services) that can contribute to the Government Reference Models as shown in Figure 11. This aspect is further elaborated and depicted in Figure 12.

A detailed discussion of the agency case study where MAGENTA was piloted is outside the scope of this chapter. However the agency's EA addressed several strategic questions like *how do core business processes impact the agency's strategic initiatives, are there common activities in this process that can be shared, which parts of the business should receive IT investments, what is the current level of application support, what could be some reengineering opportunities, what are the associated conceptual data and application models, what are the information needs for the processes, what are the potential integration needs, what governance mechanisms must be adopted,* and *how should the agency make architecture governance work.* As a result of a forward looking senior management in adopting MAGENTA and taking concrete decisions in furthering EA development, the specific agency in question is now viewed as a showcase agency for other agencies to learn from and emulate.

GOVERNMENT TRANSFORMATION WITH EA (AND MAGENTA)

Governments at all levels are being challenged to reposition, reinvent and realign themselves in the light of an increasing demand for a more cost-effective, citizen centric and networked government. It has been discussed earlier in this chapter, the criticality of EA in furthering e-government programmes. Examples of EA methodologies specifically used in the Government sector include: MITRE'S Activity Based Methodology, FEA Practice Guidance, NASCIO's EA Toolkit and MAGENTA. Though individual government agencies are encouraged to develop their respective EA, it is imperative that such agencies link their EA to their overall GEA. This ensures:

- Continued alignment between overall government goals and objectives and individual

Figure 9. Multiple views with the EA schematic

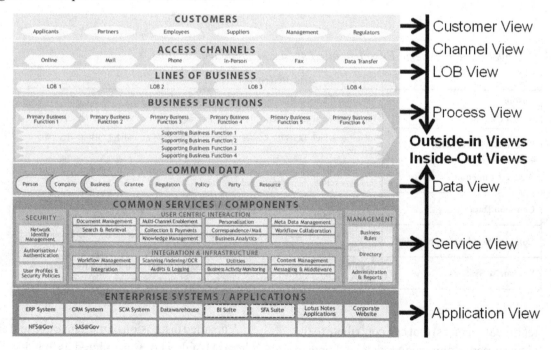

Figure 10. Line of sight with the EA schematic

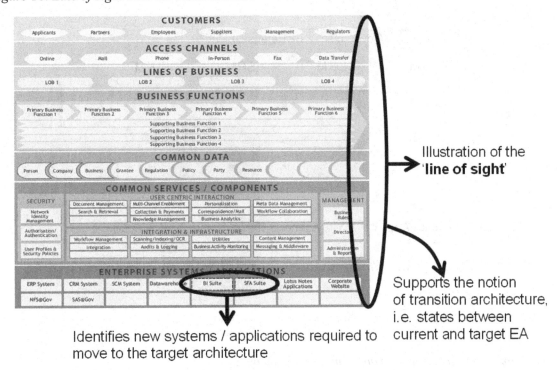

Illustration of the
'**line of sight**'

Supports the notion
of transition architecture,
i.e. states between
current and target EA

Identifies new systems / applications required to
move to the target architecture

Figure 11. Linkage to government-wide reference models with the EA schematic

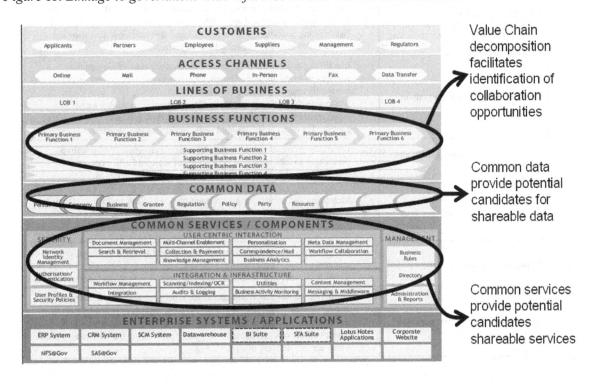

Value Chain
decomposition
facilitates
identification of
collaboration
opportunities

Common data
provide potential
candidates for
shareable data

Common services
provide potential
candidates
shareable services

Figure 12. Linking agency EA to GEA for government-wide services

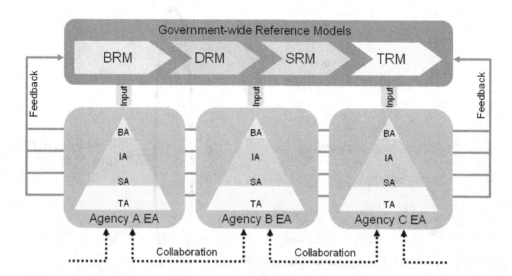

Table 8. Support for government transformation trends by EA

	Government Transformation Trend	Support Provided by EA (examples of specific mechanisms and tools)
1	**Changing the rules**	• Viewing the government in a holistic manner and as a single federated entity instead of piecemeal agency or departmental view. • Focussing on delivering core government services in an efficient manner with an outcome oriented approach. • Establishing government-wide policies and standards, but also allowing autonomy to individual agencies and departments.
2	**Using performance management**	• Identifying and constantly assessing the performance of Government services in terms of lines of businesses, functions and business processes and constantly renewing them as needed. • Evaluating the performance of the EA programme through a set of assessment criteria and linking it to the budgetary process. • Linking EA up to organizational goals, strategies and measures.
3	**Providing competition, choice and incentives**	• Establishing shared services center to cater to common administrative procedures to take benefit of economies of scale and efficiency returns. • Instituting mechanisms to support public-private partnerships.
4	**Performing on demand**	• Measuring and improving government responsiveness by having clarity on underlying business processes, data, applications, and technologies. • Focussing on core government functions and business processes.
5	**Engaging citizens**	• Providing updated government information and services in a seamless manner. • Viewing citizens and businesses as customers of government services.
6	**Using networks and partnerships**	• Furthering collaboration and cooperation between agencies and departments through common and shared processes, data, applications and technologies. • Reorganizing government services in terms of lines of businesses and business functions (irrespective of agency performing the function) to build a new service delivery system.

agency goals and objectives (some degree of vertical integration)

- Continued alignment and ongoing collaboration among the various agencies (horizontal integration)
- Agency participation and contribution to the GEA (enabling the federated governance structure)

In 2006, the IBM Center for The Business of Government published a report discussing the six trends of transforming government (Abramson, Breul and Kamensky, 2006). Table 8 delineates how EA (and MAGENTA) supports these trends.

FUTURE ENHANCEMENTS AND RESEARCH

The full potential of e-government can only be achieved by complete integration of government services across different government agencies and different levels of government. In 2000, the Harvard Policy Group at the John. F. Kennedy School of Government published the eight imperatives in ICT for Government leaders, which are:

1. Focus on how IT can reshape work and public sector strategies,
2. Use IT for strategic innovation, not just for tactical automation,
3. Use best practices in implementing IT initiatives,
4. Improve budgeting and financing for promising IT initiatives,
5. Protect privacy and security,
6. Form IT related partnerships to stimulate economic development,
7. Use IT to promote equal opportunities and healthy communities, and
8. Prepare for digital democracy.

The essence of these imperatives is to drive home the point that for successful and effective e-government, Government leaders must be deeply engaged in ICT and related issues. In an era where countries are focussing on transformation to information and knowledge society this is a critical success factor. A review of current literature clearly reveals that EA plays a very critical role in fulfilling the imperatives. Research conducted at the John. F. Kennedy School of Government and the MIT Sloan Centre for Information Systems Research further corroborate this point.

MAGENTA is now available to agencies for reference and adoption through the government intranet. Development and availability of MAGENTA for agencies to build their own EA to drive the e-government programme is the first step. Plausible areas for future enhancements and research could include:

- **Governance and regulation:** In the United States, the Clinger-Cohen Act of 1996 was cited as one of the reasons for Government agencies to develop their EA. While laws and regulations can be useful to initiate the development, it remains to be seen if they are really useful in sustaining the interest. It has been observed that agencies at times develop their EA 'just to meet regulatory requirements'. This defeats the very purpose of developing EA. Thus research on *effectiveness of regulation driven EA adoption* is clearly an area to be worked on.
- **IT engagement:** Leadership is an essential ingredient for success in EA and e-government (Ross, Weill and Robertson, 2006) and this is amply evident from the eight imperatives discussed earlier. Leadership includes Legislators, Governors, Budget Directors, Agency Heads and CIOs. For this to happen agencies need a formal IT engagement model, more so because traditionally e-government is viewed as an IT initiative that is delegated to the CIO and

the IT Department. The engagement model ensures continuous involvement of the top management leaders in EA, thus guaranteeing management attention and interest. Development of *IT engagement framework specific to e-government* is an area for future enhancement.

- **Maturity model:** This would allow agencies to be assessed and benchmarked. Properly used, such models have the potential to identify shortcomings in agency EA development and actually spur the development and effectiveness of EA. The suggestion is to have a more holistic perspective where EA is viewed not just as an engineering activity but also as an investment activity in which case real options approach can be adopted (Saha, 2006). A related area of research is to *explore and understand the interplay between EA Maturity and EA Design Models.*

- **Outsourcing:** Agencies in the Government outsource IT and IT enabled services for reasons including lower costs, variable capacity, risk mitigation, process improvement and opportunity to focus on core capabilities. The consolidation of common finance and human resource services to public agencies under VITAL.org (Centre for Shared Services) is an example of outsourcing in the Singapore Government. Of the three mutually exclusive outsourcing models, i.e. *strategic partnership, co-sourcing* and *transaction outsourcing* (Ross, Weill and Robertson, 2006), VITAL.org falls into the *transaction outsourcing* category vis-à-vis other public agencies. Further research followed by *enhancement of MAGENTA to incorporate architectural implications of outsourcing (specifically transaction outsourcing model)* would be very critical.

- **Service oriented architecture:** As seen in Tables 5 and 6, higher levels of EA (es-

pecially **business modularity**) positively influences the movement to higher levels of e-government. SOA facilitates realizing business modularity and deriving its full benefits (Ross, Weill and Robertson, 2006). Enhancing MAGENTA to incorporate elements of SOA, including development of a *Service Oriented Reference Architecture and Methodology* would allow individual agencies to adopt and take benefit of SOA. A rising interest in SOA has already been observed among Singapore agencies.

CONCLUSION

Leading countries in e-government tend to share a number of underlying characteristics. As with other leading countries, e-government in Singapore is about good governance. Good governance practices include: legitimacy, rule of law, transparency, integrity, efficiency, coherence, adaptability to new challenges, participation and engagement. As agencies realise the need to move beyond mere operational efficiencies through automation to transformation of the business of government, EA comes to the forefront as an enabling mechanism. Over the years Singapore's e-government has matured and won several accolades from United Nations, Accenture, Harvard University, Brown University, and World Economic Forum among others. iGOV 2010, its current five-year e-government plan, is poised to take it to the next level. Through an analysis of current literature on e-government stage models and EA maturity models, the chapter demonstrated close linkages between the two. Acknowledging the role played by EA to the success of e-government programme the Singapore government commissioned the development of an EA methodology, MAGENTA, for adoption by individual agencies in building their respective EA. **Nonetheless, with minor adaptations MAGENTA is generic enough to** be adopted by agencies in other governments and also organizations outside of the government sector.

MAGENTA has been designed to facilitate IT-enabled business transformation and is structured to amalgamate with IT Governance to support investment planning. Tool, technology and framework independent, MAGENTA provides agencies complete line of sight. However this is not the end. It marks the achievement of a significant milestone, but as is well known 'EA is a verb, not a noun', hence evolution and enhancement of MAGENTA must continue as more agencies start their EA journey.

ACKNOWLEDGMENT

The author would like to acknowledge the MOF and IDA who funded the development of MAGENTA and Intellectual Property Office of Singapore (IPOS) for guidance, assistance and contributions during the development.

The author gratefully acknowledges the significant contributions by Chung Mui Ken [IDA], Seleana Ng [IDA], Gan Wei Boon [IDA], Alvin Kuah [IDA], Grace Tin [IDA], David Lam [IDA] and Tan Eng Tsze [NUS] that made the MAGENTA possible.

REFERENCES

Abramson, M.A., Breul, J.D., & Kamensky, J.M. (2006). Six Trends Transforming Government. *IBM Center for The Business of Government Report*. Retrieved September 7, 2007, from http://www.businessofgovernment.org/pdfs/Six-Trends.pdf.

Armour, F. J., Emery, C., Houk, J., Kaisler, S. H., & Kirk, J.S. (2007). The Integrated Enterprise Lifecycle: Enterprise Architecture, Investment Management and System Development. In Saha, P. (Ed.). *Handbook of Enterprise Systems Architecture in Practice*. Hershey, PA: IGI Global Information Science Reference.

Baum, C., & Di Maio, A. (2000). Gartner's Four Phases of E-Government Model. *Gartner Group Research Note*. Retrieved June 15, 2007, from http://aln.hha.dk/IFI/Hdi/2001/ITstrat/Download/Gartner_eGovernment.pdf.

Bittler, R.S., & Kreizman, G. (2005). Gartner Enterprise Architecture Process: Evolution 2005. *Gartner Group Research Note*, G00130849. Retrieved July 27, 2007, from http://www.gartner.com/research/spotlight/asset_50080.jsp.

Deloitte and Touché (2001). The Citizen as Customer. *CMA Management*, 74(10), 58.

Gil-Garcia, J.R., & Pardo, T.A. (2005). E-Government success factors: mapping practical tools to theoretical foundations. *Government Information Quarterly*, 22(2), 187-216.

Government of British Columbia (2004). e-Government Plan. Office of the Chief Information Officer, Ministry of Management Services. Retrieved June 18, 2007, from www.cio.gov.bc.ca/ebc/egovplan20041215.pdf.

Government of Western Australia (2004). e-Government Strategy for the Western Australian Public Sector. Office of e-Government, Department of the Premier and Cabinet. Retrieved June 18, 2007, from http://www.egov.dpc.wa.gov.au/documents/e-government_strategy.doc.

Harvard Policy Group on Network Enabled Services and Government (2000). *Eight Imperatives for Leaders in a Networked World: Guidelines for the 2000 Election and Beyond*, John F. Kennedy School of Government, Cambridge, MA. Retrieved June 18, 2007, from www.ksg.harvard.edu/stratcom/hpg/index.htm.

Hiller, J. & Belanger, F. (2001). *Privacy Strategies for Electronic Government*. E-Government Series. Arlington, VA: PricewaterhouseCoopers Endowment for the Business of Government.

Infocomm Development Authority of Singapore (2005). Singapore E-Government 2005. *2005 Report on Singapore E-Government*. Retrieved November 13, 2007, from www.igov.gov.sg/NR/rdonlyres/C586E52F-176A-44B6-B21E-2DB7E4FA45D1/11228/2005ReportonSporeeGov.pdf.

12. Keng, S., & Long, Y. (2005). Synthesizing e-government stage models – a meta-synthesis based on meta-ethnography approach. *Industrial Management & Data Systems*, 105(4), 443-458.

Kreizman, G., Baum, C., & Fraga, E. (2003). Gartner Enterprise Architecture: A Home for E-Government. *Gartner Group Research Note*, TU-20-1831. Retrieved June 15, 2007, from http://www.gartner.com/research/spotlight/asset_50080.jsp.

Layne, K., & Lee, J. (2001). Developing fully functional e-government: a four stage model. *Government Information Quarterly*, 18(2), 122-136.

Moon, M.J. (2002). The evolution of e-government among municipalities: rhetoric or reality?. *Public Administration Review*, 62(4), 424-433.

Ross, J.W. (2006). Design Priorities for the IT Unit of the Future. *MIT Sloan CISR Research Briefings*, 4(3D). Retrieved September 7, 2007, from http://mitsloan.mit.edu/cisr/papers.php.

Ross, J.W., Weill, P., & Robertson, D.C. (2006). *Enterprise Architecture as Strategy*. Boston, MA: Harvard Business School Press.

Saha, P. (2006). A Real Options Perspective to Enterprise Architecture as an Investment Activity. *Journal of Enterprise Architecture*, 2(3), 32-52.

Saha, P. (2007a). A Synergistic Assessment of the Federal Enterprise Architecture Framework against GERAM (ISO 15704:2000). In Saha, P. (Ed.). *Handbook of Enterprise Systems Architecture in Practice*. Hershey, PA: IGI Global Information Science Reference.

Saha, P. (Ed.). (2007b). *Handbook of Enterprise Systems Architecture in Practice*. Hershey, PA: IGI Global Information Science Reference.

Tan, E.P., & Gan, W.B. (2007). Enterprise Architecture in Singapore Government. In Saha, P. (Ed.). *Handbook of Enterprise Systems Architecture in Practice*. Hershey, PA: IGI Global Information Science Reference.

The World Bank (2003). Retrieved June 18, 2007, from http://Web.worldbank.org/WBSITE/EXTERNAL/TOPICS/EXTINFORMATIONANDCOMMUNICATIONANDTECHNOLOGIES/EXTEGOVERNMENT/contentMDK:20507153~menuPK:702592~pagePK:148956~piPK:216618~theSitePK:702586,00.html.

United Nations and American Society for Public Administration (2001). Global Survey of E-Government, Retrieved June 15, 2007, from http://www.unpan.org/egovernment2.asp.

United States Federal Enterprise Architecture Programme Management Office (2006). FEA Consolidated Reference Model, Version 2.0. Retrieved June 18, 2007, from http://www.whitehouse.gov/omb/egov/a-1-fea.html.

ADDITIONAL READINGS

Australian Government Information Management Office. (2006). *Australian Government Architecture*. Department of Finance and Administration. Retrieved June 18, 2007, from http://www.agimo.gov.au/government/australian_government_architecture.

Australian Government Information Management Office. (2006). *Responsive Government: A New Service Agenda*. Department of Finance and Administration. Retrieved June 18, 2007, from http://www.agimo.gov.au/publications/2006/march/introduction_to_responsive_government.

National Association of State CIOs. (2004). *Enterprise Architecture Development Toolkit Version 3.0.* Retrieved June 18, 2007, from http://www.nascio.org/resources/EAresources.cfm.

Treasury Board of Canada. (2004). *Business Transformation Enablement Program.* Retrieved June 18, 2007, from http://www.tbs-sct.gc.ca/btep-pto/index_e.asp.

Weill, P., & Aral, S. (2006). Generating Premium Returns on Your IT Investments. *MIT Sloan Management Review*, 47(2), 39-48.

Chapter II
A Service–Oriented Reference Architecture for E–Government

Marc M. Lankhorst
Telematica Instituut, The Netherlands

Guido I.H.M. Bayens
Novius, The Netherlands

ABSTRACT

This chapter describes the development and future directions of a service-oriented reference architecture for the Dutch government. For several years now, the Dutch government has put a focus on improving the service level of public agencies. Electronic services play an important part in this, which requires a concerted effort across many organizations. A reference architecture has been created in order to guide the many different programmes and projects. In this chapter, we will describe the role of service orientation in e-government, and the creation, structure, and first results of this reference architecture for e-government. Furthermore, we will look ahead at future developments in integrated, demand-driven service provisioning in e-government.

INTRODUCTION

For several years now, the Dutch government has put a focus on improving the service level of public agencies. Electronic services play an important part in this. At the same time, the agencies involved had to be readied for electronic cooperation, to facilitate the cross-agency service delivery that is needed to provide seamless, demand-driven services to citizens. Sharing information between agencies is needed to avoid asking citizens the same information over and over again, and to create greater efficiency and less duplication in back-office processes and systems.

This requires a concerted effort across many organizations. Service orientation is an important new paradigm that can help to structure and coordinate this effort both at the level of business processes and at the level of the supporting technologies. A service-oriented reference architecture for Dutch governmental institutions has been created in order to guide the many different programmes and projects. This reference architecture comprises the overall structure of the Dutch e-government landscape, and provides a series of construction principles for e-government.

A reference architecture comprises a set of general construction principles and explanatory models to help architects in various positions to create dedicated architectures for specific business solutions. Thus, it provides a common ground for the many architects that are working on the development of the e-government targets. It is used in auditing project progress and in setting standards for the results that have to be gained.

In this chapter, we will describe the role of service orientation in e-government, and the creation, structure, and first results of this reference architecture for e-government. Furthermore, we will look ahead at future developments in integrated, demand-driven service provisioning in e-government. As such, the Dutch situation may serve as an example for others of applying the principles of service-orientation in an e-government context, and of the benefits and impact of service thinking in this situation.

BACKGROUND

Over the last decade, the pressure on public agencies to improve their services has increased sharply. Citizens and enterprises nowadays expect governmental services to be delivered in the same manner that, for example, insurance companies offer theirs. People do not want to stand in line in front of a service desk of public agencies, like municipalities, customs or social security agencies. They want to interact quickly, via modern communication channels, and obtain a high and transparent service level. And enterprises would like to develop a more sophisticated way of co-operation and interaction with public institutions than the traditional paper-based bureaucracy.

These demands and expectations did have a modest effect on Dutch governmental institutions. During the second half of the nineties, public bodies were challenged to create their own Websites. Less visible was an initiative of several big agencies in the public domain to set up a shared network for data exchange. In spite of these developments, generally speaking, real electronic services from public institutions did not appear yet.

Based on an enquiry among 1500 people, the Dutch citizen panel Citizen@Government ("Burger@Overheid" in Dutch) has drawn up a code of conduct for service to citizens (Burger@ Overheid, 2005) to which public institutions should adhere in providing e-government services. This charter consists of quality standards that define the digital relation between citizen and government (in the fields of information exchange, service delivery, and political participation). These standards are formulated as rights citizens are entitled to, and matching obligations by government bodies. They are in the interest of both citizen and government and they allow citizens to call their government to account for the quality of online contacts. Conversely, public institutions can use the charter to examine the external quality of their e-government services. Thus, the charter is an instrument to stimulate the further development of e-government from the citizen's perspective.

This code of conduct lists ten basic principles for Dutch public services:

1. As a citizen, I have the right to choose the channel for doing business with the government.
2. As a citizen, I can easily find government products and services.
3. As a citizen, I can easily understand government services, and my rights and obligations as a citizen are clear.
4. As a citizen, I have a right to accurate, complete, and actual information, and the government provides this proactively, tailored to my situation.
5. As a citizen, I only have to provide information once. The government tells me what it knows about me and does not use my personal data without my permission.
6. As a citizen, I can easily find out how the government operates, and it keeps me informed about the status of procedures in which I am involved.
7. As a citizen, I can trust the reliability of e-government. The government guarantees digital privacy, secure digital interaction, and careful digital archiving.
8. As a citizen, I can easily give feedback to the government. The government corrects mistakes, compensates shortcomings, and uses complaints to learn from.
9. As a citizen, I can compare, check and assess the performance of public bodies. The government actively provides the necessary information.
10. As a citizen, I am empowered to actively look after my interests. The government promotes participation and provides the necessary means.

Next to citizens, industry also expects an improved service level from government institutions. They would like to have a public service that produces less red tape, less regulations, less procedural complexity, and consequently, lower administrative costs.

These demands from both citizens as companies gave birth to a new governmental action programme, called "Different Government" ("Andere Overheid" in Dutch). The goal of this programme was to stimulate the transition to a modern, transparent and highly effective way of governing the Dutch state, provinces and municipalities. The main goals of this programme (which has now been subsumed by the Centre for Good Governance of the Dutch Ministry of the Interior) are:

*   Higher quality of service
*   Less red tape and regulations
*   A more comprehensive government policy
*   More cross-agency cooperation

Several sub-programmes of this action plan were developed. One of them was called "electronic government" or "e-government", which aims for a more comprehensive approach in the use of modern information technology supporting the goals of the "Different Government" programme. Some concrete goals of the e-government programme are:

*   To have 65% of the most important public services available via the Internet by the end of 2007;
*   To register data that is used by many public bodies, like data from citizens, companies, buildings, addresses and incomes in a centralized manner and provide it to official agencies when necessary and allowed, to promote reuse and data quality and to prevent asking citizens the same questions over and over again;
*   To provide every citizen and every company with a unique, electronic identity which will be used for identification and authentication purposes in public, electronic communication.

A knowledge centre was put in place for the dissemination of information about the progress of e-government initiatives, good practices, and information about ongoing projects. Programmes were set up for municipalities and provinces to stimulate the adoption of the e-government goals, and so-called "implementation teams" offer assistance to public bodies by developing project plans and the transfer of specific knowledge. In addition to these national programmes, sectoral and regional projects were also initialized. In total, many hundreds of projects, with a total budget of several hundred million euros, are aiming to improve Dutch e-government across the board.

Because of this growing number of national, sectoral and regional projects, some stakeholders became aware of the necessity of architectural guidance. The need for an interoperability framework and standards became more evident. This thought resulted in a new programme, to set up an e-government reference architecture to coordinate and guide all these developments.

REFERENCE ARCHITECTURE

In 2002, the Dutch Ministry of the Interior had a meta-architectural framework developed that would serve as the basis for further architectural initiatives. A further developed version of this meta-framework, which is based on various existing frameworks and methods, such as those of Zachman (1987), Maes (1999), TOGAF (The Open Group, 2006) and others, is shown in Figure 1.

This meta-architectural framework formed the basis for the development of the Dutch Government Reference Architecture (in Dutch: "Nederlandse Overheid Referentie Architectuur", NORA) (Bayens et al., 2007). The goal of this reference architecture is to create a common ground for the many architects that are working on the development of the e-government targets.

The initial reference architecture rested on two pillars: The first was formed by the architectural choices that had been made by the various national programmes that were going to have a

Figure 1. Meta-architectural framework (Bayens et al., 2007)

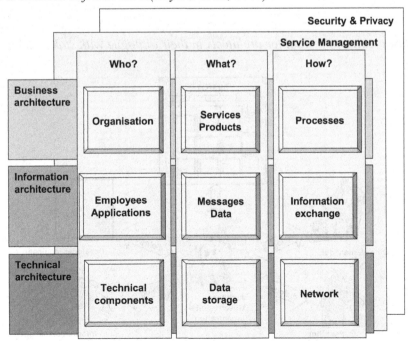

serious impact on the final architecture of the Dutch e-government, such as programmes for the development of national registrations, for e-security, and for the development and use of open standards. The second pillar was formed by the influence from several large government agencies, like the national social security agencies and the tax and customs administration. Architects from these programmes and agencies have had a great influence on the emergence of the initial draft of the Dutch Government Reference Architecture.

Creating this reference architecture was a non-trivial effort. During the development of the architecture, more and more architects from different programmes and governmental organizations took part in the discussions about the main architectural principles and models. In this way, a more robust version of the framework was developed, and the first version of the architecture was published in May 2006. Several rounds of consultation and review have lead to the current version 2.0, which was published in April 2007. At the moment, the architecture is broadly supported by both architects and decision makers in the Dutch e-government context.

Position and Role of the Reference Architecture

As we stated before, the goal of developing this reference architecture was to create a common ground for the many, many architects that are working on the development of the various elements of Dutch e-government. The idea is that architects should have a sound influence on the construction principles of e-government. From their respective positions in projects and institutions, they could take care of the necessary coherence between the many aspects of the e-government: Websites, data storage, process flow, semantics, data communication, messages, preferred technology, and so on. Architects assist in setting up e-government projects and business solutions, they advise programme and project managers about construction principles, and they play a role in giving instructions to business process analysts and software developers. Furthermore, the reference architecture is used in auditing project progress and in setting standards for the results that have to be gained.

Figure 2. Reference architecture: Tool for architects in their dialogue with stakeholders

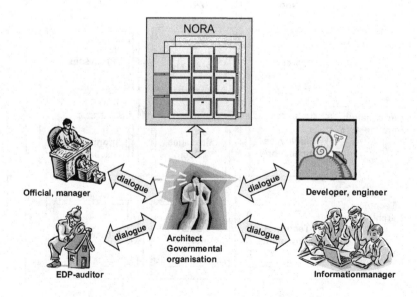

Figure 3. Hierarchy of architectures

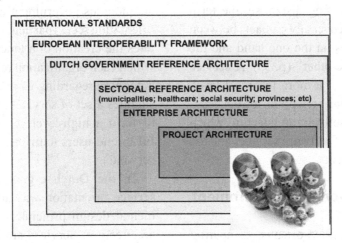

As Figure 2 shows, the idea of a reference architecture is that this set of construction principles and explanatory models helps architects in various positions to create dedicated architectures for specific business solutions. In this way, one can see a hierarchical set of architectural frameworks, ranging from international frameworks such as the European Interoperability Framework (EIF) (European Commission, 2004), via national and sectoral reference architectures, down to enterprise architectures and finally the architectures of individual projects. Just like the Russian matrushka dolls, the smaller fitting inside the larger (Figure 3).

As we saw before, demands from citizens and companies played a dominant role in the idea of what e-government should be. Therefore their demands had to be translated into architectural principles. A second influence came from the already mentioned programmes and agency's working on e-government, and developments in other countries, such as Austria (2006), Denmark (2006), Germany (2007), the UK (2005), the US (2007), and Hong Kong (2007).

For example, the eGov initiative in the USA comprises the development of a Federal Enterprise Architecture (FEA) (US, 2007), "a business-based framework for government-wide improvement."

This architecture has a broader scope than the Dutch reference architecture, since it also includes e.g. aspects of budget allocation and performance measurement, but in the core its goals are similar: to provide government architects with guidance in the form of reference models. It comprises a number of different reference models at different architectural layers. Especially interesting to the Dutch initiative is the Service Component Reference Model part of the FEA, which classifies services in a number of domains, such as customer, process automation, business management, back office, digital asset, and support. The idea is that these represent categories of services that are reusable across multiple government organizations, similar to the e-government building blocks of the Dutch reference architecture.

Another interesting example is the German SAGA architecture (Germany, 2007), which is based on the RM-ODP viewpoints (ITU, 1995). SAGA's enterprise viewpoint has a role similar to the high-level architecture principles advocated in the Dutch reference architecture, and defines a "service" as "the complete performance of a process for the citizen or business in question. A service includes processes, obligations and burdens, such as recognition as a conscientious objector, applications for unemployment benefits or the granting of an import permit. For the purposes of the following discourse, the term "service" will hence cover any contacts between citizens or businesses on the one hand and the administration on the other" (p. 35). A service concept is also used at a more technical level. SAGA's computational viewpoint introduces a multi-layer reference software architecture, which permits both the use of software services and the direct use of components.

Service Orientation in E-Government

The emergence of service-oriented computing (SOC) and Web services technology, in particular, has aroused enormous interest in the service-oriented architecture paradigm (SOA). At first, service orientation was seen as a strictly IT-related issue. However, a purely technological focus would be too limited and would fail to appreciate the value of the much more general service concept. This essentially simple concept can and should be used not just in software engineering, but also at all other levels of an architecture, to achieve ultimate flexibility in both business processes and their IT support.

What makes the service concept so appealing? First, there is the fact that the service concept is used and understood in the different domains making up an enterprise. In using the service concept, the business and IT people have a mutually understandable "language", which facilitates their communication. Second, service orientation has a positive effect on a number of key issues: interoperability, agility, cost effectiveness, and innovation power. Finally, service orientation stimulates new ways of thinking. Traditionally, applications are considered to support a specific business process, which in turn realizes a specific business service. Service orientation allows us also to adopt a bottom-up strategy, where the business processes are just a mechanism of instantiating and exploiting the lower-level services to the outside world (Steen et al., 2005).

In the context of cooperating but relatively autonomous government organizations, service orientation seems particularly attractive. It facilitates the creation of a federated architecture, in which each organization retains a high degree of autonomy regarding its internal processing, and supplies a set of services that can be integrated to form a high-level service that is meaningful to end-users (citizens, companies, and civil servants).

In the Dutch e-government architecture, service orientation was adopted as the fundamental design principle, underlying the entire architecture. Services are not only used in the narrow sense, i.e., the service as a self contained software module that performs a certain function, but in a broad sense: Not only services between a governmental body and a citizen or a company are regarded from this perspective, but also the way two or more governmental bodies are working together, and the cooperation between two or more departments of one institution.

Until recently, SOA was often understood as a technical issue and focused only on software architecture. However, the service concept is much more broadly applicable than that, which stands to reason given its original background as a business concept. Service orientation is also a very useful concept to structure the business architecture of an organization, especially in the networked institutions of e-government. It provides a conceptual basis for the entire enterprise architecture of an organization (Steen et al., 2005).

Service orientation is a concept with wide-ranging implications on more than just a technical level. From an organizational perspective, the fundamental change is that the basic unit for management and control is no longer a department with its own IT systems, but rather a much smaller entity, a business service. Monolithic, department-bound systems will disappear, and former business owners will lose control over what they thought was "their" operation. This decomposition opens up many opportunities for combining basic services into new, demand- or event-driven ensembles that really address citizens' needs. However, new management issues arise, such as control responsibility within such multi-party networks of e-government service providers.

An important consequence of service orientation for the Dutch reference architecture discussed in this chapter, was that the chosen meta-framework had to be adjusted, which lead the final version as shown in Figure 1. This adjusted meta-framework was used to develop a coherent set of construction principles for e-government.

Principles and Building Blocks

The Dutch Government Reference Architecture consists of two main types of content: architectural principles and high-level designs of e-government building blocks. The principles and models of this reference architecture have been drawn up in consultation with many architects from different programmes and governmental organizations.

The various principles are organized in the architectural meta-framework presented previously. Each cell of the architectural framework is filled with 10 to 20 architectural principles. Every principle is written down as a short statement, which is followed by a more elaborated explanation. Finally every principle has a status identification. Some principles could be derived immediately from legislation; these principles are called "*de jure* principles". The next type is called "e-government principles". These should be adopted by as many governmental bodies as possible, because they are the basis for cooperation and interoperability. Some people plead for putting these principles in a formal statute to make them more compelling. A final type of principles is called "recommendations". These are principles that only affect the internal architecture of a governmental body. This type of principles is seen as advisory, and the reference architecture in this respect serves as a body of knowledge for architects. In the appendix to this

Figure 4. Overview of Dutch e-government reference architecture (Bayens et al., 2007)

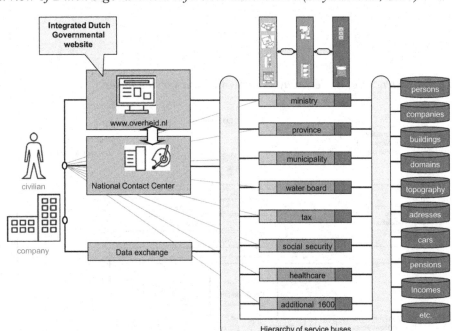

chapter, some of the main principles are listed according to the cells within the meta-framework in which they fit.

But principles alone are not enough to make an architecture usable. Guidance in applying these principles and concrete high-level designs of architectural components, the so-called e-government building blocks, are also indispensable.

One of the first steps in the development of the architecture was, therefore, to develop high-level models of the most important e-government components. In these so-called "overview maps", relevant items like national information registries, a network infrastructure, the various institutions and the common front-office channels were visualized. Figure 4 shows one result of this approach. Quite important are the symbols of both the citizen and the company as a focus point and reminder of the fact that every step and every action is devoted to these two actors.

The structure of the overall architecture, with a citizen-facing left-hand side, the various government institutions and agencies in the middle, and shared information registries on the right, is reflected in the design of the individual organizations in the middle. This is of course derived

from the common three-tier architectural pattern of presentation, business logic, and data.

In the same way, additional overview maps were developed for more specific areas of the most general overview map in order to give some more detail of under laying structures. Figure 5 shows an example: This picture shows the design of a hierarchical composition of European, Dutch, and sectoral service buses, partially based on already existing buses, but brought together and completed in an overall infrastructure architecture. Today, several parties are developing networks and service buses, based on this relatively simple architectural design.

The goal of these overview maps is to facilitate the discussion about the main architectural issues. Not only the discussions amongst architects, but also the discussion between government officials, programme managers on the one hand and architects on the other. Overview maps bridge the alignment gap between "business" and "builders".

A second important line of action is the development of common building blocks of the e-government architecture. To mention some of the most important:

Figure 5. The infrastructure: A hierarchy of networks and service buses

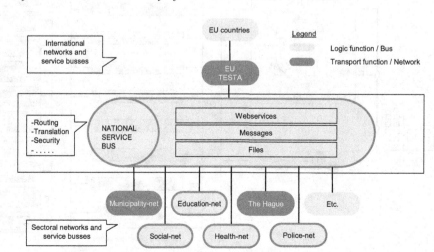

- National e-government portal for citizens, where each citizen can have his/her personalized "my government" page
- National e-government portal for companies
- National call centre for the Dutch public sector
- Unique personal number to facilitate the exchange of information and the integration of services across government agencies
- Unique number for companies and institutions
- National authentication service, with different levels of security and corresponding means for authentication
- New smartcard-based national identity card, which contains biometrical data
- National repository for all public services and products
- Mechanism providing and handling Web forms
- National infrastructure for the exchange of messages and services

This type of standard components of e-government will play a more and more dominant role in the development of comprehensive e-government solutions, especially across agencies. They will help to overcome interoperability problems and increase transparency and efficiency in the Dutch public sector.

Modelling the Architecture

The high-level descriptions of e-government building blocks presented in the previous sections need to be formalized and detailed before they can become the basis for any real implementation. These more detailed models are currently not part of the reference architecture itself, but such descriptions are made within individual projects that focus on the realization of these building blocks.

To unify these descriptions and facilitate the exchange of architectural knowledge and the integration of the various building block designs, we propose to use a standardized language for enterprise architecture modelling called ArchiMate (Lankhorst et al., 2005). This language focuses specifically on high-level modelling and inter-domain relations. With this language, we are able to model both the global structure within each domain, showing the main elements and their dependencies, and the relations between the domains, in a way that is easy to understand for non-experts. The language is rapidly gaining acceptance in the Netherlands and abroad, and architects from several Dutch governmental institutions already use it as their standard modelling technique.

ArchiMate distinguishes itself from many other languages by its well defined metamodel, set of concepts and, most importantly, its relations. Furthermore, the enterprise-level scope of ArchiMate is wider than that of languages like UML and BPMN, which focus on a more detailed description of specific domains such as software and business processes. ArchiMate's level of abstraction simplifies the construction of integrated models, where most languages appear to persuade architects to detailed modelling. Although detailed modelling of most aspects also can be performed in ArchiMate, using ArchiMate as an "umbrella language", from which links can be made to detailed models in languages such as UML or BPMN, is most useful.

ArchiMate is strongly service-oriented, not just for describing software architectures but across the entire enterprise architecture domain. This makes it very well suited for modelling the service-oriented government reference architecture at hand. Service orientation leads to a layered view of enterprise architecture models, where the service concept is one of the main linking pins between the different layers. In this context, the ArchiMate language distinguishes three main layers:

1. The *business layer* offers products and services to external customers, which are realized in the organization by business processes (performed by business actors or roles).

2. The *application layer* supports the business layer with application services, which are realized by (software) application components.

3. The *technology layer* offers infrastructural services (e.g., processing, storage, and communication services) needed to run applications, realized by computation and communication devices, and system software.

A common abstract metamodel lies behind the modelling concepts at all three layers, comprising (abstract) concepts for "structure", "behaviour", and "information", and a separation is made between "internal" and "external" concepts. In Figure 6, we see this structure of the metamodel reflected in the set of application layer concepts and the relevant relations between them, which we have used in the example models in the remainder of this chapter. The structure of this part of the metamodel is representative for the entire language and is largely repeated in the business and technology layers. The most important modelling concepts at each of the three layers are explained

as follows. For a more detailed description please refer to (Lankhorst et al., 2005).

The main structural concept at the business layer is the *business actor*, an entity that performs behaviour such as business processes or functions. Business actors may be individual persons (e.g. customers or employees), but also groups of people and resources that have a permanent (or at least long-term) status within the organizations. To each actor *business roles* can be assigned, which in turn signify responsibility for one or more *business processes*, which may manipulate *business objects*. The externally visible behaviour of a business process is modelled by the concept *business service*, which represents a unit of functionality that is meaningful from the point of view of the environment. Not shown in the figure is that services can be grouped to form (financial or information) *products*, together with a *contract* that specifies the associated characteristics, rights and requirements.

The main structural concept for the application layer (Figure 6) is the *application component*. This concept can be used to model any structural entity in the application layer: not just (reusable) software components that can be part of one or more applications, but also complete software applications or information systems. Behaviour in the application layer can be described in a way that is very similar to business layer behaviour.

Figure 6. Application layer concepts in ArchiMate

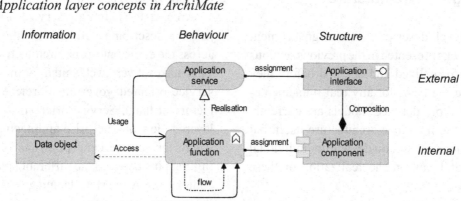

We make a distinction between the externally visible behaviour of application components in terms of *application services*, and the internal behaviour, *application functions,* that realize these services. Services are offered through the *application interfaces* of an application component. *Data objects* are used in the same way as data objects (or object types) in well-known data modelling approaches, most notably the "class" concept from UML.

The main structural concept for the technology layer is the *node*. This concept is used to model structural entities in the technology layer. Nodes come in two flavours: *device* and *system software*. A device models a physical computational resource, on which artefacts may be deployed for execution. System software represents the software environment for specific types of components and data objects. An *infrastructure interface* is the (logical) location where the infrastructural services offered by a node can be accessed by other nodes or by application components from the application layer. An *artefact* is a physical piece of information that is used or produced in a software development process, or by deployment and operation of a system. A *network* models a physical communication medium between two or more devices. In the technology layer, the central behavioural concept is the *infrastructure service*. We do not model the internal behaviour of infrastructure components such as routers or database servers; that would add a level of detail that is not useful at the enterprise level of abstraction.

Next to the concepts to model the business, application, and technology layers of an enterprise, we also need to model the different relations between these concepts. To this end, ArchiMate provides several types of relations. The access of information elements, e.g. business or data objects, by behaviour elements, e.g. processes, functions or interactions, is modelled with the *access* relation. The *usage* relation models the use of structure or behaviour elements, e.g. the use of services by processes, functions or interactions,

or the use of interfaces by roles, components or collaborations. The *composition* relation indicates that an element consists of a number of other elements, i.e., the lifecycles of the contained objects are tied to that of their container. The *aggregation* relation is used to group a number of elements within another element, but the grouped elements continue to have an independent lifecycle. The *assignment* relation links behaviour elements with structure elements (e.g. roles, components) that perform this behaviour, roles with actors that fulfil them, or artefacts that are deployed on nodes. The *realization* relation links a logical entity with a more concrete entity that realizes it, e.g. a service that is realized by an application function. The *specialization* relation indicates that an object is a specialization of another object. Temporal or causal relations between processes, function, interactions and events are modelled with the *triggering* relation. The *flow* relation describes the flow of information between elements. Finally, an *association* models a relation between objects that is not covered by another, more specific relation.

Many of these concepts and relations have been inspired by existing standards. For instance, the application component, node and device concepts and relations such as composition, association, and specialization originate from UML, while the process and event concepts and the triggering relation are used in most business process modelling languages.

Example: Personal Internet Page

The Dutch government has decided that each citizen should become a personal Internet page (PIP) called MijnOverheid.nl (translated: "MyGovernment.nl"). Citizens and businesses can use this portal to view their personal data, submit corrections or changes, receive personalized information, and manage their affairs with government in one place. Similar initiatives can be seen in other countries, such as Denmark's Borger.dk and Singapore's My.eCitizen.

The PIP will serve both citizens and government. For citizens, it will be easier to find relevant services, availability is 7x24, information can be tailored to personal preferences, information is reused across agencies, and they can get insight in their personal files and dossiers at these various agencies from one point of entry. For government agencies, this personal page makes it easier to reach more citizens with e-government services and it will provide economies of scale (build once & implement for all agencies).

The PIP thus serves as an intelligent integrator:

Figure 7. Services and data sources of the personal Internet page

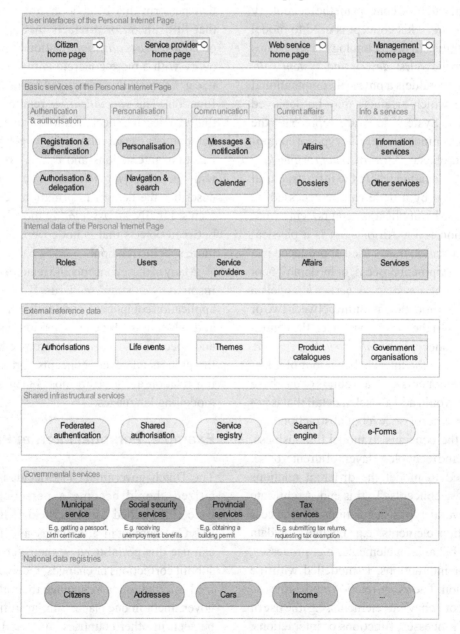

- It finds and displays e-government services
- Government agencies retain autonomy and responsibility for their services
- Services retain the identity of the government agency

Importantly, the PIP will not provide integration between (the services of) different agencies; this is left as a responsibility to these organizations themselves. On the other hand, if two or more agencies combine their services, the PIP will support the dissemination of this combined service to citizens and companies.

A first-level decomposition of the core services and data sources of the PIP is shown in Figure 7, which is based on (Ghosh, 2006, p. 20). Each of the services specified in this model can of course be described in much more detail, providing information about the functions that realize these services, the components that implement these functions, the way data is used by these functions, etc. Space limitations prevent us from showing the full detail of these designs.

As we can already see in this figure, the PIP provides a collection of services that may also be relevant outside the context of the PIP itself. Providing these services as building blocks to various government agencies for inclusion in their own e-government solutions could be a next step after deployment of the PIP itself to citizens.

First Results

First results in applying the Dutch Government Reference Architecture are encouraging. Many institutions have adopted the architecture as an important guideline in their own architectural practice and are aligning their developments with it. Sector-specific architectures, in e.g. education, social security, and healthcare, are being aligned with and based on the reference architecture. Even more importantly, the reference architecture serves to coordinate the development of a set of

common infrastructural facilities, such as service buses, shared Internet portals, authentication services, and basic information registries. To this end, the reference architecture also provides a set of over 200 relevant technology standards, which are put into context by the set of the 130 architectural principles. This combination of standards and principles for applying them puts it a step beyond comparable initiatives like SAGA (Germany, 2007) and others. In this way the architectural guidelines and the interoperability framework are intelligently combined.

Several important elements of this are already operational. A central authentication facility, "DigiD", has been developed and is currently used by many governmental institutions and more than 5 million citizens, for example to file their electronic tax returns. Basic information registries are being formed and the first of these are already operational.

FUTURE DEVELOPMENTS

Notwithstanding the important developments in Dutch e-government outlined in the previous sections, recent research has unveiled that only some 16% of Dutch citizens perceive an improvement in the quality of service provisioning by Dutch public bodies over the last few years, despite the fact that about 76% of the population has visited governmental Websites (Burger@Overheid, 2006). Apparently, there is still a large gap between governmental service offerings and the actual demand of citizens and enterprises.

A main cause of this gap appears to be that most e-government services have been designed "inside-out", based on the current structure, organization, and products of the various governmental institutions, resulting in a fragmented and ill-coordinated patchwork of services. For a single event, a citizen has to deal with many partial solutions by several organizations that hardly communicate with each other. This problem also holds for civil servants, who need to cooperate with their colleagues in different institutions, but are seldom provided with adequate means to do so. To really serve the needs of citizens, government e-services should be centred on the actual citizen demand. Such a demand driven e-government requires an integrated approach of both technical and organizational issues.

Although the reference architecture outlined before is an important step towards better integrated e-government, much more needs to be done to achieve truly citizen-centred services. This longer-term development of demand-driven e-government is the focus of a major Dutch research project "B-dossier" (B-dossier, 2007), comprising 9 partners from government, private sector, and science. In this project, we have identified requirements and designed a service architecture to make the next step towards this demand-driven perspective, in which both citizens' and civil servants' needs for better integration are addressed.

Requirements Analysis

To identify the requirements, we have studied multiple visions of different stakeholders on future e-government. These included the Dutch citizen panel "Citizen@Government" (Burger@ Overheid, 2005), the local government of the city of The Hague (Bos, 2005), a consultancy firm HEC (Mettau, 2005), and various intra-governmental projects and studies. Furthermore, visions such as "one-stop government" (Wimmer, 2002) and "virtual agencies" (Fountain, 2001) have influenced this analysis. Several user studies are carried out within the project itself, to evaluate and refine these ideas.

The requirements analysis unveiled the dominant problems that citizens and civil servants are facing. To capture these problems and the associated requirements on e-government services, we have defined a multi-dimensional framework. The first dimension of this framework is what we call the *governmental service provisioning chain*:

- **Policy:** The mission on political subjects, such as environment, health-care, taxes etc., which forms the basis for legislation and regulation
- **Legislation:** National and local laws and regulations that are implemented in accordance with policies
- **Service:** The (governmental) services that enable citizens to comply to legislation, exercise their rights, or obtain government products and benefits
- **Process:** The activities and transactions performed by the provisioning organizations to realize these services
- **Information:** Personal and public information that is involved in or required for transactions, such as the personal name and address of the requestor, or general information about a new law

Furthermore, two core issues appeared in every one of the studies we have consulted: a need for more *transparency* in how the government operates, and a need for more *control*. Both of these issues hold for citizens as well as for the civil servants involved. A further analysis revealed that these issues of transparency and control applied to four main problem categories: *fragmentation* of services across many different organizations, *compatibility* of service demand and supply, *quality* of these services, and their *accessibility*.

In our view, the development of a modern, service oriented e-government transcends the traditional way of organizing governmental processes. In the "paper age", it was accepted that one had to go from one to the other agency to collect different services or products. In the electronic service society, citizens and companies expect a one-stop shopping way of doing business with governmental institutions. So new technology enables new forms of service provision, and people simply want to have this. In the years to come, governmental institutions have to rearrange their basic functions. This is a tough assignment for senior management and politicians. Most of them have to give up a certain independent role in the public marketplace. They have to innovate, cooperate, merge, harmonize, reallocate functions and sometimes even discontinue their services. In many instances, legislation has to be adapted to make these changes possible. All this can be a painful process, with some managers gaining power and others losing. This is not just a matter of optimizing IT or business process redesign. This is giving birth to a new type of public service.

From Requirements to Services

Service orientation can be part of the solution. Since the citizen's needs and demands are seldom served by a single government agency, combining and integrating services across organizational boundaries and sharing the necessary information to deliver these services are key ingredients of demand-driven e-government.

At a high level, these requirements can (at least partially) be met by an architecture that provides at least the following elements:

- *Integrated, demand-driven e-government services*, created from sub-services delivered by the various government organizations involved
- *Cross-organizational choreography* of sub-services and -processes, to realize these integrated end-user services
- A *virtual shared information space*, an infrastructure for exchanging information between organizations and with citizens
- A *federated identity management* infrastructure for safely accessing this information
- *End-user applications* with which to access all of the aforementioned

However, this is just a high-level layering of generic elements that provides no clues to its realization. To this end, a detailed functional architecture has been developed, which fits within the context of the reference architecture described before, and existing and emerging technological solutions have been mapped onto that architecture (Lankhorst & Derks, 2007). In the next sections, we will describe in more detail which services we need to fulfil the requirements we have identified.

Fragmentation

First of all, we identified the fragmentation problem, where citizens and civil servants perceive scattered service provisioning. There is no single counter where all information or services are available. Instead, information and services are scattered around multiple governmental departments and sometimes private parties as well. This requires a substantial effort from citizen and civil servant to gather all required information and services. A particular problem for citizens is that personal data such as address, marital status, income, and social security number, are administrated by each department separately. This fragmented administration results in repeated questions to citizens to fill out forms with information that is already known to other governmental departments. This is perceived as highly frustrating. Another problem with the ever growing complexity of legislation and regulation is that citizens loose track of relevant developments, which causes them to miss opportunities, e.g. with respect to social security benefits.

Of course, one step necessary to take is to present the various governmental services in an integrated way. An example of such a *presentation service* is the Personal Internet Page described previously. However, this does not solve the problem of integrating services across agencies. To alleviate this problem of scattered service provisioning and be able to deliver integrated demand-driven services, we introduce *process integration services* that are capable of orchestrating fragmented processes. To resolve the lack of an integrated view, we introduce *directory services*, that include references to relevant information and services of different organizations. To guarantee that no opportunities or events are missed by citizens and civil servants, we introduce *subscription services* with which users and/or services are notified of relevant events. Another problem with fragmentation is the need for repeated *authentication* and *authorization*. To this end, we propose a federated infrastructure of *authentication services* and *authorization services* that can provide single sign-on.

To provide the citizen with an integrated view on the information stored by various organizations, *information services* are needed. The problems of fragmentation also plague the various organizations involved. Because they have limited or no access to the information their colleagues store, citizens are often requested to provide information that is already known to the government. These information exchange services should also help to solve this problem, by creating a transparent infrastructure where organizations and citizens can share and exchange information on an equal basis, of course respecting the applicable laws, regulations, and wishes of the owners of that information.

Compatibility

The compatibility problem involves the mismatch between demand and supply of information and services. At a business level, the compatibility problem involves the lack of an appropriate service that meets the demand. The earlier introduced process service can be used to compose and enact the required customized services. Another compatibility problem involves a mismatch with respect to compliance with standards. We consider this a language problem and introduce *adaptation services* to align messages and services between parties that use different formats and concepts.

Quality

Quality of information and services is hard to judge and control for both citizens and civil servants. Citizens may get different interpretations of the same legislation from different civil servants. Also, citizens are sometimes unaware that certain information or services are outdated. From the perspective of civil servants, the quality of information may be uncertain. Citizens may not always act truthfully, or civil servants work with outdated information. Furthermore, the complexity of forms and regulations frequently results in errors and mistakes. From the perspective of control, citizens often have no choice in what services to take. In many cases, the government acts as a monopolist, such that citizens have no control over quality of service.

To facilitate citizens and civil servants in better judging quality, we introduce *certification services*, such that the source of information can be determined accurately. Time-stamped certificates are used to denote the validity of information. Certification may encourage citizens to provide their information more accurately, because their information supply cannot be denied afterwards (non-repudiation). We introduce *archive services* to log the actual service provisioning and store previous versions of information. This way a user can verify whether newer versions of the same information are available. With the archive service, the service provisioning history can be determined objectively such that the evolution of quality over time can be tracked. Quality of service can then be controlled by selecting those services that meet quality demands. To be able to improve quality of information, *information services* are equipped with facilities so that the user of the information can report possible errors. A specific type of these services could be recommendation services, with which citizens can inform each other about the quality of e-government services, in much the same vein as e.g. the rating system of companies like Amazon.

Accessibility

The demand for access can be divided into availability of access and access privileges. With respect to availability, citizens demand access to information and services on a 24/7 basis and through multiple channels, such as a physical counter, phone, and email. Important here, is that they should receive the same information and service through all channels.

With respect to access privileges, there is an increasing demand for transparency about who has access to their personal information. In addition to this, citizens require more control over who has access to what (personal) information. Not only do they want to restrict access to certain governmental departments to protect their privacy, they also demand openness to other (semi-governmental) organizations (e.g. hospitals) to reduce administrative overhead for citizens and civil servants. In the context of the latter, the general principle of granting privileges based on understanding and accepting consequences is often referred to as *informed consent* (Hoven et al., 2005).

To maximize transparency and control, citizens demand access to the same information and services as civil services. We refer to this requirement as symmetric service provisioning, which gives citizens a high degree of self-service and the government a means to reduce cost of operations.

The accessibility problem is addressed by our approach of a service-oriented architecture where services can be replicated in order to provide the necessary 24/7 availability. Much more could be said about this, but availability problems have well-known solutions and we will therefore not address these in the remainder of this chapter.

The access problem related to access privileges is addressed in several ways. First of all, we need to be able to identify users, information and service objects. We make an important decision not to choose for global identification of objects. Instead, we allow each organization to store and reference objects in its own way. Next to the obvious practical reasons for allowing each organization to use its own practices instead of enforcing some centralized scheme, a second advantage is an improved level of security and privacy, because it becomes more difficult to combine information from different sources without having the proper authorization. In this, we deviate from the current Dutch policy, where a standardized "citizen number" is used to identify citizens across all government services (a practice that is e.g. forbidden by constitutional law in a country such as Portugal). In future, we foresee an increased pressure from private parties to connect and combine their services with governmental services. To avoid privacy and data security problems, such a federated, non-global identity infrastructure will be needed.

To be able to resolve which objects are the same and which are not, we adopt *identity services* that are able to understand this difference. The great advantage here is that new organizations can be easily integrated in the architecture without the need to adapt their internal administration. In addition to identity services, we use *authentication services* to authenticate users and *authorization services* to manage authorizations. Authorization services include functionality to handle the concept of "informed consent" described earlier. Finally, standardized *information services* should be offered by all those that administer information about the citizen, to provide access to that information. For preserving confidentiality, we use *encryption services* in a conventional way and will not further elaborate on encryption.

Future E-Government Service Architecture

The main services identified previously can be grouped into three main layers, as shown in Figure 8. On top, we see the citizen-facing services that present a unified, integrated view of the various e-government services as follows. In the middle,

Figure 8. Service layers in future e-government architecture

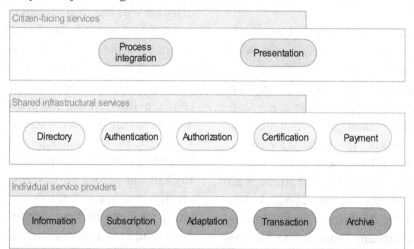

we have a layer of infrastructural services that are shared across different agencies. At the bottom, we see the services for which these agencies themselves are responsible.

An overview of the envisaged architecture that shows some more detail is given in Figure 8. The functionality needed to realize all these services, the relations between them, and the components that implement these functions have all been worked out in more detail in architectural designs. As an example of this, we show the services and functions for process orchestration in more detail.

Process Orchestration

A core element to realize the vision of integrated, demand-driven e-government services is process orchestration. End-user services to the citizen often span across multiple organizations, and their behaviour must be coordinated to deliver these services. Importantly, processes are non-atomic groups or chains of activity that present interactive behaviour to the service consumer.

We distinguish between service composition and service enactment. Service composition is concerned with the choreography of constituent

services to create an integrated whole that represents the end-user service. We envisage "step-by-step plans" as a tool to compose services in a very basic, end-user friendly way. These plans, present the various sub-services as steps in an overall scheme for delivering the integrated services.

Service enactment is responsible for executing the individual behaviours, i.e., sub-services of different service providers that realize these constituent services. Besides the generic composition and enactment primitives, process services also support secondary functions, e.g. to log the service execution, and to perform transaction management and exception handling. Furthermore, additional services may be needed to adapt these constituent services to the context in which they are integrated, and likewise, to integrate information from different sources to present this in an integrated manner to the end-user.

The main functions and services within our architecture are illustrated in Figure 9. At the top, we see the functionality for service composition. The bottom part shows the services of different service providers that are integrated into a high-level end-user service. This part, the service enactment, is presented in more detail in Figure 10.

Figure 9. Process orchestration

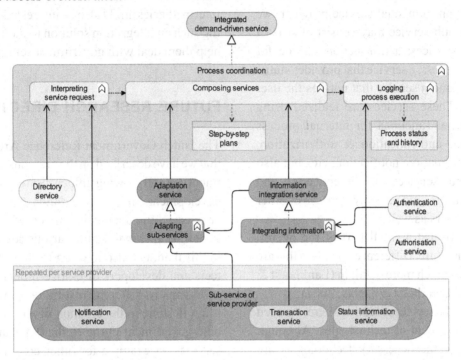

Figure 10. Realization of sub-services of service providers

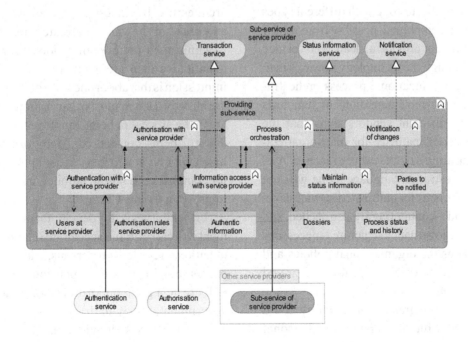

If we look in more detail at the sub-service delivered by an individual service provider, we see that this sub-service may consist of at least three other services: a transaction service for information access, a service that provides status information, and a service that notifies the user of changes. These services are realized using several internal functions for internal process orchestration, authentication & authorization, access to information, notification, etc., but also using external services for authenticating and authorizing users, and possibly services of other service providers as well.

This shows just a small part of the overall service architecture. Different elements of this are worked out in much more detail in (Lankhorst & Derks, 2006; Lankhorst & Derks, 2007).

To realize the services identified here, we need a broad complement of technologies. Although in most areas, the necessary technologies are starting to become available, there are still some important gaps to be covered. Especially in inter-organizational coordination of processes, a light-weight, easily configurable orchestration solution is needed that is able to cope with different types of services being combined, possibly from legacy systems that do not provide a clean Web service interface. Although the technology now exists to perform intra-organizational process orchestration, the different implementations of standards like BPEL by different vendors show that the necessary level of maturity for inter-organizational orchestration has not yet been reached. And a process orchestration language alone will not suffice. Mechanisms for automated service-level agreements and e-contracting are also needed, and on top of that, a governance structure is necessary that coordinates the organizational policies and actions towards the common goal of integrated service provision.

This type of integrative functionality could become part of a future version of the Personal Internet Page that was outlined in Sect. 1.4.5, although this is currently not being planned.

Commercial service providers such as financial intermediaries might also be interested in providing such an integration solution to their clients to help them deal with government services.

FUTURE RESEARCH DIRECTIONS

The Dutch Government Reference Architecture that we have described on the previous pages is an important and growing influence on e-government developments in the Netherlands. Creating such an overarching document has served not only to structure and organize the various developments in this field, but also to bring together the architects and developers of e-government solutions across many different institutions. As such, it is a milestone in the creation of a unified vision on e-government in the Netherlands and it may serve as an example for other countries of the way in which both the architecture itself and its development process may be organized.

At the moment, many government institutions are assessing their compliance with the reference architecture by investigating what the status and usage of the various architecture principles is within their own organizations. Although no quantitative data are available yet, the general impression is that about one third of the principles are already used in most organizations, one third are in the process of being employed, and the rest are still being considered. Many organizations have explicitly stated that it is their policy to strive for compliance, so these number are expected to improve in the near future.

In the next years, the development of e-government will carry on and accelerate. The availability of national registers on persons, addresses, companies, buildings, wages, pensions and the like will create a great opportunity for almost every governmental body to drastically redesign their service processes. It will create opportunities for pro-active services, quicker responses, less mistakes and less fraud. Projects are carried out to harmonize data definitions, to integrate networks, to develop sectoral and national service buses, to harmonize meta-data, to set up a national governmental call centre and to develop many, many more electronic services. And beyond this, the perspective of cross-border integration in a European context beckons.

However, much work still needs to be done on the demand side. Truly citizen-centred e-government requires close cooperation between the various agencies involved to keep up with citizens' permanently evolving expectations, questions and needs. The coordination of business processes across organizations, including the governance of these processes, is a difficult issue. As we have outlined, a service-oriented view on process orchestration can be an important step forward. However, especially in the case of autonomous organizations, it is very hard to orchestrate a cross-organizational business process that realizes a unified service to the citizen. Redistribution of tasks and responsibilities among organizations might become necessary, but this can be a painful process for the people involved.

A second important problem is the integration of information between organizations. Many different organizations use the same or very similar data, in many cases because of slightly different definitions in the regulations that are the basis of their service. Removal of these duplications would result in a considerable improvement in both efficiency and data quality. However, each of these organizations uses its own formats and concepts, and the shared infrastructure for information exchange we have described has yet to be created. The national registries outlined in previous sections are an important step in this direction, but not all data can (or should) be standardized and centralized. Although interoperability at a technical level is achievable, as has been shown in numerous practical examples, semantic interoperability is much harder to accomplish, because it requires organizations to agree on the *meaning* of the various concepts they use and not

just on their exchange format. This may require harmonization of legislation, with all the lengthy procedures this entails.

Finally, the needs of citizens are not contained within the sometimes artificial boundaries of what are considered "public" institutions, and private organizations would of course like to benefit from public infrastructural services such as the national authentication service described previously. On the other hand, citizens are fearful of misuse of their personal data if the government opens up these services to private use, and rightly so, as many incidents with e.g. identity theft illustrate. This private use of public infrastructures is therefore not just a technical or organizational issue, but requires policy makers to come up with a balanced solution, weighing privacy, ease-of-use, economic advantages, and many other issues.

ACKNOWLEDGMENT

Part of this chapter results from the B-dossier project (http://b-dossier.telin.nl) of the Telematica Instituut, a combined research initiative with partners from government and academia, comprising the Dutch Tax and Customs Administration, the Municipality of The Hague, SVB, UWV, ING, ICTU, the University of Twente, and Delft University of Technology. The project aims to bring about truly integrated, demand-driven electronic services from government institutions to citizens and companies.

REFERENCES

Alting van Geusau-Ghosh, S., Zeef, P, Toorn, H. van, & Visch, E. (2006). *Globaal Ontwerp Persoonlijke Internet Pagina*, version 1.2. The Hague, The Netherlands: Stichting ICTU. Retrieved July 17, 2007, from http://www.e-overheid.nl/data/files/PIP/Globaal_Ontwerp_versie_1[1].2.pdf.pdf

Austria (2006). *Administration on the Net – An ABC Guide to E-Government in Austria.* Vienna, Austria: Oesterreichische Computer Gesellschaft. Retrieved July 17, 2007, from http://www.cio.gv.at/egovernment/umbrella/Administration_on_the_Net.zip.

Bayens, G.I.H.M. (2006). E-Government in The Netherlands: An Architectural Approach, *Via Nova Architectura,* October 9, 2006. Retrieved July 17, 2007, from http://www.via-nova-architectura.org.

Bayens, G.I.H.M., et al. (2007). *Nederlandse Overheid Referentie Architectuur (NORA) v. 2.0.* The Hague, The Netherlands: Stichting ICTU. Retrieved July 17, 2007, from http://www.e-overheid.nl/atlas/referentiearchitectuur/

B-dossier (2007). *B-dossier project Website.* Enschede, The Netherlands: Telematica Instituut. Retrieved July 17, 2007, from http://www.b-dossier.nl.

Bos, H. (2005). *De ICT-strategie van de Gemeente The Hague (2001-2007).* Utrecht, The Netherlands: Informatiehuis. Retrieved July 17, 2007, from http://www.egem.nl/projecten/voorhoedegemeenten/kennisconferentie2006/documenten/Evaluatie%20Haagse%20aanpak%20door%20Informatiehuis.pdf?searchterm=None

Burger@Overheid (2005). *BurgerServiceCode, versie 2.1.* The Hague, The Netherlands: Burger@Overheid.nl. Retrieved July 17, 2007, from http://www.burger.overheid.nl/files/burgerservicecode_nl.pdf

Burger@Overheid (2006). *Evaluatieonderzoek 2006.* The Hague, The Netherlands: Burger@Overheid.nl. Retrieved July 17, 2007, from http://www.burger.overheid.nl/files/b@o_evaluatieonderzoek_bop_2006.pdf

Denmark (2006). *Architecture for e-Government in Denmark.* Offentlig Information Online. Retrieved July 17, 2007, from http://www.oio.dk/arkitektur/eng.

Derks, W.L.A., & Lankhorst, M.M. (2006). *Definitie en conceptualisatie van het B-dossier.* Technical Report TI/RS/2006/013. Enschede, The Netherlands: Telematica Instituut. Retrieved July 17, 2007, from https://doc.telin.nl/dscgi/ds.py/Get/File-61820

Dool, F. van den, Keller, W.J., Wagenaar, R. & Hinfelaar, J.A.F. (2002) *Architectuur elektronische overheid. Samenhang en Samenwerking.* Zoetermeer, The Netherlands: Verdonck Klooster & Associates. Retrieved July 17, 2007, from http://www.e-overheid.nl/data/files/architectuur/architectuurelektronischeoverheid.pdf.

European Commission (2004). *European Interoperability Framework for Pan-European e-Government Services,* version 1.0. Retrieved July 17, 2007, from http://ec.europa.eu/idabc/servlets/Doc?id=19529.

Fountain, J.E. (2001). *Building the Virtual State – Information Technology and Institutional Change.* Washington, DC: Brookings Institution Press.

Germany (2007). *Standards und Architekturen für E-Government-Anwendungen (SAGA 3.0).* Berlin: Koordinierungs- und Beratungsstelle der Bundesregierung für Informationstechnik in der Bundesverwaltung. Retrieved July 17, 2007, from http://www.kbst.bund.de/saga.

Ghosh, S. (2006). *PIP Architectuur white paper,* version 0.3. Stichting ICTU, The Hague, The Netherlands. Retrieved July 17, 2007, from http://www.e-overheid.nl/data/files/PIP/PIP%20architectuur%20whitepaper%20v0.3%20concept.pdf

Hong Kong (2007). *The HKSARG Interoperability Framework. Version: 5.1.* Hong Kong: Government of the Hong Kong Special Administrative Region, Office of the Government Chief Information Officer. Retrieved July 17, 2007, from http://www.ogcio.gov.hk/eng/infra/download/s18.pdf

Hoven, J. van den, Wagenaar, R., Daskapan, S., Manders, N. Kenny, S. & Eldin, A.A. (2005), *Managing Identity, Privacy & Profiles*. Technical Report TI/RS/2005/101, Enschede, The Netherlands: Telematica Instituut. Retrieved July 17, 2007, from https://doc.telin.nl/dscgi/ds.py/Get/File-52040/TUD_sotas.pdf

ITU (1995), Open Distributed Processing - Reference Model - Part 3: Architecture, ITU Recommendation X.903 | ISO/IEC 10746-3. Geneva, Switzerland: International Telecommunication Union.

Janssen, M., Gortmaker, J., & Wagenaar, R. (2006). Web Service Orchestration in Public Administration: Challenges, Roles, and Growth Stages. *Information Systems Management*, Spring 2006, pp. 44–55.

Lankhorst, M.M. & Derks, W.L.A. (2006). *B-dossier architectuur*. Technical Report TI/RS/2006/014, Enschede, The Netherlands: Telematica Instituut. Retrieved July 17, 2007, from https://doc.telin.nl/dscgi/ds.py/Get/File-61826

Lankhorst, M.M. & Derks, W.L.A. (2007). Towards a Service-Oriented Architecture for Demand-Driven e-Government. *11th IEEE International EDOC Conference (EDOC 2007)*. Los Alamitos, CA: IEEE Computer Society.

Lankhorst, M.M., et al. (2005). *Enterprise Architecture at Work – Modelling, Communication, and Analysis*. Berlin: Springer-Verlag.

Maes, R. (1999). *A Generic Framework for Information Management*, PrimaVera Working Paper 99-03, Amsterdam, The Netherlands: University of Amsterdam, Department of Accountancy & Information Management.

Mettau, P. (2005). *mijnoverheid.nl – Publieke Dienstverlening in de toekomst*. The Hague: Het Expertise Centrum.

Steen, M.W.A., Lankhorst, M.M., Doest, H. ter, Strating, P., & Iacob, M.-E. (2005). Service-Oriented Enterprise Architecture". In Z. Stojanovic and A. Dahanayake (Eds.), *Service-Oriented Software System Engineering: Challenges and Practices*, Hershey, PA: IDEA Group.

The Open Group (2006). *The Open Group Architectural Framework (TOGAF) Version 8.1.1 'Enterprise Edition'*. Reading, UK: The Open Group. Retrieved July 17, 2007, from http://www.opengroup.org/togaf/.

UK (2005). *e-Government Interoperability Framework Version 6.1*. London: Cabinet Office. Retrieved July 17, 2007, from http://www.govtalk.gov.uk/schemasstandards/egif_document.asp?docnum=949

US (2007). *Federal Enterprise Architecture*. Washington, DC: Office of Management and Budget. Retrieved July 17, 2007, from http://www.whitehouse.gov/omb/egov/a-1-fea.html.

Wimmer, M.A. (2002). Integrated Service Modelling for One-Stop Government. *Electronic Markets, special issue on e-Government*, 12(3):1–8.

Zachman, J.A. (1987). A Framework for Information Systems Architecture. *IBM Systems Journal*, 26(3):276–292.

APPENDIX: OVERVIEW OF MAIN ARCHITECTURAL PRINCIPLES

This appendix gives an overview of main architectural principles of the Dutch Government Reference Architecture, sorted by the cells of the architectural meta-framework (Figure 1).

Organization

- Governmental organizations are autonomous (subsidiarity principle).
- Governmental organizations formulate core functions.
- Governmental organizations cooperate, both horizontally and vertically.
- Service orientation is a leading principle for governmental organizations.
- Organization design supports multi-channel front offices.
- Organizations cooperate within a service-oriented architecture.

Business Services

- Organizations deliver separate and combined services towards their clients.
- "No wrong door": every starting point for governmental contact is OK.
- Multi-channel service delivery.
- The customer chooses the channel; the organization entices customers to use the best channel.
- Channel harmonization is essential.
- Pro-active services: The customer is pointed to relevant business services.
- Business services can be a combination of underlying internal services.
- Electronic identification, authentication and authorization are essential.

Processes

- Business processes produce services.
- Business processes are coupled by services.
- The customer is starting and delivery point for services and process design.
- Chain processes are controlled by the organization that has the (initial) customer contact.
- Work processes are accomplished by both employees and IT systems.
- Processes are automated unless this is not possible.
- The customer can see the work in progress (tracking and tracing).

Employees and Applications

- Applications serve only one functional domain inside an organization.
- Applications serve only one organization.
- Organizations are coupled by services.
- Applications (and employees) carry out work processes; process management (BPM) and data stores are separated from these work processes.
- Employees use "computer assisted case handling" software (WFM).

- Both workflow software and (unattended) applications controlled by business process management software.
- Front office channels can be coupled at local, sectoral and national level.

Data and Messages

- Data formats are standardized.
- There is a single point of control for data management; National registries are leading.
- The government asks data once and uses it in many situations.
- For messaging, the ebMS and Web services standards are used.
- Received data and documents are enriched with metadata and archived.
- Content and process data are differentiated.
- Every data item has an owner and an administrator.

Information Exchange

- Services and data are exchanged by a hierarchy of service buses.
- Organizations are coupled by (sectoral) buses.
- Communication protocols are standardized (ebXML, Web services, messages, fil transfer).
- The infrastructure is highly available.
- Straight through processing is preferred.

Technical Components

- The choice of technical components is left to individual organizations (subsidiarity), provided that they support the relevant standards and requirements regarding security and availability.
- Systems critical to the service delivery have to be highly reliable.

Data Storage

- National registries are leading.
- Data is reused wherever appropriate.
- Technical data model is standardized as much as possible independently of work processes.
- Data and documents are separated.
- Structured data is preferred over electronic documents.

Network Architecture

- G2G data transport uses closed, protected networks or VPNs.
- Communication with citizens and companies uses (protected) Internet.
- Organizations are coupled by one gateway (incl. firewalls, intrusion detection, virus-scanning, etc.).
- Standard exchange protocols are used, preferably TCP/IP.

Chapter III
Role of Beacon Architecture in Mitigating Enterprise Architecture Challenges of the Public Sector

Amit Bhagwat
Independent Consultant, UK

ABSTRACT

This chapter introduces the concept of Beacon Architecture as a formalized and ordered grouping of architectural elements, describing the constituents, their order, correlation and likely evolution of the grouping; and illustrating its specific value to the public sector. The first half of the chapter builds up to the concept, the reasons behind its specific nature, and its value to enterprises, especially in the public sector. For this, the chapter is split into a number of sections that may be studied separately and that also build up to introduce Beacon Architecture. The sections may be broadly divided as concepts, historical overview, illustrative case studies in public sector transformations along with a summary of peculiar architectural challenges they face, and a cyclical pattern to Architecture Development. After introducing and elucidating on concept and constituents of Beacon Architecture, the chapter delves into its correlation with architecture concepts in currency and its role in mitigating enterprise architecture challenges illustrated earlier in the chapter, before concluding on an assessment of future trends.

INTRODUCTION

Whereas the concept of *Beacon Architecture* discussed here is an invention in so far as the term, its precise definition/usage and its organization into ordered constituents go, the underlying idea in generic terms is far from novel. Reference architectures have existed in practically all successful architecture governance regimes and transformations, and in a good many of unsuccessful ones too. The precise connotation, well-defined & ordered constituents and specific relationship with architectural concepts such as Vision, Roadmap, Baseline & Target Architectures that underpin Beacon Architecture, are however not a predictable hallmark of such reference architectures. In this chapter, we shall start with aspects that define Enterprise Architecture as a *living thing*, deliberate on architecture transformation and its journey through the architecture development cycle, meander through evolution of EA frameworks (most of which have had a public-sector pedigree), discuss in some depth Enterprise Architecture challenges peculiar to the public sector, before delving into the concept of Beacon Architecture, its correlation with various architecture transformation concepts, its value to significant architecture transformations and, in particular, its significance to definition, governance and transformation of Enterprise Architecture in the Public Sector.

The chapter is organized into a number of broad sections. The first four of these lead up to the *Beacon Architecture* concept:

- The first section defines and deliberates on prevailing Enterprise Architecture concepts and relates them, under the three headings *Enterprise Architecture, Aspects of Enterprise Architecture, Transforming Enterprise Architecture*
- The second section titled *Evolution of Enterprise Architecture Concepts – An Overview*

provides a brief journey through how Enterprise Architecture concepts have developed and how sectors/industries have contributed to this. This also sets background to what is and is not covered in present day popular EA frameworks, giving context to concepts introduced under *Beacon Architecture*.

- The third section, under the heading *Public Sector Transformations*, cites three examples from the UK, which illustrate the consequences of a lack of development of concepts, grouped under *Beacon Architecture* later on in the chapter, thus establishing a background as to why Beacon Architecture is important and citing some of the oft occurring inconveniences, wastages and even outright failures that can be avoided by establishing it. The next heading in this section, *Enterprise Architecture Challenges Peculiar to the Public Sector*, expands, summarizes and generalizes on this
- The fourth section, under the heading *Progression of Architecture Development Cycle* elaborates the generic treatment followed by a number of methodologies and architecture frameworks in effecting architecturally-significant enterprise transformation

These sections provide the right background to understand why constituents grouped under the concept of Beacon Architecture are important and are sequenced as they have been. The Author, in his role as Architecture Authority / Strategist has formalized and successfully introduced in the industry these constituents. The chapter then puts these constituents together in a logical order and highlights relevance of such effort to the Public Sector. The chapter ends with a pragmatic assessment of the likely resistance to establishing Beacon Architecture and the likely scenarios of its institutionalization over the next few years.

ENTERPRISE ARCHITECTURE

Of the many and varied definitions of the word *Enterprise*, I am inclined to cite here the definition followed in TOGAF (The Open Group, 2006) FAQ – it being used in the same context as ours:

Any collection of organizations that has a common set of goals and/or a single bottom line

The immediate, implicit, and, to many of us obvious, logical progression from this is that Enterprise Architecture, which needs context of an enterprise, can only be as defined, robust, coherent and serviceable, as the enterprise itself is. Turning the statement on its head, an enterprise can be explored for its definition, robustness, coherence and serviceability, while exploring/defining its Enterprise Architecture.

Practically all enterprises are in a certain level of flux, which creates its coupled field in context of their architecture. The private sector though, usually has either a clear enough domain of operation (e.g. specific sets of financial services, goods manufactured, etc) or, in case of diversified/multi-domain groups of organizations, the practical prudence, often imposed by the variety of domain-specific regulatory regimes that different organizations within the group operate under, makes the group to be treated as a collection of enterprises, rather than a single enterprise. The private sector, being self-sustained and usually competitive, also tends to prefer individuals with experience and proven ability in the domain. Whereas achievements through individual ability may not be a safe strategy for success of an enterprise, it certainly serves better than where the leaders may lack domain expertise, vision and proven ability, and may all too often owe their position to caprice of a higher political master.

It is here, that results through definition rather than heroics, and thus the concept of architecture, assume additional significance in the public sector, over and above that elsewhere. Deriving from some of the commonly cited definitions of Architecture, as relevant in our context, including the IEEE (Maier, Emery and Hilliard, 2001) and UML (Booch, Rumbaugh and Jacobson, 1999) explorations of the concept, the following definition may be arrived at:

Architecture of «a thing», at a given point in time, is its structural and functional organization, itself decomposable as organization of components interacting through defined interfaces, recursively composed of smaller components.

Thus combining the two definitions, of *Architecture* and *Enterprise*, *Architecture of an Enterprise* is:

The (usually recursive) structural and functional composition of components of a collection of organizations, where the organizations have a common set of (essentially functional) goals

This definition therefore puts structure as a function-enabler and as such its subservient, while placing clear emphasis on functional objectives of the enterprise and of its constituents that are geared to meeting objectives (or a coherent related set of them) of the enterprise.

ASPECTS OF ENTERPRISE ARCHITECTURE

Enterprises are rarely static, either structurally or functionally. When an enterprise transforms/evolves, it can involve changes that may be superficial or that may fundamentally change the structural and functional composition/interrelation of components that make up the Enterprise. The latter are referred to as *Architecturally Significant Changes*. Structured transformation techniques analyze and mitigate such changes prior to changes that build on the changed architecture. For example, in the software/systems development/transformation world, methods such as RUP and XP refer to *the Elaboration Phase* and *the Architectural Spike* respectively, as phases in the development/transformation lifecycle where architectural changes are dealt with on priority (in other words, the new architecture is established/proven) before the rest of the development/transformation. Changing the architecture however assumes that there is a body in charge of the architecture, and to be in charge of it, they know and are able to articulate to others, what architecture is.

The following description elaborates on this by introducing and interrelating various aspects of Enterprise Architecture:

- Architecture Definition, i.e. understanding of what the structural and functional composition of components making up the enterprise (and further, recursively, components making up these components) is,

helps effective governance of Enterprise Architecture.

- Enterprise Strategy, i.e., in the long term, what broad objectives/vision, the enterprise has and in what priority, helps setting up Architecture Strategy, i.e. long term vision of functional (and, based on that, structural) organization and interrelation within the Enterprise, geared to meet its strategic objectives/vision.

In fact, in enterprises that have a well-formed Business architecture, Enterprise Strategy may be stated and elaborated as the reason of (and thus at the beginnings of) the Enterprise Architecture strategy.

- Enterprise Architecture (EA) Governance, i.e. custodianship/oversight of Enterprise Architecture, enables maintaining currency

Figure 1. Relationships among EA concepts

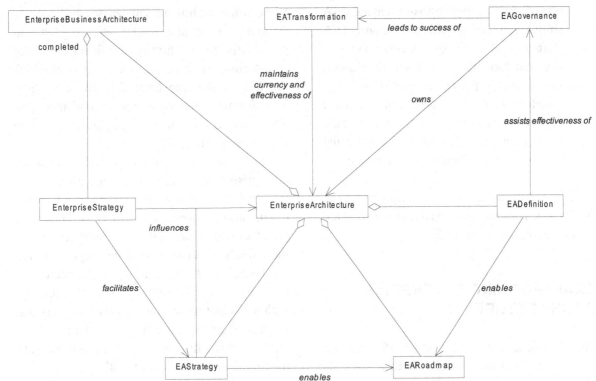

Figure 2. Dependency web of EA concepts

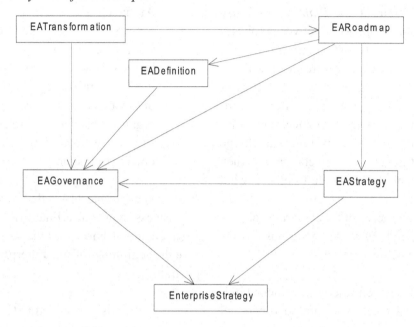

of EA and is a precursor to successful EA transformations.

- EA Roadmap, i.e. a staged, temporal description of how EA might transform to meet EA strategy, is enabled by EA definition and EA strategy, and owned by EA Governance.
- EA transformation, i.e. a clearly defined step in taking EA from an existing/initial state (often referred to as baseline state) to a desired state (often referred to as target state), in line with the EA strategy, is enabled by the EA strategy, roadmap and governance.

These relationships are pictorially represented in Figure 1. The concepts thus form a dependency Web as depicted in Figure 2.

TRANSFORMING ENTERPRISE ARCHITECTURE

We have surmised so far that transforming an enterprise might (and usually does) involve al-

tering its functional, and thus often structural, composition, including adding to or refactoring its capabilities. This can only be achieved if a body, often within the enterprise, understands its architecture, and is thus able to plan and oversee the architecturally significant aspects of transformation of the enterprise, around which the rest of the transformation might happen. Transformation needs governance, and intelligent active governance, in turn, implies efforts into definition, strategy and roadmap.

In a vast majority of successfully governed enterprise architectures, a distinct group of *elders*, called Enterprise Architects in EA-aware organizations, owns and oversees the enterprise architecture, including its transformation. These individuals, apart from well developed analytical, lateral and linear thinking skills, need to be experts in at least one of the relevant subjects, but with sufficient knowledge of other subjects that relate to their expertise subject, to be able to be circumspective thinkers and effective generalists, holding the bigger picture together.

Ownership of enterprise architecture involves responsibilities such as:

- Own business architecture
  - o Define existing business architecture
  - o Identify gaps in business architecture
  - o Evaluate opportunity for architectural improvement
    - ➤ Through robustly and effectively engineered business
    - ➤ Through automated and efficiently functioning business
  - o Objectively evaluate business *stakeholder wants* and translate them into *business needs*
  - o Define (or at least contribute to and formalize) business vision, strategy and roadmap
  - o Consider impact of business needs on existing business architecture
  - o Envisage best business architecture to meet business needs
  - o Liaise with owners of other aspects of Enterprise Architecture
- Own and similarly work on other aspects of EA (applications, information, technology), while interrelating them

Put the other way round, adaptive and responsive as they are, successful enterprises do not transform until they understand their mission and mechanism (this understanding makes them adaptive and responsive in the first place, rather than panic-struck), and have ability to govern these. Among other things, successful organizations, whatever their brand identity and generic values & goals (e.g. customer satisfaction, being among the top five of their kind, etc), know whether or not they are single enterprises, and if not, what independent or near-independent 'organizations with clear goals and separate bottom-lines' (i.e. enterprises) are they made up of.

This can further mean that successful enterprises, or groups thereof, tend to foresee, and often proactively engineer change, so as to minimize threats of sudden untested maneuvers.

EVOLUTION AND ORGANIZATION OF ENTERPRISE ARCHITECTURE CONCEPTS: AN OVERVIEW

The words Architecture and Architect have become common currency in the IT industry relatively recently, while their application outside the IT section of an enterprise (except of course to mean architect of buildings & ships, and sometimes as metaphor implying creator/visionary) is still something of a novelty. In the UK for example, about a decade ago, the role Systems Analyst was far more fashionable than say Solutions Architect is today. Most other *forms* of architects, perhaps excluding Technical Architect, but definitely including Enterprise Architect as we have discussed in this chapter, were also generally unknown.

There are some who would sneer at the changed designations, pointing out that the underlying approach and ability of the role performer have not necessarily changed, much the same way as individuals designated *administrators* a decade ago, though these days routinely called *managers*, have not necessarily *become* managers. Whereas such criticism would be apt in some cases, in general, change has occurred in the way organizations, and particularly IT organizations, approach their tasks. It has become far more routine for organizations to at least accept in principle that a component-based organization of teams (and teams of teams, etc) providing specific services and linked through defined interfaces and protocol, where the whole organizational structure and functional coordination can be easily and clearly visualized at desired level of granularity, is a better approach to running organizations. In short, *architectured organizations are good*. The concept has been led by the IT industry, or the IT function within organizations, and so whereas Solution Architects are not a replacement for analysts (including systems analysts, when systems happen to be part of the problem space), they are an important and necessary addition, now widely accepted in the IT industry/function.

Over the last few decades, the increased scope, complexity and increasing importance of information and of reliable information processing in everyday life have also helped institutionalize concepts such as object-oriented programming (and further, object-oriented analysis and design), component-based development, service-oriented architecture, etc that, as far as the underlying logic goes, may have been applies in history, but were not formalized as such; while importance of avoiding the divorce between business and IT, where the latter enables the former, has been highlighted by approaches such Convergent Engineering (and further, Convergent Architecture)

The lessons, whether on architecting systems, the business, the human organization, or the Enterprise as a whole with all that it is made of, have been learnt the hard way, often without learning from other's mistakes and usually with the IT function – an enabler – taking the lead. Further, they have been learnt best where challenges of the environment have necessitated their learning for survival of the organization and discharge of critical responsibilities that it is tasked.

This explains why in institutions relying on public money and operating in democratic societies, where, at least in theory, the budget managers can always be held accountable by the population, greater effort has been spared in developing architecture concepts and organizing them in frameworks. The best example is the defense industry, where most solutions are novel - meant to be one step ahead of the adversary, huge level of secrecy exists with far less scope for fair competition across a large number of merited suppliers, where solutions are not necessarily routinely testable in their entirety, and yet where, in principle, failure is not an option.

The lessons learnt have resulted in development of gradually sophisticated *architecture*

frameworks that have broadened, yet made precise, the definition of architecture concepts, with Enterprise Architecture concepts following one step behind (The Open Group, 2006) and eventually forming an integral part of the Architecture Framework.

Whereas an exhaustive commentary on all EA frameworks created so far may prove a candidate for a book-series, I think I may be pardoned delving briefly into some of the better and wider known frameworks.

The development of concepts of Enterprise Architecture may be likened to that of a snow-flake. While groups of water molecules/icicles are formed (and at times broken down) and are in motion through air continuing through chains of molecular interactions, a flake is recognized only when it gather sufficient mass to begin to precipitate and holds the critical mass until it has precipitated. It is generally believed that such phenomenon occurred through efforts of John Zachman in IBM in the 1980s. Whereas far from complete and with scope for differing interpretation, his framework was a widely noted and fairly comprehensive attempt at blueprinting an enterprise through a two-dimensional schema around communication interrogatives (what, how, where, who, when, why) and stakeholder groups (visionary, owner, designer, builder, implementer, worker). Whereas both the interrogatives and stakeholder classification are open to interpretation, the classification scheme has provided useful basis for further development of EA concepts e.g. architecture 'views' depending on 'viewpoints' followed, layers of abstraction, and building blocks – an omnipresent term in modern day architecture frameworks (CIO Council, 1999).

A number of 'development methods' existed and were being minted, when standards such as ISO/IEC TR 14252:1996 began appearing to assist a number of 'roles' such as consumers, systems integrators, application developer, etc in construction of information processing systems. The temporal path of context, then principles, then definition of key architecture elements, then transformational planning, was formalized in Spewak's Enterprise Architecture Planning methodology, among other places. EAP and Zachman were in turn useful sources for the Federal Enterprise Architecture Framework by the Federal CIO council; while the Federal Enterprise Architecture Practice Guide endeavored to formalize architecture transformation approaches in a variety of IS lifecycle scenarios (CIO Council, 1999).

In the meanwhile, Technical Architecture Framework for Information Management (TAFIM) was being developed under US DoD (Department of Defense, 2007). TAFIM was officially withdrawn in January 2000, where its journey into the 'Open' community began through The Open Group Architecture Framework (TOGAF) contributed extensively in its early stages by the US Defense Information Systems Agency (DISA). In particular, the TOGAF Technical Reference Model (TRM) was largely derived from TAFIM, and the TOGAF Architecture Development Method (ADM) was originally based on parts of TAFIM. The *Reference Models* aspect of the amorphous concept of *Reference Architecture* was thus first widely seen formalized in the defense pedigree of Architecture Frameworks.

The ADM and TOGAF reference models have grown in maturity version on version, though it has only been in major version 8 where TOGAF has assumed the suffix of *Enterprise Edition*. It also has fairly well defined role-based responsibilities and governance description. It provides a continuum of Reference Models (skeletal models that should be 'instantiated' and detailed to be valuable in a typical enterprise), supplemented with Standards Information Base and Platform Taxonomy, with a wider and expanding Resource Base provided as additional support. By the very nature of its contents, the level of organization diminishes from the ADM section to the Continuum section, with the Resource Base section serving simply as a receptacle. Given the evolutionary path followed by TOGAF and its 'open' nature,

it is conceivable that Beacon Architecture may be referred in future versions of TOGAF.

The Command, Control, Computers, Communications (C4), Intelligence, Surveillance, and Reconnaissance (ISR) framework (C4ISR) succeeded TAFIM as DoD EA framework and was in turn supplanted by the more comprehensive DoDAF in October 2003. C4ISR provided key abstractions and organization through its *views*, and useful EA principles, while leaving the EA transformational approach to methodology of individual organization and directing its focus on going into great detail on work products. The name C4ISR is also interesting in being one of the very few attempts at trying to be descriptive and explicit, while in reality allowing initiatives to *opt-out* of the framework and *return to the wild* on the pretext that scope of the initiative could not be *completely* covered by the four Cs, I, S & R.

DoDAF, while it retains the *views* concepts from C4ISR, is really a compendium for 'everything currently followed by various US defense bodies' with commentary on their rationale and interrelation. Whereas it has many useful sections around principles and transformational approaches, its 'collection' nature is a testimony to the fact that the US DoD is *not* an Enterprise, and so when asked to provide a consistent and reformed approach (CCA, 1996) to Information Technology Management, the best that the DoD can hope to come up with is a collection of *everything*, thus providing standards for most scenarios and a fair amount of useful wisdom, but no consistency across organizations and different scenarios, other than that they shall all follow pertinent standards set for them. The desperation with which DoD has periodically moved on with its architecture frameworks and has ended up with DoDAF (Department of Defense, 2007) – a collection of approaches followed within different organizations, is an excellent illustration of the need for the elements that have been defined and linked together in a logical order under Beacon Architecture, later in this chapter.

There too are initiatives within defense collaborators of the US to produce aligned architecture frameworks, including the UK MoDAF (with 6 rather than 4 views), and various international synchronization efforts, including the IDEAS group. Whereas such synchronization efforts allow sharing of vocabulary and proven useful concepts, they do not give rationale, nor coherence and common purpose, to the organizations involved.

PUBLIC SECTOR TRANSFORMATIONS

Unfortunately, the public sector, that is so often far closely bound to tactical interests of political leadership, does not always have the liberty of presenting itself as a domain of matured successful enterprises that know precisely their long term objectives and are geared to following a fairly well-defined roadmap, while continually making themselves efficient.

In greater part of a decade that I have spent assisting a number of public sector institutions (or privatized near-monopolies that used to be public sector institutions and still have a one-to-one governance by the government through specific regulatory mechanism) in the UK, examples of these institutions being constantly defined, refined and then, as a retrograde move, redefined, have abounded, despite the period having been under the stewardship of a single prime minister[1] and a single ruling party with comfortable majority behind it. A longer review of public sector organizations in the UK, or, for that matter, most places in the world, will show a far uncertain picture in terms of existence, let alone clear objective definition, strategy and roadmap, of a public sector institution.

Following are three examples cited from the relatively stable British socio-political scene, considering three among the highest resourced departments that are quite accessible to ordinary

people and are not bound by the kind of secrecy inherent in defense and other security establishments[2].

These are not full-fledged case studies, nor illustrative examples of Beacon Architecture in practice; rather these serve as *Illustrations by Absence* by citing situations common to the Public Sector that constituents of Beacon Architecture can address.

Transformation by Redistributing Responsibilities

On 8th June 2001, the Department of Work and Pensions (DWP) came into being by combining the employment part of *Department of Education and Employment* (DfEE) with the *Department of Social Security*. The department has a grand, albeit too amorphous to be enterprise-specific, purpose of "*To promote opportunity and independence for all through modern, customer-focused services*". The department has never been able to satisfactorily understand, let alone explain, how can it *promote opportunity* by divorcing itself from *Education*, with the result that the *Employment* segment of the department, referred to as *Jobcentre Plus*, has never quite aligned itself to the rest of the department (which largely deals with Social Security) nor quite detached itself from the remainder of the old *DfEE* (later called *Department of Education and Skills*).

In short, the DWP is not an enterprise. Its constituents have tried to cope with the politically imposed tactical change by trying to consider each of the services (such as Jobcentre Plus, The Pension Service, The Child Support Agency, etc) as a separate enterprise, making them just about workable, but unable to leverage on integrating common functions (such as payment processing, identity management, portfolio management, etc - becomes plainly evident to its customers who subscribe to more than one of these services). In fact, although clearly imprudent in terms of effectiveness of the department, budgeting and running transformational programs at individual constituent unit level has been about the only way of dealing with the disparate scene and reacting to future political whim.

In theory, it is possible to create cloned components to design and build common services and then give ownership of such cloned components to independent business units (e.g. architecting and building an identity management framework that can then be independently deployed and managed within two business units, with the option of regular synchronization of data and a common intuitive experience to the end user). However, independent political leadership of various business units makes allocation and accountability for such common budget, or even desire to do so, difficult.

Transformation by Grouping Responsibilities Together

On 18th April 2005, the Her Majesty's Revenue and Customs (HMRC) came into being by merging the Inland Revenue (IR) and Her Majesty's Customs and Excise (HMCE). The stated purpose of the merger was straightforward and admirable – to reduce administrative overhead and to leverage on mutual infrastructure/facilities.

The UK though, like many other regions the world over, lacks a simple logical revenue system. To consider just the direct tax taken out of salary, there are at least two headings – income tax and national insurance. Each heading follows its own distinct mathematical rules. In theory, Income Tax represents contribution made by a UK resident to overall governance, security and commonly used facilities, whereas the national insurance is meant to be just that – a premium paid into a common insurance pot to serve should someone lose means of livelihood or meet with an incapacitating situation requiring livelihood at least part-supported by the state. Non-European foreign nationals not yet given permanent residence in the UK (i.e. for at least the first five

years of their continuous residence in the UK, with many other whimsical get-out caveats that can indefinitely prolong this period) are however not entitled to such social security and are liable to be deported if they are unable to make positive economic contribution within a fairly rigid occupation regime. Whereas the UK has a right to decide its immigration pattern, it is against basic principles of democratic taxation – for the people by the people – to collect national insurance from foreigners not yet granted permanent residence who do not have social security and who are liable to be deported should they fail to be economically contributing in a specific way. Further, a wider accountability of where money goes from the individual pots (income tax and national insurance) in necessary if two separate pots are to be maintained.

The UK Inland Revenue never managed either to separately account for expenditure out of the two pots or to explain the rationale behind its separate National Insurance regime. It is therefore counterproductive to add to the chaos through further merger, when individual constituents of the HMRC have not yet defined their own business and when the merged business is actually expected to be two businesses running side by side collecting very different types of revenues – perhaps using separate floors of the same building with a single receptionist – which really did not need merger.

Transformation by Creating New Capabilities

The National Health Service (NHS) in the UK established the National Program for IT (NPfIT) in October 2002 to move towards standardized electronic care record for each patient, thus creating a unified patient identity accessible across ~ 30000 general practitioners and 300 hospitals.

The program however was never architecture-centric and far less emphasis was laid on defining and explaining to the end user the exact nature of the care record or associated data-relevance and protection safeguards. The program introduced additional level of abstraction, unaccountability and confusion to the governance structure by introducing the concept of Local Service Providers (LSPs) for regions of England, where each LSP provided exactly the same services in potentially very different ways, thus creating maintenance, migration and enhancement issues from the very near future, in what is, at least notionally, a unified National Health Service. Systems Transformation was planned without considering underlying Architectural Transformation, establishing an architectural pattern and considering possibility of a robust single or cloned solution to address exactly identical needs across different regions. Governance structure lacked as its key facets explicit architectural governance or end-user (clinicians and patients) requirements and expectations management.

Contractual independence and use of multiple providers for providing exactly the same services in different regions failed to manage risk, as secondary/indirect providers for separate regions happened to be the same organizations and thus risked multiple regions together, while a long chain of contractual obligations left organizations involved without a clear view of requirements (particularly non-functional requirements that are largely solved by the architecture) and architecture, and without palpable accountability that could be used constructively to deliver the program. The program cost has inflated many-folds with functional delivery still hard to predict and non-functional robustness completely unproven.

ENTERPRISE ARCHITECTURE CHALLENGES PECULIAR TO THE PUBLIC SECTOR

Our exemplified discussion about the public sector reveals many characteristic challenges including:

- Lack of definition of the enterprise as a set of organizations with a well-defined, specific (as opposed to such generic objectives as "*To promote opportunity and independence for all through modern, customer-focused services*") durable set of common objectives/purpose
- Lack of well defined, coherent business architecture
- Lack of long-term business strategy
- Lack of a transformational roadmap
- Lack of enterprise patterning to leverage on commonalities among sister functions/enterprises
- Lack of clear BAU (business-as-usual) and transformational governance

I conducted a simple non-exhaustive exercise of how various responsibilities associated with the erstwhile UK DfEE have moved across departments between 1988 and 2007, and how related departments have changed. The exercise is, as stated, not exhaustive, but even to the extent that it has been completed, it shows a myriad of function-transfers, where the only palpable motives in most transformations appear to be political, to give a Secretary of State (a politician in the upper echelons of the government – typically in charge of a department) greater or lesser power and a unified budget to go with it. The results are shown in Figure 3, which illustrate how functional cohesion can be compromised and considering the smallest atomic function (e.g. *Employment*) as a separate enterprise, though often imprudent, can end up being the most straightforward and organizationally durable way of dealing with the situation.

PROGRESSION THROUGH THE ARCHITECTURE DEVELOPMENT CYCLE

Now let's step back to what a generic enterprise might want to do having decided on an archi-

Figure 3. Considering distribution of education, employment and related functions in the British government between 1988 and 2007

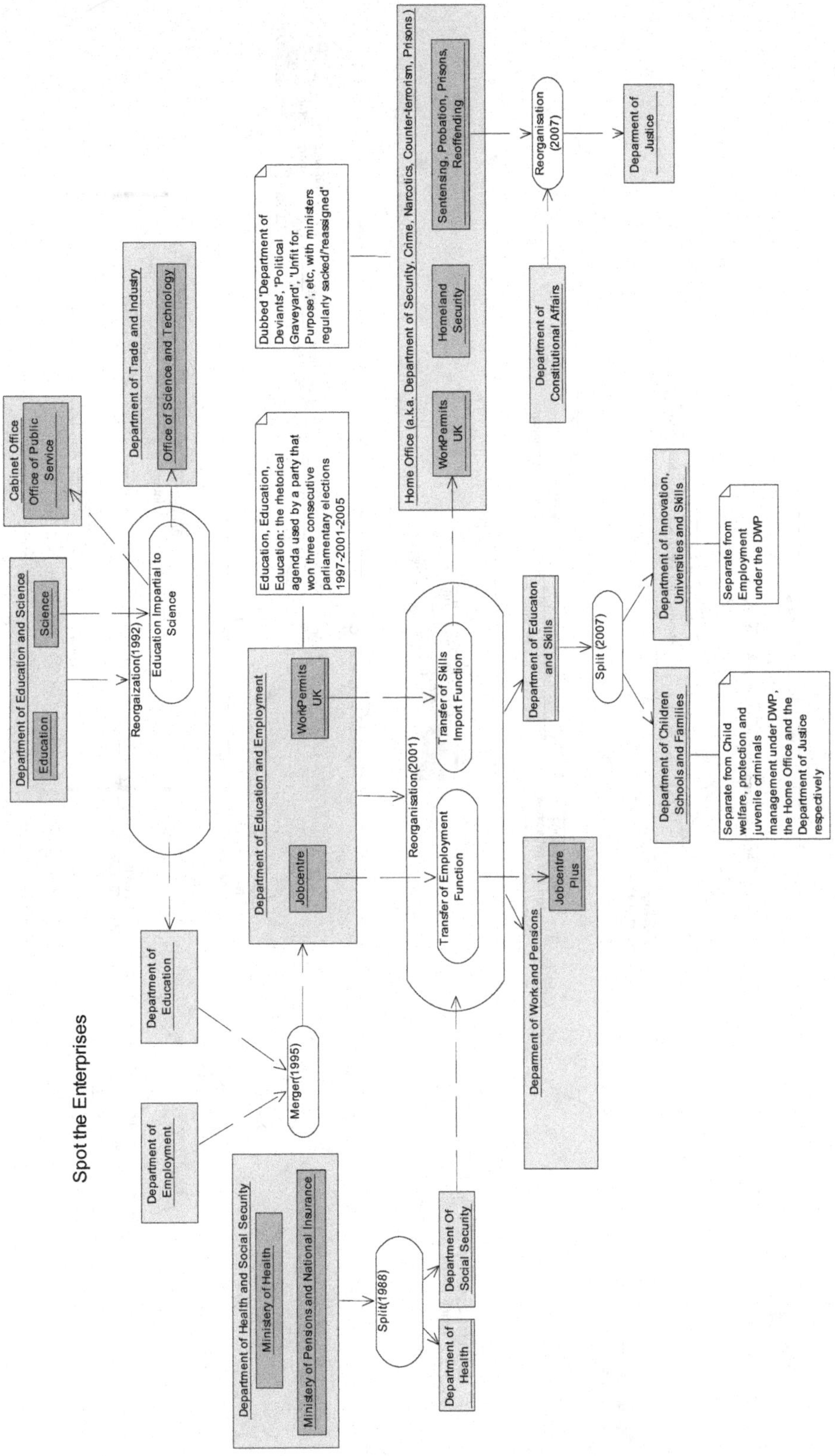

Figure 4. ADC in context of enterprise transformation

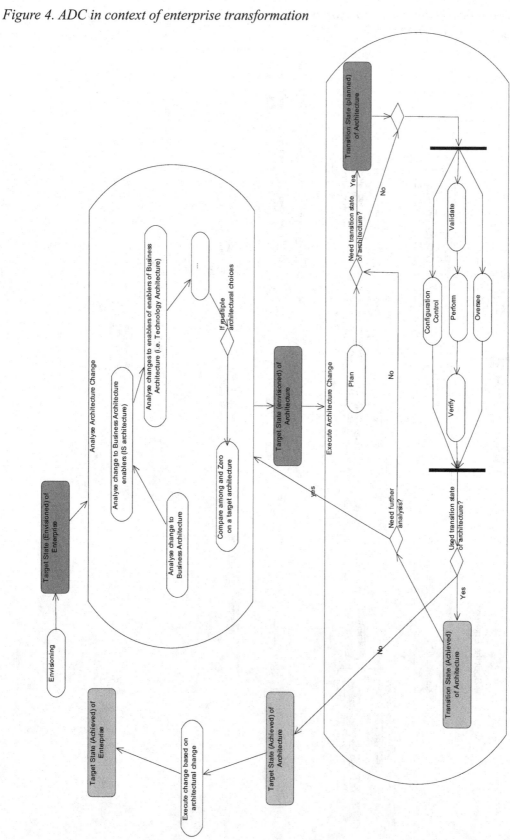

tectural transformation (presumably, having first known/understood prevalent architectural state, desired changes and their implementation orchestration and oversight).

The Enterprise undergoes a set of steps that take the Enterprise Architecture from an 'as is' to a 'to be' state. The steps form a cyclical pattern whereby the set of steps, or at least considering all and taking some of the set of steps, in a given sequence and with relevance to requirements driving the transformation, would create a repeating cycle where the *target architecture* of a cycle would be the *baseline architecture* of the next cycle. The cycle may be referred to as *Architecture Development Cycle* (ADC).

rchitecture frameworks usually formalize this set of repeating steps into a method description. For example, TOGAF refers to this by the term Architecture Development Method (ADM) and a cycle through these steps may be referred to as an ADM cycle.

The set of steps, in generic terms, go through the same treatment – envisioning the target state, analyzing changes to various aspects of the architecture (rationally going from the strategic to the tactical, from the goals to their enablers, i.e. business architecture to information systems architecture to technology architecture), comparing and zeroing down in case of options, and executing (planning, validating, overseeing, configuration-controlling, and verifying) change.

The amount of change that may be safely executed in one cycle can however be limited and may not take the architecture to a target milestone state. In such situations, a *transition architecture* (or transitional architectural state) may be defined and used for the purpose of sanity check before repeating the ADC sequence for a finite number of times (each intermediate cycle leading to a transitional state) ultimately leading to the target architecture. Here the transformation may conclude or may be followed by changes building on the architectural changes, in both cases, leading to next generation of the enterprise. Typical steps and

options involved in ADC in context of Enterprise Transformation are illustrated in Figure 4.

BEACON ARCHITECTURE

Beacon Architecture is intermediately detailed 'long-distance' architecture that an organization may define and aim to transform towards. The Beacon itself evolves; however, this is in order to fine-tune and accommodate needs of time, and not to satisfy executive/political whims. The Beacon is quite well defined in terms of Architectural Principles, Objectives/roles of constituents, definition and strategic objectives of the enterprise, and expands by citing patterns and mechanisms that can build evolutionary architectural states.

Organizational Architecture

The first input to long-distance view of enterprise architecture is definition of the enterprise, to explore whether functionally the organization represents '*a common set of goals and/or a single bottom line*'; if it does, what that is, if it does not, what enterprises or groups of enterprises (perhaps recursively) does the organization represent. In the latter case (where the organization represents more than one enterprises), the '*common set of goals and/or a single bottom line*' should be understood in case of all enterprises involved, each taking into account its interrelation with the rest of the organization and defining/designing itself based on the principle of *Design by Contract*[3].

The result of this exercise is the Organizational Architecture. We have commented earlier that architecture is function-driven and, in case of a good architecture, structure should be function-enabler. On the other hand, an enterprise having its own defined visible goals and bottom-line, when also part of the organization, may need structural elements to make it adequately self-sufficient, elements that may be dispensed with should that enterprise no longer be an enterprise, but rather an internal component of a bigger enterprise. A number of scenarios are possible here:

1. The organization is optimally architectured where there are no redundant structural elements in its compositions
2. The organization is a single enterprise and its function can be better delivered by improving its structure
3. The organization comprises of multiple enterprises, each with role complementary to others and with a level of structural redundancy where disadvantages of such redundancy are lower than the advantages it offers in managing a body with well-defined goal and optimal size.
4. The organization comprises of multiple enterprises, where each enterprise offers advantages in managing a body with well-defined goal and optimal size, but where there is substantial structural (and internal functional) redundancy.
5. The organization comprises of multiple enterprises, where there is no net functional advantage in maintaining at least some of these as independent enterprises.

This analysis should be followed by an exercise where

1. Redundant structural elements within individual enterprise, as opposed to those redundant across a number of enterprises, are identified and scenarios unifying their functions are considered
2. Redundant structural elements across a number of enterprises are identified and ways of making them efficient are considered, including:
   a. Unifying function of such elements across a number of enterprises
   b. Designing such elements centrally and cloning them with operational ownership within individual enterprise

3. Redundant enterprise(s) within the organization should be identified and
a. Either stakeholders operating at the organizational level and thus able to work beyond enterprise-level vested interests should be notified
b. Or stakeholders directing individual enterprises should be brought together to reduce the number of redundant enterprises through consensus (here it is important to attain consensus whereby enterprise leader roles can be redeployed to practical advantages rather than creating a mammoth third entity adding bottom-lines of two separately functioning entities and duplicating managerial tasks while virtually retaining the two enterprises in disguise)
c. Or a combination of the two options

Having taken these options to their logical conclusion and thus made the organization structurally efficient and geared to deliver coherent set(s) of functionality, attention should be focused on functional efficiency in terms of business process reengineering and automation, thus leading to a further refinement in organizational architecture

Business Beacon

Having obtained a structurally and functionally efficient organization of enterprise(s), to effectively meet present objectives of the organization, the next task is to detail a vision of what functional objectives and environmental position does an enterprise want to attain.

To illustrate, let's assume that the Jobcentre Plus organ of the UK DWP discussed earlier, is identified as an enterprise, which can be made efficient but can not be functionally subsumed by other enterprises or become their internal component. Its functional objective may then be stated as – to create a framework that

1. Identifies, classifies, gives ability rating to, studies trends of and forecasts pattern of
    a. Skills available in the society
    b. Professional needs of the society
    c. Members of the society in the role of single/multiple/versatile (doing one role but capable of another) /able (possibly doing one role but trainable on another) professionals
2. Establishes a matrix of potential skill-role-individual match based on
    a. Experience
    b. Ability
    c. Motivation
3. Facilitates liaison across
    a. Professionals (including prospective professionals)
    b. Seekers of professional abilities (a.k.a. the marketplace)
    c. Providers of professional training (including senior professionals needing apprentices)
4. Promotes value of equality of opportunities, while preserving human dignity, whereby
    a. Individuals in the society achieve station in life based entirely on
        i.   Ability
        ii. Motivation
        iii. Experience
    b. All humans living in the society, including foreigners resident in the society with due mandate, are treated with respect and courtesy due to every human

If an enterprise is able to set its Business Beacon with at least this clarity, there will be a realistic possibility of moving in the right direction and moving forward at all, rather than periodically going in circles. The latter syndrome is of particular significance in public sector institutions in democratic societies, where a lack of Business Beacons can make the institutions inherently inefficient, thus set in anti-incumbency sentiment, leading to another political entity coming to power and reversing changes made by its predecessor.

A clear and detailed Business Beacon drawn by the highest executive body (the cabinet, in case of the UK) and attested by the highest legislative body (the parliament, in case of the UK), among other things, gives the enterprise in question a clear enough mandate and executive powers to subsume all such functions as are necessary to discharge its role efficiently.

An example of what can happen in the absence of such Business Beacon may be elaborated by citing the difficulties of timely role-skill match in the medical profession, largely controlled by the government in the UK. In the UK, the NHS, under the Department of Health (DoH), is ultimately an almost exclusive employer of all but a few senior clinicians / specialists. The jobs include both relatively moderate-skilled jobs such as those of junior/auxiliary nurses and high-ability jobs, including those that are or are becoming highly-skilled (such as medical registrars – on their way to becoming recognized specialist consultants). At the high-end, the specialties are a sophisticated set of skills. The compartmentalization of responsibilities and the notion of higher ability = more self-reliance, means that Jobcentre Plus attracts customers and employers focusing on moderate skills, and, in turn, is unable to build profile of high-end skills / high-ability skill-sets. The NHS itself is administration-centric with managers, often of very average ability, managing clinicians of greater ability. It therefore has even poorer capability in skills measurement. The DfES that looks after education and skills, couples loosely with Jobcentre Plus and practically not at all with the DoH. Since the UK clearly has far fewer medical graduates than an inefficient-yet-effective NHS would need, a section of the Home Office – the department identified in public perception exclusively with Crime and that has a suitably negative attitude towards its interlocutors – steps in to grant visas to foreign medical graduates, to work and settle in the UK. Having done that, none of the departments are responsible for welfare of these foreigners legally immigrating and even invited into the UK. Many of them (and even British medical graduates) struggle to find jobs, not because their skills are not needed, but because no one is in charge of matching high-ability clinical skill needs with available resources, integrating unmet needs with foreign resourcing and ensuring welfare of those foreigners as equal members of the society, even in the case of errors in resource matching.

The situation is further complicated by the fact that most departments, due to historical feudal reasons and despite the moderate demographic and geographic size of the UK, operate at at least three levels:

- The union (called *the nation* elsewhere in the world)
- The nations such as England, Scotland, etc (called *states/provinces* elsewhere in the world, except that in the UK the legislative power of each *Nation* is vastly different, overlapping and inconsistent)
- The counties

with the NHS adding a fourth concept, that of region, between the nation (e.g. England) and county.

Such inconsistencies can be minimized and definition, reason of existence and achievements of a public-sector enterprise can be positively influenced by a clear-enough Business Beacon, approved and committed to by the highest set of stakeholders.

The phrase *Environmental Position* has been used in the first paragraph of this section to mean positioning with respect to other agencies / business partners and peers (which may mean similar function in another country/state etc in case of the public sector, or a similar business in the market place in case of the corporate sector).

Business Architecture Strategy

The business architecture strategy, i.e. long-term vision of functional (and, based on that, structural) organization of the business, should ideally emerge out of the exercise of defining Organizational Architecture and Business Beacon. Alternatively, should a body of Business Architects be commissioned to come up with the BA Strategy, they would need to ensure that Organizational Architecture and Business Beacon exercises are satisfactorily performed. It is also at this point that priority (including that of interactions with environment of the enterprise) and dependency (including that on elements of environment of the enterprise) should be palpable and formally laid out.

Architecture Infrastructure Capability – Engineering Practice Definition

Before moving any further with architecture artifacts and ideally even as the BA Strategy is being formulated, the enterprise should test its Architecture Infrastructure capability. Architecture is requirement-driven, involves careful management of assets, is subject to controlled change and involves management of transformations (projects). We therefore need capabilities for:

1. Requirement Management
   a. Plan
   b. Dependency Mapping
   c. Compositional Mapping (a requirement being subsidiary to another)
   d. Quantification and Parameterization (including sizing and prioritization)
   e. Traceability
   f. Articulation (including through models, charts and multimedia)
   g. Project Management Integration
2. Configuration Management
   a. Plan
   b. Asset Library
   c. Version Control
   d. Configuration Inventory and Audit
   e. Collaborative artifact development support

f.   Project Management Integration
3.   Change Management
     a.   Plan
     b.   Impact Metrics
     c.   Project Management Integration

These capabilities are collectively referred to as *Engineering/Support Capabilities* and should be articulated through *Engineering Practice definition*. In recent times, many matured interconnected tools are available to automate and better control and audit these capabilities. Building and successfully testing such infrastructure would give additional assurance and stability to progressing towards the Beacon. Only after the Engineering Practice is defined and preferably the associated infrastructure is established and tested, should development of the Beacon Architecture continue through a detailed Roadmap.

Regarding the establishment and testing of the Engineering Capability, it is often argued that tools are transformation enablers and organizations should not be shackled to a particular choice of these when what is really important is managing the transformation. Whereas there is merit in this argument and an organization need not be obsessive about a particular set of tools – they being means towards an end – organizations should nonetheless invest in proving their Engineering Capability, thus proving and beginning to institutionalize the Engineering Practice Definition, rather than keeping it in the form of an unproven thesis. The organization should then be open to changing its infrastructure, including engineering practice enablers, in a structured, evaluated, risk-mitigated and change-managed way, as defined in its Change Management Practice Definition (part of Engineering Practice Definition).

Business Architecture Roadmap

As explained while deliberating on aspects of enterprise architecture, the Roadmap is a staged, temporal description of how transformation might happen to meet the strategy. The roadmap therefore gives a sense of sequence, goes deeper into milestone states & transformational steps, and leads to resource planning and definition of transformations (projects/programs). It is preferable to have the Roadmap nailed to specific calendar dates, particularly given that external stimuli and collaborators' expectations from the enterprise may be associated with specific calendar dates. It is however possible to leave the roadmap at a 'sequence of initiatives' stage, if the utilization model of resourcing is practicable and followed (i.e. where initiatives are slotted on the calendar to utilize available resources, rather than resources are made available for calendar-bound initiatives), provided that external stimuli are not expected to invalidate key transformational states when these states are reached at a different calendar date.

Business Architecture Contingency Plan

This is really an integral part of a matured Business Architecture Roadmap. The roadmap should take into account probable, possible and ideally, every plausible scenario along the roadmap and create a sequence Web, including contingency transformations and associated transitional milestones that would not need to happen in a *happy day scenario*, thus giving robustness to the BA Roadmap. This is a lot easier with Requirement Characterization Capabilities built as part of the engineering capabilities, as that allows considering which requirements are optional or might be de-prioritized with least business impact. Additional contingency measures may exist in the form of contingency resources, either available, or acquirable from stakeholders.

Operational and Developmental Alternatives Analysis

At this point, the Business Architecture transformational path is sufficiently well understood to consider how its enablers, most notably Information Systems, evolve to meet the Business Architecture Roadmap. The first step in this is to evaluate, compare and contrast various alternatives, followed by setting out an enabler roadmap (more specifically, an Information Systems Architecture Roadmap interlinking Information with Applications) tying in with the BA Roadmap. This process also involves considering each business alternative and contingency point to evaluate whether the Information Systems evolution path will need to change to react to different business situations. Arguably, the Information Systems roadmap is less detailed and may give a set of solutions applicable under a variety of BA roadmap and contingency scenarios.

Further enablers (such as technology enabling the Information Systems) follow similar treatment. However, given the nature of changes in the technology sector and role of technology as enabler of enabler (enabler of Information Systems) rather than goal, the deliberations on technology should remain generic at continuously exploring and observing proven technologies and considering their deployments in emerging Information Systems scenarios. The Beacon Architecture should therefore confine to the processes necessary for evaluating and keeping abreast with changing technologies so as to deploy a safe, efficient and affordable solution that is available at modest timescales, rather than predicting long-distance target technologies (and further, associated brands).

Information Systems Patterns and Frameworks

Whereas Information systems are Business Enablers and thus changeable with the business, many so called 'framework services' e.g. identity management, audit trail, etc, are fairly stable, can be predicted and robustly designed beforehand. There can also be generic patterns of information operations and specific patterns of information operations attached to generic business operations, which can be designed in efficient, safe and reusable manner, so as to make the solution more predictable while also attaining economy. These

inputs are pertinent in long-term progression of the Enterprise and can form part of the Beacon Architecture.

Enterprise Governance, and Correlation to Architectural Governance and Transformation

An aspect of Enterprise definition is Enterprise Governance Definition. While those defining the Enterprise would inevitably define its Architecture (alternatively, enterprise may be defined while defining its architecture), it is imperative that Architectural Governance is formally defined, with due influence on Enterprise Governance, to keep the enterprise on its chosen path. Further, whereas vision and strategic thinking are important qualities of all leaders, Architectural governance should incorporate qualities of both a good Enterprise Architect (a relevant specialist with sufficient generalist skills and aptitude to collaborate with peers and hold the enterprise together) and a good leader. It is important to detail both the governance mechanisms, and qualities & expertise expected of key governance roles, as part of the Beacon.

The Beacon should then elaborate on definition and governance of transformations (projects/programs) to tie in with the Roadmap.

Figure 5 diagrammatically represents constituents of Beacon Architecture, also giving a sense of dependency and recommended sequence.

CORRELATION OF BEACON ARCHITECTURE WITH TARGET, TRANSITION AND REFERENCE ARCHITECTURE

The term Reference Architecture has been used quite generically by Architects and with different connotations, including meaning either present architectural skeleton to be aware of in planning transformation or a to-be broad-brushstroke state

Figure 5. Constituents of Beacon Architecture

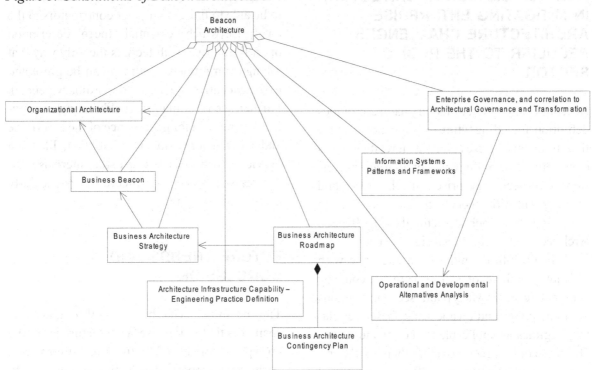

of architecture coupled with a set of principles governing the overall direction. In this latter sense, Beacon Architecture is an elaborated Reference Architecture, with specific meaning and mandating an essential set of formalized information, to be considered adequate. Its principal merit is in clearly defining what the Enterprise(s) considered is (are) and how the Enterprise should transform vis-à-vis its objectives and operational model; while the usual deliverables of typical CIO/CTO Reference Architectures in terms of Services Framework, Systems management principles, etc can be useful inclusions.

Beacon, Target and Transition are all 'to be' Architectures. As explained in context of the Architecture Development Cycle, Target Architecture is a to-be architecture state anticipated out of a transformation. If the architectural change is so significant as to consider it imprudent to be undertaken in a single ADM cycle, intermedi-

ate Transition Architectures may be defined to control the change and validate it at intermediate states expected during the transformation by spanning the transformation across multiple ADM cycles.

The Roadmap in Beacon Architecture defines at least the Target states of Business Architecture Transformations and potentially also some of the Transition states. It may provide similar treatment on Information Systems Architecture, which enables the Business Architecture, but is less likely to be fully elaborated/constraining on transition states of IS Architecture further down the line; its function being that of a Beacon and not of an administrative impediment. For this reason too, whereas it may present possible scenarios of technological evolution, it is unlikely to rigidly state Technology Architecture states during and as a result of future transformations.

ROLE OF BEACON ARCHITECTURE IN MITIGATING ENTERPRISE ARCHITECTURE CHALLENGES PECULIAR TO THE PUBLIC SECTOR

Beacon Architecture, by its very nature, provides definition, including future recommended definition, to the enterprise and helps it relate with its environment, including collaborating enterprises. In this respect, enterprises in all sectors and of all complexities benefit by defining Beacon Architecture. In public sector though, Beacon Architecture has additional significance.

To begin with, definition of an enterprise, with definite specific set of goals, is harder to come by in the public sector. Many public sector institutions are monopolies and escape sector-based regulatory regimes as applicable to the private sector. Often the only directive, rather than regulatory, disciplining influence comes from international protocols rather than binding, scrutinized and tested legislation within a sovereign nation. The legislative bodies are usually made of individuals who lack specialist understanding to precisely define enterprises in the public sector and the executive bodies usually structure and lead institutions with political motivation. In democracies, whereas the additional level of scrutiny and balance of opinion help reduce fanatical extremes of ideas, the constant pressure on both the legislative and the executive bodies to be seen to be serving and the need to win popular support for the near future, discourages serving quietly and confidently with investment in long-term strategy. As none of the executives – the chosen representatives, the indirect rulers (ordinary people) or administrative civil servants, possess adequate domain expertise, they are usually incapable of defining, designing and leading an enterprise to be of long-term effective service to them.

Beacon Architecture created by an independent body of professionals with proven domain knowledge and analytical skills, coupled with enough generalist understanding of related areas to be able to liaise with other contributors to the enterprise (which is essentially the role description of an Enterprise Architect), is the only way that a long-term rational roadmap can be presented to the executive (including the ordinary people). Further, such roadmap also deliberating on effective mechanism for governance of the enterprise and its transformation is, if applied, likely to provide effective leadership to the enterprise. For this reason, Beacon Architecture is particularly pertinent to the public sector.

FUTURE TRENDS AND CONCLUSION

The one thing that has been clear throughout this chapter is that Enterprise Architecture is not the prerogative of the IT/IS function. Information Technology supports Information Systems, which support Information Management, which has been key to smooth running, and even effective survival, of any enterprise, however far back in time we might go. What we are looking for in an Enterprise Architect is a set of well developed analytical, lateral and linear thinking skills, expertise in at least one of the subject areas relevant to the enterprise and sufficient knowledge of other subjects that relate to this expertise subject area, to be able to be a circumspective thinker and effective generalist, able to see and contribute to holding the bigger picture together. It just so happens that when we look back through the last three decades (which is minuscule time when looking at history of the concept of Enterprise), we observe that the IT industry/function has been a powerful magnet for such individuals, and, more importantly, has organically grown and retained these skills, through the type of work required of its practitioners.

This means that on the one hand, the Enterprise Architects need not be drawn exclusively, or even predominantly, out of the IT/IS function, and should definitely not be looked at by the rest of the organization as *those brainbox technologists who keep talking Latin.* On the other hand, if we are hoping to get a sizable collection of thinking minds, and more importantly, a team that can readily structure, understand, appreciate and realize its function, then there is a high likelihood that the IT/IS function might take the lead. In fact, whereas I am not at liberty to divulge specifics – the metrics leading to the conclusions being confidential – I feel at liberty to point out that there has been evidence in functions/enterprises within UK government departments I have worked with, to indicate that those functions/enterprises that have, high up in their ranks, people with the Enterprise Architect qualities (who, given history of last three decades, predominantly come from the IT/IS function) – the function/enterprise head in one case, tend to be better performing enterprises with something of their Beacon Architecture (as we have defined it here) already defined.

Taking this cue, whereas we may not be able to mandate appointment of individuals with Enterprise Architect characteristics in visionary or function-leading roles nor revolutionize the education system to identify and develop these abilities in the very near future, we can definitely get those functions where such individuals tend to exist in higher concentration to define themselves clearly and perform well, thus creating example for other functions and the larger organization/enterprise to follow.

In this respect, although steps involved in defining the Beacon Architecture have definite temporal relevance/dependency, it is possible that those steps that can be demonstrated within the IT/IS function may get demonstrated and institutionalized first.

This means that in the near term we would see greater evidence of:

- Architecture infrastructure capability – engineering practice definition
- Operational and developmental alternatives analysis

The latter may also involve unified development and separate operational deployment, where the IT/IS functions clearly see similarity and emergence of patterns in what is expected of them, but are asked to manage their systems separately and often with changing business organization, by the business owners. In general, the public sector is likely to take lead in demonstrating these two aspects alongside a formalized and repeatable approach to Information Systems Patterns and Frameworks (for which the public sector has both the time and justification of budget constraints, being less keen to substitute money for time than the corporate sector). This may be considered the first generation of Beacon Architecture Evolution.

The key role of Business Architect, with characteristics of an Enterprise Architect, is still maturing. Many aspects of Beacon Architecture that depend on this role will mature with this role. Organizational Architecture and Governance aspects would be most volatile, while also being resistant to structure and controlled-change. Therefore the remaining aspects will be demonstrably formalized first, the contingency plan developing as constituent of the Roadmap:

- Business beacon
- Business architecture strategy
- Business architecture roadmap
- Business architecture contingency plan

Here, the corporate sector, perhaps motivated by market pressures and competitor evaluation, is likely to take the lead. This may be considered the second generation (or second phase of the first generation if you like, as these developments can happen independent of the first generation/phase) of Beacon Architecture evolution.

Periodic synchronization of ideas across the Corporate and Public sector may then help establish all aspects from Business Beacon to Information Systems Patterns & Frameworks in proper order, and connect them. The dependent aspects will then fine tune with aspects that they depend on, thus improving the Beacon Architecture. The synchronization between the Corporate and Public sector is not the easiest to realize, given tendency of practitioners in respective sectors and even domains therein (such as financial services domain) to stick together and do things their own way. Once again, consultants, often branded IT-related consultants, who work independently and have sufficient recognition (or at least curiosity to check other's work) right across the business spectrum, will be key to the synchronization process.

The principal impediments to creation of effective and durable enterprises – lack of visionary ability, lack of consensus on means (and sometimes also ends) and, often, also a lack of acceptable level of sincerity among enterprise leaders, will be the principal stumbling blocks in the process of defining optimized Organizational Architecture.

There is hope on this front though. Looking at those who set out public-sector objectives in the UK over the last 100 years or so, we see palpable improvement in the maturity level of the enterprise leaders (the politicians), perhaps as a result of increased maturity of those who appoint them (the electorate). About 100 years ago, it was a norm for people of the ruling classes, irrespective of their ability, to rule with strong prejudices set by the establishment they grew-up in. Later, as the labour movement took roots, the governments alternated between regimes that were, by present day standards, extreme left or right winged. Like a dampening pendulum however, the swings have reduced in their span in successive elections, where today it is realistic for all candidate leaders to share objectives of progressive welfarism, thus not necessarily setting about undoing everything that previous government tried to do.

The means to the end however are not yet agreed on and are definitely not effective, whichever political faction is in power, while the practice of the higher executive dispensing privileges to their subordinates based on political loyalty, and reorganizing administration to redistribute patronage, continues. In fact, modern advent of mass communication has put additional pressure on top executives to be seen to be decisive and in control, while really trying out hopeful permutations. To take example of the very important and conspicuously underperforming British Home Office, we observe that in its early days, in the first 10 years under the stable and effective premiership of William Pitt the Younger (i.e. ~1783-1793), there were just four Home Secretaries, the first resigning within a week of taking office and thus really not to be counted as an enterprise leader, while the fourth continuing his service beyond the 10 years. In the 10 years that the last British Prime Minister, Tony Blair, was in office, with comfortable majority behind him, once again, four Home Secretaries served. In this case though, they all left office sincerely attempting to lead the organization and after being demonstrated not to be in sound control, or fully following the definition and interfacing of the organization they commanded; while each, in his turn, performed reorganizations within the department, without demonstrable success and often with visible failures highlighted by the media. The last of these Home Secretaries, John Reid, ended up leading three separate key departments of the government – Heath, Defense and the Home Office, is three years, with clearly no time to understand, let alone contribute to rational definition of, the organization that he was asked to lead.

Apart from challenges to definition and governance of enterprises, caused by politics (which also exists, to a degree, in the corporate sector), a greater challenge is posed by governance by non-professionals. This latter challenge too exists in the corporate sector, but manifests more vividly in the public sector, particularly where elevation to leadership position is a direct outcome of administrative seniority. Further, in such circumstances, senior administrators tend to address risk to their position caused by their lack of professional and analytical expertise, by delegating responsibilities – usually in a supplier chain mode – to other administrators, where no individual administrator takes blame for failure.

The example of the UK NHS National Program for IT (NPfIT) cited earlier, illustrates this point. Whereas the program has been variously scoped and re-scoped throughout, its basic objective has involved a functionally simple, yet architecturally substantial problem - that of creating a unified patient care record mechanism that would cope with typical non-functional requirements (volume, performance, security, availability, etc) of medical service of a medium-sized nation. The fact that this problem, relatively simple to solve for a group of professionals who design systems robust enough to address non-functional requirements (various IT architecture specialties) and who can rationally decide needs of the patient care record (clinicians and business analysts), has snowballed into one of the world's most expensive, yet uncertain and non-functionally unproven transformational program, can directly trace its roots to the number of senior roles of administrators and multiple levels of delegation involved in running the program, where few relevant professionals can be seen playing key visionary or executive roles.

Of course, it is tantamount to fortune-telling gazing into a crystal ball, to try to guess how and when will the Organizational Architecture aspect of Beacon Architecture become the norm; though when that happens, it will help fine-tune other aspects of Beacon Architecture and define the last aspect – that of prudent Enterprise Governance, and correlation to Architectural Governance and Transformation, thus taking Beacon Architecture into its fourth generation.

The fastest scenario is one of a strong and popular leader of a significant enterprise happening to possess the Enterprise Architect qualities, or at least recognize them and provide environment conducive to their application, thus providing demonstrable examples for others to follow. The slowest scenario would be of ongoing evolution-ary improvement in social maturity fostering organizational maturity. In both cases, being able to observe and communicate with the rest of the fast-shrinking world will be important.

The evolutionary path that I foresee being taken for development and institutionalization of Beacon Architecture is depicted in Figure 6. Attaching a timeline to this will need further observation of future developments.

REFERENCES

Booch, G., Rumbaugh, J., and Jacobson I. (1999). *The Unified Modeling Language User Guide.* New York, NY: Addison-Wesley Object Technology Series.

CCA. (1996). *Clinger-Cohen Act of 1996: Information Technology Management Reform*, Public Law 104-106, Fiscal Year 1996 Defense Authorization Act.

CIO Council. (1999). Federal Enterprise Architecture Framework, Version 1.1. Retrieved February 20, 2008 from http://www.whitehouse.gov/omb/egov/a-1-fea.html

Department of Defense. (2007). *The Department of Defense Architecture Framework Version 1.0.* The Department of Defense. Retrieved February 20, 2008 from http://www.defenselink.mil/cio-nii/docs/DoDAF_Volume_I.pdf DoDAF 1.5

Maier, M.W. Emery, D. and Hilliard, R. (2001). Software Architecture: Introducing IEEE Standard 1471, *IEEE Computer.* April 2001, Vol. 34-4, 107-109.

The Open Group. (2006). *The Open Group Architecture Framework Enterprise Edition Version 8.1.1.* The Open Group Architecture Forum. Retrieved February 20, 2008 from http://www.theopengroup.org/

Figure 6. The likely path of adoption and institutionalization of beacon architecture

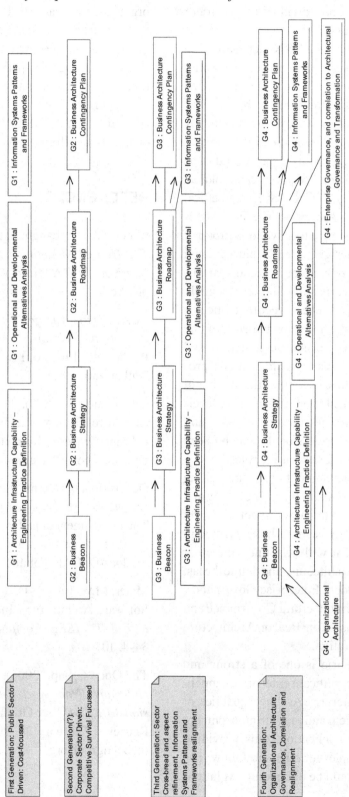

ADDITIONAL READING

Bass, L., Clements, P., and Kazman, R. (2003). *Software Architecture in Practice (2ⁿᵈ Edition)*. New York, NY: Addison Wesley.

Beck, K. & Andres, C. (2004). *Extreme Programming Explained: Embrace Change (2nd Edition) (The XP Series)*. New York, NY: Addison-Wesley Professional.

Bernard, S.A. (2005). *An Introduction to Enterprise Architecture: Second Edition*. Bloomington, IL: AuthorHouse.

Bhagwat, A. (2003). Estimating Use-Case driven Iterative Development for "Fixed-cost" Projects. *The Rational Edge*. Retrieved February 20, 2008 from http://download.boulder.ibm.com/ibmdl/pub/software/dw/rationaledge/oct03/f_estimate_b.pdf

Bhagwat, A. (2006). Enterprise Architecture in Public Sector - Observations & Considerations. *The Open Group 10th Enterprise Architecture Conference*. Retrieved February 20, 2008 from http://www.opengroup.org/london2006/program.htm

Fowler, M. (2002). *Patterns of Enterprise Application Architecture*. New York, NY: Addison-Wesley Professional.

Kroll, P (2007). OpenUP In a Nutshell. The Rational Edge, September 2007 http://www.ibm.com/developerworks/rational/library/sep07/kroll/index.html

Kruchten, P. (2003). *The Rational Unified Process: An Introduction*. New York, NY: Addison-Wesley Professional.

Ministry of Defence. (2007). *The Ministry of Defence Architecture Framework (MoDAF) Version 1.0*. The Ministry of Defence. Retrieved February 20, 2008 from http://www.modaf.org.uk/

Ross, J.W., Weill, P. & Robertson, D. (2006). *Enterprise Architecture As Strategy: Creating a Foundation for Business Execution*. Boston, MA: Harvard Business School Press.

Saha, P (2007). Handbook of Enterprise Systems Architecture in Practice. Hershey. PA: IGI Global.

Spewak, S.H. (1993). *Enterprise Architecture Planning: Developing a Blueprint for Data, Applications, and Technology*. New York, NY: John Wiley & Sons.

Whittle, R. & Myrick, C.B. (2004). *Enterprise Business Architecture: The Formal Link between Strategy and Results*. Boca Raton, FL: CRC Press.

Zachman, J.A. (1996). Enterprise Architecture: the Issue of the Century. Zachman International. Retrieved February 20, 2008 from http://mega.ist.utl.pt/~ic-atsi/TheIssueOfTheCentury.pdf

ENDNOTES

[1] Statement accurate as of mid-2007; when the prime minister changed while the ruling party remained the same

[2] Given the volatile and inadequate nature of respective official Websites, Wikipedia resources on these organizations, and reference cited therein, provide better understanding of historical events.

[3] The principle, on which Component-based development (CBD) is founded, suggests that interrelating components should adhere to a contract established between them, whereby each component is able to perform its tasks competently and deliver result expected by the contract when provided with inputs expected in the contract, verifying inputs provided to it for conformance with the contract and gracefully rejecting non-confirming inputs without itself failing catastrophically.

Chapter IV
Maturity Model Based on Quality Concept of Enterprise Information Architecture (EIA)

Hong Sik Kim
Korea Polytechnique University, Korea

Sungwook Moon
ComponentBasis, Co., Ltd., Korea

ABSTRACT

Quite a good amount of time has been spent seeking appropriate solutions to handle the giant information technology expenditure not only in government sectors but also in private sectors all over the world. Beginning with OMB, which substantially leads the U.S. governmental efforts in ITA/EA area, seems to be on the right path using process improvement concept in its ITA/EA maturity model (OMB, 2007_2). EA community still finds it difficult to introduce quality management concept into its business and practices. Therefore in this chapter, we would like to suggest a more practical ITA/EA maturity model based on the quality concept of enterprise information architecture (EIA), which is ROI–driven, practical and based on four-phased process improvement approach for the EA community. We hope that this approach could bring a substantial reduction in the costs and efforts in the entire ITA/EA area and provide sustainable development environment for the ITA/EA like the argument of the environmentalists.

INTRODUCTION

We are faced with a number of enormous complexities in this era, which represent the so-called information society. A deluge of information would be the most proper expression to the people living on this earth. This situation is as if everything is mixed in a great bowl under the name of information society. This kind of mixing would often result in the various trials of integrating everything in that society, the appearances of new paradigms for adaptation, and another chaos and the complexity arising from large-scale transitions. Since Zachman (1987) addressed the management of the complexity of information systems using an architectural metaphor, there have been a lot of efforts to address and resolve the challenges of complexities. And these efforts have resulted in a number of architectural frameworks and methodologies. The information technology architecture (ITA) and enterprise architecture (EA) is one of the various approaches in the enterprise-wide architecture horizon to manage this modern complexity caused by a deluge of information in government sectors as well as in private sectors (Figure 1).

ITA/EA, however, became another challenge to an organization because of the difficulties in the initial adaptation, utilization, continuous evolution and evaluation of its effectiveness. So the early ITA/EA Maturity Model contributors such as OMB, GAO (United States General Accounting Office), and NASCIO (National Association of State Chief Information Officers) have introduced their ITA/EA maturity models as milestones to guide the current chaotic IT situation to more manageable future complexity (GAO, 2003; NASCIO, 2003; OMB, 2007_2). But it is also extremely difficult to evaluate the progress of the ITA/EA using these maturity models because of its huge and complicated nature, the inappropriateness of the maturity models in some architectural perspectives, and the lack of proper metrics and experts for the models (EA Shared Interest Group, 2005). Furthermore, we can't even see the clear and well-prepared definition of the ITA/EA as its concept is continuously evolving over time.

With these challenges and uncertain circumstances, the future of the ITA/EA seems to be not so promising; therefore it needs to be reinforced with more sustainable approaches and assessment frameworks. Though there may not be a silver bullet as a solution for the problems, there should be a more practical approach to assess the maturity and effectiveness of ITA/EA in order for an organization to get real benefits from its huge investment in it.

Figure 1. ITA/EA and knowledge information society

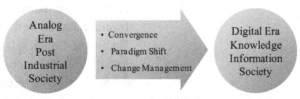

- Convergence: Capital Market Consolidation Act (2007), Bancassurance, Digital convergence

- Paradigm Shift: Plan for update law of 393 e-government implementation (2007), Sarbanes-Oxley Act (2002)

- Change Management: **ITA/EA**, TQM, Six Sigma, Process Improvement, CMMI, ITIL, COBIT

In this chapter we suggest a practical approach based on quality concept for the maturity model of the ITA/EA with some exploration to the unforeseen complexity of the future society. That is the EIAMM (Enterprise Information Architecture Maturity Model). Furthermore, we strongly recommend that organizations should borrow experiences and knowledge of the information systems development, software engineering, enterprise-wide total quality management (TQM), and incremental process improvement techniques to get really practical results through the implementation of the EIA. Especially, it is obvious that organizations will need to adopt highly sophisticated quality control (QC) circle or Kaizen (Japanese for "improvement") concept to continuously improve the entire enterprise information systems like manufacturing industries. Here we also suggest the conceptual outlines of EIA Maturity Model that is based on the practical cases of Boeing's process improvement using capability maturity model integration (CMMI) of Software Engineering Institute (SEI).

At the following background section, we are going to review some enterprise architecture definitions and compare the scopes of EA and EIA for our proposed EIA maturity model. In addition, we address some worldwide TQM models for better positioning of the ITA/EA within an enterprise. For the main thrust of this chapter, we will present a newly proposed EIA Maturity Model. After a brief description about future research, we will conclude this chapter.

BACKGROUND

The term of enterprise architecture (EA) is broadly used in the IT architecture areas worldwide. But it would be very hard for people to imagine that it is related with information technology architecture (ITA). EA also seems to have very ambiguous meaning for both IT and non IT people to understand, because the EA community could not

provide its clear definition and practical directions to obtain appropriate ROI in the reality. We understand the meaning of enterprise, but when the concept of architecture is added to it, we would need more explanation to figure out the combined meaning. Without proper interpretation, it would be difficult to understand that the architecture is mostly related to information technology related things. Here we review some of EA definitions. Furthermore the only guide of the huge ITA/EA program, the maturity model of ITA/EA, seems to be in the early stages of development without its clear definition. If we don't have a proper definition, we will not be able to produce the appropriate quality and maturity model of ITA/EA. Therefore we will suggest a desirable definition of ITA/EA, review its status within an enterprise, and provide a practical solution for the maturity model of ITA/EA, actually EIA in this chapter.

Definitions of Enterprise Architecture

Wikipedia (2007) defines enterprise architecture is the description of the current and/or future structure and behavior of an organization's processes, information systems, personnel and organizational sub-units, aligned with the organization's core goals and strategic direction. Although often associated strictly with information technology, it relates more broadly to the practice of the business optimization in that it addresses business architecture, performance management, organizational structure and as well.

Clinger-Cohen act (DoD, 2006) defines IT Architecture as "The term `information technology architecture', with respect to an executive agency, means an integrated framework for evolving or maintaining existing information technology and acquiring new information technology to achieve the agency's strategic goals and information resources management goals."

In TOGAF, the Open Group (2003) defines that there are four types of architecture that are commonly accepted as subsets of overall enterprise architecture:

- **Business architecture:** This defines the business strategy, governance, organization, and key business processes.
- **Data/information architecture:** This describes the structure of an organization's logical and physical data assets and data management resources.
- **Application (systems) architecture:** This kind of architecture provides a blueprint for the individual application systems to be deployed, their interactions, and their relationships to the core business processes of the organization.
- **Information technology (IT) architecture:** The software infrastructure intended to support the deployment of core, mission-critical applications. This type of software is sometimes referred to as "middleware", and the architecture as a "technical architecture."

OMB (2007_1) addresses the EA from the federal point of view. "The Federal Enterprise Architecture (FEA) consists of a set of inter-related *reference models* designed to facilitate cross-agency analysis and the identification of duplicative investments, gaps and opportunities for collaboration within and across agencies. Collectively, the reference models comprise a framework for describing important elements of the FEA in a common and consistent way. Through the use of this common framework and vocabulary, IT portfolios can be better managed and leveraged across the federal government."

Microsoft's Platt (2007) states that "Enterprise architecture is a conceptual blueprint that defines the structure and operation of an organization. The intent of enterprise architecture is to determine how an organization can most effectively achieve its current and future objectives."

Ross et al. (2006) describes it that "The enterprise architecture is the organization logic for business processes and IT infrastructure, reflecting the integration and standardization requirements of the company's operating model (where the operating model is defined as the necessary level of business process integration and standardization for delivering goods and services to customers). The enterprise architecture provides a long-term view of a company's processes, systems, and technologies so that individual projects can build capabilities – not just fulfill immediate needs."

Finally, IFEAD's Schekkerman (2005) states that "Enterprise architecture is about understanding all of the different elements that go to make up the enterprise and how those elements interrelate. An enterprise in this context is any collection of organizations that has a common set of goals/principles and/or single bottom line. In that sense, an enterprise can be a whole corporation, a division of a corporation, a government organization, a single department, or a network of geographically distant organizations linked together by common objectives. Elements in this context are all the elements that enclose the areas of people, processes, business and technology. In that sense, examples of elements are: strategies, business drivers, principles, stakeholders, units, locations, budget, domains, functions, processes, services, information, communications, applications, systems, infrastructure, etc."

Though there are various definitions of enterprise architecture as above, we still have difficulties in understanding what the enterprise architecture really is. In spite of the definitions as above, the EA community tends to think that EA is about the IT areas in the enterprise. But we will need to make clear that enterprise architecture is actually a framework of an enterprise for the various purposes. One of the EA communities, alEA (Association of Enterprise Architects) has recently announced that it is not recommendable for the EA community to use EA term solely except using EA with other modifiers because of its ambiguity. If we do not have even consensus in the definition of the EA and standard EA maturity model, then we may have to unnecessarily give great pains to the EA communities. When organizations practicing EA cannot find a positive way to produce reasonable ROI, eventually the entire EA industry may lose its momentum like previous giant programs that were doomed to fail.

Enterprise Architecture and Total Quality Management Models

Enterprise architecture encompasses the whole architectural aspects of an enterprise. It is not just

Table 1. Comparison of major segments for the TQM frameworks

MBNQA (U.S.A)	EFQM/EQA (Europe)	JQA (Japan)
P: Preface: Organizational Profile P1:Description/ P2:Challenges	1. Leadership	1.0 Management Vision and Leadership
1. Leadership 1.1 Senior Leadership 1.2 Governance and Social Responsibilities	2. Policy and Strategy	2.0 Understanding of Customers and Market and Action Taken
2. Strategic Planning 2.1 Strategy Development 2.2 Strategy Deployment	3. People	3.0 Strategic Planning and Development
4. Measurement, Analysis, and Knowledge Management **4.2 Management of Information, Information Technology, and Knowledge**	**4. Partnerships and Resources** **4d. Technology is managed.** **4e. Information and Knowledge are managed**	4.0 Human Resource Development and Learning Environment
5. Workforce Focus 5.1 Workforce engagement 5.2 Workforce environment	5. Processes	5.0 Process Management
6. Process Management 6.1 Work Systems Design 6.2 Work Processes Management and Improvement	6. Customer Results	**6.0 Information Sharing and Utilization**
7. Results 7.1 Products and Service Outcomes 7.2 Customer-Focused Outcomes 7.3 Financial and Market Outcomes 7.4 Workforce-Focused Outcomes 7.5 Process Effectiveness Outcomes 7.6 Leadership Outcomes	7. People Results 8. Society Results 9. Key Performance Results	7.0 Results of Enterprise Activities 8.0 Customer Satisfaction

for the IT area. From the view point of architectural quality, total quality management (TQM) models are suitable for the enterprise architecture. We will look over several TQM models here; MBNQA (Malcolm Baldrige National Quality Award of U.S.A), EFQM (European Foundation for Quality Management) Excellence Award and JQA (Japan Quality Award). Table 1 shows the comparison of the major segments of the TQM frameworks.

IT-related area in MBNQA (Table 1): Among the components of MBNQA model, IT area is directly shown in the section '4.2 Management of Information, Information Technology, and Knowledge.' But it is still a relatively small portion of the entire organization's components. The contents of each category in the MBNQA framework seem to be a lot different from IT perspective based on the EA concept we have used, that consists of business architecture, data architecture, service architecture, technical architecture, and security architecture.

IT-related area in EFQM/EQA (Table 1): From the components, we can also find IT related areas as in the sections '4d. Technology is managed and 4e. Information and Knowledge are managed.'

IT related area in JQA (Table 1): One of the eight high-level categories, 6.0 Information Sharing and Utilization, is directly allocated to the IT-related area. JQA model gives a relatively larger portion to the IT area than MBNQA and EFQM. JQA also directly uses the word *enterprise* in the section '7.0 Results of Enterprise Activities.' In this context, the meaning of enterprise seems to imply the entirety of a company or an organization.

Among three TQM models, MBNQA was the first model pursuing the excellence initiated by the NIST (National Institute of Standards and Technology, U.S.A). As MBNQA showed great success for the economy of the U.S.A, EQA and JQA followed the way of MBNQA to learn the new competitive scheme known as the management text book. All three models are very similar to each other. We can see the relationship between the enterprise and the IT area through the detailed description of section '4.2 Management of Information, Information Technology, and Knowledge' in the MBNQA TQM model.

In the section 4.2, applicants are supposed to answer the question "how do you manage your information, information technology, and organizational knowledge?" The companies applying MBNQA also should describe how they ensures the quality and availability of needed data, information, software, and hardware for their workforce, suppliers, partners, collaborators, and customers

The detail of this category directly says about the information areas in the enterprise and we may write about the more specific information for ITA/EA as an answer to these questions. With this approach, we can avoid any confusion in positioning the ITA/EA within the enterprise concept.

Considering the above, if we still want to use the term EA, we, in the first place, need to define the scope of enterprise by utilizing the above well-known TQM national models and then define the scope of the IT area and necessary components in order to correctly describe the term EA. Otherwise, It would be recommendable to find other appropriate terms rather than using EA, like enterprise information architecture or enterprise information technology architecture, etc, which will clearly convey to stakeholders a right scope of IT area framework that we are going to handle out of enterprise framework. This direction will lead us to the correct domain of the work we are going to handle. In line therewith, we here divide enterprise architecture into three main areas which are IT related area, non - IT area and interface area between those two areas. With this basic concept of the EA, we discuss further developments towards the direction, maturity path - EIA maturity model from which we will be able to get the practical benefits.

Figure 2. Proposed scope of the enterprise architecture

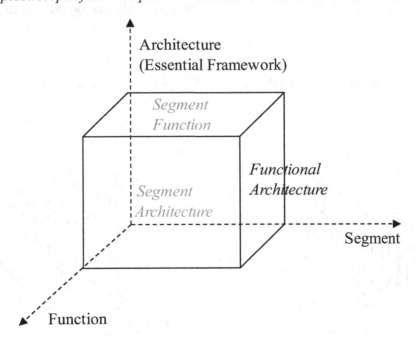

Figure 3. Proposed detail description of enterprise architecture

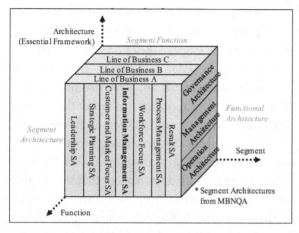

PROPSED SCOPE OF THE ENTERPRISE ARCHITECTURE

With the above relationship for the enterprise and its information management, we can further develop the scope of the ITA/EA/EIA step by step through the four consecutive figures (from Figure 2 to Figure 5) as follows. This approach could help the ITA/EA community to overcome the complexities of the information resources management.

Figure 2 shows the proposed scope of the desirable enterprise architecture which has three aspects (segment architectures, functional architectures, and segment functions). The concept of this enterprise architecture shows the essential framework of an enterprise and provides a milestone to the specific decision of the enterprise at a glance.

Figure 3 shows the proposed detail description of the enterprise architecture defined in this chapter. Each segment of the segment architecture is adopted from the first level categories of the MBNQA. In OMB case, completion, use, and results are categorized as segment architecture. These segment architectures are supposed to be determined in accordance with the need of the enterprise. And the other facets show the general functions of the enterprise like the line of business and the hierarchy of the enterprise. The terminology "Architecture" used in the figure represents the current fashion, a kind of "buzz word." With this kind of proposal for the enterprise architecture, we can clearly show a framework of the enterprise architecture and its components from the three important perspectives.

Figure 4 shows the proposed scope of the enterprise information architecture. We replace

Figure 4. Proposed scope of enterprise information architecture

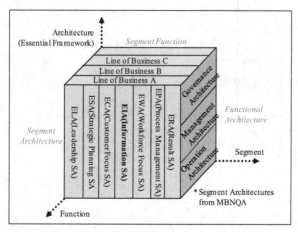

Figure 5. Proposed scope of segment architectures of EIA

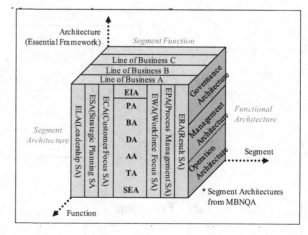

the information management segment architecture with the EIA within the enterprise architecture. Here we can conclude that the enterprise architecture currently applied in the EA community is equivalent to the area of the EIA in this chapter. With this approach using TQM model, we are going to show that there can be other segment architectures besides the EIA like enterprise results architecture, enterprise process management architecture, etc.

But existing enterprise architects may not be interested in other enterprise segment architectures because they are not their domain areas for the job. Then it would be very important that enterprise architects understand the status and position of ITA/EA or EIA within the enterprise. With this clear scope of the EIA, enterprise architects and relevant stakeholders can better respond to the requirements of the ITA/EA or EIA. Unclear scope of the ITA/EA or EIA will only prevent the enterprise from utilizing the beneficial side of the ITA/EA or EIA.

Figure 5 shows the proposed scope of the segment architectures of the EIA. These general terms in the existing EA are performance architecture (PA), business architecture (BA), data architecture (DA), application architecture (AA), technology architecture (TA), and security architecture (SEA) within the EIA. From this point of view, it is very clear to distinguish the scope of the EA and the EIA with their segments architectures. Therefore, for this reason, we propose that EIA be used as a better terminology to handle the complexities of information management in the enterprise instead of the enterprise architecture. With this in mind, we are going to explore the main topic of this chapter, the maturity model of EIA.

Enterprise Information Architecture: Concept and Maturity Model

For a better and more practical definition of enterprise architecture, it would be necessary to find a definition to cover an overall and basic framework of an enterprise so that we may see its status at a glance including IT area. This should have broader concept than EA community has thought it would have. For such purpose, we would like to take the information area out of the enterprise architecture, which is enterprise information architecture, and this will lead us to clearly see the differences between the EIA (Enterprise Information Architecture-IT related area) and the EA (Enterprise Architecture-total). In this sense, enterprise architecture should probably provide overall management and evaluation function to the enterprise like a TQM model and EIA does the similar function to the information technology area of the enterprise.

Definition of Enterprise Information Architecture

Here, we would like to suggest a better term and definition of EA in this chapter, namely EIA rather than the ambiguous EA. Our definition of EA is "An essential architectural framework for an enterprise to make a better decision about the future activities of its own." The definition of EIA is "the essential framework for an enterprise to effectively invest for and manage information technology resources to satisfy its goals and objectives."

Previously, we defined the enterprise as what has comprehensive domain areas not just for the information technology areas. Therefore with enterprise architecture, we will have to deal with entire enterprise domain areas like factories, materials, machineries, and all kinds of technologies directly. We usually, however, deal with things only relevant to the information systems and technologies within the so-called EA in reality. So it will be a little bit more practical to use EIA rather than EA in order to avoid any confusion derived from the terminology "EA."

Enterprise Information Architecture Maturity Model

With the introduction of EIA, we will be able to aim at a right target and focus on next process for the practical maturity model to avoid the tremendous unnecessary trial and errors. The goal of the EIA maturity model is to assess the maturity level of information systems and technologies within an enterprise. Here enterprises could be companies, government agencies or non-profit organizations including agencies which have geographically distributed branch offices connected with networks.

In order to make the EIA alive, we need to link the EIA activities to the real world all the time. Unfortunately we could say that the current software engineering technologies still have a long way to go because the relevant industry is still immature. It is obvious that the core EIA technologies depend upon software engineering, continuously changing and evolving information technologies, and sophisticated project management, which shows its success rate just limited to around 30 % at most (Standish Group 2003). Under such circumstances, it would be extremely difficult to create practical frameworks to effectively control the IT resources. Therefore, we would need a better maturity model to support the current ITA/EA community and to guide any kinds of organizational entity to a foreseeable future. Here our definition of EIAMM is *"A milestone to assess the maturity level of the information systems and technologies within an enterprise, and guide its ITA/EA Progress to the **practical** and**sustainable** direction with ROI driven results based on quality (**P-D-C-A Cycle** and **process improvement techniques**) of EIA regardless of the countries, enterprise entity (Public or Private sector), and enterprise size."*

We also need to define the quality concept of ITA/EA or EIA here based on the above definition. In line therewith we suggest the definition of quality, quality management system (QMS), and quality reference model (QRM) of EIA in total as *"Depending on the ITA/EA maturity model used by an enterprise and QMS or quality model used by the enterprise, a systematic approach using best EIA practices to meet the objectives and goals of EIA and enterprise business and to satisfy the final customers and stakeholders of EIA."*

EIA MATURITY MODEL APPROACHES

This chapter tries to focus on the result-oriented EIA implementation in the real world to practically get direct benefits from the EIA programs. As the basic purpose of introducing EIA is to satisfy the relevant stakeholders with expected results from the starting project, it is strongly recommended to find practical solutions and implement them in the enterprise using EIA project. Basically without such a strong support of the people involved in the EIA program, it will confront great difficulties in proceeding. Therefore EIA maturity model puts great emphasis on mitigating the aspects of the cultural conflicts at the same time. EIA maturity model also tries to provide generic approaches regardless of the countries, public or private sectors, and size of the enterprises ranging from large, medium to small sized one, so that any organizations can adopt this EIA maturity model to enhance their performances in the knowledge-oriented information society.

Practical EIA Maturity Model

There are various maturity models for the ITA/EA such as *Enterprise Architecture Management Maturity Framework (EAMMF)* of United States General Accounting Office (GAO, 2003), *Enterprise Architecture Assessment Framework (EAAF)* of United States Office of Management and Budget (OMB, 2007_2), *Enterprise Architecture Maturity Model (EAMM)* of National Association of State Chief Information Officers

Table 2. Levels of proposed EIA maturity model

Level	Description	Remark
Level 5: Continuous Improvement	EIA process improvement activities should be continuously executed yearly through the formal organization of the entire enterprise and include the incentive rewarding system for the EIA program	Creative and continuous improvement of EIA over the whole enterprise
Level 4: Standardizing Enterprise-wide	Enterprise initiates standardization of EIA and official EIA process improvement activities should be applied to the entire enterprise	Effective and efficient standardization of EIA
Level 3: Deploying EIA Solutions	Enterprise deploys formal EIA improvement program based on the EIA solutions elicited for the whole enterprise incrementally	Introducing EIA solutions to the major parts of the enterprise
Level 2: Finding EIA Solutions	Enterprise needs EIA and finds out practical solutions through EIA pilot project using process improvement methods	Finding practical IT management solution
Level 1: Initial	No necessary of EIA and lack of IT investment management	No control of IT investment

(NASCIO, 2003), *Advancing Enterprise Architecture Maturity (AEAM)* of US Industry Advisory Council's Enterprise Architecture Shared Interest Group (IAC EA SIG) and *Government Information Technology Architecture-Maturity Model* of National Information Society Agency of Korea (NIA, 2006). But multiple EA maturity models

that overlap and do not consistently measure the goodness, the impact and the completeness of enterprise architectures can be confusing and very frustrating to the staffs of agencies and departments that are trying to use them to improve EA maturity. (EA Shared Interest Group, 2005)

Here we introduce a practical EIA maturity model (EIAMM) as an experimental case from the initial level to the continuous improvement level. The key point of EIA maturity model is trying to focus on the practical benefits based on the findings of actual solutions in real enterprise environment through incremental process improvement supported by highly sophisticated IT project management and process management.

EIA Maturity Model Level 1

This level includes every enterprise without any solution for the EIA.

EIA Maturity Model Level 2

In CMMI Level 2, project management is supposed to be an infrastructure to be mastered. But in case of the EIA, there are many distinct differences between CMMI maturity model which first introduced the maturity concept into the informa-

Figure 6. Four phases of process improvement model (Vu, 2004)

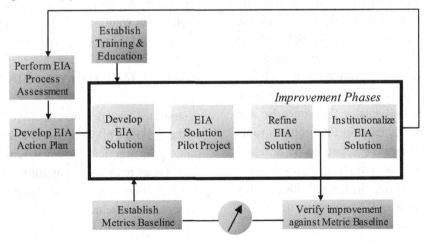

tion technology areas, and EIA maturity model from the perspectives of maturity concept. One of the differences could be the ROI-oriented approach to the EIA implementation. EIA maturity model level 2 pursues early stage benefits from the initiatives of the EIA like finding problem solutions in the field. This level also tries to divide the process of finding EIA solutions into 4 process improvement phases and seriously follow the process improvement (PI) guideline to get the EIA solutions.

At this level, without finding an appropriate solution, it is very dangerous to go on further to level 3 because its direction of EIA introduction may not be verified and approved by the stakeholders at this stage. Finding proper practical EIA solutions supported by stakeholders will be a premise to go up to the next level 3. If any EIA solutions are not practical enough to implement, the enterprise will have to hold going on further and spend more time and efforts until finding EIA solutions to be good enough for the real world.

Maturity in EIAMM means that an enterprise should follow a right direction which can lead to building a good foundation of the EIA and which will solve the problem of the enterprise through the introduction of the EIA. In another perspective, the maturity in EIA maturity model includes a natural way for the enterprise to follow step by step with enough ROI. One more difference from CMMI maturity concept will be the satisfaction of stakeholders with the EIA program. Performing the EIA program in a reasonable way, the visible output of EIA will be provided to the stakeholders so that they can be satisfied with the program.

Currently the problem of the so called EA is that it doesn't secure enough commitments from the people inside and outside the enterprise and that it doesn't clearly explain EA program to its stakeholders. There even seems to be no clear definition of the EA, which has raised much confusion in performing the EA activities. In this ambiguous situation of EA programs, the reason why we focus on the satisfaction of stakeholders is that it will secure their commitment and lead them to managing the complex IT investment including the reduction of total costs of the IT investments, enhancing the efficiency, effectiveness, and reusability of the IT assets, and the interoperability between the IT systems, and finally achieving the business goals of the enterprise using IT.

Figure 6 shows the four phased process improvement models during the level 2 of EIAMM which is the core part of the entire EIAMM. With this mechanism of process improvement, EIAMM can access to the practical ITA/EA/EIA and provide substantial benefits to the stakeholders in the real world.

Phase 1: Develop EIA Solution

Within the major problem area, an organization assigns its personnel to develop a solution for 3 months and manage this process as a formal project. If the solution is satisfactory to the organization, then go to the next process 'Pilot project' to see whether the solution is good enough in reality or not.

Phase 2: Pilot Project for EIA Solution

Assigned personnel to the pilot project run this process as a project for 3 months. And if the final evaluation of this process is good enough for the organization, then it goes to the next process 'Refine the solution'. If not, it goes back to the Phase 1 and 'Find solution' process again.

Phase 3: Refine Proven EIA Solution

A small team works together to refine the results of the previous pilot solution for 3 months. If the outcome is practical enough in real environment, then it goes to the next 'Institutionalize Solution' process. If not, the team needs one more refining project to get the actual solution.

Figure 7. Development of EIA action plan (Vu, 2004)

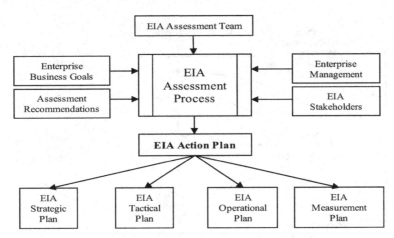

Phase 4: Institutionalize EIA Solution

This process is to deploy the proven solution to the organization for 3 months. A team also prepares the deployment plan and incrementally executes the plan to the organization. This phase prepares the initial foundation of the standardizing of the solution enterprise wide for the EIAMM Level 4.

Supporting Activities

Training and education should be supported by the organization and measurement scheme should be established and applied to the entire 4 phases of process improvement. Verification process is needed to check the status of process improvement.

Figure 7 shows the development of the EIA action plan. The EIA action plan is a set of plans;

Figure 8. EIAMM implementation and standardization strategy

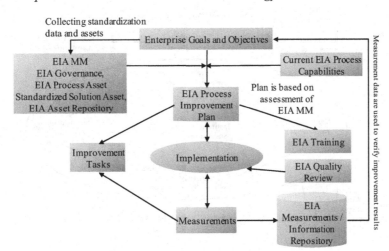

Figure 9. Level 3 deploying EIA solution overview

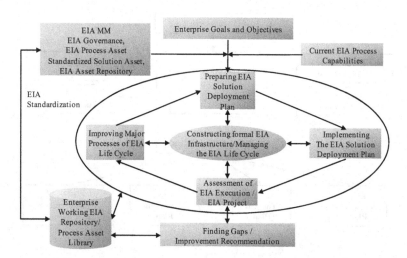

EIA strategic plan, EIA tactical plan for each processes, EIA operational plan for each action task, and EIA measurement plan to measure progress. Consistent alignment of EIA enterprise goals and objectives (strategic plan) to implement tactical & operational plans is the key.

EIA Maturity Model Level 3

With the ROI-oriented maturity concepts and EIA solutions obtained from the EIA maturity model level 2 activities, the next step is the deploying of the EIA solutions to the entire enterprise. Our maturity concept could be said to adopt a bot-

Figure 10. Level 4 deploying EIA solution overview

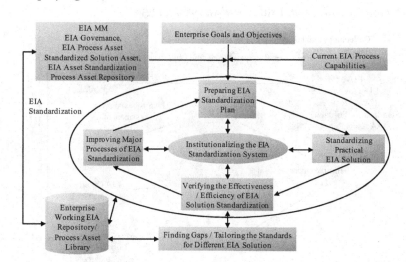

tom up approach. However, we also try to apply the top down approach together at the level 3 (Figure 9). For example, enterprise headquarter may continue to support good investment into the EIA with belief including enterprise-wide education, training and the planning of better strategies with various supporting resources in order to effectively and efficiently deploy the EIA solutions to the enterprise.

At this level, the enterprise may need standardizing mechanism (Figure 8), process improvement techniques, and tailoring guidelines with various IT resources like Web EIA repository, EIA tools and techniques. These must be supported from

Figure 11. Level 5 continuously improvement EIA

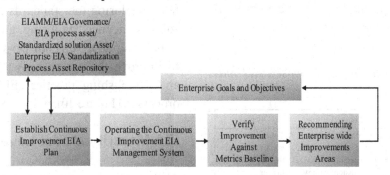

Figure 12. EIAMM overview

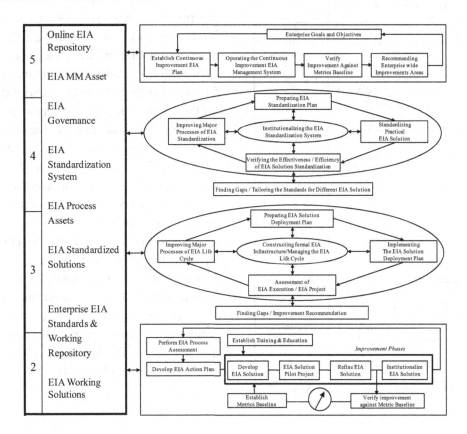

the top management. In this sense, these kinds of top down approach must be applied with bottom up at the same time.

We may also need certain kinds of change management as new technologies and concepts always require some sort of innovation and improvement in the organization. We need ever evolving strategic planning, execution, evaluation, and feedback in order to get better results. We need to assess all the EIA activities during level 3, to find gaps and improve the areas until the business goal is met.

Table 3. Major processes of proposed EIA maturity model

Level	Description	Remark
Level 5: Continuously Improving EIA	• Establishing formal system of EIA process improvement team in local organization • Measuring continuous improvements' effectiveness and efficiency • Providing incentive rewards to the every organization in the enterprise	Continuous improvements of the EIA solutions to be made
Level 4: Enterprise-wide standardization	• Standardizing the practical EIA solutions in the field • Tailoring the standards for different EIA solution needed (tailoring guideline) • Institutionalizing P-D-C-A cycle to improve the standardization enterprise-wide. • Establishing Practical EIA measurements • Processes	Establishing practical EIA standardization System
Level 3: Deploying EIA Solutions	• Preparing enterprise deployment planning • Constructing formal EIA infrastructure • Implementing the EIA deployment plan • Managing the EIA life cycle • Assessment system implemented to evaluate the EIA status or project	Assessment of the EIA executions/Finding gaps/ Improving major processes of EIA life cycle
Level 2: Finding EIA Solutions	• Verify the benefit of the solution • Find EIA solution to solve business problems • Execute EIA pilot project • Tuning the results of pilot project • Preparing the practical EIA solutions	Finding practical EIA solution for 1 year and with 4-phased process improvement
Level 1: Initial	• No necessary of EIA and lack of IT investment management	No control of IT investment

EIA Maturity Model Level 4

At this level, the enterprise may achieve remarkable improvement of the EIA practice and figure out transparent relationship between the practical EIA standardization and the business goal. Therefore enterprise-wide EIA standardizing systems are a very important identifier of this level. Among those standardizing EIA systems, there are many practical EIA solutions in the fields; tailoring the standards for different EIA solution needed (tailoring guideline), institutionalizing PDCA (Plan-Do-Check-Act) cycle to improve the enterprise-wide EIA program, and establishing practical EIA measurements processes (Figure 10).

EIA Maturity Model Level 5

At this level 5, every organization in the enterprise may establish a formal EIA process improvement team or one with other names of the enterprise architecture in order to continuously improve the EIA system through the measurements of the effectiveness and efficiency of the EIA program. Another key feature of this level 5 is to invest appropriate overhead and resources for the continuous improvement activities of the EIA program all the time like the QC circle, six-sigma and enterprise-wide TQM activities in the manufacturing industries (Figure 11).

The most important concepts behind of the EIAMM are natural, cycling, continuing, sustainable, and self survival idea in any enterprises. There is a brief overview of these concepts that all the 5 levels connect each other through the EIA repository and standardization mechanism (Figure 12). And these concepts also apply to an overview diagram for the role of the EIAMM within an enterprise as the alternative solution mechanism for the business and IT alignment problems (Figure 13 and 14).

Major Processes of the EIA Maturity Models

The Basic Characteristics of EIA Maturity Model

This is one of the experimental drafts of the EIA maturity model to find out a real practical approach among various trials in the ITA and EA world.

At the same time, on account of the various reasons, there is no practical standard definition existing in this community and furthermore it is too difficult to define the quality of the EIA (or EA) in this situation. Even with huge investments in the EIA, we may still have difficulties in figuring out the ROI of the EIA projects without appropriate quality criteria. Therefore, based on this EIA maturity model which is a more practical guideline being different from other approaches, EIA community may try a practical EIA approach and verify whether it is good or not.

Finally, EIA maturity model could provide a basis to find out the ROI-oriented maturity criteria to verify and validate the EIA program and projects in the real world. Further description of the quality of EIA will be mostly dependent on the various concepts of this EIA maturity model.

The Comparison between EIAMM and CMMI

The basic differences between enterprise information architecture maturity model (EIAMM) and CMMI show different perspectives for the maturity development. From the view of the CMMI, it provides step by step approaches to institutionalize from the low level key processes

Table 4. Comparison of the levels between EIAMM and CMMI

Maturity Level	EIAMM	CMMI
Level 5	Continuous Improvement	Optimizing
Level 4	Standardizing Enterprise-wide Solution	Quantitatively Managed
Level 3	Deploying EIA Solutions	Defined
Level 2	Finding EIA Solution	Managed
Level 1	Initial	Initial

Table 5. Comparison of the characteristics between EIAMM and CMMI

Category	EIAMM	CMMI
ROI	Strong ROI oriented approach	Indirect ROI approach
Practicality	Practical approaches to find solution at early improvement level	Focusing on Institutionalization of the defined processes at each level rather than practicality
Leveling up	Without applicable solutions, enterprise units can't go up to level 3.	Institutionalization of lower level allows going to next level.
Standardization	Strong mechanism like the Standardization of TQM model	Strong Standardization required
Stakeholders Satisfaction	Stakeholders satisfaction is essential	Stakeholders satisfaction is not directly commented

to the higher level key processes. Although we need to verify the effectiveness and efficiency of the activities which CMMI introduces to an enterprise, it seems to be difficult to prove the return on CMMI investment because there is not such a function in this model. We may need to invest in creating new verifiable processes for this. And this may be another burden to the modern CEOs trying the CMMI.

For the EIAMM, we put the self-verification processes into level 2 as "Finding EIA Solution." Here the solution means "actionable and concrete solutions for specific problems" in the real world that could provide tangible and intangible benefits to the customers of the EIA. It is also designed to aim at the practical support of the business including complex IT environment. Once we find out an appropriate solution through the 4-phased process improvement method, then we distribute the EIA solution to the rest of the organization for the improvement of quality and the enhancement of productivity during the level 3 "Deploying EIA Solutions." This could enable the enterprises to avoid "unnecessary trial-and-errors," and achieve the least beneficial results with "positive expectation for the new changes." (Table 4)

At level 3, the enterprise will experience more or less benefits through the distribution of the EIA solutions and draw the proved solutions with the best practices based on the realities of enterprises. We focus on the standardization of the enterprise-wide EIA solutions at level 4 and construction of continuous improvement systems for the EIA at level 5.

The scheme of the EIAMM is to try to provide real and practical solutions to the Enterprise-wide stakeholders even at level 2 and to guide the enterprise to the right way from the very beginning of the EIA, which is so difficult and complex in nature. Therefore, the core level of the EIAMM would be the level 2. This means that it could be a kind of waste to spend the limited resources and efforts in the wrong direction without clear solution.

EIA Maturity Model for Enterprise Business and Enterprise IT Alignment

Basically the modern management of an enterprise always has the most difficult alignment problems between its business and IT area. ITA/EA is sup-

Figure 13. EIAMM as enterprise business and enterprise IT alignment

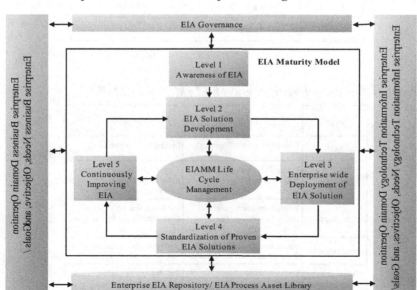

Figure 14. EIAMM for enterprise business and enterprise IT alignmentwithin enterprise architecture

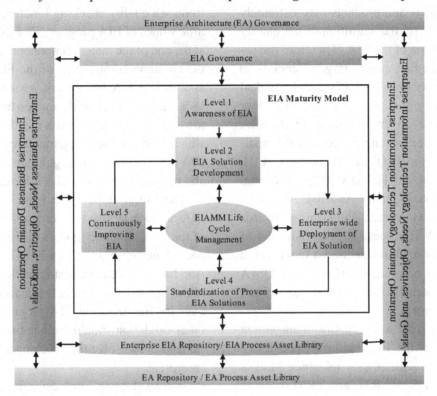

posed to provide the alignment function to the enterprise including online EA Web repository. In this chapter, we suggest a theoretical proposition that the alignment between business and IT could be achieved if we appropriately use the EIAMM as an intermediary interface tool. EIAMM actually should reflect the enterprise business needs and its related IT needs as well. Therefore if EIAMM is positioned in the middle of the two and provides its smooth communication to the enterprise like Figure 13, we expect that aging alignment problems could be solved and that enterprise architect serves its role better to the enterprise.

In this point of view, Figure 14 clearly shows the differences between EA and EIA with the EIAMM for enterprise business and enterprise IT alignment within EA. The biggest difference is that EA will govern the entire enterprise and EIA will coordinate the alignment problem between business and IT (not other technology or

areas) according to the continuous improvement strategy, EIAMM by the Figure 14.

Quality of EIA

Quality areas are basically well established in various industries and coverage perspectives including quality control (QC), quality assurance (QA), quality management (QM), quality management systems (QMS) (BSI DISC, 1998) and total quality management (TQM). The definition of the quality varies from industry to industry, from scholar to scholar, and from perspective to perspective. The quality in new budding industries like software engineering often follows the proven way of quality management from matured industries like manufacturing. The best practices in the EIA could be considered as one of the quality concept.

However, the concept ranging from EIA programs to projects and products may extremely vary depending on the definition of the quality and the definition of the EIA. Therefore the assumption of the EIA quality largely depends on the EIA maturity model described above to deal with the quality area. And it seems that other important focus on the definition of the EIA quality should reflect the concept of the quality reference model (QRM) including CMMI, SPICE, ISO 9001, TickIT, and MBNQA (Malcolm Baldrige National Quality Awards). Also JQA (Japanese Quality Awards) and Deming Awards in Japan, EQA (European Quality Awards) of EFQM (European Organization for Quality)and EC (European Commission) in Europe and QMA (Quality Management Awards) in Korea are well known in the world.

There should be some quality management function within the EIA maturity model like QRM aligning with other 5 reference Models (PRM, BRM, DRM, SRM, and TRM of FEA) initiated by the Federal Enterprise Architecture activities and other functions. Examples of QRM might be CMMI, SPICE, ISO 9001/TickIT, or a specific quality model for a target organization. If the QRM is not proper enough to handle the EIA quality, it may be improved to a more suitable shape for the EIA QRM.

Also, one of the direct customers of the QRM should be the CIO (Chief Information Officer) of the organization as CIO has lots of interests in the quality status for the Information Systems managed by IT people. Qualified stakeholders can also find out the quality status of the EIA program at anytime through the QRM. At the same time, management from IT people and customers may want to know the quality status and practical work forces too. So like other reference models, a column for the QRM may be provided to accommodate the quality area from high level to detailed level besides the 5 reference models (PRM, BRM, DRM, SRM and TRM).

In addition to the QRM concept, we may introduce a quality checking function to the major mile stones of EIA program. The milestones are at the end of the major components and basically the common components of the EIA can be an appropriate EIA framework, as-is view of EIA, to-be view of EIA, transformation from as-is view to to-be view, management of the EIA information which are standard management procedures for the EIA information including the storing, changing and representing of the EIA information.

The initial steps toward the quality of the EIA are to establish the verification procedures of the five reference models of the EIA and the consistency checking procedures between them. And finally we can validate that the final results of the EIA activities meet the goals of the objectives for the pertinent EIA program or project. Final validation should include finding a practical solution to solve the problems of the current enterprise.

We can also apply process improvement techniques to the EIA program in order to early find out the practical benefits from the EIA program. Basically using EIA and process improvement together may be one of the ways of realizing substantial benefits from the EIA program. If we apply the process improvement concept of the CMMI to the assessment of the as-is view of a target organization or system, we can find out more accurate information of the current status in terms of maturity concept.

There are big processes for transformation from current EIA views to future EIA views. If we manage these processes with process improvement concepts of CMMI or some other quality scheme, the quality status of the projects will be consistently secured at the intended maturity level at least. Later we can adjust and improve the outcome at reasonable time continuously. This process should be dealt with like a project. Then this process will secure minimum quality status according to the QRM specified.

Table 6. Annual assessment process of FEAP EAAF 2.2 (OMB, 2007_2)

Rating	Content
Green	Score equal to or greater that 4 in the "Completion", 'Use", and 'Results" capability areas
Yellow	Score equal to or greater than 4 in the "Completion" capability area and; A score equal to or greater than 4 in either the "Use" or "Results" capability areas
Red	All other score

Table 7. EIAMM 1.0 vs. EAAF 2.2 comparison

Category	EIAMM	EAAF 2.2 (OMB)
Common areas	• Process improvement approaches. • Practical results-oriented approaches.	
Standardization areas	• Standardization scheme is put into place in the model level 4.	• OMB itself is supposed to do its standardization role as a formal program.
Variety of maturity model	• Single maturity model	• Multiple maturity models of segment architectures for reference model of an architecture
Target	• Public or private sector • Large, medium or small sized enterprise • Federated countries or a country	• Public sectors (usually government areas)
Quality System	• PDCA cycling scheme • QRM (Quality Reference Model) or QMS (Quality Management System) aligned with EIAMM • V&V for major work in process of EIA	• No specific quality scheme for EA other than maturity model
Cultural Conflicts	• Mitigate cultural risks to introduce new improvement program with 4-phased process improvement	• Aligning the level of achievement for EA with quarterly EA performance review of FEAP EAAF2.2

And other things left for the quality will be how quality status for the jobs processed will be verified or validated and fixed before going to next stage. The big jobs may be current EIA views, future EIA views, and enterprise information architecture repository (EIAR) and securing the quality of the resulting artifacts from this model or small architecture may be very important for the quality of the entire work. First, we revise the milestone for the quality; the usual processes are review, inspection, verification and validation depending on the degree of requirement of the quality and putting them into places with well known procedures for these activities. Then all components appearing on the EIA seem to be theoretically secured by the above descriptions.

Last thing we will check about the quality is the process improvement and integration. It can be managed by adding these elements into QRM. Therefore QRM should handle all the process improvement matters like CMMI for the major processes including if necessary, the addition of specific processes and while the other five reference models (PRM, CRM, DRM, SRM, and TRM) should be under quality control, the quality related results should be reflected as a part of the QRM.

FUTURE TRENDS AND RESEARCH

More practical process improvement techniques, methods, and tools with accurate maturity models are expected to be available through a lot of experience with various maturity models. What is important will be that EIA industry finally has to ensure more practical ROI to successfully perform the transition activities through the maturity models of the process improvement for the unforeseen future.

The process improvement strategic efforts of FEA maturity model initiated actively by the OMB's Federal Enterprise Architecture Program EA Assessment Framework 2.2 (OMB, 2007_2) provide representative examples of the new trends seeking practical EA maturity model to find out the substantial ROI in the EIA industry. In the FEAP EAAF 2.2 (Federal Enterprise Assessment Program EA Assessment Framework 2.2), OMB provides two different types of process assessment and improvement framework. One of the process assessment types is three rating scale (Table 6) for the agency's overall performance for annual EA assessment process. The other process assessment type is five rating scale for the agency's quarterly EA performance review.

The three scale rating of annual assessment process is based on the five rating scale self assessment by the agencies and provides a comprehensive review of the state of an agency's enterprise architecture program. On the other hand, the five rating scale similar to the maturity phases of the CMMI is applied to the assessment of the segment architectures for the "Completion", "Use", and "Results" area.

Here we can see much diversified approaches to the application of the maturity models under an enterprise. OMB uses an overall process improvement model-3 rating scale, 3 different general maturity model in the segment architectures of three scoring area for the quarterly EA assessment, and 6 maturity models for "Completion" capability scoring area including performance architecture, business architecture, data architecture (or information architecture), application architecture, technology architecture, transition strategy, four maturity models for "Use" capability scoring area including EA governance and EA program management, EA change management and EA deployment, collaboration and reuse, and CPIC(Capital Planning and Investment Control) integration, four maturity models for "Results" capability scoring area including cost savings and cost avoidance, performance improvement, measuring EA program value, Internet protocol version 6 (IPv6)" OMB creates and applies total 18 different kinds of maturity model of its own version to manage its EA activities.

In case of OMB maturity model, we find that there is a clear trend of diversified maturity models used in an enterprise (Federal Enterprise) to handle complexities of its EA.

Other trend in OMB case is that the concept of segment architecture was introduced. "The purpose of development of segment architectures is to promote and accelerate a substantial reduction in IT project implementation cost, as legacy IT applications are redesigned and replaced. The use of segment architectures will also eliminate enterprise-wide data duplication and the necessity of reconciling the differences that occur when the same data is collected and stored by multiple stove-piped processes." From the OMB case, segment architecture seems to be other representation for the target architecture focused on obtaining the practical ROI and early benefits. Therefore this is other obvious trend for the EA maturity model of OMB towards the practical ROI focusing on the segment architectures of target architecture and various kinds of process improvements technique.

For our research proposal, we have found that common area between EIAMM and FEAP EAAF 2.2 is focusing on practical ROI from the EA investments. But the differences between them would be that EIAMM has a standardization scheme, 4 phased process improvement processes, and general application guideline regardless of the enterprise properties. We would like to study further research, apply our model in real enterprise architecture programs, and analyze the results to see what the critical success factors (CSF's) for the application of EIA maturity model are.

Table 7 shows some prospective trend and insights of ITA/EA maturity model through the comparison between EIAMM 1.0 and EAAF 2.2. However EAAF of OMB represents the current practice of Federal Enterprise Government area and EIAMM is a theoretical proposal for the improvement of the ITA/EA practice. Therefore we need to consider this as a research purpose with certain degree of limitation.

CONCLUSION

Since the final decade of the last century, every organization, which has suffered from the handling of a deluge of information generated from business activities, has been interested in the ITA/EA. Beginning with Zachman's enterprise architecture framework (Zachman, 1987), a number of enterprise architecture frameworks have been introduced. Especially in public sectors, United States federal governmental organizations have sought to obtain strategic advantages through the successful establishment and operation of their own ITA/EA. Coming over the 21st century, a lot of countries have made laws and regulations that force every governmental organization to establish infrastructures and processes to manage its information resources effectively and efficiently. And a galactic amount of budgets is invested in the ITA/EA programs all over the world every year.

But from the past experiences of AD/Cycle Architecture program, we learned a valuable lesson that only the products and thoughts making a practical contribution in giant programs could be served for future stage. And one of those products having outlived the AD/Cycle Program is still playing a major role in the ITA/EA market as shown in the example of System Architect of Telelogic, but all the other major products and vendors did not outlive because they were not practical enough for the business and technological environment and hardly gave benefits to their clients. To avoid the precedent of the AD/Cycle, ITA/EA programs should be executed in a way of effectiveness and efficiency from the start.

For that reason, many governmental organizations and standard bodies have proposed several maturity models to assess ITA/EA maturity during the establishment and operation of the relevant programs. The benefits, however, of the ITA/EA and the effectiveness of the maturity models are still questionable because the models have difficulties in application and they are still immature to measure the economic indexes such as ROI except a few cases. So we need a new approach to assess the ITA/EA maturity model from a quality and economical efficiency view.

In this chapter, firstly we reviewed a number of definitions of enterprise architecture and suggested a new definition of Enterprise Information Architecture to stress that our maturity model focused on the information technology area of an enterprise. And we explored several worldwide total quality management (TQM) models which have relations in their framework with information area, and discussed the possibilities of applying the techniques that those models can contribute to the ITA/EA maturity model.

In the proposal section of a new EIA maturity model, we adopted two major schemes of process improvement area. One was the maturity level scheme of SEI's CMMI. We classified the maturity level of the model in five steps, and specified characteristics and processes for each level. The other was the four-phased process improvement scheme of Boeing. Its practical approach for the process improvement gave us an inspiration to devise a mechanism to improve the ITA/EA processes and assess the progress and quality of them. In order to find the future direction of the ITA/EA maturity model, we definitely need to take a process improvement way using four-phased process improvement, accumulate the resultant solutions and improvement experiences as enterprise assets with the standardization mechanism in an enterprise, and use those capabilities to achieve operational, tactical and strategic business goals. We hope the proposed EIA maturity model will be an incremental and practical approach to assess the accurate maturity level and make sure the effectiveness of ITA/EA.

REFERENCES

Bernard, S. A. (2004). *Enterprise Architecture Management Maturity (EAMM) – Enterprise Architecture Development, Documentation and Measurement.* Lecture notes for the enterprise architecture course sponsored by Korea IT Industry Promotion Agency, Seoul, Korea.

BSI DISC. (1998). *The TickIT Guide – A Guide to Software Quality Management System, Consturction and Certification to ISO 9001.*

Chrissis, B. M., Konrad, M., & Shrum, S. (2007). *CMMI – Guidelines for Process Integration and Product Improvement.* 2nd Ed. Addison-Wesley.

DoD. (2006). *Department of Defense Chief Information Officer Desk Reference. Vol.1 Foundation Documents.* United States Department of Defense,

EA Shared Interest Group. (2005). *Advancing Enterprise Architecture Maturity, version 2.0.* American Council for Technology/Industry Advisory Council.

EFQM. (2006). *The EFQM Excellence Award, Information Brochure for 2006, Version 2.* European Foundation for Quality Management.

GAO. (2003). *A Framework for Assessing and Improving Enterprise Architecture Management, version 1.1.* United States General Accounting Office.

Hall, M. (2005). *Building and Enterprise Architecture Website and Repository.* Lecture notes for the enterprise architecture course sponsored by Korea IT Industry Promotion Agency, Seoul, Korea.

Japan Quality Award Committee. (2000). Japan Quality Award – Award Criteria: Innovation and Creation for Competitiveness – 2000 Ed. Japan Quality Award Committee. Tokyo.

NASCIO. (2003). *NASCIO Enterprise Architecture Maturity Model, Version 1.3.* National Association of State Chief Information Officers.

NIA. (2006). *Government Information Technology Architecture-Maturity Model, Version 1.0 (Draft).* National Information Society Agency. Korea.

NIST. (2007). *Baldrige National Quality Program. NIST. Technology Administration.* Department of Commerce.

OMB. (2007_1). *FEA Consolidated Reference Model Document, Version 2.2.* Office of Management and Budget.

OMB. (2007_2). *Federal Enterprise Architecture Program EA Assessment Framework 2.2*. Office of Management and Budget.

Platt, M. (2007). *CIO Definitions – Enterprise Architecture*. Retrieved August 13, 2007, from http://searchcio.techtarget.com/sDefinition/0,,sid19_gci1081274,00.html

Ross, J. W., Weill, P., & Robertson, D. C. (2006). *Enterprise Architecture as Strategy: Creating a Foundation for Business Execution*. Harvard Business School Press.

Schekkerman, J. (2005). *Trends in Enterprise Architecture 2005: How are Organizations Progressing? 1st Ed*. Institute for Enterprise Architecture Developments (IFEAD).

The Open Group. (2003). *TOGAF (The Open Group Architecture Framework) version 8.1*.

Vu, J. (2004). *Process Improvement Journey*. Lecture notes for the CMMI course sponsored by Korea IT Industry Promotion Agency, Seoul, Korea.

Zachman, J. A. (1987), *A Framework for Information Systems Architecture*. IBM Systems Journal, 26(3), 276-292.

Chapter V
Measuring the Benefits of Enterprise Architecture:
Knowledge Management Maturity

Alan Dyer
EWA, Australia

ABSTRACT

Enterprise Architecture is the organising logic for business processes and Information Technology infrastructure, the purpose of which is to create a more effective organisation in the context of the business's strategy and goals. However, the ability to measure the effectiveness of any activities initiated under the guise of Enterprise Architecture is limited, even more so in those organisations, such as government agencies, that do not recognise financial return on investment. In this chapter the author introduces the concept of Knowledge Management, linked to the strategic outcomes of Enterprise Architecture and proposes a maturity model framework for the measurement of Enterprise Architecture implementation. The aim of this chapter is to provide a basis for discussion of a wider Capability Maturity Profile with architectural frameworks to help develop and measure the benefits of implementing frameworks and architectures.

INTRODUCTION

Enterprise Architecture is a business strategy tool; one that should be used in the operation of the enterprise as well as the initial design. In the commercial environment, where success is easily measured in financial terms, enterprises must "grow" and improve (remain competitive).

But Enterprise Architecture is not just a tool for use in a financially competitive world; it is a tool that can help improve the efficiency of organisations that do not measure success by the financial "bottom line". Government agencies represent just that environment and those who make the critical, strategic, decisions within the enterprise must understand the level of improvement; they must be able to measure such changes in their enterprise.

During this chapter I will provide some background by briefly discussing the concept of Enterprise Architecture and its link to decision-making. One aspect of decision-making is Knowledge Management, a concept that I will then explore and briefly discuss the measurement of such. This discussion is not intended to be an authoritative tome on Knowledge Management, the discipline is still too young for such a case to be presented; however, the introduction and linkage of the concept will allow for future research into the ideas presented.

A previous concept for evaluating Knowledge Management Projects exists, and I will use this to develop a Knowledge Management Maturity Model such that it can be used as part of an architectural view – enhancing the design and operation of the enterprise. Finally, I will discuss how a maturity model can be used in the context of an architecture.

These discussions are intended to show how the strategic audience (Chief Information Officers, Business Analysts, Managers, etc.) can use maturity models to determine if new approaches are achieving the desired aims. But, such discussions are not the sole purview of the strategic decision-makers. Academics and professionals can use maturity models for insights into processes and knowledge transfer. Technologists will be more interested in some of the maturity offshoots, but will still benefit from the strategic understanding of what their tools should support.

Ultimately, this chapter is intended to engender further discussion on the evolution of enterprise architecture as a business strategy tool and how the architecture extends beyond "design" to the "operation" of the enterprise.

EA FRAMEWORKS

What is Enterprise Architecture?

The seed for enterprise architecture can be traced as far back as 1987, when Zachman (1987) provided a framework for information systems architecture (ISA). The first shoots, however, didn't really appear until Sowa and Zachman's paper (1992) which extended the 1987 framework.

The extended Zachman framework is based on a matrix of entities which can be used to describe particular perspectives and relationships. The columns represent the "what", "how", "where", "who", "when" and "why", and the rows represent models such as "scope", "enterprise model", "system model", "technology model", "components", and "functioning systems". Even at that early stage, the ISA was not seen as "the enterprise" architecture, but as an "information systems" architecture.

The identification of such architectures with enterprise was not seen until Barnett et al (1994) used the term "Enterprise Architectures" in their paper on architecture for the virtual enterprise. In there, the authors described enterprise architecture as a "blueprint" or "picture" which assists in the design of an enterprise; a blueprint that considers three issues: what activities are performed, how activities are performed and how the enterprise should be constructed. However, the authors took a business modelling approach and did not appear to have the full range of perspectives that Zachman (with Sowa) had suggested.

Study into this new field continued and Bernus and Nemes (1996) identified the emergence of a number of enterprise reference frameworks, including the Purdue enterprise reference architecture, the GRAI integrated methodology, Computer Integrated Manufacturing Open Systems Architecture (CIM-OSA) and Toronto Virtual Enterprise (TOVE). These Australian researchers produced the generic enterprise reference architecture methodology (GERAM) to describe the different types of architecture that were appearing. GERAM was not a framework within itself, although the authors described it as being applicable to potentially all types of enterprise.

Even by this stage, "enterprise architecture" was not a common theme; Bernus et al (1996) noted keywords such as "enterprise integration", "reference architecture", "enterprise engineering methodology", and "enterprise modelling" – but not "enterprise architecture".

During the mid-1990's, Zachman produced three relatively short papers (1996; 1997; 1997a) which re-introduced the work done previously on ISA. It was at this point that Zachman (1996) introduced the concept of EA by remarking on his original framework: "... it was clear that it should have been referred to as a 'Framework for Enterprise Architecture'".

These latter papers did not change the original framework, but did clarify the context and provided a stepping stone for further work.

Chen et al (1997) used "enterprise architecture" (inter alia) as a key word for their paper on mapping the GRAI integrated methodology onto GERAM. This is not the only instance of mapping onto the GERAM, Noran also mapped the Zachman and C4ISR frameworks (2003; 2005). The theme of mapping these diverse frameworks shows the underlying commonality, at least in purpose if not in method.

Since the inception of EA, the frameworks have proliferated. According to Gartner (Allega, 2005) and The Institute for Enterprise Architecture Developments (IFEAD)[1] there are at least nine architectural frameworks (although not all of these have been blessed with the title of "Enterprise", they can be linked to EA).[2] Many of these frameworks are not in competition, but are evolutions or variations on a theme. A description

of individual frameworks is outside of the scope of this chapter; the referenced papers provide descriptions in great detail.

The proliferation and evolution of frameworks presupposes a large degree of research and work, but, as the literature review reveals, most of this work has only scratched the surface.

Wikipedia[3], to some extent, maps some of the evolving thinking about EA, with an earlier definition of "[a] comprehensive framework used to manage and align an organization's structure, processes, information, operations and projects with the organization's overall strategy" (November 2005) and then a revised definition that encapsulates the current essence: "[e]nterprise architecture is the practice of applying a comprehensive and rigorous method for describing a current and/or future structure and behaviour for an organization's processes, information systems, personnel and organizational sub-units, so that they align with the organization's core goals and strategic direction" (October 2006).

Schekkerman (2006) provides an overview of existing architectures and quotes some definitions (notably from the Open Group, US Federal CIO Council and the former Meta Group Inc.). He doesn't provide a succinct definition of his own, but does define various elements that make up the phrase "Enterprise Architecture" (including "architecture", "elements" and "enterprise"). From here we can deduce that an Enterprise Architecture is the structure of people, processes, business and technology, their interrelationships and the principles and guidelines governing their design and evolution over time; in the context of a collection of organisations with a common set of goals/principles or a single bottom line.

Finally, the most recent succinct definition has come from Ross et al (2006), who state that "Enterprise Architecture is the organizing logic for business processes and IT infrastructure reflecting the integration and standardization requirements of the company's operating model".

EA and the Enterprise

Enterprise Architecture is less than a decade old and the concepts and underlying knowledge appear to be maturing, including the generation of standards such as ISO15704:1998 (Requirements for Enterprise Reference Architecture and Methodologies), preEN/ISO19440:2003 (Enterprise Integration - Constructs for Enterprise Modelling) & 19439:2003 (Enterprise Integration - Framework for Enterprise Modelling).

Earlier papers (Chen et al, 1997; Allega, 2005; Bernus et al, 1996; Schekkerman, 2004) concentrated on the mechanisms (the industrial aspects) of EA but do not detail how much benefit an organisation can gain from implementation. Part of this issue, and certainly outside the scope of those documents, is that each implementation of a framework or architecture is highly dependent on the enterprise context. While the authors could describe a general framework, they could not describe how each element of the framework affects individual businesses, especially as each business may operate in a different environment (e.g. some may be in a financial environment, some may be political and others may be traditional trade-based). This perspective was reinforced by Schulman (2004) who noted that frameworks should be matched to the organisation.

The number of available frameworks and the need to match generic frameworks to the organisation leads to the premise that no single framework is fully complete (Schulman, 2004). As such, any chosen Architecture will have to be developed – a process discussed by Lapkin (2004). In doing so, the advice of Allega (2005) should be heeded in that proponents should not become entangled in taxonomical debates and should concentrate on "what is important", especially as taxonomical classifications appear to evolve or change about every 15 months.

Enterprise Architecture is not an end unto itself, in that it is a tool for dealing with the complexities and dynamics of the Enterprise (Zach-man, 1997), and a means of describing the look and feel (Lapkin, 2004). Lapkin's pattern-based approach is by no means unique; other authors have expounded on mechanisms to ease the burden on enterprises, such as the language described by Jonkers et al (2003), the Universal/Unified Modelling Language (UML) approach taken by Armour et al (2002), and the viewpoint oriented approach taken by Steen et al (2004).

As such, EA is only an enabler to enterprise efficiency and enterprises must consider which framework to adopt. The process of developing architecture (including the tools and training required) is an investment by an enterprise; each enterprise, thus, must consider how much to invest in building the architecture, how much to invest in ensuring implementation or compliance and how much to invest in maintaining the architecture.

Architectural Returns

The return on any investment is an important consideration for the enterprise. Gartner authors (Lopez, 2002; Allega, 2005a) have noted that the traditional accounting method of "Return on Investment[4]" is not valid when measuring EA. Lopez suggests that "Return on Assets[5]" (ROA) should be used, while Allega notes that the application of EA is where the benefits lie, not in the architecture itself. Allega's paper, while not providing any real insights into how returns can be measured, notes that predicting the results of EA is not feasible – unlike the predictability of traditional investments in the enterprise. Unfortunately, Lopez links the ROA approach only to IT asset productivity, and not enterprise productivity as a whole.

Saha (2004) provided some insight into a "real options" approach, which is not so much a means of evaluating EA, but as a way of looking at investments in the architecture. This approach looks at the options (defer, explore/pilot, scale, compound, growth) and maps these to the conditions for viability and risks. These elements may give some insight in how to judge the value of the architecture in the context of the enterprise. Saha acknowledges that "[a]ssessing the value of EA initiatives is imprecise and still evolving." Under current understanding, the benefits appear to be intangible.

The literature reviewed thus far suggests that EA is still hard to describe, especially in enterprise-specific terms, and even harder to measure. While frameworks exist to build architectures, these frameworks do little to describe the benefits and costs, unless tailored by experts within the enterprise; even then the overall value may be indeterminate. That EA is being accepted is not being contested, but EA is still evolving (Schekkerman, 2004).

Quantifying architectural benefits using financial measures may be hard enough, but quantifying these benefits in organisations that do not rely on the financial position as the ultimate measure of success (such as Government agencies) is even more difficult. Moore (2005) highlights the different drivers for the government; the ability to relieve budget pressures remains key. Whereas commercial organisations can find solace in the cold hard bottom line, government departments rely on public perception of the efficiency of service within the nominated budgets.

A measure that highlights efficiency rather than one that depends on financial metrics is thus necessary to ensure that the implementation of the architecture is providing benefit. Maturity models are one mechanism to provide this measure. Maturity models also have added benefit of identifying a progression from the current state to the desired state when the maturity model is properly tailored to the enterprise.

Enterprise Architectures, though, cover many facets of an organisation. Technology, decision-making, information and capability are four examples of such facets. A single maturity model would not be able to cover all the facets effectively, and an aggregated view may hide opportunities for further improvement. A suite of maturity models, forming a Capability Maturity Profile (CMP), would enable the necessary level of granularity.

Thus, the CMP is an important mechanism to measure the progress of evolution of the implementations resulting from the architecture. The CMP is not a measure of the architecture itself; but of those elements that are described by the architecture.

A profile addressing maturity of capability is not a common feature amongst the architectural frameworks previously discussed and further study is required to validate any benefits, as well as which facets are suitable for inclusion. However, the CMP has been considered in the past, albeit in a very limited form.

The C4ISR Architectural Framework initially considered a CMP, but this artefact was not included in the published version (C4ISR Architecture Framework, 1997). Reference to this consideration can be found in the Department of Defence Architectural Framework (DoDAF) Deskbook (2003), which notes that the "... Capability Maturity Profile can aid in the transition from an As-Is to a To-Be architecture ..." (p 2-106), measuring the rate of progress of change and evolution. The DoDAF itself did not include a CMP.

The Australian incarnation of the DoDAF (the Defence Architecture Framework - DAF), however, did include the CMP as a "Common View" (DAF Resources CD, 2005). The DAF noted the "Capability Maturity Profile aids in describing the transition from the current state (as-is) to a mature state (to-be) of an architecture. The CV-3 supports other products by providing a roadmap or profile of the areas that need to change to achieve a mature capability". The DAF version of the CMP was a direct replica of what was suggested for the C4ISR Architecture Framework (C4ISR Architecture Framework, 1997).

Unfortunately, the DAF description of the CMP does not put the same emphasis on tailoring and adapting the CMP to meet the needs of the architecture. Whereas the C4ISR AF product (as described in the DoDAF) provides example categories to demonstrate the view, the DAF provides the same categories as absolutes (termed information system components). While these components are useful at the technology level, they add little to understanding the enterprise. To this end, the DAF CMP provides little benefit in measuring the effects of the overall architecture.

A generic CMP could look at the many facets of an architectural particularly those that address business processes, behaviours, and operating models. An integral part of business execution is "decision-making" and the results of decision making can be seen in the behaviours and outputs of processes. Decision-making is built on a foundation of knowledge; knowledge is an important base for processes and decisions. As such, the ability for the organisations knowledge management to influence the business execution is one of those facets that should be measured as the enterprise evolves.

KNOWLEDGE MANAGEMENT AND CURRENT MEASUREMENT OF KM

An Explanation of Knowledge Management

Formalised approaches to managing knowledge are recent phenomena, although these approaches are influenced by several, more traditional, disciplines. As such, definitions for Knowledge Management (KM) are only now emerging and can hardly be called mature. KM is about managing knowledge processes to support both business processes and organisational knowledge bases; connecting intellectual assets and business growth (Furlong, 2001; Paulzen & Perc, 2002).

As well as emerging definitions, the character of KM is also developing. Knowledge is a ubiquitous entity that is applicable in new environments and a catalyst (in that knowledge is not a direct agent or end result of itself) (Furlong, 2001;

Paulzen & Perc, 2002). KM encompasses much more than the technological processes to support business outcomes; the people, organisation and processes, and content are critical facets (Paulzen & Perc, 2002). Some of these basic processes include creating, storing and retrieving, transferring and applying knowledge (Kankanhalli & Tan 2004).

KM differs from Information Management (IM) in that KM aids the creation of innovative knowledge, the application of knowledge to increase "value", and results in actions that reflect changes in human behaviour. IM, however, is an important enabler for KM and the links between Data – Information – Knowledge are important aspects of KM; employees routinely transform knowledge into information and information into knowledge (Furlong, 2001). Information Technology (IT) is a related enabler, IT can be used to enforce rules or to empower knowledge and information processes; however, the emphasis on IT should not be technology for technology's sake, but a supporting mechanism for work practices (Furlong, 2001).

IT and IM are not the only enablers for KM; others include business strategy, leadership issues, cultural concerns, content management, organisational structure, technology and innovation (Furlong, 2001). The knowledge workers have specialised skills and intellect, albeit they may be recognised through different perspectives; these skills directly influence the organisation's growth and competitiveness. Competitiveness in a government context goes beyond the fiscal management and into the realm of being more capable than the adversary (however so defined); the concept of "business" is different between the government and commercial worlds although the underlying lessons and processes may have more than just a passing similarity.

Managing knowledge, itself, is not new, but as a discipline KM is a young, growing, field that can assist organisations to improve their business processes and increase competitiveness. However,

KM depends on expressing many underlying constructs within the organisation and understanding the connectivity, not just from a technology sense, but also from a social and value network context. This level of understanding implies a fresh look at the business architectures, a better understanding of how the different perspectives and views are connected.

Measuring KM

KM is a strategic initiative and that measurement is necessary to understand success and failure (Metainnovation, 2004). Knowledge Management can be measured in a variety of ways; success indicators can be artefact-, activity-, cultural- (behavioural-), and intellect-centred; another perspective on these elements identifies the number of new claims, rate of generation, quality of claims and impact of the knowledge (Standards Australia, 2005) (Metainnovation, 2004). Likewise, metadata (an enabler to knowledge management) should be checked for meaning, maturity (in terms of consistency and enduring integrity), manage-

ability, maintainability and migrate-ability (shared across different environments through sharing, interoperating and porting) (Duttaroy, 2005).

The facets of KM that can be measured are numerous (Metainnovation, 2004; Kankanhalli & Tan, 2004; Furlong, 2001; Martin, 2006; Roberston, 2003; Standards Australia AS:5037, 2005); Table 1 identifies broad areas; the headings have been taken from the Australian Standard.

Knowledge audits should measure the role of structure; technology experience, perceptions, requirements; the impact of culture; the nature of process management; sources of innovation; models of communication; strategy; and perceptions of the current KM initiative (Furlong, 2001). Many mechanisms exist to measure KM, or the impacts of KM initiatives. Some that have been discovered through the literature include (from (Kankanhalli & Tan, 2004; Roberston, 2003), etc):

- House of Quality (development of a metrics matrix to find correlations and focus priori-

Table 1. Measurable areas of KM as summarised from the literature review

Artefact	Activity	Behavioural	Intellect
Rate of knowledge acquisition Predictive Accuracy of Knowledge Claims Explanatory power of knowledge claims Rate of knowledge production (includes papers produced, lessons learned, databases created, etc) Knowledge production quality Parsimony measure of knowledge claims (minimum number of symbols required to convey relevant knowledge) Technical aspects for Enterprise Knowledge Repositories (EKR) (system run-time metrics, number of users, number of accesses etc) Originality of knowledge claims	Staff efficiency Process efficiency Staff learning Knowledge transfer or diffusion (requiring a knowledge broadcaster and a knowledge receiver) "Community of Practice" contributions and accesses Organisational Awareness (knowing policy and procedures, standing operating procedures etc) Outcomes (impact on the organisation key performance indicators) Consistency of advice Organisation's leverage of knowledge claims	Implementation of knowledge initiatives Selected behaviour and interactions (participating in KM-related activity) Comparing future performance with benchmarks Effectiveness of knowledge claims Staff morale	Quality of knowledge acquired Change in intellectual capital Predictive power of knowledge claims Information quality (including techniques such as user rankings, expert evaluation, useability testing) User feedback on the knowledge provided Anecdotal evidence Intellectual property
			(Quality: accuracy, timeliness, granularity, currency)

ties on those elements that will have the best effect)

- Balanced Scorecard (a tool to translate high-level strategies to real targets)
- American Productivity Center benchmarking approach (a process classification framework that can be used to benchmark and assess impact on business processes)
- Skandia Navigator (a series of metrics in five focus areas which could be considered as an extension of the Balanced Scorecard)
- Intellectual Capital index (an extension to the Skandia metric)
- Intangible Assets Monitor (largely focussed on the financial perspective of intellectual capital and reputation – groups the indicators {e.g growth, renewal, efficiency and stability/risk} into three distinct categories {external structure, internal structure and individuals competence})
- Knowledge Capital Valuation techniques such as:
  o Market value to book value,
  o Tobin's Q,
  o Calculated intangible value,
  o Baruch Lev's knowledge capital valuation,
  o Paul Strassmann's knowledge capital valuation,
  o Measuring intellectual assets, and
  o Accounting methods for measuring intellectual capital.

These techniques are designed for use in the commercial world and are not easily tailored, if at all, for use within the non-commercial (e.g. Government) environment where costs and resources are measured in dimensions other than the dollar. The use of techniques is somewhat hindered by a lack of consistency of vocabulary; although most of the techniques overlap in their approach to measures and metrics (Kankanhalli & Tan, 2004).

Measuring Knowledge Management, like KM itself, is a maturing discipline and appears to currently be "soft around the edges". Techniques exist to subjectively measure the effect that knowledge has on an organisation; the ability to confidently objectively measure such effects (and hence, confidently enhance business processes) are yet to be fully developed. Most of the techniques hinge on "scorecards" to quantify the activity levels of an organisation, a means to indicate an organisation's knowledge management maturity level.

Maturity Models

A maturity model is a means of simplifying the description of an organisation's level of development, and the stages of development that an organisation can be expected to pass through as part of its continuous improvement strategy (Weerdmeester et al, 2003). Models are simple, with a limited number of maturity levels which have certain requirements. The levels themselves form a continuous progression (from an initial level to a perfect "ideal"), in that an organisation has to pass through them sequentially (Weerdmeester et al, 2003). Essentially, maturity models are designed to be easy to understand and use, thus suitable for presentation to the higher-level decision-makers in an organisation (Marco, 2002).

A well known maturity model is the Software Engineering Institute's "Capability Maturity Model" (CMM), which has 6 levels (not performed, performed informally, planned and tracked, well-defined, quantitatively controlled, continuously improving) and 5 orthogonal concepts (consistent, repeatable, transferable, quantitative and qualitative) (Marco, 2002). Some additional models, of which many are extensions, or variations of the CMM, are (Weerdmeester et al, 2003; Mohanty & Chand, 2005; Paulzen & Perc, 2002):

- The Knowledge Management Framework Assessment Exercise which uses a five level "knowledge journey" covering key areas of knowledge management (awareness and commitment, strategy, culture, external focus, incentives, IT, maintenance and protection, ongoing assessment, organisations, and using and applying knowledge). The key areas of KM can also be defined though people, process, content and technology.

- The Quality Management Maturity Grid with 5 "stages" across six measurement categories (management understanding and attitude, information quality organisation status, information quality problem handling, cost of information quality as percent of revenue, information quality improvement actions, and summation of company information quality posture).

- The Siemens Knowledge Management Maturity Model which defines five levels of maturity across key areas (strategy, knowledge goals, environment, partnerships, staff, competencies, cooperation, culture, leadership, support, knowledge structures, knowledge forms, technology, infrastructure, processes, roles, organisation). However the model is applied across four perspectives (time horizon, knowledge, actor, rules) leading to eight key distinctions (strategic, operative, external, internal, people, technology, informal, formal).

- The KMM Model from Infosys Technologies which uses five levels of maturity. These levels can be applied across people, process and technology and have defined key result areas.

- TATA consultancy services provide another five level maturity model addressing the three basic pillars of capability (people, process, technology).

- The Knowledge Process Quality Model (KPQM) is based around the dimensions of maturity stages, knowledge activities (those business activities in which the handling of knowledge is of particular importance; characterised by the types identify, generate,

use, store, distribute and evaluate), management areas and assessments; with the understanding that knowledge processes can be improved by enhancing the corresponding management structures. The KPQM assessment structure places process attributes in a matrix of maturity stage versus organisation/people/technology; each process attribute can be described through activity-specific or activity-independent practices.

The maturity of Information Management (as an enabler to KM) practices is also an important aspect of any KM System; management of information is most effective when data and information is treated as assets (Ladley, 2002). Again, a variety of models, the key principals of which parallel those of any capability maturity model, are available, with corresponding levels ("operate, consolidate, integrate, optimise, innovate" or "reporting, analysing, predicting, operationalising, active warehousing") that may work across types of activity (primarily batch with pre-defined queries, increase in ad hoc queries, analytical model grows, continuous updates and time sensitive queries gain importance, event based triggering takes hold). Hybrids are also available such as those suggested by Ladley which aligns levels of maturity (transactions, reporting, analysing, predictive, operationalise, collaborative, closed loop, foresight) with the DIKX hierarchy (in this case data, information, knowledge, action) (Ladley, 2002).

LINKING KM TO ENTERPRISE ARCHITECTURE

Knowledge and knowledge management do not currently have an explicit link to Enterprise Architecture or to any of the previously mentioned architectural frameworks. The indirect linkages can be found by examined the purposes of the Enterprise Architecture and understanding the nature of the enterprises. EA should document business processes and organisational knowledge bases, while KM should manage the knowledge processes that support these. Certainly, an indirect link was noted earlier in this chapter where I stated that "KM depends on expressing many underlying constructs within the organisation and understanding the connectivity, not just from a technology sense, but also from a social and value network context." Additionally, the Australian Standard (Standards Australia AS:5037, 2005) acknowledges two principal benefits of undertaking knowledge management: to improve productivity and organisational efficiency, and to promote innovation. Enterprise Architecture is the frame within which those benefits can be elicited.

Snyman et al (2004) looked to Drucker in noting that the knowledge and knowledge workers are the most valuable assets for enterprises in this modern day. An appropriate fit between the overall strategy and an organisation's knowledge management is critical. From an architectural viewpoint, business processes are (or should be) an extension of the flow of information through the organisation; determining this flow of information will enable strategists to assess the flow and exchange of knowledge.

The understanding and expression of the enterprise vision and strategy remains a critical function of ensuring the enterprise can be successful. Enterprise content management, which takes place in a collaborative environment and supported by enabling technology and tools, is essential to create an organisation that is transparent, extended and intelligent (Klein, 2005). Although Klein takes a low-level perspective on Enterprise Architecture (equating EA with data or information management), the linkages between the strategy and the need to manage content remain valid. This is particularly so for those organisations who measure their assets in the content and services they provide, rather than the direct financial equation of the products of commercial entities.

Nothing in the literature easily distinguishes the importance of decision-making, knowledge management or enterprise architecture between commercial and government interests. However, government interests do not have financial shareholders to please; the implementation of policy depends on the strength of their decision making. In this sense, there is little difference between the non-profit and profit based organisations, as these decisions affect the operating capital (public perception or operating budget). While the importance of decision making may be no less, the outcomes of decisions in the government sector are more visible than that of the commercial sector.

Knowledge Management is an integral support activity for decision-making, along with the information held within the intellectual capital and enterprise environment (Vandegriff, 2006). Certainly, KM helps connect the intellectual assets and business growth (Furlong, 2001; Paulzen & Perc, 2002). An Enterprise Knowledge Architecture (as a form of Information Systems Architecture) permits integration of knowledge management systems (including necessary processes) into a knowledge network (Iyer et al, 2006).

Enterprise Architecture and Knowledge Management are very closely tied to the enterprise's strategy. Ultimately, Zachman makes a direct link between EA and KM; "… Enterprise Knowledge Management is very, very closely tied to, if not the same as, Enterprise Architecture Management" (Zachman, undated). The upshot of Zachman's thoughts is that the expression of the architecture is an expression of the underlying management knowledge of the organisation. The measurement of the effectiveness of Knowledge Management is an indirect measurement on the effectiveness of the use of knowledge within the organisation.

A KM MATURITY MODEL

In the previous section, I noted that KM is a concept that assists human decision-making; improvements in KM maturity indicate an improvement in the feedback from the system, and a greater understanding of the overall business (including strategies). KM can be measured through artefacts, activity, intellect, behaviours or maturity; although, techniques to extract useful metrics are still being evolved.

The "hard" measures (such as those advocated through the Australian Standard (Standards Australia AS:5037, 2005), require careful selection and presentation to ensure integrity of meaning. A measure of the rate of production of artefacts (for instance) means nothing in isolation; causal factors (such as changes in the environment and rates of knowledge error) must also be considered. In the context of EA, partial measures will be open to interpretation and the flow-on effect of creating the architecture may not be directly visible or attributable to any improvements in the measures until well after the fact. In addition, such measures may need to be "seasonally adjusted"; a process that may not be possible if the information is not available, especially through lack of historical collection.

Maturity Models have the benefit of providing a "snapshot" of the organisation at a particular point in time. Such models can be subjective, the data provided depending on the interpretation of the questions by the respondent. However, the design of a Maturity Model is intended to be static throughout the life of the initiative (however that may be described) and comparisons at various points in time should be valid.

In the previous section I noted a number of existing Maturity Models that could be used, but these either provide a limited overview (the categories are too aggregated to be useful), or are proprietary and require resources (both financially and time) to tailor and complete. Certainly, the CMM is extremely complex and requires a degree of training to complete properly. However, (from my own observations) the nature of Government staffing precludes the widespread employment of highly specialised personnel, and the necessary

expertise to exercise the Maturity Model for full effect would not persist within a department; let alone across Government. For these reasons, the previously listed Maturity Models would not be suitable for implementation in a living Architecture.

To this end, I am proposing a framework for a persistent maturity model to form one leg of the CMP. Rather than commence this work from scratch, I have decided to build on the work of Iftikhar et al (2003) from their paper "Developing an Instrument for Knowledge Management Project Evaluation", in which the authors developed an instrument of evaluation for knowledge projects.

The Knowledge Management Maturity Model framework

Iftikhar et al (2003) noted that "[e]valuation is important [...] to determine whether the organisation's investment pays off in terms of demonstrable performance improvements. In many domains, however, changes in performance are difficult to measure because of uncontrollable factors that exist within the larger organisational context." (p57) The authors defined a series of questions that can be applied to a knowledge project. The questions are divided into four key categories, each with significant sub-categories:

- Organisational Environment. Sub-categories include Social Aspects, Culture, Incentives and Trust Issues.
- Technical and Managerial Support. Sub-categories include Organisational structure and Awareness and Commitment.
- Strategy and Goals for KM Projects. Iftikhar et al did not list any particular sub-categories for this section.
- Utilisation of Knowledge and Technology. Sub-categories include Information Technology, Maintenance and Protection, and Using and Applying Knowledge.

Iftikhar et al did not include a "Quality section" in their questions, but the quality of the outcomes when dealing with knowledge and decision-making is as important as the fact that an outcome has been achieved. Likewise, an overall statement reflecting the organisation's perception of their own KM was not considered by Iftikhar et al.

Within the following sections I follow the intent of Iftikhar et al (2003) who posed a series of questions (or made a series of statements) within each of the categories. After a brief discussion on each of the categories I will develop a table which will link the questions (or statements) posed by the authors to a maturity marker. I have not fully developed the maturity model within this chapter – validation of the framework within an active architecture is still a work in progress. In addition, I do not intend to discuss the authors' work in any detail; this can be sourced from their original paper.

Organisational Environment

Iftikhar et al (2003) noted the importance of a knowledge friendly atmosphere for business to succeed.

Social Aspects

Knowledge is not just a technical artefact but is part of the social environment within which it is used. In the knowledge realm organisational culture and interpersonal communications have an important role to play in the non-technical information system. (Iftikhar et al, 2003).

Internodal communication is an important element within any enterprise architecture. At the technical or information level, this communication may exist from system to system, technology to technology; however, within an enterprise architecture, the nodes are more likely to include personal communications.

Culture

Iftikhar et al (2003) noted that "[o]rganisational culture reflects the behaviour within an organisation, which either enables or hinders effective KM" (p58). The enterprise architecture frameworks highlight organisational behaviours and important processes. Development of the architecture should invoke discussion about these behaviours and the desired outcomes.

Incentives

The development of the architecture itself is unlikely to provide impetus to staff to give maximum output because the Architecture does not provide any direct recognition or appreciation. However, improved efficiency may manifest itself as a result of programs introduced through the improved awareness promoted by the architecture.

Trust Issues

Iftikhar et al (2003) note that "[k]nowledge sharing and willingness to take the time to help others is based on trust and confidence" (p58). Trust and confidence is often built on personal relationships, but these factors can be enhanced by using the architecture to formalise the interactions that are necessary in the development of trust. Common knowledge of processes, outcomes and communication methods will help build the trust and confidence that is needed.

Technical and Managerial Support

"KM initiatives can be started based strictly on the availability of new technology. However, if the managerial support is missing even a successful project might fail when it comes to utilisation of the system in the long run" (Iftikhar et al, 2003, p59). Architectural frameworks may not necessarily show the support (both technical and managerial) needed to ensure success, but they can formalise the mechanisms for support as shown in the next two paragraphs. The form will depend on the architectural framework chosen.

Organisational Structure

The "command and control" (C2) structure is an essential view in the frameworks evolved from the C4ISR AF. Sowa & Zachman (1992) had not specifically identified a C2 hierarchy in his model, but such a wireframe would sit comfortably at the intersection of System Model and People. When discussing the resultant organisational structure, the term "maturity" may be misleading as some of the elements reflect business choices rather than "growth". As an example, an organisation may decide to not have a full-time Chief Knowledge Officer, but instead to ensure the role is spread across other staff.

Awareness and Commitment

Effective use of the workforce depends on the awareness that can be built by the ability for business functions to link and share information (Iftikhar et al, 2003). The developed architecture documents the linkages, through processes and information, between the business functions.

Strategy and Goals for KM Projects

The relationship between EA and strategy has been previously discussed and architecture should clearly demonstrate linkages between strategies and goals. In addition, the architecture will help identify current gaps and act as an initiator for various projects (through the "as-is" and "to-be" representations).

Utilisation of Knowledge and Technology

The Information Sciences origin of enterprise architecture (c.f. Zachman, 1987, 1997) reinforces the linkages between knowledge and technology. Importantly, any measurement of the architecture should show if the tools exist to properly support decision making in the organisation. Iftikhar et al (2003) had noted the important relationship between collecting and extracting information and the need to turn that which is collected into knowledge.

Information Technology

Technology provides the tools necessary to support the KM processes. The Architecture should highlight the range of tools or technology needed, and promote their effective use.

Maintenance and Protection

Like any physical asset, data, information and knowledge (and the tools and processes that manipulate them) must be maintained, otherwise the resultant deterioration will render them worthless (Iftikhar et al, 2003). The development of the architecture allows the important aspects of the organisation to be documented along with the needs of the organisation; facilitating processes to ensure protection and maintenance.

Using and Applying Knowledge

Collecting information and exploiting it to produce knowledge is of no avail if these products are not used in an effective manner. Amongst other things, the role of the architecture is to document processes to ensure that such knowledge is used efficiently and effectively.

Quality

Wikipedia[6] notes that the "Quality Management Maturity Grid is used by a business or organisation as a benchmark of how mature their processes are, and how well they are embedded in their culture, with respect to service or product quality management." The architecture documents the processes within the backdrop of the organisation. As such, any maturity model reflecting the organisation should also include a section on "quality". To some extent, these elements are covered within the previous elements; but explicit statement of the elements will help clarity and understanding.

Tailoring the Model

The following table (Table 2) summarises the link between the instrument of evaluation mooted by Iftikhar et al (2003) and a KM Maturity Model Framework. Naturally, the associated maturity levels or stages (not listed in this table) must be tailored for each organisations; failure to do so

will reduce the relevance and hence the acceptance and utility.

USING THE KM-MM IN AN EA CONTEXT

Despite the level of work to reach an effective maturity model, the model is not an end within itself and is a tool to support the processes of the enterprise as well as supporting the development of the Architecture. Like all tools, it will only be effective when used in the right manner and context. Four broad uses of this maturity model exist in the context of EA: identifying the baseline (as-is), identifying the goal (to-be), identifying

Table 2. A KM maturity model framework

Sub Category	Iftikhar et al (2003) Question (sic) (pp58-61)	Resultant Maturity Area Description
	Social Aspects	
Social Aspects	All employees are ready and willing to give advice or help on request, from anyone else in the company.	This area identifies the extent that employees give advice or help, on request from anyone else in the company.
	Informal networks across the organisation are encouraged.	This area identifies the effect and support of informal networks within the organisation
	Multi-disciplinary teams are formed and managed.	This area identifies how multi-disciplinary team are recognised within the organisation.
	Staff is rotated to spread best practice and ideas, or the natural internal staff turnover is actively capitalised upon in this regard.	This area identifies how the organisation utilises staff movements to spread best practice and ideas.
	Training is available for those who want to improve their communication skills.	This area identifies the organisation's approach to communications training.
	Management uses different means to facilitate knowledge dissemination and creation e.g. mentoring programs, project debriefing, learning games, training programs, story telling etc.	This area identifies the management's approach to different means to facilitate knowledge dissemination and creation. e.g. mentoring programs, project debriefing, learning games, training programs, story telling etc.
	There is a strategic program in place to collect and analyse business intelligence information to assist with business strategy development.	This area identifies the organisation's approach to the use of business intelligence to assist with business strategy development.
	Technology is shared with suppliers/clients where appropriate to enhance relationships.	This area identifies how technology is shared by the organisation.
	There is a program of active participation in business conferences and other discussion forums to share and learn ideas and experience.	This area identifies the organisations approach to participation in business conferences and other discussion forums.

continued on following page

Table 2. continued

Sub Category	Iftikhar et al (2003) Question (sic) (pp58-61)	Resultant Maturity Area Description
Culture		
Culture	Failure is not stigmatised, rather it is seen as an opportunity to learn.	This area identifies the organisation's approach to failure.
	Recording and sharing knowledge is routine and second nature to promote continuous knowledge exchange.	This area identifies the organisation's approach to recording and sharing knowledge.
	Looking for the best practice or work that can be re-used is a natural, standard process.	This area identifies the organisation's approach to re-use of work and practices.
	Knowledge sharing is seen as a strength, knowledge hoarding as a weakness.	This area identifies the organisations approach to knowledge hoarding and sharing.
	Time is allowed for creative thinking.	This area identifies the organisation's approach to creative thinking.
	Employees are encouraged to learn more and develop themselves.	This area identifies the organisation's approach to employee development.
	There are no restrictions on access to information unless it is confidential or personal.	This area identifies the organisation's approach to access to information (allowing for privacy or confidentiality provisions).
	A common language exists for exchanging and clarifying information to people with different backgrounds.	The area identifies the ability of the organisation to use a common language for exchanging and clarifying information to people with different backgrounds.
	Efforts are made to combine the ideas of different cultures within the organisation.	This area identifies the organisations efforts to combine the idea of different cultures within the organisation.
Incentives		
Incentives	Good KM behaviour (e.g. sharing, reusing etc.) is actively promoted on a day-to-day basis.	This area identifies how the organisation promotes good KM behaviour.
	Bad KM behaviour (e.g. hoarding, not using best practices etc.) is actively discouraged.	This area identifies how the organisation deals with bad KM behaviour (e.g. hoarding, not using best practices etc.).
	Good KM behaviour is monitored and built into the appraisal system.	This area identifies how the organisation monitors the KM behaviours of the organisation's personnel.
	Individuals are visibly rewarded for teamwork, knowledge sharing and re-use, and re-use of knowledge.	This area identifies how the organisation rewards good KM behaviour (e.g. teamwork, knowledge sharing and re-use, and re-use of knowledge).
	Training and development programs in KM behaviour and procedure are encouraged from point of recruitment onwards	This area identifies the KM training and development programs within the organisation.
Trust Issues		
Trust Issues	People are engaged in decisions that directly affect them.	This area identifies how the organisation engages personnel in decision-making.
	Explanation is given about why decisions are made the way they are.	This area identifies how the organisation explains decisions to personnel.
	Expectations from the employees after changes are stated clearly.	This area identifies how well the organisation communicates changes in expectations.
	Work groups see themselves as interdependent with others outside their team.	Work groups see themselves as interdependent with others outside their team.
	When it comes to problem solving, groups and/or individuals regard themselves as part of a larger, integrated entity.	This area identifies how groups and/or individuals regard themselves, in relation to a larger, integrated entity.
	People are genuinely interested in helping one another to develop new capacities for decision making.	This area identifies how personnel are interested in helping develop new capacities for decision making.

continued on following page

Table 2. continued

Sub Category	Iftikhar et al (2003) Question (sic) (pp58-61)	Resultant Maturity Area Description
	There are different personality types within the organisation that allow people to cluster into groups of compatible types.	There are different personality types within the organisation that allow people to cluster into groups of compatible types.
	Usage issues (e.g. experts' willingness to use databases or share their knowledge) are understood by management.	This area identifies how well the management understands usage issues (e.g. experts' willingness to use databases or share their knowledge).
Organisational Structure		
Organisational Structure	Formal networks exist to facilitate dissemination of knowledge effectively.	This area identifies the use of networks to facilitate dissemination of knowledge.
	A flexible, well-structured, up-to-date knowledge map exists to point staff in the direction of the knowledge they seek.	This area identifies the use of knowledge maps within the organisation.
	Information useful for different units is available to a number of different users in different formats.	This area identifies how information may be available in different formats to improve usefulness.
	A Chief Knowledge Officer (CKO) is in place, and effective with the appropriate degree of authority to facilitate knowledge creation.	This area identifies the role a CKO plays in the organisation.
	There are a number of dedicated knowledge workers in place to support and assist the knowledge processes (i.e. creation, storage, dissemination etc.).	This area identifies the role that knowledge workers play in the organisation.
Awareness and Commitment		
Awareness and Commitment	At all levels there is a general understanding of KM, with respect to how it is applied to the business.	This area identifies the general level of understanding of KM within the business.
	Business functions e.g. Customer Service and Support, Human Resource, Information Technology, Learning and Training, Project Management etc. are related with KM.	This area identifies how business functions e.g. Customer Service and Support, Human Resource, Information Technology, Learning and Training, Project Management etc. are related with KM.
	KM is given representation at the board level by creating an extra seat on the company's board of directors.	This area identifies how KM is represented at the board level.
	Senior management demonstrates commitment and action with respect to KM policy, guidelines and activities.	This area identifies senior management commitment with respect to KM policy, guidelines and activities.
	Senior management supports knowledge sharing, learning and other desired 'KM' behaviour.	This area identifies how senior management supports knowledge sharing, learning and other desired KM behaviour.
	At the senior level there is an ongoing review of the effectiveness of KM for the whole company.	This area identifies the approach to reviews of KM effectiveness.
	Intellectual assets are recognised and valued.	This area identifies how intellectual assets are recognised and valued.
	Senior management has a good understanding of the skills of their staff.	This area identifies how senior management understand the skills of their staff.

continued on following page

Table 2. continued

Sub Category	Iftikhar et al (2003) Question (sic) (pp58-61)	Resultant Maturity Area Description
	Strategy and Goals	
Strategy and Goals	KM projects have already been initiated.	This area identifies if KM projects have already been initiated.
	There is a vision for how KM should integrate into the business.	This area identifies if there is a vision for how KM should integrate into the business.
	It is clear how KM initiatives support the business plan.	This area identifies how KM initiatives support the business plan.
	There are defined responsibilities and a budget set for KM initiatives.	This area identifies how responsibilities are defined and budgets are set for KM initiatives.
	KM principles are set (e.g., definitions of key knowledge and guidelines for knowledge creation and management).	The area identifies if KM principles are set.
	There is clear ownership of KM initiatives, either by the business unit or the whole business.	This area identifies the ownership of KM initiatives, either by the business unit or the whole business.
	There is a program of initiatives in progress to improve KM.	This area identifies if a program of KM initiatives exist.
	There is a close relationship between the strategic program and the learning program within the organisation.	This area identifies the relationship between the strategic program and the learning program.
	Information Technology	
Information Technology	People use existing IT effectively as normal working practice.	This area identifies how staff use the existing IT.
	IT is leading edge and is fully supported.	This area identifies the currency of the IT.
	Technology is a key enabler in ensuring that the right information is available to the right people at the right time.	This area identifies how the technology enables the passage of information throughout the organisation. This area does not include technology's role in creating or storing information.
	IT makes the search for information easier.	This area identifies how IT assists searching for information.
	IT allows effective communication across boundaries and time zones.	This area identifies how IT eases communications across boundaries and time zones.
	Process tools and technologies are related to KM.	This area identifies how process tools and technologies are related to KM.
	There is investment in infrastructure development to support groupware and collaborative computing tools.	This area identifies how investment for groupware and collaborative computing tools is managed.
	Information is used to make sense of changes in the environment, create new knowledge and/or make decision about a course of action.	This area identifies how information is used to make sense of the environment, create new knowledge and/or make decisions.
	Maintenance and Protection	
Maintenance and Protection	There are regular reviews to delete out of date information and ensure regular updates from designated information owners.	This area identifies the frequency of reviews of corporate information.
	Effective cataloguing and archiving procedures are in place for document management, whether held electronically or not.	This area identifies the organisation's approach to cataloguing and document management.
	Key information to be protected, such as customer information, is identified and measures are in place to ensure it stays in the company should key employees leave.	This area identifies how key information might be protected if key employees leave.
	Intellectual assets are legally protected.	This area identifies how intellectual assets are protected.
	There are complete IT security procedures in place (backup, recovery etc).	This area identifies the organisation's attitudes to security practices.
	Regulatory and compliance requirements are clearly published and understood; they are monitored to ensure compliance.	This area identifies the organisation's approach to regulatory and compliance requirements.

continued on following page

Table 2. continued

Sub Category	Iftikhar et al (2003) Question (sic) (pp58-61)	Resultant Maturity Area Description
	Using and Applying Knowledge	
Using and Applying Knowledge	To improve decision making, critical knowledge is elicited and prioritised.	This area identifies the organisation's attitude to the use of critical knowledge in decision making.
	Ideas to exploit pools of information are reviewed and acted on for potential business benefit.	This area identifies how the organisation acts upon ideas to exploit pools of information.
	Best practice in internal methods are reviewed and propagated.	This area identifies how the organisation manages best practice in internal methods.
	Knowledge provision is targeted towards major decision points in key business processes.	This area identifies how knowledge provision is targeted.
	Use of knowledge and information is controlled in line with regulatory and compliance requirements.	This area identifies how knowledge and information is controlled.
	Quality	
Quality		This area identifies the organisation's ability to use quality measurements as a management tool
		This area identifies the visibility of "quality" within the organisation
		This area identifies how the organisation deals with problems.
		This area is an indication of investment in quality
		This area identifies how proactive the organisation is towards improvement. When tailoring this maturity model, replace the 14-step program with whichever quality improvement program that is applicable for the organisation.
		This area is a single statement that sums up the organisation's approach to quality
	Knowledge Management	
Knowledge		This area is a single statement that sums up the organisation's approach to KM

the road to reaching the goal, and measuring progress.

Working out the "As-Is"

As previously discussed, the primary role of the CMP is to highlight those elements that need to change in order to achieve an appropriately mature capability. Knowledge Management is only one leg

of the profile; further models should be developed to ensure a full Capability Maturity Profile.

Additionally, I had noted that KM is a strategic initiative and that measurement is necessary to understand success and failure. Measuring progress is to understand the difference between the origin and the current situation. To this end, the maturity model can be used to form a snapshot of the current position. The appropriate levels should be recorded to reflect the current environment within the enterprise.

However, using the maturity model to document the baseline is not likely to be simple as completing a survey or filling in forms. The Observer and Hawthorne Effects[7] note that the mere act of observation may cause changes to that which is being observed.

Completing the maturity model becomes a journey of discovery, which (in part) links to the other uses of the maturity model, to be discussed shortly. The discovery of unnoticed initiatives, or unrecognised benefits from current initiatives, will affect the maturity model. This may not be a bad thing – but their level of integration and understanding could be overstated. Individual perceptions will cloud the selected levels or will ascribe a maturity level based on their understanding of knowledge boundaries, rather than of the enterprise as a whole. Finally, the maturity model may not necessarily be tailored properly to the Enterprise, and the non-specific language may confuse the participants who may ascribe unrealistic values.

Defining the "To-Be"

Far easier is to use the maturity model to describe the future, especially when the detail has not yet been determined. Part of defining the "to-be" must be the tailoring of the maturity model to describe clearly the "to-be" maturity level. Such a description allows recognition of when the Enterprise has reached the goal. A perfect maturity across the board may not be attainable, at least not in the lifetime of the selected Architecture.

The tailoring of the maturity model may be a cyclic process, where an understanding of the "as-is" may change based on the new understanding of the "to-be". Generally, this understanding may place the "as-is" at a lower maturity level as the understanding of current initiatives is redefined.

Developing the Roadmap

Having identified the current situation and the goal, the maturity model can also be used as signposts on road to attaining the goal. A maturity model is usually too coarse to definitively express the steps through which an enterprise can reach a higher level of maturity, but the intervening maturity levels can be used as markers.

Importantly, the maturity model the KM-MM can be used a learning or elicitation tool; a tool to ensure full coverage of the aspects the architecture is supposed to support. This could be seen as duplication of the purpose of the Framework; but it should be better seen as a means of tailoring and refining the requirements of the framework to suit the needs of the organisation.

Through this process, the maturity model will be further tailored so that the interim maturity levels can be used for measurement.

Measuring Progress

Finally, a fully tailored maturity model noting the "as-is", "to-be" and interim maturity levels can be used to monitor progress along the roadmap. A maturity model is not a substitute for proper project management, but provides a simplified mechanism for presenting the necessary information to the higher-level decision-makers.

CONCLUSION

Within this chapter I have provided descriptions for EA (the organizing logic for business processes and IT infrastructure reflecting the integration and standardization requirements of the company's operating model) and KM (managing knowledge processes to support both business processes and organisational knowledge bases; connecting intellectual assets and business growth). In both cases, the definitions are not yet authoritative, but provide a very clear context for the progress of the disciplines.

EA and KM are important for all manner of Enterprises; the imperative for governments is borne by the visibility of the results of decision-making.

While neither EA nor KM provide explicit references to each other, the indirect linkages can be seen through the commonality of purpose. Both disciplines respond to the overall strategy of the organisation, and both rely on structure and information flows.

But neither EA or KM are an end, each are a means to ensure the goals and strategies of the enterprise are achieved. To ensure that investment in EA is warranted, the effect that the architecture has on business outcomes must be measured. The management of knowledge is one such facet that can be measured.

But knowledge management maturity is a versatile tool within any architecture. The KM maturity level form part of the "as-is" baseline, and the desired levels of maturity form part of the "to-be goal. As important is the role that the determination of tailored maturity levels plays in the discovery of important aspects of the architecture. Finally, a maturity model can act as a road map and monitoring tool.

Further study is required to validate the maturity model and to confirm the usefulness as a means of measuring the effect creating the architecture has on enterprises. In addition, a full Capability Maturity Profile should be developed to be added as a useful perspective to architectural frameworks. These studies will only serve to enhance the utility of EA.

REFERENCES

Allega, P.J. (2005); *Architecture framework debates are irrelevant*; Gartner report G00127331, 07 Jun 2005.

Allega, P.J. (2005a); *Enterprise Architecture will never realize a return on investment*; Gartner report G00128285, 24 Jun 2005.

Armour Dr. F., Kaisler Dr. S., Getter J., & Pippin D. (2003); *A UML-driven Enterprise Architecture case study*; Proceedings of the 36th Hawaii International Conference on System Sciences (HICSS) 2003.

Barnett, W., Presley A., Johnson M., & Loles D.H. (1994); *An Architecture for the Virtual Enterprise*; 1994 IEEE International Conference on Systems, Man, and Cybernetics, 1 (pp. 506-511)

Bernus, P. & Nemes, L (1996); *A framework to define a generic enterprise reference architecture and methodology*; Computer Integrated Manufacturing Systems, Vol 9, No3 pp 179-191, 1996.

C4ISR Architecture Framework (Version 2.0) (1997); C4ISR Architectures Working Group (USA) ; Department of Defense (USA)

Chen, D., Vallespir, B., & Doumeingts, G. (1997); *GRAI integrated methodology and its mapping onto generic enterprise reference architecture and methodology*; Computers in Industry, Vol 33 (1997), pp 387-394.

Collison, C., & Parcell G. (2005); *KM Self-Assessment*; Retrieved 01/04/2007 from "Learning to Fly" Website (http://www.chriscollison.com/l2f/whatiskm.html#assessment)

Defence Architecture Framework – Resources (CD) (Version 1.0) (2005); Australian Government, Department of Defence (Chief Information Officer Group)

DoD Architecture Framework – Deskbook (Final Draft) (Version 1.0) (2003); DoD Architecture Framework Working Group; Department of Defense (USA)

Duttaroy, A. (2005); *Five Ms of Meta Data*; DM Review (http://www.dmreview.com) April 2005.

Federal EA Framework (V 1.1) (1999); CIO Council (USA)

Furlong, G. (2001); *Knowledge management and the competitive edge*; University of Greenwich Business School; 2001, revised May 2003.

Iftikhar, Z., Eriksson, I.V., & Dickson, G.W. (2003); *Developing an Instrument for Knowledge Management Project Evaluation*; Electronic Journal of Knowledge Management, Vol1, Issue 1, 2003, pp55-62

Iyer, B., Shankaranarayanan G., & Wyner, G. (2006); *Process Coordination Requirements: Implications for the design of Knowledge Management Systems*; The Journal of Computer Information Systems; Volume 46, Issue 5; 2006

Jonkers, H., van Buuren, R., Arbab, F., de Boer F., Bonsangue M., Bosma, H., ter Doest, H., Groenewegen L., Scholten J.G., Hoppenbrouwers S., Iacob M., Janssen W., Lankhorst M., van Leeuwen D., Proper E., Stam A., van der Torre L., & van Zanten G.V. (2003); *Towards an Language for Coherent Enterprise Architecture Descriptions*; Proceedings of the Seventh IEEE International Enterprise Distributed Object Computing Conference (EDOC) 2003.

Kankanhalli, A., & Tan, B.C.Y. (2004); *A review of Metrics for Knowledge Management Systems and Knowledge Management Initiatives*; Proceedings of the 37th Hawaii International Conference on System Sciences – 2004.

Klein, J; *ECM best practices for the Enlightened Enterprise*, KM World; Vol 14, Issue5, May 2005

Ladley, J. (2002); *Beyond the Data Warehouse: Information Management Maturity*; DM Review (http://www.dmreview.com) August 2002.

Lapkin, A. (2004); *A users guide to architectural patterns*; Gartner Report G00124049, 22 October 2004

Lapkin, A. (2004); *Architecture Frameworks: How to Choose*; Gartner Report G00124230, 19 November 2004

Lopez, J. (2002); *Return on Enterprise Architecture: Measure it in Asset Productivity*; Gartner Report: RPT-0702-0119, 19 July 2002

Marco, D. (2002); *Meta Data & Knowledge Management: Capability Maturity Model*; DM Review (http://www.dmreview.com) August/September/October/November 2002.

Martin, P. (2006); *Measuring KM-Based improvements in decision-making*; personal communication through the ACTKM forum (http://www.actKM.org) March 2006.

Metainnovation (2004); *KM Concepts Module 8: Metrics*; Retrieved May 2006 from Metainnovation KM Concepts course (www.metainnovation.com)

Mohanty, S., & Chand, M. (2005); *5iKM3 Knowledge Management Maturity Model*; TATA Consultancy Services 2005.

Moore, A. (2005); *What makes government different?*; KM World Vol 14 Issue 6; Jun 2005

Noran, O. (2003); *A systematic evaluation of the C4ISR AF using ISO1504 Annex A (GERAM)*; Computers in Industry vol 56 (2005) pp 407-427.

Noran, O. (2005); *An analysis of the Zachman framework of enterprise architecture from the GERAM perspective*; Annual Reviews in Control Vol 27 (2003) pp 163-183.

Paulzen ,O., & Perc, P. (2002); *A maturity model for quality improvement in knowledge management*; Proceedings of the 13th Australasian Conference on Information Systems (ACIS 2002).

Robertson, J. (2003); *Metrics for knowledge management and content management*; Step Two Designs (www.steptwo.com.au) February 2003, accessed May 2006.

Ross, J.W., Weill, P., & Robertson, D.C. (2006); *Enterprise as strategy: creating a foundation for business execution*; Harvard Business School Publishing; 2006.

Rosser, B. (2002); *Architectural styles and Enterprise Architecture*; Gartner report AV-17-4384, 13 August 2002.

Saha, P. (2004); *A real options perspective to Enterprise Architecture as an investment activity*; (accessed 24 Aug 05 through The Open Group Architecture Forum http://www.opengroup.org/ architecture).

Schekkerman, J. (2004); *Enterprise Architecture Validation*; Institute for Enterprise Architecture Developments, August 2004.

Schekkerman, J. (2004); *Trends in Enterprise Architecture: How are organizations progressing?*; Institute for Enterprise Architecture Developments, 2004.

Schekkerman, J. (2006); *How to survive in the jungle of Enterprise Architecture Frameworks: Creating or choosing an Enterprise Architecture Framework*; Trafford Publishing; 3rd Edition 2006 (First published 2004).

Schulman, J. (2004); *Architecture Frameworks provide system road maps*; Gartner Report G00125007, 29 November 2004.

Snyman, S., & Kruger, CJ; *The interdependency between strategic management and strategic knowledge management*; Journal of Knowledge Management; Vol 8, Issue 1, 2004).

Sowa, J.F., & Zachman, J.A.(1992); *Extending and formalizing the framework for information systems architecture*; IBM Systems Journal, Vol 31, No 3, 1992.

Standards Australia (2005); *Australian Standard 5037-2005: Knowledge management – a guide*; Standards Australia, September 2005.

Steen, M.W.A., Akehurst, D.H., ter Doest H.W.L., & Lankhorst M.M.(2004); *Supporting Viewpoint-Oriented Enterprise Architecture*; Proceedings of the 8th IEEE International Enterprise Distributed Object Computing Conference (EDOC) 2004.

Vandegriff, L.J. (2006); *Unified approach to agile knowledge-based enterprise decision support*; VINE Vol 36, Issue 2; 2006)

Weerdmeester, R., Pocterra, C., & Hefke, M. (2003); *Thematic Network/Roadmap: Knowledge Management Maturity Model*; Information Societies Technology Programme, June 2003.

Zachman, J.; *The Physics of Knowledge Management*; undated, retrieved 29 Apr 2007 from http://www.zifa.com

Zachman, J.A (1987); *A Framework for Information Systems Architecture*; IBM Systems Journal, Vol 29, No 3, 1987

Zachman, J.A. (1996); *Enterprise Architecture and legacy systems. Getting beyond the legacy*; accessed from Information Engineering Services Pty Ltd via http://members.ozemail.com.au/~visible/ papers/zachman1.htm on 25/07/2005

Zachman, J.A. (1997); *Concepts of the framework for enterprise architecture. Background, description and utility*; accessed from Information Engineering Services Pty Ltd via http://members. ozemail.com.au/~visible/papers/zachman3.htm on 25/07/2005

Zachman, J.A. (1997a); *The challenge is change: a management paper*; accessed from Information Engineering Services Pty Ltd via http://members. ozemail.com.au/~visible/papers/zachman2.htm on 25/07/2005

ENDNOTES

1 http://www.enterprise-architecture.info/
2 The listed frameworks are: Zachman Framework; The Open Group Architecture Framework (TOGAF); Command, Control, Communications, Computing, Intelligence, Surveillance and Reconnaissance (C4ISR); Treasury Information Systems Architecture Framework (TISAF); Federal Enterprise

Architecture Framework (FEAF or FEA); Treasury Enterprise Architecture Framework (TEAF); Department of Defence Architecture Framework (DoDAF); Extended Enterprise Architecture (E2A); Object Management Groups Model Driven Architecture (MDA). The Australian Defence Force (ADF) has adapted the DoDAF to produce the Defence Architecture Framework (DAF).

[3] http://en.wikipedia.org/wiki/Enterprise_architecture

[4] According to Wikipedia, return on investment (ROI) is a calculation used to determine whether a proposed investment is wise, and how well it will repay the investor.

[5] According to Wikipedia, the Return on Assets (ROA) percentage shows how profitable a company's assets are in generating revenue. Investopedia (http://www.investopedia.com/terms/r/returnonassets.asp) notes ROA as a useful indicator of how profitable a company is relative to its total assets. Interestingly, Investopedia notes ROA as sometimes being known as ROI.

[6] http://en.wikipedia.org/wiki/Quality_Management_Maturity_Grid (accessed 25 March 2007) but the original source is cited as (Crosby, P. (1979); *Quality is Free*; McGraw Hill)

[7] http://en.wikipedia.org/wiki/Observer_effect and http://en.wikipedia.org/wiki/Hawthorne_effect (accessed 12 Aug 07)

Section II
Leadership, Governance, and Management

Chapter VI
The Criticality of Transformational Leadership to Advancing United States Government Enterprise Architecture Adoption

William S. Boddie
National Defense University, USA

ABSTRACT

An effective enterprise architecture (EA) capability enables an organization to develop sound enterprise plans, make informed human, materiel, and technology resource investment and management decisions, and optimize key business processes. Despite U.S. Congressional legislation, U.S. Office of Management and Budget guidance, and U.S. Government Accountability Office reports and recommendations, many U.S. government leaders struggle in advancing EA adoption in their organizations. U.S. Government leaders must embrace transformational leadership to advance EA adoption. The author presents the Vision, Integrity, Communication, Inspiration, and Empowerment Transformational Leadership Model that describes competencies U.S. Government leaders need to advance EA adoption. The author also presents the Transformational Leadership and Enterprise Management Integration Framework that describes the relationship between transformational leadership and enterprise management functions. U.S. Government leaders must adopt this framework to realize improved enterprise performance.

INTRODUCTION

Many U.S. government organizations struggle in implementing effective enterprise architecture (EA) capabilities. Despite Congressional legislation, U.S. Office of Management and Budget guidance, and U.S. Government Accountability Office recommendations, many U.S. government leaders struggle in advancing EA adoption in their organizations. The U.S. General Accounting Office (GAO) (2001) concluded that an EA is critical to modernizing enterprise business processes, information technology (IT), and improving enterprise performance effectiveness. The GAO (2004) found EA was critical to improving organizational performance in the private and public sectors. The U.S. Office of Management and Budget (OMB) (2006) stated "Architecture is a management practice to maximize the contribution of an agency's resources to achieve its mission. Architecture can establish a clear line of sight from investments to measurable performance improvements whether for the entire enterprise or a portion (or segment) of the enterprise" (p. 1 – 2).

An EA describes an organization's current capabilities and constraints, the organization's desired capabilities, and the organization's plans to transition from the current to the desired capabilities. Enterprise architectures provide "to people at all organizational levels an explicit, common, and meaningful structural frame of reference that allows an understanding of (1) what the enterprise does; (2) when, where, how, and why it does it; and (3) what it uses to do it" (GAO, 2003, p. i). An effective EA enables organizations to develop sound enterprise plans, make informed human, material, and technology resource investment and management decisions, and optimize key enterprise business processes. "Enterprise architectures are essential for organizations to effectively and efficiently develop new and evolve existing information systems" (GAO, 2000, p. 4). The GAO also found, "If defined properly, enterprise architectures can assist in optimizing the interdependencies and interrelationships among organizations' business operations and the underlying information technology supporting these operations" (GAO, 2000, p. 4). An effective EA capability can enable government organizations to realize improved performance.

Advancing an effective EA capability requires organizational leaders to adopt an enterprise perspective rather than focusing exclusively on sub-enterprise activities. The GAO (2004) "repeatedly identified the lack of an enterprise architecture as a key management weakness in major modernization programs at a number of federal agencies" (p. 1). Many government organizational leaders struggle to embrace an enterprise perspective and consequently miss significant opportunities to improve their organization's performance. Additionally, many government leaders lack the necessary leadership competencies to advance EA adoption. Kotter (1995) reported, "A paralyzed senior management often comes from having too many managers and not enough leaders" (p. 60). Kotter found "Change, by definition, requires a new system, which in turn, always requires leadership" (p. 60). Government organizations need strong leaders to advance EA adoption. The U.S. Government Accountability Office (2006) stated, "The key to these [U.S. government] departments and agencies building upon their current status, and ultimately realizing the benefits that they cited architectures providing, is sustained executive leadership, as virtually all the challenges that they reported can be addressed by such leadership" (p. 1). Transformational leadership is critical to government leaders advancing EA adoption and improving their organization's performance.

The objectives of this chapter are to review U.S. government efforts to advance EA capabilities, define the current EA state in U.S. government organizations, emphasize the criticality of transformational leadership to advancing government-wide EA adoption, situate the relationships between transformational leadership and enterprise management functions, and highlight the outcomes the U.S. Department of Labor realized from its adoption of transformational leadership, EA, and enterprise management.

REVIEW OF U.S. GOVERNMENT ENTERPRISE ARCHITECTURE

U.S. Government EA efforts were originally grounded in information technology (IT). The U.S. Senate Governmental Affairs Committee (1994) found that billions of U.S. taxpayer dollars were wasted buying federal government computer systems. The committee also found that many government organizations' efforts to modernize their computer systems were characterized by poor management, inadequate planning, and failed execution. To address these challenges, the committee recommended government-wide IT management reform.

The U.S. Senate Governmental Affairs Committee report resulted in the Information Technology Management Reform Act (ITMRA) of 1996. The IRMRA of 1996 was combined with the Federal Acquisition Reform Act and was renamed as the Clinger-Cohen Act of 1996 (CCA). CCA established the position of the Chief Information Officer (CIO) for government departments and agencies and mandated that the CIO was responsible for "developing, maintaining, and facilitating the implementation of a sound and integrated information technology architecture for the executive agency" (U.S. Congress, 1996, p. 685). CCA defined an IT architecture as "an integrated framework for evolving or maintaining existing information technology or acquiring new information technology to achieve the agency's strategic goals and information resources management goals" (p. 686). OMB established several initiatives to advance government-wide EA adoption.

U.S. OFFICE OF MANAGEMENT AND BUDGET ENTERPRISE ARCHITECTURE INITIATIVES

The OMB oversees U.S. government organizations, assists the President in overseeing the preparation of the federal budget and supervising its administration in Executive Branch agencies, and oversees and coordinates the Administration's procurement, financial management, information, and regulatory policies (OMB, 2007b, para. 1). OMB initiated programs to advance government-wide EA adoption. Key OMB initiatives included the Federal Enterprise Architecture and the Enterprise Architecture Assessment Framework.

Federal Enterprise Architecture

OMB began developing a Federal Enterprise Architecture (FEA) in 2002 (OMB, 2007). The purpose of the FEA is to "identify opportunities to simplify processes and unify work across the agencies and within the lines of business of the Federal government" (History and Background, para. 1) and to be a "more citizen-centered, customer-focused government that maximizes technology investments to better achieve mission outcomes" (para. 1). OMB based the FEA on the principles of:

- **Business-driven:** The FEA is most useful when it is closely aligned with government strategic plans and executive level direction. Agency mission statements, presidential management directives and agency business owners give direction to each agency's enterprise architecture (EA) and to the FEA.
- **Proactive and collaborative across the Federal government:** Adoption of the FEA is achieved through active participation by the EA community in its development and use. The FEA community is responsible for the development, evolution and adoption of the FEA.

- **Architecture improves the effectiveness and efficiency of government information resources:** Architecture development is an integral part of the capital investment process. No IT investment should be made without a business-approved architecture. (OMB, 2006, p. 4)

The OMB (OMB, 2007) also established the Performance, Business, Service Component, Data, and Technical reference models to enable government organizations to develop effective EA capabilities. The Performance Reference Model enables organizations to anticipate and measure the impact of organizational inputs to processes, outputs, and enterprise performance outcomes. The Business Reference Model enables organizations to identify business functions used to deliver services to citizens. The Service Component Reference Model enables government organizations to describe the services they use to perform enterprise business functions. The Technical Reference Model enables organizations to describe the technical standards upon which their technology assets are based. The Data Reference Model enables organizations to describe the data they process to deliver services to citizens. These reference models were established to enable organizations to advance EA capabilities and, by extension, to use the EA capabilities to improve enterprise performance. Further, OMB developed an EA Assessment Framework to evaluate organizational EA capabilities.

Enterprise Architecture Assessment Framework

The OMB established the Enterprise Architecture Assessment Framework (EAAF) to evaluate government organization EA capabilities and to "advance the use of enterprise architecture (EA) across the Federal government" (OMB, 2006a, p. 1). The EAAF is based on EA Completion, Use, and Results categories. The Completion category examines the extent to which organizations describe their current and target architectures and describe their plans to transition from the current to the target architecture. The Use category examines the extent to which organizations use the EA for enterprise planning, resource investment decision-making, and management. The Results category examines the extent to which organizations realize performance goals as a result of its EA. OMB (2007a) reported greater government-wide EA adoption in 2007 than it reported in 2006 and reported increased EA adoption since 2004. Although OMB reported improved government-wide EA adoption, the GAO found less promising results.

U.S. GENERAL ACCOUNTING OFFICE/GOVERNMENT ACCOUNTABILITY OFFICE AND

Enterprise Architecture

The U.S. Government Accountability Office (GAO) is the U.S. Congress' agency for monitoring and reporting U.S. government organization management performance information. "The U.S.

Table 1. GAO EA Reports (1998-2007)

U.S. Government organizational enterprise architecture report year	Number of reports by year
1998	1
1999	1
2000	11
2001	14
2002	30
2003	36
2004	45
2005	32
2006	27
2007	24
Total reports	221

Government Accountability Office (GAO) is an independent, nonpartisan agency that works for Congress. GAO is often called the "congressional watchdog" because it investigates how the federal government spends taxpayer dollars" (GAO, 2007, para. 1). The GAO was established in 1921 by the Budget and Accounting Act, is independent of the executive branch, and investigates how federal funds are spent. The GAO's name was later changed to the Government Accountability Office (GAO) in 2004 (GAO, 2007a, para. 1). The GAO publishes reports of its investigations of government executive branch organizations' management effectiveness and efficiency. The GAO published numerous reports regarding government-wide EA management.

The GAO began evaluating government-wide EA management in 1998 and, since then, conducted 221 reviews of government organizational EA programs. Table 1, GAO EA Reports From 1998 – 2007, reports GAO's EA reports in this period.

The GAO reports consistently found that government organizations were significantly challenged in EA management. For example, the GAO found "The Customs Service does not have a complete enterprise information systems architecture to guide and constrain the millions of dollars that it spends each year to develop and acquire new information systems and evolve existing ones" (GAO, 1998, p. 1). In another example, the GAO found that the Immigration and Naturalization Service (INS) struggled in developing an EA, that the INS EA was incomplete, and that the INS lacked a target architecture (GAO, 2000, p. 1).

The GAO concluded effective EA management was critical to improving organizational performance (2002). The GAO (2004a) reported that an effective EA was needed to enable the Department of Homeland Security to integrate 22 previously independent federal agencies. The GAO (2006) found that the U.S. Department of Defense's (DoD) EA management was deficient

and reported that the DoD's EA was incomplete. To influence government-wide EA adoption, the GAO published an EA assessment instrument.

The GAO (2002a) published an EA assessment framework to evaluate government organizational EA management. The GAO "developed a maturity framework for enterprise architecture management and reviewed architecture use in the federal government, specifically determining agencies' development, implementation, and maintenance of these architectures, and OMB's oversight" (p. 1). The framework, titled, the *Enterprise Architecture Management Maturity Framework (EAMMF) version 1.0*, enabled government organizations to earn EA management maturity ratings based on a maturity stages 1 through 5. Stage 1 represented the least maturity and Stage 5 represented the greatest maturity. Using its EAMMF version 1.0, the GAO found that only four percent of organizations had effective EA management (p. 1).

The GAO (2003) published version 1.1 of the EAMMF framework in 2003 and based the version on the 31 core EA elements found in the Chief Information Officer Council *A Practical Guide to Federal Enterprise Architecture* (CIO Council, 2001). In its 2004 report, the GAO (GAO, 2004b) found "the lack of an enterprise architecture as a key management weakness in major modernization programs at a number of federal agencies" (p. 1), found "little change in overall maturity between 2001 and 2003 (p.1), and found that "Only 20 of 96 agencies examined had established at least the foundation for effective architecture management" (p.1).

In its 2006 report, the GAO found that only four of the 27 assessed organizations had advanced to Stage 3 on the EAMMF and reported that no organizations had matured beyond Stage 3. GAO's report title, *Leadership Remains Key to Establishing and Leveraging Architectures for Organizational Transformation*, emphasized the criticality of strong organizational leadership to advancing government-wide EA management. The GAO stated "The key to these departments and agencies building upon their current status, and ultimately realizing the benefits that they cited architectures providing, is sustained executive leadership, as virtually all the challenges that they reported can be addressed by such leadership" (p. 1). This review of U.S. government-wide EA adoption leads to a very clear and concerning conclusion.

Despite extensive U.S. government oversight including Congressional legislation, OMB policy guidance, and GAO's assessments and recommendations, many U.S. Government leaders struggle in advancing EA adoption. It is evident that government oversight alone is insufficient to advance government-wide EA adoption. U.S. Government leaders must adopt transformational leadership to advance EA adoption in their organizations.

TRANSFORMATIONAL LEADERSHIP

Leadership is influencing others to action. Transformational leaders persuade individuals to achieve group goals (Bass, 1990, p. 11). Transformational leaders enable organizations to realize long-term organizational performance improvement (Bass, 1990). Various researchers found that transformational leaders improve long-term organizational performance.

The transformational leader broadens and elevates the interests of their followers and motivates followers to consider the greater good of others rather than their own self-interests. Transformational leaders inspire and motivate others to do more than the followers originally intended to do or thought possible (Bass, 1998). "The transformational leader asks followers to transcend their own self-interest for the good of the group, organization, or society; to consider their longer-term needs to develop themselves, rather than their needs of the moment; and to become more aware of what is really important" (Bass, 1990, p. 53).

Anderson (1998) found that transformational leaders build leadership organizations and make positive differences in organizations and in the lives of others wherever they go. Transformational leaders climb the heavens, reach beyond the ordinary, the predictable, the average, and chart new territories and possibilities. These leaders reach, motivate, inspire, and pull others below them upward to greater, unseen heights on the way (1998). Egan (as cited in Anderson, 1998) stated, "By stimulating, modeling, advocating, innovating, and motivating, they [transformational leaders] mold this culture, to the degree that this is possible, to meet both internal and environmental needs" (p. 48).

Transformational leaders achieve the desired results through charisma, inspiration, intellectual stimulation, and individualized consideration. They use charisma to influence others to high performance levels. They inspire and motivate their followers by providing meaning and challenge to the objective (Bass, 1998). This inspiration increases team spirit, enthusiasm, and optimism. Transformational leaders engage followers in viewing meaningful attractive visions of the future. "Transformational leaders stimulate their followers' efforts to be innovative and creative by questioning assumptions, reframing problems, and approaching old situations in new ways" (p. 5). The transformational leader pays special attention to each individual follower. The leader's individualized consideration helps develop successive higher levels of potential.

The transformational leader enables organizations to realize long-term goals and objectives rather than just immediate results. As a result of a compelling sense of urgency, vision, and strong interpersonal communication skills, these leaders generate a sense of urgency and excitement for the followers and colleagues to contribute richly to their environment. Boddie and Newman (2006) identified vision, communication, inspiration, and empowerment as competencies needed to advance government-wide EA adoption. The author developed the Vision, Integrity, Communication, Inspiration, and Empowerment Transformational Leadership Model to describe the competencies government leaders need to advance effective EA capabilities.

VISION, INTEGRITY, COMMUNICATION, INSPIRATION, AND EMPOWERMENT

Transformational Leadership Model

The Vision, Integrity, Communication, Inspiration and Empowerment (VICIE) Transformational Leadership Model consists of vision, integrity, communication, inspiration, and empowerment. These elements collectively represent the essence of transformational leadership. The VICIE Transformational Leadership Model functions analogous to an electrical circuit.

An electrical circuit produces the expected output if the required elements are present. For example, the typical electrical light switch operates in an on and off manner. If the required elements are present, the light bulb will light. If any of the required elements are missing the light bulb will not light. The electrical circuit is based on the electrical engineering AND state principle. The AND state principle requires that each required input element be sufficiently present for the circuit to fire. As a result, using the light switch example, if any required input element is missing, the light fail to light.

The VICIE Transformational Leadership Model requires each input element to be sufficiently present. If a required element is missing, transformational leadership will not result. Figure 1, the Vision, Integrity, Inspiration, Communication, and Empowerment Leadership Model, illustrates this perspective.

Vision

Vision is a critical transformational leadership competency. Transformational leaders articulate a clear and compelling vision of the future desired state. Whether the leader is the informal leader of a group of playground children or the formal leader of a very large and complex transnational organization, the leader articulates a clear and compelling vision of the desired future state. Ozaralli (2003) found that "transformational leaders create a dynamic organizational vision that often

Figure 1. Vision, integrity, communication, inspiration, and empowerment transformational leadership model

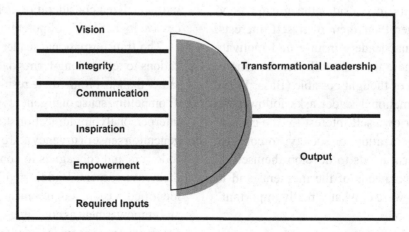

necessitates a metamorphosis in cultural values to reflect greater innovation" (Transformational leadership, para. 3). Forrester (2006) found that government "Change agents see new possibilities and know how to create and communicate a clear, compelling vision" (p. 6). Forrester cited Retired Vice Admiral Art Cebrowski, former Director of the DoD Office of Transformation, as an example of a transformational leader (p. 6). Rothwell (as cited by Forrester) concluded transformational leaders establish a vision, assemble the right teams, articulate the vision such that everyone embraces the vision and the priorities to achieve that vision (p. 6).

Stephenson (2004) found transformational leaders "must have a vision and purpose for their organizations, and that this vision and purpose must be tied to the organization's impact on society" (p. 4). Stephenson found that "leading CEOs around the world have visions for their companies that go well beyond making sure that projections are met for the next quarter. This makes good sense" (p. 4). Stephenson further stated, "A strong sense of vision and purpose is especially important to employees" (p. 4). The *Globe and Mail* reported (as cited by Stephenson, 2004) "the best employers as the ones who articulated a clear and consistent vision, starting with the CEO [Chief Executive Officer]. This vision kept their employees focused on the company's goals" (p. 5). Stephenson further found "that a vision and commitment to social responsibility is a strategic imperative for companies and business in general" (p. 5).

Vision is a critical transformational leadership competency. U.S. government leaders must establish a clear and compelling vision and encourage their employees to embrace this vision to advance EA adoption. U.S. government leaders must also demonstrate impeccable integrity to advance EA adoption.

Integrity

Integrity is about doing the right thing. Banutu-Gomez (2006) identified integrity as the most important leadership attribute and found "A leader with integrity provides consistent responses that show a sense of equal respect for everyone. . . . A leader who behaves consistently exhibits the integrity necessary to nurture the growth of trust" (p. 157). Simmons-Welburn and Welburn (2006) found strong leaders acted with integrity "as a way of suppressing self-interest for the good of the community-in other words, making decisions with an appreciation of the broader social context and institutional and professional values" (p. 468). They also described leaders with integrity as leaders whose "decisions are predicated upon a leaders' understanding that integrity involves looking out for the common good of the institution over self-interest or self-promotion" (p. 468).

Zablow (2006) found integrity was integral to establishing a productive organizational environment and reported "Employees are very sensitive to situations that impact their workplace and base much of their perceptions of the organizational culture on what they hear senior management say and, more importantly, what they see senior management do" (p. 27). Cloud (as cited by Udechukwu, 2007), found that integrity enhances the formation of appropriate character and that character, "(1) creates and maintains trust, (2) is able to see and face reality, (3) works in a way that brings results, (4) embraces negative realities and solves them, (5) causes growth and increase, (6) achieves transcendence and meaning in life" (p. 106). Sayer, Wright State University professor and Department of Communication chairman and president of the university faculty, emphasized integrity as an integral aspect of personal character. Sayer stated:

It used to be said that a "man's word was his bond," that you could take what a person said and trust it completely. Now we say to get it in writing and have it notarized. We live at a time where personal integrity seems to be more the exception than the rule, as greed and avarice control so much human behavior. Trust is a critical element in all human interaction, but how can we trust anyone when there is an absence of integrity behind a person's words and actions? Another old axiom fits perfectly here: "Say what you mean, and mean what you say." If all of us did just that, then our society would be better and we might be able to trust one another again. (p. 114)

Motorola Corporation's corporate values are based on integrity. Motorola (as cited by Gorman, 2007) stated, "Motorola has had two enduring core values through the years. The first is uncompromising integrity. The second is constant respect for the individual. What the leaders wanted to do was to keep those values, build on them and evolve them into statements that reflected the more competitive, performance-based culture they wished to encourage" (p. 24). Darling & Beebe (2007) identified trust as a key predictor of leadership integrity, found that trust was critical to an organization's functional effectiveness, and found that trust provided the foundation that maintains organizational integrity. They also found that there was no greater need in entrepreneurial leaders than the need for integrity and defined integrity as the integrated ethical framework from which a person functions. They further found that "integrity in the entrepreneurial leadership position leads to trust by those individuals counted on to facilitate achievement of excellence in the operational development of the organization" (p. 80).

Integrity is a critical transformational leadership competency. U.S. government organizational leaders must demonstrate impeccable integrity to advance EA adoption. These leaders must also communicate effectively to advance EA adoption.

Communication

Communication involves sharing meaningful information with another or others. Kotter (1995) found that long-term organizational performance improvement is especially challenging and is even more so unless hundreds or thousands of people are willing to help, often to the point of making short-term sacrifices. Kotter found that employees will not make needed sacrifices unless they believe that useful change is possible. Kotter concluded, "Without credible communication, and a lot of it, the hearts and minds of the troops are never captured" (p. 64).

Kotter (1995) found that transformational leaders incorporate messages into their daily activities, communicate how proposed solutions fit into the large enterprise perspective, and discuss how follower performance is critical to accomplishing the vision. Transformational leaders use one-on-one opportunities, small group sessions, water-cooler opportunities, staff and team meetings, and formal presentations to communicate the vision. Transformational leaders turn boring company newsletters into lively articles about the vision, transform management meetings into exciting transformation discussions, and replace generic management education with courses that focus on business problems and the new vision. Kotter found transformational leaders "use every possible channel, especially those that are being wasted on nonessential information. (p. 64)

Beebe, Beebe, & Ivy, 2004 (as cited in Darling & Beebe, 2007), found that entrepreneurial leaders communicate and inspire individuals to pursue organizational goals. Darling & Beebe (2007) found that transformational leaders communicate through their vision, their verbal and nonverbal messages, the trust symbolized by their positioning, and their respect for their associates. They also found that entrepreneurial leaders communicate through appropriate means to create shared meanings with followers, provide information about the underlying rationale, motive and context that empowers and enables followers to accomplish the enterprise goals. They further found that effective communication empowers followers to align their actions with the organizational goals. These authors also found that leaders gain respect through listening to others. Of the 90% of the time a leader spends communicating, almost half of that time is spent listening to others (Klemmer & Snyder, 1972; Nichols, 2004). Darling & Beebe (2007) found "listening and leadership go hand in hand. Listening, more than speaking, is what leaders do; at least what good leaders should do" (p. 81).

Harris (2007) found that transformational leaders provide numerous communication feedback mechanisms such as face-to-face meetings, roundtable discussions, meals with organizational staff members where the "leader is available to talk to employees in a more casual and informal setting" (p. 12). Harris found that transformational leaders, in addition to face-to-face meetings, also provided opportunities for organizational members to provide feedback in anonymous manners as some members might be uncomfortable being totally frank with the leader. Garrett & Watson (2007) studied transformational leadership during the Farm Credit Canada (FCC) multi-year cultural transformational program. They reported that FCC's significant transformational progress was based on leaders who were taught to "speak from the heart, listen to other perspectives, be open and responsive to feedback and encourage personal and professional growth" (p. 21). Garrett and Watson reported that strong organizational leaders focused on delivering clear, consistent messages about strategic enterprise outcomes and corporation priorities and related individual actions to business outcomes.

FCC tracked key organizational messages, adopted a multi-challenge approach, and reduced information overload (Garrett & Watson, 2007). FCC leaders hosted monthly lunches for organizational members, established an online capability in which organizational members could anonymously ask questions regarding the transformation program and posted the responses for organizational members to review, authored more organization-wide e-mails, were more visible at corporate events, and delivered presentations relating the criticality of employee activities to the transformation. The FCC President and Chief Executive Officer stated that:

communication is at the heart of building a high-performance culture - a culture where people are fully engaged. Communication is vital. Without it, leaders cannot effect positive change. Our internal strategy recognizes employees as a primary audience and a key conduit to the customer, the media, stakeholders and communities. Our strategic approach to internal communication significantly contributes to business results. (p. 23)

Communication is a critical transformational leadership competency. U.S. government leaders must communicate effectively to advance EA adoption. These leaders must also inspire their organizational members to advance EA adoption.

Inspiration

Effective leaders inspire followers to meaningful performance. Bass and Avolio (as cited in Higgs, 2003) defined inspiration as "encouraging individuals to challenge the status quo, to consider problems from new and unique perspectives and to be innovative and creative" (p. 276). Bass (as cited in Higgs, 2003), defined inspiration as "the ability of leaders to provide a clear sense of mission, which leaders in turn convey to members and develop a sense of loyalty and commitment" (p. 278). Griffith (2004) found that high school principles in large metropolitan area, suburban school districts who inspired their teachers consistently realized significant school performance outcomes.

Posner and Kouzes (2002) included inspiration as a key aspect in their work *The Leadership Challenge.* Posner and Kouzes believed leaders needed to "describe their dreams and their [leader] ability to life others' spirits" (p. 144). These authors concluded, "It's not necessary to be a famous, charismatic person to inspire a shared vision. What is necessary is believing and developing the skills to transmit that belief" (p. 144).

An example of inspiring leadership is former U.S. President Ronald Reagan. Baldini (2007) cited Reagan as an example of inspiring leadership and concluded:

Few could rouse audiences as well as President Reagan. Consider his speech in the wake of the Challenger disaster when he praised the bravery of the astronauts but also made it very clear that space travel would continue because it was important to our national identity. A more stern Reagan lectured the Soviet Union in Berlin by challenging the Soviet premier: "Mr. Gorbachev, tear down this wall." He was reflecting the hopes and dreams of free people everywhere. (para. 3)

Kerfoot (2001) found that transformational leaders inspired organizational members to effective long-term action. Kerfoot reported that transformational leaders:

instill an intrinsic drive that is fueled by a higher purpose, a sense of mission, and a commitment to a vast array of possibilities. Inspiring leadership unleashes creativity, enthusiasm, and passion that motivational leadership cannot. The passion an inspirational leader has is authentic, and surges throughout the organization. These leaders truly believe that their role is to serve the people and to enable them to reach their innate potential. When people are inspired, they feel the fire of passion that will drive them intrinsically and independently to achieve the right thing. People in an inspired organization feel passionate about the values and purposes, the commitment of the

leaders to a higher good, and to the people of the organization and the significance of their work. They model the leader who lives and breathes passion for others and consequently see their work as serving others. (p. 530)

Kerfoot also found that transformational leaders establish bonds between themselves and their followers based on trust, are passionate about the vision, unleash potential by inspiring people from within, truly love what they do, and care about their followers. Kerfoot found transformational leaders care about people, reawaken and open hearts, listen to their followers, and commit to making differences in the lives of their followers.

Sir Winston Churchill, former English Prime Minister, is an excellent example of inspirational leadership. Throughout Germany's blitzkrieg against England in World War II, Churchill inspired England to overcome the onslaught. Longstaffe (2005) reported "Churchill unquestionably communicated vision and encouraged innovation; he inspired a nation, perhaps the world, with his passion and determination" (p. 80). Churchill would "explain the current realities, then inspire the team by offering them a vision for how things could be, then tell them how to achieve this and finally mobilize them into action" (p. 80). Longstaffe concluded "Churchill communicated vision with passion and determination, inspiring those he led by action and example with courage and integrity" (p. 83).

Transformational leaders inspire their followers to performance excellence. U.S. government leaders must inspire their members to advance EA adoption. These leaders must also empower their members to advance EA adoption.

Empowerment

Transformational leaders empower their organizational members to realize extraordinary accomplishments. These leaders empower organizational members with "power, information, knowledge and rewards" (Raelin, 2004, p. 7). Raelin (2004) found that transformational leaders share key information with organizational members, dialogue openly with these members, encourage members to challenge leadership decisions without adverse repercussions, and empower members to make understandable mistakes. Raelin (2004) also found that transformational leaders encourage participative management, establish decentralized organizational structures, and emphasize employee development. Herb Kelleher, former Southwest Airlines CEO, reflected (as cited by Raelin, 2004) that "he hopes that when people think back about their time at work, "they say that Southwest Airlines was one of the finest experience they ever had; that it helped them grow beyond anything they though possible" (p. 8). Gilbert Fairhold, *Perspectives on Leadership* author (as cited by Raelin, 2004), found that people feel empowered when they are "thinking contributors, not just physical extensions of the managers' capacities, ideas and creativity" (p. 9). Other researchers reported similar findings.

"Empowered employees have greater authority and responsibility for their work that they would in more traditionally designed organizations" (Conger & Kanungo, 1988, as cited in Ahearne, Mathiew, & Rapp, 2005, p. 945.) Organizational member empowerment is an important driver of organizational effectiveness (p. 945.) Transformational leaders create organizational cultures that increase employees self-efficacy and control, eviscerate conditions that foster feelings powerlessness, and are as flexible as circumstances allow (Ahearn et al. 2005). Transformational leaders empower organizational members by delegating "responsibility down the hierarchy so as to give employees increased decision-making authority in respect to the execution of their primary work tasks" (Leach, Wall, & Jackson, 2003, as cited in Ahearn et al. 2005, p. 946.). Individuals with higher self-efficacy levels produce greater effort, are better able to manage challenging work envi-

ronments, and have greater job performance (Sujan et al. (1994), as cited in Ahearn et al., 2005).

Transformational leaders encourage collaboration with organizational members to realize enterprise performance effectiveness outcomes. "Collaborative leadership emphasizes consensus building through engaging diverse individuals in dialogue and in building relationships by facilitating communication, nurturance, inspiration, and the mobilization of teams" (Bryson & Crosby, 1992; Chrislip & Larson, 1994, as cited in Fischback, Smerz, Findlay, Williams, & Cox, 2007, p. 30). Transformational leaders energize and focus people through and across organizational boundaries (Avery, 1999, as cited in Fischback et al. 2007). Rogers, Pace, & Wilson (2002) studied 21 remarkable organizational transformational experiences and found that empowering employees was critical to effective organizational transformation. Rogers et al. (2002) found that employee empowerment was critical to contact lens maker Wesley Jessen's dramatic transformation. Wesley Jessen's leaders empowered organizational members with critical information and delegated decision-making to the lowest organizational levels. As a result, Wesley Jessen transformed a $40 million annual loss into profit in the first month of the new CEO's leadership and maintained profits in each subsequent quarter (Rogers et al. 2002).

"Empowered employees have freedom to choose, think and respond, as appropriate, to communication from others in the organization" (Darling, 2005, as cited in Darling & Beebe, 2007, p. 85). These authors found that "Empowered employees are fundamental to facilitating an entrepreneurial spirit throughout a developing organizational setting" (p. 85).

Transformational leaders empower organizational members to accomplish organizational goals. U.S. government leaders must empower their members in their organizations to advance EA adoption. U.S. Government leaders must adopt the VICIE Transformational Leadership Model to advance EA adoption.

The author presented the VICIE Transformational Leadership Model at 12 conferences in 2006 and 2007 including the 17th Information Resources Management Association International Conference in 2006, the ArchitectureGOV 2007 Conference, and the 2007 Human Resources Government 2007 Conference. The model resonated greatly with these audiences. The author also presented the model to various U.S. Government organizations in 2006 and 2007 including the U.S. Defense Intelligence Agency, U.S. Army Undersecretary for Financial Management, U.S. Army Chief of Staff for Intelligence, U.S. Department

of Homeland Security, and the U.S. Government Accountability Office. The model also resonated greatly with these audiences. Further, the U.S. National Defense University (NDU) incorporated the VICIE Transformational Leadership Model into the curriculum in five of its academic programs and the model was presented to over 400 NDU students in 2006 and 2007. The model also resonated greatly with the students.

The VICIE Transformational Leadership Model describes the competencies needed to advance EA adoption. In addition to understanding these competencies, U.S. Government leaders must understand how EA is situated within the context of enterprise management. The author

Figure 2. Transformational leadership and enterprise management integration framework

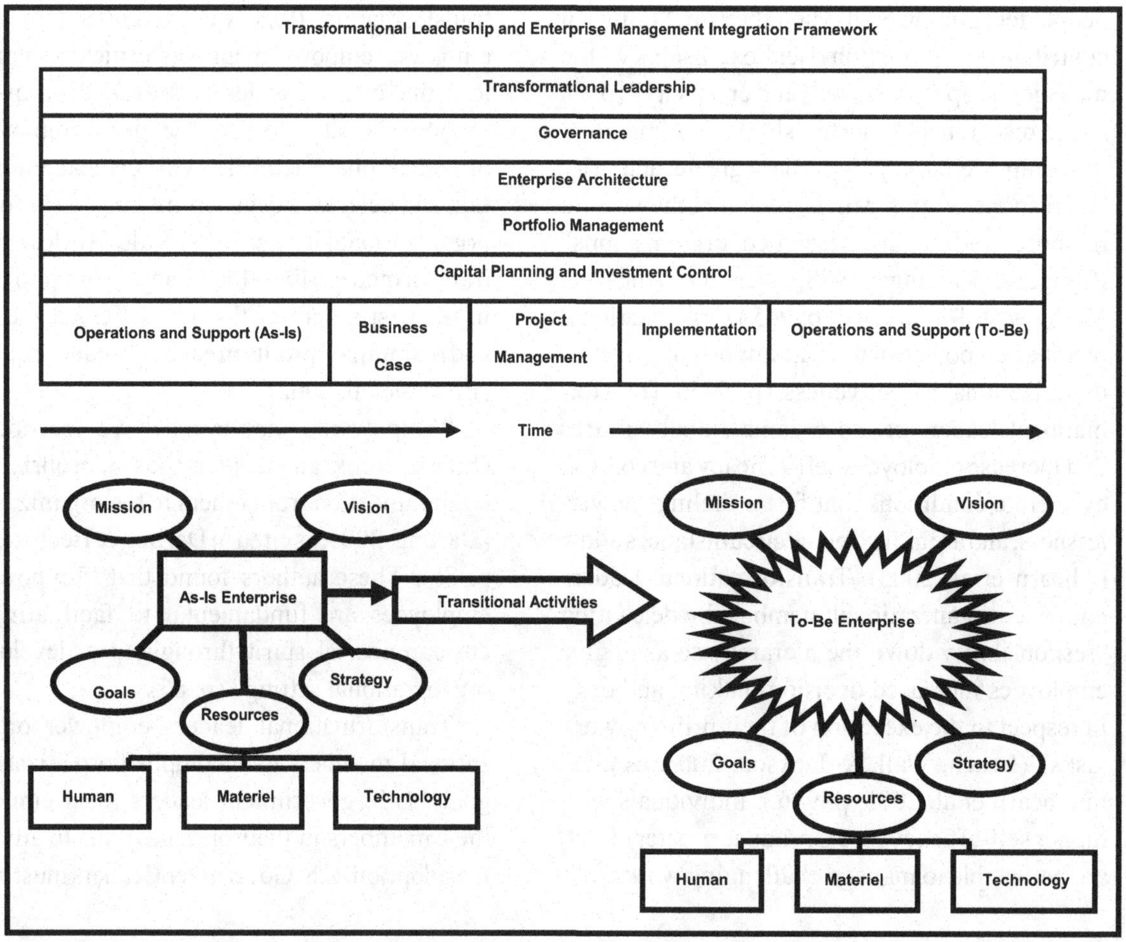

developed the Transformational Leadership and Enterprise Management Integration Framework to enable U.S. Government leaders to understand this context.

TRANSFORMATIONAL LEADERSHIP AND ENTERPRISE MANAGEMENT INTEGRATION FRAMEWORK

The Transformational Leadership and Enterprise Management Integration Framework situates EA within the context of enterprise management activities and describes the relationships that exist between transformational leadership and enterprise management functions. Figure 2, Transformational Leadership and Enterprise Management Integration Framework, depicts these relationships.

Transformational leadership enables organizations to realize their long-term performance goals. The transformational leader provides vision, integrity, communication, inspiration, and empowerment to enable improved enterprise performance. The criticality of transformational leadership to advancing government-wide EA adoption was discussed earlier and is not discussed in this section. Each enterprise has an overarching business mission with a related vision and goals.

Key enterprise management functions include governance, enterprise architecture, portfolio management, and capital planning and investment control. Governance involves establishing the rules, roles, and responsibilities for enterprise decision-making. The U.S. Food and Drug Administration (FDA) leveraged governance to enable the FDA to develop an effective EA capability. Governance is the process by which the organizations establish and adopt rules, roles, and responsibilities for enterprise decision-making. The FDA embraced governance to meet the U.S. Department of Health and Human Services mission (OMB, 2005). Governance enables the

organization to advance an effective EA capability. The EA describes the enterprise "As-Is" and "To-Be" states and the transition plan. The FDA "turned to Enterprise Architecture (EA) to serve as the methodology to achieve its desired state of efficiency and effectiveness" (OMB, 2005. p. 2). The EA reveals information that enables enterprise portfolio management.

Portfolio management involves making decisions regarding enterprise human, materiel, and technology resource investment decisions. These decisions involve existing and/or desired resource investments. The FDA used EA to inform and manage its portfolio of resource investments (OMB, 2005). Enterprise portfolio management then informs the enterprise Capital Planning and Investment Control (CPIC) process. The CPIC process implements enterprise portfolio management resource investment decisions. Finally, organizations develop business cases to substantiate enterprise investments, manage investments as projects and, over time, implement new capabilities to improve enterprise performance. The U.S. Department of Labor adopted the framework elements and dramatically improved its performance.

U.S. DEPARTMENT OF LABOR AND THE TRANSFORMATIONAL LEADERSHIP AND ENTERPRISE MANAGEMENT INTEGRATION FRAMEWORK

Under its Secretary, Elaine Chao, the U.S. Department of Labor (DOL) adopted the Transformational Leadership and Enterprise Management Integration Framework elements and realized significant performance outcomes. Chao (2007) cited leadership as the key critical enabler for DOL's performance outcomes and stated, "The single most influential factor guiding any agency or organization is the quality of the organization's leadership and core values. Leadership and values determine organizational culture. And a management culture that puts a strong emphasis on performance is one that promotes responsibility and accountability" (para. 5). Chao (2007a) stated that "Leaders advance and defend the interests of their organization and their colleagues. So executives need to be articulate, both in written and in oral presentations. That's why skillful communication is absolutely essential to career advancement and becoming a leader" (para. 24).

Chao (2007a) cited vision, integrity, communication, inspiration, and empowerment as key leadership competencies. She further observed that everyone can become a better leader through practice and stated "learning how to be an effective leader is not easy. In fact, it's one of the hardest things I've had to learn in life. And, it's a never ending process" (para. 28). Tom Weisner, former DOL Chief Information Officer (CIO), (as cited in Mosquera, 2005), stated, "There's always been leadership and commitment from the secretary [Elaine Chao] herself, throughout the senior management and through the entire department in trying to achieve success in the five PMA areas" (para. 16).

The DOL implemented governance as a critical performance enabler. Wiesner (as cited in Mosquera, 2005) reported that strong governance contributed to the DOL's performance outcomes and stated, "It starts from the management review board level, and the agency heads within the department drill down to our technical review board, which is made up of senior IT representatives from DOL agencies, and then we spin into the various subcommittees on capital planning and investment, enterprise architecture and security" (para. 18). Wiesner further stated:

Higher than that is a matter of using what you've developed in terms of everyday management of your programs, business processes and IT investments. We have a strong governance process to address the EA requirements of the department. We've developed an enterprise architecture for

universal functions that go across all of DOL and are starting to use the EA process in making IT investments. We've used enterprise architecture in our unified DOL technology infrastructure. The EA helps identify the redundancies. (Mosquera, 2005, para. 14)

The DOL performance outcomes were quantified in its President's Management Agenda scorecard results.

The President's Management Agenda (PMA) is a key instrument through which government organizational performance is measured. The U.S. Executive Office of the President established the PMA in 2001 to improve "the management of the Federal government. It focuses on five areas of management weakness across the government where improvements and the most progress can be made" (OMB, 2007c, para. 1). The PMA desired outcome is improved government performance in Human Capital, Competitive Sourcing, Financial Performance, Expanded Electronic Government (which includes EA), and Budget and Performance Integration management (OMB, 2007c). OMB evaluates each government organization in each area quarterly and assigns a color-coded rating of Green, Yellow, or Red for each area. A Green rating represents success in meeting the evaluative area criteria, Yellow represents mixed results, and Red represents unsatisfactory performance.

The DOL earned Green ratings in each evaluation area in the June, 2005, report and earned all Green ratings in subsequent reports through March, 2007. DOL Assistant Secretary for Management and former DOL CIO Patrick Pizzella (as cited in Miller, 2005), stated, "We got to green on human capital first and the rest just fell into place. Human capital impacts every other agenda item, and you can connect the dots" (para. 11). Pizzella (as cited in Miller, 2005), further stated that Chao emphasized the criticality of leadership throughout the department and reported "Chao held monthly meetings on nothing but management issues. In four years, she missed only one meeting—on Sept. 11, 2001" (para. 14). The DOL was the single government organization to earn Green in all five PMA evaluative areas until the December, 2006, report, when the State Department also earned Green ratings in all five evaluative areas (OMB, 2007c). OMB Deputy Director for Management Clay Johnson (as cited in Miller, 2005), stated, "The Department of Labor is the leader, the best, per the PMA scorecard. . . . They are the first and only department ... to have installed all the management disciplines and habits which the president established as priorities back in 2001" (para. 9). Johnson further reported that Chao made the PMA a department-wide priority and "had tremendous follow-through with her deputy and assistant secretaries" (as cited in Miller, 2005, para. 13).

Under Chao's leadership, the DOL realized additional significant performance outcomes. The DOL earned six consecutive clean financial audit opinions through 2006, four U.S. President's Quality Awards through 2005, and an unprecedented four consecutive years as the number one ranked U.S. government organization on George Mason University's annual government performance report. The DOL was one of only four government organizations to earn Stage 3 on the GAO 2006 EAMMF assessment report (GAO, 2006) and was one of only six government agencies to earn the highest scores on OMB's 2007 EA assessment (FCW, 2007). Given the performance outcomes the DOL realized from adopting the Transformational leadership and Enterprise Management Integration Framework, other U.S. Government leaders must also embrace transformational leadership to advance EA adoption and must adopt the framework to improve their organization's performance.

CONCLUSION

Many U.S. government leaders struggle in advancing EA adoption. Despite U.S. Congressional legislation, OMB guidance, and GAO reports and recommendations, many U.S. government leaders struggle in advancing EA adoption and, as a result, miss opportunities to significantly improve their organization's performance. Transformational leaders enable their organizations to realize long-term enterprise performance goals. These leaders establish and encourage shared visions, have extraordinary integrity, are strong communicators, inspire others to excellent performance, and empower followers. The U.S. DOL, by embracing transformational leadership and by adopting the Transformational Leadership and Enterprise Management Integration Framework elements, realized dramatic and unprecedented performance outcomes. Other U.S. government leaders must also embrace transformational leadership to advance EA adoption and must also adopt this framework to realize dramatically improved long-term performance.

REFERENCES

Ahearne, M., Mathiew, J., & Rapp, A. (2005). To empower or not to empower your sales force? An empirical examination of the influence of leadership empowerment behavior on customer satisfaction and performance. *Journal of Applied Psychology*, 90(5), 945-955.

Anderson, T. D. (1998). *Transforming leadership* (2nd ed.). Boca Raton, Florida: CRP Press, LLC.

Baldini, J. (2007). *How to master professional speaking*. Retrieved on June 1, 2007, from http://www.cio.com/article/print/104611.

Bass, B. M. (1990). *Bass & stodgill's handbook of leadership, theory, research, and managerial applications (*3rd ed.). New York: The Free Press.

Bass, B. M. (1998). *Transformational leadership*. Mahwah, New Jersey: Lawrence Erlbaum Associates, Publishers.

Banutu-Gomez, M. B. (2006). Great leaders know that all change must start both at the top and the bottom: The whole system must change. *The Business Review*, Cambridge, 6(1), 157-161.

Boddie, W. S., & and Newman, E. M. (2006). *Stan Boddie and Matt Newman defining effective leadership*. Retrieved on June 1, 2007, from http://www.gcn.com/cgi-bin/udt/im.display.printable?client.id=gcn_daily&story.id=41598

Chao, E. L. (2007). *Speeches by secretary Elaine l. Chao*. Retrieved on June 1, 2007, from http://www.dol.gov/_sec/media/speeches/20070130_Summit.htm

Chao, E. L. (2007a). *Speeches by secretary Elaine l. Chao*. Retrieved on June 1, 2007, from http://www.dol.gov/_sec/media/speeches/20070503_APA.htm

Chief Information Officers Council (2001). *A practical guide to federal enterprise architecture*. Version 1.0. Washington, DC.

Darling, J. R., & Beebe, S. A. (2007). Effective entrepreneurial communication in organizational development: Achieving excellent based on leadership strategies and values. *Organizational Development Journal*, 25(1), 76-93.

FCW (2007). OMB rates agency EAs higher than ever. Retrieved on July 15, 2007, from http://www.fcw.com/article103177-07-09-07-Web&printLayout

Fischbach, L. M., Smerz, C., Findlay, C. W., & Cox, a. (2007). Co-CEOs: A new leadership paradigm for social service agencies. *Families in Society*, 88(1), 30-34.

Forrester, D. P. (2006). *The government's new breed of change agents, leading the war on terror*. Retrieved on June 1, 2007, from http://www.governmentchangeagents.com/documents/GovernmentChangeAgents.com_WhitePaper.pdf

Garrett, K., & Watson, C. (2007). Defining the role of strategic comms at farm credit Canada. *Strategic Communication Management*, 11(2), 20-23.

Gorman, B. (2007). Building the buzz, the brand and the business at Motorola. *Strategic Communication Management*, 11(4), 24-27.

Griffith, J. (2004). Relation of principal transformational leadership to school staff job satisfaction, staff turnover, and school performance. *Journal of Educational Administration*, 42(3), 333-355.

Harris, S. (2007). Supporting leaders through change. *Strategic Communication Management*, 11(4), 12.

Higgs, M. (2003). How can we make sense of leadership in the 21st century? *Leadership & Organizational Development Journal, 24*(5/6), 273.

Kerfoot, K. (2001). On leadership: From motivation to inspiration leadership. *Pediatric Nursing*, 27(5), 530-531.

Kotter, J. P. (1995). Leading change: Why transformation efforts fail. *Harvard Business Review*, 73(2), 59-67.

Longstaffe, C. (2005). Winston Churchill, a leader from history or an inspiration for the future. *Industrial and Commercial Training*, 37(2/3), 80-83.

Miller, J. (2005). PMA yields turnaround at mismanaged agencies. Retrieved October 15, 2007, from http://www.gcn.com/cgi-bin/udt/im.display.printable?client.id=gcn&story.id=36519

Mosquera, M. (2005). Tom Wiesner: Labor's e-gov guide. Retrieved October 15, 2005, from http://www.gcn.com/cgi-bin/udt/im.display.printable?client.id=gcn&story.id=36769

Osaralli, N. (2003). Effects of transformational leadership on empowerment and team effectiveness. *Leadership & Organization Development Journal*, 24(5/6), 335-344.

Posner, B. Z., & Kouzes, J. M. (2002). *The leadership challenge* (3rd ed.). San Francisco, CA: Jossey-Bass Inc.

Raelin, J. (2004). The "bottom line" of leaderful practice. *Ivey Business Journal Online*, Jan/Feb, 1-9.

Rogers, P., Pace, S., & Wilson, P. (2002). Making change stick. *European Business Journal*. 14(1), 2-7.

Simmons-Welburn, J. & Welburn, W. (2006). Leadership Lessons in a Climate of Social Transformation, *Libraries and the Academy*, 6(4), 467-470.

Stephenson, C. (2004). Rebuilding trust: The integral role of leadership in fostering values, honesty and vision. *Ivey Business Journal Online, 1.*

Udechukwu, I. I. (2007). Integrity: The courage to meet the demands of reality. *Journal of Applied Management and Entrepreneurship*, Fort Lauderdale 12(2), 106-107.

U.S. Congress (1996). Public Law 104-106, 110 Stat. 186.

U.S. General Accounting Office (1998). *Customs Service Modernization: Architecture Must Be Complete and Enforced to Effectively Build and Maintain Systems AIMD-98-70*. Retrieved on June 1, 2007, from http://www.gao.gov/archive/1998/ai98070.pdf

U.S. General Accounting Office (2000). *Information Technology: INS Needs to Better Manage the Development of Its Enterprise Architecture AIMD-00-212*. Retrieved on June 1, 2007, from http://www.gao.gov/archive/2000/ai00212.pdf

U.S. General Accounting Office (2001). *DLA should strengthen business systems modernization architecture and investment activities*. Retrieved June 1, 2007, from http://www.gao.gov/new.items/d01631.pdf

U.S. General Accounting Office (2002). *Information Technology: OMB Leadership Critical to Making Needed Enterprise Architecture and E-government Progress GAO-02-389T*. Retrieved on June 1, 2007, from http://www.gao.gov/new.items/d02389t.pdf

U.S. General Accounting Office (2002a). *Enterprise architecture use across the federal government can be improved*. Retrieved June 1, 2007, from http://www.gao.gov/new.items/d026.pdf

U.S. General Accounting Office (2003). *A framework for assessing and improving enterprise architecture management*. Retrieved June 1, 2007, from http://www.gao.gov/new.items/d03584g.pdf

U.S. General Accounting Office (GAO) (2004). *Information technology: The federal enterprise architecture and agencies' enterprise architectures are still maturing*. Retrieved June 1, 2007, from http://www.gao.gov/new.items/d04798t.pdf

U.S. General Accounting Office (2004a). *Leadership remains key to agencies making progress on enterprise architecture efforts*. Retrieved June 1, 2007, from http://www.gao.gov/new.items/d0440.pdf

U.S. Government Accountability Office (2004b). *Homeland Security: Efforts Under Way to Develop Enterprise Architecture, but Much Work Remains GAO-04-777* Retrieved on June 1, 2007, from http://www.gao.gov/new.items/d04777.pdf

U.S. Government Accountability Office (2006). Leadership remains key to establishing and leveraging architectures for organizational transformation. Retrieved June 1, 2007, from http://www.gao.gov/new.items/d06831.pdf

U.S. Government Accountability Office (2007). *The GAO: An introduction*. Retrieved on June 1, 2007, from http://www.gao.gov/about/history/introduction.htm

U.S. Government Accountability Office (2007a). *GAO's name change and other provisions of the GAO human capital reform act of 2004.* Retrieved on June 1, 2007, from http://www.gao.gov/about/namechange.html

U.S. Office of Management and Budget (2005). *FDA uses ea to standardize and save with consolidation effort.* Retrieved June 1, 2007, from http://www.whitehouse.gov/omb/egov/documents/FDA_FINAL.pdf

U.S. Office of Management and Budget (2006). *FEA practice guidance.* Retrieved June 1, 2007, from http://www.whitehouse.gov/omb/egov/documents/FEA_Practice_Guidance.pdf

U.S. Office of Management and Budget (2006a). *Federal enterprise Architecture program EA assessment framework version 2.1* Retrieved June 1, 2007, from http://www.whitehouse.gov/omb/egov/documents/OMB_EA_Assessment_Framework_v21_Final.pdf

U.S. Office of Management and Budget (2007). *FEA consolidated reference model document version 2.2.* Retrieved July 15, 2007, from http://www.whitehouse.gov/omb/egov/documents/FEA_CRM_v22_Final_July_2007.pdf

U.S. Office of Management and Budget (2007a). *Results of FY 2007 federal enterprise architecture assessment.* Retrieved July 28, 2007, from http://www.whitehouse.gov/omb/egov/documents/2007_EA_Assessment_Results_Summary.pdf

U.S. Office of Management and Budget (2007b). *OMB's mission.* Retrieved June 1, 2007, from http://www.whitehouse.gov/omb/organization/role.html

U.S. Office of Management and Budget (2007c). *President's management agenda.* Retrieved June 1, 2007, from http://www.whitehouse.gov/omb/budintegration/pma_index.html

U.S. Senate Governmental Affairs Committee (1994). *Computer chaos: Billions wasted buying federal computer systems. Investigative report of Senator William S. Cohen.* Retrieved June 1, 2007, from https://acc.dau.mil/CommunityBrowser.aspx?id=22163

Zablow, R. J. (2006). Creating and sustaining an ethical workplace. *Risk Management*, 53(9), 26-29.

Chapter VII
Adaptive IT Architecture as a Catalyst for Network Capability in Government

Jay Ramanathan
The Ohio State University, USA

Rajiv Ramnath
The Ohio State University, USA

Anand Desai
The Ohio State University, USA

ABSTRACT

Public institutions that are organized in hierarchies find it difficult to address crisis or other unique requirements that demand networked solutions. This chapter first provides a prescriptive transaction-based method for achieving such networking organizations with information technologies (IT) and then discusses how the organization becomes more effective in non-routine responses to citizen requests. We illustrate how the prescriptive transaction-based enterprise architecture[1] framework[2] was used for decision-making in a multi-year interdisciplinary industry-university collaboration resulting in a successful 311 system.

INTRODUCTION

Public institutions are organized in hierarchies making it challenging for them to address *non-routine* problems that demand networked solutions. This chapter first provides a prescriptive method for achieving such networking organizations with information technologies (IT) and then discusses

how the resulting capabilities may be used for crisis-management. We illustrate how the underlying transaction-based *enterprise architecture[3] framework[4]* was used for decision-making in a multi-year interdisciplinary industry-university collaboration[5] with the City of Columbus, Ohio which has implemented a successful 311[6] system. The collaboration reported here is based on two related projects: 1) the Department of Technology's Strategic Plan [Ramnath and Landsbergen 2005] and 2) the Independent Evaluation of the 311 system [Ramnath and Desai 2007].

Finally, we also introduce an *Adaptive Complex Enterprise*[7] (ACE) architecture framework that treats organizations and IT in a holistic manner to create networked service capability. Figure 1 shows how our basic unit of analysis, *the RED transaction* tuple consisting of *Requirements, Execution of transaction and Delivery* arising from Requests in its contextual environment. The ACE consists of a number of nested *dimensions*. The outermost dimension of ACE is the *strategic* dimension where the external context and environment is scanned and external requirements are assessed. The *business* dimension is where the investments and value creation of ACE are aligned to respond to this assessment of the external requirements. The costs and the production aspects of ACE are aligned in the *operations* dimension and the transactions are finally executed in the *infrastructure use* dimension where the Requirements are operationalized into actual transaction tasks and deliverables are produced.

In ACE, service-providing agents (that is organizations, applications and processes) are dynamically assembled to provide adapting responses to specific routine and non-routine Requests. Our focus in this chapter, however, is on the collaboration across silos that must be established in order to manage *non-routine Requests*, which are the defining characteristics of crises. Hence the underlying *ACE* framework offers a *Requirements-Execution-Delivery* based prescription for planning and execution of a strategy through the alignment dimensions where IT plays a catalyst role in building networks that cut across organizational silos. We illustrate how the ACE-based analysis also succeeds in justifying the networking and the prioritization in complex organizations.

A common criticism of a complex systems characterization of an organization, particularly in the public sector, is that because of the complexity and its emergent properties it is difficult to establish clear lines of responsibility. Therefore accountability is not readily established. However, in this fine-grain monitoring of the requests and execution of transactions-deliverables it is possible to provide accountability and to establish a history, on a Request basis, even in highly uncertain and dynamic crisis management contexts.

This chapter is organized as follows. We begin with a discussion of the networking research and trends in government along with the related IT challenges that demand an interdisciplinary approach. We then present the ACE framework itself. We apply this framework to our case study of the implementation of the city's 311 non-emergency response system. Finally, we present the IT deployment process, the results of the 311 deployment and their success in building an adaptive capability for responding to and managing crises.

Figure 1. ACE architecture framework for building network capability on existing silos

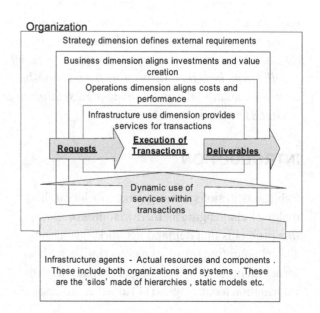

BACKGROUND IN GOVERNMENT AND IT CHALLENGES

Historically, most public enterprises have been organized around hierarchical principles with decision-making concentrated at the apex of the organization. Centralization has been the typical organization pattern for several reasons, including ensuring fairness of treatment for both service recipients and employees; creating clear chains of accountability; and minimizing the exposure of service delivery to political forces. In response to criticisms that centralized hierarchies are stultified and inefficient, some public organizations have devolved discretion downwards through decentralization or by creation federations by separating large multi-service bureaucracies into loosely coupled units. Recently, organizational boundaries in the public sector have become porous as service delivery becomes the responsibility of a *network* of organizations – government agencies, private firms, non-profit organizations – bound together by contracts, grants, with a common commitment to addressing relevant policy problems [Agranoff and McGuire 2003; Nohira 1992, O'Toole and Meier 2000]. Large metropolitan municipal governments with wide-ranging service responsibilities are thus typically conglomerations of all three of these organization patterns, hierarchies, federations and networks.

We next present our conceptual model of a networked organization and discuss the challenges encountered in achieving full networking.

Conceptual Model of a Networked Organization and Non-Routine Requests: Any organization can be logically conceptualized as in Figure 1. On the left we characterize the *Requests* for services originating from the customers in the Strategy dimension. We also characterize each Request type as being *routine or non-routine*. Regular trash pick-up, maintaining the regular flow of traffic in city streets and regular policing are routine municipal activities,

however, ad hoc requests for bulk trash pick-up or closing a city street to shoot a movie or for a block party or a bank hold-up are examples of non-routine Requests.

Responding to non-routine requests requires considerable expenditure of effort in navigating across organizational silos [Kling et al. 2001]. Traditional public institutions are organized in hierarchies, however, agencies increasingly face difficult, non-routine requests that demand networked solutions and require managers to weave strong hierarchies into effective networks. While we know that the innovative processing of non-routine services is the future [Landsbergen 2001, Longstaff 2005], it is also true that managers in the public sector do not have a tradition of dynamic on-demand cross-silo collaboration, and have not developed the necessary competencies, simply because the need for such activity has not existed during their professional lifetimes. What is needed is, firstly, a strategic catalyst for, and secondly, a foundation on which to build network capability. We show that a key catalyst is crises-management planning since *all levels* are being required to (and more importantly are receiving federal and state funds to) develop crisis management plans and capabilities, and as they are doing so are beginning to at least talk about the networks required [Schwartz 2003].

Non-routine Requests often generate many sub-Requests that require complex coordination across multiple government units [Groenlund 1997]. Given the growth in non-routine requests for service delivery, the IT systems that support public enterprises must become adaptive, integrated, and flexible [Bovens and Zouridis 2002; Ho 2002; Moon 2002]. Based on a long history of working relationships with public enterprises, we believe this new generation of demands on public enterprises requires a concomitant evolution of IT [Teisman and Klijn 2002].

Complexity of Network Enabling IT: Existing IT systems and Websites are designed to enable hierarchical public enterprises are not built to adapt to each request. Geared currently towards optimizing repetitive routine requests, these systems assume predictability and process stability. This assumption has commonly led to redundant yet distinctly separate organization and IT elements. The presence of organization and IT silos makes coordination and information sharing difficult [Malone and Crowston 2001]. This arrangement has proved effective for simple requests. However, the environment of public enterprises is increasingly more dynamic and often turbulent [Salmela and Spil 2002; Thietart and Forgues 1995]. Large bureaucratic organizational systems based on stable models are not designed to be nimble and become effective in the presence of rapidly changing environments. It is our contention that it is possible to create organization-IT alignment that yields effective performance even under dynamic uncertain conditions.

Relationships Between organization Patterns and Technology Patterns: Organization theorists – contingency theorists in particular – argue that organization performance is a function of the fit between organizational patterns, their environment, internal processes and technology [Child 1972; Donaldson 1999]. Organizations that adopt the pattern or forms that best fit the relevant combination of task, technology, and environment are likely to perform at a high level. While the connection between organization patterns and environment has been studied extensively [Laurence and Lorsch 1967; Drazin and Van de Van 1985], research is needed to examine how interactions between organization and technology patterns affect performance [Gresov 1989].

As characterized previously, IT must in the near future support the networking of public organizations so they can embrace externally-driven variation and non-routine Requests. Recent IT technological advances [Agha 2002, Anderson 2001, Bauer 2004, DAML[8], Digtalgovernment] now allow us to build Service-Oriented Architec-

tures (SOA) within which existing applications can be treated as agents and components providing specific WebServices that is accessed within contexts [Gortmaker et al 2004]. With these advances in place, services of agents (human services and application services) can be invoked dynamically by a logical workflow layer to deliver on the requirements of a Request [WFMC]. Thus, with workflow and SOA, IT has evolved from being merely a mechanism in a programmer's productivity tool-kit into an electronic Business Process Management (eBPM) which is a logical business modeling and execution tool [BPMI, Ramanathan 2099, Ramanthan and Ramnath 2004]. Along with dynamic binding of Requests to services, execution-level monitoring and accountability of service and resource utilization is now possible. Thus upon completion of a response to a Request, performance-related measurements – task span time, resource time used, quality incidents. - can be readily captured electronically.

Patterns for Enterprise Architectures: Enterprise architectures are typically considered to have high-level definitions of the processes, data, applications, and technology needed to support the business. However, there are several challenges with current approaches. The links among business planning, organizational patterns and implemented software architecture is often missing. Thus, high-level plans often flounder for lack of a clear connection to actual system development guided by a detailed strategy implementation plan [Cross 2002].

More generally, as the world becomes demand-driven and linear models become obsolete[9], we look to principles from Complexity theory to reassure us that complex behaviors can result from a small number of simple recursively applied patterns [Peitgen et al 1992]. Others have shown [Kelly and Allison 1998] many complex enterprises are composed of nested organizations that are similar in structure; exhibiting SELF-SIMILARITY. The study of patterns itself has had a long and varied history in fields such as fractals [Mendelbrot 1982], architecture [Alexander 1977], and pattern template for object-oriented business and e-Commerce modeling [Eriksson and Pennker 2000, Adams 2001], and simulation along the value chain [Mackenzie 2002]. Based on these works, the ACE framework was introduced to integrate the treatment of organization and IT agents. [Ramanathan 2005].

More specifically, guided by the contingency theory of organizations and the potential of emerging service-oriented IT architectures, we identify across the enterprise the points of interaction between Requests and enabling agent services to produce deliverables. At the same time we retain the leverage the services of existing enterprise applications where it has successfully enabled routine processing within hierarchies. We accomplish this with the decision-making guided by the conceptual ACE representation.

Adaptive Complex Enterprise (ACE) framework objectives for Networking: The objective of the *ACE* architecture framework is to help adapt each response by managing underlying agent service interactions. These interactions can become non-linear, emergent and complex [Morçöl 2002, Desai 2005]. The framework leverages concepts of complexity theory and recent evolutions in Internet technologies to implement ACE architecture as a logical layer using existing agent and new services (Figure 1).

Consequently we can now implement an IT infrastructure that can take traceability to its ultimate goals of networking across the organization and technology layers. As non-routine events occur, the specific organization and IT services are identified and dynamically invoked to provide the most efficient response. Thus the agent services *adapt* to handle non-routine events – or shocks– from the external environment and respond to requests efficiently even though these processes are not incorporated into the models of existing IT systems.

ACE FRAMEWORK

At a high level, the organization responds to external forces through its vision, by projecting citizen requirements, investments and operations. Within its operations, the organization also takes in Requests and produces deliverables. This 'black-box' view of the organization is illustrated in Figure 2 A. The objective of B and C illustrations of the figure is to progress to a 'white-box' view of the organization. That is, visualize for improvement all aspects of agent interactions and resulting performance from the perspective of each stakeholder of that interaction.

When applied in analysis the patterns[10] explicate value-chain interactions between agents, namely, organizations, IT components and applications, in the infrastructure as they service different REDs. Thus the ACE framework's RED pattern informs and guides the architecture team to 1) produce a conceptual representation of the organization focused on Request types and related RED transactions within the enterprise, and 2) use this ACE representation and structure to monitor and analyze the performance and develop strategies for overall improvement.

ACE Framework Concepts: The underlying concepts are first motivated and then presented in detail.

- **Dimensions:** This structures the various stakeholders of the organization and aligns them into an external-focused *business* planning-and-execution value chain.
- **RED transaction pattern:** Identifies each *Request Type* its RED transaction - the **R**equirements, **E**xecution and **D**elivery - milestones at which service performance contribution (i.e. $\triangle$) of its *roles*[11] are measured from the perspective of each dimensional stakeholder as shown.
- **Triage pattern:** Applies policies that *dynamically* assign specific agents to service

Figure 2. ACE concepts at-a-glance

A: The external forces and service requests addressed by an organization

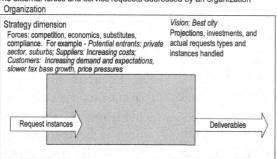

B: Introducing the 1) the Dimension pattern to visualize the organization's value chain of stakeholders and 2) the RED pattern to identify the contributions of each transaction to the stakeholders in each dimension.

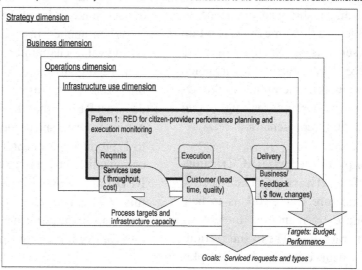

C: Introducing the 1) Triage execution pattern that assigns infrastructure agents to RED roles, and 2) Roles as an abstraction of agents to achieve dynamic assignment.

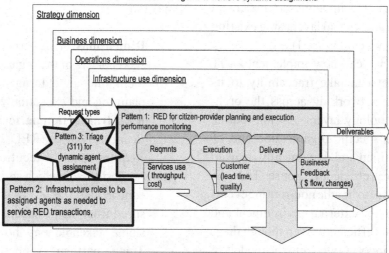

roles based on the requirements of a specific Request. And,

- **Infrastructure roles pattern:** Identifies the prototypical agent service or service clusters required to service and execute each Request and RED *type*. In addition, these roles allow dynamic assignment, if needed, to achieve delayed binding between the RED transaction and the underlying *infrastructure* (agents that are either internal or external to the organization).

The concepts, patterns and their relationships are in Figure 2 and discussed in detail as follows.

Dimension: The *dimensions* illustrated in Figure 2 B structures the organization's planning and execution value-chain of stakeholders. The performance of each dimension *is aligned with* (represented as '↔') neighboring dimensions. This *alignment* is also external-environment-focused. The forces identified on the organization in Figure 2 A as in [Porter 98] are addressed by structuring the organization's internal stakeholders and what they need to achieve effective responses and customer satisfaction for each Request. That is:

Infrastructure services and use and Request satisfaction ↔ *Operations* performance of groups of requests ↔ *Business* value ↔ *Strategy* satisfaction.

This alignment (similar to the balanced scorecard [Kaplan and Norton 1996]) along the internal value-chain between the customer-and-provider organizations of the public enterprise is as required by contingency theory. This alignment is also enabled through the performance of each and every Request by the 'RED' transaction discussed next.

RED Analysis12 Pattern: Strategy is devised for each Request type originating from the external dimension using the RED pattern for analysis. The RED structure guides the interactions between the customer-provider agents so that the transaction can complete successfully with a satisfactory deliverable. The transaction captures both the service *roles* needed for response and the resulting execution performance. That is, the same pattern structure is used both for planning and execution. Finally, note that at the milestones R, E, D contributing performance to the corresponding dimensions are as follows:

RED execution begins with the Request from the customer (a citizen, a government official, or any entity that can make a demand of the system). The arrows from the transaction execution of Figure 2 B, illustrates the relationship between the RED execution and the ACE dimensions or perspectives. We see the performance contribution starting from the infrastructure use dimension and working outward. We next see how the scale and scope of planning and execution interest in RED performance is different in each dimension to meet the needs of its specific stakeholders:

- **Strategy:** The external environment that encourages or discourages the growth of certain types of Requests is monitored and trends identified from the organization's strategic perspective.
- **Business:** The value provided by collections of Request types and instances is of interest from the perspective of creating value and determining investments.

Table 1.

RED Transaction Milestones	1. Dimensions
Requirements negotiated between the customer and provider and identification of service capacity to be used, costs, and response time	Operations Dimension
Execution results in value creation for the customer measured through customer satisfaction and related quality assurance	Strategy Dimension
Delivery in the customer's environment resulting in cost accounting and value to the organization, performance feedback to the infrastructure	Business Dimension and Infrastructure Dimension

- **Infrastructure use:** The roles needed to service each RED transaction type are identified. These roles are assigned actual shared or dedicated resources such as people, IT components etc. Upon assignment, the RED transaction executes to complete the response. Note that the roles have associated *operating-level agreements* (or OLAs) required to successfully complete the RED transaction and *service-level agreements* (or SLAs) that are of interest to the stakeholders in the different dimensions[13]. The stakeholders in the infrastructure dimension must ensure value is provided to operations.

- **Operations:** The performance of each specific *type* of Request and all its instances is of interest to the department (team, group) and its director (leader). The operational stakeholders ensure value is provided to business.

Finally, a RED transaction step can initiate other RED transactions at any time. Note also that while delivery completes the response transaction, there can be a variety of reasons why transactions do not complete. (This is due to various reasons – lack of capacity, customer dissatisfaction etc. We will not address such issues here due to limitations of space.)

Triage pattern: This pattern is a fundamental dynamic interaction pattern between the incoming non-routine Requests and the infrastructure needed for servicing that Request. While it provides the customer with a single interface into the organization, it also handles the assignment of initial resources for execution and provides the networking capability.

The arrival of a Request causes the triage organization (examples of triage pattern include the help desk, customer support center) to first understand requirements, clarify the Request and apply rules to assign initial resources to RED roles. In this context it is important to note:

- Triage implements policies by which agents within the organization are assigned to RED roles and prioritizes Requests. Since this makes it is possible to delay the assignment of roles till the RED execution, there is flexibility in determining which agents are engaged. This flexible scheduling ability allows for the flexible use of existing resources.

- The agents can be from different organizations and yet be assigned to the roles of a RED to form a temporary coalition to complete the transaction. For example, the roles may be supplied by departments or agencies across political jurisdictions such as the corporate municipal boundaries, and across geographic communities such as neighborhoods and precincts.

- RED transactions that network across boundaries can be audited (for example, to identify cost implications) providing insights into questions such as: How often do non-routine Requests involve multiple boundaries? (Note, while this can be implemented [Holowczak 2003], such information is difficult to obtain with current IT systems.)

Infrastructure Roles Pattern: This final pattern focuses on the individual and shared agents in the infrastructure that perform potentially multiple roles within multiple REDs. To ensure quality of service (i.e. meet OLAs) that in turn ensures RED SLAs, each service or cluster of services is treated as a whole and monitored as it is used within the specific REDs. The result of the monitoring is a precise measure of use, quality delivered and feedback for improvement of agents and the overall infrastructure.

Together the patterns provide flexibility to assemble response systems that network across organizations and agencies. For example, the delayed binding of RED roles to the underlying infrastructure at triage provides dynamic capability. Within a larger crisis-management context

Figure 3. The ACE framework products needed for a dynamic networked enterprise

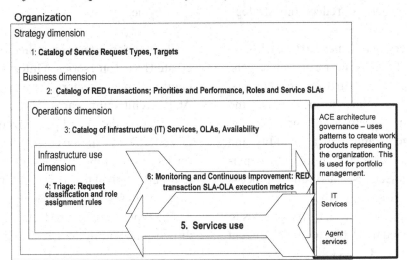

[Arens 2002, NIMS]), the interaction with actual infrastructure agents required to address the needs of an incoming Request is determined by policies implemented at triage. These policies can begin with the rules determining which Requests should be handled first and who should handle them.

Current customer relationship management and enterprise systems have simple customer-specified priorities to determine when a Request should be handled. In such systems there is also a tendency to mark Requests as critical or high. Requests with lower priorities or secondary Requests are typically not entered because they are unlikely to be addressed anyway. Policies should also be designed, for example, to create a learning environment or even build an organization's capacity.

THE CITY'S STRATEGIC TECHNOLOGY PLAN

The illustrative case used here is based on the City of Columbus which serves as the state capital of Ohio. As a result of significant population growth, the City is now the most populous in Ohio and 15th largest in the country. Population growth has been facilitated by a liberal annexation policy – the City services over 200 square miles of territory. An expanding service area and a growing population have combined to place stress on existing response systems. The current Mayor has instituted a "covenant" that includes a guiding principle that technology will be a key tool to achieve city objectives, namely improving service responses. To this end, the City consolidated its IT operations under a Department of Technology (DOT) and began implementing a series of IT improvements. However, the rate of IT solution deployment slowed when, for example, tax revenues declined. The City used our team to help develop a strategic plan to guide the IT implementation. We next illustrate how the ACE framework informed the architecture team as they developed the DOT strategy.

ACE team and Work products: The ACE architecture team made up of IT architects and customer facing account managers govern by using the patterns to create the enterprise-specific architecture representation and *work products* (Figure 3) through following steps:

1. Catalog external *Request types* and *performance targets* to reflect the strategy perspective.

2. Catalog of service roles needed for each RED type, identify SLA performance targets. Consolidate and prioritize *across* Requests, from strategic value, business value and investment perspectives (aligning with 1).

3. Plan the agents and their availability and capability to fill roles and meet SLA performance objectives - a business process perspective (aligning with 2).

4. Execute responses driven by triage rules to bind the needed RED roles to available agent services to meet OLAs (aligning with 3).

5. Identify services used for each transactions (aligning with 4).

6. Continuous improvement - for each RED monitor service performance feedback and use that to inform the next improvement cycle.

The work products identified in Figure 3 were created based on a series of interviews of the various department directors and team members by the ACE Architecture teams. The *ACE architecture team* consolidated and prioritized across all the city's RED transactions using the work products for decision making. We show how these prescriptive steps applied to the city. The responses were captured in spread sheets as illustrated in Figure 4. The types of work products aligning the ACE dimensions within the city are discussed next.

1. **Request types and performance targets; strategy Dimension:** As with many organizations, the city had already defined its strategy - primary citizen Request types

Figure 4. At-a-glance work product spreadsheets and sample responses corresponding to Figure 3

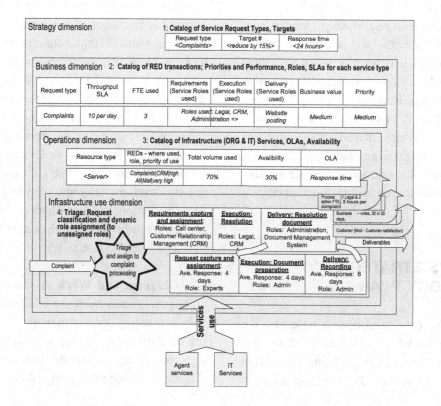

handled by its departments. With each type there were numbers and targets which were stated as $\triangle$ improvements. Here the $\triangle$ could be a positive or negative number. For example, 'weed abatement target' was a negative number that implied a reduction was desirable to control undesirable elements, but might need additional service capacity and investment to accomplish it. The catalog of Request types is identified in the strategy/environment dimension.

2. **Catalog of RED transactions; Priorities and Performance, Roles, SLAs for each service type; business Dimension:** This planning step created the logical RED structures that relate the Request types initiated in the environment to the responding roles and desired performance within provider's enterprise. As in the business dimension of Figure 4, for the complaint Request type, the RED milestone and Roles specifics (i.e. CRM, administration etc.) and business value are all identified.

3. **Catalog of Infrastructure (IT) Services, Availability and OLAs; operations Dimension:** Using the output of step 2, this step takes the perspective of each agent and service and determines where it is used by specifically identifying the RED roles satisfied. For example from the perspective of the CRM service, it is use in the complaint transaction but it also used in many others.

Within the business process dimension, the objective is to manage agent OLAs to achieve the performance SLAs at each RED milestone (e.g. 10 per day for complaints).

4. **Triage: Request classification, role assignment, RED execution perspective:** As in Figure 4, the as-is RED type's overall execution performance $\triangle$ towards each dimension is identified. Also each RED's roles, sub-REDs and needs were explicitly captured and related to the value to business. Flexibility in role assignment is identified.

5. **Service Monitoring and Continuous Improvement: RED transaction execution metrics; an improvement perpective:** Since the basic goal of an IT strategic plan is to develop a precise road map that takes the city from as-is to to-be with a prioritized set of projects, we needed to take individual department work products and consolidate and prioritize across all departments. This was accomplished by the ACE team as follows.

Analysis and Decision-making leading to 311 Implementation: As mentioned before, the ACE architecture team was composed of selected business analysts, system architects, and departmental directors. The use of the strategic IT planning process is illustrated in Figure 5. The primary role of the ACE team is to develop the application portfolio for investments through

Figure 5. Governance process using ACE framework

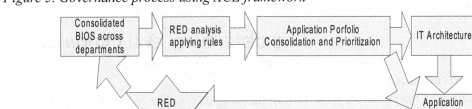

consolidation of inputs from individual departments and through the RED analysis.

From the city's perspective many suggestions were made to the account management teams. The reduction of time or the need for a new IT service was often requested. However, there was a need to objectively select projects of maximum impact to the external environment and to the business. This was accomplished through the following rules to consolidate and prioritize the IT projects:

Rule for RED analysis and prioritization: From a strategy and environment perspective, prioritize primary RED transactions for improvement based on the following:

- High competitive value to the organization,
- High Request volume,
- Lower than desired throughput,
- High queue times,
- Use of shared services with other REDs, and finally
- Identify the sub-transactions of the high-priority transactions and also assign these a high priority.

Rule for identifying maximum return on investment: List all the IT needs and projects, prioritize by maximum impact to business value by looking across REDs (prioritized previously). This gives us the maximum service level impact through the investment in the IT services and operating improvements.

The aforementioned process actually led to the prioritization of the 311 project since many high-value non-routine Requests identified the needed IT support in many different ways. For example:

- Case management,
- Status reporting to customer,
- Order coordination and management with other departments,
- Project management,

- Document management, and
- Consolidation of call-centers.

At the start of our engagement, there was on-going discussion about implementing a single call-center interface; however the justification for this – the benefits and the costs - were not clear. The ACE framework - work products and RED analysis - gave a precise justification in terms of value to the organization and through identifying across departments where the positive effects would be of this shared service. For example, we identified that of the 17 City service departments, about 30% of the Requests were non-routine nature, often requiring interactions with up to three other departments. Previously, interdepartmental response processes were all handled in an ad hoc fashion with manual procedures (such as phone calls) and hand-offs (via email). In these instances, the absence of an efficient means of coordinating across boundaries resulted in slow and sometimes incomplete responses to citizens, affecting satisfaction.

Consequent to the strategic IT planning project, the City of Columbus implemented a one-stop approach to the placement of orders for city services. The 311 Project entailed centralizing the city's entire call center structure into one common call center that can be contacted through the use of one number (311). This centralized call center utilizes a common supporting type of software which is the repository for Requests for city services as well as the performance management of those requested services. The City of Columbus decided to develop its own supporting software and manage this project with its internal resources.

INDEPENDENT EVALUATION OF THE 311 SYSTEM

In the *Independent Evaluation of the 311 system* project we had two tasks 1) to evaluate the system as-is and 2) to evaluate the impact of 311 on crises-management at the City of Columbus. Part of the funding for the 311 Project was obtained from the Department of Justice via a grant. As a requirement of the Federal grant, an impact evaluation on crises-management had to be conducted.

Evaluation Approach

Approach to Direct Impact: Three areas of direct 311 impact on crises management were identified using guidelines from the Office of Community Oriented Policing Services outlined in [COPS03-1]. These are listed as follows, in order of importance:

- *Workload reduction* of public-safety-related departments and divisions: The impact of 311 in enabling departments and divisions in the first line of support with respect to safety (Department of Public Safety, Department of Health) to improve their performance by taking away the distraction of handling non-emergency requests and thus allowing them to focus on emergency operations. (Note that this ties to the Triage pattern enables different policies to be designed and applied.)
- *Information clearing-house:* The ability for 311 to serve as an information clearing-house, i.e. as a unified contact and information dissemination point to assist in the management of crises. (This ties to the requirements gathering for each Request and then information sharing.)
- *Community Policing:* The ability of 311 to provide data to pinpoint trends (such as trends in crime, or population demographics), detection of unanticipated events (such as the prototypical Baltimore example of the detection of a West Nile virus outbreak from increasing bird deaths) and the ability to identify correlations among trends (such as the correlation of vacant homes to crime) is important in order to *anticipate* crises.

(This is the expected result of traceability due to capturing of metrics). .

Approach to Indirect impact: In addition to evaluating the direct impact of 311, we believed that a very important benefit of 311 would be as an integrative capability for creating effective informal networks within the City. We decided to investigate this integrative capability through the specific lens of emergency and crisis management. In particular, we sought to evaluate whether and how a 311 system, its stakeholders and its supporting services architecture would serve as a catalyst for creating network competencies for delivering critical, non-routine services. As described in [Mendonca 2007] non-routine response requires emergent improvisation by dynamically created "adhocracies." Thus, we were looking for how 311 may catalyze competencies such as:

- Activation: i.e. enlisting participation in networks;
- Framing: influencing the operating rules, prevailing values, and norms while altering the
- Perceptions of the participants, in response to emergent phenomena;
- Mobilizing: developing a view of the strategic whole and an ability to develop and achieve a set of common objectives based on this whole; and
- Synthesizing: creating the environment for interaction among network participants by blending perceptions [Agranoff 2001]. Instead of legal authority as the factor that binds actors, we wished to see if managers now rely on trust when managing across silos.

Tool used: Both structured interviews and collected data were used in our evaluation. We used information collected by 311 in terms of addresses mapped to GIS coordinates for each Request. We correlated these records with either existing data available through census tract or publicly available demographic data indexed by zip code.

The interviews consisted of questions asked in a setting intended to encourage discussion rather than precise answers. Certain questions were repeated in order to elicit a broader range of answers. All departments were asked the following questions:

1. Have you heard of the City's ColumbuStat 311 system?
2. In a few words, could you describe it to us?
3. What is your evaluation of 311?
4. How are your Dept.'s processes and roles integrated with 311?
5. Give examples of how 311 data has benefited or could have benefited your organization?
6. What additional features should exist or what additional data can be collected in 311 to assist in the execution and improvement of your processes?
7. What change management or cultural aspects have needed addressing because of 311?
8. How has 311 been integrated into your department's systems, especially its work-order system?
9. How have you incorporated 311 into your Crisis Management and Disaster Recovery plans?
10. What other benefits do you see from 311?
11. What integration issues do you see with 311 and existing systems in your organization?
12. Has your knowledge about the operations and capabilities of other departments increased over the past year? In what manner?
13. In what manner, other than 311, does your Dept. get citizen Requests for service? How many such Requests do you get?

The Department of Public Safety was asked the following specific questions:

1. Has there been a reduction in 911 overtime or budget during this past year?
2. Has there been an increased ability for 911 operators to take on additional calls because there are less non-emergency calls?

The following Departments were interviewed:

3. Public Safety
4. Health
5. Public Service
6. Public Utilities
7. Community Relations
8. Recreation and Parks
9. Department of Development

We summarize as follows the direct, indirect, and potential impact.

Evaluation of Direct and Indirect Impact

Overall the evaluation concluded that the City of Columbus has established a successful 311 program, and that the 311 call-center is now an established asset of the City. The 311 system has successfully transitioned from a technology project in the Department of Technology (DoT) to a service-delivery asset managed by the business – specifically the Department of Public Service (DPS). The specifics are as follows.

Evaluation of direct impact: The City has begun to make progress in integrating 311 more deeply into the City's day-to-day business processes, and making it a key source of data in measuring and managing the City's service delivery. In particular, DPS and DoT are working towards:

1. Safety related cost and workload reduction: Leveraging 311 to reduce costs and personnel workloads in City departments that have a direct responsibility for public safety: Instead of calling 911, residents are being encouraged to route non-emergency calls to 311. Additional service Request types have been added to suitably characterize these calls within 311, so they may be tracked appropriately.

2. Information clearing house: 311 is being utilized as clearing-house for resident-relevant information. Processes have been established to be able to rapidly update the 311 knowledge-base and also to quickly get new information to 311 operators at short notice.

3. Maintaining high-level support for 311: Continuing to remind the Mayor and key stakeholders of the City of 311 and ensuring sufficient DoT representation in all strategic and any City-wide or cross-Departmental operational planning and execution.

4. Raising awareness among users and stakeholders: Marketing it both with residents and internally within the City. The desire is to make sure 311 stays front and center of stakeholders' consciousness, and being able to confirm 311 penetration by incorporating systematic feedback mechanisms into the awareness raising process.

5. Integrating 311 into internal Departmental business processes: The work-order systems used by Departments and Divisions are being integrated with 311. A range of integration architectures must be designed to deal with the different paradigms by which work is allocated in different departments. A next step will be to integrate 311 data into the performance reporting systems within each department.

6. Extending the capabilities of 311: The capabilities within the technical and organizational architecture of 311 need to be extended to deal with special needs – in particular needs of crises management: This is being done by extending the capabilities of 311 (for example, by moving to a 24x7 operation) and by adding the necessary variation points within the 311 processes and competencies and its organizational architecture to (a) deal with areas of citizen concern – such as health and safety – where specialized expertise needs to be made available and (b) develop flexibility and extensibility in the software, as well as the personnel, needed to handle the ad-hoc information intake and dissemination that will be the requirement during a crisis.

7. Integrating it with Crisis-Management Planning: Once (6) has been addressed, DoT and DPS plan to actively promote the use of 311 in crisis-management – through incorporation into the Citywide crises-management, business continuity and disaster-recovery plans.

8. Phase-out of other access to City services: As 311 became established; the diverse call-centers within the City have been merged into 311 and eliminated. Listings of several direct-access numbers from Government section of the telephone directory (the Blue Pages) have been removed and replaced by 311. The phasing-out of additional direct lines is in the planning stages.

9. Building a data warehouse: The City plans to create a data warehouse with 311 data integrated with data from other call centers. This data warehouse is an essential enabler for data-driven community policing initiatives.

10. E-Gov: In the recent E-Government initiative, 311 has been identified as a foundational component. The E-Government initiative has been prioritized by citizen-facing requirements, which will mean that 311 will become the point of support and assistance for the electronic services delivered.

Generally speaking, 311 has had a positive impact. All the personnel we interviewed were aware of it and encouraging with respect to its continued and expanded use. For example, the Department of Health expressed interest in using 311's after-hours capability to extend availability of services. 311 has helped to understand operations of other departments in cross-over areas (such as rodent control between Health and Public Service, and in cross-departmental business continuity discussions). Interviewees have also stated that 311 has helped to systematize internal processes.

Issues highlighted with 311 were generally concrete and backed by considered and thoughtful opinion. For example, Health had (a) not proceeded to transfer their after-hours call center to 311 because it was not currently available 24x7 and (b) had not transferred its normal call center operations to 311 either, because of concerns that regular 311 operators would not be able to disseminate health-related information because of their lack of medical expertise. Certain departments, for instance, Health and Utilities continue to use their separate lines. A 311 call is transferred to these lines, which remain active and are directly called by service requestors.

Our evaluation is summarized as follows:

10. The general impression of 311 is good. 311 is seen overall as a success, and is now an established asset of the City.
11. Progressing beyond its non-emergency call center focus to evolve into an integral part of a crises-management process remains a challenge.

Evaluation Indirect Impact of 311: As aforementioned, the indirect impact of 311 was evaluated through structured interviews and the discussions generated during the sessions. Our evaluation is as follows:

- Capability of 311 and its service architecture of being used in an ad-hoc manner: There is currently no ad-hoc capability in 311, such as support for online collaboration, and for emergent processes. Thus, new information to be disseminated is typically supplied through email to the call center coordinator to be broadcast to all call center operators.
- Use and support of 311 for continuous improvement in Departmental processes, including those implemented within the 311 system. Use of 311 metrics in continuous improvement: We were unable to discover what Departmental processes existed for continuous improvement. However, 311 metrics were extensively used for continuous improvement in certain departments (Public Service and Public Utilities), but not yet in others (Health).
- Change in support of City value systems for increased inter-Departmental collaboration as a result of 311: All the interviewed Departments that already collaborated prior to 311 and stated that they continued to do so. Few departments reported that this had changed at a Department leadership level due to 311. However, knowledge may be spreading at the operational levels within the City. For example, Department of Public Utilities reported that staff's knowledge of other departments had increased due to 311.
- Changes in relationships and linkages across departments attributable to 311: Departments that typically collaborated prior to 311 (such as Health, Safety and Public Service) reported a better understanding of others' processes and constraints after 311.
- Increased internal collaboration within Departments due to 311: This was reported by the Department of Public Service only.
- Changes in City and Departmental operational plans after 311: The Department of Public Service was the only Department reporting changes in such plans after 311.
- Use of increased visibility of intra- and interdepartmental processes for exposing

and resolving accountability and coordination issues within City Government: The Department of Public Services reported increased accountability due to visibility in the assignment of City personnel to service Requests.

• An increased ability to re-purpose resources, such as call-handlers and responders – for example, 911 operators switching to 311, and City staff being made available for activities associated with emergency response: There was discussion around this topic, but no concrete action has been reported.

• Enablement of more appropriately tailored responses to crises due to 311: We were unable to evaluate this, although it was anecdotally claimed that 311 was used to tailor a response to ice storms.

Our major recommendations:

12. Maintain high-level support for 311: Continue to remind the Mayor and key stakeholders of the City of 311. Ensure sufficient DoT representation in all strategic and any City-wide or cross-Departmental operational planning and execution.[14]

13. Raise awareness: Actively continue to market it both with citizens and showcase it internally within the City, to make sure it stays front and center of stakeholders' consciousness. Note that while marketing and publicity campaigns to date have managed to a lot with very little, a big failing is that they do not appear to have incorporated systematic feedback mechanisms into the process.

14. Integrate 311 into the internal processes of City Departments and Divisions: Integrate 311 into internal Departmental work-order systems. Note that a range of integration architectures must be designed to deal with the mismatches in paradigms of the 311 system and the work-order system. Integrate

311 data into the performance reporting systems within each department.

15. Develop the necessary capability within the 311 technical architecture, variation points within the 311 processes, and competencies within an organizational architecture to deal with the specialized areas of citizen concern – such as health, safety and neighborhood services. Develop the flexibility and extensibility needed to handle ad-hoc information intake and dissemination into 311. Establish a Disaster Recovery Plan for 311.

16. Integration with Crisis-Management Planning: Once (4) has been addressed, actively look to promote the use of 311 in crisis-management, by incorporation into the City-wide crises-management, business continuity and disaster-recovery plans.

17. Data warehouse: Create a data warehouse with 311 data integrated with data from other call centers. This data warehouse is an essential enabler for data-driven community policing analysis and initiatives [Fayyad et al 02].

CONCLUSION

We identify the contributions from the perspectives of the city and from the underlying methodology which is widely applicable.

Case Contributions: We illustrate through two projects that while crises-management gives the environmental context to building network capability, a 311 system and its associated organizations, processes and IT components serves as an adaptive foundation for capability development. As in e-Government literature [NIMS; Punia et al , Governance, FirstGov] the implemented 311 systems played the expected roles within public safety, as follows:

- Alleviating loads on the emergency response system (i.e. 9-1-1) through offloading non-emergency calls,
- Enabling advancing community policing, by serving as a location-based database for reporting and identifying incident hotspots, and thereby facilitating the targeting of responses,
- Being available as an established, accepted, and standardized resource for information dissemination to the public.

Several 311 improvements were identified, to the 311 call center, its processes supported by 311, as well as the 311 application itself. These improvements were as follows:

- The ability to graphically "rubber-band" an area of interest, and access relevant 311 information, as well as related GIS-based information in additional mapping layers (such as the water resources of a selected area).
- Reverse-311, i.e. an ability to use 311 to make automated telephone calls and send automated emails to user-selectable addresses.
- Speedup in taking customer information during the process of creating a service Request
- Additional reporting available on-line.
- Remote access via VPN
- Ability to route calls to operators with special capabilities – such as operators that are Somali speaking, are medically trained, understand utility bills and so on.
- Direct connection between service delivery and 311 (such as integration with the refuse collection truck).
- Collection of additional information specific to certain service Requests (e.g. The Department of Health identified the need for time, date, name, address, and jurisdiction of call, and expressed a desire to involve their epidemiologist in the identification of

additional information to be collected).

- Selective incorporation of information currently provided by other call centers (specifically in areas where lay CSRs can reliably provide correct information). These included providing directions to medical resources (while keeping in mind that most medical information should not be disseminated by lay operators).
- Integration of 311 and other data sources into a data warehouse. This data warehouse will provide integrated information for data analysis for purposes such as community policing.
- An increased availability – ideally 24x7

Methodology Contributions: Traditional modeling techniques are hyper-rational and focus models and analysis on the most efficient way to build an enterprise IT system. Yet, the most efficient system may not be the best performing if it ignores new externally-generated requirements, multiple stakeholder priorities, need to handle variation in service Requests and service providers; and political, business and resource constraints. We introduce the Adaptive Complex Enterprise (ACE) architecture framework based on patterns that guide the architecture team to isolate and represent points of interactions between Requests and the service provider roles that complete the Requirements-Execution-Delivery transaction with performance that is monitored. This approach not only represents the as-is but also the ways in which the representation can evolve. Resource agents can be dynamically assembled into coalitions, new sub-requests can be dynamically spawned and new request types can be added. Thus the model begins to provide the representational ability and organization to implement networks across existing silos. Further, with the emerging Internet technologies, services that are local or remote can be assembled into coalitions to deliver on requests. These ACE characteristics, we have shown through the Case projects, provide the architecture team with the methodology for decision-making which leads to systems such as 311 for triaging Requests. Furthermore, by building the 311 system to adapt to the needs of each Request, we build in adaptability needed for crisis-management type scenarios.

In summary, we believe that using triage data and simulation techniques [Jain 2003] to provide information needed for decision-making [Page 2003], and very effective crisis and overall IT-enabled capability [Scholl 2003].

ACKNOWLEDGMENT

We wish to acknowledge the many valuable contributions from Gary Gavin, Jeff Clause, and Paul Carlson from the City of Columbus; Joe Bolinger, Brett Gerke, David Landsbergen, Kelly Yakovich and other participants of Center for Enterprise Transformation and Innovation.

REFERENCES

Agranoff, R. and McGuire, M. (2001). Big questions in public network management research. *Journal of Public Administration Theory and Research 11*(3), 295–326.

Alexander, C; Ishikawa, S., Silverstein, M., Jacobson, M., Fiksdahl-King, I., and Angel, S. (1977). *A pattern Language*. Oxford University Press.

Arora, A., Ramnath, R., Ertin, E., Sinha, P. (2005). ExScal: Elements of an Extreme Scale Wireless Sensor Network," 11th IEEE International Conference on Embedded and Real-Time Computing Systems and Applications, Hong Kong, China.

Adams, Jonathan; Koushik, Srinivas; Vasudeva, Guru; and Galambos George. (2001). Patterns for E-Business: A Strategy for Reuse. Mc Pr Llc, ISBN: 1931182027.

Agha, Gul, A. (2002) . Adaptive Middleware. *Communications of the ACM, 45*(6).

Arens, Yigal; and Rosenbloom, Paul. (2002). *Responding to the Unexpected*, USC/Information Sciences Institute, NSF Workshop.

Ambite, José Luis; Giuliano, Genevieve; Gordon, Peter; Decker, Stefan; Harth, Andreas; Jassar, Karanbir; Pan, Qisheng; and Wang, LanLan. (2005). *Argos: An Ontology and Web Service Composition Infrastructure for Goods Movement Analysis*, Information Sciences Institute School of Policy, Planning, and Development, Digital Gov. Website.

Anderson, Ross (2001). *Security Engineering: A Guide to Building Dependable Distributed Systems*. New York: Wiley.

BPMI. *Business Process Management Initiative*, www.BPMI.org.

Bauer, Johannes M. (2004). Harnessing the Swarm: Communications Policy in an Era of Ubiquitous Networks and Disruptive Technologies. *Communications & Strategies, 54*, 2nd quarter.

Bovens, M.; and Zouridis, S. (2002). From Street-Level to System-Level Bureaucracies. *Public Administration Review 62*(2): 174-184.

Clements, P. et. al. (2003). Software Architecture in Practice, (2nd ed.) New York, NY: Addison Wesley.

CMG. Capacity Management Group

Cross, Cross, S. et al. (2002). *SEI Independent Research and Development Projects*, TECHNICAL REPORT CMU/SEI-2002-TR-023 ESC-TR-2002-023.

Child, J. (1972). Organizations, Structure, Environment, and Performance: *The Role of Strategic Choice. Sociology, 6* 1-22.

COPS 03-1. http://www.cops.usdoj.gov/txt/fact_sheets/e01060007.txt

DAML. www.daml.org. The DARPA Agent Markup Language (DAML).

Deming W. E. (1982). *Out of the Crisis*, Cambridge, MA: MIT Press.

Desai, Anand. (2005). Special Issue: Adaptive Complex Systems. *CACM 49*(5).

Digtalgovernment. Government agencies affiliated with dg.o, are known as the "Digital Government Consortium." Member agencies often partner with NSF research performers and the private sector to leverage information technology research and identify financial resources to help build the Digital Government of the 21st Century. www.digitalgovernment.org

Donaldson, L. (1999). *The Normal Science of Structural Contingency Theory, in S.R.*

Drazin, Robert; and Van de Van, Andrew H. (1985). Alternative Forms of Fit in Contingency Theory. *Administrative Science Quarterly, 30,* 514-539.

Gamma, E., R.; Helm, R. Johnson; Vlissides, J. (1995). Design Patterns, Elements of Reuseable Object Oriented Software. New York, NY: Addison Wesley.

Eriksson, H; and Penker, M. (2000). Business Modeling with UML: Business Patterns at Work. New York, NY: John Wiley.

Fayyad, Usama; and Uthurusamy, Ramasamy. (2002). Into Evolving Data Mining Solutions for Insights. *CACM, 45,*(8).

Firstgov. To facilitate efforts to transform the Federal Government to one that is citizen-centered, results-oriented, and market-based, the Office of Management and Budget (OMB) is developing the Federal Enterprise Architecture (FEA), a business-based framework for Government-wide improvement. www.firstgov.gov.

Gortmaker, Jeffrey; Janssen, Marijn; and Wagenaar, René W. (2004). *The Advantages of Web*

Service Orchestration in Perspective. ICEC'04, Sixth International Conference on Electronic Commerce Edited by: Marijn Janssen, Henk G. Sol, and René W. Wagenaar. Copyright ACM 1-58113-930-6/04/10.

Governance and Performance: New Perspectives Washington, DC: Georgetown University Press pp. 263-291.

Gresov, C. (1989). Exploring Fit and Misfit with Multiple Contingencies. *Administrative Science Quarterly 34*, 431-453.

Groenlund, A. (1997). Public Computer Systems – A New Focus for Information Systems Research. *Information Infrastructure and Policy, 6*, 47-65.

Alfred Tat-Hei. (July/August 2002). Reinventing Local Government and the E-government initiative. *Public Administration Review, 62*(4): 434-444.

Hammer, M.; and J. Champy. (1993). *Reengineering the Corporation: A Manifesto for Business Revolution.* New York, NY: Harper.

Holowczak, Richard D.; Soon, Ae Chun; Artigas, Francisco J.; and Atlurit, Vijayalakshmi. (2003). "Customized Geospatial Workflows for E-Government Services," *Proceedings of the IEEE/WIC International Conference on Web Intelligence, IEEE.*

Jain, Sanjay; and McLean, Chuck; (2003). *Modeling and Simulation for Emergency Response*, NISY Technical Report, NISTIR 7071.

(ITIL) http://www.itil-officialsite.com/home/home.asp

Kaplan, R. S.; and D. P. Norton. (1996). *The Balanced Scorecard*. Boston MA: Harvard.

Klijn, Erik-Hans. (1996). Analyzing and Managing Policy Processes in Complex Networks. *Administration and Society, 28*(1), 90-119.

Kelly, S.; and Allison. M. A. (1998). *The Complexity Advantage*. New York, NY: McGraw Hill.

Kling, R. et al. (2001). *Transforming Coordination: The Promise and Problems of Information Technology in Coordination*. In G. Olson, T. Malone, J.B. Smith. The Interdisciplinary Study of Coordination. Mahwah, NJ: Lawrence Erlbaum Associates.

Warmer, Kleppe A, J.; and Bast, W. (2003). *MDA Explained: The Model Driven Architecture--Practice and Promise*. New York, NY: Addison-Wesley.

Lakoff, G.; and Johnson, M. (1980). *Metaphors we live by*. Chicago, IL: University of Chicago Press.

Laurence, P.R. and J.W. Lorsch. (1967). *Organization and Environment (Boston: Division of Research*, Graduate School of Business Administration, Harvard University.

Landsbergen, D. and Wolken, G. (2001). *Realizing the Promise: Government Information Systems and the Fourth Generation of Information Technology*, Public Administration Review.

Longstaff, P.H. (2005). *Security, Resilience, and Communication In Unpredictable Environments Such as Terrorism, Natural Disasters and Complex Technology Program for Information Resources Policy*, Harvard University.

Mackenzie, D. (2002). The Science of Surprise - Can complexity theory help us understand the real consequences of a convoluted event like September. *DISCOVER, 23*(2).

Mendonca, D., Jefferson, T., Harrald, J. (March ,2007). Collaborative Adhocracies and Mix-and-Match Technologies in Emergency Management. *Communications of the ACM*.

Malone, T.; and K. Crowston. (2001). The Interdisciplinary Study of Coordination. In Coordination Theory and Collaboration Technology, Gary M. Olson, Thomas W.

Mandelbrot, B. B. (1982). *Fractal Geometry of Nature*. New York, NY: W H Freeman.

MIPT. (2004). *Responder Knowledge base, National Technology Emergency Plan for Emergency Response to Catastrophic Terrorism, MIPT* (National Memorial Institute for the Prevention of Terrorism), April, www.rkb.mipt.org. .

Moon, M. Jae. (2002). *The Evolution of E-government among municipalities, Rhetoric or Reality* Public Administration Review (July / August), 62:4: 424-433.

Morçöl, G. (2002). *A New Mind for Policy Analysis* Westport CT: Praeger.

NIMS. *National Incident Management System*, www.fema.gov.

OAG. Open applications group. *Uses XML for every where to every where integration.*

OASIS: www.oasis-open.org, OASIS (Organization for the Advancement of Structured Information Standards) is a not-for-profit, international consortium that drives the development, convergence, and adoption of e-business standards

OGC: The Open Geospatial Consortium, Inc. (OGC) is a non-profit, international, voluntary consensus standards organization that is leading the development of standards for geospatial and location based services. www.opengeospatial.org.

OMG: http://www.omg.org.

OSI. The Open Source Initiative (OSI), a non-profit corporation responsible for the management and promotion of the Open Source Definition (OSD). www.opensource.org.

Nohria, N. (1992). *Is a Network Perspective a Useful Way of Studying organizations?* In N. Nohria and R. G. Eccles (eds.), Networks and organizations: Structure, Form and Fit (Boston: Harvard Business School Press).

O'Toole, Laurence and Meier, Kenneth. (2000). Networks, Hierarchies, and Management: Modeling the nonlinearities, in Heinrich, C. and L. Lynn (eds.).

Page, S. (2003). Entrepreneurial Strategies for Managing Interagency Collaboration. *Journal of Public Administration Research and Theory, 13*(3), 311-340.

Peitgen, H.; Jurgens, H.; and Saupe, D. (1992). Chaos and Fractals: New Frontiers of Science. Berlin: Springer Verlag.

Porter, M. E. (1998). Competitive Strategy: Techniques For Analyzing Industries And Competitors. New York, NY: Free Press.

Punia, Devendra K.; and Saxena, K. B. C. (March 2004). E-government services and policy track: Managing inter-organizational workflows in eGovernment services, *Proceedings of the 6th international conference on Electronic commerce.*

Ramanathan, J. (1999). *Enterprise Integration with NIIIP Protocols, SME, ASME* Autofact Proceedings.

Ramanathan, J.; and Beswick, R. (2000). *Imperative: Why Process-based Architecture is Essential for Successful Supply-Chain Participation. EAI Journal.*

Ramanathan, J. (2005). *Fractal Architecture for the Adaptive Complex Enterprise*, Communications of the ACM, May.

Ramanathan, J. and Ramnath, Rajiv. (2004) *IT Architecture and the Case for Lean eBusiness Process Management,* Knowledge Supply and Information Logistics in Enterprises and Networked organizations, Fraunhofer-Institute for Software and Systems Engineering ISST.

J Ramanathan and R. Ramnath. (2006). *Co-engineering Business, Information Use, and Operations Systems for IT-enabled Adaptation.* Book

chapter in "Adaptive Technologies and Business Integration: Social, Managerial and organizational Dimensions", Publisher IDEAS.

Ramnath, R., Landsbergen, D. (May, 2005) IT-enabled sense-and-respond strategies in complex public organizations. *Communications of the ACM, 48*(5).

Ramnath, R. and Desai, A. (2007). *City of Columbus, 311 Impact Evaluation, Final Report.*

Rosetta Net. http://www.rosettanet.org/.

Scholl, H.J. (2003). E-government: A special case of IT-enabled Business Process Change, *Chapter presented at the 36th Hawaiian Conference of Systems Sciences*, Hawaii.

Schwartz, Peter. (2003). *Inevitable Surprises: Thinking Ahead in a Time of Turbulence.* New York: Gotham Books.

SCOR. http://wwwsupply-chain.org.

Teisman, G. and E.H. Klijn. (2002). Partnership Arrangements: Governmental Rhetoric or Governance Scheme? *Public Administration Review, 62*(2), 197-205.

Thiétart, R.A. and B. Forgues. (1995). *Chaos Theory and Organization Science, 6*(1):19-31.

Salmela, H.; and Spil, T.A.M. (2002). Dynamic and emergent information systems strategy formulation and implementation. *International Journal of Information Management, 22*, 441-460.

Williamson, O. E. (1975). *Markets and Hierarchies.* New York: The Free Press.

Winograd, T. and Flores F. (1987). *Understanding Computers and Cognition - A New Foundation for Design.* Reading: Addison Wesley.

TOGAF. http://www.opengroup.org/architecture/togaf8-doc/arch/.

W3C. www.w3c.org. (August 2003). *WSA, Web Services Architecture.* W3C working Draft 8.

WfMC. www.wfmc.org.

ENDNOTES

[1] Architecture: the fundamental organization of a system embodied in its components, their relationships to each other and to the environment and the principles guiding its design and evolution. (ANSI/IEEE Std 1471: ISO/IEC 42010, http://www.iso-architecture.org/ieee-1471/index.html). We interpret the components to be both organizational and technology components in order to enable a uniform system for decision-making, across all the stakeholders of the organization.

[2] An architecture framework" is a tool or method which can be used for developing a broad range of different solution architectures. It describes a method for designing a system of organization and information components in terms of a set of building blocks, and for showing how the building blocks fit together. It should contain a set of tools and provide a common vocabulary. It should also include a list of recommended standards and compliant products that can be used to implement the building blocks.

[3] Architecture: the fundamental organization of a system embodied in its components, their relationships to each other and to the environment and the principles guiding its design and evolution. (ANSI/IEEE Std 1471: ISO/IEC 42010, http://www.iso-architecture.org/ieee-1471/index.html). We interpret the components to be both organizational and technology components in order to enable a uniform system for decision-making, across all the stakeholders of the organization.

[4] An architecture framework" is a tool or method which can be used for developing a broad range of different solution architectures. It describes a method for designing a system of organization and information components in terms of a set of building blocks, and for showing how the building blocks fit together. It should contain a set of tools and provide a common vocabulary. It should also include a list of recommended standards and compliant products that can be used to implement the building blocks.

[5] The Collaborative for Enterprise Transformation and Innovation (CETI) at The Ohio State University has been deeply engaged with Information Technology initiatives at the City of Columbus. It is also a research site for the CERCS IUCRC at Georgia Tech.

[6] A 311 system is a central, one-stop-shop for requesting non-emergency City services (such as bulk trash pickup), reporting non-emergency information (such as potholes, water leaks, and dead animals) and receiving information – such as open routes to Fourth of July fireworks displays.

[7] An "enterprise" is a collection of organizations that has a common set of goals. An enterprise can be a government agency, a whole corporation or distinct organizations linked together by a common problem.

[8] Program officially began in August 2000. The goal of the DAML effort is to develop a language and tools to facilitate the concept of the Semantic Web. Mark Greaves, DARPA Program Manager for DAML.

[9] The rapid obsolescence of static plans – project plans, process models, workflow execution models, budgets and business models – is a testimony to this phenomenon. For example, re-engineering efforts started during the '90's and '00's resulted in a variety of different process models [Hammer and Champy, 1993]. However, as the environment changed, many of the models became obsolete and never found their way into practice.

[10] The term pattern has multiple meanings in literature. In object-oriented literature [Gamma et al, 1995] it means documenting the problem solving process based on object interactions in a standardized form. A generic definition of patterns in design

is given by Alexander (2002). Here we will use the term to mean a problem solving template. In complexity theory [Mandelbrot, 1982], it also refers to a recursively-applied structure.

11   We use the term roles to refer to the prototypical service description that has to be delivered by any agent that performs the role.

12   The main concept consists of the primary 'RED' transaction pattern between a *customer and provider* organization. This pattern is quite ubiquitous and is proposed in the Speech Act Theory [Winograd, 1987]; the Plan-Source-Make-Deliver process pattern between customers and suppliers in any Supply–Chain pattern [SCOR]; the Rosetta Net [Rosetta] for Request and delivery exchange; and lastly the basis for approaches to process

improvement and measurement [Burk 1994; Demming, 1982; Jones, 2003; Kaplan 1996; Porter, 1998]. ACE uses customer-provider transactions that are fractals (recursive patterns applied in different scales) to allow dynamic non-linear interactions between a non-routine Request and the resources and services used in satisfying that Request. RED transaction is similar to and maps to the concept of a 'transaction' as discussed in the transactions costs literature [Williamson 1975] and nested transactions in Speech Act Theory [Winograd 1987; Lackoff and Johnson 1980].

13   Note that the agreements can be formal or informal.

14   Perhaps 311 data could be made available to candidates during mayoral campaigns.

Chapter VIII
Design Integrity and Enterprise Architecture Governance

Chris Aitken
Queensland Health, Australia

ABSTRACT

This chapter describes a design integrity framework for developing models of any entity of interest at various levels of abstraction. The design integrity framework presented describes and defines contextual, conceptual, logical and physical model types. The framework also defines a set of alignment attributes for each model type and explains how these are to be used to demonstrate alignment from initial concept and requirements through to actual physical implementation. These concepts are then applied in an organisational context to identify the roles necessary to support an EA governance framework and strong alignment from idea to implementation.

INTRODUCTION

Operational agility is a hallmark of contemporary enterprise management in both the private and public sectors. Agility in the marketplace implies an ability to quickly and effectively undertake significant controlled change at all levels within an enterprise. Change is increasingly a characteristic of modern government agencies. The requirement

for change and flexibility is driven by changing public expectations of government provided services, budget constraints and rationalisation of government resources. Furthermore, machinery of government changes and whole-of-government consolidation frequently require agencies to merge, split or re-align to better meet government objectives and service requirements. The impact on individual agencies may range from relatively minor technology-based modifications through to wholesale changes where the enterprise is transitioned to become something entirely new.

The requirement for change inevitably means that consideration has to be given to design integrity. Whenever we are concerned with the alignment between an initial idea and the way in which it is implemented we are dealing with the issue of design integrity. In a change driven environment, design integrity assists us to understand whether the changes undertaken are required and whether they have been implemented as intended. Furthermore, such an approach reinforces modularity of design allowing incremental change or partitioning of change initiatives in a manner that is more likely to achieve the overall objective or outcomes. Clearly, design integrity is closely related to the concept of governance. Governance is the ability to control change within an enterprise. In this respect design integrity is a key enabler of governance. Within the day-to-day practice of enterprise architecture this relationship between governance and design integrity is arguably even closer. This is particularly true in environments which employ agile system development methodologies (Ambler 2002, Beck 1999). Such methodologies involve short iterative cycles of development and modelling, and are more likely to be successful where there is attention to maintaining design integrity. A common misconception is that such approaches to system development do not require high levels of rigor in modelling. This chapter will argue that in fact upfront effort in developing a set of well referenced models greatly assists rapid development methodologies.

This chapter describes a framework for design and modelling integrity. Although the framework is generic enough to be applied to the design of any entity of interest, throughout this chapter the framework will be applied in the context of government agencies. The framework provides a means for describing the measures for ensuring design integrity from an initial idea through to its actual physical implementation. In order for the enterprise architect to be confident that the transition from current to future states occurs as intended, within any system development methodology (eg. Agile, XP, Waterfall) he or she must be sure that the necessary governance roles and responsibilities within the enterprise have been identified and exercised. The second half of the chapter applies the framework in an organisational context, identifies governance roles and illustrates why and at what point they are required in the process of enterprise architecture.

DESIGN INTEGRITY

Design integrity needs to be understood at both the level of individual enterprise components as well as at the broader level of the enterprise transition from current to future state. Enterprise architectural design integrity addresses the following questions:

- Does the design of an entity satisfy a set of initial requirements?

This question relates to whether the design is the right one given the context, constraints and requirements of the entity in question. It is possible to design a solution that delivers a desired outcome but does not do so in a way that is consistent with the restrictions in which the component must be operated. For example, an application that provides the desired output but does so in a way that does not comply with legislative requirements. Therefore, design integrity must assess the alignment between the requirements of the broader context and the characteristics of a given design.

- Does a given design contain all the relevant elements of an entity?

This question highlights the need to ensure that a design is complete. The design must adequately represent all the specified aspects of the entity of interest. To have integrity a design must completely represent the entity of interest. Alternatively, a design must be limited to only include those aspects that are considered to be 'in scope' for the entity. This problem is at the heart of the all too common phenomenon of systems or applications which provide functionality, typically paid for by the user, that is never used. Completeness however, does not necessarily mean that all aspects must be represented to the same level of detail.

•   Is a given design consistent with the desired approach or strategy?

A design must also be able to be assessed for conformance to intent. It is possible to develop a design that meets external requirements, represents all aspects of the entity, but does not represent the desired approach or design strategy. For example, it is possible that a given outcome might equally be achieved via a stand alone application or by adopting a Service Oriented Architecture (SOA) based solution involving the orchestration of multiple services. However, the two approaches represent fundamentally different approaches in design. Therefore, design integrity must also address the degree to which a design can be said to reflect a particular desired approach to meeting an initial set of requirements.

•   Has the design been implemented as intended?

Design integrity also refers to the need to ensure that designs and changes to designs at a conceptual or logical level are accurately translated into physical implementation. Without a way to measure and assess this alignment it is not possible to determine whether a given physical implementation is consistent with a given design. Again, the design of an SOA solution can look great on paper, only to be let down through poor implementation and inconsistent adherence to SOA design principles.

Only by considering design integrity at each of the levels addressed by the questions listed before is it possible to assess the degree to which an implemented entity is consistent with what was originally intended. The following section sets out an initial framework of definitions designed to assist the enterprise architect to understand the magnitude of a given change, which of the aspects of design integrity are affected, and how the implications might best be represented.

Design Integrity from Idea to Implementation

The process of undertaking enterprise architecture inevitably requires that there be some level of abstraction from physical reality. Within the discipline of enterprise architecture, levels of abstraction are typically managed through the development and use of models. For example, a value chain model might provide a high level overview of a set of processes, which in turn might be the subject of more detailed process models. The use of a model enables the enterprise architect to represent ideas, concepts and their respective relationships and explore the inter-dependencies and the impact of changes to both concepts and their relationships.

Enterprise architects frequently refer to the terms physical, logical and conceptual models to represent ideas at increasing levels of abstraction. By aligning models across levels of abstraction the architect is able to represent the same entity in a way that is suitable for a variety of audiences and types of analysis. A similar need for alignment across levels of abstraction is evident in the discipline of Science. Table 1 illustrates a compelling comparison of similar hierarchies of abstraction found within both the positivist scientific method and the discipline of enterprise architecture. What the comparison suggests is that the need for design integrity is similar both for the scientist designing and conducting experiments as it is for the enterprise architect attempting to model and ultimately effect change in an enterprise. In order for the scientist to be able to claim that a given experiment either proves or disproves a theory or hypothesis, the scientist must be able to demonstrate alignment between theoretical constructs, the variables representing the constructs, and the measures used to measure change in the variables of interest. Similarly, an architect must be able to demonstrate that the ideas contained in conceptual level models are also reflected the associated logical models, and are ultimately translated into physical level models and implementation. A similar comparison between the disciplines of mathematics and science was famously popularised by Pólya (1971) who suggested that although they might differ in how they are outwardly described, the two disciplines resemble each other in the problem solving processes they employ (ie. how practitioners think about things). The framework presented in this chapter is a further extension of this idea.

To achieve design integrity requires that the terms 'conceptual model', 'logical model' and 'physical model' be unambiguously defined. However, although the terms conceptual, logical and physical are frequently used within the field of enterprise architecture they are not always used or defined in a consistent fashion. The concepts appear most well developed in the area of data modelling (Tsichritzis & Klug, 1978). However, even here there are plenty of examples of a lack of consistent application (Simsion, 2006). Often the terms 'conceptual model', 'logical model' or 'high level model' are used interchangeably to mean a model with 'some level' of abstraction.

Table 1. Comparison of levels of abstraction

Scientific method	Enterprise architecture	
Hypothesis or theory	Contextual model	⟸ Alignment ⟹
Construct	Conceptual model	
Variable	Logical model	
Measure	Physical model	

This lack of specificity significantly limits the architect's ability to claim that the ideas or concepts as they are modelled have in fact been implemented as intended or that a given logical design accurately reflects the original idea or intent. Furthermore, a not uncommon scenario in the author's experience is for two analysts to independently model a solution component (eg. a process model, a use case model) only to find that they are not able to be meaningfully brought together or compared due to differences in detail, scope or abstraction.

Clearly, what is required is a framework which defines model types and characteristics which enables the practitioner to reference lower level detailed models within higher level conceptual or contextual ones. In this way the more abstract models provide a frame of reference for the more detailed models. Such a framework would greatly assist developers in agile system development environments by allowing them to model or even implement different solution components at different rates and provide some certainty that the end product will work as in tended and remain true to the original concept.

The comparison in Table 1 also suggests a definitional framework for the terms 'contextual', 'conceptual', 'logical', and 'physical'. The following sections present a suggested framework of model types to represent the various levels of abstraction.

THE DESIGN INTEGRITY FRAMEWORK

The following design integrity framework borrows ideas from the ANSI conceptual data model definition (Tsichritzis & Klug, 1978). The framework also draws heavily on ideas found in the following EA frameworks:

- Zachman framework (Zachman, 2005)
- Generalised enterprise reference architec-

ture (Bernus, Nemes & Schmidt, 2003)
• EA cube (Bernard, 2005).

In order for the architect to achieve alignment from idea to implementation each model or level of abstraction needs to be appropriately referenced in relationship to the other levels. The framework presented here provides definitions of each model type, purpose, and relationship to other models or levels of abstraction. The framework also describes features of the models at each level that are required to ensure design integrity.

The framework can be applied to the design of any entity. Where the entity is an enterprise the model types and levels of abstraction approximately correspond with the rows of the Zachman Framework (Sowa & Zachman, 1992). Furthermore, the columns of the Zachman Framework suggest at least six domains in which the modelling framework might be applied (ie. data, process, roles, business rules, logistics and events). Similar to the Zachman Framework the framework presented here is recursive and can equally be applied to any given cell within the Zachman Framework. However, there are some important differences. Firstly, whereas the cells in the Zachman Framework are 'loosely' vertically related, the purpose of the design integrity framework is to provide a means of achieving strong vertical alignment by referencing lower cells in those with higher levels of abstraction. Secondy, although both frameworks represent the concepts 'contextual', 'conceptual', 'logical' and 'physical' as rows, these concepts are differently defined in each framework. This means that the cell contents are likely to differ between frameworks. Zachman claims to have derived the rows or views within his framework from careful observation of design practices in other design and engineering domains. The rows or 'model types' in the framework presented in this chapter are derived by applying a set of strict definitions to the terms

'contextual', 'conceptual', 'logical' and 'physical' and a defined set of alignment attributes.

In the following sections each model type is described and a set of criteria provided to assist the practitioner in identifying the category to which a given model belongs, and for determining the characteristics required of a model of a given type. It is not uncommon to encounter models which include characteristics of two or more of the types listed here. In these cases it is usually beneficial to deconstruct the model into two or more separate models. For example, implementation details might be included in a logical process model for reasons of expediency. However, such an approach means that changes in the physical implementation model of the process (eg. work instruction) are also likely to require re-work of the logical level process model (eg. procedure). Furthermore, such an approach does not promote logical model re-use.

Although consistent modelling notation is important, the most important aspect of the following framework is that subordinate models clearly reference themselves within their super ordinate or parent model type. The alignment between models is top down as it is typically not possible to deduce a higher order model from a lower level one. This approach promotes modelling modularity which means that components of a given entity or solution are able to be developed relatively independently of one another while still achieving consistency and overall integrity. For example, once a conceptual level model has been developed it provides a frame of reference for lower level logical models, allowing the possibility of them being developed by different design teams, or at different iterations of an agile system development process. The following sections define each model type and provide a listing of modelling criteria which help distinguish one model type from another.

CONTEXTUAL MODEL (REQUIREMENTS)

Purpose: To describe requirements and external related entities. The model identifies the external constraint requirements, the overall goal of the entity (ie. its purpose), and the outcomes it will need to achieve.

Definition: A contextual model treats the entity of interest as a 'black box'. A contextual model describes external entities, their relationship to the entity of interest, and the requirements that must be met to satisfy the relationship. It does not however, contain a description of the entity itself. The IDEF0 Top-level Context diagram (Computer Systems Laboratory of the National Institute of Standards and Technology, 1993) is an example of a contextual model. A change in a contextual model is likely to require changes to the conceptual models which reference it. Changes at the contextual level will represent changes to requirements or constraints.

Modelling criteria: A contextual model will have the following characteristics:

- The entity of interest is depicted as a 'black box' (ie. no description of the entity make up is provided); and
- Describes only those entities external to the entity of interest and their relationships to it.

CONCEPTUAL MODEL (SCOPE)

Purpose: To define the entity's construct[1] domain.

Definition: A conceptual model is 'stateless' in the sense that it is independent of current or future state. The conceptual model is comprised of all the constructs and relationships required to fully represent the entity. The relationships between constructs must be consistent with external constraints identified in the parent contextual model. A conceptual model can be thought of as a template against which state based descriptions are subsequently mapped. A conceptual model must be able to support the mapping of both current and future state logical representations. A reference model is an example of a conceptual model (eg. MacKenzie, Laskey, McCabe, Brown, Metz, 2006). Business process and technology patterns are further examples. Value chain models (Porter, 1985) are also an example of a conceptual level model. A value chain model describes broad sequential categories of activities within an organisation that turn inputs into value-added outputs. Note that the model typically does not describe the detailed processes of which these categories are comprised.

Changes in a conceptual model are likely to require changes in the logical models which reference it. Changes at the conceptual level will represent the introduction of new constructs and therefore new characteristics (eg. functionality) that need to be captured in any logical level design. For example, in the case of business process modelling, changes at the conceptual level will represent new business functions not previously considered as falling within the entity specification. Such a change may mean that there are no current state logical level process models which are able to reference the new construct and that the logical process models associated with another area in the business may now become associated with this entity.

A conceptual model provides a point of reference that allows partitioning and management of logical level models. This means that logical models can be developed for discrete 'sections' of the overarching conceptual model while retaining the correct relationship between one logical model and another. Such an approach inherently promotes the principle of modularity of design.

Modelling criteria: A conceptual model will have the following characteristics:

- Defines the domain of constructs and their relationships that specify the make up of the entity;
- Is independent of state such that both current and future state logical level descriptions can be mapped to it;
- Does not describe the entity's environment or context;
- Does not include state based descriptions; and
- References a single parent contextual model.

LOGICAL MODEL (DESIGN)

Purpose: To describe a design through the application of entity constructs to particular states (ie. current or future state). A logical model translates conceptual level constructs into logical components. The model selects and arranges these components according to design principles.

Description: A logical model represents a particular design strategy and the associated configuration of logical components and relationships between them. A logical model is independent of any physical implementation. A logical data model (Tsichritzis & Klug, 1978) is an example of a logical level model. Changes in a logical model will require change to the physical models which may reference it. Changes at the logical level will represent changes to the components for which physical implementation will be required.

Modelling criteria: A logical model will have the following characteristics:

- References a single conceptual level model and represents all constructs within that model;

- Does not introduce new constructs;
- Provides a state specific description of logical components; and
- Does not include implementation detail (eg. technology descriptions).

PHYSICAL MODEL (IMPLEMENTATION)

Purpose: To describe an actual physical implementation and measures for a given logical description. The physical model is the critical link between abstract design and the real world.

Description: A physical model is implementation and state specific. It describes the way in which a given logical model will be or is implemented. A physical model translates logical components into specific physical components, and provides a comprehensive listing of all required physical components that make up the implemented entity (ie. a bill of materials).

Modelling criteria: A physical model will have the following characteristics:

- Includes implementation specific detail (eg. make, version, condition etc);
- Does not include physical components that cannot be mapped to a logical model component; and
- References a single (state specific) logical model.

IMPLEMENTING DESIGN INTEGRITY

The previous section outlined model type definitions for a design integrity framework. The model types within the framework can be used to represent any entity at any of four levels of abstraction. In this section we will identify types of attributes associated with each model type that are required

Table 2. Alignment attributes summary

Model type	Purpose	Alignment attribute type
Contextual	Requirements	• Goal • Requirements
Conceptual	Scope	• Objectives • Constructs
Logical	Design	• Design principles and assertions • Logical components and implementation criteria
Physical	Implementation	• Measures • Physical components

to ensure design integrity from idea through to implementation. The attribute type framework presented here allows subordinate model types to be correctly referenced and aligned to their parent model type. Table 2 provides a summary listing of the attribute types for each model type. The following sections describe each attribute type in detail.

CONTEXTUAL MODEL

A contextual level model must contain an attribute or attributes that provide a description of the goal or purpose of the entity of interest (ie. the 'black box' entity). Such goal alignment attributes are typically referred to as the 'mission' or 'vision' when applied in an organisational context. However, it is important that the goal alignment attribute does not describe anything internal to the entity (eg. internal processes, roles, strategies). A contextual model must also specify a complete listing of requirements. This alignment attribute type includes outcomes the entity must achieve or provide, constraints within which it must be implemented, or other externally driven specifications. The listing of requirements is derived from consideration of each external entity and the requirements of the relationship between it and the entity of interest. Together both the goal and requirements alignment attribute types when

documented in a contextual model provide a frame of reference for a sub-ordinate conceptual level model.

CONCEPTUAL MODEL

The first alignment attribute type within a conceptual model are a set of documented objectives which describe what the entity must achieve in order to satisfy the contextual level model's stated entity goal. The objectives may be stated in absolute or relative terms but must be quantifiable. The second alignment attribute type that must be documented in a conceptual level model are the constructs contained within it. Each construct within a conceptual level model must reference one or more of the contextual model requirement attributes. These linkages to contextual requirements provide the 'reason' for including the construct as part of the conceptual model.

LOGICAL MODEL

The first alignment attribute type documented in a logical model are the logical components of which it is comprised. Each logical component of the model must reference at least one construct within the parent conceptual level model. The full specification of any logical component also includes a description of implementation criteria. These criteria (eg. performance criteria) describe in an implementation neutral way, the criteria any given physical component must satisfy to be said to implement the logical level design. For example, in a logical model where the design principle of efficiency has been applied the implementation criteria for logical components might include a cost criteria. This would most likely be a comparative measure in terms of throughput or other relevant characteristic of the model. The development of the implementation criteria requires careful consideration to ensure that there is not a mismatch later on between the demands of the logical design and the ability of the physical implementation to support it.

The logical level models are primarily concerned with design. Therefore, the second alignment attribute type to be documented within a logical model are a set of design principles and an associated set of assertions. The design principles indicate the design approach or design strategy to be adopted (eg. the principle of modularity of design, the principle of re-use of components, or the principle of limiting unnecessary variation). Each design principle should reference one or more objectives within the parent conceptual model. This provides the level of justification for adopting a given design principle. Each principle should also be associated with one or more assertions. The assertions are statements which can be answered affirmatively if a given principle has been applied to a given model. For example, an assertion for the principle of modularity of design might be that components should be able to be replaced by alternative components without compromising the operation of the entity. Alternatively, the design principle of maximising performance speed applied to a logical data model could be evidenced by the assertion that the model represented the minimum number of logical data table lookups required per logical transaction.

PHYSICAL MODEL

The physical components within a physical level model provide the first alignment attribute type. The full specification of the physical components documented in the model must include an exact description of the technology to be implemented (eg. brand, model, version etc). Each physical component must reference one or more of the logical level components in the parent logical model, and satisfy the implementation criteria documented in the relevant logical component.

The second alignment attribute type that a physical model should include are measures. Each measure documented within the model must reference one or more of the design principles and associated assertions in the parent logical model. The alignment between measures and design principles is discussed further in the following section.

USING THE DESIGN INTEGRITY FRAMEWORK

This section briefly outlines how the design integrity framework covered in previous sections might be used within the broader process of enterprise architecture. A well aligned set of models that translate a set of requirements through to physical implementation represents a thorough description and decomposition of a given entity. A fully specified set of models allows the enterprise architect to powerfully demonstrate that they have correctly understood the business context, concepts and requirements. Such a set also allows the architect to describe the design strategy or approach adopted with respect to business concepts, and how this strategy will be translated into a tangible implementation.

Figure 1 illustrates the capacity of the design integrity framework to provide a means to reference and align models of varying levels of abstraction. This allows the enterprise architect to possibly compartmentalise the development of lower order models. For example, in Figure 1 several implementation models (eg. Physical 1 (b)) might be evaluated against the implementation criteria and design assertions in a higher order logical model (eg. Logical 1 (b)). Figure 1 also highlights the ability of the framework to capture and reference changes in logical design between current and future states of an entity with reference to a single conceptual parent model.

Figure 1. Referencing across levels of abstraction

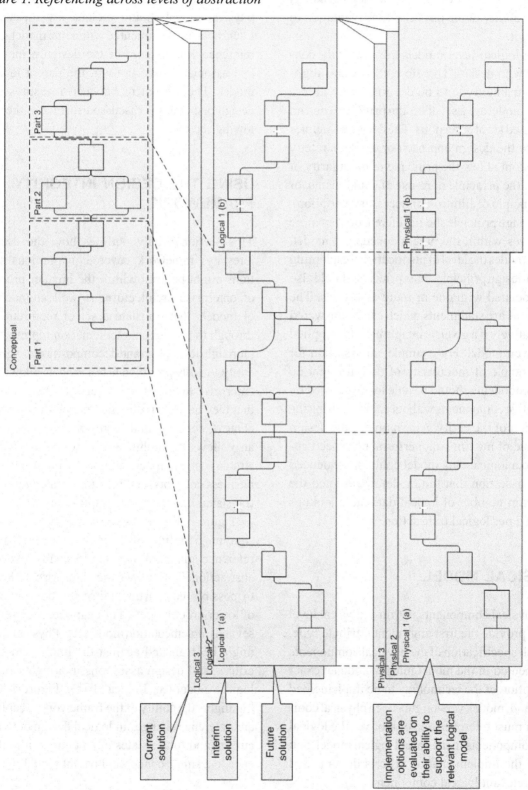

Design integrity also provides a means for the effect of changes to a design to be evaluated. Furthermore, design integrity allows the completeness of modelled entities to be tested and in this way also assess whether all relevant aspects of a design or concept have been captured. The following section examines some of these issues further.

CHOOSING MEASURES

The alignment attribute type framework outlined previously provides a means to measure alignment at all levels of abstraction. However, the framework is dependent on the appropriateness of the measures included in the physical level model. Careful consideration should be given to the selection of these measures in terms of:

- **The purpose of the measure.** Measures should be designed and selected on the basis of their ability to test the design principle assertions documented in the logical model. There need not be a one-to-one relationship between measures and design principles, as some measures may be more global and provide overall feedback about a number of principles. Conversely, a single design principle may be measured using a number of measures. The key point is that the measures need to be designed and selected ahead of time on the basis of their ability to provide information about the implementation of a given design principle (ie. their construct validity[2]).
- **Performance.** Measures that do not attract a performance cost should be chosen in preference to those that do. This usually means selecting as a first choice those measures which are provided as a natural consequence of the operation of the implemented entity.

PERFORMANCE ASSESSMENT

The design integrity framework presented in previous sections provides a means to assess performance at the following four levels of abstraction

- **Contextual:** Whether the entity as implemented supports the overall goal.
- **Conceptual:** Whether the entity achieves its objectives.
- **Logical:** Whether the entity has been designed according to a particular strategy or design principle.
- **Physical:** Whether the entity meets particular implementation criteria.

At the contextual level all measures within the physical model are ultimately a measure of the fit between implementation and the entity goal. At this level the measures can be considered to represent a type of entity profile. The degree to which one implementation of the entity meets this goal compared to another can be determined by a comparison of measurement profiles.

At the conceptual level measures will relate to specific objectives and provide a global measure of the extent to which the objective has been achieved by the entity as implemented. At this level it is possible to compare implementations of a given entity in terms of their ability to satisfy the entities objectives (eg. comparison of the ability of current and future state implementations to meet the same set of objectives).

In order to assess the performance of a logical design we must be able to identify the separate contributions of design and physical implementation to overall performance. Where designs are implemented using the same number and type of physical components, any improvement in performance[3] can be attributed to differences in design. Where the same physical components are not used the contribution of design differences becomes more difficult to determine. However, within the alignment attribute type framework outlined previously, the measures in the physical model are designed to measure application of design principles or strategies. They therefore provide a means to evaluate the effect of changes in design. However, their ability to provide this measure is dependent on their construct validity. Construct validity is a concept borrowed from the social sciences. It describes the ability of a measure to reflect changes in a concept or construct. Construct validity is usually determined through the application of explicit logical argument regarding what is understood about the mechanisms thought to underpin the construct, and the comparison (or correlation) of the measure with other measures also thought to be related to the construct. Usually for logical design models this determination is readily made with respect to design principles. However, there may be occasions where the relationship between selected physical measures and the relevant design principle may need to be tested and evaluated before including it in the physical model.

At the physical level measures are concerned with determining whether individual physical components meet or exceed the implementation criteria specified in the parent logical model components.

GAP ANALYSIS

Gaps may exist in all models at the various levels of the design integrity framework. As illustrated in Figure 2 [4] there may be contextual level requirements for which no conceptual constructs exist, or conceptual constructs for which there are no logical or physical level mappings. Each one of these situations highlights a significant lack of alignment or gap in the design integrity of the entity of interest. Experience has shown that an analysis of gaps across all four levels of abstraction usually results in the identification of fruitful insights or new aspects of the entity of interest.

Figure 2. Gap analysis across levels of abstraction

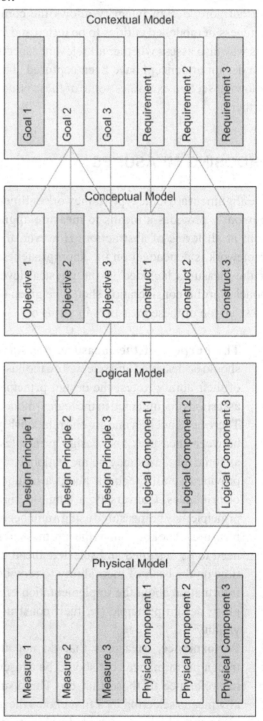

Therefore, it is recommended that a thorough gap analysis is conducted.

Gaps at the contextual, conceptual, logical or physical levels should be resolved before moving to actual implementation. A gap at the contextual level may mean that there is a mismatch in scope between the contextual level requirements and conceptual model. This suggests that there are external entities and relationships that the conceptual model does not address. In this situation either the contextual level model external entities need to be deemed out of scope by the project sponsor (or similar role) or the conceptual model needs to be revised to satisfy the additional contextual level requirements. Alternatively, there may be conceptual constructs which do not map to any contextual level requirements. This suggests possible missing external entities in the contextual model or unnecessary constructs within the conceptual model. Finally there may be conceptual level objectives which do not relate to the entity goal. This suggests that there is a mismatch between the overall purpose of the entity and the conceptual model thought to support it.

A gap at the conceptual level means that there are conceptual constructs or objectives for which there are no logical level components or design principles. Or alternatively logical level components or design principles which do not relate to any conceptual level construct or objective. This situation suggests either an incomplete logical model, or unnecessary logical level components.

A gap at the physical level suggests that either the implementation contains physical components that are not specified in the design, or that the physical implementation will be incomplete.

IMPACT ANALYSIS

Impact analysis is concerned with understanding the consequences of change. The design integrity framework presented in this chapter allows impact analysis to be conducted at each of the four

levels of abstraction. Changes at the contextual or conceptual levels will typically represent large wholesale changes to the purpose or constructs by which the entity of interest is represented or identified. Within the government agency context these changes are typical of 'machinery of government' changes where whole departments may be created, abandoned or merged. Conceptual level changes are represented by those situations in which functionality is moved from one agency to another to better meet the needs of the public. Contextual level changes represent those situations where the agency acquires new customers and an associated set of new requirements. The consequences of these changes can be mapped to current logical level and associated physical level models. From this mapping the extent of any gaps can be identified. This analysis then allows some understanding of the consequences of the changes in terms of physical implementation (eg. costs, training, personnel, information systems).

Changes at the logical level will represent changes in design strategy or approach. Again, the impact of these changes can be understood by determining the ability of existing physical models to support the design change, and identifying and quantifying the gaps where the current physical model is unable to support or accommodate the change. The design level change can also be assessed in terms of its ability to support the conceptual level objectives and the entity's context level purpose. From the perspective of an individual government agency, logical level change is typical of internal 're-structuring' initiatives. Here the requirements and overall functionally are likely to remain the same whereas the internal configuration of resources, roles and processes are likely to change significantly to align with a new strategic approach.

The design integrity framework also allows for a more holistic understanding of the consequences of changes at the physical implementation level. Using the measures in the physical model, changes at this level can be assessed in terms of their overall impact on the entity goal and objectives. Changes at this level usually reflect changes in technology or personnel.

GOVERNANCE ROLES

This section adds to the design integrity framework by introducing a set of governance roles. This section does not provide a complete enterprise architecture governance framework, however it does provide a description of the key roles and the levels at which these are important within the overall governance process and across levels of abstraction. For a comprehensive treatment of IT governance frameworks and approaches the reader is referred to Weill & Ross (2004) and Betz (2006). Each role described here has a unique contribution to the governance over the implementation of the models within the framework. The roles are described at a conceptual level (ie. do not include design or implementation detail). Therefore, in reality there may be many positions within a given organisation which might fulfil these roles. Table 3 illustrates the alignment between role and level of abstraction or model type. It also highlights the key model attributes that each role is responsible to define or approve. Table 3 provides the enterprise architect with a conceptual framework for categorising actual roles and stakeholders for a given context.

THE ENTERPRISE ARCHITECTURE STEERING COMMITTEE

Most government agencies that have an enterprise architecture program will have a committee or board which oversees the implementation of the program and its initiatives. The level of influence the committee has will vary depending on the maturity of the organisation and its enterprise architecture program. In a mature enterprise the committee will include its most senior executive managers. In less mature organisations the committee is likely to sit within the IT section and be chaired by the CIO or CTO. Irrespective of the level of maturity every enterprise architecture program will require such a committee as it forms the point of accountability for program decision making. Most committees of this type soon discover that it is not possible to exercise all aspects of enterprise architecture governance. This is particularly so at the contextual and conceptual levels where the decision making typically has nothing to do with technology. Most committees require instead that evidence be provided of verification by business representatives of contextual or conceptual issues. The discussion in the following sections assumes the existence of a committee such as the Enterprise Architecture Steering Committee or similar.

Table 3. Governance roles

Model type	Purpose	Alignment attribute type	Governance role
Contextual	Requirements	• Goal • Requirements	Customer
Conceptual	Scope	• Objectives • Constructs	Sponsor
Logical	Design	• Design principles and assertions • Logical components and implementation criteria	Designer
Physical	Implementation	• Measures • Physical components	Implementer

THE DESIGN INTEGRITY GOVERNANCE ROLES

It is important to realise that the roles listed, although similar, are not the same as the roles associated with the horizontal views within the Zachman Framework. The purpose of the roles listed in Table 3 is to reinforce strong alignment between levels of abstraction within the design integrity framework. The roles are described in a generic or logical sense in terms of the various aspects of the design integrity framework to which they apply. The actual positions within an enterprise which might fulfil the roles will be determined by the nature of the entity of interest. Although most if not all the models within the design integrity framework will be developed by the enterprise architect, each model will have specific governance requirements that must be met before the architect can be sure that proper governance has been exercised. Each role and its responsibilities are discussed in detail as follows.

CUSTOMER

Purpose: To identify the purpose and requirements to be met by the entity.

Responsibilities: To approve the goal statement and requirements as documented within the contextual model.

Actor: This role represents any external stakeholder or recipient of the services or outputs from the entity of interest.

Within the design integrity framework the role of customer is responsible for clearly articulating and determining the purpose and requirements of the entity of interest. The concept of customer might equally apply to an agency CEO or alternatively service recipients or citizens in the wider public depending on the nature of the entity of interest. Customers might be directly involved in

the governance process in any number of ways. For example, the Enterprise Architecture Steering Committee may include customer representatives within its membership. Alternatively, in the private sector shareholders exercise a gross contextual level governance at a corporation's AGM. Similarly, within the public sector governance is exercised by the community through public forums, submissions and ultimately their vote at election time. For smaller internal change initiatives the customer role may be fulfilled by a functional area situated within an agency. Obviously however, it is sometimes not possible for the customer to provide direct governance. Nevertheless, in these situations there are a variety of customer feedback mechanisms (eg. questionnaires, complaints processes) that might be deployed or accessed by the enterprise architect to ensure that the requirements are sufficiently described and validated. Irrespective of the level of direct involvement of the customer the enterprise architect will need to demonstrate adequate validation of the goal statements and requirements described in the contextual model. This may require the architect to work with consumer or customer groups or stakeholders to specifically identify the goals and requirements. It is typically the validation of goal and requirements statements that is provided to the Enterprise Architecture Steering Committee for endorsement. Not providing sufficient priority to this role or opportunity for it to exercise governance frequently leads to the all too common scenario where solutions are identified well before for the problem is fully understood.

SPONSOR

Purpose: To set the objectives to be achieved by the entity of interest, and to identify the scope and constructs to be defined within the entity.

Responsibilities: To approve the objectives and constructs as documented within the conceptual level model.

Actor: Any position which has the ability to initiate change to the entity of interest in response to changes in purpose or requirements.

In practice this role is usually fulfilled by a senior position within an organisation. Nonetheless, any position can potentially fulfil this role where the position is responsible for defining the scope and objectives of the entity of interest. The development of objectives and definition of the constructs may in reality fall to the enterprise architect working in collaboration with the sponsor. However, the sponsor's approval of the objectives and constructs should probably be presented to the Enterprise Architecture Steering Committee prior to design work commencing.

DESIGNER

Purpose: To identify the design to be adopted to meet the stated objectives.

Responsibilities: To approve the logical model design principles and assertions. To approve the logical model components and implementation criteria.

Actor: Any position responsible for design (eg. Enterprise architect, business planner, engineer)

The enterprise architect is employed within most organisations to act as an authority on what constitutes good design. It is therefore, the role of the architect to provide approval of the design selection. The level of maturity of the organisation and its enterprise architecture program will determine the extent to which this is actually where the accountability for design decisions will sit. In less mature organisations some or all of this responsibility will be subsumed by the sponsor.

All too often this results in 'siloed' initiatives that are not well designed to support the wider context or purpose they are intended to achieve.

The designer role will determine from the logical and physical level models, a program of work to be completed to transition the entity from current to future state. The Enterprise Architecture Steering Committee oversees and monitors progress with this program of work.

IMPLEMENTER

Purpose: To instantiate the physical model.

Responsibilities: To provide or report measures as defined in the physical model. To ensure that physical components selected meet the relevant logical component implementation criteria.

Actor: Any position responsible for implementing a design (eg. project manager, builder).

There is an important hand-off between the Designer and the Implementer. The hand-off needs to include the logical model component implementation criteria. For a more detailed treatment of this issue the reader is referred to Phase G – Implementation Governance of The Open Group Architecture Framework (The Open Group, 2006) .

Although the Designer might determine which projects are required, it is not the role of Designer to undertake individual projects. The build process should be the responsibility of the Implementer. Ideally there should be very few design decisions left to the Implementer. The physical level model can be used to provide a 'bill of materials' to the Implementer. The implementation criteria for each component within the logical level model can also be used to provide guidance to the Implementer where there are a number of alternative physical components that might equally be deployed. In practice the development of the physical model is likely to be a joint collaboration between the enterprise architect and the relevant project managers.

While it is common to have a Program Delivery Committee or Board to oversee the coordination and implementation of a portfolio of projects, it is the role of the Enterprise Architecture Steering Committee to see that the hand-off between enterprise architect and project manager occurs and to track project completion in order to determine the status of transition. The implementer role has responsibility for providing the measurements as specified in the physical model which allow implementation to be tracked, and verification that the logical model and its design principles has been accurately implemented.

CONCLUSION

This chapter has outlined a design integrity framework which allows the enterprise architecture practitioner to readily identify a range of models required to fully describe and represent any entity of interest. The framework is centred around a set of definitions of four levels of abstraction. These definitions together with a set of defined alignment attributes provide a means for ensuring strong alignment between initial idea through to actual physical implementation.

The design integrity framework has been developed using the scientific method rather than the 'construction industry' as the underlying analogy or metaphore. Adopting such an analogy poses some interesting questions for the future maturity of the discipline of enterprise architecture. The adoption of a scientific paradigm would represent a similar shift as the adoption of Six Sigma (Pande & Holpp, 2002) was for the field of process improvement. The author believes that such an approach might represent a significant step away from the dominant and possibly too rigid engineering and construction industry paradigm. Such a shift suggests new processes or method-

ologies for undertaking enterprise architecture based on experiment and observation, and easier integration or collaboration with disciplines such as organisational psychology.

The final section in this chapter has attempted to identify the organisational roles required to implement the framework. The roles are discussed with reference to contemporary enterprises and government agencies in particular. By defining governance roles for each level of abstraction the framework provides a means for realising strong alignment between layers necessary to ensure accurate translation from idea to implementation.

REFERENCES

Ambler, S. W. (2002). *Agile Modeling: Effective Practices for Extreme Programming and the Unified Process*. New York, New York: John Wiley & Sons.

Beck, K. (1999). *Extreme Programming Explained: Embrace Change*. Boston: Addison-Wesley Professional.

Bernard, S, A. (2005). *An Introduction To Enterprise Architecture: Second Edition*. Bloomington, Indiana: AuthorHouse.

Bernus, P., Nemes, L., & Schmidt, G, (Eds.). (2003). *Handbook on Enterprise Architecture*. Berlin : Springer.

Betz, C. T. (2006). *Architecture and Patterns for IT Service Management, Resource Planning, and Governance: Making Shoes for the Cobbler's Children*. San Francisco, CA: Morgan Kaufmann.

Computer Systems Laboratory of the National Institute of Standards and Technology. (1993). FIPS Publication 183.

MacKenzie, C.M., Laskey, K., McCabe, F., Brown, P. F., & Metz, R. (2006). *Reference Model for Service Oriented Architecture 1.0*, OASIS Committee Specification. OASIS Open 2005-2006.

Pande, P., & Holpp L. (2006) *What is Six Sigma?*, New York, NY: McGraw-Hill.

Pólya, G. (1971). *How to Solve it: A New Aspect of Mathematical Method.* Princeton, NJ: Princeton University Press.

Porter, M. (1985). *Competitive Advantage: Creating and Sustaining Superior Performance.* New York, NY: The Free Press.

Simsion, G. (2006). *Conceptual, Logical, Physical: Clearing the Confusion.* The Data Administration Newsletter, No. 36. Robert S. Seiner.

The Open Group, The Open Group Architecture Framework. (2006) , Version 8.1.1, Enterprise Edition.

Tsichritzis, D., & Klug, A. (Eds.). (1978). *The ANSI/XWSPARC DBMS framework report of the study group on database management systems.* Information Systems, 3(3), 173-191.

Weill, P., & Ross, J. (2004). *IT Governance: How Top Performers Manage IT Decision Rights for Superior Results.* Boston, Massachusetts: Harvard Business School Press.

Zachman, J. A. (2005). *The Zachman Framework for Enterprise Architecture: A Primer for Enterprise Engineering and Manufacturing.* Zachman International, www.ZachmanInternational.com.

ENDNOTES

[1] Definition: an image, idea, or theory, esp. a complex one formed from a number of simpler elements. *Random House Unabridged Dictionary.*

[2] This term is defined in the following section.

[3] In this discussion the word performance is used in its most general sense.

[4] Coloured elements represent potential gaps in the logic of the models

Chapter IX
Policy Mapping:
Relating Enterprise
Architecture to Policy Goals

Dwight V. Toavs
National Defense University, USA

ABSTRACT

Few government executives can explain the enterprise architecture of his or her agency, and it is rare to find a political executive who is able to explain how their political objectives are furthered by a government-wide enterprise architecture (Holmes, 2007). This low level of awareness translates to enterprise architecture efforts that are often undervalued and under funded because the budget priorities of political and functional executives rarely include enterprise architecture. Unsurprisingly, many points of tension exist as the CIOs and architects work to translate political goals into resources and architectural plans supporting the agency's programs. This tension, between the rational orientation of enterprise architecture advocated by the CIO and the political nature of policy goals sought by executives, often puts a CIO at odds with his or her organization's political and functional executives. This chapter discusses that tension, and advocates that CIOs and enterprise architects develop a "Policy Map" to bridge the gap between the political and the rational perspectives. A policy map provides the "Purpose Reference Model" missing from present architecture models and policies, and visually portrays and communicates key relationships between policy goals and functional programs on the one hand, and the enterprise architecture and its implementing IT initiatives on the other hand. A well-crafted Policy Map is a visual reference for aligning resources, effort, architecture, and the policy goals of political executives.

PARADOX OF GOVERNMENT ORGANIZATIONS

We spend most of our lives in organizations. Although we rarely think about it, the formal organizations with which we are familiar are abstract concepts. We see the building and think of the organization; we see the people and think of the organization. Despite the physical evidence, the notion of the organization exists primarily in our minds. At this conceptual level organizations are created and exist in order to serve specific purposes that is, they are instrumental entities. Typically these purposes are defined by the organization's leaders, individuals who may be the organization's creators, its owners, or perhaps its managers. For example, businesses are created by an individual or a group of individuals with an idea, a product they wish to sell, or a service they wish to offer. These organizations are instrumental in helping fulfill the intent of their creators. Business organizations use rational approaches in the conduct of their activities, that is, approaches based on reasoning that produce goods and services as efficiently and effectively as possible. Therefore, it would be rational for the business owners to expect a profit from their endeavors, and to run their business organization as effectively as they reasonably can. They may even create and implement an enterprise architecture, one of the latest rational and comprehensive approaches to structuring efficient and effective organizational action.

Government organizations are simultaneously similar to and yet different from the generic business organization noted previously. Government and business organizations are similar in that government organizations also seek to perform their missions or fulfill their goals as effectively and efficiently as they can—in this respect government organizations are also instrumentally rational. But government and business organizations differ in that government organizations are established through a political process that seeks to satisfy political goals. They are established to serve political purposes and address societal challenges that have been defined and justified in political terms, challenges such as reducing illiteracy, improving air and water quality, or providing a level playing field for businesses seeking to sell their goods and services to government organizations. In working to fulfill political goals, government organizations are clearly political in character, yet in pursuing these political goals through rational organizational actions they are rational in nature and instrumental in pursuing their purpose. This dual nature of government organizations, that is, an organization that simultaneously serves a political purpose (has a "political face") as well as a rational purpose (has a "rational face") creates an organizational paradox – and a significant challenge for enterprise architects and the CIOs as they try to implement their enterprise architectures. This chapter encourages CIOs and enterprise architects to create a "Policy Map" for their organizations to help resolve this organizational paradox. Your "Policy Map" can effectively serve as the "Purpose Reference Model" for your enterprise architecture, and serve to relate political goals to rational organizational activities with the goal of educating political and functional executives, congressional overseers, managers and technical specialists, and citizens.

Organizational Faces

Depending upon where you are within the organization you may see one or the other of the "faces" of government organizations. For example, legislators, parliamentarians, elected and appointed political executives devote most of their attention to the "political face" of government organizations. This perspective views organizations as political and instrumental in nature, as mechanisms for turning political ideas into societal realities.[1] The political face of a government organization is turned toward society, and exhibits its organizational strengths and capabilities as resources to address societal problems and achieve politically defined societal goals. As a result the public typically sees the political face of the government organization, such as when they need assistance in recovering from a disaster; when they seek to qualify for some entitlement program; or when they are dissatisfied with the actions or decisions of an agency and seek to affix blame. Never far from this political view of government organizations are issues of competence and trust; of political promises and citizens' hopes and dreams; and of our individual and collective ideas for a desirable and democratic society.

Functional executives, managers, IT professionals and enterprise architects see the "internal face" of the organization and thus view the government organization quite differently. These professionals constitute the rational face of government as they perform the assigned missions and seek to achieve the goals of their agencies. From this rational perspective, the organization is a purposeful entity with people and processes designed to carry out the assigned mission, implement policies, and deliver desired results. Action oriented, this view of government organizations is focused on the rationality and objectivity needed to produce organizational results efficiently and effectively. The government organization, from this point of view, is an instrumental organization. As one would expect, this face is turned inward on the organization, and focuses on managerial concerns such as acquiring resources and creating organizational results through its money, people, processes, techniques, and technologies.

The paradox of governmental organizations arises from these seemingly contradictory states, where the organization is simultaneously a political entity and yet is an objectively rational entity. Government organizations are creatures of the political system, brought into being by political processes, and intended to solve societal problems that have been defined through the political process. In this way government organizations bear the deep imprint of political authority (Bozeman

and Straussman, 1990). Simultaneously these organizations are expected to apply their capabilities and resources in a rational and objective manner to perform their missions, be they to rescue the victims of disasters, to restore some semblance of public order in the affected communities, or to stimulate the economic recovery of the area. A failure to live up to this model of "citizen's expectations" results in harsh criticism. Critiques of government organizations in the wake of the September 11, 2001 attacks on New York and Washington, D.C. demonstrate the imprint of political authority on government organizations, and the need to affix blame when things go wrong. Comptroller General of the U.S. David Walker (GAO, 2002) noted that the government organizations under scrutiny had been established in a very different era to solve a rather different set of societal problems. Upon the logic of this argument legislators justified the need to create the Department of Homeland Security (DHS) in response to this new societal need. The DHS' new composite form aggregated capabilities from twenty-two previously existing government agencies to address the homeland security threat. Yet when Hurricane Katrina devastated the Gulf coast of the U.S. in August 2005, the inadequate response from the Department of Homeland Security brought an immediate and blistering critique.

Government organizations, departments, agencies, or bureaus, are assigned responsibility for implementing the policy pronouncements of political leaders, policies which may be either substantive or procedural in nature. Substantive policies outline the "what" of public policy, the goals and challenges in society that are being addressed. Implementation or procedural policies provide the "how" of public policy, and focus on translating political goals into organizational responsibilities and guidance to organizational leaders and functional experts. Policies are translated into the functional programs and the resources used by managers to create desired organizational outcomes. CIOs marshal the organization's information technology (IT) resources and capabilities to support these functional programs. Organizational effectiveness, and a program's ability to deliver results can thus be evaluated from two very different points of view, one of them substantive in nature and the other focused on procedural concerns. Political executives in government departments and agencies typically focus on political utility, that is, the ability of the organization and its programs to achieve the substantive and politically desired goals of the administration to which they owe allegiance. Career executives and managers of functional operations in organizations, on the other hand, are focused on rational goals and the procedural concerns necessary to achieve results – attentive to cost, schedule, performance and reliability concerns – the focus of contemporary management. And while each of these perspectives is equally valid, it should be emphasized that they originate from and are justified in vastly different terms. The challenge comes in trying to rectify the differing perspectives where the enterprise architecture is concerned.

ENTERPRISE ARCHITECTURE ENTERS GOVERNMENT

Information technology was introduced into the US Federal government through two venues, first as number-crunchers for agency financial managers, and later to support functionally-oriented programs. Functional programs initially acquired their own unique IT support systems, a process that simultaneously grew increasingly expensive and opaque to congressional overseers (Commission on Federal Paperwork, 1977). As information technology became increasingly ubiquitous it was obvious that the tipping point was approaching; by approximately 1986, agency programs were so reliant on information technology they could no longer function without their

integral IT support (Toavs, 2004). Early research in information systems focused on technical or systems architecture approaches (Zachman, 1987). Eventually functional stove-piping, cost, and duplication in program support arrangements led to demands for increased use of organization-wide information technology (Sowa & Zachman, 1992) to promote efficiency and effectiveness in organizations (Gore, 1993). By the mid-1990s process reengineering was a new skill requirement in IT organizations (Hammer & Champy, 1994), and new approaches to managing information focused on innovation (Davenport, 1992) and improving the processes central to functional programs. Additional efficiency and productivity gains could be achieved, it was believed, by crafting an enterprise-wide architecture for holistic management of an organization's information systems (Spewak, 1993). Building on these efforts, advocates of enterprise architectures convinced political leaders that architectures could deliver additional efficiency and effectiveness gains by eliminating arbitrary program boundaries, stovepipes, and organizational barriers. In 1996 all these innovations became agency requirements by their inclusion in the Information Technology Management Reform Act of 1996, later renamed the Clinger-Cohen Act of 1996, Public Law 104-106, in honor of its legislative sponsors. This substantive policy required agencies to implement enterprise architectures; they proceeded with caution as little in the way of implementation or procedural policy guidance was available or provided to agencies.

The notion of enterprise architecture in government was positively advanced by the government reform initiatives launched by the Bush administration in 2001. "Rather than pursuing management reforms based on a legislative agenda or on the recommendations of an expert commission, the Bush administration intended to implement a management reform agenda within the framework of existing legislation and policy. Electronic government was envisioned as the delivery mechanism, and enterprise architectures established the conceptual framework for efficient and effective service delivery." (Toavs, 2004, p. 299). The administration's e-government efforts began with an interagency task force (OMB, 2001) of knowledgeable individuals drawn from a wide representation of agencies. As the e-government strategy evolved and candidate initiatives identified, it became apparent that significant redundancies existed. In addition to the obvious redundancies across agencies, existing enterprise architecture efforts made few if any provisions for inter-agency activities such as resource sharing or information transfer (OMB, 2002). These insights led to developing an overarching Federal Enterprise Architecture (FEA) to which each of the agency enterprise architectures would relate. As noted in the Federal Enterprise Architecture home page, development of the FEA began in early 2002 and refinement of the architectural concepts, guidance and tools continues today (OMB, 2007a). The development and evolution of both substantive and procedural policies for the Federal Enterprise Architecture and its implementation in agencies has continued as conceptual knowledge and practical experience have advanced. The cur-

rent FEA Reference Model is shown at Figure 1 (OMB, 2007b).

The notion of enterprise architecture is a relatively recent innovation in thinking about organizations and government functions. Viewing an entire sovereign government as an enterprise, that is, the concept of a government-wide architecture is even more recent, and arises principally from the literature of disciplines associated with information technology, business, and management. Enterprise architecture concepts and practices are motivated primarily by the search for lower costs and additional profits through increased business efficiency and effectiveness. Traditionally the study of government organizations was informed by older and well established disciplinary perspectives such as organizational theory, political theory, and public administration. These traditional voices are notably absent from the discussion of enterprise architecture. Public administration and political science, the principal disciplines focusing on government, have largely ignored the potent effects of information technology (Toavs, 2004, p. 36) and enterprise and government-wide architectures. Rather, researchers in these disciplines appear to have narrowed their

Figure 1. Federal enterprise architecture reference model (OMB, 2007b)

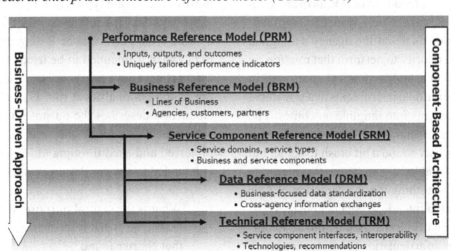

investigations to less-technical treatments such as transforming government via e-government. Topics such as the underlying structure or architecture of the organization and its information-technology enabled capabilities are not often researched and consequently not well understood in many parts of academia that study organizations. For example a text search conducted in July 2007 for the term "enterprise architecture" in the database of Public Administration Review articles for the past seven and one-half years (2000 to the present) resulted in only two articles; the search term "e-government" yielded thirty-two citations for the same time period. Anecdotal evidence suggests that mid-level program managers in government are aware of the concept of enterprise architecture; however even they often lack an understanding of the operational impacts of architecture concepts on their programs and on the agency's IT infrastructure. This uneven level of knowledge about enterprise architecture by political leaders, functional experts and managers, and academic researchers suggests that the traditional communications methods lack effectiveness and could benefit from new approaches.

The Missing Link: The Purpose Reference Model

A policy map is intended to help inform and educate executives, stakeholders, managers, and technical professionals about the agency's assigned mission, its authority to perform that mission on behalf of citizens, and its political goals – all in relation to the rational instruments that transform mission statements into tangible outcomes. The policy map is essentially a "purpose reference model." This may sound a bit brash to some, but in modern IT-enabled organizations the enterprise architecture is nothing if not a depiction of *how* the organization intends to conduct business.

Missing, and typically assumed to be understood by all, is an articulation of *what* your agency is doing and *why* it is engaged in that activity.

Your policy map is a visual depiction of your organization's charter - what your organization is charged with doing and why. It should show political goals and expectations on the one hand, and the relationships to parts of the agency's rational enterprise architecture and implementation plans, thus describing the connection between purpose, rationale, and instrument. A policy map such as this provides a number of instant benefits: first, and foremost, a policy map is explicit, giving reality to substantive legislation and procedural policies; secondly, a policy map is visual, giving memorable form, texture, and color to the agency's mission; thirdly, a policy map is descriptive of reality, showing what the agency does and why; and fourthly a policy map identifies important relationships thus allowing individuals to locate themselves and relate their contributions to the organization's overall effort. Placed in a public area, a policy map quickly becomes a conversation magnet as members of the organization inform themselves and their colleagues about the enterprise architecture; about the functional programs the architecture supports; about government and organizational policies; and about the political goals they work to support.

Readers will note the continued use of the term "policy map" rather than the term "purpose reference model." Using the latter term is tempting, however, terms are typically abbreviated in daily usage and the FEA reference model already has a PRM – the Performance Reference Model. A policy map is intended to be used at the level of a department, an agency, or at sub-agency level, not at the national level (the U.S. Constitution eloquently describes the purpose of the Federal government), therefore the term policy map is preferred and used throughout. The policy map is intended to answer three key questions:

- What is the central purpose of this organization, i.e., what is its charter, and where is that charter found?

- What substantive programs is the organization charged with managing, and what is the authority for those programs? portfolio
- Who are the key stakeholders and who are the program's clients?

Answers to these questions should clearly define and describe the mission and goals of the organization, identify its authority to pursue these activities on behalf of the county's citizens (and the limits of this authority) and authorize the use of public funds to pay for these activities, and identify the stakeholders and program clients in order to better the understand the priorities of various mission and program components.

POLICY MAPPING: WHY, WHAT, AND HOW

The second half of this chapter focuses on the why, what, and how of policy maps. First, a few reasons why one might want to consider a policy map are examined in light of the earlier discussion of the two organizational faces. This discussion examines several arguments for a policy map from a CIOs' or enterprise architect's point of view. Similarly, a few reasons why political executives might find a policy map useful are examined. Secondly this discussion defines and describes a policy map, examining its attributes and the "what" of a policy map. Reasons that visual approaches like policy mapping are considered effective approaches to communicating are discussed. Then thirdly the "how to" of a policy map is addressed. Here, I must be candid. I've not had the opportunity to craft a true policy map in real-world circumstances. I have however, used many of Horn's (1998) visual language techniques to communicate in a variety of other venues, and have experienced the challenges of trying to convey technical concepts such as enterprise architecture to government executives. The preeminent challenge one faces in creating a policy map is the considerable thought

and deliberation required to convey the precise idea and nothing more.

In any communication, knowing your audience and knowing the message you want to convey are essential to your success. Most CIOs and technical professionals working with architectures are comfortable with the objectivity, rational logic, and language used in information systems and enterprise architectures. They are, very likely, notably less comfortable in political and policy contexts characterized by politics, political coalition building, subjectivity, tradeoffs, compromise, and negotiation. This is not to fault their experience, dedication, or education, but simply to point out that the political side of government organizations uses a skill set and vocabulary quite different from that with which most CIOs and enterprise architects are familiar.

Why Create a Policy Map?

Chief Information Officers and enterprise architects in government organizations are confronted with at least a quartet of fundamental challenges, each of which has the potential for clashes between the rational approach of the enterprise architecture and the political orientation of the organization's political executives. First and foremost is the continual challenge of estimating, justifying, and finally acquiring resources. Secondly, CIOs must communicate with diverse constituencies to convince them of the usefulness of the enterprise architecture and supporting IT projects. Third, CIO's must demonstrate performance in their own organizations while simultaneously identifying the contribution IT makes to individual programs and to the organization's overall outcomes. And fourth, the CIO is challenged to create agile and "adaptation tolerant" capabilities in the face of changing circumstances. Let's examine these challenges in more detail.

The first challenge, acquiring and justifying resources, is an ever-present concern given the annual budget cycle of most governments. CIO's and their staffs typically work across at least three fiscal years as they plan, implement and operate IT capabilities for their agencies. The present year's budget is being executed through its projects and daily operations, even as next year's budget request is being estimated, justified, defended and prioritized. Simultaneously, planning is underway for projects and operations in the out-years, long-lead time infrastructure items, and consolidation projects identified in the architecture. A policy map can help sustain a concerted focus on the goals, and keep the multitude of necessary conversations focused on achieving desired organizational outcomes rather than becoming jargon-filled discussions about technical details. When reprioritization of effort and resources occurs, as it typically does in projects of this nature, the policy map can help focus attention toward those projects that contribute most to achieving both political goals and desired organizational performance and outcomes.

Secondly, CIOs have a responsibility to inform as well as educate organizational members about the role of information technology and the enterprise architecture in achieving desired organizational performance and outcomes. Since the CIOs' and architects' activities cut across all internal organizational units, they are expected to understand each of the agency's functional programs and the role and contribution of information technology in each program. They should be able to discuss the enterprise architecture, and its supporting IT projects, with people at all levels of the organization, helping individuals understand the relationship of their individual efforts to organizational effectiveness. As a result of the CIO and architect's policy mapping activities, IT professionals should increase their understanding of architecture implementation and supporting IT projects. Functional and program executives should more clearly understand how the architecture provides more effective and efficient IT support for their programs. And

political executives in the agency should better understand EA activities and be able to explain how their enterprise architecture contributes to achieving political goals.

A third fundamental challenge facing the CIO is to demonstrate that the enterprise architecture positively contributes to organizational performance and to achieving desired organizational outcomes. Simultaneously the CIO must demonstrate that his or her organization is performing effectively. While it is imperative that the CIO assist functional programs in improving their outcomes by innovative uses of information technology, that of itself is not enough; the IT organization itself must demonstrate the desired level of performance, and demonstrate innovative approaches to implementing the architecture and boosting the effectiveness and efficiency of the organization's programs. Again, the policy map can be effective by keeping all parties focused on and working toward producing the desired outcomes. Despite the different roles of organizational components, they all face the single imperative of working together to achieve the desired outcomes – a condition called strategic alignment.

The need to become agile and "adaptation tolerant," the fourth challenge, is a new requirement for 21st century organizations as they encounter a variety of challenges such as globalization (Friedman, 2005). While government organizations are more indirectly affected by global economic change than are their business counterparts, they face a parallel challenge of global political reform (Kettl, 2000) that challenges their relevancy and viability. Developing organizational capabilities that are agile and adaptable are the usual responses to these external forces of change. Frequently overlooked as a source of turbulence in government organizations, however, are the election cycles that go hand-in-hand with political executives' time-limited tenure. Frequent executive turnovers are a significant source of organizational turbulence. Agility and adaptation to a new leader or a new leadership team are important qualities for CIOs and program executives. Policy maps can help ease the steep learning curve facing new executives by identifying essential relationships between political goals and organizational actions. By familiarizing new executives with the policy map CIOs and program executives can demonstrate their support for their new political bosses.

The previous paragraphs have suggested some of the contributions a policy map can make from the CIOs point of view. From that perspective, a policy map can provide a resource focus; inform and educate members of the organization; support efforts to achieve alignment for performance improvement; and promote agility and adaptation in the face of external as well as internal organizational turbulence. As generically listed before, these benefits seem rather similar to the capabilities and insights political executives might desire of their organizational decision environments. In other words, a policy map may serve to not only convey the logic, approach, and intent of the rationally focused enterprise architecture, but may also serve broader politically oriented goals of the organization's leaders. Political executives certainly need to understand the challenges of resource acquisition, allocation, and prioritization in their agency and be able to relate resource requests to the goals and missions addressed. Informing, educating and communicating are leadership functions supported by policy mapping, however much of political executives' efforts in this regard might be expected to focus on external stakeholders and key players in political processes. Influence plays large in political environments, and policy maps provide strong visual illustrations of the desired "to-be" state articulated by the architecture, all intended to positively influence stakeholders. Intended performance improvements incorporated into the enterprise architecture can be depicted in relationship to the organization's mission, goals and political agenda. Lastly, well developed policy maps used in conjunction with an enterprise architecture can be used to create

organizational adaptability and agility, a significant asset to leaders involved in organizational change (Lawrence, Dyck, Maitlis, & Mauws, 2006). Knowledge of the structural and informational attributes and relationships displayed on policy maps can assist in creating and evaluating sophisticated scenarios of organizational change. And given that today's organizations were crafted in another era to address a different set of challenges, significant opportunities exist to reshape today's organizations to new purposes.

As CIOs address each of the challenges noted before, *resource acquisition, communication, performance,* and *agility,* they carry out an implicit translation in which they relate the context and technologies of functional programs and processes to the priorities and information needs of political executives. Skillful and successful CIOs perform this implicit "mental mapping" and translation in real time as they address their audience's concerns. Individuals less aware of organizational politics or less skilled at addressing issues in executive contexts, typically watch in awe as functional concerns, political issues, and technological details are addressed with seeming ease by seasoned CIOs. Such performances demonstrate that his or her success is not accidental. Rather, successful CIOs have taken the time and effort to understand the political or functional executive's interests, and have mentally mapped the relationships between the executive's interests and the CIO's knowledge of enterprise architecture and IT projects. He or she has already created a mental policy map representing the CIO's tacit knowledge of the relationships between executive and CIO environments. In order to make this knowledge more widely available and useable, CIOs and enterprise architects need to create explicit and visual policy maps, incorporating and displaying the wisdom of their implicit mental "policy maps." Such policy maps should become a component of the agency's enterprise architecture, be a standard feature of the organization's architecture presentation, and be converted to poster-sized hallway displays.

When included as part of the EA, a policy map has the potential to help all interested parties understand the translation of political goals into agency implementation actions enabled by information technology.

A Policy Map Shows Relationships

What exactly is a policy map? At its simplest, a policy map is and does what any map does – it depicts and describes relationships. A geospatial map of the Mid-Atlantic region of the US, for example, shows the relationship between Washington, D.C. and Philadelphia expressed in terms of distance and direction. Depending upon its properties, this map might also display terrain, hydrographic information, transportation systems, and points of tourist interest. Similarly, a policy map for an e-government application in the U.S. Federal government might show the relationship between the citizen-centered services goals of the President's Management Agenda and the Recreation One-Stop e-government initiative. It might show, for example the Department of Interior as the lead egovernment agency for this initiative and list each of the agencies collaborating to make Recreation One-Stop a successful egovernment initiative. It could depict how Recreation One-Stop is integrated into the department's architecture framework, and depending upon the level of detail desired, might show OMB's egovernment and security policies and how the policies are implemented in the initiative. By creating a policy map, one creates a line-of-sight between the political goals that are sought (the ends), and the processes and delivery mechanisms within the architecture that are designed to deliver citizen services (the means). Within an enterprise architecture, a policy map brings together the policies, procedures, and guidance that provide justification and rationale for the enterprise architecture and its implementing initiatives. In articulating policies and creating a clear view of accountability, a policy map provides significant

insights for functional programs and processes, and highlights the usefulness of EA efforts for political, functional, and technical executives.

The notion of a policy map is, of course, metaphoric. And to truly understand it, if the metaphor is a useful one, the attributes or "entailments" of the metaphor's "source domain" (the map) should transfer to the metaphor's "target domain" (the policy map) and help explain the nature of the target domain (Horn, 1998, p. 113). To illustrate the entailments of a map, Mark Monmonier's "How to Lie With Maps" (1996) is recommended. In a witty yet brutally truthful volume, Monmonier discusses maps and mapping as well as the ways in which maps both portray and distort reality. Since we desire to portray the intersection of a rational enterprise architecture with the reality of political executives, we need to be able to deal with both distortion and reality, as we understand and perceive them. "Maps have three basic attributes: scale, projection, and symbolism. Each element is a source of distortion. As a group, they describe the essence of the map's possibilities and limitations. No one can use maps or make maps safely and effectively without understanding map scales, map projections, and map symbols." (Monmonier, 1996, p. 5).

Transforming the attributes of a map – scale, projection, and symbolism – into their counterparts in a policy map completes the metaphor and lends some needed definition to the concept of a policy map. First, the attribute of scale focuses on describing the ratio of reality to representation. Inherent in determining scale is the question of what are the boundaries of the reality being represented? Does this policy map represent the enterprise architecture for the entire agency, or does it represent the architecture of a single functional program? Scale, in a policy map, identifies the portion of the enterprise architecture represented in that particular map. One might address the scale issue by representing only the top-most portion of the enterprise architecture, that part associated with the performance reference model. Scale can be indicated by a short descriptive sentence: "This policy map depicts the relationship of political goals and policy initiatives to the agency's performance reference model." While two other methods of stating the scale exist, ratios and graphs, they are less appropriate for policy maps.

Projection, the second attribute of a map, is the means by which the planet's three-dimensional surface is converted into a flat two-dimensional plane. This notion is analogous to the notion of "perspective" used in the information systems architecture framework (Sowa & Zachman, 1992, p. 601), Bernard's "EA Framework" (2004, p. 38), or the hierarchical set of five reference models that comprise the Federal Enterprise Architecture (OMB, 2007b) shown as Figure 1. Using the FEA reference models for example, the projection of a policy map might incorporate the Performance Reference Model (PRM) or the Business Reference Model (BRM), the two most likely policy map projections used to construct policy maps for use with political executives. Functional executives

are likely to be interested in both the PRM and BRM, with the BRM receiving perhaps greater scrutiny due to its relation to program activities as shown in Figure 2.

Symbolism, the third map attribute, is the system of map symbols, the mechanisms for encoding information on a map. Maps typically use three geometric symbols – points, lines, and areas – which can then be varied by size, shape, graytone value, texture, orientation, and hue (Monmonier, 1996, pp. 18-22). Most of use are quite familiar with the typical map conventions: points on maps typically denote towns or places of interest, with the size of the point providing an indication of the size of the town; lines typically denote roads, railroads, streams and rivers; size and hue (color) are added to provide a descriptive dimension to line symbols; and area symbols typically suggest contiguous areas, such as incorporated cities, parks, or specially designated areas. Descriptive richness is then added to map symbols by using size, hue, and texture. As shown on Figure 2, lines are used to show relationships

Figure 2. Policy map depicting scale and projection

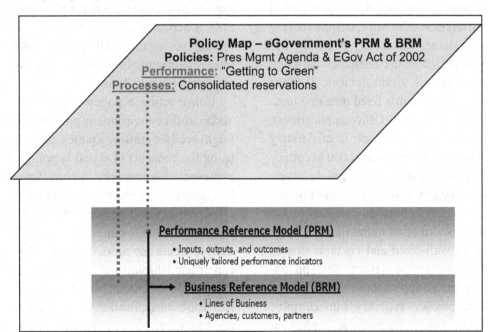

between political goals – shown as the performance initiative "Getting to Green" (Emery, 2003) – and the PRM portion of the enterprise architecture. Here the policy map illustrates the linkage between a political initiative and the relevant portion of the enterprise architecture, the Performance Reference Model. In the same manner, the goal of creating a consolidated reservation system for Recreation One-Stop is shown as a process related to a portion of the Business Reference Model. A side annotation could have listed the two IT projects planned for next year that will enable the process to deliver the desired outcome – a consolidated reservations capability. A note of cautionary is in order. It is important to remember that when creating policy maps, the map characteristics just described are not part of the enterprise architecture, but can be overlaid on a portion of the architecture to show the underlying relationships. In all cases, however, ensure you craft your enterprise architectures in accordance with extant guidance.

In summarizing the discussion of what constitutes a policy map, it is important to emphasize that a policy map is a means to communicate. Policy mapping uses visual depictions of relationships to aid communication between groups that have very different vocabularies, despite sharing a common language. Visual language combines words, images and shapes to communicate through four general types of visual devices: 1) icons are a simple graphic with a fixed meaning (e.g., toolbar icons on Microsoft Office applications); 2) concept diagrams use a simple to moderately complex graphic and a sentence or two to convey a single concept; 3) an information graphic, typically a page-sized illustration, combines images, shapes and text into a complete communication unit; and 4) an information mural that can range from poster to wall-sized and contains one or more information graphics (Horn, 1998, pp. 55-64). Visual language approaches have been used effectively to provide visibility into complex issues, to illuminate cross-boundary issues, to

keep discussions focused while surfacing various points of view, and to produce creative and non-intuitive approaches to persistent challenges. The few research efforts into the effects of visual language show interestingly positive results. Horn reports (1998, p. 234) a study conducted at the Wharton School of Business found that visual language aids decision making; makes a better impression; shortens meetings; promotes group consensus; and is persuasive.

Crafting Your Policy Map

Earlier we described successful CIOs as having an implicit mental model that allows her or him to (seemingly) effortlessly and effectively address the challenges and concerns of the political executives with whom they are dealing. Expertise, experience, judgment, and timing are all hallmarks of effective performance. Crafting and presenting a policy map that defines and illustrates the relationships between an enterprise architecture and political goals and objectives requires a stage-worthy performance. Know the context, the environment, and the message you are delivering; know your lines and responses to the likely questions; and practice your delivery until it becomes natural. Practice sessions with an audience are especially valuable, as their questions provide important clues to topics or concepts requiring greater clarity.

Constructing a policy map is not difficult. Today's office environment provides the tools one might need for crafting a policy map, especially if using the concepts of visual language. Graphics or presentation programs, such as PowerPoint can be effectively employed to create the content for a policy map, and newer versions of MS Word provide most of the same capabilities. Clip art can used to create any needed images, shapes can be constructed through the drawing features of both Word and PowerPoint, and text capabilities are native to both applications. Icons have been developed for many physical items and for some commonly used concepts. A remaining challenge is the lack of useful graphic representations of more complex conceptual constructs, those notions that do not yet have a defined visible form. Some conceptual constructs have been given generally recognizable form, such as the lighted bulb over a person's head to indicate an idea, or getting an idea, or a sudden new awareness. In some places this notion has been turned into an icon, using just the outline of a bulb to represent the idea. Other concepts, however, are a bit more difficult to visualize. Consider, for example, the concept of federalism which is important in egovernment applications and which may figure prominently in some enterprise architectures. Federalism is an agreement by which a central and superior state with prescribed powers is created from several states which retain limited powers in their own right. This concept is particularly interesting because it contains two sets of paradoxes, the first in the notions of sovereignty and dependency; and the second in the notions of exclusivity and inclusivity. These complexities notwithstanding, the preeminent challenge to creating a policy map

is the abstract thinking and contextual creativity to extract essential ideas and relationships, and then synthesize and present them a coherent manner. A notional policy map for "Getting to Green" is shown at Figure 3.

To summarize, a policy map expresses the relationships between political goals and agendas and the enterprise architecture. It is intended to bridge the gap between political goals and ideas and rational organizational planning. In form it is intended to be context dependent and visual, and like its geographical counterpart, has the attributes of scale, projection, and symbolism. Scale refers to the portion of the enterprise architecture represented in the policy map. Projection, or perspective, indicates the viewpoint within the hierarchy of architecture reference models. And symbolism is concerned with the presentation of information content. Policy maps can be created with standard office software suites using visual language constructs (images, shapes, and text) and communication units (icon, concept diagram, information graphic, and information poster and mural).

Figure 3. Notional policy map for "Getting to Green"

E-Government Implementation Policy Map

Goal: Get to Green in E-government on the President's Management Scorecard

Scale: Architecture for Recreation One-Stop

Perspective: Business Reference Model (BRM)

Symbolism: Overlaid on this portion of the architecture are line symbols showing traceability from the President's Management Agenda (E-Government initiative) through the Business Reference Model portion of the architecture (key processes) to the President's Management Scorecard. Folder symbols represent approved Form 300 Business Cases for projects that implement our architecture (expected completion 4QFY07).

This space contains architectural components annotated to show the policy goal traceability and the areas of ongoing projects. Clearly indicated is the timeline for "Getting to Green" by the end of 4QFY07.

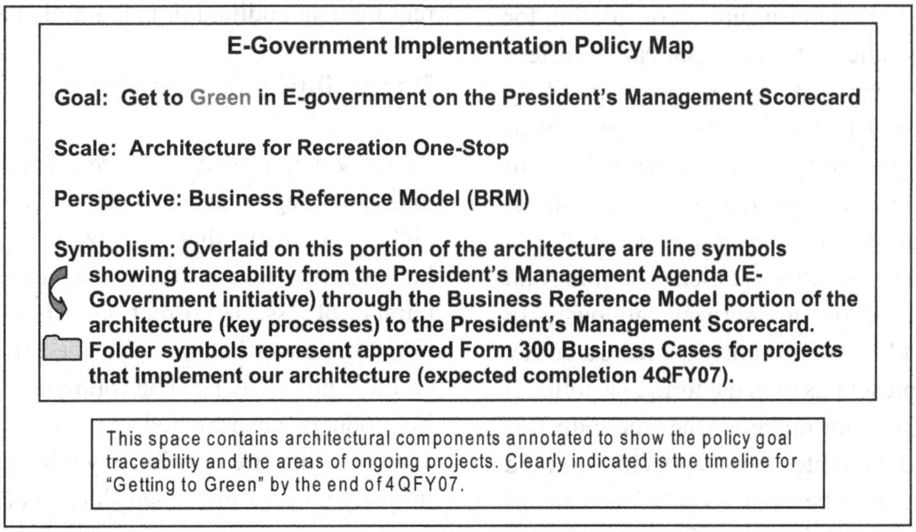

CHALLENGES TO POLICY MAPPING

Earlier we discussed a quartet of sound rational reasons to undertake policy mapping, citing the benefits and payoffs to the CIO and architect and highlighting the insights offered to political executives. However, human behavior is frequently other than completely rational, and in many instances is more like political behavior. Policy mapping at this time should be considered an experimental venture, with all the risks and rewards associated with experimental work. Some individuals will see the promise and payoff of a new idea such as policy mapping and be excited about exploring the possibilities of linking policy goals to organizational endeavors. Other individuals will be less able to see a payoff and instead will find it difficult to surmount what they perceive as the additional effort and the risky possibility of being less than successful. As excited as I am about the possibilities for strategic alignment that policy mapping offers, due diligence and responsible argumentation necessitate examining some of the difficulties one is likely to encounter.

Policy mapping as described here is a cross-disciplinary endeavor, in both an academic context as well as in an operational context. Researchers are unlikely to find much support or funding for conducting studies of the communications effectiveness of policy mapping. Operators are likely to be told to stick to doing what they know how to do and cautioned to "go through channels" with the intent of keeping this "idea guy" from contact with political executives. Secondly the challenge of crossing the line between rational planning and political goals is one to approach cautiously. In an ideal world, the opportunity to create a policy map would present itself in the form of a political executive expressing interest in the time and effort being expended on enterprise architecture. Skilled entrepreneurs may be able to arrange such an opportunity by collegial staff contact. A third challenge to policy mapping is more technical, in that policy mapping tries to bridge a "level-of-detail" gulf likely to raise analytic eyebrows. Whereas architecture analysis focuses on decomposition and fine-grained assessment, political analysis tends to be more holistic and rather course-grained by comparison. Critics using this argument may tend to unreasonably demand predictability and precision from qualitative and speculative political analysis, and fault such analysis as being messy and non-rational. A fourth criticism of policy mapping is that it is new and different and because of this is suspect. New ideas, like new adventures always face a wide array of obstacles, mostly from the established order. Closely associated to the newness objection is the fifth challenge. Here opponents cite the necessity to learn new skills and develop new processes, there being a dearth of training available for such activities. And of course this argument is absolutely right! Having disposed of these five arguments, opponents will now present you with their showstopper. You are likely to be told that, should you proceed with your policy mapping effort, you had better get it right the first time or you can kiss your career goodbye. Yet experience shows that new ideas and approaches do indeed survive and thrive. The notion of enterprise architecture was just such an idea in the late 1980s, yet by late 1996 it was a requirement codified in U.S. public law.

Possibilities to Consider

A policy map provides coherence and promotes understanding at the intersection of the enterprise architecture with other organizational mandates, both explicit and implicit. One can foresee a number of less than direct benefits to organizations that have their roots in the effort to craft credible policy maps. The following "beneficial by-products" are provided for your consideration, and since they are only loosely related, the order in which they are presented should not be viewed as particularly significant.

First, from a performance management point of view, outlining the relationship of political goals to architecture components and IT initiatives may help organizations to better define program success, a difficult proposition to describe in objective terms. The tough question, "what does success look like?" is brought more clearly into focus when policy ends are viewed in concert with the process-based means and the policy ideas that energize government activities.

The effort invested in crafting a policy map may help relocate the organization's effectiveness vs efficiency debate into a more productive venue. Whereas enterprise architectures in business organizations have a primary concern – efficiency – enterprise architectures in government organizations have several simultaneous and sometimes conflicting drivers. For example, US Federal acquisition policies are crafted to promote not only efficiency, but to also simultaneously create a level playing field for those offering goods and services to the government. Small business set-asides and programs to give preferences to minority and women-owned businesses are driven by concerns over equity, not efficiency. Success, as noted previously, may mean promoting such societally desirable programs at the expense of efficiency.

Cross-agency collaboration can be both eased and enhanced through the use of policy mapping. Most political goals cannot be achieved by a single organization operating in an agency-centric manner. The need for multi-agency collaboration, essential for achieving effective outcomes is more easily seen when looking at the big picture provided by a policy map. Even the most parochial executive must at some point admit that the broad policy objectives can only be achieved by collaborative effort. The lessons of Hurricane Katrina and the rebuilding of New Orleans provide useful examples.

Federalism, collaboration that extends vertically to link national endeavors with sub-national and local endeavors serving the same purpose, can benefit greatly from policy mapping. In these instances policy maps should be created at each level of government to ensure end-to-end compatibility. Policy mapping could be especially useful to e-government efforts in the fields of health care, housing, and welfare.

Policy maps provide an opportunity to educate professionals within the IT organizations, functional programs, and within the political layers of agencies. It is becoming increasingly important that all professionals understand enterprise architecture and how it both affects and benefits political initiatives, functional programs, and the CIO's office. A creative and enlightening policy map enlarged to the size of an information poster or information mural could provide a hallway conversation focus that benefits all members of an organization.

And lastly, communication with executives is enhanced when policy maps provide a point of reference around which to array architectural and functional initiatives. Policy maps provide essential references to overarching goals, creating a point of departure for discussing decisions, tradeoffs, and implementation planning.

CONCLUSION

This chapter has posited the idea of creating policy maps to help bridge the gap between the politically oriented face of government typified by political executives, and the rational face of government as typified by the organization's Chief Information Officer, its enterprise architect, and its enterprise architecture. A policy map in concept allows one to stretch a string from the political goals and agendas through the enterprise architecture to the implementation and the organization's desired outcomes. This concept is an extension of the practice of ensuring requirements traceability, the extension being into the goals and agenda items of political leaders.

Many, while acknowledging the positive benefits of policy maps, may be tempted to forego the investment in time and research needed to develop useful policy maps. A variety of excuses will be presented, including all of the following: a) we assume that the policy environment is static and will remain so; b) we assume political executives will embrace the architecture because it is required by statute; c) we assume the architecture will be funded because it is required; and d) we hope that someone else will recognize the importance of the architecture and take steps to get the necessary resources to develop and implement it. Rather, CIOs and architects might do well to view policy as being nearly as dynamic as information technology, and with a similarly short "product cycle."

As this is written in the fall of 2007, intense political maneuvering is already underway for the election that will be held in 12 months. The political cycle for the 2008 election in the US is well underway. Between mid-November 2008 and the end of June 2009 a sea change will occur at the top of most Federal agencies. A new crop of political executives, full of energy and ideas on what is broken and what needs fixing will replace today's political executives. As the CIO or architect you will eventually prepare a series of information briefs and position papers for the new crop of political executives. Consider developing a policy map to demonstrate how the work you've been doing will help achieve the political goals your new executives have pledged to support.

REFERENCES

Bernard, S. A. (2004). *An introduction to enterprise architecture*. Bloomington, IN: AuthorHouse.

Commission on Federal Paperwork. (1977). *Information resources management: A report of the commission on federal paperwork*. Washington, D.C.: Government Printing Office.

Bozeman, B., and Straussman, J.D. (1990). *Public management strategies: Guidelines for managerial effectiveness*. San Francisco, CA: Jossey-Bass, Inc.

Davenport, T. H. (1992). *Process innovation: Reengineering work through information technology*. Boston, MA: Harvard Business School Press.

Emery, G.R. (2003, July 21). It ain't easy getting to green: Most agencies making progress but management goals yet to be achieved. WashingtonTechnology. Retrieved Oct 25, 2007 from http://www.washingtontechnology.com/print/18_8/21225-1.html

Office of Management and Budget. (2001, July 18). Citizen-centered e-government: Developing the action plan. (OMB Memorandum 01-28). Retrieved June 10, 2007, from http://www.whitehouse.gov/omb/memoranda/m01-28.html

Office of Management and Budget. (2002, February 27). E-government strategy. Retrieved June 10, 2007, from http://www.whitehouse.gov/omb/inforeg/egovstrategy.pdf

Office of Management and Budget. (2007a, July). FEA consolidated reference model document version 2.2. Retrieved June 10, 2007, from http://www.whitehouse.gov/omb/egov/documents/FEA_CRM_v22_Final_July_2007.pdf

Office of Management and Budget. (2007b, July). FEA reference model mapping quick guide (FY09 budget preparation). Retrieved June 10, 2007 from http://www.whitehouse.gov/omb/egov/documents/FY09_Ref_Model_Mapping_QuickGuide_July_2007.pdf

Friedman, T.L. (2005). *The world is flat: A brief history of the twenty-first century*. New York, NY: Farrar, Straus and Giroux

Gore, A. (1993). *Creating a government that works better and costs less: The report of the national performance review.* New York, NY: Penguin Books.

Hammer, M. & Champy, J. (1994). *Reengineering the corporation: A manifesto for business revolution.* New York, NY: HarperBusiness.

Holmes, A. (2007). *Gov. Perdue knows IT.* Government Executive. Retrieved August 8, 2007, from http://blogs.govexec.com/techinsider/archives/2007/08/gov_aligns_it_with_government.php

Horn, R. E. (1998). *Visual language: Global communication for the 21ˢᵗ century.* Bainbridge Island, WA: MacroVu.

Kettl, D. (2000). *The global public management revolution: A report on the transformation of governance.* Washington, D.C.: Brookings Institution Press.

Kettl, D. (2002). *The transformation of governance.* Baltimore, MD: The Johns Hopkins University Press.

Lawrence, T. B., Dyck, B., Maitlis, S., & Mauws, M. K. (2006). The underlying structure of continuous change. *MIT Sloan Management Review,* (2006, Summer), 59-66.

Monmonier, M., 2ed. (1996). *How to lie with maps.* Chicago, IL: University of Chicago Press.

Sowa, J. F., & Zachman, J. A. (1992). Extending and formalizing the framework for information systems architecture. *IBM Systems Journal.* 3.

Spewak, S. H. (1992). *Enterprise architecture planning: Developing a blueprint for data, applications, and technology.* New York, NY: Wiley.

Toavs, D. (2004). *Pixelating policy: Issue transformation in real and virtual worlds.* (Doctoral dissertation, Virginia Polytechnic Institute and State University, 2004). Retrieved June 10, 2007, from http://scholar.lib.vt.edu/theses/available/etd-12222004-094635/

U.S. General Accounting Office. (2002). *Homeland security: Proposal for cabinet agency has merit, but implementation will be pivotal to success.* (GAO Publication No. GAO-02-886T). Washington, D.C. Retrieved June 9, 2007, from http://www.gao.gov/new.items/d02886t.pdf

Zachman, J. A. (1989). A framework for information systems architecture. *IBM Systems Journal.* 3.

ENDNOTE

[1] Throughout this chapter the U.S. Federal model of governance is used. Within the U.S. context this key principle was established in the Constitution and articulated best by James Madison. Madison, Kettl notes, "built a political theory in which administration was subservient, in practical operation and in theoretical understanding, to political power" (2002. p. 38).

Chapter X
Enterprise Architecture Management and its Role in IT Governance and IT Investment Planning

Klaus D. Niemann
act! Consulting GmbH, Germany

ABSTRACT

A comprehensive enterprise architecture management has strategic and operative aspects. Strategic tasks cover the identification of appropriate fields of activity for information technology (IT) investments in accordance with business strategy and portfolio management. Enterprise architecture management is cross-linked with other IT management processes and delivers the necessary information for a sustainable governance. The continuous analysis of the IT landscape, the deduction of measures for optimization and its controlling also belong to the tasks of architecture management. Standards for development and infrastructures are made, e.g. reference architectures and a "book of standards", whose implementation is overseen by solution architects throughout the operative architecture management.

INTRODUCTION

In many companies the role of architecture management amounts to nothing more than drawing up plans of the actual IT landscape and putting them at the disposal of target groups like IT management, project leaders, or IT steering committees. Sometimes there is also the role of a project- or solution architect, who designs appropriate architecture concepts for single projects. Thus, architecture management concentrates on the modelling of the actual status and, through project support, on the accompanying of change processes evolving from the business.

Yet, are there no other big opportunities for a more comprehensive version of architecture management?

- Could the actual model not serve as the basis for a target-oriented evaluation with which weaknesses in the grown IT landscape can be identified? (s. section 5.2, Figure 8)
- Could this as-is model not also serve a better controlling of a company's IT investments? (s. section 5.2, Figure 9)
- Could there be standards and guidelines for transformation processes evolving from the business which guarantee an efficient development, maintanance, and safe operations? (s. section 5.3.1)
- Finally: is it not possible to cross-link the work of solution architects with planning tasks more tightly? (s. section 5.4)

By dealing with these questions this chapter tries to show approaches for the development of a more comprehensive enterprise architecture management

BACKGROUND

Enterprise Architecture Management

Enterprise architecture (see Figure 1) is a structured and coordinated collection of plans for the design of the IT-landscape of a company,

- Which represent in various details and views,
- Focused on special groups of interest (e.g. managers, planners, clients, designers)
- Different aspects of IT-systems (e.g. data, functions, interfaces, platforms, networks)
- And their embedding within the system (e.g. goals, strategies, business processes)
- In past, present, and future specifications (Niemann, 2006).

Enterprise architecture management combines all those processes, methods, tools, and responsibilities which are necessary to make things work, to ensure that IT-systems do just what they must do – cost-efficient, smoothly, and elegantly. Simply said: architecture management is a process resulting in enterprise architecture.

Enterprise architecture management is the instrument with which to run the household: to cul-

Figure 1. Enterprise architecture

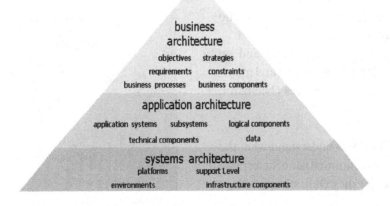

tivate application- and infrastructure landscapes, maintain and improve the value of existing assets, seamlessly integrate new components, adjust everything and make it work. "Housekeeping" is in high demand when budgets for new prospects decrease!

This continuous analysis of application- and infrastructure portfolios belongs to the tasks of an enterprise architect. For this the ongoing maintenance of the enterprise architecture model is indispensable. On this basis weaknesses can be identified and potentials for optimization detected, then measures can be taken and incorporated into change processes. For an enterprise architect this means to focus his work on these requirements and consider enterprise architecture as a means of IT-governance. In this context enterprise architecture

- Must generate transparency and be understood by the management; be the RADAR of the Chief Information Officer (CIO) and a management information system,
- Must be analytically useable and derive new information from known facts, must react on new demands, be flexible and, better still, actively prepare for changes,
- Must open perspectives on the future; may not only be a static representation of the actual state, but must be the basis for scenarios and plans for the to-be,
- Must be realizable and operatively effective, and with methods, organisation forms and architecture management tools strongly support the tranformation of strategy into operative reality,
- Must be measurable and binding and an effective basis for the controlling and monitoring of strategic IT-measures (Niemann, 2005).

An analogy will help us understand what the key steps are for construction and use of enterprise architecture. As for a journey we firstly need maps and documentation of the area we want to travel in. This would be the enterprise architecture which consists of elements of existing models: business process models, organization models, IT-product lists, IT infrastructure catalogues, and the like.

As soon as we have the maps for our travel area we want information on places of interest, hotels, road conditions. Likewise, an enterprise architecture displays its true value if not only seen as a static picture but if actively used for analyses and as the management information system of the CIO.

The analysis of our maps is followed by the planning of the route. The analysis of enterprise architecture, too, must be followed by the development of planning scenarios which address detected weaknesses and show problem solutions. The "to-be image" and transformation planning are then incorporated into the project portfolio and program management to realize the strategic plan. Within the implementation of the transformation plan enterprise architecture functions as a governance instrument.

An initial version of the enterprise architecture emerges from a project with a duration of 3-6 months and must then be imported into an ongoing architecture management process.

An enterprise architecture designed for immediate use in the context of an IT-governance program thus originates from a cycle of docu-

Figure 2. The enterprise archi-tecture cycle

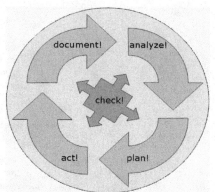

mentation, analysis, planning, imple-mentation, and control (see Figure 2).

An enterprise architect focuses on the continuous devel-opment and optimization of the application- and infrastruc-ture landscape oriented at the business strategy. On the one hand architecture management as an enabling process sup-ports the demand processes of order- and portfolio man-agement. On the other hand, as a governance instrument it has standardizing and controlling effects on the supply processes of project-, program-, and service management.

Architecture management is responsible for the planning, development, use, and maintenance of enterprise architecture. It organizes associated processes, controls and monitors the development. Therewith architecture management describes procedures for the close interlocking of business, IT-applications, and IT-infrastructure.

Architecture management is concerned with:

- The strategic processes for documentation, analysis, and planning of enterprise architecture
- The operative processes for the consistent implementation of enterprise architecture, the conformity check against reference architectures, and defined infrastructure "shopping carts",
- The definition of documentation procedures,
- Analysis- and planning methods,
- Evaluation procedures,

- Tools and their integration into the tool-box,
- Procedural methods and responsibilities,
- Key figures and controlling.

Architecture management has both an operative and a strategic dimension. Documentation, analysis, and planning of enterprise architecture on a strategic level must result in measures which are to be operatively implemented into projects or line functions.

Here, too, architecture man-agement must give support, e.g. develop reference archi-tectures in the fields of ap-plication- and system archi-tecture, monitor their use and implementation, ac-tively help, get things started.

IT Governance

Searching for definitions of the term Corporate Governance, we find (e.g. in Germany's Corporate Governance Code) (DGI, 2003) that corporate governance contains essential legal directives to the direction and supervision of listed companies and defines international and national standards of good and responsible business management. The board of directors is responsible for the appropriate risk management of the enterprise Furtherand develops the strategic alignment of the business and provides for its implementation.

Good and responsible management, strategic focus of the company and its implementation, appropriate risk management and –controlling: the top managers of our companies are committed to

Figure 3. Operative and strategic architecture management

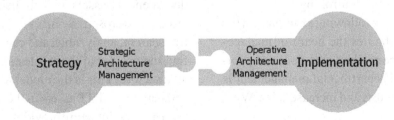

these principles. Facing this list which IT-manager would not react enthusiastically if asked for his contribution to the realization of these principles? And surely he would indicate that information is the key to success of the corporate governance program, that all kinds of management need transparency, that each implementation of strategies needs a clearly defined course of action developed on the basis of all pieces of information, that risk management and –controlling can not be realized in the dark but only in the light of a transparent basis of information. And he would finish his remarks by adding that it is no other than IT which, with the help of its information systems, produces the light without which no controlling, navigation, monitoring or correction of course would be possible.

To follow governance principles also means to make informed decisions. Governance presupposes planning, organization, controlling, and monitoring – in short: management – on the basis of comprehensive information.

But what exactly does the IT department do to support the other specialist departments in their planning-, controlling-, and monitoring tasks and to contribute to the implementation of corporate governance principles? It delivers precisely this comprehensive information: with data warehouse systems, business intelligence suites, management or executive information systems. The management of the departments use just these systems to improve the business, save costs, open new markets, develop or place new products. With the information provided by these systems they support good and responsible corporate management, the strategic orientation of the company and its realization, an appropriate risk management and –controlling.

Let´s have a look at following example: On the basis of their key figures the board of management finds that one product area does not operate profitably. The departmental management is required to reduce costs and increase sales. What

are they going to do to meet these requirements? The first action will probably be an analysis of the current status to generate a detailed list, e.g., of the distribution of costs across the departments, or of the series of operations, or to thoroughly understand the distribution of costs across the distribution channels. The figures for this analysis are obtained from the information systems of the company. IT-systems will likely play an important role in the controlling of the measures derived from the analysis.

Thus IT plays a significant role in corporate governance issues. This is often demonstrated by legal specifications such as the Sarbanes Oxley Act, Section 404 which make high demands on internal company controlling and therefore on the IT. But what about governance of the IT department itself?

Let´s have a look at another example: The management board decrees cost savings which for the IT department mean a budget decrease of 15%. Now our CIO is in a similar situation as his colleague in aforesaid example. Which IT system can the CIO use to generate an initial analysis as a preparation for this strategy? Where do we find information on IT applications, IT infrastructure components, their dependencies on the business (organization units and business processes), and which in addition to this identifies and makes analyzable the costs, risks, ongoing projects and available IT staff? Does the IT department deliver the key information for the implementation of corporate governance for all other company areas but has no own tools to develop and control IT governance processes?

Where do we find the management information system of the CIO? Where is the model which documents IT assets with all their dependencies, effects, and cross-references in a way that they are transparent, analyzable, and can be planned? We find the answer to these questions in enterprise architecture. This is the model which documents and networks all IT assets in the necessary form; enterprise architecture provides support for analysis and planning indispensable for an effective IT governance.

The installation of an IT governance program asks for measures on three areas of activity: processes, organization, and information (Mandler, Niemann and Henning, 2007). Typical topics of these areas are:

Process

- Networking of IT management processes
- Business–IT Alignment
- Workflow
- Result types and templates
- Quality Gates
- Ways of decision making (monarchic, dual, feudal, or federal structures)
- Stakeholders
- Use Cases

Organziation

- Bodies
- Roles (task, competence, responsibility)
- Escalation- and steering committees
- Communication (acceptency, commitment, perforation)

Information

- Goals and strategies
- Focus (scope)
- Assessment and benchmarks
- Transparency (dependencies and effects)
- Information model and tool environment
- Weakness analysis (e.g. heterogeneity, complexity, cost drivers, value creation)
- Standards and reference architectures
- Principles, compliance rules & policies
- Decisions
- Metrics and KPIs

All three areas of activity of IT governance are addressed and supported by the implemen-

tation of an enterprise architecture model and the development of an „enterprise architecture practice" within the company.

The IT Governance Institute (2000) defines IT government as follows: "IT governance is under the responsibility of the board of directors and the management and is an integral part of company management. IT government consists of leadership, organization structures and processes which ensure that IT supports the company strategy and goals. IT governance ensures that

- The expectations on IT are fulfilled,
- IT-resources are continuously planned, controlled, and optimized,
- The performance of IT is measured
- And risks are minimized."

So this is about effectivity, efficiency, and reliability. To do the right things correctly and reliable. Enterprise architecture provides the necessary overview, the understanding for the relation of company goals, business processes, technical requirements, projects, IT applications, IT platforms, and IT infrastructure. It interconnects these elements, demonstrates effects and dependencies, documents costs, risks, availabilities, stability, and a lot more attributes.

But enterprise architecture can do significantly more: it can not only document a given situation, but also delivers procedures for the analysis of weaknesses. Where are the cost drivers in the application landscape? Where are redundant development technologies? Where the support of business processes is inadequate or redundant? This as-is analysis is the basis of an effective IT governance process and, as part of corporate governance, indipensable.

What is the next step after the analysis? It is the planning and implementation of measures. Enterprise architecture helps us plan, it is the basis for the development of planning scenarios in which alternative ways of IT application portfolios are evaluated. Enterprise architecture therefore is a central instrument of any kind of governance program. How could we lead, direct, and control without knowing where we stand, how the route looks like and where it leads to?

IT Investment Planning

The point of IT investment planning is to direct IT budgets onto the right areas, i.e. to ensure the effectivity of investments. Finance management supports IT investment planning by defining, administering, and monitoring IT cost centres. From our experience IT investment planning is often equated with project portfolio management, which - usually annually - balances business requirements with the budgets available for the projects. To this end projects are e.g. evaluated regarding their monetary and strategic importance for the business. The monetary importance is derived from the business case of the project, the strategic significance is derived from the support this project provides for the actual business strategy, e.g. an impact on the improvement of the market position in relation to the competition.

On this basis projects are positioned within a port-folio, for example (see Figure 4), where the ex-pected project costs are indicated by the size of the symbol, too. The allo-cation of available budg-ets on projects which are economically and strate-gically important results in a "red line" and the assignment of those pro-jects which are above/right of this line in the portfolio.

The term IT investment planning used here has further meaning, though. The IT budget as a whole covers significantly more than just the part which is available for new projects and controlled purposefully and according to business strategy by the project portfolio management.

An examination of the distribution of costs of big IT areas helps to find out how big the share of the whole IT budget needed by portfolio management is to ensure a target-oriented investment to the benefit of the business.

Figure 5 shows an exemplary distribu-tion. As in recent years for many eco-nomic fields a significant reduction of new developments as opposed to main-tenance has been obvious, this example on development assumes 30% correc-

Figure 4. Project portfolio (example)

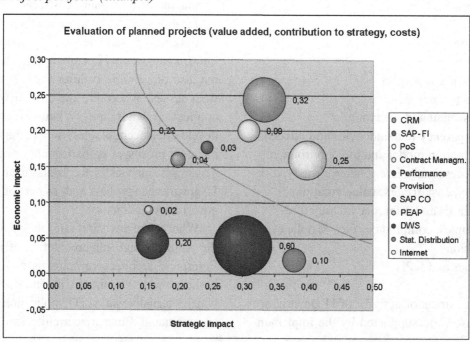

Figure 5. Distribution of IT costs

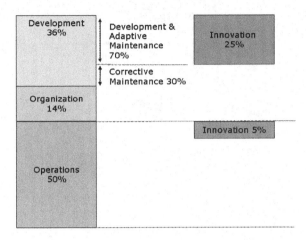

tive maintenance and 70% for new de-velopments and adaptive maintenance.

If we assume that the business invests a share of 10% on innovations of technology projects, for example, we find that only about 30% of the whole IT budget is spent on real innovations. Only this share is used to increase the value of the IT for the business.

Portfolio management concentrates on the evaluation of IT investments in new projects and sometimes also directs part of investments into adaptive maintenance. This then depends on the scale of maintenance activities. Often enough, though, the controlling of adaptive maintenance, i.e. the adaptation to changes of business require-ments or legal conditions, is done by dedicated maintenance activities.

Usually, investments in corrective maintenance and the operation of the existing landscape are not included into investment controlling through portfolio management or similar concepts, but are seen as must-investments. But is it not especially this grown landscape which is full of technical challenges and therefore a true cost-driver?

ENTERPRISE ARCHITECTURE, IT INVESTMENT PLANNING, AND GOVERNANCE

Primary Objectives

How can we ensure that while planning our IT initiatives we address the right fields of activity, that means pushing those activites which optimize the contribution IT to the business value? How can we ensure that our IT systems, our develop-ment and operation processes run optimally, i.e. cost-efficient, well-performing and without fric-tion? How can we ensure that the expectations on IT are continually and safely met, namely that processes are continually supervised, measured, and monitored?

The subject of enterprise architecture managment is to identify the right fields of activity, to support them appropriately, and to continually accompany the process and monitor it. The overall objective of enterprise architecture management: to do the right things efficiently and reliably (see Figure 6).

Figure 6. Use of enterprise archi-tecture man-agement

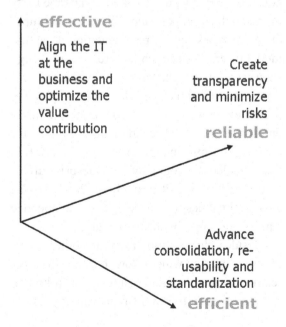

Enterprise architecture creates transparency and control-lability of IT transformation processes. It identifies the proper IT services by expert knowledge and technically driven application portfolio management and directs IT investments for maintenance and optimization into the correct fields of activity ("housekeeping"). To do this efficiently heterogeneous structures within the applica-tion- and technology portfolio must be consolidated and successful solutions must be standardized and re-usable. Governance requires reliability and accountability, transparency of IT assets and –processes. This serves risk management and compliance, increases the safety of the development and supply of applications. The use of enterprise architecture management therefore can be evaluated by its impact on the dimensions effectivity, efficiency, and reliability of IT.

Figure 7. Cluster map

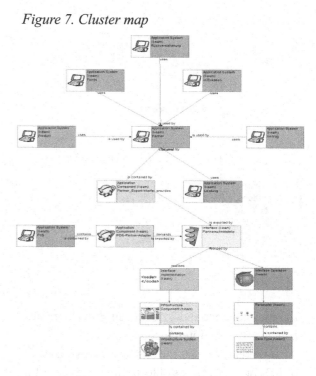

Finding the Right Fields of Activity

An important task of architecture management is to design and cultivate the as-is model of enterprise architecture regarding purposes of analysis and planning in a suf-ficiently current status. The analysis of the actual landscape indicates potentials for optimization and is thus the basis of the application portfolio. There are a number of figure types for the representation an actual model of enterprise architecture. Figure 7, e.g., shows a so-called cluster map in which application systems and their interfaces are graphically presented. Such displays can highlight many enterprise architecture attributes relevant for analysis, for example in terms of colour. Often this is called "cartography" of enterprise architecture (Matthes and Wittenberg, 2004). Costs, availabilities, business criticality, and compliance can be examples for such at-tributes.

Besides cluster maps there are other forms of representation which allow to establish direct relations to the supported business. A well-known sample for such a form of representation is the "business support matrix" (see Figure 8), which e.g. juxtaposes the main processes of the organization with the main services provided by the organization within a matrix (Matthes and Wittenberg, 2004; Niemann, 2006). The supporting applications are then entered into the matrix and may be coloured regarding cost of production or maintenance, availability, compliance or indicating white spots, for example. Often instead of the main services organization units or locations are juxtaposed with the processes.

The business support matrix offers the possibility to set application systems in direct relation to supported business processes and their importance for the business, or to services and their volume share. With this it becomes possible to operationalize the IT support for the business. For the analysis of enterprise architecture this form of representation has been well tried. The placement of application systems within such a matrix allows the analysis of costs, of the technical coverage regarding gaps or redundancies,

Figure 8. Business support matrix (example: public administration)

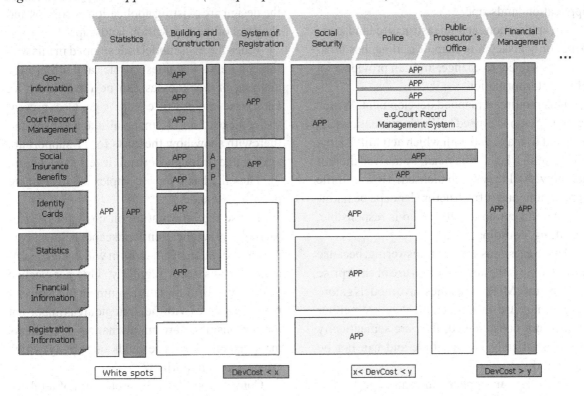

and to examine interfaces regarding complexity or heterogeneity.

The placement of application systems in a structured application landscape is based on references between the architectural levels business and application. Application systems support business processes and the handling of products. The visualization of a product/process matrix already enables some evaluation, but even more can be achieved by a documentation of the application landscape in a data bank and/or a special tool for the modelling of enterprise architectures.

Such a documentation of the application landscape is an efficient basis for analyses and sets the stage for the optimization of existing enterprise architecture. The visualization of the application landscape is also prerequisite for navigation and communication. In projects, steering committees, coordination meetings: everywhere a visualization is necessary. Our daily practical experience

with projects shows that such visualizations are often drawn up according to situation, but rarely comprehensively across different areas of interest, and not combined with necessary maintenance and adaptation processes.

As soon as the objects in our application landscape are mapped one can begin with the evaluation regarding costs, redundancies, gaps, and breaks. Did we analyze the number of interfaces, run scenarios? Do we really use the data of the application landscape or do we merely look at it instead of into it?

The representation of the application landscape needs attributes. If the objects within the enterprise architecture have no attributes the analysis of the application landscape will not result in a proper statement. Costs, strategic impact, dependencies, performance indicators, efforts, age, capacities – all these are sets of information required for a complete enterprise architecture, and to be able to analyze them throughout the references in the application landscape.

An application- and infrastructure landscape is not only a sketch or map. It is alive, has attributes, is subject to change, and can provide a lot of useful information.

This requires a planned development. Which references do we need? Which evaluations do we want to make and with which actuality? How often? Which key figures shall be derived thereof and how shall they be condensed? How will the application- and infrastructure landape be maintained and kept up to date? Who is responsible, partaking, coordinating?

These questions are worth answering, because the outcome is the key to the real use of enterprise architecture. Most companies have models galore but can not use them because they are neither aligned nor consolidated; they are semantically and syntactically incompatible and can not be compared.

To design an application landscape by answering the aforementioned questions requires a syntactic and semantic alignment, a synchroniza-

tion of the models, and referencing. Sources for the design are existing application portfolios and sketches of the application landscape.

When the as-is model is developed in this way the coherence becomes visible and a thorough analysis of weaknesses can be made. Such an enterprise architecture can, e.g., also present the context of an IT financial management and therewith show how the costs for IT support are aggregated through several levels (see Figure 9). Thus the basis for a complex IT investment planning is made.

To use the information on costs for the cartography of application landscapes allows, e.g., the identification of hotspots in which high maintanance costs occur regularly. This perspective (see Figure 10) allows the alignment of IT investment procedures with the strategic areas important for the business: are maintenance investments made exactly for those fields of activity which are presently important?

Considering that only about 20% of total application costs throughout the complete life cycle are spent on the initial development, but 80% on

Figure 9. Finance management in enterprise architecture

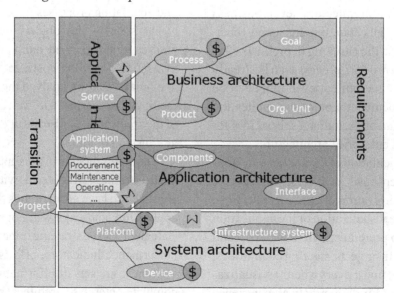

Figure 10. Maintenance & integration costs

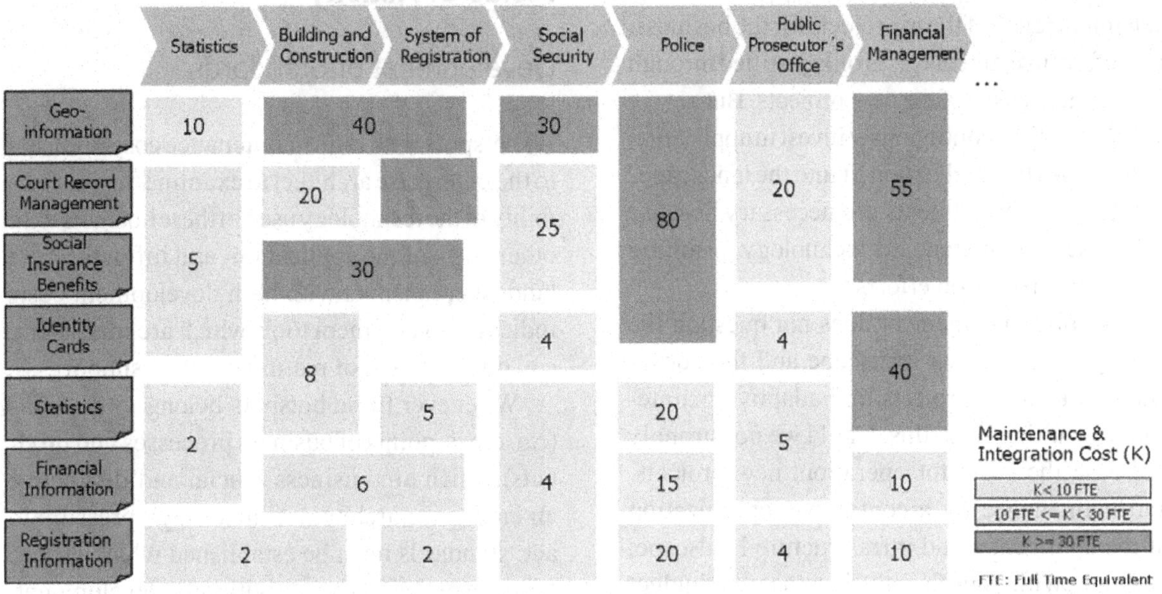

	Statistics	Building and Construction	System of Registration	Social Security	Police	Public Prosecutor's Office	Financial Management	
Geo-information	10	40		30				...
Court Record Management		20			80	20	55	
Social Insurance Benefits	5	30		25				
Identity Cards		8		4		4	40	
Statistics	2		5		20	5		
Financial Information			6	4	15		10	
Registration Information		2	2		20	4	10	

Maintenance & Integration Cost (K)

| K < 10 FTE |
| 10 FTE <= K < 30 FTE |
| K >= 30 FTE |

FTE: Full Time Equivalent

cur-rent maintenance and especially inte-gra-tion, this question becomes more important (see Figure 11)

Can we ensure with the help of known and existing mechanisms such as IT portfolio management that IT invest-ments are made in coherence with the business strategy?

Portfolio management as the interface between business and IT is responsible for the decision from which projects the company derives the most benefit – and which therefore must be implemented. Can portfolio management ensure that IT investments are made for those fields of activity which support the strategic direction of the whole company?

The following situation shall serve as an example: the annual evaluation of the project portfolio defined n new projects. Each of these projects has calculated its own individual business case, is conform to the strategy, and was allocated with a budget. In a grown application landscape we can presume that each of the n projects must deal with integration issues with other existing systems. Let's say that the application system ABC shown in Figure 11 will have to be integrated into m projects (with m <= n), and that each project must invest a share of its budget into the integration with ABC. The investment for the integration of ABC is thus the result of $I_{ABC} = \sum P_i (0 < i <= m)$. The total investment of all m projects is ensured by portfolio management. But all these projects invest parts of their budgets into application ABC and thereby contribute to the 80% maintenance and integration costs shown in Figure 11.

Figure 11. Lifecycle costs of an application system

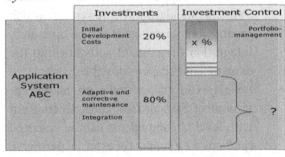

Portfolio management did not assess investment I_{ABC} against system ABC but against the actual importance of the m projects for the business. Therefore investment I_{ABC} is only justified through the business cases of the new projects. But are we really willing to continuously invest in application ABC? Does the application fit into the landscape? Maybe these investments are necessary because ABC uses a non-standard technology, resulting in higher integration efforts?

Portfolio management does not question the quality of the grown landscape and the consequences for new projects and adaptive maintenance resulting from this. Could we not strongly decrease the costs for operation, new projects, and mainanance by a continuous optimization of the application and infrastructure landscape, and therewith significantly increase the budget for innovation?

We have already looked upon the role of architecture management in the context of housekeeping. Why is housekeeping so important? In many economic sectors IT has become a primary means of production: banks, insurance companies, energy brokers, and telecommunication companies produce their services and products almost exclusively with IT; logistics, transportation and trading firms highly depent on IT.

Thus the grown application- and infrastructure landscape has an immense value for a company and must be taken care of and maintained just like real assets and means of production. This facility management for the IT department requires planning and controlling: do we still invest in the proper IT production facilities, or do we maintain applications, interfaces and development technologies for products which are no longer the focus of our business strategy? Do we have badly adapted or developed IT systems which disturb smooth business operations or prevent the establishment of new systems and thus have a negative impact on the time to market?

The Right Support of the Right Fields of Activity

Development of Standards

As hotspots with high maintenance costs indicate to the enterprise architect to examine the compatibility of the technology used in these hotspots with other parts of the application- and infrastructure landcape, hotspots with high development costs indicate development tools which are inefficient, e.g. due to a lack of maturity or bad support.

Whenever these hotspots belong to domains (e.g. cross-points of business processes and products) which are business crucial and distinctive an enterprise architect is under high pressure to act: standards must be established which ensure efficient and effective activities for development, maintenance, and operations.

Often standards are generated bottom-up: a book of standards is developed which lists products and technologies for development, maintenance, and operations. Sometimes we find additional information on products, e.g. life cycle attributes, which tell us how long a specific product is usually supported. It is even more effective to classify products regarding the level of support they are given by the company. To determine technological cornerstones such levels of support or standard levels are defined for available or planned components of the book of standards (see Figure 12):

- Level A is supported as produc-tion- and development environ-ment.
- Level B is supported as produc-tion environment. Standard software systems which require components of B can be oper-ated. Integration of standard software into the existing land-scape is possible.
- Level C is only supported as production environment. Standard software only conform with level C components can be operated (perhaps with support of external partners),

Figure 12. Standard level

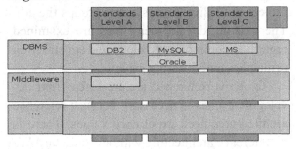

but must be run on its own and can not be integrated into the existing landscape.

There are quite a few more standards, though (see Figure 13):

*   Superior standards: principles, rules, and IT decisions
*   Standardization of ap-plications by an infrastructure portfolio ("shopping cart") in the book of standards
*   Standardization of development and sup-ply of applications through reference ar-chitectures

The following example of reference architectures shall help to clarify the use of standards in architecture management.

Setting Standards Through the Development of Reference Architectures

Hardly any company can keep open all options, can support all conceivable principles, master all possibilities of software architecture design: that would be too complex and expensive. It makes sense to have guard rails, make commitments, exclude options. It makes more sense to define reference architectures. A reference architecture is a construction pattern for software systems which defines principles for

*   The creation of components and levels and their responsibilities,
*   The vertical and horizontal structure of a system,
*   The design of interfaces and their intercommunication,
*   The integration of surfaces,
*   The integration of components and services, e.g. error management, reporting, workflow.

A specification of a reference architecture contains the resources necessary for its implementation such as the infrastructure for development,

Figure 13. Standards

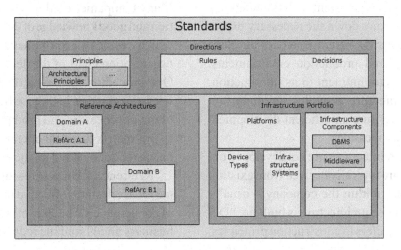

testing, and operation, as well as skills and procedures (e.g. data saving, deployment). Heuristics to fulfill functional and non-functional requirements and for development costs, dates, and risks also belong to a reference architecture.

Usually there are several reference architectures for a company. The popular vision of just the one target or reference architecture for a big company could in practice not be realized. The requirements on back office systems, mobile distribution support, Web applications, production controlling or dispositive systems are too diverse. Also, the business scenarios which serve as the basis for system development differ too much. Usually several reference architectures are needed because just one can not serve all business areas, products, and distribution channels of a complex company. So do not keep open all kinds of options for development but use an instrument of defined reference architectures which is target oriented at the business!

A reference architecture delivers construction plans for new systems. To define such construction plans one can fall back on patterns for software development; reference architecture itself is a pattern for the design of whole systems. To this belongs the determination of development technologies to be used and of tokens from the shopping cart of system architecture.

Reference architecture is an extract of the complex diversity of all thinkable principles for the design of software systems. Thus a reference architecture narrows down the necessary expert knowledge, limits the heterogeneity of development-, testing- and production environments. Once there is a commitment to its introduction, reference architecture provides an important contribution to ensure an efficient development and supply of applications.

Reference architectures are not developed out of the blue but are typically derived from existing developing lines within the company – usually while an enterprise architecture is built up. "Development line" refers to construction principles, development tools, and infrasctructure used in a project or application system or groups thereof. The existing development lines are examined regarding common technology and construction principles, and differing criteria.

To derive reference architectures from development lines is necessary because reference architectures need experience values. There is no reference architecture without heuristics! We need this experience to check architectural drafts and choose the reference architecture appropriate for a concrete task, and to be warned in time if threshold values, e.g. of transaction rates or availiabilities, are exceeded. We also need these heuristics to assert governance into the operative environment. Also, conformity checks are based on experience values.

Each reference architecture is tied to an operational scenario, for example mobile sales support, development of Internet portals, back office services. A reference architecture describes a technical solution pattern for such an operational scenario and defines the principles on which a company builds and supplies application systems which support this operational scenario. From a technical perspective the term "architecture domain" is often used to describe the fields in which the construction principles necessary for a specific operational scenario are specified in a reference architecture.

How are operational scenarios identified? Many companies do this with a sense of proportion and good knowledge of the technical incidents which result in requirements on IT. Often an organisation chart of the departments is helpful. One procedure for the methodical derivation of operational scenarios is based on the juxtaposition of major processes and products of the company. In this matrix fields for operational scenarios can be easily defined and analysed.

Reference architectures and operational scenarios are the most effective instruments in terms of convergence. The step-by-step convergence of business and IT and the reduction of heterogeneity and complexity require governance extending to the operational level. The things defined in an application portfolio are operatively implemented by the use of reference architectures. Operational scenarios and their reference architectures generate the basis for compliance checks.

Usually, with the outlined procedures, reference architectures providing the necessary heuristics are derived from existing development lines. But reference architectures can not always be de deduced from existing development lines, sometimes new ways have to be found. The standardization of reference architectures must not slow down innovations. When a reference architecture does not become obvious, an architecture planning must be carried out within the framework of the project or a pilot study. In the context of this architecture planning and based on sytem requirements and conditions several architecture scenarios must be developed and evaluated. In these cases new development lines are drawn, assumptions are made and supported by prototypes, and pilot projects will be made.

If a new development line proves successful it will enable the fulfillment of expectations, because a new reference architecture will emerge from this. Only after a successful implementation of at least one system a reference architecture for this operational scenario can be derived, and the experience with it is then taken into account for the application portfolio. This is why one should always refer to experience when developing reference architectures. One needs information on volumes, performance, availability, reliability, scalability, number of users, and security. To a certain extent the experience gained out of one´s own company can be used, too. Information exchange with other users, architecture management days, congress reports, and benchmarking can be the sources. Yet, for a reference architecture heuristics are imperative!

There are other sources for the development of new reference architectures, new technical impulses, and innovation:

- While examining project specific architecture drafts an architecture board finds gaps in the builiding of reference architectures and orders or initiates the testing of a new development line, which is then, after a possible modification, included into the number of eference architectures.
- The planning of strategic application portfolios leads to the realization that there are fields to which no reference architecture can be applied. In this case, too, the trying out of a new development line and its inclusion into the number of reference architectures must be initiated.

Both cases presuppose that there is a department in charge of the project. Any architectural development solely motivated by technology remains unfocused.

The examples show that reference architectures play a role in various contexts of architecture management processes:

- Architects of operative software make use of reference architectures as patterns for project work.
- Within the framework of evaluating architecture drafts – be it in a project, review, or by an architecture board – reference architectures serve as a measure. Without them there would be no reference figures for the usefulness of architecture drafts. Only a reference architecture which has already proven its value for a defined and documented number of requirements, e.g. quantity structures, allows us to evaluate another architecture draft.
- Reference architectures are used in the context of application portfolio planning to determine the kind of "building" for a lot which is empty or in need of refurbishment. Thus the prevalence of reference architectures can already be specified during the planning of application portfolios.

Then requirements e.g. regarding needed qualifications can be derived, and human resources development and staff planning are provided with another planning basis.

- The specification of reference architectures is accompanied by the determination of components of the "shopping cart". The total of all infrastructure components needed for the implementation of reference architectures is the actual shopping cart for development and production. Development lines no longer enforced eventually need further infrastructure components, but these find production support only until the development line is ended. Other infrastructure components may be supported with the productional help of external partners.

Reference architectures belong to most powerful instruments of enterprise architects: they deliver standard patterns for the controlling of new developments and maintenance. They are based of efficient development technologies based of a set of tools reinforced in the infrastructure portfolio. They deliver the initial acceleration for development projects and provide guidance for the solution architects. Also, they define a standard which can be checked on the conformity to the architecture.

Controlling of the Standardization Process

The controlling of the standardization process prevents the enterprise architect from slipping into the role of a policeman enquiring into the conformity with regulations which are inadequately specified, communicated, and supported. How can we focus the process of development and maintenance of standards and ensure that the necessary standards for development, maintenance, and operation are available for precisely those areas in which IT investments result in a high contribution to the business success? Especially in big IT organisa-

tions with many and diverse requirements the enterprise architect in charge is faced with the question which areas he should focus on. Ideally, standards are created for exactly those functional domains which are currently important for the business strategy, and which then can ensure an efficient development and efficient operations.

An example shall clarify this: Let us assume that a public IT service provider pursues the strategy to gain market leadership in terms of providing statistics. The objective is to create a statistics department which later on shall act as a service provider for several public organizations. Thus the IT support for the domain of processing statistics becomes very important (see Figure 14 and Figure 15). This domain needs standards for development, maintanance, and operation: the reference architecture for data collection and processing of statistics must be derived from the experience values of existing systems. The book of standards must be maintained and advanced accordingly, and solution architects, project managers and developers must be made familiar with these standards. The strategy of our IT service provider is to enter a market segment in which the price, i.e. the costs of statistics processing, determines the position of a company.

The service provider wants to modify its business and be more cost efficient in commodity issues than the competition. Figure 16 shows a rating matrix with a positioning of the service provider's strategy in the upper left quadrant.

The industry specific mapping of technologies to matrix cells within this matrix supports the development of standards conform with the business strategy.

Thus in addition to the bottom-up catalogization and classification the standardization can be made top-down.

For our example Figure 16 repre-sents data warehouse technologies in the upper left quadrant, which should be included with high pri-ority into the standardization proc-ess in accordance with the business strategy of the services provider. With

Figure 14. Diverse systems and technolo-gies within functional domain (example)

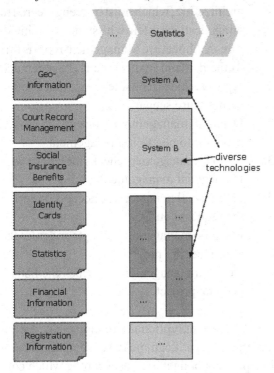

Figure 15. Standardization within func-tional domain through reference archi-tecture (example)

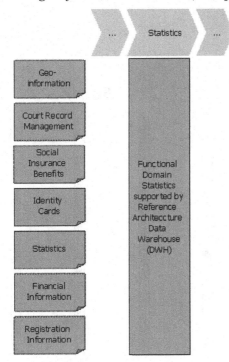

Figure 16. Technology standardization priorities based on business strategy

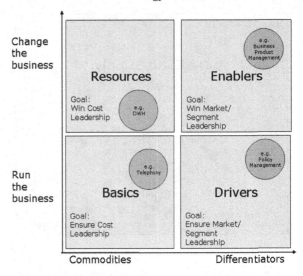

the help of this rating matrix depicting technologies which are to be standardized, the enterprise architect ensures that at first those standards are established which support the development and operation of business critical ser-vices.

To Support the Right Fields of Activity Right and Reliably

The measures derived from the running analysis of the application- and infrastructure landscape must be implemented. This presupposes that the enterprise architect is able to launch these housekeeping project out of his office in the IT department. Herefore an independent housekeeping is needed – or a "jump on the bandwagon" of project portfolio management.

What do we need to establish such a housekeeping process as a major part of strategic architecture management, and as primary task of the enterprise architect? We must classify architecture management into the context of IT management processes. Demand-, supply-, and enable-proc-

Figure 17. Big Picture of IT-Management Processes

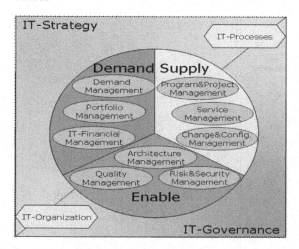

esses must be categorized and cross-linked into the big picture (see Figure 17).

In this big picture we will find the connection between architecture management and port-folio management, which allows the enter-prise architect to initiate housekeeping pro-jects (see Figure 18).

The process (simplified here) is run by following steps:

1. Architecture Management has identified an application system with non-standard architecture, which must be reengineered to an application system with standard architecture. Architecture Management reports this to the demand management. This demand report includes a business case and a rough architecture scenario.
2. Demand management presents a project proposal to portfolio management.
3. Porfolio management checks the budget with IT financial management.
4. IT financial management accepts or denies the requestd budget.
5. Portfolio management accepts or denies the housekeeping project.
6. Demand management launches the housekeeping project.

There are exceptional situations, e.g. during a merger, when it can make sense to allocate an independent budget to housekeeping which covers the consolidation measures. Then it can be regarded as a strategic action for renovation and optimization rather than being subject to portfolio

Figure 18. Initialization of housekeeping project

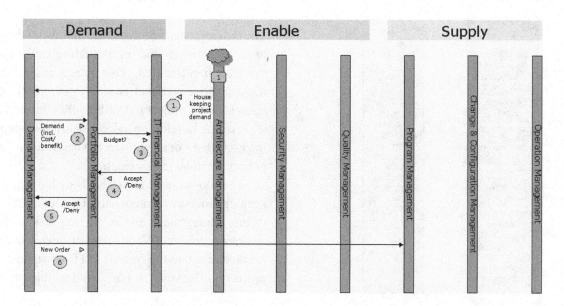

management. Usually, though, the housekeeping business case initiated by the enterprise architect should prevail against other business projects.

As soon as architecture management is cross-linked with the other IT management processes and the enterprise architect is able to directly launch housekeeping projects the measures in progress must be supported. Standards such as infrastructure portfolio or reference architectures must be included in housekeeping activities. This is the task of solution architects, which pursue the operative architecture management processes.

The office of the enterprise architect is in charge of the identification of the right fields of activity and for the definition of necessary optimization measures. Also, by the portfolio of standards it delivers the required guidance for the implementation, which must then be accompanied by the solution architects. Thus, the enterprise architect is responsible for the strategic architecture management process, which must go hand in hand with the operative architecture management of the solution architects.

The teamwork of strategic and operational architecture management is key for the reliable implementation of the strategy into stable and functioning IT systems.

CONCLUSION

In the given context, the importance of architecture regarding impact and focus is increasing. The road trends from IT architecture to enterprise architecture: to develop, standardize, plan, and controll architecture (see 19).

Driven by requirements, the development of architecture is based on projects. Primarily efficiency and security benefit from this: in the reusablility, initial acceleration, reduction of set-up times through conventions, patterns, frameworks, and industry standards.

The standardization of architecture is concerned with the conception of shopping carts for infrastructure, and reference architectures for the development. This requires a cross-project perspective. Here, too, the immediate use of architecture lies in efficiency and security. Yet, the standards set the stage for a business-based application portfolio, the objective of which is IT alignment throughout the business.

Architecture planning requires an analysis of weaknesses of the IT landscape. First steps are analysis and mapping: among others, heterogeneity, complexity, gaps, value creation, costs must be analyzed to obtain a basis for planning. Application portolio is focused on the wish to optimize

Figure 19. The growing importance of IT architecture

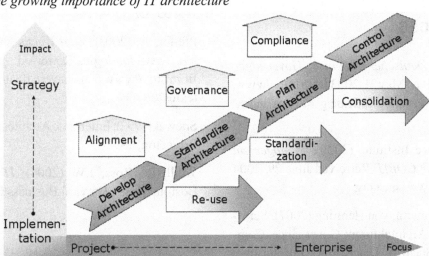

the application- and infrastructure landscape regarding the technical quality and orientation at the business.

The business oriented and strategy driven controlling of architecture requires an all-embracing transparency and operationalization. Measurability through key performance indicatiors, compliance checks, embedding into IT management processes, and the value oriented optimization of the IT portfolio are the building blocks of a strategic architecture management which is business focused.

The short programme is the alignment of IT the business sectors, and as the freestyle event a CIO will continuously take over the responsibility for the process optimization thoughout the corporation.

Such a strategic architecture management has not in view single project architectures but an enterprise architecture which makes transparent the connections between objectives, strategies, business processes, IT services, and platforms. For informed decisions such a navigational help is called for, so that enterprise architecture becomes the information system of a functioning IT governance. In a comprehensive IT planning process ensuring an effective use of means architecture management and portfolio management act complementary – guided by IT governance.

REFERENCES

DGI. (2003). *Deutscher Corporate Governance Kodex*. Retrieved May 21, 2003 from http://www.corporate-governance-code.de/ger/kodex/index.html.

IT Governance Institute. (2000): *Management Guidelines for COBIT*. Retreived June 29, 2004 from http://www.isaca.org

Mandler, Niemann, von Henning (2007). Servi-ceorientierte Architekturen: Governance, Compliance und Security. Duesseldorf, Euroforum.

Matthes, F., Wittenburg, A. (2004). *Softwarekarten zur Visualisierung von Anwendungslandschaften und ihren Aspekten – Eine Bestandsaufnahme*. Retrieved December 19, 2004, from http://wwwmatthes.in.tum.de/de/main.htm.

Niemann, K. (2005). IT Governance and Enterprise Architecture - Impact of IT cost reduction on innovation power. *The Journal of Enterprise Architecture*, 1 (1), 31-40.

Niemann, K. (2006). *From Enterprise Architecture to IT-Governanc*e. Wiesbaden: Vieweg.

ADDITIONAL READING

Benson, R.J., Bugnitz, T.L., Walton, W.B. (2004): *From Business Strategy to IT Action*. New Jersey, N.J.: Wiley.

Keller, Wolfgang (2004): Perfect Order versus the Timeless Way of Building, Lecture at the EAI Congress sponsored by TU Berlin 2004 (Internet download from http://www.sysedv.tu-berlin.de, December 2004)

Lutchen, M.D. (2004): *Managing IT as a Business*. New Jersey, N.J.: Wiley.

Niemann, K. (2007): Enterprise Architecture: From Business Strategy to IT-Service. *SAP Info*, 143, 33-35.

Pfeifer, A. (2003): *Zum Wertbeitrag von Informationstechnologie*. Retreived June 24, 2005 from http://www.opus-bayern.de/uni-passau/volltexte/2004/34.

Spewak(1992): Enterprise Architecture Planning, Princeton, 1992

Weill, R., Ross, J.W. (2004): *IT Governance*. Boston, Mass.: Harvard Business School Press.

Chapter XI
The GEA:
Governance Enterprise Architecture–Framework and Models

Vassilios Peristeras
National University of Ireland, Ireland

Konstantinos Tarabanis
University of Macedonia, Greece

ABSTRACT

Departing from the lack of coherent and ready-to-use models and domain descriptions for public admin-istration, we present here our effort to build a set of generic models that serves as a top-level, generic and thus reusable Enterprise Architecture for the overall public administration domain. We have called this set of models Governance Enterprise Architecture (GEA). GEA has deliberately remained technology independent and following the Model Driven Architecture approach, GEA constitutes a computationally independent model for the domain. GEA has been derived from multi-disciplinary influences and insights and identifies two broad modeling areas, called governance mega-processes: Public Policy Formulation and Service Provision. These two, together with the object versus process perspective, form a four-cell matrix that defines four modeling areas for the GEA models. To populate these cells with models we use a challenging metaphor: we model the society - public administration interaction as a discourse to identify important elements and functions of the governance system. Until now, a large number of services has been modeled using GEA and more recently, an extended modeling effort has started with GEA being chosen for use by a national EU-country project. GEA can be also used as a knowledge infrastructure for applying semantic technologies. In this line, it has been used for creating a public administration specialization of a formal Semantic Web Service ontology, namely WSMO.

1. INTRODUCTION – MOTIVATION

In the era of a highly networked world, public administrations (henceforth: PAs) worldwide are facing similar types of problems and challenges:

- Re-inventing government in a client-focus approach
- Improving performance & quality through measurements
- Changing organizational boundaries and structure
- Building partnerships with the private sector
- Delegating decisions and responsibilities to independent agencies
- Globalization & competition
- Information Technology (IT) enabled services

The use of IT to facilitate the major efforts of reorganization, modernization and reinvention of governance has proven not to be a simple task. There is an increasing pressure on PA organizations to manage information systems and information technology as an enterprise key capital resource (Tapscott & Caston, 1994). IT-based solutions need to overcome a series of negative PA specific characteristics in order to add value to the administrative outcome:

- High complexity of the administrative procedures since many actors, many interests, and many goals are intertwined.
- Sparse, hierarchical (vertical) and low quality communication amongst PA agencies, leading to "stovepipe" or "legacy" systems both organizationally and from an information viewpoint.
- Diverged views, definitions and terminology for the same piece of information.
- Vague business processes.

Through historical analysis, we conclude that contemporary PA systems have gradually developed a great degree of internal differentiation in order to cope with a turbulent and complex external environment. However, this progress was not supported with the required level of integration, through the development of adequate internal PA interfaces amongst agencies. The result has been a highly fragmented administrative space. In addition and despite major changes in PA size, output and culture during the last century, the external PA-society interface remains mostly the same. Thus, we identify a dual communication /integration problem:

- Internally among PA agencies and
- Externally between PA and its external environment.

This has been called the "dual PA integration deficit" (Peristeras V. & Tarabanis K., 2006). Related to this, a clear business need for all PA systems emerges:

In order to manage the volume and diversity of social needs and at the same time avoid fragmentation, dissolution and a legitimacy deficit, PA systems should be reengineered and a paradigm shift of today's modus operandi should be introduced in order to facilitate the necessary PA internal and external systemic adjustment. Specifically, PA systems should develop advanced internal and external interfaces to address the dual PA integration deficit; that is, to achieve internal integration at the administrative intra- and inter- agency level, external integration with society.

Thus, the need for inter- and intra- organizational exchange of information becomes indispensable: PAs must shift the proportion of resources dedicated to maintaining existing stovepiped systems to architected systems focusing on enterprise-wide data, processes and technology based on open architectures.

The ability to analyze and document the processes performed by each agency and identify the information flows has become a key feature towards this direction. The discipline of Enterprise Architecture (e.g. (Zachman, 1987; Zachman & Sowa, 1992)) provides the enabling framework in which to integrate process & data models into one enterprise-wide representation. These representations, if built, constitute a valuable asset. They document the current state of the system and can be used in various types of organizational development initiatives related to e.g. IT acquisition, information systems development, Business Process Re-engineering, Total Quality Management, Activity Based Costing, Benchmarking, etc. An Enterprise Architecture (EA) is expected among other things to:

- Serve as a common language for all terms and relations in PA (Klischewski, 2004),
- Assist decision making, policy formulation and citizen information,
- Provide common semantics for the development and representation of life-events and one-stop portals (Tambouris, 2001)
- Provide the necessary infrastructure to organize collective discussion, effective and efficient action and all the services needed to support e-Government (Rosati, Lai, & Gnoli, 2004).

There are already some EA frameworks that could be used as a basis for EA development. Among the most famous are the Open Group Architecture Framework (TOGAF)[1], the Zachman Framework (Zachman & Sowa, 1992), the C4ISR Architectural Framework (C4ISR Integration Task Force, 1997), the Enterprise Architecture Planning (EAP) (Spewak & Steven C. Hill., 1992), and the Federal Enterprise Architecture Framework (FEAF) (TopQuadrant, 2005b). The latter is discussed in more details below as it is relevant to public administration.

As an EA can be used to provide and organize sets of domain models it can also be linked with ontological engineering projects where ontologies are drafted to express several organizational characteristics. These ontologies could then populate different perspectives in an EA framework (e.g. actors, data, processes, events). Domain models and ontologies are perceived as a key concept for employing semantic technologies (e.g. (Berners-Lee, Hendler, & Lassila, 2001; Fensel D., C. Bussler, & Maedche, 2002)). Governmental domain models recently attracted a lot of interest in eGovernment research (e.g. (Brahim Medjahed, Abdelmounaam Rezgui, Athman Bouguettaya, & Ouzzani, 2003; Klischewski, 2004; Klischewski & Jeenicke, 2004; Missikoff, 2002; Motta, Domingue, Cabral, & Gaspari, 2003; Semantic Interoperability Community of Practice (SICoP), 2005; Tambouris, Kavadias, & Spanos, 2004; Vitvar T., Kerrigan M., Overeem v. A., V., & K., 2006)).

Identifying the lack of suitable and ready-to-use models and domain descriptions for public administration, we gradually built a set of generic models that documents the operation of the system under analysis. We have called this set of models *Governance Enterprise Architecture* (GEA). GEA is a top-level, generic and thus reusable Enterprise Architecture (EA) for the overall governance domain. We have tried to keep GEA as technology independent as possible. Following a Model Driven Architecture approach, we may say that GEA constitutes the Computational Independent Model (ATHENA Project, 2005) for the governance system. In the following parts, we present an overview of this work.

We have organized this chapter as follows: In part 2 we present the background (literature review). The foundations of GEA are presented in part 3. In part 4, we present an overview of all the existing GEA models. Part 5 provides conclusions and future direction of work.

2. STATE OF THE ART

In this part, we briefly present a set of relevant initiatives. We have included not only purely EA initiatives but more general attempts to create generic models for the Governance domain. The following relevant initiatives have been identified.

- Three spheres in eGovernance (Gronlund, 2005)
- Gartner Government Performance Framework (Gartner, 2003)
- Faceted Classification of Public Administration (Rosati et al., 2004)
- SAP Public Sector Solution Map (SAP, 2000)
- Government Process Classification Framework (Inter-Agency Benchmarking & Best Practices Council, 1996)
- ONTOGOV project service ontology (D. Apostolou, L. Stojanovic, T. Pariente Lobo, & Thoenssen, 2005)
- UK Government Common Information Model (Office of e-Envoy UK, 2002)
- WebDG Ontologies (Brahim Medjahed et al., 2003)
- DIP eGovernment Ontology (DIP Project, 2004)
- Federal Enterprise Architecture (FEA) Ontology (TopQuadrant, 2005a)

We rate all the above initiatives based on the following five criteria:

- Their *relevance* to the PA domain: Low (domain independent), Medium (partly PA domain specific), high (PA domain specific)
- The *depth* of analysis (e.g. number of concepts): Low (up to 10), Medium-Low (10-30), Medium (30-50), Medium-High (50-100), High (over 100)
- The part of the public administration *domain* modelled: Support Operations (S), Public Policy Formulation (P), Service Provision (O)
- *Perspective*: Technical, Conceptual/Business
- *View*: Focusing on Process, Object or Holistic (attempts to combine both views).

The results are presented in the table below, with some additional comments including their relationship with our approach (GEA).

3. THE GOVERNANCE ENTERPRISE ARCHITECTURE FRAMEWORK

In this part, we present the GEA framework and its theoretical foundation.

3.1 Theoretical Foundation

For constructing the GEA framework and populating the GEA models, we followed a multi-disciplinary approach and used theories and concepts from several areas:

(a) Public administration and public policy theory in order to comprehend the domain of interest (e.g. (Bevir & Rhodes, 2001; Hogwood & Gunn, 1984; Lane, 1995; Rhodes, 1997; Riley, 2003; The World Bank, 1992)). We have used these theories to define the governance system, delineate the scope of our initiative and propose a broad categorization of relevant concepts to be used.

(b) Speech Act Theory (e.g. (Searle, 1969)) and Language Action Perspective (LAP) (e.g. (Dietz & Mulder, 1998; Goldkuhl, 1996; Johannesson, 2001)) has been used to model specific parts of the domain. We consider the relationship between public administration and society as a *discourse*. This metaphor has been proven a

Table 1. Relevant literature review

Initiative	Relevance	Depth	Domain	Perspective	View	Relationship-to-GEA
Three spheres in eGovernance	High	Low	S-P-O	Conceptual	Holistic	It provides a top-level categorization of the overall domain, identifying its primary actors and their functions. It is compatible to the GEA overall process model. The functions performed are not further elaborated.
Gartner Government Performance Framework	High	Medium-Low	S-P-O	Conceptual	Holistic	It provides a top-level categorization of the overall governance domain, compatible with the GEA overall process model. These categories are further elaborated but in lower levels it becomes clear that the model constitutes an evaluation and assessment tool and not an attempt to analyze and model the domain.
Faceted Classification	High	Medium-Low	S-O	Conceptual	Holistic	It provides a reference eGov ontology using concepts of the faceted theory. It looks like ongoing work that currently provides more details only for the procedure/process concept. The classification of eGov processes is interesting but lacks clear definitions.
SAP Public Sector Solution Map	Medium	Medium-Low	S	Conceptual	Process	This is a blueprint of generic processes that are executed by every PA agency. The focus is on the service provision but stemming from a rather introvert ERP approach only the supportive and not the operational functions are analyzed.
Government Process Classification Framework	High	High	S-P	Conceptual	Process	This initiative is quite close to the above. A very detailed organization of all governmental processes is proposed, but again the focus remains on the supportive functions, then at the policy related functions and excludes the analysis of the operational (service provision) functions
ONTOGOV	Medium	Medium	O	Technical	Holistic	It is an attempt to present an OWL_S specialization for the PA service. The PA domain specific semantics introduced are rather limited. The strong point here is the compatibility with a standardized and well-accepted service description/ontology. The modeling covers only service provision and has technological emphasis.
UK-GCIM	High	Low	O	Conceptual	Object	This is a pure PA service modeling attempt. It provides an interesting view of the service, but remains at a very high level of description. GEA elaborates on the concepts introduced here.
Web DG-Ontologies	Low	Medium-High	O	Technical	Holistic	The proposed ontology aims at facilitating Web Service composition. It uses the eGovernment domain as a test bed and does not provide any type of domain specific conceptual modeling.
DIP-eGov Ontology	Low	High	S-O	Conceptual	Object	This is a taxonomy of terms used by PA agencies rather than a reference PA domain description model.
USA-FEA (Business Reference Model)	High	Medium-High	S-O	Conceptual	Process	This model is the only FEA PA domain specific model that provides an articulated categorization and description for the service provision process (but not for the policy process). It uses a functional approach and roughly follows the ministerial departmentization of government.
USA-FEA (other models)	Low	Medium-High	S-O	Technical	Holistic	With the exception of BRM, all the FEA models are domain independent.
GEA	High	Medium	S-P-O	Conceptual	Holistic	It is a pure PA modeling effort claiming to be technology independent. It provides a holistic view for the overall governance system and constructs PA domain models based on two axes: objects and processes.

valuable asset both at the initial stage of scoping and at latter stage when specific models were developed. Specifically, we used concepts from these disciplines to:

- Construct the overall object model of the governance system (part 4.1)
- Identify the main type of goals performed by the governance system (part 4.1.3).
- Model the service provision mega-process by distinguishing its informative and performative parts (part 4.6).

(c) Moreover for specific parts of GEA, we have employed concepts from fields like:

- Organizational theory (e.g. defining the operational/support layers (H. Koontz, Donnell, & Weihreich, 1980)).
- Upper ontologies (e.g. DOLCE, (Claudio Masolo, Stefano Borgo, Aldo Gangemi, Nicola Guarino, & Oltramari, 2003)) for identifying e.g. the two core dimensions of the GEA framework (process-object).
- Semantic web services (e.g. (Battle et al., 2005; Hepp, Leymann, Domingue, Wahler, & Fensel, 2005)) for proposing e.g. a model as the PA domain specific service ontology.
- Deontic modelling and patterns analysis/design (e.g. (Fowler, 1997; Hay, 1996; Johannesson & Wohed, 1998; Lind M. & Goldkuhl, 2001; Wieringa & Meyer, 1993)) for e.g. adding a knowledge layer to an existing transaction model.

The models were built in a combined top-down and bottom-up fashion: for the first, theories and concepts from the above-mentioned disciplines were used; for the second, a number of real public administration cases were analyzed and studied.

3.2 The GEA Framework

The GEA Framework is based on a two-dimensional framework which consists of a vertical and a horizontal dimension.

- In the first, the governance system mega-processes have been included.
- In the second, we introduce the process versus object modelling view.

These two dimensions define a number of cells. Each cell constitutes a modeling area.

Vertical Dimension: Governance System Mega-Processes

In this dimension, we present the two mega-processes of the governance system (see also part 4.2). A mega-process is defined as the aggregation of all governmental functions, services and processes which are related to one of the two main interaction types that take place in the citizen-state discourse. These are:

- Public Policy Formulation. During this mega-process, the demand from society for state action is identified and political processes such as prioritizing public needs take place. The main actor is the political system.
- Service Provision. The production and distribution of public services takes place in this mega-process. The main actor is the public administration system.

Thus, the GEA framework defines two modeling areas, namely the "Public Policy Formulation Area" and the "Service Provision Area" (Figure 3-1).

Some administrative areas are still left out of scope for our analysis:

- Following Montesquieu's fundamental separation of the three administrative powers, our analysis remains at the executive power, and we deliberately leave out of scope the legislative and judiciary powers.
- We also do not consider here a third mega-process that has been called Support Services/Operations (see also part 4.2). In this, we group all the supporting functions to the above two core layers (e.g. logistics, financial/taxation services, information and human resources management). This supportive mega-process has not attracted our interest, as it does not acquire significant PA domain specific characteristics, which means that analysis and modeling performed for the private sector can be easily reused and transferred with small customization to the support operations of PA.

It is important to make a clarification with regards to the usage of the terms "government" and "governance" in this chapter. "Governance" is used to refer to the aggregation of the two mega-processes presented above. Thus as examples, the governance system contains both the political and administrative subsystems and the governance EA refers to models relevant to both mega-processes. We use the term government to refer to the administrative system (public administration). As a consequence of this, when we mention "eGovernment", we refer to the use of ICTs by public administration to facilitate the service provision mega-process. When we use "eGovernance", we refer to the use of ICTs to facilitate both mega-processes. As such "governance" can be also perceived as a super concept of "government". This definition remains compatible with common PA literature, e.g. (Rhodes, 1997).

Horizontal Dimension: Objects and Processes

In the horizontal dimension, we accommodate the distinction between *objects* and *processes*. These are fundamental concepts in the upper level ontology and the enterprise architecture literature:

- In SUMO (Niles & Pease, 2001), physical entities may be *Objects*, or *Processes*.

Figure 3-1. The complete GEA framework

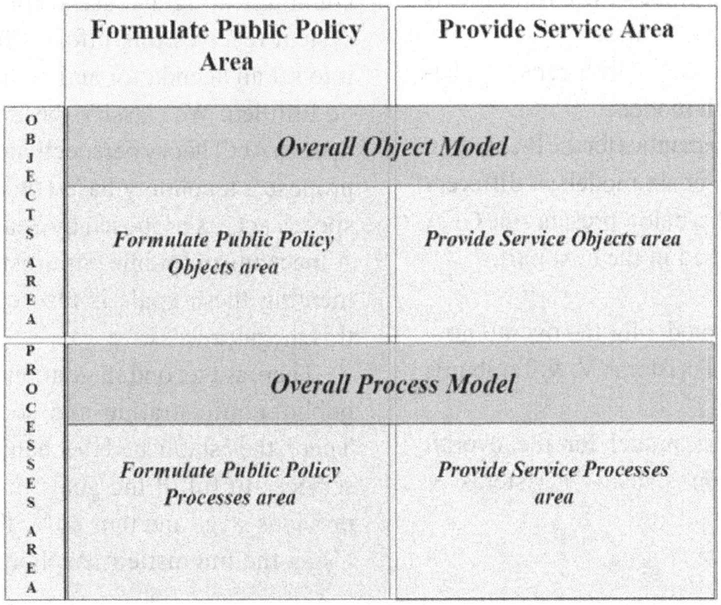

	Formulate Public Policy Area	Provide Service Area
OBJECTS AREA	*Overall Object Model*	
	Formulate Public Policy Objects area	*Provide Service Objects area*
PROCESSES AREA	*Overall Process Model*	
	Formulate Public Policy Processes area	*Provide Service Processes area*

- In DOLCE (Claudio Masolo et al., 2003; Oltramari A., Gangemi A., Guarino N., & Masolo C., 2002) the most fundamental division is between *perdurants*, entities that unfold in time (*processes*) and *endurants*, entities that are present all at once in time (*objects*).
- MITRE discusses the concepts of *continuant (process)* and *occurrent (objects)* (Semy, Pulvermacher, & Obrst, 2004).
- In the Zachman Enterprise Architecture Framework ((Zachman, 1987; Zachman & Sowa, 1992)) the WHAT and HOW columns correspond to *objects* and *processes*.

The matrix defined by these two dimensions is presented in Figure 3.1.

The four cells correspond to separate modeling areas. These areas are the following:

- Formulate Public Policy Objects area
- Formulate Public Policy Processes area
- Provide Service Objects area
- Provide Service Processes area

For each of these areas/cells, we propose models. Moreover, we have added two models: one as a top-level representation of all the objects and the other for all the processes. These models ensure consistency of the framework.

Thus developing GEA actually means populating the framework with models.

GEA provides rich semantics for the PA domain as it currently consists of six models at different levels of analysis. The list below presents the GEA models that are discussed in the next part.

1. The GEA object model for the overall governance system (Peristeras V. & Tarabanis K., 2004b)
2. The GEA process model for the overall governance system (Vasilis Peristeras & Tarabanis, 2000)

3. The GEA object model for public policy formulation (Tarabanis, Peristeras, & Fragidis, 2001)
4. The GEA object model for service provision (Peristeras V. & Tarabanis K., 2004a)
5. The GEA process model for public policy formulation (Vassilios Peristeras, Tsekos, & Tarabanis, 2003)
6. The GEA process model for service provision (Peristeras V. & Tarabanis K., 2005)

4. THE GOVERNANCE ENTERPRISE ARCHITECTURE MODELS

4.1 The Overall Object Model for the Governance System

The core of this model has been basically derived in a top-down fashion. The basic model's entities, instances and relationships emerged by employing the linguistic metaphor and perceive the interaction between society and the governance system as a *discourse*. Following this metaphor, we identify a constant dialogue going on between society and the governance system.

During the Public Policy Formulation mega-process, society is the initiator of the discourse communicating needs, while the governance system receives this information and processes it to set an agenda for action, as a set of goals to be fulfilled. We classify these goals following a Speech Act Theory perspective (Searle, 1969), and propose a taxonomy based on the main types of speech acts as proposed by Searle (Searle, 1975). A mechanism (public administration) for implementing these goals is also established during this mega-process.

Then, at a second stage a conversation between public administration and society takes place. There, the established mechanism (PA) provides services to fulfill the goals that were set in the previous stage and thus cover the societal needs. Using the linguistic metaphor, we may say that public services are "sentences" uttered by PA in order to perform the necessary changes in the world (speech acts).

In language, the types of speech acts intended by an interlocutor are not identical with the types of the sentences uttered to perform these acts. The first is related to *What* the interlocutor want to do (e.g. to declare something or to direct a behavior), while the second *How* the interlocutor tries to do it (e.g. by command, statements, questions). We may say that speech acts and sentences are loosely coupled. This means that speech acts and sentences are classified in different typologies with an existing but loose relationship between the various types of acts/sentences.

In a similar way in the governance-society discourse, the types of public services used to perform a goal should not be identified with the type of the goals they try to fulfill. The goals concept presents *What* the governance system want to do (e.g. promote social justice), while the public service represent *How* PA has decided to fulfill the goal (e.g. by providing unemployment benefits). Public service is the technical means

to the goals accomplishment. Goals and public services are again loosely coupled and classified in different typologies with an existing but loose relationship. Thus, in addition to the typology of goal, here we also propose a separate typology for public services. All the above are discussed in detail below.

We organize this section as follows. First, we present the participating actors (subjects) in the model (4.1.1). Then, we introduce the "Need" and "Goal" objects (4.1.2). In 4.1.3, we present a typology of governance goals, using the discourse metaphor. In 4.1.4, the "Public Service" object is introduced. A public service typology is presented in 4.1.5. We discuss the relationship between "Public Service" and "Goal" (4.1.6). Last, the overall model appears in 4.1.7.

4.1.1 The "Subject" Object

We use the object *Subject* to cover all the participating actors in the Governance-Society interaction. At the first level, *Subject* may consist of *Governance Entities* and *Societal Entities*. *Governance*

Figure 4-1. The participating "Subjects" (actors) in the governance system

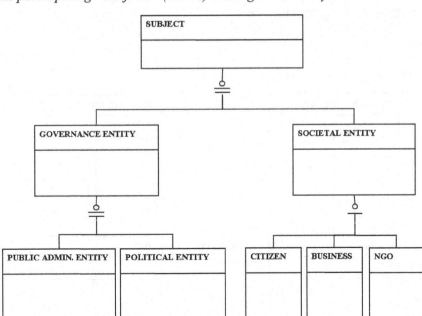

Entities refer to all entities participating in the governance system. *Societal Entities* refer to any actor existing out of the governance system boundaries that (may) exercise any kind of influence on the latter. These two are the main types of actors that participate in the governance domain. *Governance Entities* may be *Public Administration Entities* (e.g. PA agencies) and *Political Entities* (e.g. Ministers). *Societal Entities* may be decomposed into several types of entities (e.g. *Citizens*, *Businesses* and *NGOs*) (Figure 4-1).

4.1.2 The "Goal" and "Need" Objects

As already presented in the introduction of this section, societal entities have *needs*. Needs are deficits that society feels Governance Entities as the appropriate actor to address them. These needs are communicated to the governance system through the Public Policy Formulation mega-process. The governance system receives this need, processes and prioritizes them and sets *goals* to be fulfilled. Goals refer to the desired outcome of the governance action. These governance goals should be ideally set in line with the needs of the society.

Not all needs expressed by societal entities are eligible to be handled by governance enti-

ties. The process of defining goals (e.g. issue filtration and agenda setting (Hogwood & Gunn, 1984)) is quite complicated in public policy, as amongst others things drafting goals is directly linked to the ability of realizing them (Browne & Wildavsky, 1984).

4.1.3 Typology of Governance Goals

Regardless of the encountered difficulties, governance entities come up with a concrete and usually long list of goals to pursue. Some examples are prevent criminal actions, prevent pollution, promote exports.

Taking into account the large number of all possible goals, a challenging task is to classify them. Researchers in public policy and PA theory usually address this issue by proposing various classifications (Lane, 1995; Lowi, 1979; Musgrave, 1959). One of the more common is based on the functional notion of the public policy field and administrative function is classified along categories such as transportation, foreign affairs, social services, health, etc.

In order to present more advanced typologies of governance goals and goal-seeking behaviour, we present two types of typologies (Figure 4-3):

Figure 4-2. The "Goal" and "Need" objects

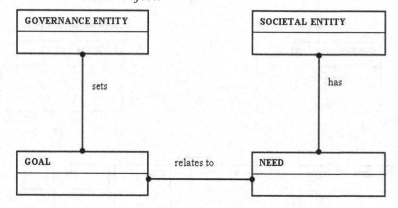

Figure 4-3. Typology of goals

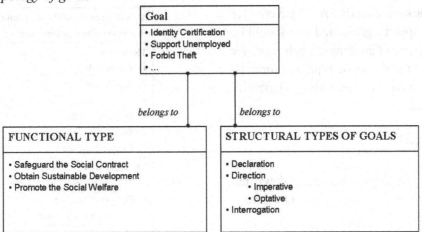

Functional Typology

The identification of the top nodes of a functional hierarchy/typology of governance goals is a challenging exercise. We propose the following three top nodes:

- Safeguard the Social Contract; meaning obtain the peaceful coexistence amongst the members of the society.
- Obtain Sustainable Development; meaning direct and streamline the macro-economic development taking into account sustainability concepts (e.g. environment).
- Promote the Social Welfare; meaning enhancing the social cohesion by fighting exclusion and poverty.

Structural Typology

Speech Act Theory (SAT) studies the speech acts and is part of pragmatics, which forms part of linguistics. Pragmatics is about the language use. According to this, a speaker uses language to

- The first is based on the goal's functional type.
- The second is based on structural characteristics and concepts from Speech Act Theory.

perform a set of speech acts, which could be also perceived as types of societal behavior.

A speech act implies that by each utterance a speaker not only *says* something but also *does* certain things: giving information, stating a fact or hinting an attitude.

Searle identified the following classes of speech acts (Searle, 1975):

- Assertives, statements that may be judged true or false because they aim to describe a state of affairs in the world.
- Directives, attempts by the speaker to get the addressee to do something.
- Commisives commit the speaker to some future course of action.
- Expressives express a psychological state.
- Declarations attempt to change the world by "*representing it as having been changed*".

Austin (Austin, 1962), Vendler (Vendler, 1972), Alan (Allan, 1994) and Bach (Bach & Harnish, 1979) have also proposed similar or slightly different speech acts categorizations.

Through setting goals, the governance system exhibits a particular goal-seeking behavior: not only does it *says* something but also *does* certain things (acts). The governance goals pertain to specific types of governance acts and are the equivalent to the speech acts in SAT. A governance entity pursues specific goals, and this should be perceived as a type of governance behavior. We use a similar to the linguistic typology for classifying these governance goals/acts and identify four main types:

- Declarative
- Assertive
- Directive, which is further broken down into two categories: Imperative and Optative.
- Interrogative

As governance goals are central in our analysis, we further elaborate on these structural goal types and present them in detail.

4.1.3.1.1 Declarative Goals

Through declarative goals, governance entities want to change the world by *"representing it as having been changed"*, to use the linguistic equivalent. Through declarative goals, the governance entities pursue changes in the states of the world.

Social entities need a third party to officially register and keep records of important world changes (events). PA entities are considered to be the most reliable and official "registering" actor

Table 4-1. Indicative list of declarations

An indicative list of the world changes that Public Administration keeps records of
The citizen   • Birth   • Marriage   • Death   • Personal and professional capacities (e.g. issuance of driving license)
The enterprise   • Company establishment and shut down
The land and its use
Commodities, Vehicles, Others…

Table 4-2. Indicative list of certifications

An indicative list of the state information that governance entities certifies
The citizen   • Personal data   • Family status   • Health issues   • Property status   • Professional capacity   • Criminal records
The enterprise   • Tax and insurance compliance   • Economic situation   • Environmental conformity
The land and its use
Commodities, Vehicles, Others…

in society: a kind of "honest broker" recording world change in a neutral manner.

Nowadays, public administration registers an extended set of world changes as can be seen in Table 4-1.

4.1.3.1.2 Assertive Goals

Through assertive goals, governance entities inform and certify the existence and the truth of certain world states. This behaviour is referential and descriptive, meaning that no changes in the real world happen.

Social entities need to interchange certified information during their interaction. Governance entities are considered to be the most reliable certification actors in society: a "honest broker" arbitrating private transactions in a neutral manner.

Governance entities certify an extended set of information as can be seen below.

4.1.3.1.3 Directive Goals

Through directive goals, the governance system directs society to certain states. This goal and behaviour is constructive and deontological. The governance system leads society towards certain "desired" states that are politically defined.

Public administration uses two types of means to promote these desired states:

- By command, this means by imposing compulsory the behaviour towards the desired state *(Imperative)*.
- By providing incentives, by trying to persuade society to voluntarily adopt the behaviour that leads to the desired state *(Optative)*.

4.1.3.1.3.1 Imperative Goals

As imperative, we define the goals through which the governance system tries to mandates or forbids special types of societal behaviours.

Interestingly, imperative goals appear in two forms:

- *Absolute command*, when the prohibition or obligation is general and without exception (e.g. theft, kidnap, rape)
- *Conditional command*, when the prohibition or obligation can be lifted under specific

circumstances (e.g. not to build without a building permit).

The latter category refers to *permissive* goals. We define as *permissive*, the goals/acts through which governance entities recognize special rights and allow behaviours otherwise prohibited. Through permissive acts, exceptions are activated in situations where a universal prohibition has been enforced.

4.1.3.1.3.2 Optative Goals

In this broad category, we define the set of goals through which governance entities offer guidance and support in order to *promote specific behaviors*. Historically, public administration fully developed these functions after the 2nd World War, with the emergence of the Welfare State.

Optative goals are promoted though providing either *Incentives* or *Support*.

- *Incentive*: Through incentive acts, the governance entities promote specific behaviours

Figure 4-4. Types of directive goals

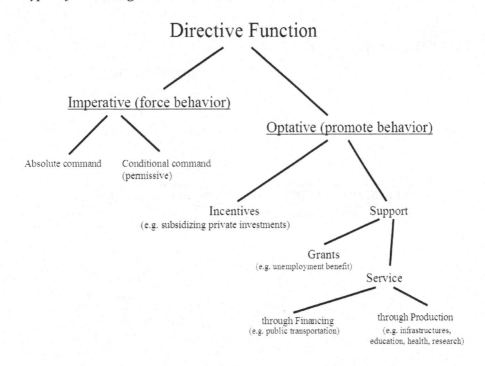

by offering a special "bonus" to persuade and urge society towards these behaviours (e.g. subsidizing investments, providing a grant for having a third child or for employing people previously unemployed).

- *Support*: Governance entities support access to goods and services that are considered as vital and for which exclusion is considered unacceptable. This may happen by:
  - Directly *providing grants and benefits* to reduce social exclusion (e.g. unemployment benefits)
  - *Facilitating* access to vital services and goods. This may occur in two ways, that is, through:
    - *Internal Production*, when governance entities offer for free (or below the production cost) infrastructure and services that have been produced internally (e.g. public goods).
    - *Financing*: The internal production of services is not always considered a suitable approach and outsourcing is preferred. Recently with the support of New Public Manage-

ment this has become a significant trend (Yergin & Stanislaw, 1998).

Figure 4-4 depicts the various types of Directive goals.

4.1.3.1.4 Interrogative Goals

Through its interrogative function, the governance system collects societal needs. Contrary to the declarative and directive goals, this type of acts/goals is directly linked to the Public Policy Formulation mega-process and not to that of Service Provision.

Concluding this part, it is important to stress that the governance goals may vary in strength and frequency depending on the particular type of governance system in place, e.g. in non-democratic regimes the interrogative function may become weak and volatile. Nevertheless, all these goals are practically pursued by all contemporary states.

4.1.4 The "Public Service" Object

In this part, we introduce the *Public Service* object which is considered central in the Service Provision mega-process.

Figure 4-5. The "Public Service" object

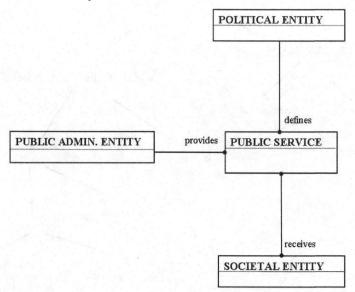

There are three main actors that are related to the *public service* object. These are (Figure 4-5):

- *Political entities* decide and define the public services to be provided to society in order to address the identified needs.
- *Public administration entities* provide (execute) public services to society.
- *Societal entities* ask for and receive (consume) public services.

The relationships between public services and political-societal entities are important in our analysis. We summarize these relationships in Figure 4-6. The model reads:

Societal entities have *needs*. By collecting, processing and prioritizing these needs, *political entities* set *goals* (through the Public Policy Formulation mega-process) to be fulfilled. In order to pursue these goals a set of *public services* are defined and become available by *public administration entities*. *Societal entities* have *needs* and these needs are fulfilled (or covered) by the provision of *public services*.

4.1.5 Typology of Public Services

Focusing our analysis on the *"Public Service"* object, we have tried to create a typology of public services, similar to the typology of goals presented in previous part.

Again the most commonly used classification is based on the policy field criterion (transportation, health, education, etc). This classification has the same problems as the functional classification of goals. To use the linguistic analogy, the functional categorization of sentences would result in classifying the sentences: *"This is a dog"*, *"Do you have a dog?"* and *"I don't like dogs"* under the same *"sentences that speak of dogs"* category. This classification is based on the semantics of the sentence but not on their structural characteristics. Similarly, the policy field based classification of public services is also based on the semantics of the service e.g. set of services that promote health, education, etc.

Taking a different stance, we emphasize on the structural (e.g. process patterns) and not on semantic/functional characteristics of public services. We employ again the *discourse* metaphor.

Figure 4-6. Public services relationships with political/societal entities

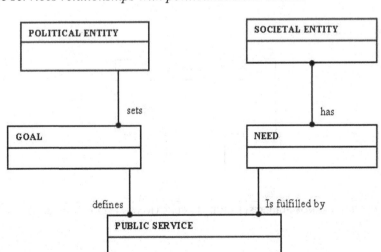

In linguistics, a quite common categorization gives three types of sentences (R.E. Asher (ed.), 1994):

- Statements
- Questions
- Commands

Interestingly, a speaker may use different types of sentence in order to perform the same type of speech act e.g. to declare something or direct the behavior of its interlocutor. Similarly, PA may alternatively use different types of public services to fulfill a given governance goal. We present this idea in detail below.

Can we classify the hundreds of public services provided by public administration into general types with common structural characteristics? By addressing this question, we then can identify generic types of public services. These generic types could be described once and these descriptions could then be used either to analyze existing or to create new instances of services by just reconfiguring the generic types appropriately. A generic process model could also be proposed for each such type of public service.

We tried to identify such generic types of public services in two ways:

- Top-Down. Using as a starting point the PA goals described, we examined the ways in which public administration realizes them. The hypothesis has been: "Each type of government goal is *mainly* realized by one generic type of public service".
- Bottom-Up. Studying a great number of public services, we focused on the type of action the administration performs each time. The verbs used in describing the service were used as a guide. The hypothesis has been: "A few verbs can describe all public services and each of these verbs is associated with one generic type of public service"

Following this perspective, we identified five generic types of public services. These are:

- Declaration
- Certification
- Control
- Authorization
- Production

We describe these types below.

Figure 4-7. Types of public services

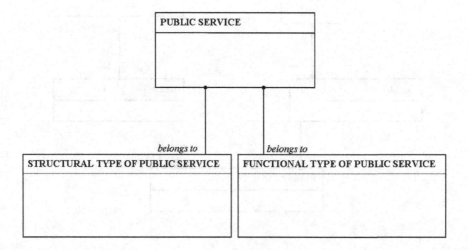

4.1.5.1 Declarations

There is a characteristic public service type for fulfilling declarative type of goals and this is "*Declaration*". Through providing public services of declaration type, PA declares and registers changes in the state of the world (e.g. marriage). The typical process model followed by public administration for performing declarations is composed of the following steps:

- A societal or public administration entity asks for registering a world change.
- A set of evidence needed to be validated is gathered.
- The service provider checks completeness and correctness of all evidence.
- The service provider may ask for additional evidence, information and clarifications.
- The service provider declares or justifies the refusal to declare the new state.

4.1.5.2 Certifications

There is a characteristic type of public service for fulfilling assertive type of goals and this is "*Certification*". Through certifications PA certifies existing states of the world (e.g. issuing birth certificate). The typical process model followed by public administration in order to perform certifications is similar to that presented above for declarations, with the difference that at the first step the societal entity applies for a certification. At the end, PA either certifies or justifies the refusal to certify.

There are cases where PA simply informs society about certain states of the world (e.g. weather report, statistical reports). These *informational PA services* can be also perceived as a special type of certifications, where the process and PA commitment is much looser than in formal certifications.

4.1.5.3 Controls

How does public administration realize the goals of imperative type, through which it either pro-hibits or forces upon society specific behaviours? And how does public administration secure the compliance to the rules? At the practical level, PA has to secure that society adheres to all prohibitions and obligations posed. The main role of PA in this case is to "suppress and control".

PA uses a specific type of public service in order to address this: "*Control*". As the offender tends to hide his/her behaviour from PA, the most ordinary type of control is inspections on a periodic or on an impromptu basis.

In order to perform controls, PA follows a process model with the following steps.

- PA performs various types of controls (e.g. inspections).
- PA arrives at a decision regarding compliance or not.
- In case of non-compliance, PA passes sentences.

4.1.5.4 Authorizations

There is one prevailing type of public service through which public administration realizes both *permissive* and *support* goals. We call this type of public services "*Authorization*".

Public administration has to set up an entire mechanism to exercise this type of services. In general, either universal prohibition should be relaxed (permissive) or support should be awarded (supportive), if special conditions are met.

The process model for authorization is similar to that of declarations/certifications.

4.1.5.5 Production

In the description of the optative type of governance goals, support through the production of services was identified to be one of the possible implementations of the governance goals. The type of public service that is employed in order to fulfil this goal is unique. Public administration has organized internally a production mechanism and *"Production"* thus becomes a new type of public service. Examples of this type of services

Table 4-4. Multiplicity in the "Speech Act – Sentence" relationship

> *Goal: to have the window opened by someone else*
>
> *Speech Act Type: Directive*
>
> *Sentences uttered to fulfil this Speech Act:*
>
> *a. "Could you please open the window?" (Question)*
>
> *b. "Open the window!" (Command - **characteristic**)*
>
> *c. "It is hot here with the window closed" (Statement)*

may include services related to health, education, defence, police, transportation, etc.

Production as a generic type of public service cannot be easily depicted using a generic description. *Production* as performed by PA is quite similar to production of services by the private sector. We can even question whether production is a straightforward public administration type of public service, or just a private sector function that has been historically transferred for several reasons to PAs. The similarities with production in the private sector, regarding the organization of work, are so apparent that it would be difficult to identify significant differences. As a result, well-known criteria (e.g. effectiveness, productivity, quality) can be transferred from private sector management with little customisation.

4.1.6 Relationship between Goals–Public Services

In the table below, the correspondence is shown between the types of governance *goals* and the *characteristic* types of *public services* typically employed for the implementation of each type of goal. Characteristic here means most common. Interestingly, the authorization type of public service is employed to fulfill both permissive and optative types of goals.

In language, there is a many-to-many relationship between a speech act and a sentence. Different types of sentences may be used to perform a specific type of speech act. For example, an

Table 4-3. Characteristic types of public service and governance goals

Governance Goal	Characteristic Type of Public Service
Declarative	Declaration
Assertive	Certification
Imperative (absolute command)	Control
Permissive	Authorization
Optative	Authorization
Production	Production

affirmative or an interrogative sentence may be used for directive, declarative or another type of Speech Act. An example of the relationship between speech act and type of sentence is presented in table 4-4. Although there is a characteristic type of sentences to utter speech acts of directive type, other types can be used as well.

Similarly and despite the characteristic relationship between the types of governance goals and the types of public services (table 4-3), each type of governance goals can be realized by different types of public services.

The choice of the specific public service, through which PA addresses a goal, depends on various factors, such as administrative capacity, information technology, existing organizational and institutional infrastructure, administrative culture etc. Thus, in order to meet goals of e.g. imperative type, PA could alternatively use public services of certification, authorization, control and/or of the production type.

Table 4-5. Multiplicity in the "Goals – Public Services" relationship

Goal: Prohibition of polluting the atmosphere Goal Type: *Directive-Imperative* Public services provided to fulfil this goal: a. Periodic control of pollutant emission from factory flues (Control – characteristic) b. Issuance of an operating license for factories (Authorization) c. Issuance of a certificate asserting that no pollution is caused (Certification)

We demonstrate this "multiplicity" feature between goals and public services using an example (table 4-5).

In this case, the goal (prohibition of polluting the atmosphere) is of *"directive – imperative"* type. PA realizes this goal by exercising public services of *control*, *authorization* and *certification* type according to circumstances. Although there is a *characteristic* relationship between imperative => control, PA can use other types of services as well, in order to meet the goal posed.

4.1.7 Model Overview

Here we present an overview (Figure 4-8). This reads:

We identify two major actors in Governance: Governance Entities and Societal Entities. Governance Entities are either Political Entities or PA Entities. Societal Entities may be Citizens, Businesses and NGOs (not depicted in figure for simplicity).

Societal Entities have Needs. Political Entities take into account these Needs and set up Goals to be fulfilled.

In contemporary states, the Governance Goals belong to three broad functional categories. These are:

- Safeguard the Social Contract
- Obtain Sustainable Development
- Promote the Social Welfare

Moreover, Governance Goals belong to structural types. These are:

- Declarative
- Assertive
- Directive
- Interrogative

Societal Needs are fulfilled by the provision of Public Services. These services are defined by the Goals set by Political Entities and are realized by PA Entities. Societal Entities participate in the provision of Public Services by asking for and/or receiving these services.

Public services exhibit some common structural characteristics that allow the identification of certain types of public services. These are:

- Declaration
- Certification
- Control
- Authorization
- Production

In the table that follows, we summarize the analogy we have found between linguistics and governance.

4.2 The Overall Process Model for the Governance System

In this part, we present the overall process model for the governance system. This description is a high level abstraction (black-box view) that identifies the basic processes of the overall governance system. These are called *mega-processes*.

Figure 4-8. The GEA object model for the overall governance system

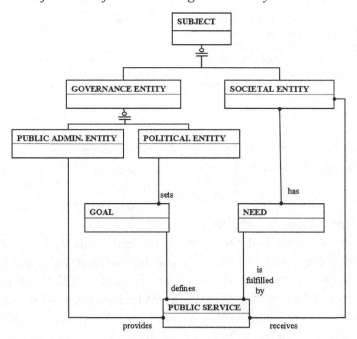

Table 4-6. The Linguistic Metaphor in modeling Governance-Society interaction

LINGUISTICS	GOVERNANCE
Types of Speech Acts	Governance Functions
- Declaration	- Declarative
- Assertive	- Assertive
- Directive	- Interrogation
- Commisive	- Directive
- Expressive	o Imperative
	o Optative
Sentence	Public Service
- Statement	- Declaration
- Question	- Certification
- Command	- Authorization
	- Control
	- Production
m:m relationship between Speech Act - Sentence	m:m relationship between Goals – Public Service

The governance system performs three mega-processes:

- Public Policy Formulation
- Service Provision
- Support Services

This separation of the overall governance domain was introduced in (Vasilis Peristeras & Tarabanis, 2000) and has been followed by Gartner in the Gartner Government Performance Framework™. Gartner refers to these three dimensions as political management, service supply management and support services (Gartner, 2003).

During the first mega-process, the governance system collects, processes and prioritizes the emerged social needs. It also organizes a mechanism - public administration - to address these needs. The study of this mega-process is the research area of political theory and public policy literature.

In the second mega-process, the established mechanism (public administration) produces and delivers services to society.

In the third layer, all the supporting functions to the above two core layers are held (e.g. logistics, financial, information and human resources management).

Putting these three mega-processes together, we depict governance as a system that receives

Figure 4-9. The GEA overall process model

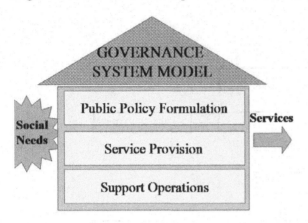

Figure 4-10. The main actors participating in Governance

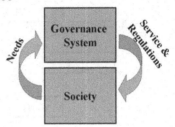

societal needs as input, processes and prioritizes them and then designs, produces and delivers services to address these needs as output (Figure 4-9).

This model constitutes the GEA overall process model and at the same time it defines the two separate, core domains for the modeling exercise in the GEA framework: Service Provision and Public Policy Formulation.

The overall governance process incorporates two basic actors and their interactions. These actors are identified to be (Figure 4-10):

- Society
- The Governance System as the aggregation of Administrative System (PA) plus Political System

4.3 THE OBJECT MODEL FOR PUBLIC POLICY FORMULATION

In this part, we present the object model for the Public Policy Formulation mega-process.

The concepts used for the construction of this model are basically based on concepts employed in business strategy models as adapted to a PA perspective. This adaptation becomes possible since the differences between business and public

administration are decreasing (Hughes & Owen E., 1994).

In the following figure, we present the model (Figure 4-11). A description of its entities follows.

- *Political Entity.* Political Entities receive Needs from Societal Entities and process them according to their Knowledge and Values to develop Vision and Mission. In doing so, they are influenced by their Power Structure.
- *Values.* They refer to attitudes, beliefs, outlook, ideology and philosophy of Political Entities.
- *Mission.* The concept of Mission refers to long-term and high level target of Political Entities. Mission is considered to incorporate all enterprise goals in high level of abstraction. Despite the fact that it is very significant, it is often not made explicit and is taken for granted.
- *Vision.* It refers to the desired situation that Political Entities imagine Societal Entities to be in the long term.
- *Power Structure.* It refers to diverged set of interests, conflicts and power that affects and even shapes all political activities. In modern democracies, this is a very complex, contradictory and ever changing set.
- *Societal Entity.* It refers to any force existing out of political system boundaries that

249

Figure 4-11.The GEA object model for public policy formulation

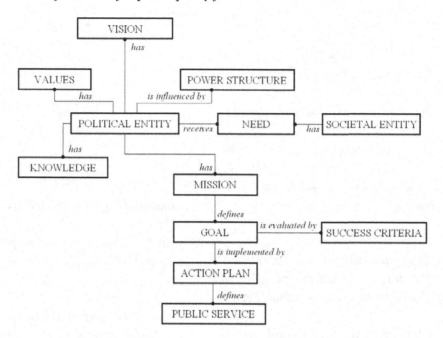

(may) exercise any kind of influence on the latter.

- *Need.* It is a deficit that society feels Political Entities as the appropriate actors to address it.
- *Knowledge.* It refers generally to knowledge acquired by Political Entities and utilized during Mission and Goal setting processes.
- *Goal.* It is a central object in the model. It refers to the desired outcome of governance action. Mission is considered to be at a more abstract level of analysis while goals form its detailed specification. Goals are considered to describe more concrete and specific governance objectives, rather than generic expressions of the future of governance system.
- *Success Criteria.* It refers to pre-defined criteria according to which the achievement of goals of Political Entities is measured.
- *Action Plan.* It may be considered in two levels:

  o Level 1 refers to strategic plan, *what* a Political Entity should do in order to attain its goals, not *how* to do it.
  o Level 2 describes in detail *how* a Political Entity implements the strategic plan.
- *Public Service.* The Action Plan defines Public Services to be executed. These services are provided by PA Entities.

4.4 The Object Model for Service Provision (PA Service Model)

This model comes from in-depth analysis of the Service Provision mega-process. It is of particular importance for eGovernment applications and implementations as it can serve as the conceptual basis for constructing a PA service ontology. This is why we alternatively call it, the *PA Service Model*.

The model is PA domain-specific but at the same time, it remains compatible to generic service ontologies (e.g. OWL-S and WSMO). The model may cover many different (ideally all) application areas in PA. This makes it reusable in different cases of public service provision.

It is worth mentioning that a large number of services have been already modeled using this model for verification purposes. Moreover, the model has been recently adopted by the central PA Unit in an EU member state to be used in an extended national project. The goal of this project is to document in a rigid way a large number of PA services (>100).

A detailed presentation of the model follows.

4.4.1 The Core Objects

The *"Public Service"* object is placed at the center of the PA Service Model. The core of the model consists of three more objects (Figure 4-12). These are:

- Input
- Outcome
- Law

All Public Services are executed according to a Law (or Rule) that governs the execution process. This object provides the execution/control logic for the service provision.

Each Public Service uses Input and produces Outcome. The types of input/outcome with their characteristics are discussed below.

4.4.2 The "Outcome" Object and its Types

We use the term Outcome to refer to all different types of results a PA service may have. Public Services produce Outcomes. This is a fundamental assumption in GEA, which can be found also in PA models like GCIM (Office of e-Envoy UK, 2002) or in generic service models like OWL-S and WSMO.

We define three types of service Outcome (Figure 4-13):

- Output
- Effect
- Consequence

The two first concepts are used similarly but not identically as in OWL-S Process Model (OWL Services Coalition, 2004), while the third is an extension added due its particular importance in PA domain.

In OWL-S, *Output* is related to the acquisition of information by the client. Accordingly, we use the same definition and define as PA service *Output* the acquisition of information related to the PA service execution by the client (e.g. citizen, business). This information is currently embedded in administrative documents, which officially present (and document) the decision of the Service Provider regarding the service asked by the client.

Figure 4-12. The core objects

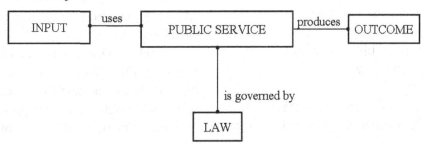

Figure 4-13. The "Outcome" object and its types

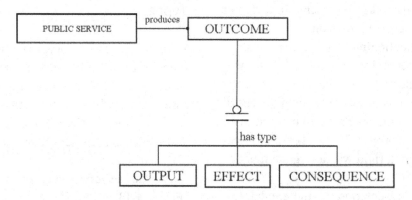

The execution of a service may result in a change in the state of the world (e.g. transferring money to an account). This is the *Effect* of the service as defined also in OWL-S. In the PA domain, the service *Effect* is the actual permission, certificate, restriction or punishment the citizen is finally entitled with. In cases where administration refuses the provision of a service, there is no effect.

Consequence is defined as the forwarding of the information related to a service execution to parties with an interest in the event. Clients usually are not directly interested in the service consequences. Consequence may be:

- Internal, when the same agency providing the service has to inform its own organization and/or information system for the service execution.
- External, when information related to the service execution must be communicated to other agencies to ensure information consistency amongst agencies.

4.4.3 The "Input" Object and its Relationship with "Law"

Public services are controlled by *Laws* (e.g. legislation, administrative decisions). *Laws* provide the service execution logic by setting *Preconditions* for service provision.

Public services need *Input* to be executed. *Input* is information needed to be checked or used in any way in order for a service to be executed. *Evidence placeholder* is the part of Input that contains *Piece of Evidence*, that is piece of information that the service provider should have access to in order to check the validity of the Preconditions. There is a many-to-many relationship between the evidence placeholders and the pieces of evidence depicting the fact that an *evidence placeholder* (e.g. ID-Card) usually "stores" many *evidences* (e.g. date of birth, surname) and a *Piece of Evidence* might be found in numerous different placeholders.

Various types of evidence placeholders exist. For example, they may be physical (e.g. documents) and electronic (e.g. databases, XML documents).

Information that is used by the service for other purposes is not considered evidence and is modeled here as *Other Input* (e.g. the applicant's address to be used for communicating a document/decision).

In each service, a piece of evidence has a *Purpose*. The evidence purpose is related to the underlying business logic that explains the reason for which the service provider wants to have access to the specific piece of information.

Figure 4 14: The "Input" and "Law" objects

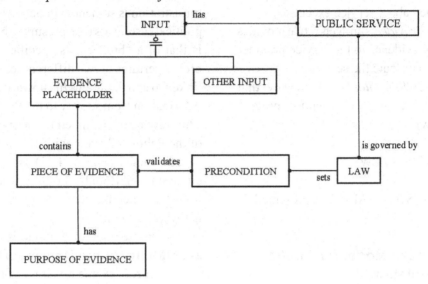

For example, the purpose of the ID card number (evidence) serves for checking and validating the identity of the applicant. It is interesting to mention that in different countries, different pieces of evidence may serve the same purpose e.g. the Social Security Number and/or the passport number may be used for identification purposes as alternative to ID-card number. The *"Evidence Purpose"* is a valuable concept in cross-border public service provision.

The different types of service *"Input"* and its relationship with the concepts of *"Law"* and *"Precondition"* are presented in Figure 4-14.

4.4.4 The "Public Administration Entity" object

There are four types of roles that PA agencies can acquire during the service execution process. These are (Figure 4-15):

- *Service Provider* is the agency that produces and provides the service. Sometimes, it makes sense to separate the *service producer* (the entity that produces the service) from the *service distributor* (the entity that delivers the output of the service).

Figure 4-15. The roles of the "Public Administration Entity"

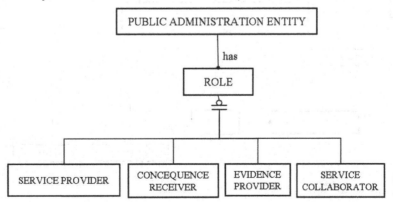

- *Consequence Receiver* is a third agency that is informed about service execution.
- *Evidence Provider* is an agency that provides necessary evidence to the service provider in order to execute the service.
- *Service Collaborator* is an agency that participates in service execution process (workflow).

4.4.5 Model Overview

The overall PA Service Model is presented in Figure 4-16.

4.5 The Process Model for Public Policy Formulation

Societal entities are the ultimate *"client"* of the governance system. Society has delegated power to the Political System, acknowledging the latter as the primary "server" of society. Public administration is somehow in between society and political system. Its role, presumed by its position, is that of a "broker". Its specific function as a broker pertains to two different roles. The first is linked to and facilitates the upward movement of information from society to the Political System. The second role is linked to the implementation of the Political System will.

The model (Figure 4-17) is presented as a circle starting from the bottom, where the social need for collective action triggers and activates the whole system.

A simplified view of the model is also presented as a UML Interaction Diagram, in Figure 4-18.

In Figure 4-18, the upper part of the model is related to the Public Policy Formulation mega-process. Accordingly, the bottom part - which is shaded and discussed in the next part - corresponds to the Service Provision mega-process.

Figure 4-16. The PA service model

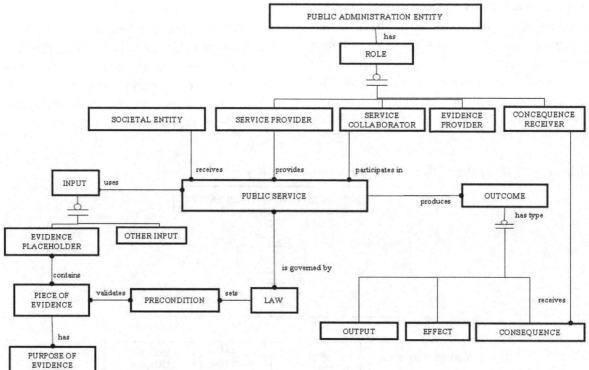

Figure 4-17. The GEA process model for public policy formulation

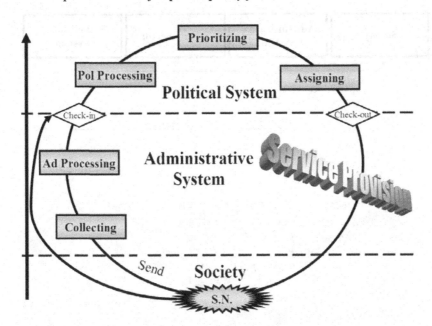

The description of the model follows:

Everything starts with societal needs to be addressed by governance system. These needs should reach political entities (political system). Generally, society has two ways for communicating needs to the political system: the formal, bureaucratic channel through public administration, and a number of alternative channels which bypass bureaucracy in order to directly reach the political system. These channels may vary from a formal political party or NGO to informal conversations of political appointees with "ordinary citizens".

Focusing on the formal administrative channel, the first role of administrative system (PA entities) is the collection of societal needs and a whole system should be set up for this purpose. In order for this system to operate effectively, the capacity of not only reactively collecting but also proactively "sensing" societal needs is critical.

After this first step, "administrative processing" follows. This processing is the first attempt by the administrative system to organize un-structured information that it collects, during the "collection" phase. Categorizing this information, translating it to the language of public administration and codifying it are some aspects of this administrative processing.

At the "check-in" point the processed information reaches political bodies. It is here that we usually find supporting offices of political personnel. They try to filter all the information they feel important and transfer it to key people. Information processing by the political layer though is different to administrative processing. Since we have entered the realm of the political sub-system, choice based on political criteria is enforced. These offices exclude needs as inappropriate (e.g. not compatible with the political agenda) and draft a final list of issues to be addressed.

Then we reach the phase of prioritizing, which is a critical function for the political system. The placement of the "Prioritizing" step at the head of the model emphasizes its importance. The elected political personnel are the main actors in this intensive decision-making process. The output is

Figure 4-18. The process model for public policy formulation

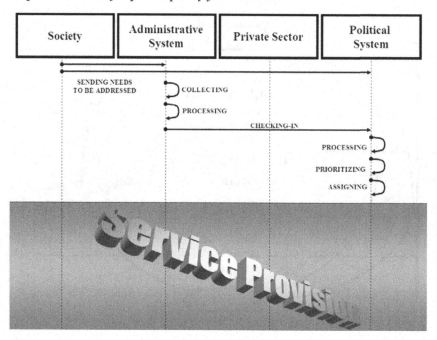

a hierarchically ranked list of political To-Dos, which forms a political Action Plan.

After that, information starts moving downwards. The upward movement was the flow of needs towards decision makers; the downward movement is related to realization of political decisions.

The prioritizing phase is followed by the "assigning" phase. While the former clearly expresses political values, the second deals with technical arrangements. At this step the political subsystem delegates its mandate to PA to realize its political action plan. Nevertheless, an alternative implementation channel exists: the private sector can act as an alternative provider of public services to society.

Through its legislative power, the parliament assigns duties to entities (public/private) to realize the political action plan. The political will becomes a concrete plan, with actors, budget, accountability and management mechanisms.

At the "check-out" point, information leaves the political realm and returns to the adminis-

trative subsystem (or the private sector). What PA personnel usually receive from this stage is a law or a decree that has to be enforced and practically implemented. PA has to organize and execute what has been decided. The "check-out" point is the point, where we pass from the Public Policy Formulation to the Service Provision mega-process.

Society has initially asked for collective action to solve emerged issues/problems and finally receives services that address the initial needs.

Closing the description of this process, we present some interesting feedback mechanisms that could be used to monitor the overall process. These are:

1st Control – *Political Awareness*: Checks the divergence between what society needs and what the political system thinks society needs.

2nd Control – *Administrative Accountability*: Checks the divergence between what the political system wants to provide to society and what society finally receives from the administrative system.

3rd Control – *Political Accountability*: Checks the divergence between the demand from society as received by the political system and the final plan that is communicated by the political system to the administrative system for addressing this demand.

4th Control – *Governance Responsiveness*: Checks the divergence between what society has asked for and what society receives at the end of the process.

4.6 The Process Model for Service Provision

This model depicts the main steps performed each time a client (citizen, business) asks for PA service execution. That is, it covers the path that leads from the conceptualization of a client's atomic need eligible to be addressed by PA, to the execution and delivery of the service in the real world.

To deploy this model, we borrowed concepts from Speech Act Theory in order to define two the informative and performative parts of the service provision process. Specifically we have identified:

* The planning phase, which constitutes the *informative* part of the citizen-administration conversation: citizens ask the *who, why, what, how, when, where* of a service. Actions included here pertain to discovering the type of service needed, the type and specific instance of the service provider, the specific location where the service is available and information about the service behaviour.

* The execution phase, which constitutes the *performative* part of this conversation. During this phase public administration executes the service and provides outcome.

Table 4-7. The GEA process model for public service provision

Informative Phase (Planning)
1. An atomic need/obligation eligible to be addressed by the government emerges to a Client.
2. The Client identifies the type of Public Service (Service) available from the administrative system that addresses the emerged atomic need/obligation.
3. The Client finds the type of PA agency that provides the Service needed (e.g. the proper administrative level with the mandate to provide a type of service).
4. The Client finds the specific instance of the PA agency that acts as the actual Service Provider for the specific case (WHO provides the Service).
5. The Client finds the Location (physical or electronic) from where the Service is available by the specific Service Provider (WHERE the Service is provided).
6. The Client visits/contacts the Location from where the service is available. At this point, a communication channel between the Client and the Service Provider is established.
7. The Client gets information regarding various aspects of the service (HOW the Service is executed – behaviour).
Performative Phase (Execution)
8. The Client initiates the Service execution.
9. The Service Provider receives and processes all the service input and validates the Logical Preconditions of the service (iterative). During this process, external agencies may be communicated either to provide additional evidence (evidence providers) or to participate in the workflow (service collaborators).
10. The Service Provider checks the overall service Procedural Preconditions. Although, all Evidence's checks have been performed in the previous step, some additional check of the service as a whole takes place in this step (e.g. eligibility, quality of service).
11. The Service Provider comes up with the final decision regarding the case.
12. Output: The Service Provider prepares the administrative document, which is the output of the service. The administrative cument includes the official decision made by the Service Provider.
13. Consequence: The Service Provider updates archives kept internally (local consequence) and may inform other agencies (global consequence).

Several GEA defined objects participate in the process of PA service execution (part 4.4). A brief description is presented in table 4-7. More detailed description can be found in (Peristeras V. & Tarabanis K., 2005).

5. CONCLUSION / FUTURE WORK

The work presented here constitutes a domain analysis effort for public administration. It has resulted in a set of models that constitute the Governance Enterprise Architecture (GEA). GEA is a top level, generic and thus reusable enterprise architecture for the overall governance system and covers its two core mega-processes, namely Public Policy Formulation and Service Provision.

These models are valuable and exploitable per se as business modeling constructs can be used as blueprints for designing and documenting PA systems. So for example, when a PA agency decides to provide a new service, the service model presented in part 4.4 could be used as a template to allow the designers of the service discuss and decide the various aspects and characteristics of the service. The same model could be used to document existing services and provide uniform description/language for cross-agency and reengineering projects. This is what has already been planed in a large scale national project in an EU country. More than 100 public services will be modeled using the GEA service model.

We also place emphasis on the potential to use these models for information systems analysis and development based on semantic technologies. In such technological environments, the GEA models provide the basic knowledge infrastructure (domain models) to make real the potential of semantic technologies.

Our future work includes mainly two directions:

A.   Further verification/elaboration through real world and extended application of the

GEA models. Towards this goal, we aim at elaborating and applying improvements to the GEA models. This may take the following directions:

- *Bottom-up experience* by analyzing and modelling a great number of real PA services following the proposed models in order to identify possible improvements and further validate them. Although we have modelled a great number of services for verification purposes we are currently applying some of the models to a project run by an EU Member State Administration to document national PA services. We anticipate that this down-to-earth extended experience will provide further insights to our modelling effort.
- *Top down insights* which may come by studying and putting side by side GEA models and the ever evolving, contemporary public policy and public administration theory.
- *Elaborating and extending the discourse metaphor* that we used to model the Society-Governance interaction.

Taking the above into consideration, we foresee that at a future time there may be a need for developing a second version of the GEA models to incorporate all the improvements and amendments.

B.   We have already started working towards the direction of using GEA in order to build a full Semantic Web Service based execution environment. This environment is based on GEA defined semantics, models and ontologies. We have combined the formal service ontology semantics provided by WSMO and proposed a WSMO-PA specification as a specialization of WSMO for the PA domain. WSMO-PA uses and builds heavily on GEA concepts and models. Some related work that links WSMO and GEA can be found in (Peristeras V., Goudos S., Vitvar T., Mocan

A., & Tarabanis K., 2006) and (Xia Wang et al., 2007).

As a further step, we intent to use this PA Service Ontology (WSMO-PA) in a Semantic Web Service execution environment that could be tailored to the PA semantics, practices and special characteristics.

Last but not least, we try to propose the GEA reference enterprise architecture and modeling perspective to several national and international bodies and work towards the creation of a community of practice that adopts and uses GEA descriptions for eGovernance systems development, documentation of PA services, re-engineering projects, etc. In the future this line of work could further lead to a standardization activity. Taking into consideration the complexities of such an effort substantial support is sought by important actors in the eGovernance field, including big information systems and consulting vendors.

REFERENCES

Allan, K. (1994). Speech act classification and definition. In R. Asher (Ed.), *Encyclopedia of Language and Linguistics* (Vol. 8, pp. 4124-4127): Oxford: Pergamon Press.

ATHENA Project. (2005). *D.A6.1, Specification of a Basic Architecture Reference Model.*

Austin, J. L. (1962). *How to do things with Words.* Cambridge, MA: Harvard University Press.

Bach, K., & Harnish, R. M. (1979). *Linguistic Communication and Speech Acts.* Cambridge MA: MIT Press.

Battle, S., Bernstein, A., Boley, H., Grosof, B., Gruninger, M., Hull, R., et al. (2005). *Semantic Web Services Framework (SWSF).*

Berners-Lee, T., Hendler, J., & Lassila, O. (2001). The Semantic Web. *SCIENTIFIC AMERICAN, May 2001.*

Bevir, M., & Rhodes, R. A. W. (2001). *A Decentered Theory of Governance* (Working Paper 2001-10). Berkeley: Institute of Governmental Studies, University of California.

Brahim Medjahed, Abdelmounaam Rezgui, Athman Bouguettaya, & Ouzzani, M. (2003). Infrastructure for E-Government Web Services. *IEEE Internet Computing, 7*(1), 58-65.

Browne, A., & Wildavsky, A. (1984). *Should Evolution become Implementation*: Pressman and Wildavsky.

C4ISR Integration Task Force. (1997). *C4ISR Architecture Framework, Version 2.0.*

Claudio Masolo, Stefano Borgo, Aldo Gangemi, Nicola Guarino, & Oltramari, A. (2003). *Wonder-Web: Deliverable D1.8, Ontology Library (IST Project 2001-33052).*

D. Apostolou, L. Stojanovic, T. Pariente Lobo, & Thoenssen, B. (2005). Towards a Semantically-Driven Software Engineering Environment for eGovernment. In (Vol. 3416, pp. 157–168): LNAI.

Dietz, J. L. G., & Mulder, J. B. F. (1998). *Organisational transformation requires constructional knowledge of business systems.* Paper presented at the 31st Annual HICCS.

DIP Project. (2004). *D9.3 e-Government ontology.*

Fensel D., C. Bussler, & Maedche, A. (2002). *Semantic Web Enabled Web Services.* Paper presented at the ISWC 2002.

Fowler, M. (1997). *Analysis Patterns*: Addison-Wesley. New Performance Framework Measures Public Value of IT, Research Note, 8 July 2003 2003).

Goldkuhl, G. (1996). *Generic business frameworks and action modeling.* Paper presented at the 1st International Workshop on Communications Modeling - The Language/Action Perspective.

Gronlund, A. (2005). *What's In a Field – Exploring the eGoverment Domain*. Paper presented at the 38th Hawaii International Conference on System Sciences.

H. Koontz, Donnell, C. O., & Weihreich, H. (1980). *Management* (7th Edition ed.): McGraw Hill.

Hay, D. (1996). *Data Models Patterns*. NY: Dorste House Publishing.

Hepp, M., Leymann, F., Domingue, J., Wahler, A., & Fensel, D. (2005, October 18-20). *Semantic Business Process Management: A Vision Towards Using Semantic Web Services for Business Process Management*. Paper presented at the IEEE ICEBE 2005, Beijing, China.

Hogwood, B. W., & Gunn, L. A. (1984). *Policy Analysis for the Real World*. Oxford: Oxford University Press.

Hughes, & Owen E. (1994). *Public Management and Administration: an introduction*. New York: St. Martin's Press.

Inter-Agency Benchmarking & Best Practices Council. (1996). Government Process Classification Scheme.   Retrieved Dec. 2001, from http://www.va.gov/fedsbest/index.htm

Johannesson, P. (2001). A Language/Action based Approach to Information Modeling. In Rossi M. & Siau K. (Eds.), *Information Modeling in the new Millenium*: IDEA Publishing.

Johannesson, P., & Wohed, P. (1998). *Deontic Specification Patterns - Generalisation and Classification*. Paper presented at the International Conference on Formal Ontologies in Information Systems, Trento, Italy.

Klischewski, R. (2004). Semantic Web for e-Government - a Research Agenda. *AIS SIG SEMIS Newsletter Volume 1, Issue 1*.

Klischewski, R., & Jeenicke, M. (2004). *Semantic Web Technologies for Information Management within e-Government Services*. Paper presented

at the 37th Hawaii International Conference on System Sciences.

Lane, J.-E. (1995). *The Public Sector: Concepts, Models and Approaches* (2nd ed. ed.): Sage Publications.

Lind M., & Goldkuhl, G. (2001). *Generic Layered Patterns for Business Modeling*. Paper presented at the 6th International Workshop on the Language-Action Perspective on Communication Modeling, Montreal, Canada.

Lowi, T. J. (1979). *The End of Liberalism: The Second Republic of the United States*. New York: W.W. Norton.

Missikoff, M. (2002). Harmonise – an ontology-based approach for semantic interoperability. *ERCIM News, 51*, 33-34.

Motta, E., Domingue, J., Cabral, L., & Gaspari, M. (2003). *IRS II: A Framework and Infrastructure for Semantic Web Services*. Paper presented at the 2nd International Semantic Web Conference.

Musgrave, R. A. (1959). *The Theory of Public Finance*. New York: McGraw-Hill.

Niles, I., & Pease, A. (2001, October 17-19). *Towards a Standard Upper Ontology*. Paper presented at the 2nd International Conference on Formal Ontology in Information Systems (FOIS-2001), Ogunquit, Maine.

Office of e-Envoy UK. (2002). e-Services Development Framework Primer v1.0b.   Retrieved Noe 2002, from http://www.govtalk.gov.uk/documents/eSDFprimerV1b.pdf

Oltramari A., Gangemi A., Guarino N., & Masolo C. (2002, October 2002). *Sweeting ontologies with DOLCE. Ontologies and the Semantic Web*. Paper presented at the 13th International Conference, EKAW 2002, Siguenza, Spain.

OWL Services Coalition. (2004). OWL-S: Semantic Markup for Web Services.   Retrieved March 2005, from http://www.daml.org/services/owl-s/1.1/

Peristeras, V., & Tarabanis, K. (2000). Towards an Enterprise Architecture for Public Administration : A Top Down Approach. *European Journal of Information Systems, 9*(Dec. 2000), 252-260.

Peristeras, V., Tsekos, T., & Tarabanis, K. (2003, 31 Jul.-2 Aug.). *Building Domain Models for the (e-) Governance System.* Paper presented at the International Conference on Politics and Information Systems: Technologies and Applications (PISTA '03), Orlando, Florida, USA.

Peristeras V., Goudos S., Vitvar T., Mocan A., & Tarabanis K. (2006). *Towards Semantic Web Services for Public Administration based on the Web Service Modeling Ontology (WSMO) and the Governance Enterprise Architecture (GEA).* Paper presented at the 5th EGOV International Conference, DEXA Krakow, Poland.

Peristeras V., & Tarabanis K. (2004a). Advancing the Government Enterprise Architecture - GEA: The Service Execution Object Model. In R. Traunmuller (Ed.), *Electronic Government, DEXA, 3rd International Conference EGOV 2004, Zaragoza, Lecture Notes in Computer Science 3183* (pp. 476-482): Springer.

Peristeras V., & Tarabanis K. (2004b). The Governance Enterprise Architecture (GEA) Object Model. In M. A. Wimmer (Ed.), *Knowledge Management in Electronic Government, Lecture Notes in Computer Science 3035, (5th IFIP International Working Conference, KMGov 2004, Krems, Austria, May 27-29)* (pp. 101-110): Springer.

Peristeras V., & Tarabanis K. (2005, 22-24 April 2005). *The GEA Generic Process Model for Public Administration Service Execution.* Paper presented at the 8th International Conference for Business Information Systems (8th BIS 2005), Poznan, Poland.

Peristeras V., & Tarabanis K. (2006, Mar. 27-29). *Reengineering the public administration modus operandi through the use of reference domain models and Semantic Web Service technologies.*

Paper presented at the 2006 AAAI Spring Symposium, The Semantic Web meets eGovernment (SWEG), Stanford University, California, USA.

R.E. Asher (ed.). (1994). *The Encyclopedia of Language and Linguistics.* Oxford: Pergamon.

Rhodes, R. A. W. (1997). *Understanding Governance*: Open University Press.

Riley, B. T. (2003). *e-Government vs. e-Governance* (International Tracking Survey Report, No 4). Ottawa: Commonwealth Centre for E-Governance.

Rosati, L., Lai, M. E., & Gnoli, C. (2004, 10th December). *Faceted Classification for Public Administration.* Paper presented at the Semantic Web Applications and Perspectives (SWAP) - 1st Italian Semantic Web Workshop, Ancona, Italy.

SAP. (2000). R/3 System SAP Solution Map. Retrieved Dec. 2000, from www.sap.com

Searle, J. R. (1969). *Speech Acts. An Essay in the Philosophy of Language.* London: Cambridge University Press.

Searle, J. R. (1975). A taxonomy of illocutionary acts. In Gunderson K. (Ed.), *Language, Mind and Knowledge.* Minneapolis: University of Minesota.

Semantic Interoperability Community of Practice (SICoP). (2005). *Introducing Semantic Technologies and the Vision of the Semantic Web, White Paper Series Module 1.*

Semy, S. K., Pulvermacher, M. K., & Obrst, L. J. (2004). *Toward the Use of an Upper Ontology for U.S. Government and U.S. Military Domains: An Evaluation* (No. 04B0000063): The MITRE Corporation.

Spewak, S. H., & Steven C. Hill. (1992). *Enterprise Architecture Planning: Developing a Blueprint for Data, Applications and Technology*: John Wiley & Sons.

Tambouris, E. (2001). *An Integrated Platform for Realising One-Stop Government: The eGOV project*. Paper presented at the E-Government Workshop within DEXA01.

Tapscott, D., & Caston, A. (1994). *Paradigm Shift : The New Promise of Information Technology*.

Tarabanis, K., Peristeras, V., & Fragidis, G. (2001, June 2001). *Building an Enterprise Architecture for Public Administration: A High Level Data Model for Strategic Planning*. Paper presented at the 9th European Conference on Information Systems, Bled, Slovenia.

TopQuadrant. (2005a). FEA Reference Models Ontologies v.1.1.   Retrieved 16 Mar., 2006, from http://www.topquadrant.com/documents/TQFEARMO.pdf

TopQuadrant. (2005b). *FEA Refererence Model Ontologies (FEA RMO) v1.1*.

Vendler, Z. (1972). *Res Cogitans*: Ithaca: Cornell University Press.

Vitvar T., Kerrigan M., Overeem v. A., V., P., & K., T. (2006, Mar. 27-29). *Infrastructure for the Semantic Pan-European E-government Services*. Paper presented at the AAAI Spring Symposium, The Semantic Web meets eGovernment (SWEG), Stanford University, California, USA.

Wieringa, R., & Meyer, J. (1993). *Applications of Deontic Logic in Computer Science: A Concise Overview*: Wiley.

The World Bank. (1992). *Governance and Development*. Washington: World Bank.

Xia Wang, Goudos S., Peristeras V., Vitvar T., Mocan A., & Tarabanis K. (2007, 4-10 Jan.). *WSMO-PA: Formal Specification of Public Administration Service Model on Semantic Web Service Ontology*. Paper presented at the 40th HICSS, Hawaii.

Yergin, D., & Stanislaw, J. (1998). *The Commanding Heights: The Battle Between Government and the Marketplace That is Remaking the Modern World*. New York: Simon & Schuster.

Zachman, J. A. (1987). A framework for information systems architecture. *IBM Systems Journal, 26*(3).

Zachman, J. A., & Sowa, J. F. (1992). Extending and formalizing the framework for information systems architecture. *IBM Systems Journal, 31*(3).

ENDNOTE

[1]   http://www.opengroup.org/architecture/togaf8-doc/arch/

Chapter XII
Enterprise Architecture and Governance Challenges for Orchestrating Public–Private Cooperation

Bram Klievink
Delft University of Technology, The Netherlands

Wijnand Derks
Telematica Instituut, The Netherlands

Marijn Janssen
Delft University of Technology, The Netherlands

ABSTRACT

The ambition of the Dutch government is to create a demand-driven government by means of effective use of information and communication technology. This requires not only public, but also private parties to interact with each other. This is a complex endeavour as private and public organizations have their own goals, systems and architectures that need to be coordinated. Within this setting, a new architecture should be created for managing and orchestrating the interactions among governmental and private organizations. In this chapter we present an architecture aimed at supporting the coordination of public and private parties for creating a one stop shop and the main challenges therein. We found that a public-private service network poses higher requirements on the architecture of a service network, whereas the variety in systems of the various organizations and different aims make it more difficult to develop such an architecture. Furthermore, it is difficult to isolate architectural challenges from governance aspects, as many architectural issues need to be complemented by governance mechanisms. Architecture and governance cannot be considered in isolation.

INTRODUCTION

It is the ambition of many governments to improve service-delivery to citizens. One way to do this is by ensuring a widespread and effective use of information and communication technology to create a demand-driven government. Many governmental organizations offer products and services to citizens. From the citizen's perspective, the services provided by one organization are often only one part of the total service process they require. From their point of view, their situation involves multiple steps to be taken, and some of these steps have to be fulfilled by services performed by various governmental organizations. This is especially true in countries with highly fragmented governments where the government consists of many agencies and organizations that each have a relatively high degree of autonomy. To fulfil the objective of demand-driven e-government, the focus should shift from services offered by a single organization to an integrated service-delivery process fulfilling citizens' needs. From the citizen's perspective, these services do not stop at organizational boundaries. Therefore, many citizens' requests require multiple organizations to interact with each other. These cross-agency service-delivery processes need to be coordinated.

In the Netherlands, this call for coordination recently gave rise to the development of a national reference architecture (for a comprehensive description see the chapter 'A Service-Oriented Reference Architecture for E-Government' by Lankhorst and Bayens in this book). The Dutch Government Reference Architecture (abbreviated as NORA (Nederlandse Overheid Referentie Architectuur) in Dutch) provides a common ground for developing the electronic government (Kenniscentrum, 2007). It consists of design principles arranged by an architecture framework based on the Zachman framework and models for the (re)engineering of (electronic) government service

delivery (ICTU, 2007). The NORA is based on a Service Oriented Architecture (SOA), which is a fundamental principle, but it also includes very specific guidelines. Some of those principles are mandatory (by law), some are advisory. The task of this reference architecture is to guide public organizations in the direction of a responsive, demand-driven and efficient government.

Demand-driven service-delivery does not stop at the boundaries of individual organizations, nor does it at the boundaries between the public and the private sector. Private parties might be involved in the service provisioning, in several ways. Sometimes governmental services are funded by public money, but are in fact executed by private organizations. This might be considered a form of outsourcing. Furthermore, services provided by private parties can be closely related to governmental services, even so close that from the citizen's perspective, it is part of the same service-delivery process. Health care is a good example, in countries that publicly fund basic health care services, the actual care may be provided by privately held organizations. From the citizen's perspective this does not consist of separate processes at the government and the health care provider, but it is one and the same process. Finally, governmental organization might deliver their services using channels operated by private parties (Janssen, Kuk, & Wagenaar, 2008). For example, when buying a car, the car dealer also registers the car and the new owner at the responsible governmental agency. In these cases, truly demand-driven e-government requires cooperation with private organizations as well. In this chapter, the cooperation between public and private organizations will be denoted as public-private service networks, or service networks for short.

Given these public-private service networks, there is a need to go beyond a governmental reference architecture and to design an enterprise architecture that supports the cooperation between public and private organizations for integrated service delivery. The national reference architecture provides directions in governmental enterprise architecture, while private organizations have their own strategies, enterprise architectures, systems and interests. Since these organizations are (semi-)autonomous, it is often not possible to enforce a unified enterprise architecture or process-specifications that should be adhered to. The diversity of key stakeholders and their interests makes service networks very complex (Provan & Milward, 2001). Within this institutional and organizational setting, new architectural guidelines are needed for managing and orchestrating the interactions among the public and the private partners to offer integrated services. This demands an enterprise architecture facilitating the public-private cooperation and governance mechanisms to ensure that the enterprise architecture is used.

The *objective* of this chapter is twofold. The first objective is to identify and present guidelines for an architecture enabling cooperation between public and private partners. The second objective is to identify architectural and governance challenges that should be dealt with. The architecture has been developed using action research, and we derive architectural and governance challenges from the implementation of the architecture and literature.

This chapter is structured as follows. In the next section we describe the background, the complexity of the situation and the key concepts. In section three the research approach is presented. In section four the case study and the developed architecture are briefly discussed. In the section thereafter we analyze the main architectural and governance challenges. Finally, we offer future trends and conclusions about architecture as a management instrument and the need for effective governance mechanisms guiding a public-private service network.

BACKGROUND

The introduction of enterprise architectures encompassing several actors is a complex undertaking. This is complicated as there is often no uniform view on architecture and every organization has its own strategies, interests and systems. Despite the agreement that the development of enterprise architectures is a complex undertaking, there is little insight in the specific challenges that need to be dealt with, nor theories that provide support for this. The literature available draws attention to aspects that should be investigated. For example Janssen and Hjort-Madsen (2007) found that in such complex architectural efforts at least five elements should be considered; (1) policies, actors and structures, (2) governance, (3) architecture models, (4) architecture principles and standards and (5) implementations. This literature is of help to investigate the aspects that are needed, but does not provide insight into the types of problems that need to be dealt with when designing enterprise architecture for public-private service networks. This chapter aims at fulfilling this gap by investigating the development of an enterprise architecture for demand-driven e-government in which both public and private parties are involved.

The Role of Architecture

Integrated service delivery requires integrating the single fragments that make up a service delivery process. These parts can either be provided by public or by private parties and the dependencies among these parts need to be coordinated in a coherent and consistent manner. In the past, many organizations within the Dutch government have implemented their own systems and procedures. To coordinate ICT efforts within government, the NORA was introduced as a reference architecture. The national reference architecture may link ICT efforts of governmental organizations, but this does by no means align them with the

Figure 1. The need for architecture

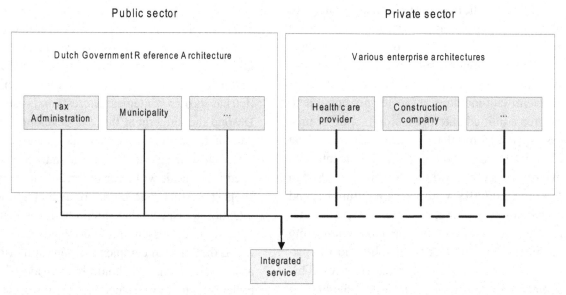

architecture of private organizations that are (or could be) involved in the delivery of specific services. Furthermore, the national enterprise architecture was only recently developed, there is no obligation for organizations to use it, and it may take organizations years to comply with its principles.

Given this background, integrated service delivery needs to deal with heterogeneous systems and business processes of public and private organizations. In order to integrate services and truly focus on citizens' demands, some kind of coordination is necessary. The problem of public-private cooperation for integrated service delivery is schematically sketched in Figure 1. All the organizations provide one or more elements that should be managed to provide an integrated service.

In this complex multi-actor environment, enterprise architecture should help to coordinate the services provided by the individual organizations. Furthermore, there is a need for governing the relationships and architecture among these organizations. Therefore, we explore the concept of enterprise architecture and governance in the following subsection.

Enterprise Architecture and Governance

In order to orchestrate the public-private service network, a frame of reference is needed. This frame of reference can be created using enterprise architecture. Many definitions of enterprise architecture (EA) can be found in the literature (e.g. Lankhorst, 2005; Richardson, Jackson, & Dickson, 1990; Ross, 2003). As yet, there is no generally accepted definition on architecture (Ross, 2003). Conceptually, architecture is about defining the structure and functions of a design at an abstract level, often used in construction. One of the first definitions of enterprise architecture in information technology (IT) was by Richardson, Jackson and Dickson (1990). Recently, the city plan concept has given birth to a type of architect that develops detailed drawings of the interactions between various systems (Ross, 2003). With enterprise architecture, the concept is not just applied to technology and information, but also to the entire organization or enterprise. Therefore, enterprise architecture can be defined as the "coherent whole of principles, methods and models that are used in the design and realisation of an enterprise's organizational structure, business processes, information systems, and infrastructure" (Lankhorst, 2005, p. 3). An architecture can be descriptive, prescriptive or both. In a descriptive sense an architecture shows the existing relationships among the elements which can be used to analyze weaknesses and opportunities. In a prescriptive sense it can be used as a blueprint that needs to be realized within a certain timeframe. If both descriptive and prescriptive architectures are available, a roadmap from the current to the envisioned future situation can be realized. In this chapter we take a prescriptive view on EA, as the objective is to move towards a situation in which public and private parties cooperate seamlessly. This needs to be complemented by governance mechanisms to take aspects like differences in interests and systems into account.

IT governance represents the framework for decision rights and accountabilities to encourage desirable behaviour in the use of IT resources (Weill, 2004). In analogy, architecture governance can be viewed as the practice and orientation by which enterprise architectures are managed and controlled. The governance of architecture is complicated due to the heterogeneity of network partners and their various strategies, interests and systems. Each organization might have different strategic objectives, capabilities and resources. Moreover, potential partners may have different processes and levels of IT sophistication that needs to be taken into account before services can be shared.

Organizations can make use of three kinds of governance mechanisms: (1) decision-making structures, (2) alignment processes and (3) formal communications (Weill & Ross, 2005). Allocating decision-making responsibilities, roles and organizational committees are part of the decision-making structures. Reaching effective IT governance by formal communications includes two-way communication and a good relationship between business- and IT people. Alignment pro-cesses as governance mechanisms involve management techniques for securing widespread and effective involvement in governance decisions and their implementation, for example by service level agreements (SLA's). This is especially important in public-private service networks, because we're dealing with existing autonomous organizations, each with existing decision making structures, processes and systems. Governance should help to manage the development and practice of an architecture that coordinates the dependencies among public and private organizations.

The Need for Orchestration

The dominant architectural paradigm is currently the Service Oriented Architecture (SOA). In a SOA, the focus is on services that offer functionality, thereby uncoupling functionality from the technical implementation of the functionality. The focus on services offers a way to align processes in public-private service networks, while leaving the underlying organizational structures, processes and systems untouched. Demand-driven service-delivery processes can be composed of various services at various public or private organizations. Citizens currently select and invoke services themselves. Consider the following situation: first, a citizen searches for information and selects the appropriate services. Next, the citizen requests the service at each organization, uses the response to request a subsequent service at another organization and so on. Finally, the citizen monitors the status, submits reminders, collects the responses and integrates them. Due to the complexities involved in governmental service-delivery, the coordination of the dependencies among the activities and systems of the individual parties is a major challenge.

The effective coordination of the dependencies among various organizations with the aim of creating an integrated service-delivery requires process orchestration, or orchestration for short. Process orchestration is the goal-oriented coordination by a single responsible entity in a cross-organizational process flow (Janssen, Gortmaker, & Wagenaar, 2006). In the situation described before, the citizen performs the role of orchestrator because they select and invoke services themselves. To improve service-delivery, the orchestration role should be performed by the government instead of by the citizen. This should result in a reduction of administrative costs for citizens.

The transition of this orchestration role from the citizen to the government is depicted in Figure 2. In this figure, the orchestrator role is visualized by adding a layer on top of the individual organizations. The introduction of this role is aimed at reducing the administrative burdens for the citizen, as only one request needs to be made. The orchestrator handles all activities necessary for the coordination of the cross-agency service process and returns one answer. Basically, the orchestrating process orchestrates the services at various organizations into one single request by and one single response to the citizen.

The basic concept of orchestration provides a simplistic view which is useful for explanation purposes, but does not capture the full complexity of reality. There are many orchestration variants possible. Essential parts of any orchestration vari-

ant are determining which organization is overall responsible for the service and which organization handles the customer interactions. Figure 3 shows a schematic overview of these basic variants of roles that handle interactions with clients. When considering other design variables, many more specific variants of orchestration can be derived. The basic models on the allocation of the primarily role of orchestration are the following:

- **First-in-chain:** The agency that delivers the service is responsible for the orchestration of the entire chain and returns a single answer to the user. This can be a different agency depending on the point of entry in the service chain;
- **Pass-the-buck:** The agency that delivers the service shifts the responsibility for (parts of) the execution of the process to the agencies directly involved in executing the next process step (or part);
- **Director:** Agencies in the partnership create a separate process orchestration role and allocate this role to one actor. This could be a new organization or any of the organizations most qualified to perform this job. The actor fulfilling this role is orchestrating the

Figure 2. Basic concept of orchestration (Based on: Gortmaker, 2008)

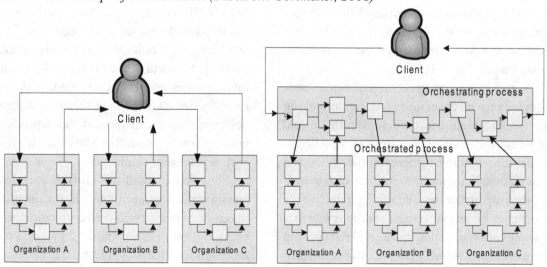

Figure 3. Schematic overview of basic orchestration variants

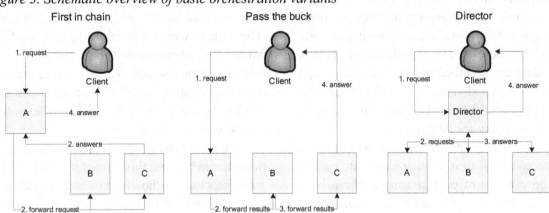

cross-agency process; thereby becoming a specialized director.

Previous research on orchestration of electronic governmental services (e.g. Janssen et al., 2006) shows that this is not just a technical challenge, governance-related issues should be considered as well. In order to successfully orchestrate these service delivery processes, agreements need to be made on issues such as lead-times, accountability and information sharing (Gortmaker & Janssen, 2007). We elaborate on this research by stressing the role of agreements and other components of governance that become even more important if private organizations are among the service partners.

Public-Private Cooperation

Cooperation between public and private partners has a long history. Already back in the 1970's, and again in the 1990's, public-private partnerships (PPP) were established to strike a balance between the entrepreneurial spirit and public interest considerations (Linder, 1999). Research on public-private partnerships identifies both strengths and weaknesses in the practice of having private parties execute projects concerning public

interest. Strengths include possible financial gains, while weaknesses include possible conflicts of interests and concerns on privacy.

Research in the United States and the United Kingdom show the performances of these partnerships are mixed, often resulting in short-term financial gains at the expense of long-term public costs on accountability, transparency and equal access to services (e.g. Flinders, 2005; Rosenau, 1999). The Internet and SOA paradigm might provide new incentives to come to successful public-private cooperation. ICT may play a role in shaping this cooperation. In the introduction we already argued that including private partners in public services may be necessary to achieve the vision of a truly integrated, demand-driven and citizen oriented e-government. Orchestrating these public-private service networks is necessary to come to successful cooperation.

An important part of these orchestrations are agreements, contracts, procedures, etc. that specify the relationship between the partners in a service network (Pongsiri, 2003). The downside of strictly formalized relationships is that the service network loses some of its flexibility and becomes more tightly coupled, while a loosely coupled network would suit the orchestration model best. An important instrument in orchestrating these service networks is the Service Level Agreement (SLA), in which agreements on response time, management information, availability, etc. are specified at the level of the organizational services. This should be specified in such a way that enough freedom is provided to the participants, but the main conditions for effective cross-organizational service-delivery are guaranteed.

The clear allocation of roles, responsibilities and accountability is another important part of the governance of orchestrating public-private service networks. Who takes the initiatives in case of failure? How are decisions made and enforced if they concern more than one organization? The difference in interests might complicate these kinds of decisions. Governmental agencies have a primary (social) responsibility towards the public, whereas private organizations have a primary (economic) allegiance towards management, owners, and stakeholders (Rosenau, 1999). The aforementioned public-private partnerships were mainly aimed at increasing public service's efficiency by introducing the entrepreneurial spirit of private organizations. However, this may lead to democratic, public and political costs, like privacy and public responsibilities on failures of private parties (Flinders, 2005; Rosenau, 1999). The clear allocation of responsibilities and roles and introducing other types of governance mechanisms may help to avoid the occurrence of these negative aspects. Clear responsibilities, in combination with SLA's creates a setting in which trust can develop between partners.

RESEARCH APPROACH

In this chapter we present enterprise architecture guidelines for integrated service delivery and identify the main architectural and governance challenges therein. Based on the literature survey in the previous section, a case study in the Dutch public sector was conducted. This case concerned the design of an architecture for the allocation of

household care to needing people. Such a project involves both public and private organizations. The authors were involved in the design of the architecture, therefore the type of research can be labelled action research. We confront our findings with the literature and identify specific architectural and governance challenges for orchestrating public-private service networks.

Action research or applied case study research was chosen because this type of research instrument is focused on 'how to' questions (Checkland, 1981). This enabled the investigation of the design and development process of the application of the enterprise architecture to this case. The authors were involved in designing the architecture for demand-driven e-government. In addition, the case study aspect came from the interviewing of a number of key persons from different organizations and disciplines to identify the main challenges.

CASE: AN ARCHITECTURE FOR INTEGRATED SERVICE DELIVERY

The motivation for the development of the architecture stems from the observation by several larger governmental institutions and private parties in the Netherlands that cooperation is necessary to meet the demands of citizens and enterprises, in order to bring about a truly demand-oriented e-government (Lankhorst & Derks, 2007). This resulted in the 'B-dossier' project (http://www.b-dossier. nl), a joint research initiative with partners from government, academia and business. The project aims at establishing requirements and solutions for public-private service networks. In this setting a generic functional architecture and a demonstrator have been developed. Both the architecture and the generic end-user interface were applied to the case study in the Netherlands.

Part of social security facilities in the Netherlands is the household care. People can apply for this facility in case they cannot take care of their household themselves. In these cases, these persons apply for a personal budget, which can be used to buy the necessary care. This has the advantage that people can choose the care they need themselves, but this comes at the cost of considerable administrative overhead. In the context of the Social Support Act (abbreviated as WMO (Wet Maatschappelijke Ondersteuning) in Dutch) the social security facility of household care has been decentralized by the government from the national level to the municipal level. This act combines several laws on care entitlements. As a part of this law, municipalities have become responsible for providing their citizens with appropriate services to support them. In our case we investigate the application of our architecture to a new portal initiated by the City of The Hague to facilitate the WMO. The City of Hague sees public-private service networks as a powerful means to provide demand-driven, integral services to citizens. This is demonstrated by her initiative to start Residentie.Net, an internet portal for citizens of The Hague that connects citizens to public and private services in one portal. This portal supports citizens of The Hague in acquiring and managing their personal budget for household care. The following public and private stakeholders are involved:

- **City of The Hague:** The Hague is the seat of the Dutch Parliament and serves as the International City of Peace and Justice. As a municipality it is responsible for the implementation of the WMO, including household care.
- **Residentie.Net:** Residentie.net is a public-private partnership creating a digital portal for the community of The Hague. The mission of Residentie.Net is to connect citizens of The Hague to public and private parties to encourage use of public and private facilities.
- **Centre for Care Entitlement (CIZ):** This institute decides how much care somebody is entitled to, based on the degree of disability.
- **Social Insurance Bank (SVB):** SVB provides (among others) services to holders of a personal budget to relieve them from administrative overhead. SVB is a large organization, with over 4000 employees.
- **Dutch Tax and Customs Administration:** The tax office provides income details on which the budget is based.
- **Care providers:** Organizations offering household care.

Generic Process

In order to research how a demand-driven electronic portal could be realized in the WMO case, a prototype of such a portal was developed by Residentie.Net and was branded 'WMO-portal'. A typical process consists of the following main steps.

1. **Application:** If a client thinks he/she may be entitled to household care, the client can apply for this care him/herself, using the WMO-portal. The portal features a process plan that consists of a number of sequential steps;
2. **Check entitlement:** One of these steps is the application for household care. Part of the application form is a field with the clients' income. This data can be provided by the Dutch Tax Office. Whether the client is entitled to care, is decided by the Centre for Care Entitlement (CIZ);
3. **Contract:** If the application is accepted, the client can search for a household care provider. Once a provider is selected, a formal contract will be made using a template provided by the portal. Both the client and the provider can sign the contract digitally, from their computers;
4. **Receive and consume care:** Household care is provided for the period and amount of care the client is entitled to;

5. **Manage budget:** During the period the household care is effective, the client can manage his/her budget in the portal. The SVB can help the client in administrative overhead.

The main steps of this process are schematically shown in Figure 4. The client passes through the individual steps in the process that is facilitated by the portal. The actors presented in the previous paragraph are also shown; the City of The Hague is overall responsible, Residentie.NET offers the portal and the other organizations are shown in the lower layer, each offering services that are part of the overall process. It is clear that this case suits our description of service-delivery by a network of public and private organizations, thereby illustrating the fragmentation.

The Architecture

The enterprise architecture for demand-driven e-government was applied to the WMO case in a functional architecture specific for this case, the functional architecture was developed in the B-dossier project (Lankhorst, Derks, Fennema, Iacob, & Joosten, 2006). Figure 5 provides an overview of the most important services and functions of the architecture. This figure is drawn in

the Archimate language, which is an architecture description language derived from several other languages and shows the dependencies between architectural layers (Lankhorst, 2005).

Figure 5 shows that services and functions related to authentication and authorisation are seen as part of the shared infrastructure, and are delivered by separate providers. Those third party organizations are shown in the left block ('shared infrastructure'). The delivery of sub-services, adapting these services to the client's question and the integration of information from several sources all are examples of functions that are executed by the service providers involved in the cross-agency process. These service providers are the organizations that provide (parts) of the service-delivery. Integrating all required services and the supply of user information is done by an application, which in turn may be provided by a third-party. This is shown in the upper part of Figure 5 and may be seen as the core functionality of a demand-driven architecture, and therefore under the direct responsibility and supervision of the client (Lankhorst et al., 2006, p. 55).

The architecture supports the generic process of the user, which starts when the user logs-on and is authorized. The user can browse and/or search the directory of services and information and create and update a step-by-step plan. The

Figure 4. Generic WMO-portal process

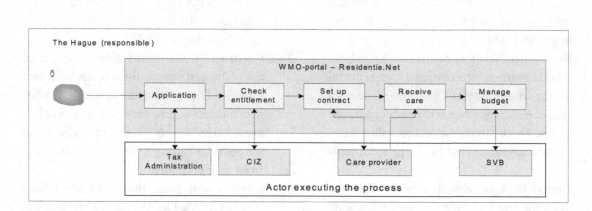

Figure 5. An overview of the service architecture blueprint (Lankhorst & Derks, 2007; Lankhorst et al., 2006, p. 55)

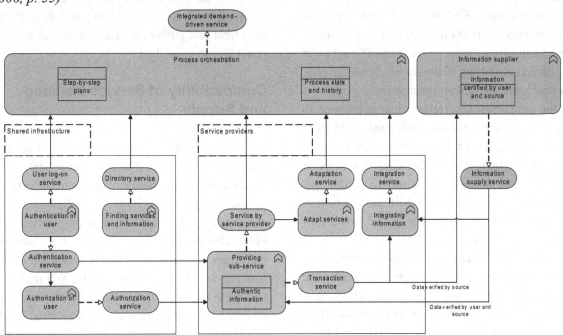

user can also configure and manage the application, for example to authorize access to his file. In these steps, various application services are used, like those for authentication and authorization (Lankhorst et al., 2006, p. 53).

The functional architecture is based on the service-oriented architecture paradigm and consists of a set of requirements and guidelines for an architecture for public-private service networks. These guidelines are divided into four categories: (1) fragmentation, (2) compatibility, (3) quality and (4) access. Those requirements are derived from the enterprise architecture and translated to the case at hand. For a full list of guidelines and requirements we refer to Lankhorst and Derks (2007). We limit our description to those requirements that proved to be challenges in the public-private service network we investigated.

Solving the Fragmentation of Services Across Many Different Organizations

Process orchestration. End-users are faced with the fact that services are dispersed over multiple organizations. End-users need support for the management of scattered service provisioning. The proposed solution to this fragmentation follows the lines of the B-dossier functional architecture (Lankhorst et al., 2006). This means that the basic infrastructure of all service providers (in this case the City of The Hague, CIZ, SVB and the Dutch Tax and Customs Administration) remains in place. Residentie.Net plays a central position; it provides a broker function that facilitates the operation of the public-private service network. As such, Residentie.Net provides a generic orchestration service that is able to execute the step-by-step plans. In this application, The Hague provides the step-by-step plan to Residentie.Net, in such a way that its users can orchestrate the process.

Single identity. End-users and employees have different accounts at different service providers. Users and entities are registered in different ways at different registries. There is a need for managing these identities in order to create a uniform identity. In the case, each service provider is allowed to maintain its own registration of identities, in order to provide maximum flexibility. When a service provider exchanges data, the identity service at each provider generates pseudonyms for the keys of the data items, such that third parties cannot easily combine data. This way, the privacy of users is guaranteed.

Single authentication. End-users and employees have to authenticate themselves for most of the service providers separately and each organization has its own facility and user administration. Therefore, a single sign-on facility is desirable for true integrated service delivery. A single sing-on is created by accepting the authentication at one of the service provider by the other service providers in the service network. This means that users that are authenticated at Residentie.Net are also authenticated (indirectly) at The Hague. Similarly, authentication of employees by SVB is accepted by Residentie.Net.

Single authorization. Exchange of information among service providers is often cumbersome. Either service providers cannot access the information of the client such that the client needs to provide the same information over and over again, or information is exchanged without the consent of the owner. Each service provider has its own access control infrastructure, including policy enforcement, decision, administration and information points (Demchenko et al., 2005). Each of the service providers has a policy enforcement point that controls the transaction service on the end-user's records. At Residentie.Net there is an integral transaction service that has access to the transaction services of the other service providers. The integral transaction service is allocated

to Residentie.Net's access control. The client controls access to his/her data stored at different service providers from Residentie.Net. In addition, the client can authorize other users and service providers to view data.

Compatibility of Service Demand and Supply

Translation support. Terminology used by service providers and end-users is often idiomatic. This increases the chance of errors in the service provisioning process. In the case, the translation of terminology is performed by the service providers that interact with the client. They address the target group in their own terminology. The generic architecture foresees in a translation service to facilitate the necessary interoperability on syntactic, semantic and organizational levels (Lankhorst et al., 2006). However, this has not been implemented yet.

Quality of Services

Choice of services. In many cases, service providers are pre-selected by some party. Often, the reason for this is not regulation, but operational efficiency. Therefore, end-users should have the freedom to select and execute services they find most suitable. In the WMO case, a directory of household caretakers is maintained, which allows a client to select one of those caretakers. A client may also decide to choose another service provider.

Accessibility of Services

Access. Service provisioning in our case study involves many providers, many services and much data. This requires access control and consistency preservation. In the WMO case, access to the records of a client is controlled by the client his/herself through Residentie.Net's authorization services, and by the service providers through their authorization services. Consistency can be achieved by direct access to the client's records at other organizations, trough Residentie.Net. Still, the client is in control and he/she may decide to supply data him/herself, e.g. fill in a net income, rather than importing the data from the Dutch Tax and Customs Administration.

Informed consent. An end-user may desire or need to share information with other users or service providers, for example to get assistance. A requirement is that users should be able to explicitly grant access to this data. In the architecture and demonstrator for this case study, a client can explicitly authorize an employee of a service provider to remotely access his/her information, in order to assist the client in a step.

Context-sensitive role-based access. A user or service provider may provide others with access to services and data. For example, a user may grant another user to perform some service for him and therefore grants access to all data that is required to complete the service. This access should be context-sensitive and based the role the user that gets access should play. An example from the case is that a client could allow (registered) household caretakers access to the application form. The access is only allowed in the context of the household care request (context-sensitive) and only granted to household caretakers (role-based). The context and role are both captured in the authorization records stored at Residentie.Net.

Logging of access. For acquiring management information for control purposes, it should be logged who had access to what data and services at what point in time. Also the requests and outcomes of services should be archived. Each public and private service provider has a logging service. Aggregating this variety of data is necessary for creating an overview of the management information. In the case, Residentie.Net monitors the access by the client and other users of the information of the client. This allows for tracking use by service providers of client's records.

CHALLENGES

In the previous section, a number of requirements on the enterprise architecture for public-private service networks and their fulfilment in the WMO case are described. The requirements are implemented in a demonstrator and various choices concerning the implementation were made. Many other ways to implement these requirements are possible and we do not know the best way yet. As such, each of the aforementioned requirements can be viewed an architectural challenge in developing a public-private service network.

The overall challenge is to design an enterprise architecture that allows public and private partners to cooperate in a service network. Besides the architectural challenges, this overall challenge also puts challenges on the governance of the architecture. We describe the main architectural challenge first and then turn to the challenges on the governance aspects in a public-private service network.

Architectural Challenges

The overall architectural challenge is to allow public and private partners to cooperate in a service network. The requirements discussed in the preceding section are at the same time the challenges that need to be met by the enterprise architecture. Partners can connect to the architecture by using standardized interfaces in the developed enterprise architecture. To reach the ideal of a flexible architecture for public-private service networks, the interfaces should be further decoupled from organizational processes and systems. This allows partners to plug-in or -out of the service network, in analogy to the electricity network where you just connect using the power plug and eventually use adapters to translate one format in another format. This plug-in principle is schematically depicted in Figure 6.

All of the requirements described in the previous section can be directly translated into challenges for such a plug-and-play architecture. For this case, the most notable challenges are resolving a lack of standardization, coping with legacy systems and designing a scalable architecture.

The involvement of different service providers deals with a lack of standardization among various service partners. Technologies like Web Services can solve technical problems of interoperability, but terminology used by service providers and end-users is often incompatible. This increases the chance of errors in the service provisioning process. In addition, incompatibility may result in inefficiency at the service provider's side. The architecture should be able to translate service provider's and end-user's terminology. The challenge of overcoming incompatibilities grows as more different organizations are included in the service networks.

Coping with legacy systems is another interoperability challenge. As the number of partners grows, so does the number of legacy systems involved in the cross-agency process. Standardized interfaces can help in making legacy systems

accessible, but this doesn't solve the fact legacy systems are involved.

The ability of a system to adapt to the number of partners involved, the volume of data and transactions, etc. is referred to as scalability (Medjahed, Benatallah, Bouguettaya, Ngu, & Elmagarmid, 2003). The demand-driven architecture is very high-level (as shown in Figure 5) and has only been specified to a few cases. Since the architecture deals with a number of partners, the service networks are complex. Scaling the architecture to include more services or a wider variety of service providers increases this complexity even more. Service oriented architectures are better at this than 'traditional' architectures are, but scalability remains a challenge nonetheless.

The architectural challenges cannot be resolved without governance of the architecture. The success of a plug-and-play architecture depends on the compliance to governance mechanisms and principles. Especially accountabilities and responsibilities need to be clearly allocated to partners in the service networks. In the case, the overall

Figure 6. Orchestration by standardized sockets

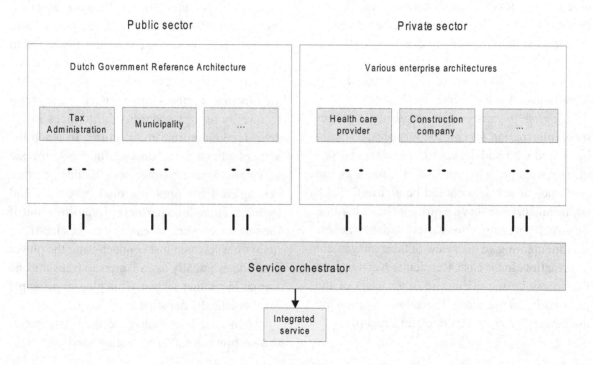

responsibility was assigned to the municipality, in this case the City of The Hague, as required by law. The City of The Hague is innovative and already uses Web service technology to allow for communication with partners. Combining these technological standards with Service Level Agreements should result in an architecture with standard sockets for partners to plug-in (or out).

Governance Challenges

The view on process orchestration, as depicted in Figure 2, assumes that a cross-agency processes can be centrally orchestrated. In reality, the situation is often much more complex. For various parts of the process there can be different orchestrators. Moreover, there can be a nested structure in which an orchestrator coordinates sub-processes that are each managed by their own orchestrator. The challenge is to gain insight in layered or distributed orchestration mechanisms, which enables the client to orchestrate the high-level service according to his needs, but also enables the actual coordination of all sub-services in order to provide that service.

This is a challenge that is not specific for public-private service networks, but is relevant to cross-governmental processes as well. Including private partners adds to this relevance and complexity. It is usually not possible to predefine a cross-organizational process and actually enforce it. Private partners often have their own specific processes and orchestrators and need an orchestrated interaction with governmental agencies, without being forced into an orchestrated overall process. This adds to the challenge.

From the case study and the literature review, we identify a number of governance challenges that can be seen as requirements on the coordination or orchestration of the enterprise architecture for public-private service networks.

Availability of Management Information

If a process is executed by various partners and includes many services and data, acquiring management information is a challenge. Some questions can only be answered if data sources of multiple organizations are combined. In the case, the logging of access is standard facility for providers and disclosure is considered not a problem. The challenge remains to track back the executive data among different service providers to create a complete picture of a service-process that has already been completed.

Including Private Partners

The creation of demand-driven electronic government requires the inclusion of relevant private partners. These partners could improve the overall quality of the service by adding functionality or by completing a chain of related services by integrating sub-services with public providers' services (thus, realizing a one-stop-shop). Specifically for public-private cooperation there is an implicit assumption that private organizations do certain things best while public organizations are better at other things. Cooperation between these sectors should ideally bring the best of both worlds (Pongsiri, 2003; Rosenau, 1999).

Although partnering with private organizations offers the possibility of integrating services and thereby bringing about demand-driven service-delivery, cooperation with private organizations can also have disadvantages for government. Public values like the uniformity of the channels used, the equality of rights and access for citizens and the privacy of citizens might not be warranted and depend on the quality of a private organization. Focus on profits may lead private organizations to address only those clients that are profitable. Agreements about service levels, the monitoring of quality, allocation of responsibilities, and how to deal with problems have to be made to guarantee these public values. The exact role and responsibilities of each of the partners (public and private) should be specified to facilitate public-private cooperation.

On the issue of privacy, the case shows concerns by public organizations for sharing privacy sensitive information with private partners. Citizens expect their government to handle their confidential information with care. This requires agreements on what information is shared among partners, and these agreements should be transparent in order to demonstrate that information is shared only if necessary for the provision of the service. A citizen should have a (last) say in what information is shared with private partners.

Developing Trust Between Partners

Differences in interest may occur between public and private organizations, for example a conflict of interest; "Business is in the business of selling us as much as it possibly can", says Mintzberg (1996, p. 77). The objective is making a profit, while governments use public money to achieve public goals. Another example is transparency; businesses may want to disclose the least possible information in order to keep or gain a competitive advantage. Public organizations on the other hand must be transparent. These types of conflicts of interests cannot always be avoided; they have to be dealt with (Flinders, 2005; Rosenau, 1999). This calls for a mechanism to govern cooperation between public and private partners, in order to cope with conflicts of interests. One way to achieve this is by reducing conflict potential, allowing partners to develop trust relationships. In the case, we found a number of examples that stress the importance of trust between partners, both public and private.

One of those examples derives from the architectural challenge of creating a single identity. Service providers appear to be biased towards the adoption of a global customer identification mechanism. In the Netherlands this means that organizations would like adopt the governmental citizen service number (abbreviated as BSN (Burger Service Nummer) in Dutch), rather than introducing their own identification within each service provider. The citizen service number can be viewed as one of the building blocks of the enterprise architecture. Private parties also like to adopt this BSN, but it is still unclear if this is going to be allowed. Thus, using a single identity may be blocked if private parties are involved.

In line with the adoption of BSN, governmental parties as well as private parties favour a global authentication service for citizens over federated authentication. A challenge service providers face with federated authentication is insufficient trust of authentication by third parties. Both government and private parties would like to adopt the global authentication service 'DigiD' that is offered by the Dutch government.

A problem with the current global authentication facility is that private parties are not allowed to use it. Another problem regarding a global authentication service are concerns on availability, for example, the fear to become too dependent on the central authentication service for its service provisioning. Therefore, despite the preference for global authentication, federated authentication is still present in some organizations and single authentication remains a challenge.

The considerations not to trust authentication services of third parties are also seen in the context of authorizations. Organizations are generally reluctant to trust authorization services by other parties, for example because of the responsibility public institutions have with respect to citizens' privacy. Security is extremely important in order to enable the service network to build relations based on trust. This requires a security mechanism, for example in authentication and authorization services, certification and verification functionality.

Orchestrating Interactions

The concept of orchestration as presented in this chapter is overly simplified. For explanatory purposes, Figures 2 and 3 illustrate a situation in which one of the partners handles the interactions with the client. In reality, individual service providers often have contact with the client themselves, and with other partners. They independently run parallel processes that sometimes interact on a common case. On top of that, sub-services are seldom of the simple request-response type. More often than not, the services that are delivered by a partner are too complex to refer to them as one sub-service. In reality, this often involves a set of services and a complex pattern of interactions, often including both technical and human components.

These complex interactions in an orchestration require an extension of the simplified model of orchestration as is discussed in this chapter, because orchestration comprises not just responsibility and contractual relations between service partners and/or the client, but also the operational coordination of their service processes (which may run in parallel) and the interactions between partners and/or the client. Designing such a generic model for orchestration is a challenge.

Establishing Service Level Agreements

If organizations decide to open up their records to partners, they like to maintain some level of control to whom information is provided. Allowing partners access to the records of an organization requires trust and strong authentication and authorization mechanisms, since all organizations need to rely on it. Besides these mechanisms, this requires strict agreements that rule the roles and responsibilities of each of the partners.

Contrary to these strict agreements is the desire to create loosely-coupled service networks, which ideally results in a flexible infrastructure.

This shows a trade-off in building public-private service networks. On the one hand, there is more security by clear and strict contracts; on the other hand there is more flexibility by loosely-coupled networks. It is a challenge to design SLA's that enable a flexible network, while providing enough security for all parties involved.

These SLA's are extremely important, for example because in organizational networks the costs and benefits are often spread over the various organizations. The interdependency of costs and benefits over organizations causes a unique challenge. The organizations that need to invest in the architecture may not gain return on their investments. For example, in our case study, The Hague is responsible for creating integrated service delivery and bears most costs associated with the infrastructure of Residentie.Net. As a result, there is no or only a limited incentive for partners to develop or improve the enterprise architecture. Furthermore, the unequal division of benefits may cause opposition to necessary changes.

Riggins and Mukhopadhyay (1994) found that for electronic interactions, unequally distributed benefits affect the initial adoption decision negatively. Furthermore, they found that how organizational partners implement and use the system internally and externally may directly affect the level of benefits. An organizational modification may result in specific benefits for that organization, but not necessarily for the network.

Prior to the architectural efforts, it may be necessary to negotiate the division of the costs and benefits among participating organizations. This might not be easy, as the cost of implementing a system can be relatively easily assessed, but the benefits are much more difficult to assess and often comprise qualitative and/or non-tangible benefits.

Accountability and Responsibility

In cross-agency service-delivery processes, allocating accountability for the combined service is a challenge (Gortmaker, Janssen, & Wagenaar, 2005). In complex orchestrations, it is necessary to specify who is accountable for failures like exceeding lead-times. This also extends to determining which partner can provide accountability information to stakeholders or clients, if requested. It should be specified who takes the lead and who is responsible for monitoring the cross-agency process and the quality of the services provided. These accountability issues and the allocation of responsibilities in a cross-agency process have to be dealt with before an orchestration becomes effective (Gortmaker & Janssen, 2004).

Maintaining transparency and accountability while including private partners, increases the challenge. A focus on efficient public service delivery by public-private service networks, may lead to costs on democracy and equity (Flinders, 2005; Rosenau, 1999). Central to democratic governance is the ability to hold public officials and government responsible for public services (Rosenau, 1999). Therefore, the governance of public-private service networks should also be held responsible for the performance of these networks. However, there is some evidence in our case that the costs for public-private service networks are in large parts or even completely paid by the public partners. In the literature it is even argued that this goes for responsibility as well; if public-private service networks fail, the democratic costs are 'paid' for by government (Flinders, 2005; Rosenau, 1999). It is therefore necessary to clearly allocate responsibilities in a public-private service network. This can for example be done by assigning orchestration roles (Janssen et al., 2006).

Flexibility

Networks are not static and will likely change over time. Consequently, flexibility is necessary to add new partners to the network and remove existing partners without letting the service network fail. This requires at least a loosely coupled architec-

ture and clear interfaces with the partners. This is visualized in Figure 6 by providing a platform that allows for 'plugging in' partners. Besides the technical implementation, it is a challenge is to determine governance principles and conditions to add and remove partners to the network. For example, an intuitively appealing governance mechanism is that one partner must not be removed before there is a suitable replacement. This may be contradictory to a private partner's interest, thus calls for governance.

Orchestrating Over Multiple Channels

Many organizations have implemented a multi-channel strategy, or are considering to implement one. Channels like the Website, the telephone and a counter desk require synchronisation of information across channels. For service networks, this means that not only various organizations need to be taken into account, but also the various channels at the organizations. Orchestrating across channels is a challenge that adds to the complexity.

FUTURE TRENDS AND RESEARCH

In order to realize demand-oriented e-government, services related to governmental processes are more and more executed by private organizations and these private organizations need to be included in the service-delivery process. This stresses the importance of further expanding the knowledge about developing and using enterprise architectures for public-private service networks. The developed architecture deals with some of the challenges and further research is necessary to deal with them all.

Since public-private service networks are rarely static, private providers will likely come and go. Takeovers, bankruptcies, changing strategies and specialization may lead to new providers of certain services or to the disappearance of some providers. It may even lead to the disappearance of all providers. Therefore, governments must be able to fill this void, even if it is very unlikely to happen, in order to warrant the continuation of public services. The versatility in providers of (partial) services requires the enterprise architecture to be flexible and adaptive; partners must be able to plug-in to the network and play. The creation of a flexible and adaptive plug-and-play architecture requires further research.

Orchestration of public-private networks becomes more and more important and influences public sector efficiency and effectiveness. Orchestration has gained limited attention by researchers. There is a lack of theory concerning which orchestration arrangement is the best for which situation, especially concerning the specificities of public-private cooperation. Moreover, orchestration has had a central focus, which does not match the layered or even decentralized nature of the investigated public service network. These issues are addressed by an ongoing research programme at the Delft University of Technology that focuses on the orchestrations of complex public-private service networks. We need more insights into the requirements on public-private service networks, which coordination mechanisms are able to meet the complexity of such networks and what type of architecture fits these complex networks.

Although enterprise architecture is a single research area, it is more and more interwoven with governance, which gives rise to the future research direction 'architectural governance'. Architecture and architectural descriptions needs to be governed by rules, where governance can be supported by architecture as an instrument for communicating the current situation, potential future situations and the long term vision. Our case study demonstrated the interplay between governance principles guiding the development of the architecture and we conclude that architecture and governance should be considered simultaneously. Research investigating the dependencies

among the two areas and how they can strengthen each other is still scarce.

Since we have only studied one case, albeit extensively, this research's main purpose was to identify typical challenges in a public-private service delivery architecture and governance. Our findings call for additional research in this field to rise to the challenges identified here and to further develop and test the architectural and governance principles of public-private service networks.

CONCLUSION

Cooperation by different partners in government and the private sector makes it increasingly difficult to design an architecture for integrated service delivery. Many challenges need to be bridged and some of them require trade-offs to be made. A uniform way of dealing with those challenges does not exist yet. In our case study, the main elements of the service network were outlined by an architecture. Architecture needs to be complemented by governance mechanisms to help communicate it to the various organizations and to ensure that it will be used. Even the division of challenges in architectural and governance challenges proved to be difficult, because the architecture cannot do without governance, and vice versa.

Orchestration is viewed as the management of the dependencies among public and private organizations with clear allocation of responsibilities. Our case study showed that taking the view of one stakeholder, that is a too narrow view as each organization orchestrates its own activities and various orchestration roles might be located to different organizations. More layered or decentralized forms of orchestration are subject of further study by the authors. The architecture presented in this chapter is a step in the right direction, but still many challenges need to be bridged.

Architecture serves as a means for the communication and prescription on how the goals of such a project could be reached. It deals with challenges on orchestration, authentication, authorization, interoperability and scalability. Governance is necessary to deal with clear responsibilities, ensuring public values like privacy and accountability and to interact with private parties. Even flexibility, which might initially be considered as primarily a hard issue, needs to be accompanied by governance mechanisms. In order to realize effective service networks, a trade-off must be made in flexibility, thus allowing partners to plug in (or out), and strict contracts, that help in aligning parties and avoiding conflicts. Combining organizations in a service networks requires agreements and contracts, standards for technology, implementation and governance of the network, the allocation of roles and responsibilities, the building of trust relations and the alignment of processes and technologies. Only after these measures are taken, we can create effective public-private service networks, and truly focus on citizen's demands, instead of government processes.

ACKNOWLEDGMENT

Part of this chapter results from the B-dossier project (http://b-dossier.telin.nl) of the Telematica Instituut, a combined research initiative with partners from government and academia, comprising the Dutch Tax and Customs Administration, the Municipality of The Hague, SVB, UWV, ING, ICTU, the University of Twente, and Delft University of Technology. The project aims to support integrated, demand-driven electronic services from public and private organizations to citizens and companies.

REFERENCES

Checkland, P. (1981). *Systems Thinking, Systems Practice*. Chichester: Wiley.

Demchenko, Y., Gommans, L., De Laat, C., Oudenaarde, B., Tokmakoff, A., Snijders, M., et al. (2005). *Security Architecture for Open Collaborative Environment*. Paper presented at the European Grid Conference - EGC 2005, Amsterdam, The Netherlands.

Flinders, M. (2005). The Politics of Public-Private Partnerships. *The British Journal of Politics and International Relations (BJPIR), 7*, 215-239.

Gortmaker, J. (2008). Designing a Reference Architecture for the Accountable & Adaptive Orchestration of Public Service Networks. Unpublished doctoral dissertation (forthcoming). Delft University of Technology.

Gortmaker, J., & Janssen, M. (2004). Business Process Orchestration in e-Government: A Gap Analysis. *International Resources Management Association (IRMA)*.

Gortmaker, J., & Janssen, M. (2007). Automating Governmental Cross-Agency Processes Using Web Service Orchestration: A Gap Analysis. In L. Al-Hakim (Ed.), *Global E-Government: Theory, Applications and Benchmarking*. Hershey: Idea Group Publishing.

Gortmaker, J., Janssen, M., & Wagenaar, R. W. (2005). Accountability of Electronic Cross-Agency Service-Delivery Processes. *EGOV2005, 4th International Conference on Electronic Government*, 49-56.

ICTU. (2007). Flyer NORA v2. Retrieved June, 15, 2007, from http://www.e-overheid.nl/data/files/architectuur/flyer-nora-v2.pdf

Janssen, M., Gortmaker, J., & Wagenaar, R. W. (2006). Web Service Orchestration in Public Administration: Challenges, Roles, and Growth

Stages. *Information Systems Management*(Spring 2006), 44-55.

Janssen, M., & Hjort-Madsen, K. (2007). *Analyzing Enterprise Architecture in National Governments: The cases of Denmark and the Netherlands.* Paper presented at the Hawaii International Conference on System Sciences (HICSS), Hawaii, Big Island.

Janssen, M., Kuk, G., & Wagenaar, R. W. (2008). A Survey of Web-based Business Models for e-Government in the Netherlands. *Government Information Quarterly, 25*(2) (forthcoming).

Kenniscentrum. (2007). *NORA 2.0 (Nederlandse Overheid Referentie Architectuur)*: Stichting ICTU.

Lankhorst, M. M. (2005). *Enterprise Architecture at Work: Modelling, Communication and Analysis.* Berlin: Springer.

Lankhorst, M. M., & Derks, W. L. A. (2007). *Towards a Service-Oriented Architecture for Demand-Driven e-Government.* Paper presented at the 11th IEEE International EDOC Conference (EDOC 2007).

Lankhorst, M. M., Derks, W. L. A., Fennema, P., Iacob, M. E., & Joosten, S. (2006). *B-dossier architectuur.* Enschede: Telematica Instituut.

Linder, S. H. (1999). Coming to Terms With the Public-Private Partnership: A Grammar of Multiple Meanings. *American Behavioral Scientist, 43*(1), 35-51.

Medjahed, B., Benatallah, B., Bouguettaya, A., Ngu, A. H. H., & Elmagarmid, A. K. (2003). Business-to-business interactions: issues and enabling technologies. *The VLDB Journal The International Journal on Very Large Data Bases, 12*(1), 59-85.

Mintzberg, H. (1996). Managing Government, Governing Management. *Harvard Business Review*(May-June 1996).

Pongsiri, N. (2003). Public-Private Partnerships in Thailand: A Case Study of the Electric Utility Industry. *Public Policy and Administration, 18*(3), 69.

Provan, K. G., & Milward, H. B. (2001). Do Networks Really Work? A Framework for Evaluating Public-Sector Organizational Networks. *Public Administration Review, 61*(4), 414-423.

Richardson, L., Jackson, B. M., & Dickson, G. (1990). A Principle-Based Enterprise Architecture: Lessons From Texaco and Star Enterprise. *MIS Quarterly, 14*(4), 385-403.

Riggins, F. J., & Mukhopadhyay, T. (1994). Interdependent benefits from interorganizational systems: opportunities for business partner reengineering. *Journal of Management Information Systems, 11*(2), 37-57.

Rosenau, P. V. (1999). Introduction. The Strengths and Weaknesses of Public-Private Policy Partnerships. *American Behavioral Scientist, 43*(1), 10-34.

Ross, J. (2003). Creating a strategic IT architecture competency: Learning in stage. *MISQ Quarterly Executive, 2*(1), 31-43.

Weill, P. (2004). Don't Just Lead, Govern: How Top-Performing Firms Govern IT. *MIS Quarterly Executive, 3*(1), 1-17.

Weill, P., & Ross, J. (2005). A Matrixed Approach to Designing IT Governance. *MIT Sloan Management Review, 46*(2), 26-34.

Section III
Realization and Deployment

Chapter XIII
People–Led Enterprise Architecture

Neil Fairhead
Fujitsu Services, UK

John Good
Serco Consulting, UK

ABSTRACT

This chapter provides an approach to Enterprise Architecture that is people-led, as a contrast to being led by technology or modelling methodology. It identifies the major stakeholders in Enterprise Architecture and suggests where in the organisation they may be found and how they may be connected with the Enterprise Architecture. It highlights the roles of stakeholders throughout the process of defining and implementing an Enterprise Architecture. The view of stakeholders managing the EA effort is described through the complete lifecycle, from setting the EA mission to sustaining the benefits after implementation. In proposing the adoption of such an approach, we aim to encourage a more direct link between Enterprise Architecture, the needs of the stakeholders it serves, and the pubic policy outcomes it enables.

INTRODUCTION

This chapter highlights the need to ensure that enterprise architecture, as both a discipline and set of deliverables, recognises the need to focus on people before technology. Based on the authors' experience working in both the public sector and commercial organisations, it posits that the value of enterprise architecture comes from making it easier to introduce successful change into organisations and that this requires leadership by key stakeholders. A key conclusion is that identifying, engaging and gaining real commitment by relevant groups of stakeholders is a critical success factor for an enterprise architecture team.

BACKGROUND

Over recent years there has been an increasing focus in Government and the wider public sector on technology and transformation. For example, the UK Government published 'Transformational Government – Enabled by Technology' (Cabinet Office, 2005) as a key strategy for the reform of public service provision and managing the relationship between citizens, organisations and Government. However, while technology does enable transformation, it does not cause it. People have to decide what transformation is needed and why. They have to think through all the steps which lead from current situation to desired state – and build the plans to implement those steps.

People have to communicate to everybody impacted by the proposed change that the change

Figure 1.

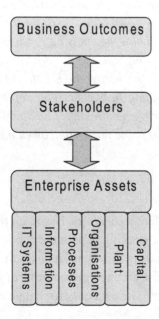

is necessary, that it is possible and that it will happen – again and again. In short, People have to lead the change – if they want other people to follow it.

However, there are still many government organisations where enterprise architecture is led by a choice of method or framework, or a desire to model the enterprise, before an understanding of the problem, from the problem owner's perspective, is obtained. Coupled with a typically long distance from the determination of public policy and the delivery of public services to the chief architect (if one even exists), enterprise architecture has a long way to go to realise its potential in the public sector.

This chapter, based on our experience of doing enterprise architecture in the public sector, describes how enterprise architects can deliver an approach in which people lead, and technology enables, real business transformation. We propose a "both/and" world not an "either/or" one. Both people and technology are necessary but the sequence is important. There are still far too many large change programmes which come close to failure because the people affected were not involved early enough and so are not committed. It is not the technology that successfully delivers transformation, it is people using the technology. Beginning enterprise architecture with this simple recognition and ensuring that people are at the centre of the architecture – the big picture of change – is a strong first step towards successful transformation.

This approach, and therefore this chapter, is as much about choices and values as it is about specific techniques. Enterprise architecture is about change. Change is driven by a need to improve the business outcomes. The current outcomes are not satisfactory or are not sustainable. Stakeholders in these outcomes, i.e. people, have to choose what needs to change in order to achieve the improved outcomes. The changes are implemented though changes to the enterprise assets which are the subject of the enterprise architecture. Hence the key link between the target outcomes and the enterprise architecture is the stakeholder. Enterprise architecture must therefore be people-led and people-focused to make a lasting and positive impact.

Which People - Know your Stakeholders

Architecture is about change, which means that it is about people. It is often stated that people do not like change. This is not necessarily true but it is certain that they hate having change forced upon them without their understanding and involvement. Done well, enterprise architecture can help ensure that change is actively adopted. As the U.S. General Accounting Office (2003, p. 2 - our emphasis) states, Enterprise Architectures provide:

*to **people** at all organisational levels an explicit, common, and meaningful structural frame of reference that allows an understanding of (1) what the enterprise does; (2) when, where, how, and why it does it; and (3) what it uses to do it.*

Recognising that communication is part of the service that EA delivers, and that the value of any service is measured by the recipients, leads us naturally to placing stakeholders at the centre of our approach to developing, implementing and maintaining an organisation's enterprise architecture. In this people-led approach, stakeholders become subjects not objects. Stakeholder management is no longer about how the enterprise architecture function "sells" to or "manages" stakeholders but rather about identifying who has real and significant needs that the enterprise architecture approach can help to meet, and how the EA function delivers to those stakeholders. We must ensure that stakeholders actively manage the process rather than being passive players responding to the EA specialists. It is a team approach.

The stakeholders of the enterprise architecture function provide the guidance and direction for the function to ensure that it is focused on the highest value priorities, that the architecture is developed in the most efficient and effective manner and that the resulting products are fit for purpose and use. Understanding who needs what from enterprise architecture, and why, is a critical step in ensuring that the enterprise architecture gets used and so delivers real value. In this way we can ensure that stakeholders are active team members who are inside the EA process. ("Further, committee experience indicates that progress is best made with the top-level management team supported by an architecture team composed of a small number of full-time professionals dedicated to the task." National Research Council (2004).)

What Do We Need From Stakeholders?

Stakeholders have a variety of contributions to make. Understanding clearly what we need from them is a first step to ensuring that we have the right ones. The following items are typically important to the success of enterprise architecture.

1. The first thing we need from stakeholders is direction in targeting the highest value and most important issues as perceived by the business stakeholders. Developing enterprise architecture has significant cost since it requires high calibre, multi-talented people. Most organizations find this type of individual both valuable and scarce so it is essential that we make the best use of them. But what is that best use? Enterprise architects need to get clear guidance on the priorities for improvement and the value they will deliver from people involved in all business functions. By ensuring that all architecture work is focused on supporting high value improvements, we can ensure

Table 1.

Focus on Value
The value of EA is related to its impact on the total, net, present, probable, realised value of the changes that it is guiding. To improve this we need to focus on:

1. The highest potential value changes	2. How to achieve them at minimum cost	3. Delivering that value as soon as possible	4. While identifying, reducing and managing the risks	5. And ensuring that the processes by which the benefits will be harvested are in place.

that we are maximising the value of what we do.

2. Stakeholders need to provide real business insight into the business opportunities, challenges and constraints in the specific areas that have been prioritised. While good architects have an understanding of the business, this is no substitute for being immersed on a daily basis. This insight can often require the involvement of stakeholders with management responsibility for the subject area. They will be leading the people most directly impacted as well as carrying the responsibility for achieving the business improvements and harvesting the benefits.

3. Architects need to ensure implementation plans are realistic by getting user contributions. We need to avoid the situation where the architecture has been developed but cannot be implemented because it is considered too theoretical and does not respond to operational realities. We need to involve stakeholders who understand the day-to-day details, including history, attitudes, skills and capabilities. In this way, the architecture will demonstrate understanding and can be made tangible to the people whose activities will be changed.

4. The fourth contribution needed from stakeholders is building the intent to implement. As we look at architecture work, how often do we see examples that were never implemented? This often occurs because the ar-

chitecture was built without the involvement of the key people who can make it happen. If there is no adequate intent to implement then the architects are wasting their time and the organisation is wasting valuable resources.

For example, when helping a government department to design its enterprise architecture function we went to visit another organisation. We were very impressed by their knowledge, their models and their tools. Then we asked "who is using this?" The silence was eloquent. The lack of intent to implement was obvious. The value of all their efforts was questionable.

5. However, even when an architecture is implemented, built out through changes to processes and systems and people, that is not the end. To quote Winston Churchill, it is perhaps the end of the beginning. The success of the architecture depends on it having a sustained impact and delivering continuing improvement. This requires commitment at all levels rather than mere acquiescence. Help in building this ongoing commitment is another key contribution that we need from our stakeholders. They can ensure that we build commitment through responding to deep felt needs.

6. To be effective, we need our stakeholders to generate respect and to show it publicly. (This could be construed as a statement of the obvious but experience shows that

many EA functions are not respected, often being considered ivory tower theorists who are disconnected from business realities.) However, we cannot just demand respect, we need to earn respect, delivering value by significantly helping key stakeholders who themselves are respected through the organisation.

Stakeholder Roles

Looking at the contribution that we need from our stakeholders leads to the recognition that we can segment our stakeholders into different groups. This will make it easier to identify the set of stakeholders required for success and make it easier to explain their roles and associated responsibilities and contributions to them. There are three main segments; Customer, Builder and User stakeholders. Each of these has clearly different roles. Note that this segmentation is by role so one person may be in more than one segment – but different contributions are required in each role. This is a pattern that is regularly seen in government where the same people or even group may have two quite different roles. (For example, from the Canadian Province of Ontario, "Treasury Board/Management Board of Cabinet is a joint committee of Cabinet established under the Treasury Board Act and Management Board of Cabinet Act. In its capacity as Treasury Board, it sets policy direction as the architect and manager of the government's fiscal plan, makes ongoing decisions about operating and capital expenditures and ensures consistency and coordination. In its capacity as Management Board, it sets policy direction as the government's employer and makes decisions about the government's people, land, buildings, technology and information." (Government of Ontario, 2006).)

Customer stakeholders: They need the output of EA to achieve bigger business ends. Here you will find the sponsors, people with the need and the authority, both positional and personal, to make

things happen. Typically they are important line-of-business and programme managers, however having authority, visible "respect" and owning a priority task are also attributes of other key staff and influencers who can link EA to business plans, strategies and budgets.

Customer stakeholders are focused on achieving significant business improvements and driving any required changes. Typically therefore, they are managing many moving parts in order to achieve specific, tangible and compelling improvements in the performance of their areas. They need enterprise architecture to provide structure, to simplify where there is complexity and to ensure a consistent common understanding of what needs to change, how and why. However, they are not necessarily familiar with enterprise architecture (which tends to come from within the IT organisation) nor do they always understand how enterprise architecture can deliver this service. Hence, a key part of obtaining their agreement to becoming a stakeholder is making tangible to them the contribution that enterprise architecture can make. We need to show them that we can help to increase their probability of success in ways for which they are willing to pay. Only then are .they likely to contribute their own time and involvement in developing the EA. Without that insight, they will probably remain outside the process whose value will be severely diminished.

Builder stakeholders: They will create architectural artefacts. They are not necessarily located in a formal architecture function, but they are using architectural methods and creating architectural products. For example, they may be business analysts inside an operating division, modelling processes and designing improvements. Bring them into the architecture community and share both deliverables and best practices – and broaden the knowledge base being applied to developing the enterprise architecture. Note that they may also be outside the organisation too as partners working with your organisation together (for example, to create a shared service for a single point of contact for citizens), or they may be vendors (for example, an outsourced service provider).

Builder stakeholders are also valuable because of the network they have. Often they are embedded in the organisation in a way that the enterprise architecture function is not, since it often resides in the IT function. The aim is to create a virtual team which uses the same basic approach, follows the same standards and contributes products to a single, logical, repository of architectural information. In this way enterprise architecture can help to simplify the complexity of a large organisation and make it easier for knowledge and information to flow across the silos that still often form barriers to change.

User stakeholders: They will use the products of enterprise architecture in the implementation of change, be it to processes, to systems, to business relationships or to people and their goals, skills and performance. This group typically includes a rich variety of people, for example:

- Business improvement directors looking to change key performance indicators who will need the business view products.
- Programme and project managers and their solution designers who will use the architecture to drive change.
- Planners, such as an IT strategist looking to simplify an organisation's application portfolio who will clearly need the products of the information systems view of the enterprise architecture.
- Corporate compliance manager concerned about privacy who will need outputs from the data/information view.

User stakeholders are significant because if the products of enterprise architecture do not get used then they have no value. It is not the architecture itself that is important but its use, and user stakeholders have enormous influence on that. From the beginning, enterprise architects need to be thinking about the users, their needs and wants and how to help make them more productive.

Balancing the Needs of our Stakeholders

By now it should be obvious that the needs and contributions of our stakeholders can vary considerably. This fact alone justifies spending time and thought on segmenting them and understanding those differences rather than just treating them as a homogenous group. In addition, a key challenge of developing enterprise architecture is finding solutions that meet all their needs. There is no point in planning an architecture that perfectly meets the requirements of one "vertical" in the organisation if it causes problems in another. There is no point in designing an architecture which perfectly meets the needs of the Customer stakeholders if we do not have the ability to build it. Similarly there is no point on developing a new enterprise architecture if the User stakeholders do not take it and implement it. We do not merely need knowledge of our stakeholders and a relationship with them, we also need a mechanism for resolving all their different requirements and capabilities to the benefit of the organisation as a whole. The following diagram (Good and Fairhead, 2007) shows how we can approach this.

This diagram shows the different types of stakeholder, gives examples of each and the primary community that they represent. It also shows the forum in which these differences can be resolved and a common direction provided to the enterprise architecture development. This forum is the Enterprise Architecture Governance Board. It is the core team of Executives, across all the functions of the organisation who drive the enterprise architecture function and focus it on the areas of highest value to the enterprise. The Board sets priorities for enterprise architecture work, approves key architecture guidelines, standards and products, oversees the quality assurance of enterprise architecture work and is

Figure 2.

Source: Serco Consulting

the point of escalation for issues concerning the implementation of architecture products. The "Customer" members are responsible for ensuring both business buy-in and business priorities and guidance.

How Do You Find Your Customer Stakeholders? - Who has a Need?

Building the base of stakeholders is one of the most important tasks in enterprise architecture. Identifying potential Customer stakeholders is the first step. We suggest that the following questions will guide the search. The initial objective is to build a sufficient base to get started and to ensure that we are focused on the most important issues, not to be exhaustive.

- Where is the business stress?
- Who feels real pain from lack of an architectural approach?
- Where is the complexity and cost of systems causing a problem?

- Where is the cost and poor quality of information causing a problem?
- Who is hurt by the time and cost of development and change of business systems?
- Who has big change strategies and programmes impacting many people, processes and systems?
  o How do you know if the projects and programmes will/are achieving the target improvements? If you do not, what problem does that cause, to whom?
  o How do you ensure that your programmes and projects complement and enhance the value of each other rather than conflict and confuse? If you cannot, what problem does that cause, to whom?

How Do You Find Your Builder Stakeholders - Creating a Virtual Team of All the Architects

We have noted that many different groups can be involved in building components of the architecture, and not all of them need be, or often are, in the line-management of the Chief Architect. It is highly beneficial that this be done in a coherent, consistent and coordinated manner. To achieve this we recommend that all the builders be seen as members of a virtual team who work together to create the single overall architecture that reflects the organisation as a whole while delivering to the individual business units within.

Even though we are now focused down on the Builder stakeholders, the architects themselves, they are in many places – and may not consider themselves architects. These include the IT function (including centralised, decentralised or outsourced), major change programmes and line-of-business delivery units. Within each category there may be many instances (e.g. line-of-business units). In short, the virtual team will be much larger than you originally expect.

It is valuable to carry out a reasonably comprehensive search for builders for two reasons. First, you will have a broader influence and, as the coordination improves, a bigger resource base. Second, the other architects will carry on doing their job. Doing so in isolation increases the possibility of duplication of effort and may result in incompatible approaches that are only discovered at the implementation phase. As we know, any rectification gets more costly the later it is done.

In summary, People-Led Enterprise Architecture ignores organisational boundaries to create the community. Obviously this means working relatively closely across organisational boundaries which can be problematical. Four key things can help:

1. **The Enterprise Architecture Governance Board:** Should represent, at a senior level, most of the organisational units involved. They can provide a remit that prescribes this collaborative approach as well as defining the constraints within which it must be carried out (e.g., no transfer of budget);

2. **A mission of service:** for the function not the organizational unit. Enterprise Architecture can be viewed as a profession, like engineering. Professions typically have a number of key characteristics such as agreement on the purpose of the profession, its mission of service. It highlights that the enterprise architecture does something really valuable - and places value on you, the architect. The mission of service typically also highlights the principles that you live by (e.g., as demonstrated by the Hippocratic Oath);

3. **Agreed common methods and tools:** Having a common set of methods, standards, formats and tools will make it much easier to share information across all the different groups involved in creating enterprise architecture components and bringing them together to create a single overall architecture. A key part of creating a community is involving all the different teams in agreeing the standards and choosing the tools;

4. **A sense of community:** A community is made up of people, not organisational units. Ensuring that people want to work together requires trust. Share the success. Be generous - it will multiply and come back. Make sure people know of successes and that you are promoting other people's success.

How Do You Find Your User Stakeholders - Meeting the Needs of the Implementers

The third group are equally important and much more diffuse – the users of your architecture. Reaching them is a classic marketing exercise. They need to be identified, segmented, understood and communicated with. We need to think about what we can do to make it easier for them:

1. To recognise that the deliverables of architecture can help them do their jobs better;

2. To know that appropriate deliverables may exist (i.e. it is worth looking for them);
3. To find those appropriate deliverables (or be reasonably sure that they do not exist);
4. To retrieve the deliverables;
5. To give access to the builders to get a deeper understanding of the deliverables if necessary;
6. To use the deliverables in the daily execution of their jobs.

Thinking about how our deliverables can be used helps to both identify prospective users and ways of segmenting them. In particular, it can be helpful to start with considering the typical users of that major portion of the EA deliverables, the major architectural viewpoints that are typically defined. (It is not the purpose of this chapter to define the EA deliverables, as these should be defined by each team in accordance with the requirements of, and to meet the concerns of, the relevant stakeholders. We have used a typical set of viewpoint names that have common currency in EA to illustrate the point.)

Signing Up Your Stakeholders

Of course at this point we have merely described how you identify the stakeholders that you need, which is not the same as getting them committed and signed up. Two elements are crucial to this. First, do you have a heavy-weight sponsor? One who believes that having an enterprise architecture is important? Who really cares - and why?

Again going back to U.S. Government experience, the General Accounting Office reports that making IT investments without putting them into the context of architecture often results in

Table 2.

Architecture Viewpoint	Typical Users (examples, not exhaustive)
Performance	• Programme managers focused on outcomes not just outputs • Management Information Office focused on measuring and reporting performance
Business	• Line managers focused on improving their processes • Business analysts focused on designing and implementing improved processes • Human Resources focused on people, skills, training • Organisational development focused on how people and responsibilities should be structured and organised • M&A focused on acquiring new high value capabilities or disposing of existing non-core activities
Application / Service	• Developers building or maintaining applications • ICT financial management focused on overall lifecycle costs and their reduction • Shared service centres working to maximise the return on their investment through reuse of functionality • Line managers looking to improve the productivity of their people through using applications and services already available
Information / Data	• Marketing management focused on "what do we know about our customers?" • Risk managers focused on being able to identify and measure key risks • Compliance managers focused on being able to prove the efficacy of key controls
Technology	• Operations managers focused on simplifying the infrastructure that they run to make it easier to manage, identifying single points of failure to reduce risk or finding consolidation opportunities to reduce costs • Procurement looking to reduce licenses or increase buying power • Legal focused on ensuring that all software is legitimate

systems with requirements that are not clearly and succinctly derived from business objectives, processes and targeted improvements as well as unnecessary repetition of functionality and components which can result in excessive complexity and lifecycle costs.

Examples include the FBI Trilogy program of which the National Research Council (2004) report stated: "the FBI must *first and as a matter of its highest priority* in its IT efforts formulate an enterprise architecture." (page 3). When a key part of the programme, the Virtual Case File (VCF), was cancelled in March 2005 after costing $170 million it was described in IEEE's Spectrum journal as follows: "...This cavalier approach to software development would prove fatal to the VCF. Today, many organizations rely on a blueprint—known in IT parlance as an enterprise architecture—to guide hardware and software investment decisions.......The problem was, the FBI didn't have such a blueprint, ..." (Goldstein, 2005)

The key step in signing up stakeholders is making them aware:

- Of the contribution that enterprise architecture can make;
- Of the risks of not having an architecture.

Stakeholder Management Principles

One of the attractive components of TOGAF™ is the structured approach it applies to principles. We suggest that this can be applied by the enterprise architecture team to its stakeholders as follows.

You will need your sponsor to step forwards and personally request other stakeholders to take part, i.e. to get stakeholders first have a stakeholder. Any enterprise architecture needs a senior sponsor who understands the difference the structured approach can make and is willing to press the case to their peers. This case is based on the contribution that enterprise architecture can make to helping senior executives to achieve tangible, significant and compelling improvements. That contribution includes:

- Addressing complexity. Complexity slows diagnosis (what's happening), slows design

Table 3.

Name	Stakeholder Roles
Statement	The role of every identified stakeholder will be defined in terms of both what they require from the enterprise architecture and what they will contribute to the enterprise architecture.
Rationale	Reasons for implementing the principle • Three types of role can be stakeholders in the enterprise architecture function, those who have a need for the enterprise architecture in order to achieve bigger business objectives ("Customers"), those who will build enterprise architecture products ("Builders") and those who will consume the enterprise architecture products in their job ("Users"). Knowing why a role is a stakeholder will make the enterprise architecture function more responsive to the stakeholder's requirements • Enable tuning of information flows to match individual stakeholder's role, e.g. meetings will have a narrower, more effective scope • Focus stakeholders on the contribution expected from them (i.e. being a stakeholder implies responsibilities as well as rights.) Impact of not implementing the principle • Overlapping responsibilities leading to confusion or discord
Implications	• Need to make very clear what the different roles are (and why), the selection criteria, the authority of and the contributions expected from each role. • Need to identify the key stakeholders and gain their agreement to being a stakeholder • Need to maintain regular communications with the stakeholder community

(what's got to change), slows development and slows implementation. Unnecessary complexity also adds cost and risk. As the CTO of Microsoft, Ray Ozzie wrote "Complexity kills. It sucks the life out of developers, it makes products difficult to plan, build and test, it introduces security challenges, and it causes end-user and administrator frustration." (Lohr, 2006)

The enterprise architecture will provide knowledge and tools to identify where how and why complexity can be taken out of the infrastructure and processes (including ICT) hence helping to identify unnecessary duplication of function, information and effort as well as ensuring that differences in methods reflect real differences in requirements not just preferences.

- Addressing uncertainty. Uncertainty can stem from changes in needs, changes in priorities and surprises (changes not predicted). The objective is to think through the sources of uncertainty, plan how to respond to possible alternatives fast (as opposed to planning for just one alternative) and recognise that a change is arriving in advance so we have enough time to implement the necessary actions in response.

- Providing corporate memory. In large organisations, including governments, there is constant movement of people. In particular, high calibre personnel who are expected to achieve high rank and authority are often moved relatively swiftly to give them a broad experience as well as enabling them to climb fast in organisations with many layers. In addition, in many commercial organisations the ranks of middle management have been significantly reduced over the last two decades. For example the US Federal Government reduced its middle management ranks by over 20% (from 161,000 to 126,000) between 1993 and 1998 (Light, 1999). As a result there can be rela-

tively little continuity of decision makers with concomitant difficulty in recreating how and why decisions were taken. This causes two problems. First we can waste time and resources recreating information that has already been captured because the people who knew the information have moved. Second, we fail to learn from previous work, whether successes or failures, because we do not remember how that work was approached. Enterprise architecture can make a very useful contribution to the corporate memory provided that we set out to do so and hence plan to capture relevant information and hold it in our architecture repository for use by our stakeholders.

Remember: Stakeholder Management = stakeholders managing EA

REALISING THE ARCHITECTURE, FROM A PEOPLE-LED POINT OF VIEW

Essential to the people-led objective in realising the architecture are *motivated*, *skilled* and *informed* senior stakeholders with a demonstrated consensus on the objectives and purpose of the architecture. The architecture team then has the responsibility to motivate, skill and inform the participants to deliver the right things for the business.

As enterprise architects, we have to continuously ensure that we are undertaking our work in response to a clear customer requirement, using tools, methods and products that our stakeholders can understand and use, to a plan that fits with their own plans (from strategic enterprise objectives through to tactical departmental ones).

To provide a framework for describing our approach to implementation, we have used a simple 5-step method as follows:

1. Identify the purpose for the architecture ("WHY")
2. Develop a focused architecture framework that will serve as a means for people to deliver the value set out in the purpose ("WHAT")
3. Develop a migration path and associated plan of activities ("HOW")
4. Implement the architecture approach
5. Review, measure success and revise.

The formulation of a complete and rigorous method is not our purpose here, and we encourage the use of a more robust method as appropriate (e.g., such as TOGAF™). However, we do commend the people-led messages in each of the 5-steps be applied to whichever method you choose.

Identify the Purpose

At this initial step, we identify the purpose of the architecture. Without a clear and agreed understanding of this purpose, we will not be able to provide focus and measure success. From our people-led perspective, the main objective here is to align ourselves with the *motivations* of our customer stakeholders and so provide a motivation for all stakeholders for engagement in the enterprise architecture.

We have often observed a mission statement for the enterprise architecture derived from a definition of enterprise architecture itself, rather than from the purpose to which a customer wishes enterprise architecture to be put. Compare the following types of mission statement:

To provide an explicit and cohesive description of our business from the perspectives of the business strategy, operations, information systems and technical infrastructure;

To achieve maximum value from investments in IT services and the efficient and effective delivery of change programmes through the design of optimal enterprise and solution architectures.

In the first there is no sense of why the EA should exist, other than to be created for itself. In the second, we understand the purpose to which the enterprise architecture is to be put and can see in this the influence of customer stakeholders (in this case the purchasers of IT services and the sponsors of change programmes).

In order to understand the needs of the stakeholders you first have to identify them (see the Stakeholder Roles section). Stakeholders are always working and operating in a particular context, defined by the drivers of change they face. Such drivers include competitive pressures, customer preferences, and other political, economic, social, technological, legal or environmental, "PESTLE" (Prime Ministers Strategy Unit, 2004), external drivers. As people, they choose a response to those drivers that will (it is hoped) effect an improvement in their situation. This response is expressed variously as a requirement, resolution of an issue, realisation of an opportunity or acceptance of a constraint. Together these will form the stakeholder concerns that will drive our mission statement.

Figure 3.

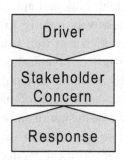

The output of this exercise can be captured in a simple matrix with four items as follows (Good and Fairhead, 2007):

- Vision statement. A broad picture of what the future will be like. This statement need not be constrained to the enterprise architecture. It is often wise to paint a broad vision for the enterprise from the perspective of the stakeholders in the enterprise architecture. This will then capture something of the ambitions of the stakeholders, rather than of the enterprise architecture. It is useful to complete the sentence "A world in which..." to get the right sense of a visionary outcome!
- Mission statement. A statement of the contribution that enterprise architecture will make

to the delivery of the vision. It is useful to think of this in three parts:
- o A first clause describing the core, customer stakeholder focused, outcome-based purpose;
- o A second clause describing how to achieve motivated, informed and skilled customers, builders and users, and
- o A third relating to the nature of the resulting EA itself.
- Goals. For each element of the mission statement, a defined set of goals that will contribute to the achievement of the mission. There may be many goals, but around 3 to 4 per clause in the Mission statement will

Table 4. An Example of public-service enterprise architecture purpose matrix

Vision	Mission	Goal	Success Factor
A world in which each citizen can choose the method, location and timing of their access to government services (e.g., renewing a driving licence, applying for a grant or submitting their tax return)	To define a cost-effective, channel independent, government service access architecture that provides for a measurable, incremental migration path to realisation through the maximum use of shared components and services	To align implementation of the architecture with the local development plans of all stakeholders	Access to development plans and alignment of dependencies
		To rationalise the component architecture, re-using existing building blocks where possible	All components and service building blocks must be defined to the same architecture description standards
	To enable the goals of Transformational Government (Cabinet Office, 2005) directed by the CTO Council (Cabinet Office, 2007) and in partnership with strategic information systems suppliers	To have the stakeholders in Transformational Government adopt the enterprise architecture	Alignment between the Transformational government milestones and the implementation of the enterprise architecture
		To have the members of the CTO Council use the enterprise architecture in cross-government and local initiatives	Enterprise Architecture to provide for abstraction and localisation where necessary to enable both uses.
	through the definition of an enterprise architecture description that is tuned to the needs of its users, easy to search and use, accurate and complete.	develop and deliver a repository that serves as the single source of information relating to the enterprise architecture	repository meets the needs of all stakeholders, is trustworthy and simple to use
		develop and deliver a consistently used EA method and framework that is people-led in its derivation and use	EA is integrated and aligned with change programme delivery methods

be sufficient (any more will be difficult to track and manage);

- Success Factors. For each goal, a definition of the things that have to be done, and done well, to assure success. It is important here to focus on only those things that are critical, so as to provide for management attention in the high priority areas.

This model is motivated mainly by the customer stakeholders, and provides for linkages to user and builder stakeholder concerns. In order to reflect this purpose back and provide motivation for its delivery for the people involved, we would expect these goals to be translated into performance objectives agreed in the performance appraisal and development plans of each stakeholder, be they customers, builders and/or users.

Develop Architecture Framework

The people-led objective in developing our EA framework and methodology is to develop stakeholders who are *skilled* to use the architecture to best effect. For the customer stakeholders, this is not so much of an issue, but for the users it means defining what they will have to be able to do to carry out their responsibilities, and for the builders it is about enabling them to deliver

The people-led approach starts with the users. What architecture views do they need, and what services have to be provided by the EA team to enable this use? Once you know what the users need, you can look to off-the-shelf frameworks and methods to adopt and adapt. In short, if you cannot identify a user with a need, don't develop the architecture artefact or the service that goes with it.

Consideration should be given to creating an architecture service that defines how each architecture product is created, used and maintained. These services will be a lifeline for users and builders in the wider architecture community. In the initial stages of developing and using enterprise architecture, users and builders may not be familiar with the artefacts and how to use them. A useful principle is that "architecture models come with people". This proposes that if a user or builder needs a model, it is always delivered in person by an architect who can explain the model and its use, assist the user to use it and provide ongoing assurance to ensure that the best value is obtained from the product. With a wider perspective, this engagement also ensures that updates are captured to enrich the model for the next user and that the models remain relevant as the architecture implementation progresses.

Plan

The people-led objective in planning is to ensure that we are *informed* about our stakeholder needs and take them into account in planning our work. We then use our plan to *inform* our stakeholders of what we will do. This is crucial to obtaining their support and involvement. Clearly this stage is also about good planning, but a plan is worth nothing if it is not relevant to those it serves and communicated to those it affects.

The key factors in our approach to planning are direction and balance.

Direction

As noted previously, the focal point in giving direction is the EA Governance Board. In particular they will need to choose between different opportunities for applying the limited enterprise architecture function resources. While there will be ongoing enterprise architecture services (e.g., management of policy and standards, management of architecture change) major enhancements will be delivered via projects focused on supporting specific business requirements.

Projects will mostly be initiated by senior sponsors with whom the enterprise architects should engage to agree their contribution through jointly defining a Statement of Architecture

Work. A request to develop such a Statement would be assigned to either the core enterprise or appropriate domain architecture teams. The nominated architect should ensure that the Statement responds to the specific requirements of the project, but also wider concerns from any parent Change Programme (which typically exist to drive the achievement of the most strategic goals and will be concerned that the results of many projects are cohesive in that context) and other enterprise architecture stakeholders.

Once agreed, the Statement should be submitted to the EA Governance Board for review and approval. The criteria to be applied to reviewing the Statement would be expected to include:

1. The Statement is compliant and has been approved by the project/programme and architecture team management;

2. The Statement considers the direct needs of the programme/project and also the wider concerns of other related stakeholders. These would be expected to include related governance boards (e.g., an IT or information security committee), standards bodies (e.g., involvement in related inter-Governmental or industry standards groups), departmental steering groups (in related functions of the enterprise, including in IT), business partners (e.g., in the case of ministry or departmental collaboration), architecture user groups (e.g., there may be a corporate data model or business process special interest group) and product vendors (perhaps through membership of a user group);

3. The work proposed is commensurate with the objectives, timescales, risks and resources of the programme/project and architecture team;

4. All related impacts have been identified and there are no remaining assumptions (having all been signed-off by an owner or reflected in the project risk register where they have been mitigated);

5. The products to be developed have been fully identified and provision for their lifetime management beyond the initial project has been identified. This is crucial as typically these products will define and impact the architecture for a period some time after the project has ended;

6. There is a plan for the inclusion of the EA Governance Board at the appropriate key milestones to provide review and assurance on the architecture products developed.

Balance

When the enterprise and the domain architecture teams create the overall plan for developing and implementing the architecture, there needs to be balance between the local requirements of projects and the broader requirements of wider stakeholders. This is an architecture for people to use, rather than for compliance with a comprehensive classification or taxonomy.

In general terms we therefore propose that a broad architecture view is developed that models the current and target enterprise at a high, but specific, level. This initial view serves to provide context for all the detailed work that follows, and helps us identify overlaps and gaps in the completed architecture description. It enables usage as it allows the users to see where, in navigation terms, they are in the architecture at any point.

For each of the prioritised purposes we then drill down to provide "complete" pictures that meet the business needs of a particular programme, project or other group of stakeholders. We do not drill down in each interrogative dimension separately (e.g., by completing a standalone data architecture) as this is of little use without the context of the related models in other dimensions. Typically we achieve this by managing two sets of models: a series of composite models that meet the needs of the users, and a series of atomic models that meet the needs of the architects to ensure cohesion and completeness across all the composites.

We balance this pragmatic development with periodic reviews, where we identify gaps and overlaps and resolve these, validating the relationships between the elements, to improve the coverage, cohesiveness and standardisation of the architecture. These exercises are not just "academic", but also assist in identifying opportunities for further value (e.g., by identifying overlaps in application functionality that may be rationalised).

It is often useful to represent this balance between short-term project implementation-focused delivery and longer-term strategic development using two-track planning, where tactical delivery is tracked on one plan, and the achievement of strategic milestones on another. In this way, when there is a preponderance of tactical requirements (as there always is!) the architect can demonstrate the risk to strategic milestones and make the case for retaining some effort in the plan for furthering strategic goals as well as supporting immediate delivery.

Further, such a two-track plan helps the EA Governance Board as it enables two checks; 1) is the project proposed in line with the strategy and 2) is the strategy being furthered in as best a way as possible by the project. This later check is often the more difficult, as it suggests the ability to amend the scope of the project to ensure that strategic benefits are delivered, which may not have the immediate approval of a project sponsor focused on short-term benefit.

Implementation, Realising the Architecture

The people-led implementation approach looks for the most value from the least impact on the people. This is not to say that we shy away from change, major change can be achieved without negative impact provided that the stakeholders

are engaged with and the people-factors in change dealt with.

This requires the enterprise architecture programme to have an explicit understanding of the culture, people, communications and how-things-get-done-around-here, as much as the more procedural and structural elements of the organisation such as governance and management structures, delegated authorities, approvals processes, management processes etc.

The enterprise architecture programme should therefore formulate explicit strategies for how it will engage with the organisation to ensure the definition, delivery and implementation of the architecture.

Using and Enhancing Existing Governance and Management Approach

The stakeholders we have identified will already know and be accustomed to their existing governance and management. We should not seek to burden them with new modes of governance and management, but rather inject appropriate elements into the existing approach. The following are examples of this approach:

- Enhancing the review criteria of existing OGC Gateway reviews (as defined by UK Government) to include review criteria from the enterprise architecture function (e.g., for compliance with corporate data or technology standards);
- Providing architecture input into issue resolution processes to bring a comprehensive view of the impact of alternative resolution tactics for consideration by the stakeholders;
- Provide alignment between the service management metrics of IT services with the performance indicators of the customer stakeholders.

It is important in all these examples to identify unique and compelling criteria for the enterprise architect that cannot be adopted by any other role. Often this is in the enterprise architects view across the enterprise in terms of breadth (i.e., takes a view across many business domains) and time (i.e., balances short and long-term thinking).

Using and enhancing existing programme and project delivery and management methodologies and frameworks.

The same argument is applied to the work of the enterprise architect with the solutions delivery change programmes of the enterprise. The introduction of new processes and techniques can be

Table 5.

Start-Up	Feasibility	Initiation	Delivery	Closure
Strategic Critical business change projects delivering major elements of the enterprise architecture				
Provide the project team with access to the repository Core EA team provides advice on what information may be most relevant	Core EA team works with project team to develop architecture products Core EA team develops request for waiver if required and works through EA Governance Board to get approval	Core EA team provides certification that project is compliant with EA and/or terms of EA waiver	Core EA team reviews and certifies that the design is compliant with EA and/or terms of EA waiver Core EA team identifies content for loading into the repository	Core EA team works with project sponsor to review EA and EA contribution for review Core EA team prepares RFC to EA content or process if justified by post project review
Standard Important, domain-based, projects, building on major EA elements.				
Provide project team with access to repository Domain or infrastructure team provides advice on what information may be most relevant	Domain or infrastructure team works with project team to develop architecture products Domain or infrastructure team develops request for waiver if required and works through EA Governance Board to get approval	Domain or infrastructure team provides certification that project is compliant with EA and/or terms of EA waiver	Domain or infrastructure team reviews and certifies that the design is compliant with EA and/or terms of EA waiver Domain or infrastructure team identifies content for loading into the repository	Domain or infrastructure team works with project sponsor to review EA and EA contribution for review Domain or infrastructure team prepares RFC to EA content or process if justified by post project review
Minor Smaller projects with no material impact on the enterprise architecture				
Provide access to repository to project team	Domain or infrastructure team provides ad-hoc support on request by project team (no waiver should be required by a minor project)	Domain team provides certification that project is compliant with EA	n/a	n/a

disconcerting for some people. The involvement of the enterprise architect can benefit all stakeholder types (from the programme perspective) as follows:

- The programme customers may benefit from an improved value opportunity as the architect identifies cross-programme opportunities for re-use, sharing solution elements and simplification of systems and processes;
- The programme builders may benefit from reduced cost and risk if they re-use existing enterprise architecture assets (such as a corporate process model) and this in turn prompts the re-use of existing solution building blocks;
- The users of the programme deliverables may benefit from a more cohesive and consistent systems architecture that maximises the investments in systems and therefore in their own training, and reduces complexity.

It is useful for the programme and project managers to be able to define the architects responsibilities to them, and their obligations back to the architects, and the enterprise architecture. The following table of definitions and modes of engagement (Good & Fairhead, 2007) provides examples as the basis for developing such an engagement model between project types and project phases:

In addition, there are general techniques that would be shared between projects and enterprise architects. Again, we recommend adopting and enhancing the standard practices where possible. For example refer to Table 5.

- Re-use of the PRINCE2 (OGC, 2005) product quality review technique for the enterprise architect's reviews of the architecture artefacts produced by the project (assuming a PRINCE2 working environment);

- Providing common tools and processes for the delivery and management of project artefacts, and a repository service that outlives the project to serve as corporate memory of the project and the solution;
- Enhancing the requirements management process by linking requirements to the relevant architecture views describing the solution to enable change impact assessment and configuration control (e.g., in release management).

In these and any other examples, we suggest keeping the enterprise architect's own methods and techniques hidden from the stakeholders as far as possible. Exposure to "architecture-speak" alienates stakeholders, sets barriers to communication and can create the impression of architecture for architecture sake.

Work with the Culture

There are many sources of guidance as to the patterns of enterprise architecture to adopt that are based on the nature of the problem to be solved, the business sector or the in-vogue technology paradigm of the day amongst others. Our people-led approach suggests that an examination of the culture of the enterprise, that is, of the way the people work with each other, communicate and organise themselves and are led and managed, will provide the driving influence both to how to go about implementing the enterprise architecture and what sort of architecture to adopt.

Table 6 represents a simplified view of three cultural metaphors for enterprises, selected for their contrasting suggestions as to the how and what of an enterprise architecture.

(This table is derived from the results of a workshop run by the author (Good, 2004) which itself was inspired by the writings of Morgan (1986) and the BBC's Leadership Programme

Table 6.

Type of organisation	Indicators of this type	Examples of this type	How to do EA	What EA to consider
Process-driven	Strategy by structured analysis Management focus on process Decision-making by numbers Systematisation of work	Back-office processing-unit (e.g., processing benefits claims). Operational service-delivery agencies	Decree Centralised Formalised	Process-centric Centralised Integrated
Organic	Strategy follows Vision Leadership not management Consensus-based decision-making around a shared direction Focus on working together	Policy Unit Charitable Organisation Overarching government departments that set the context for delivery via various agencies School	Visions Standards Project-focus	Federated Standards-based Interoperable
Networked	Strategy by gut-feel Leadership focus on having conversations Autonomous and local decision making Ideas driven by the people network	Research department Scientific or product R&D University	Subversively Networking By-Example	Localised Distributed Low-level

designed and delivered by Ashridge Management School.)

Viewed another way, the table suggests that there are some approaches, which might be thought of as standard for enterprise architecture (such as defining enterprise-wide single function services as might be defined from an SOA approach, in a networked culture) that are simply not suitable in a given culture because the people will not back them or work with them.

Monitoring, Measurement and Continuous Improvement

If we have established our vision, mission and goals as suggested at the top of this section, and in particular developed these into individual objectives, then we must ensure that the measurement activities are planned to monitor, review and take action on progress towards achieving these.

Table 7.

Stakeholder	Customer	Builder	User
Key Criteria	Did it deliver value?	Did we do it well?	Was it useful?
Example Questions	Did the EA enable the preferred business outcomes? Is the EA resilient to other business scenarios? Is it easier to judge which investments to make?	Were our own processes effective and efficient? Were we more productive? What is the level of customer satisfaction in our work?	Am I able to access and use the EA? Does the EA enhance productivity? Is the enterprise easier to understand, more accurately?

To reinforce the people-led approach to enterprise architecture, we suggest organising the terms of reference for the quality assurance reviews carried out according to our three stakeholder groups. This form of review ensures that the findings are directly relevant to our stakeholders and engages them in addressing their issues and concerns. This is in contrast to other approaches, defined by the step in the process (e.g., define purpose, or create plan), architecture view (e.g., performance, business, information etc) or other based on the structure of the architecture itself which can often appear introverted (EA review for EA) and meaningless for stakeholders.

Of particular importance is the linking of User quality criteria to Customer criteria. For example, if a business/systems analyst on a major change programme is able to quickly and consistently gain access to information regarding the business processes in the enterprise and the applications that support them, then there should be a link to reducing the cost and risk of the programmes in which the customer stakeholders are investing.

Opportunities for measurement can take many forms and the following should be considered as good candidates:

- At any enterprise architecture review of a project, the use of a shared checklist to measure common objectives and criteria such as compliance, product quality and error rates, customer satisfaction, resource deployment, timeliness of delivery will build up a picture relating to the engagement of the architecture team with the project, usefulness of the architecture products and the effectiveness of the architectural processes;
- Periodic EA plan reviews will enable wider measures such as stakeholder engagement and communication, success in hitting strategic milestones, resource utilisation and deployment, risk mitigation success to be measured;

- Periodic repository reviews will present opportunities to measure how up-to-date the products are (against review and archival dates), how used the products are, where demand lies (e.g., by capturing search criteria) and therefore measure the usefulness of the architecture.

SUSTAINING THE EFFORT, BEING READY FOR THE FUTURE

In this section we look forward, to how we can anticipate and prepare for the future demands our stakeholders will place upon us. Much of the work we need to do on an ongoing basis is described previously. We need to plan, execute, review and revise our approach and architecture on a continuous basis. We need to ensure that our architecture governance is embedded in our day-to-day procedures and practices.

When looking to the future and planning our future capability, we ask slightly different questions of ourselves, our customers and our users. The following pragmatic questionsn (Table 8) can be asked, reflecting that we often have a view of the specific changes planned by the organisation over the next 18 months or so, but only a strategic view for the longer term after that (Good and Fairhead, 2007).

Using the quality assessment matrix presented previously (Table 7) you can assess your capability maturity in a way that is innately tuned to the needs of the stakeholders. Within each stakeholder assessment, maturity is driven by the following factors:

- **Repeatability:** The extent to which the requirements of the stakeholders are met on an ongoing basis, not just in "one-off" project delivery;
- **Resilience:** The extent to which the capability is flexible and adaptable to changes in circumstances;

Table 8.

- Realisation. Am I getting the benefits from what I've already delivered?
- Optimisation. Am I getting the most out of what I'm currently doing?

  - Prioritisation. Am I going to do the right things?
  - Preparedness. Have I the right resources?
  - Planning. What are my opportunities/constraints?
  - Leverage. What can I re-use?
  - Benefits. Am I realising my business case?

    - Implementation. Is my strategy right?

      - Positioning. Is my vision right?

| Now | 18 months | 3 years | 5 years |

- **Value recognition:** The extent to which there is explicit recognition of value achieved and ongoing measurement of outcomes;
- **Coverage:** The scope of implementation of the enterprise architecture;
- **Usage:** The extent to which all the artefacts of the enterprise architecture are used by all relevant stakeholders.

Using the understanding of our stakeholder needs, now and into the future, the assessments of enterprise architecture quality and the maturity assessment, you can plan required capability going forward.

We should always remember that perfection often fails (as it is generally measured in technical terms rather than by the opinions of the stakeholders) and constant improvement works. By listening and responding to our stakeholders in ways that they direct and find most appropriate, we will continue to improve our service and the value we generate for the organisation. If there is a single long-term goal, it is to make it easier for our stakeholders to do the right thing, first time.

CONCLUSION

We have proposed that when considering all aspects of enterprise architecture, we take a people-led approach. Unless there is an explicit alignment between the interests of the stakeholders and the proposed architecture, there is a high probability that the architecture will not be implemented and that the value of the enterprise architecture programme will fail to be understood and realised. This stands regardless of the feasibility of the underlying IT from a technical perspective.

We have proposed that stakeholder management means stakeholders managing us. That we specifically recognise, understand and be led by our customers, involve the whole of the builder community and address the needs of our users.

We have seen how the general steps of defining our purpose ("why"), our approach ("what") and our plans ("how") is not only an intuitive approach but also addresses motivating, skilling and informing our stakeholders.

We have suggested techniques for defining our mission statement and objectives and our implementation plan in the context of this people-led approach, not least through the explicit recognition of the enterprise culture.

Finally, we have suggested that a people-led approach to quality assessment would be one that would engage more directly with all our stakeholders, by being tuned to their original requirements and needs as we should have identified them at the start of the enterprise architecture process. This in turn will lead us to plan the enhancement of the enterprise architecture capability in line with our stakeholders' needs and better serve them over time.

REFERENCES

Cabinet Office (2005), Transformational Government, Enabled by IT. Retrieved 31st July 2007 from http://www.cio.gov.uk/documents/pdf/transgov/transgov-strategy.pdf

Cabinet Office (2007), Chief Technology Officer Council. Retrieved 31st July 2007 from http://www.cio.gov.uk/chief_technology_officer/index.asp

Goldstein, H (2005) *Who Killed the Virtual Case File?,* IEEE Spectrum September 2005, http://www.spectrum.ieee.org/print/1455

Good, J (2004) *Defining an Architecture Roadmap that talks to the Enterprise Culture*, EA Conference Europe 2004, London, IRM UK Ltd

Good, J and Fairhead, N (2007) *Getting started in Enterprise Architecture* EA Conference Europe 2007, London, IRM UK Ltd (copyright Serco Consulting, used with permission)

Government of Ontario, Office of the Premier (2006). Description of the role of the Treasury Board/Management Board of Cabinet. Retrieved 30th July 2007, from http://www.premier.gov.on.ca/team/Committee.asp?Team=2

Light, Paul C (1999). *The Changing Shape of Government* The Brookings Institute, Policy Brief # 45

Lohr, Steve and Markoff, John (in press) Windows Is So Slow, but Why? *New York Times; March 27, 2006*

Morgan, Gareth (1997) *Images of Organisation*, 2nd Edition, London. Sage Publications

National Research Council (2004). McGroddy, James C., and Lin, Herbert S., Editors, *A Review of the FBI's Trilogy Information Technology*, Committee on the FBI's Trilogy Information Technology Modernization Program, Computer Science and Telecommunications Board, Division on Engineering and Physical Sciences, National Research Council of the National Academies, . ISBN:0-309-09224-8. Retrieved on August 6 2007 from http://www.nap.edu/catalog/10991.html

Office of Government Commerce (2005). *Managing Successful Projects with PRINCE2 Manual 2005*, 4th Ed. TSO (The Stationery Office).

Prime Minister's Strategy Unit (2004). Strategy Survival Guide v2.1. Retrieved 31st July 2007 from http://www.cabinetoffice.gov.uk/strategy/downloads/survivalguide/skills/s_pestle.htm

U.S. General Accounting Office (2003). *Information Technology: A Framework for Assessing and Improving Enterprise Architecture Management (Version 1.1)*, GAO-03-584G, April 1, 2003. Retrieved 3rd August 2007 from http://www.gao.gov/new.items/d03584g.pdf

ENDNOTE

[1] TOGAF is a trademark of The Open Group in the US and other countries

Chapter XIV
Using Enterprise Architecture to Transform Service Delivery:
The U.S. Federal Government's Human Resources Line of Business

Timothy Biggert
IBM Global Business Services, USA

Kunal Suryavanshi
IBM Global Business Services, USA

Ryan Kobb
IBM Global Business Services, USA

ABSTRACT

This chapter provides a case study on how the U.S. Office of Personnel Management has led the establishment of the Human Resources Line of Business (HR LOB). It explains how the HR LOB program has used enterprise architecture to drive transformation to a new Human Resources service delivery model across the United States Federal government. The authors propose that the common view and vocabulary that EA artifacts provide, along with the collaborative governance that took place to create the artifacts, has produced a solid business foundation for this extensive business transformation effort.

INTRODUCTION

Enterprise architecture synthesizes a business entity – and much of its complexity – into a single integrated set of structures that can be used as a basis for strategy and planning. "In a large modern enterprise, a rigorously defined framework is necessary to be able to capture a vision of the '*entire system*' in all its dimensions and complexity. Enterprise architecture (EA) is a framework which is able to coordinate the many facets that make up the fundamental essence of an enterprise. It is the master plan which '*acts as an integrating force*' between aspects of business planning" (Stevenson, 1995, para. 2).

The **United States Office of Management and Budget** has formulated an enterprise architecture strategy for the U.S. government that can help government agencies manage complexity and move toward innovation and transformation – informed and enabled by enterprise architecture. This chapter is about the U.S. Federal government's transformation of service delivery for Human Resources using enterprise architecture and reinforced by collaborative governance.

The **Human Resources Line of Business (HR LOB)** is *driving transformation* of Federal Human Resources service delivery *via enterprise architecture*. The HR LOB enterprise architecture provides a common, government-wide view and vocabulary for the HR function – a view and vocabulary that provide a basis for common, government-wide solutions that agencies will implement to realize the vision and goals of the Federal government's HR transformation.

Using broad-based collaboration as a fundamental governance principle, the **HR Line of Business** program at the U.S. Office of Personnel Management was able to achieve consensus on its enterprise architecture and use that EA to define shared services-based service delivery expectations for the future Federal HR operation. Under the leadership of the HR LOB program, hundreds of HR professionals representing three

dozen agencies came together in dozens of work sessions over a four year period to define a government-wide HR enterprise architecture.

The results of this collaboration are presented in the pages that follow. This chapter is organized into the following sections:

- **BACKGROUND:** Provides environmental and historical context for the U.S. Government's electronic government initiatives and the events that led to the formation of the HR LOB program.
- **ENTERPRISE ARCHITECTURE:** Describes how the HR LOB EA helped achieve the vision of standardization of HR processes across the Federal HR function.
- **GOVERNANCE:** Explains how HR LOB used collaborative governance to develop an EA necessary to standardize and modernize HR services delivery.
- **TARGET REQUIREMENTS FOR SHARED SERVICE CENTERS:** Describes how the HR LOB EA has been used to drive implementation – by compiling and developing the solution-level target requirements for shared service centers.
- **LESSONS LEARNED:** Outlines critical lessons learned while developing an EA for the HR LOB.
- **FUTURE TRENDS AND RESEARCH:** Provides insight into how EA can be used to help government calibrate how it delivers shared services to its customers.

BACKGROUND

Innovation in the use of technology is driving a revolution in business today, enabling the creation of new businesses and business structures. Homeowners can shop for refinance loans from their own homes. Businesses can integrate suppliers and customers into their own end-to-end business processes with seamless precision. Companies can outsource functions to other companies located on the other side of the planet.

Fueled by technology, the pace of change is in fact accelerating. According to McDavid (1999):

Technological innovations give rise to increased opportunities: new ways to do old things better and whole new things to do. These opportunities give rise to business innovations, and companies move in to take over new niches and sub-niches. These changes in the way of doing business create new ideas and expectations of even better, more innovative performance on the part of technology. In turn, pressure is put on technology providers to support still more new and innovative forms of business behavior. (Purpose of a business system architecture section, para. 7)

Expectations about innovation do not stop with business; the public expects innovation to thrive throughout government as well. "Polling data from the Pew Foundation, for example, show that over 40 million Americans went online to look at Federal, State and local government policies and over 20 million used the Internet to send their views to governments about those policies. This and similar data show that if the U.S. Government can harness the power of technology, it will be meeting expectations of an increasingly wired citizenry" (Office of Management and Budget [OMB], n.d.a, What the Public Expects section).

According to the **U.S. Office of Management and Budget (OMB)**, the goal of the United States Government "is to be the best manager, innovator, and user of information, services, and information systems in the world… There continue to be great opportunities to apply existing and emerging business best practices to government to achieve increases in productivity and delivery of services and information. We remain focused on the customer instead of our traditional approach of focusing on departments and agencies" (OMB, 2006, December, p.1).

In his February 2002 budget submission to Congress, the President of the United States proposed his strategy for achieving this shift to a customer focus. The President stated that "our success depends on agencies working as a team across traditional boundaries to better serve the American people, focusing on citizens rather than individual agency needs" (OMB, n.d.a, The President Urges Agencies to Work Together section). According to **OMB** (n.d.a) the *President's Management Agenda* proposes that this can be accomplished through expanding **electronic government** – or *E-Government* – which leverages advances in technology to:

- Make it easy for citizens and businesses to interact with the government
- Save taxpayer dollars
- Streamline citizen-to-government communications

The United States Government has been a particular beneficiary of information technology:

The United States Government continues to be one of the largest users and acquirers of data, information and supporting technology systems in the world, by investing approximately $65 billion annually on Information Technology (IT). The Federal Government has made improvements but continues to strive to be the world's leader in managing technology and information to achieve the greatest gains of productivity, service and results (OMB, 2006, December, p. 1).

The **E-Government** Act of 2002, signed by the President on December 17, 2002 and made effective on April 17, 2003, codified 24 E-Government initiatives into legislation. The initiatives have already achieved tangible progress. Following are just some of the benefits OMB (2007, February) reported to Congress in the second annual *Report to Congress on the Benefits of the E-Government Initiatives.*

- **GovBenefits.gov:** The GovBenefits.gov initiative provides a single point of access for citizens to locate information and determine potential eligibility for government benefits and services. It receives an average of approximately 300,000 visits per month by citizens and to date has provided nearly one million citizen referrals to benefit programs.

- **IRS Free File:** For the 2006 filing season to date, more than 3.9 million citizens have filed taxes online for free using the Free File E-Government solution.

- **Grants.gov:** With over 1,000 grant programs offered by all Federal grant making agencies, Grants.gov provides a means for navigating through the complexity of finding and applying for U.S. Government grants. The initiative has seen a substantial increase in the number of grant application packages posted on Grants.gov since the beginning of fiscal year 2005. In the first quarter of FY05, 252 packages were posted on Grants.gov. By the last quarter of fiscal year 2006, 4,523 packages were posted on Grants.gov, almost 17 times the number at the beginning of fiscal year 2005.

- **SAFECOM:** SAFECOM provides research, development, testing, and evaluation, guidance, tools, and templates on communications-related issues to local, tribal, state, and Federal emergency response agencies. In 2006, the initiative increased the number of urban areas that can establish interoperable communications at the command level within one hour of a major event from 10 to 75. Additionally, 66% of public safety agencies report using interoperability to some degree in their operations.

- **E-Travel:** E-Gov Travel is a collaborative interagency program the purpose of which is to realize the cost savings and increased service associated with a common, automated, and integrated approach to managing the travel function of the United States Government's civilian agencies. The Department of Labor, one of the first agencies to complete its migration to an E-Travel service provider, reported a decrease in travel voucher costs from approximately $60 per voucher to approximately $25 per voucher (a decrease of about 60%) and a reduction in voucher processing time from seven to three business days. Additionally, both the Department of Transportation and the Department of the Interior are realizing savings of over $1 million per year through the use of online booking.

- **e-Training:** The e-Training initiative is transforming learning by creating a premier e-Learning environment to support the development of the Federal workforce and to advance the accomplishment of agency missions through simplified and one-stop access to high quality e-Learning products, tools, and services. To date, over 840,000 Federal employees have registered in the GoLearn.gov Learning Management System. Federal employees have completed more than 2.7 million courses provided through the E-Training initiative. E-Training is assisting the United States Government in maintaining a highly skilled workforce at a fraction of the cost of classroom training alone.

- **E-Payroll:** The E-Payroll initiative is consolidating 26 Executive branch Federal payroll providers to just four providers, standardizing payroll policies and procedures, and simplifying and better integrating payroll, human resources, and finance functions. Through migration to one of the four payroll service providers, agencies are able to realize cost savings and improved efficiencies. For example, the Department of Health and Human Services has reduced the annual costs of payroll processing for its more than 65,000 employees from $259 to $90 per employee (an annual savings of almost $11 million) while the Environmental Protection Agency has reduced the cost from $270 to $90 per employee for its staff of 18,000 (an annual savings of approximately $3.2 million).

- **Recruitment One-Stop.** Each month, over 100,000 resumes are created on USAJobs. gov, the branded Web site of Recruitment One-Stop (the Federal online recruitment service). USAJobs.gov receives over 240,000 visits daily from job seekers looking for information regarding career opportunities with the United States Government.

Working across traditional government agency boundaries to achieve business benefits of this magnitude requires a common view that spans government boundaries, a view that enables cross-agency conversation, debate, and collaboration. This common view is achieved through enterprise architecture. Recognizing this, **OMB** commissioned the **Federal Enterprise Architecture** (FEA) Program on February 6, 2002. The FEA Program provides specifications for building a comprehensive business-driven blueprint of the entire United States Government.

In 2004, OMB appointed the **U.S. Office of Personnel Management** (OPM) to lead five of the 24 **E-Gov** initiatives. That appointment constituted a White House challenge to OPM: assume a key role in supporting the transformation of the United States Government – with 1.8 million employees deployed across multiple disparate agencies – into an efficient, cost-effective, performance-driven business. **OPM** is meeting that goal through its **Human Resources Line of Business** (HR LOB) – an initiative that is creating a modern, standardized, and interoperable HR function throughout the Federal government. Up to now, each Federal agency has handled its own HR operations, resulting in duplication and waste across hundreds of agency locations. The **HR LOB** program is driving consolidation of HR

data and processes. It has the potential to produce cost savings of hundreds of millions of dollars.

At the onset, OPM convened a task force comprised of 24 Federal agencies to chart the vision and goals for the HR Line of Business. The vision of the **HR LOB** is "*government-wide, modern, cost-effective, standardized, and interoperable HR solutions providing common, core functionality to support the strategic management of human capital and addressing duplicative HR systems and processes.*" The goals of the **HR LOB** program include:

- Improved Government-wide Strategic Management of Human Capital
- Operational Efficiencies
- Cost Savings / Avoidance
- Improved Customer Service

Two dimensions that underlie the **HR LOB** vision are *standardization* and *common solutions*. Standardization implies that solutions are to be developed through a set of common and repeatable processes and tools. This standardization will be a basis for government-wide common solutions that not only provide economies of scale, but also address measurable business improvements. Enterprise architecture has provided the means for making tough decisions around standardization and common solutions.

The concepts of standardization and common solutions will in large part be operationalized by the introduction of HR **shared services**. A small number of agencies have been identified to deliver HR services to other agencies via shared service centers (SSCs). Additionally, private sector providers will also deliver HR services to Federal agencies. Over time, this will enhance competitive market forces in the HR Line of Business, supporting another tenet of the President's Management Agenda.

Shared services is traditionally defined as an operational model in which services are delivered by business entities that are internal to an organization but operate independently – **shared service centers** (SSCs). **SSCs** operate as a business and have dedicated resources to provide well-defined, process-based or knowledge-based services for more than one unit of a company (division, business unit, or agency). SSCs are fully responsible for managing costs, quality, and timeliness of services. The concept of shared services is not new; the private sector embraced it ten to fifteen years ago. It is just now gaining momentum in the public sector.

The **HR LOB** Concept of Operations states that these HR **shared service centers** will take a phased approach to delivering HR services. At a minimum, all SSCs will offer the same common core functionality. The solutions that operate at these SSCs will be evaluated and recommended by a multi-agency steering committee that stresses scalability, interoperability, and portability. Agencies will select SSCs on a competitive basis and have choices; they can shop around for the SSCs that best meet their needs. The shared service centers will leverage "plug and play" architecture concepts.

In his report on innovation in government, Borins (2006) of the University of Toronto reports that, interestingly, "frontline staff and middle managers are the most frequent initiators of public management innovation" (p.5). The results of his study also reveal that "innovative organizations draw ideas from people at all levels" (p.5). Borins' conclusions are quite consistent with the **HR LOB** Program experience: collaboration is key. Since 2004, over 400 participants from 24 Federal agencies have collaborated to produce the business and technical architectures that define this new HR service delivery approach. The **HR LOB** program is a model for leveraging cross-government expertise and collaboration to develop an enterprise architecture that standardizes business processes, data, performance measures, business services, and technical infrastructure.

The Human Resources Line of Business is using enterprise architecture to innovate and

transform the HR function throughout the United States Government. The next section of this chapter, **ENTERPRISE ARCHITECTURE**, describes how the HR LOB EA helped achieve the vision of standardization of HR processes across the Federal HR function.

ENTERPRISE ARCHITECTURE

The **Human Resources Line of Business** Program established enterprise architecture (EA) as one important means of achieving the vision and objectives of the program. EA provides the common view and vocabulary across 24 United States Federal agencies that enables dialog, debate, and collaboration around standardization, common solutions, and the new shared services-based HR delivery model.

Over the course of four years, various workgroups were convened to build out the models. Each workgroup was comprised of government *human resources professionals* representing the human resources point of view of the HR LOB member agencies. The **HR LOB** approach to EA was based on a fundamental tenet that would drive the multi-year effort: EA deliverables would comply with **OMB's Federal Enterprise Architecture** guidelines and, more important, would provide real *business value* to agencies. The objective was to produce artifacts that were both compliant and useful.

The United States General Accountability Office (2003, November) reports that there are seven EA frameworks in use at various agencies across the United States Federal government. The frameworks in most widespread use are:

- Federal Enterprise Architecture Framework (FEAF) - 61 agencies
- Federal Enterprise Architecture Program Management Office (FEAPMO) Reference Models - 56 agencies
- Zachman Framework - 36 agencies

Other frameworks in use, albeit less popular, include:

- Treasury Enterprise Architecture Framework (TEAF)
- National Institute of Standards and Technology Framework (NIST framework)
- Command, Control, Communications, Computers, Intelligence, Surveillance, and Reconnaissance (C4ISR) Framework
- Department of Defense Architecture Framework (DoDAF)

The **Office of Management and Budget** strongly encouraged the various lines of business to develop their segment architectures using a common framework, the FEAPMO Reference Models. The rationale behind this is simple: the lines of business have been established to consolidate services across the government, reducing or eliminating duplicative services and systems. Having a common framework allows for the segment architectures to roll up to a government-wide view. This provides for discovering duplication of processes, services and /or systems and for recognizing best of breed that are recommended for use across the government.

And although the framework may be specific to the U.S. Federal government, the modeling methods that underlie the framework are not uncommon. **FEA** Practice Guidance, published by the FEAPMO (2006, December), states that "Segment architecture work products are developed using standard formats and content... Standard work product content and formats promote collaboration and reuse by facilitating the reconciliation of segment architecture work products with the agency EA and relevant cross-agency initiatives found in the *Federal Transition Framework*" (section 2, p.8).

The program facilitated the development and validation of all five models put forward by FEAPMO Reference Model guidelines (Figure 1.).

These models are described in more detail in the pages that follow.

Figure 1.

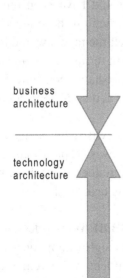

business architecture

technology architecture

1. The *HR LOB Business Reference Model* provides an end-to-end view of the human resources processes that take place in departments and agencies across the United States Government.

2. The *HR LOB Performance Model* proposes a set of performance measures for core HR functions and provides linkages between measures and program objectives.

3. The *HR LOB Service Component Model* provides a services view and identifies and defines the business services that can be put into place to support the BRM business processes. It also describes methods for delivering services to the consumers of those services.

4. The *HR LOB Data Model* provides a view of the data necessary to perform the BRM activities. At the conceptual level, it provides a complete view of data objects and their relationships. At the logical level, it identifies and defines data elements for those data objects that will be shared across agencies.

5. The *HR LOB Technical Model* provides a view of the technology required to enable business services plus the standards that can be put into place to promote interoperability.

HR LOB Business Reference Model

The first EA artifact developed by the HR LOB EA workgroup was the **Business Reference Model** (BRM), an end-to-end process model for the Human Resources function of the United States Government. Although previous efforts had been made to build a government-wide HR process model, this was the most comprehensive to date in terms of the extent of agency participation and the completeness and breadth of the result. Over 300 participants representing 33 agencies met to develop and validate the HR LOB Business Reference Model.

According to OMB (2007, July) **FEA** guidelines:

The **BRM** provides a framework facilitating a functional (rather than organizational) view of the Federal government's lines of business, including its internal operations and its services for citizens, independent of the agencies, bureaus and offices performing them. The **BRM** describes the Federal government around common business areas instead of through a stove-piped, agency by agency view. It thus promotes agency collaboration and serves as the underlying foundation for the FEA and **E-Gov** strategies (p.6).

The **BRM** is structured into a multi-tiered hierarchy. Business areas appear in the topmost tier and include:

- Services for citizens
- Mode of delivery
- Support delivery and services
- Management of government resources

Business areas are comprised of lines of business. For example, the business area Management of Government Resources is comprised of the following lines of business:

- Supply Chain Management
- **Human Resources Management**
- Financial Management

- Administrative Management
- Information Technology Management

And lines of business are comprised of sub-functions, the lowest level of granularity in the government-wide **BRM**. The entire government-wide Business Reference Model can be found on OMB's Web site at:http://www.whitehouse.gov/omb/egov/a-2-EAModelsNEW2.html

Using the government-wide BRM as the context, the HR Line of Business constructed a BRM for the Human Resources function, taking the government-wide model down to a greater level of detail. The HR LOB Business Reference Model, first published on December 31, 2004 and re-validated and re-published in January 2006, provides an end-to-end process view for Human Resources Management.

The model consists of ten Human Resources sub-functions, organized by HR life cycle phase. The model is three layers deep. For each line of business, the sub-function layer represents the top layer. Underlying the sub-function is the process layer and underlying the process layer is the activity layer. The HR LOB model was not defined below three layers for three important reasons:

- First, it would have been quite impractical and difficult to decompose to the next (task) level; the model would have become unwieldy in terms of size and complexity.
- It would also have been quite difficult to get agreement across 24 agencies on task level detail.
- And the downstream business purpose of the model was to be a management tool, not a design document; there was no need to go to the task level.

The HR LOB **BRM** provides a level of detail that is flexible enough to be applicable to the entire Federal government while remaining tangible enough to be relevant for individual agencies.

Box 1.

Using EA to drive workforce analytics –
the U.S. Department of Health & Human Services

Just after the HR LOB Business Reference Model was first published in 2004, the Department of Health & Human Services (HHS) leveraged this artifact to make strategic workforce decisions and build a business case for moving to a new HR operational model.

Using the process framework of the BRM, HHS HR personnel developed an analytical tool to determine the number of full-time equivalent employees (FTEs) who performed each HR process and to estimate the percentage of time each FTE spent on each process. The tool was designed to provide an order of magnitude view of labor costs currently allocated to each business process. They then made decisions about whether these processes would, in the future, be delivered directly by HR personnel, via the Web, or via a call center. Given these new service delivery methods, they projected future staffing requirements.

This data became the basis for a business case that projected investment costs versus cumulative benefits over a ten year period. This business case was used to justify the new operational model and to provide a basis for planning the deployment of the service delivery methods.

For HHS, the HR LOB Business Reference Model served as a useful business planning tool.

Figure 2. HR LOB BRM – end-to-end process view

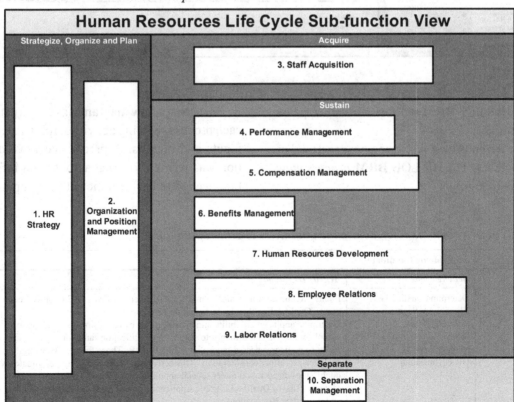

Figure 3. HR LOB BRM – sub-function view

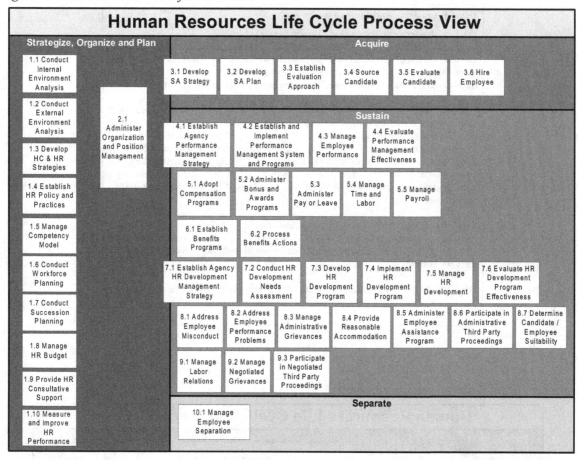

The HR LOB **BRM** *sub-function view* appears in Figure 3.

The ten sub-functions decompose to a total of 45 processes. The HR LOB **BRM** *process view* appears in Figure 3.

An activity flow diagram was constructed for each process showing activities, roles, and major inputs and outputs. A precise narrative definition was written for each activity and information needed to perform the activity (inputs) and

Table 1. Activity definition for determine qualified / eligible applicants

Process	3.5 Evaluate Candidate	
ID	**Activity Name**	**Activity Definition**
3.5.1	Determine Qualified / Eligible Applicants Role: Management HR Organization	*Inputs:* Recorded Applicant Documentation, Selection Criteria, Eligibility Requirements, Qualification Standards, Selection Factors Determine applicant eligibility and qualifications by reviewing applications for completeness and conformance to eligibility, qualifications and / or legal requirements (e.g., degree accreditation) including ICTAP. Those found to be ineligible are provided no further consideration. This activity includes identifying candidates who qualify for consideration under special appointing authorities. *Outputs:* List of Qualified/Eligible Applicants, List of Special Authority Candidates, and Candidate Notifications.

information produced as a result of the activity (outputs) were also listed. Table 1 below provides a sample definition for the activity *Determine Qualified / Eligible Applicants*.

The HR LOB **BRM** – and the work that led to it – is significant for a number of reasons.

- First, the simple structure, along with the thorough information behind it, provides an easily understood view of HR that could be developed and validated – and subsequently used – by HR professionals with no knowledge of enterprise architecture.

- The initiative was the most comprehensive collaboration that ever took place regarding U.S. Federal HR process, and over the course of the collaboration HR professionals came to the realization that there is a large degree of commonality across the government.

- The HR LOB **BRM** is a springboard for process innovation. Workgroup members were encouraged to be innovative and create a future view of the human resources process in the United States government. However, since the process is driven by legislation and policy, it was quite difficult for them to think outside the current view. Because of its widespread acceptance since its introduction, we can expect the BRM to become a starting point, over time, for innovation. (The BRM does contain kernels of innovation. For example, although the concept of competency management is not well established in the government, it appears as a thread throughout the model.)

- The **BRM** is a basis for the subsequent models built and thus serves as the *integrating artifact*. The activity inputs and outputs provided an important starting point for the HR LOB Data Model. It provided a structure for the HR LOB Performance Model. And it established the basis for identifying the HR services that appear in the HR LOB Service Component Model.

- Most important, it has become a useful management tool. At the HR LOB program level, for example, all collaborative work sessions are organized by BRM sub-functions. And at the agency level, the General Services Administration has used the **BRM** to drive transformation of its hiring processes.

The entire HR LOB **BRM** can be found at the U.S. Office of Personnel Management Web site: http://www.opm.gov/egov/documents/architecture/#brm

HR LOB Performance Model

In January 2006, a workgroup convened to develop the HR LOB **Performance Model** (PM). The HR LOB **PM** proposes a common set of performance measures for use throughout the Federal government. These performance measures will gauge how effectively government HR resources are used to support agency mission results, support the effective management of human capital across the government, and provide for effective human resources service delivery to employees, managers / supervisors, and other HR constituents. A total of 49 participants representing 12 agencies met to develop and validate the HR LOB Performance Model.

According to **FEA** guidelines, the **PM** will ultimately have three main uses:

1. Help produce enhanced performance information to improve strategic and daily decision-making.
2. Improve the alignment – and better articulate the contribution of – inputs to outputs and outcomes, thereby creating a clear "line of sight" to desired results.
3. Identify performance improvement opportunities that span traditional organizational structures and boundaries.

Table 2. Total compensation as a percent of agency budget

Measure Name	Definition	Purpose
Total Compensation as a percent of agency budget	Percent of budget allocated to compensation. Compensation Cost includes salary, student loans, benefits, recruiting / retention / relocation incentives	Shows the percentage of budget allocated to compensation; useful for market comparison. Useful for year over year comparison and trend analysis.

The first version of the HR LOB PM focuses only on the end-to-end processes of the core Business Reference Model sub-functions – Compensation Management and Benefits Management – and those BRM activities that result in a personnel action. These areas are the first to be supported by the new shared service centers because they are highly transactional and administratively intense.

FEA guidance describes a hierarchical construct for the **PM** that has four levels.

- *Measurement area* is the broadest area and is the high-level organizing framework capturing aspects of performance measures at the output level. The HR LOB falls under the *Management of Government Resources* Measurement Area.

- The *measurement category* level reflects collections within each measurement area describing the attribute or characteristic to be measured. This aligns with the Lines of Business.

- The *measurement grouping* level is a further refinement of the measurement category. The groupings align with the **BRM** sub-functions.

- The *measurement indicator* level defines those specific measures identified for the specific sub-function. The indicators evaluate the results of the sub-function's contribution to agency business results. According to the FEA guidance, each Measurement Grouping (HR LOB sub-function) should have at least one measurement indicator

(performance measure) that addresses each of the outcomes and objectives.

For each BRM sub-function (measurement grouping), the workgroup identified and defined a set of performance measures (measurement categories). The group was very careful to identify *pragmatic* measures, i.e., measures for which results data exists and can be collected. To illustrate the model, for the sub-function Compensation Management the workgroup identified a total of 13 performance measures, one of which is named *total compensation as a percentage of agency budget*. This measurement indicator is defined as follows:

The **PM** provides a framework that links measures to government-wide HR strategic outcomes[1] – as defined by the **Office of Personnel Management** – and to the strategic objectives of the **HR LOB** program. These linkages are important as the government-wide HR strategic outcomes and **HR LOB** strategic objectives link to specific agency business objectives. Thus, the PM measures, when implemented, provide tangible evidence of agency business results.

To continue the aforementioned illustration, all 13 of the measurement indicators that support the BRM sub-function Compensation Management were linked to HR LOB objectives as shown in table 3 below. This mapping is important because it provides "line of sight" between performance and desired results.

The concept of moving highly transactional and administratively intense activities to **shared service centers** to reduce costs, increase efficiency

Table 3. Performance indicators mapped to strategic objectives

Strategic Objectives	Compensation Management Measures
Improved Mgmt	• Total compensation as a percentage of agency budget • Average compensation per agency FTE • Employee satisfaction with compensation • Compliance
Operational Efficiency	• On time project performance • Retroactive payroll adjustments • Electronic access • Amended / corrected time records • Payroll certifications • Timeliness: time to disburse off-cycle payroll transactions • Cycle time: W-2 distribution • Quality: W-2 corrections as a percent of total W-2s
Cost Savings / Avoidance	• On budget project performance • Cost / price per W-2
Improved Customer Service	• Quality: Personnel Action corrections – bonus & awards • Timeliness: Change Notification • Customer Service: Time to resolve / respond to inquiry

and even improve employee satisfaction appears on the surface to be a good idea. And the notion that this could free up agency HR personnel to do more valuable HR work is intuitively appealing. However, this new operating model could have *negative value*. It could in fact cost U.S. taxpayers twice as much, create more inefficiency and create employee dissatisfaction – given the possibility that when agencies migrate to the new model, there is a very real likelihood that they will retain *shadow staff* to duplicate the work of their service providers.

It is thus imperative to baseline current performance and track performance over time as more and more agencies migrate to this new operational model. Having a common set of measures across the government will provide benchmarks that will enable comparative analysis across shared service centers, across agencies, and with private sector enterprises. Having this performance data will help identify high performers whose practices can be replicated. It will also help identify performance issues and provide a basis for improvement programs.

The entire HR LOB **PM** can be found at the U.S. Office of Personnel Management Web site: http://www.opm.gov/egov/documents/architecture/#pm

HR LOB Service Component Model

In March 2006, a workgroup was formed to begin to develop an approach to building the HR LOB **Service Component Model** (SCM). The **SCM** lays the groundwork for the new services-based approach to HR service delivery described in the HR LOB Concept of Operations – in a very tangible way. The **SCM** formalizes a government-wide view of services by proposing the *universe of business services that could be put into place to support the HR processes depicted in the HR LOB BRM*, and provides the construct that can be used to realize the shared services vision proposed by the HR LOB.

The **Service Component Model** identifies all the services that could be provided by HR service providers to support **BRM** processes – the list of potential services from which providers will select to establish their portfolio of services. These portfolios of services, in turn, provide the menu of services options that customer agencies will have when shopping for services. The HR LOB SCM, thus, provides a brand new services view that is crucial to defining this new line of business.

FEA guidelines provide a hierarchical construct for the **SCM**. *Service domains* appear at the top of the hierarchy. Service domains are comprised of *service types* and service types in turn are comprised of *service components*. The service domain Back Office Services, for example, is comprised of five service types:

- Data management
- Human resources
- Financial management
- Assets / material management services
- Human capital management

The HR LOB SCM workgroup, which included 97 participants representing 14 agencies, identified 17 service components under the service type Human Resources (e.g., Pay Administration, Payroll Processing, Benefits Enrollment, Benefits Counseling, Recruiting) and 16 service components under the service type Human Capital Management (e.g., Competency Management, Workforce Planning, Succession Planning, Staffing). They also identified 30 service components outside the service types HR and HCM that support HR processes (e.g., Customer Support, Call Center Management, Knowledge Management, Consultative Support, Project Management).

The entire HR LOB **SCM** can be found at the U.S. Office of Personnel Management Web site: http://www.opm.gov/egov/documents/architecture/#scm

The SCM workgroup also constructed a *service delivery model*. The workgroup identified user types: generic customers or constituents that might take advantage or use a service. The group mapped service component to user types to identify viable usage instances. For each usage instance, the group decided the most appropriate delivery mode:

- **Tier 0 direct access:** Enables the user to perform an action related to the task or activity without any direct involvement or guidance from another person (e.g., Web, IVR)
- **Tier 1 call center:** Enables the user to speak to a Human Resource generalist who utilizes scripts and a knowledge base to respond to a wide variety of questions and issues
- **Tier 2 subject matter expert:** Interprets policy to respond to escalated issues and questions
- **Tier 3 decision maker:** Interprets policy and has decision-making authority around complex issues, questions and critical incidents

The **service delivery model** provides a useful planning tool for service providers to understand the skills, resources, and infrastructure required at each tier.

The SCM and its companion **service delivery model** demonstrate in a very real way how *enterprise architecture is being used to shape HR service delivery for the United States government.* Previously, the processes and activities in the BRM were used as a basis for discussing services. This was quite useful, but imprecise because many of the activities are collaborative (i.e., both provider and customer have a role in the activity). The SCM provides a common view of services that will provide the basis for providers' portfolios of services. The narrative definitions provide a vocabulary for discussion services. This common view and vocabulary around a *common set of services* will allow providers to more easily differentiate their services from other providers and will allow customers to compare offerings across providers.

It will also conceivably provide a more solid basis for customers and providers to negotiate service level agreements (SLAs). Since **Target Requirements** (described in a subsequent section) will be mapped to service components, those requirements help set expectations between the customer agency and service provider regarding how the provider is expected to meet each requirement that is linked to each service being negotiated. Thus, very specific expectations can be set.

According to the OPM HR LOB **SCM** Report (2007):

The HR LOB Common Solution(s) White Paper and Concept of Operations (CONOPS), developed by the HR LOB Common Solution and Target Architecture Workgroup under the multi-agency HR LOB Task Force in 2004, discussed two dimensions that would be very important to any Federal line of business: common solutions and standardization.

The concept of *common solutions* is based on a model that provides a business-driven approach to deliver standardized, scalable, and portable HR services across the Federal Government. **Shared service centers** would be a keystone for common solutions, producing economies of scale and supporting the four goals of the **HR Line of Business**: reduced cost, better efficiency, improved customer service, and improved management of human capital.

Standardization defines common and repeatable processes that make common solutions possible. Enterprise architecture provides the framework and vocabulary for deciding what is to be standardized.

Two desirable outcomes result from building out these dimensions – *reusability* and *interoperability*.

• *Reusability* is the ability to utilize a business asset in more than one context – by multiple organizations or across multiple processes.
• *Interoperability* is the ability to exchange assets for like assets without undue impact. It enables the purchaser of an asset to trade out one asset for another. And because the asset is self-contained and independent in terms

of what it accomplishes and the resources it needs, there is minimum rippling effect when the trade-out occurs.

Identifying these assets is one step toward achieving the concepts of *reusability* and *interoperability* (pp. 4-5).

The HR LOB **Service Component Model** identifies and defines reusable assets at the *business services* level.

The real value of the **SCM** is that it promotes the concept of reusable asset at the business services level. The various lines of business will submit their models to OMB and OMB will consolidate the models into a consolidated government-wide reference model. This government-wide model will be available to help agencies identify opportunities for collaboration and sharing of assets. Thus, this EA artifact has real potential to *contribute directly* to innovation and cost savings throughout the United States Government.

HR LOB Data Model

In July 2005, a workgroup of 42 participants representing 10 agencies convened to launch the HR LOB **Data Model** (DM) initiative. Using the activity inputs and outputs in the **Business Reference Model** as a starting point, the DM workgroup identified and modeled the data required to perform the **BRM** activities.

According to OMB (2005, November) **Federal Enterprise Architecture** guidelines, the **DM** can provide value to agencies by:

• **Providing a means to consistently describe data architectures.** The **DM**'s approach to Data Description, Data Context, and Data Sharing enables data architecture initiatives to uniformly describe their data artifacts, resulting in increased opportunities for cross-agency and cross-COI data sharing.
• **Bridging data architectures.** The **DM** provides a "Rosetta Stone" to facilitate com-

munications between enterprise and data architects about data and data architecture in their efforts to support the business/mission needs of the enterprises that they support.

- **Facilitating compliance with requirements for good data architectures.** The **DM**'s standardization areas provide a foundation for agency data architecture initiatives to put forth requirements that can result in increased compatibility between agency data architectures. (p. 4)

The objectives of the HR LOB **DM** initiative were to:

- Promote common identification, use, and appropriate sharing of HR LOB data and information across the United States government. Since existing data structures do not allow for easy data exchange between agencies, shared service centers, and the Office of Personnel Management, this standardized data structure will facilitate information sharing. It will also define common data elements and structures needed to share data across BRM processes.
- Provide a standard for service providers and point solutions. It will delineate a vision for a standardized version of how the data is stored and transmitted, providing for the ability to share information.
- Specify future solution design data format. It will provide a standardized data structure that provides a basis for future detailed design documents, including government-wide standard reports.

The HR LOB **DM** provides two levels of detail. The *conceptual data model* consists of an entity relationship diagram (ERD) for data that supports the entire breadth of the end-to-end human resources process depicted by the BRM. The ERD shows data objects and it names and defines

relationships between data objects. Additionally, a definition was written for each data object.

A *logical data model* was also created for a subset of the above – data that is likely to be shared between agencies and shared service centers. For this subset of data objects, data elements were identified and defined. The logical data model also identified *information exchange packages*, specific recurring data exchanges between a shared service center and an agency or a shared service center and a third party. These information exchange packages lay the groundwork for interoperability. They are groupings of data attributes from various data entities that come together for a particular business purpose. Examples include:

- Personnel action
- Approved time and attendance
- Thrift savings plan enrollment
- Payroll disbursement

All of these information exchange packages contain data elements from multiple data entities that are compiled into a single grouping of data that serves a business purpose.

This model is important because data sharing is a key element of interoperability. Technology components cannot work together unless those components can send and receive data in a coherent fashion. The **DM** provides a view of data and the common data definitions that will be the basis for this data sharing. And again, *HR professionals* were recruited to participate in the workgroup and business-oriented facilitators worked with the workgroup to build the models. A technical architect was also assigned to the workgroup to ensure the model was technically viable.

The entire HR LOB **DM** can be found at the U.S. Office of Personnel Management Web site: http://www.opm.gov/egov/documents/architecture/#dm

HR LOB Technical Model

The HR LOB **Technical Model** (TM) initiative was launched in June 2007 to establish a common view of technology for the line of business and to compile a set of standards for each of the technology services that appear in the model.

According to OMB (2007, July) **Federal Enterprise Architecture** guidelines, the **TM**:

is a component-driven, technical framework categorizing the standards and technologies to support and enable the delivery of Service Components and capabilities. It also … provides a foundation to advance the reuse and standardization of technology and service components from a government-wide perspective. Aligning agency capital investments to the **Technical Model** leverages a common, standardized vocabulary, allowing interagency discovery, collaboration, and interoperability. Agencies and the Federal government will benefit from economies of scale by identifying and reusing the best solutions and technologies to support their business functions, mission, and target architecture. (p. 7)

The HR LOB **Technical Model** along with standards profile and best practices will facilitate the reusability of service components at both business and technical levels and promotes interoperability of technical service components. Conceptually, the **TM** provides two things. First, it provides a *model* of technology that proposes a view of and vocabulary for technology services and interfaces. It also provides a set of *standards* for the technology. This is important because common standards are an important means for achieving interoperability across disparate technologies.

OMB (2007, July) **FEA** guidelines specify a hierarchical construct for the **Technical Model** comprised of three layers:

- *Service areas* represent a technical tier supporting the secure construction, exchange, and delivery of service components. Each service area consists of multiple service categories, which in turn group technologies and standards that directly support the service area.

- *Service categories* classify lower levels of technologies and standards with respect to the business or technology function they serve. Each service category is comprised of one or more service standards.

- *Service standards* define the technologies and standards that support the service category. To support agency mapping into the TM, many of the Service Standards provide illustrative specifications or technologies as examples.

The HR LOB **Technical Model** is a component-driven, technical framework that identifies the standards, specifications, and technologies that support and enable the delivery of service components and capabilities. It is not a specific system or solution design. Rather it establishes a common vocabulary and defines a set of services and interfaces common to the solutions. The **Technical Model** will also identify and organize the standards that apply to the technology components that appear in the model. It will provide a standards profile, which is a database of facts and guidance relative to technology standards. The standards profile will point to standards that come from many sources: from formal standards bodies such as NIST, ANSI, ISO or IEEE; from authoritative consortia, like the World Wide Web Consortium and the Object Management Group; and from internal sources, such as agency HRIS development standards. Over time, this compendium of standards will become an important basis for interoperability across disparate systems and technologies (Prabandham, 2007).

Unlike the other four artifacts, the HR LOB **Technical Model** has been developed by technical architects. It has, however, traceability to the HR LOB business architectures via the HR LOB **Service Component Model**. The **SCM** shows that *service components* are delivered to *user types* using a *delivery structure*. The **TM** shows the *technology components* that enable this service delivery, directed by a *standards profile*. This business to technology view is called the delivery process-action chain. The delivery process-action chain is not an implementation design or a solution specification; rather, it is a traceability and linkage structure between the SCM and the TM. The concept of process-action chain is illustrated in Figure 4 (Prabandham, 2007).

The **Technical Model** will contribute to efficiency and cost reduction by enabling interoperability across systems that support the line of business. In the absence of a Technical Model, systems interfaces are based on ad hoc efforts leading to rigid information infrastructures, duplicate efforts, continual reinvention of the wheel, and as many systems with interfaces as potential partners. According to Prabandham (2007) the goal of the **TM** is to ensure services components achieve effective levels of reusability and interoperability by promoting:

- A consistent and common lexicon for description of interoperability requirements between diverse systems,
- A means for consistent specification and comparison of system/service architecture,
- Support for commonality across systems,
- The consistent use of standards, and
- Comprehensive identification of information exchange and interface requirements

Over time, HR LOB architects will work with architects across other lines of business to compile a government-wide technology model and standards profile with the goal of achieving these objectives on an even broader scale.

HR LOB Enterprise Architecture

The HR LOB EA was developed in alignment with FEA guidelines and consists of the five models: Business Reference Model, Performance Model, Service Component Model, Data Model, and

Figure 4. Delivery process-action chain

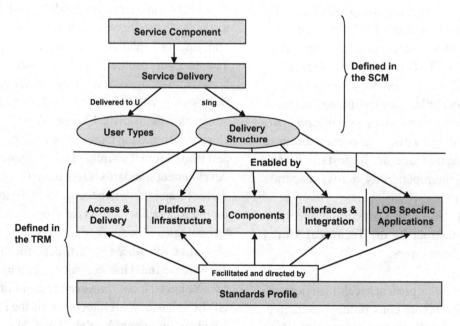

Technical Model. Agencies and **shared service centers** use these models as useful business tools for business planning, performance measurement, and IT investment. The next section of this chapter, **GOVERNANCE**, explains how HR LOB used collaborative governance to develop an EA necessary to standardize and modernize HR services delivery.

GOVERNANCE

The dynamics of innovation are enormously complex. Innovation changes continuously, while the pace of innovation change accelerates. Innovation is more open, spans virtually all disciplines, is increasingly global, and starts in more places. Understanding the dynamics of innovation is a first step toward exploiting it to make the government more effective. What approaches to human capital management foster innovation? What management systems and cultures support a climate that accepts innovation? What business processes are conducive to innovation? As increasing economies of scale and use of IT encourage more partnering, what approaches foster getting more innovation from those partners?

Most governments have been actively reforming their operations for several decades. Initially, these efforts were relatively straightforward ones of improving efficiency, reforming management practices, streamlining program operations, and outsourcing commercial or non-core activities. Public sector organizations are now under ever-increasing pressure for more profound changes to better address growing fiscal pressures, terrorism, and new requirements of contemporary society.

Transforming Government. Governments at all levels – Federal, state, local, and especially defense and homeland security organizations – are challenged to reposition, reinvent, and realign themselves in light of an increasing demand for a more cost effective, citizen-centric, and networked government. A combination of economic, politi-

cal, strategic business and technical advances has positioned the public sector to transform the way it orchestrates the business of government. Can a public sector organization truly reinvent itself? Do transformation efforts work? If so, what are the critical success factors and lessons learned?

E-Government. Information technology continues to trigger disruptive change in the U.S. economy. Many business processes can be incrementally improved but many need to be completely transformed to capture the full benefits. Areas of interest include: electronic delivery of information, programs, and services; web 2.0 and the expansion of social networking, blogging, wikis, etc.; electronic communications to increase citizen engagement; and the use of new cross servicing arrangements. What issues occur when the government adopts private sector practices?

Inter-departmental / Inter-agency Collaboration. Government lines of business are realigning traditional agency boundaries. Areas of interest include the enhancing of public sector performance or mission-centric operations through end-to-end operating models that extend traditional organizational boundaries and models for effective integration of organizations and processes.

Shared Services – **Beyond the Back Office.** The private sector has increased efficiency and effectiveness through the use of **shared services** for many internal operations. Public sector organizations are increasingly following suit. What are the best practices? Which private sector approaches work in the public sector and which do not? What governance frameworks are needed for success (Breul & Morales, 2007)?

Human Capital Management. A more effective back office frees up resources to do the more strategic work of HR. Areas of interest include: the strategic alignment of human capital with organizational objectives; workforce planning and deployment; the recruitment, retention and development of talent; results-oriented performance culture; leadership and knowledge management; e-learning; workforce development; workforce security; human resource service delivery models; accountability; and use of contractors versus government employees.

According to Breul (2006), to *drive innovation*, governments need more sophisticated strategies for *governing transformation* than they have generally had to date. This section describes the governance strategy employed by the **U.S. Office of Personnel Management** (OPM) to address the challenges incurred in leading the Human Resources Line of Business.

OPM is the Managing Partner agency responsible for the **HR LOB**. The Office of the HR LOB, a division within OPM, serves as the Program Management Office (PMO) for the HR LOB. The PMO brings focus and provides momentum for the HR LOB. The HR LOB PMO is staffed with senior executive staff personnel steeped in HR services and payroll delivery expertise. These senior Federal managers are supported by IBM consultants with expertise in program management, facilitation, change management, and Federal HR and enterprise architecture principles.

The HR LOB **governance** was set up in early 2004 to establish the vision, goals, and objectives of the HR LOB. The Director of the Office of HR LOB, in conjunction with the Heads of OPM and the E-Government Directorate of the **Office of Management and Budget** (OMB), invited 22 agencies to join OPM and OMB in a task force that set the vision and timeline for transformation of the Federal HR function.

The success of the 2004 HR LOB Task Force in building consensus and acceptance of the vision and timeline for HR transformation provided impetus to the Director of HR LOB to establish, in 2005, a permanent governance body of the 24 agency coalition. This permanent chartered body, referred to as the Multi-Agency Executive Strategy Committee (MAESC), reports to the Director of OPM and the Director of E-Government and IT Reform at OMB.

The HR LOB **governance** structure comprises of three broad tiers:

Strategy / Policy, Planning and Oversight. The 24-agency MAESC is the primary decision making body that sets the strategic direction for the HR LOB. The MAESC meets regularly to take key decisions – on human resources strategy, architecture, and concept of operations – that will impact the 1.8 million civilian employees of the Federal government.

The MAESC is co-chaired by the Director of HR LOB and the OMB Portfolio Manager for the **e-Government** portfolio of Internal Efficiency and Effectiveness (IEE). The *Strategy / Policy, Planning and Oversight* tier of the HR LOB governance structure also includes the Requirements Board which is led by OPM's Strategic Human Resources Policy (SHRP) Division. The Requirements Board is the ultimate arbiter of the target requirements for the shared service centers from an HR policy perspective.

User Requirements. This tier of the governance structure is comprised of workgroups or sub-committees focused on developing requirements from the customer or user perspective. These sub-committees of HR subject matter experts (SMEs) are typically employees at or between levels 12 through 15 on the Federal General Schedule (level 15 is the highest level) and have been recommended by the MAESC members for their specialized HR skills and expertise. The User Requirements workgroups have played a seminal role in developing HR LOB deliverables. Some of the notable workgroups under the User Requirements tier are as follows:

- Customer Council. This standing council is comprised of members from agencies that are or will receive HR services from HR service providers and represents the "voice of the customer". This council also plays an important role in evaluating and selecting public and private sector shared service centers.

- Business Reference Model (BRM) Workgroup. This ad-hoc workgroup developed the first ever government-wide end-to-end business process mapping of the HR sub-function. This workgroup comprised of HR subject matter experts from over 30 agencies defined the ten sub-functions of the HR LOB and mapped out the processes, activities, definitions, and inputs and outputs of the HR function.
- Target Requirements Workgroups. These ad-hoc workgroups developed the detailed business and technical requirements for the shared service centers. These workgroups took policy inputs from the Requirements Board and developed detailed requirements for government-wide delivery of HR functions.
- Service Component Model (SCM) Workgroup. This ad-hoc workgroup developed standardized definitions for HR services and the service delivery channels that

deliver those services to customers of the services.

The architecture and requirements workgroups met in many sessions over the past four years to establish a body of knowledge that is visionary and evolve-able. When developing these models, agencies focused on their similarities rather than their differences. The notable feature of all the aforementioned workgroups has been their dedication to improving Federal HR and their passion for standardizing definitions, processes, and requirements under the HR function.

Operations and Delivery. This tier of the HR LOB governance provided the "voice of the provider" and was comprised of operationally-focused members from the Federal designated shared service centers and e-Payroll providers. The Shared Service Center Advisory Council (SSCAC) meets on a regular basis to discuss the operational challenges of delivering the HR and payroll services and other issues related to

Figure 5. HR LOB governance structure

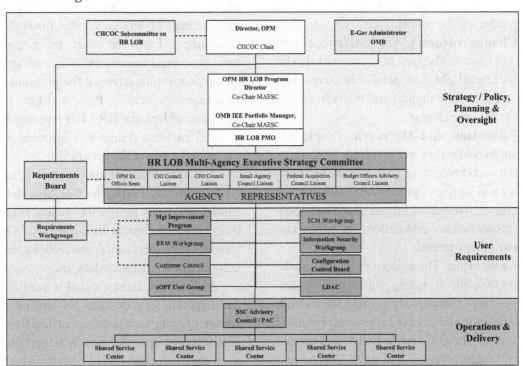

meeting the target requirements established by the HR LOB. Figure 5 shows the three tiered HR LOB **governance** structure.

The HR LOB organizational structure provided a forum for collaborative **governance** that led agencies to put aside their differences and work together to modernize and standardize HR services delivery. This HR LOB model of collaborative **governance** produced some valuable insights:

- **Perspective.** Through asking the HR LOB governance bodies to review and comment on strategic and architectural deliverables, the HR LOB was able to gain information and insight from many different points of view. This enabled agencies to have a "seat at the table" in making strategic decisions and provided OPM with a government-wide perspective to set HR policy.
- **Buy-in.** The model of collaborative governance worked because we involved people who are going to be affected by the vision in defining the vision. People buy into results when they feel they have been involved in producing the results.
- **Change Advocacy.** Any governance body will have its skeptics, but there will also be the bright lights that "get it". Initiatives must leverage their support and really use them to advocate change.
- **Education and Outreach.** People get smart when they get involved. Encourage the stakeholders on your governance bodies and workgroups to take what they learn and tell it to others. Provide them with tools (presentations, newsletters, etc.) they can use to do outreach.
- **Leadership.** The objective is to be collaborative, but ultimately you are going to ask your governance body to make some tough decisions and resolve cross-organizational issues. The governance body must consist of leaders who are willing to step up and make tough decisions and then represent those decisions to their stakeholders.

Governance is critical to the success of any EA program. The HR LOB used governance to achieve stakeholder buy-in from the beginning; this is one of its key triumphs. The next section of this chapter, TARGET REQUIREMENTS FOR SHARED SERVICE CENTERS, describes how the HR LOB EA has been used to drive implementation – by compiling and validating the solution-level target requirements for shared service centers.

TARGET REQUIREMENTS FOR SHARED SERVICE CENTERS

The HR LOB EA artifacts were produced with a very particular business outcome in mind: the successful adoption of a new **shared services**-based HR delivery model. This new delivery model has been put forward with some very real objectives in mind: reduced costs, increased efficiencies, improved customer satisfaction, and enhanced management of human capital throughout the government. From the onset, the EA artifacts have been used to conceive this new operating model and in turn advance the program toward its business objectives. Presented here is an illustration of how the HR LOB leveraged its EA to yield business results in alignment with the vision and goals of the program.

One of the first real uses of the HR LOB EA artifacts involved using the **Business Reference Model** as a basis for discussing and organizing business and technical requirements. While EA provides the *conceptual* framework for standardizing business processes, data, and services across the government, there existed a need to define more specific expectations for **shared service center** operations. Government legislation and policy is very specific about how certain operations are conducted, including human resources.

A comprehensive set of business and technical requirements was compiled and validated to document **SSC** operational expectations.

According to OPM HR LOB (n.d.), the HR LOB *Target Requirements for Shared Service Centers* represents the first-ever government-wide set of detailed business, technical, and data requirements for human resources. The **target requirements** report provides the detailed requirements outlining the expectations of **shared service centers** (SSC) by describing the role of the SSC in the HR process and providing specifications for the efficient and successful delivery of services and solutions. The **target requirements** also outline the expectations the Federal government strives to achieve through the implementation of the HR LOB **service delivery model** (OPM HR LOB, 2006). The HR LOB *Target Requirements for Shared Service Centers* is publicly available on the OPM Web site at: http://www.opm.gov/egov/documents/requirements/

Scope of the Target Requirements

The HR LOB Business Reference Model (BRM) provided the overall framework to define the scope of the requirements effort and to develop the target requirements. Every BRM activity was scrutinized to determine whether it should be supported by a shared service center in the future or continue to be performed at the agency. Each BRM activity was then given one of the following designations:

1. The activity will be performed in the future by the agency only.
2. The activity will be performed in the future by an SSC only.
3. The activity may be collaboratively performed in the future by some combination of both the agency and an SSC.

These designations provided the basis for the scope of the **target requirements**. Since the intention of the target requirements is to set *expectations of shared service centers*, requirements were

gathered and linked to those activities that will or could be supported by SSCs (2 and 3). Agency-only requirements (1) were not included.

Development of the Target Requirements

The HR LOB *Target Requirements for Shared Service Centers (SSCs)* is the result of landmark cross-agency collaboration between hundreds of HR subject matter experts working over a two-year period to define target requirements for both "core" and "non-core" services that may be offered by HR LOB SSCs. The HR LOB leveraged a phased approach to the development of the requirements by addressing in FY 2005 the requirements that **SSCs** *will* provide ("core") to agencies, deferring to FY 2006 the development of the requirements that **SSCs** *may* provide ("non-core") to agencies.

According to OPM HR LOB (2006) in January 2005 an initiative was launched to define business and technical requirements around the BRM. The HR LOB program designated three highly transactional, administratively intense areas to be the focus of this effort. Eighty-eight representatives from 24 agencies validated these requirements in a series of work sessions completed in the second half of 2005 and produced "core requirements" that specify services and supporting technology for:

*   Personnel Actions
*   Compensation Management sub-function (Payroll related)
*   Benefits Management sub-function

In Fiscal Year 2006, the HR LOB completed the development of the target requirements by addressing the remaining sub-functions for requirements not defined in the version 1.0 report. One hundred and seventy-one representatives from 29 agencies participated in a series of work sessions to validate the "non-core requirements" that specify services and supporting technology for activities that fall within the remaining BRM sub-functions:

- Human resources strategy
- Organization and position management
- Staff acquisition
- Performance management
- Compensation management (beyond payroll)
- Human resources development
- Employee relations
- Labor relations
- Separation management

THE TARGET REQUIREMENTS REPORT

The HR LOB **Target Requirements for Shared Service Centers** provides SSCs and agencies with two views of the target requirements. The first view, the Conceptual Design, provides a descriptive view of the role of the **shared service center** in the end-to-end HR process depicted by the HR LOB BRM. It also describes SSC innovation, outlining how SSC performance will change agencies' service delivery.

The report also provides a very detailed view, listing all the business and technical requirements that support each BRM sub-function. The requirements are presented in a matrix format as seen below in table 4.

Each requirement is linked to the activity(s) it supports. This linkage serves to further define the requirement; some requirements are more easily understood when the process context is understood.

Downstream Use and Next Steps

Changing Requirements. Defining the target requirements for service delivery was an important achievement but is only a first step. The requirements defined and validated in version 2.0 of the report (September 2006) reflect the current state of HR service delivery as it pertains to existing Federal HR policy, technology, and best business practices. The reality is that the Federal HR landscape is continually changing as new policies are written and old policies revised, and as innovation drives business practices forward.

To meet the challenges of the continually changing Federal HR landscape, the HR LOB has defined a requirements change process to provide over time the same level of participation that took place when the requirements were initially defined. The change process is outlined in the HR LOB *Target Requirements for Shared Service Centers version 2.0*. The change process is currently being operationalized as the HR LOB is validating a series of changes based on requirements use and changes to Federal HR policy. The results of this update to the target requirements will be reflected in version 3.0 to be published in September 2007. It is expected that updates to the target requirements will be published on annual basis into the future.

Design Documentation. Requirements describe business outcomes that a shared service

Table 4. HR LOB requirements format

Primary Reference	Unique ID	Requirements Description	Type	Priority	Who	Process Linkages
Lists policy references for each requirement	The ID by which requirements are identified	The requirements statement	Policy, Service, Technology, Performance	Mandatory, Critical, Useful	SSC, SSC / Agency	The BRM activities the requirement links to

center could produce for each BRM sub-function and are not meant to provide design-level detail. SSCs will be responsible for translating target requirements into design-level blueprints that meet customer expectations. The expectation is that this approach was taken to foster innovation among SSCs, to encourage competition, to encourage customer involvement, and to decrease the need for maintenance over time. (OPM HR LOB, 2006, September)

SSC Selection. The **target requirements** support the evaluation and selection of SSCs at two levels: at the program level and at the agency level. At the program level, HR LOB **shared service centers'** ability to deliver the target requirements to agencies is part of the criteria to *become* shared service centers. To be selected as an HR LOB SSC, the candidate SSCs provided self-evaluations of their ability to meet the target requirements. SSCs that do not fully meet the target requirements are subject to ongoing improvement reviews from the HR LOB Customer Council, a group consisting of customer agencies that ensures that customer needs are addressed by the SSCs.

At the agency level, the self-evaluation results are an important set of criteria supporting an agency's selection of an **SSC** to provide services to the agency. In defining its future HR operational model, each agency will identify which services to migrate to an SSC and which HR processes to retain within the agency. Having identified the scope of services for the SSC, the agency will leverage the results of the self-evaluations to identify the appropriate SSCs to compete for its HR services and to justify its best value selection of an SSC.

SCM-Requirements Mapping. Based on agency and SSC recommendations, the HR LOB is undertaking an initiative to map the requirements to **Service Component Model** (SCM) service components. According to OPM HR LOB (2007, September), understanding the collection of requirements that supports each service component would help to define that service component in terms of customer expectations (requirements) for the service. It could be a very important basis for negotiation between customer and provider. A number of benefits could be achieved from this mapping:

- It will provide detailed content to the SLA and be a very tangible basis for SLA negotiation.
- It will reduce risk because expectations will be clarified and thus surprises will, conceivably, also be reduced.
- It will provide a means for delineating basic service (defined by those requirements designated as SSC only) and premium service (defined by those requirements designated as SSC/agency).
- It will enable providers to better predict their involvement in the whole process and thus be better able to project staffing, infrastructure, and other resource requirements.
- It will afford a real basis for providers to price their services.

The **Target Requirements for Shared Service Centers** serve as a tangible example of how the HR LOB used EA to develop detailed business and technical requirements that will serve as the cornerstone for the successful implementation of shared services across the Federal government. The next section of this chapter, **LESSONS LEARNED**, outlines critical lessons learned while developing the EA for the HR LOB.

LESSONS LEARNED

The HR LOB program has taken an innovative approach to make EA a relevant and useful tool for conceiving and managing this new line of business. The potential fiscal benefits of the program are staggering; it has the potential to save U.S. taxpayers many millions of dollars through consolidation of services and supporting technology and infrastructure. The business case, however, is long-term; agencies will not begin to migrate to service centers until year five of the program and benefits will not begin to accrue for at least three years beyond that.

Maintaining the momentum of any government program that does not have demonstrable short-term benefits can be a struggle, even if the long-term business case is clear. The **HR LOB** program continues to exist in part because of the experience and insight of the program management team. Some of that insight is shared below.

Sponsorship

No EA initiative can survive without a credible executive sponsor who is willing to visibly and vocally support it. The HR LOB program's sponsor reports directly to the Director of the U.S. Office of Personnel Management. The placement of the program at this high level provides the program with a credibility that would not exist had the program been buried in the organization.

The program director came from the private sector, bringing his 40+-year career experience to this directorship. During his tenure, he reached out to a variety of stakeholders and interests – including the Office of Management and Budget, participating agency HR executives, shared services providers, and professional organizations – on the relevance of EA to the overall HR LOB transformation effort. This program has made great progress in four years in large part due to the experienced leadership of this director.

Lesson learned: Engage an executive sponsor who is both capable and willing to take on an active leadership role to drive the EA initiative to succeed.

Relevance

The HR LOB EA artifacts (with the exception of the Technical Model) were produced by HR profes-

sionals with a very particular business outcome in mind: the successful adoption of a new shared services-based HR delivery model. The agencies that provided resources to participate in EA workgroups saw the link between these artifacts and the outcome. They knew that, because the EA artifacts were intended to be the blueprints for the new operating model, participating in the construction of these blueprints gave them an active voice in designing the new model.

The artifacts were never meant to be an abstraction of a theoretical to-be state but are blueprints for very real impending change. This relevance motivated solid participation and this participation resulted in deliverables that reflect a broad government-wide point of view on an unparalleled scale. This broad participation also strengthened buy-in into a program that had many skeptics at the inception of the program.

Lesson learned: Find relevant *business reasons* to do EA; make sure people understand the links between EA and those business outcomes and involve them in the development of the solution to increase buy-in and win hearts and minds.

Political Correctness

Working with a consortium of 24 diverse government agencies to produce defined EA deliverables with limited resources in a specific time frame was a tremendously complex undertaking. Cultivating their support and soliciting meaningful involvement required significant resources and more than a little tenacity. It also required a thoughtful approach to communicating certain concepts and plans. Although program managers made efforts to communicate as much as possible as frequently as possible, sometimes the messages were necessarily shaped by political correctness: certain topics were understated and certain words were avoided. Communication was some times watered down and messages, at times, became mixed. Communication frequently required a balancing act to address disparate concerns. Certainly, candor is discouraged in many environments – in both the private sector and the public sector – but the public sector can be particularly restrained.

For example, an early version of the HR LOB *Target Requirements for Shared Service Centers* referred to shared service centers providing business process and technology support for selected core functions. There was disagreement among the stakeholders concerning the mention of business process support because the original HR LOB business case was based on savings from technology consolidation and the original Concept of Operations therefore also focused on technology consolidation. Most stakeholders agreed to the SSCs taking on administrative process support as well as technology support, but the concerns were addressed by deleting the words "process and" from the report narrative, leaving just "technology support". Ironically, there remained target requirements in the addenda of the report that spoke to business process support.

Lesson learned: Work hard to communicate clearly and openly, but political correctness may at times triumph over candid, open communication.

Change Management

The EA efforts of the HR LOB program demonstrate that business enterprise architecture can drive transformation. However, business professionals can be quite skeptical of EA and claim it is time consuming, irrelevant, and esoteric. Even when you can demonstrate true business relevance, you have to convince your stakeholders. A formal change management program can help.

In the beginning, HR LOB EA efforts did not have the support they eventually came to have. The HR LOB Business Reference Model was the first of the EA artifacts to be developed and many BRM workgroup participants told us they attended BRM work sessions "because they were told to". In some instances, participants told subordinates to attend.

A formal change management program identifies the potential change issues and addresses them in a holistic way. A change management program identifies pockets of resistance, strategies about how to overcome this resistance, and puts actionable plans into place to achieve the strategy. It also provides a coherent communication program that orchestrates the various messages that are provided to various stakeholder groups. And it encourages broad-based participation that produces both results and buy-in into the results.

Lesson learned: Don't assume everyone understands the value of EA. Implement a formal change management program to educate stakeholders on the value of EA, address resistance to doing EA, and increase the probability of having a successful, relevant result.

Developing an EA across a broad-based community such as the U.S. Federal government requires innovation and enthusiasm to maintain momentum. The next section of this chapter, **FUTURE TRENDS AND RESEARCH**, provides insight into how EA can be used to help government calibrate how it delivers shared services to its customers.

FUTURE TRENDS AND RESEARCH

A widening resource gap in government has produced an imperative for challenging any and all government budgets that do not contribute directly to government services. The issue is global in nature and based on a fundamental reality: demographics. As nations' populations age, tax bases taper down thereby reducing funds available for government programs. At the same time, aging populations have basic health and welfare needs that increase the need for government spending. Costs go up while revenues go down. In this climate, administrative budgets are certainly likely to be reduced. High cost operating models for administrative services are becoming a phenomenon of the past.

Furthermore, the maturing of government workforces is producing a drain on government talent resulting in a shrinking knowledge base around policies and practices. It is estimated that over the next ten years, 60% of the United States Federal government workforce will become eligible for retirement (Springer, n.d.). The inevitable loss of experience and intellectual capital could dramatically degrade government services.

Agency Transformation through Shared Services

In this era of funding constraints and diminished intellectual capital, we must find innovative ways to effectively deliver government services with the resources that remain. The **Human Resources Line of Business** has chosen to adopt a shared services-based HR **service delivery model**, an operational model that has yielded profound benefits in the private sector for quite some time and is now gaining ground in the U.S public sector: EquaTerra and the International Public Management Association for Human Resources (2006) report that 58% of Federal agencies surveyed already employ some shared services to deliver HR services. The **HR LOB** is working toward expansion of this operating model throughout the United States Federal government to:

- Reduce costs by moving transactional and administrative processes to shared service centers
- Leverage the knowledge and experience of HR professionals that remain at the agency level to do the more valuable, strategic work of Human Capital Management for the agency

The UK government embraced the concept some time ago, having identified shared services as a *key enabler* of "Transformational Government". They believe that shared services... "offers the opportunity to accelerate change in the culture of Public Sector organizations and improve the delivery of services to citizens. Unless taxes and other revenues rise dramatically (one unacceptable, the other unlikely), it follows that maximizing Public Value requires not only greater efficiency but genuine and significant Public Sector transformation. This must not only occur within individual organizations but critically across organizations; removing unnecessary complexity and duplication at all levels. The move to shared services will greatly improve the main focus of Public Sector Transformation – improved citizen service – through delivering Efficiency, Effectiveness, and Employee Experience." And since the

Figure 6. Transformation of the HR function — resources will shift

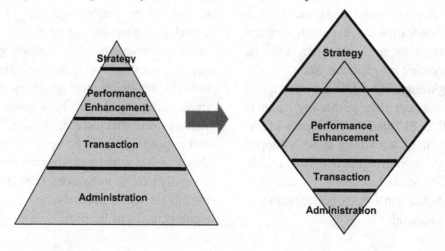

cost of a public sector back office in the U.K. is estimated to be two and a half times the cost of its private sector counterpart, shared services also has the potential to significantly reduce cost (BuyIT Best Practice Network & Shared Services Advisory Group, 2006).

The **HR Line of Business** is looking at **shared services** as a strategy for realizing comparable benefits through transforming the Human Resources function across the United States government. Agencies currently apply a majority of their HR resources to administrative and transactional work and far fewer resources to performance enhancement and strategic work. If a preponderance of administrative and transactional activities were moved to shared service centers, resources that remain at agency HR departments could be shifted to more valuable work. A **shared services**-based operating model would have fewer agency HR personnel doing administrative and transactional work, allowing a major shift of resources to performance enhancement work and strategy. This new operational model will enable agency HR departments to do more with less (see figure 6).

Enterprise Architecture proved invaluable to devising the new operational model. The HR LOB **Service Component Model** has identified the reusable *business services* that have been proposed to be candidate *shared services*. The collaboration that took place to build this model provided an objective technique and forum for discussing those services that could become part of a provider's *portfolio* of services. The **Business Reference Model**, similarly, provides a government-wide reference for those more value-adding processes that will remain with the agency HR operations. And the **Technical Model** provides a common government-wide abstraction of the technology that will enable these services plus the standards and specifications that will promote reusability and interoperability at the *technical services* level.

Future of Enterprise Architecture in the U.S. Federal Government

The FEAPMO (2006, December) advocates the concept of *segment architecture*. A segment architecture is "a shared vision for business and IT transformation within a core Mission area or common service." Segment architectures have been formed around each of the Federal lines of business, including the **HR Line of Business** (section 2, p.9).

Over the years, resource management at the individual agency level has resulted in a stove-piped approach to agency business processes, services and technology. One might surmise that adding the segment layer opens up an opportunity for a whole new layer of stovepipes! The **FEA** framework, however, works to prohibit this. Segment architectures roll up to government-wide reference models which provide visibility across segments and thus serve to identify and help manage redundancy. More important, this government-wide perspective helps identify opportunities for collaboration and sharing across lines of business. This has the potential for a *fundamental shift* in the management of government resources in the future.

And just as government-wide reference models provide a means for consolidating segment architectures, segment architectures provide a means for consolidating solution level architectures – and the means for identifying opportunities for cross-agency collaboration and sharing at this level. Figure 7, published by the FEA PMO (2006, December), "illustrates the relationships between enterprise architecture, segment architecture, and solution architecture" (section 1, p.9).

Plug and Play: The Future of Shared Services

Given funding and time constraints, shared service providers will not have the luxury to

Figure 7. Architectural levels and attributes

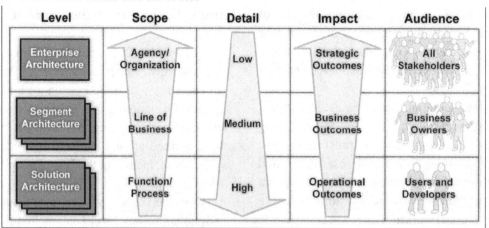

design and build solutions. Public sector providers will likely not be appropriated the funds for these capital outlays; private sector providers will not have the time or expertise to develop new solutions. Providers will likely partner with best of breed providers to link together best of breed composite solutions. The ability to rapidly provide these solutions to customers on demand will be critical to the success or failure of any shared service provider. Segment architectures will be the key to identifying these partnerships and defining these solutions for rapid deployment to a provider's customer base.

Box 2.

Partnering to deliver –

the GoLearn model

As part of the E-Training initiative established by the E-Government Act of 2002, the Office of Personnel Management (OPM) established an online training capability, branded GoLearn. GoLearn was intended to be "a catalyst for transforming the way government manages human capital by effectively and efficiently implementing solutions that align workforce development with organizational goals, resulting in improved mission attainment" (GoLearn, n.d., para.1).

GoLearn provides a learning management system (LMS) with online course content and access to government-mandated training. To provide for rapidly changing demands of agency training needs, GoLearn also provides a wide variety of content from multiple vendors and serves as a contracting vehicle for agencies to obtain training as needed. GoLearn provides the following highly technical contracting services:

- development of statements of work (SOWs) and task orders
- coordination of activities between GoLearn vendors and client agencies
- management of task order award competitions
- awarding task orders (GoLearn, n.d.).

This approach to establishing a portfolio of services is a viable model for creating the best composite solutions on demand from any number of suppliers in the marketplace.

CONCLUSION

This chapter demonstrated how the HR LOB is *driving transformation* of Federal Human Resources service delivery *via enterprise architecture*. The **Office of Management and Budget** formulated an enterprise architecture strategy for the U.S. government to help government agencies manage complexity and move toward innovation and transformation. The HR LOB used this strategy and developed an enterprise architecture that provides a common, government-wide view and vocabulary for the HR function – a view and vocabulary that provide a basis for common, government-wide solutions that agencies will implement to realize the vision and goals of the Federal government's HR transformation.

Using broad-based collaboration as its fundamental governance principle, the HR LOB program achieved consensus on its enterprise architecture and is using that EA to define shared services-based service delivery expectations and drive agency transformation to this new operational model.

THOUGHTS ON FUTURE RESEARCH

1. As enterprise architecture programs mature throughout the U.S Federal government, opportunities may exist to identify services for reuse that span lines of business. Future research could explore how other public sector enterprises have leveraged EA across lines of business to realize process improvements, cost savings, and reuse of assets.

2. Shared service centers will likely seek to partner with other public and/or private sector providers to supply best of breed solutions quickly and effectively. Future research could explore how shared service centers have used EA to build partnering capability and to manage the multi-provider supply chain.

REFERENCES

Borins, Sandford. (2006). *The Challenge of Innovating in Government* (2nd ed.). Retrieved 5 June 2007 from IBM Center for the Business of Government Web site: http://www.businessofgovernment.org/pdfs/BorinsReprint.pdf

Breul, J.D. (2006). What is Transformation?. In M.A. Abramson, J.D. Breul, & J.M. Kamensky (Eds.), *Six Trends Transforming Government* (p. 7). Retrieved 16 April 2007 from IBM Center for the Business of Government Web site: http://www.businessofgovernment.org/pdfs/SixTrends.pdf

Breul, J.D., & Morales, A. (2007, June). 2007-2008 Research Announcement: Providing Cutting Edge Knowledge to Government Leaders. Retrieved 16 July 2007 from IBM Center for Business of Government Web site: http://www.businessofgovernment.org/pdfs/Research_Announcement_07.pdf

BuyIT Best Practice Network & Shared Services Advisory Group. (2006). "Shared Services in the Public Sector: Vision." Retrieved 27 April 2007 from BuyIT Best Practice Network Web site: http://www.buyitnet.org/Best_Practice_Guidelines/SharedServicesPubSect/docs/G1%20Vision.pdf

EquaTerra & International Public Management Association for Human Resources [IPMA-HR]. (2006, June). *Human Resources Transformation in Public Sector Organizations*. Retrieved 2 May2007 from the IPMA-HR Web site: http://www.ipma-hr.org/pdf/TransformationWhitePaper.pdf

McDavid, D.W. (1999). A standard for business architecture description. IBM Systems Journal, 38 (1), 12-31. Retrieved 20 April 2007 from IBM Systems Journal Web site: http://www.research.ibm.com/journal/sj/381/mcdavid.html

Prabandham, S.M. (2007, June). *A Case Study in Service Component Reusability and Interoperability: HR LOB Technical Reference Model*. Unpublished manuscript.

Springer, L.M. (n.d.). Retirement Systems Modernization. Retrieved 1 August 2007 from the OPM Web site: http://www.opm.gov/rsm/index.asp

Stevenson, D.A. (1996, April). Positioning Enterprise Architecture. In D.A. Stevenson, *Component Based Enterprise Architecture*. Dissertation presented to the Department of Information Systems, University of Cape Town, South Africa. Retrieved 10 August 2007 from the IS World Net Web site: http://users.iafrica.com/o/om/omisditd/denniss/text/eapositn.html

United States. Executive Office of the President. Office of Management and Budget [OMB]. (2005, November). *The Data Reference Model Version 2.0*. Retrieved 10 August 2007 from the OMB E-Gov Web site: http://www.whitehouse.gov/omb/egov/documents/DRM_2_0_Final.pdf

United States. Executive Office of the President. Office of Management and Budget [OMB]. Federal Enterprise Architecture Program Management Office [FEAPMO]. (2006, December). *FEA Practice Guidance*. Retrieved 22 October 2007 from the OMB E-Gov Web site: http://www.whitehouse.gov/omb/egov/documents/FEA_Practice_Guidance.pdf

United States. Executive Office of the President. Office of Management and Budget [OMB]. (2006, December). *Expanding E-Government: Making a Difference for the American People Using Information Technology*. Retrieved 30 April 2007 from the OMB E-Gov Web site: http://www.whitehouse.gov/omb/egov/documents/expanding_egov_2006.pdf

United States. Executive Office of the President. Office of Management and Budget [OMB]. (2007, February). *Report to Congress on the Benefits of the E-Government Initiatives*. Retrieved 16 May 2007 from the OMB E-Gov Web site: http://www.whitehouse.gov/omb/egov/documents/FY07_Benefits_Report.pdf

United States. Executive Office of the President. Office of Management and Budget [OMB]. (2007, July). *FEA Consolidated Reference Model Document Version 2.2*. Retrieved 16 July 2007 from the OMB E-Gov Web site: http://www.whitehouse.gov/omb/egov/documents/FEA_CRM_v22_Final_July_2007.pdf

United States. Executive Office of the President. Office of Management and Budget [OMB]. (n.d.a). E-Gov Background. Retrieved 8 May 2007 from the OMB E-Gov Web site: http://www.whitehouse.gov/omb/egov/g-1-background.html

United States. Executive Office of the President. Office of Management and Budget [OMB]. (n.d.b) Federal Enterprise Architecture. Retrieved 22 May 2007 from the OMB E-Gov Web site: http://www.whitehouse.gov/omb/egov/a-1-fea.html

United States. General Accountability Office [GAO]. (2003, November). *Information Technology: Leadership Remains Key to Agencies Making Progress on Enterprise Architecture Efforts*. Retrieved 10 October 2007 from the GAO Web site: http://www.gao.gov/new.items/d0440.pdf

United States. Office of Personnel Management [OPM]. GoLearn. (n.d.) The Office of Personnel Management's GoLearn Program. Retrieved 24 October 2007 from the GoLearn Web site: http://www.golearn.gov/MaestroC/index.cfm?room=welcome&roomaction=about

United States. Office of Personnel Management [OPM]. (n.d.). Human Capital Assessment and Accountability Framework [HCAAF]. Retrieved 18 May 2007 from the OPM Web site: http://www.opm.gov/hcaaf_resource_center/2-2.asp

United States. Office of Personnel Management [OPM]. Human Resources Line of Business [HR LOB]. (2006, January). *HR LOB Business Reference Model version 2*. Retrieved 23 April 2007 from the OPM HR LOB Web site: http://www.opm.gov/egov/documents/architecture/BRM_Report_V2.pdf

United States. Office of Personnel Management [OPM]. Human Resources Line of Business [HR LOB]. (2006, February). *HR LOB Data Model version 1*. Retrieved 23 April 2007 from the OPM HR LOB Web site: http://www.opm.gov/egov/documents/architecture/HRLOB_DM.pdf

United States. Office of Personnel Management [OPM]. Human Resources Line of Business [HR LOB]. (2006, June). *HR LOB Performance Model version 1*. Retrieved 23 April 2007 from the OPM HR LOB Web site: http://www.opm.gov/egov/documents/architecture/HRLOB_PM_6.30.06.pdf

United States. Office of Personnel Management [OPM]. Human Resources Line of Business [HR LOB]. (2006, September). *HR LOB Target Requirements for Shared Service Centers version 2.0*. Retrieved 23 April 2007 from the OPM HR LOB Web site: http://www.opm.gov/egov/documents/requirements/Reqv2.pdf

United States. Office of Personnel Management [OPM]. Human Resources Line of Business [HR LOB]. (2006, September). *HR LOB Service Component Model version 1*. Retrieved 23 April 2007 from the OPM HR LOB Web site: http://www.opm.gov/egov/documents/architecture/HRLOB-SCMv1.pdf

United States. Office of Personnel Management [OPM]. Human Resources Line of Business [HR LOB]. (2007, September). *HR LOB Service Component Model version 2*. Retrieved 15 November 2007 from the OPM HR LOB Web site: http://www.opm.gov/egov/documents/architecture/HRLOBSCMv2.pdf

United States. Office of Personnel Management [OPM]. Human Resources Line of Business [HR LOB]. (n.d.). HR LOB Benefits and Accomplishments. Retrieved 30 May 2007 from the OPM HR LOB Web site: http://www.opm.gov/egov/HR_LOB/benefits/

ENDNOTE

[1]   See Office of Personnel Management [OPM] (n.d.), for more information on these outcomes defined in the HCAAF.

Chapter XV
Enterprise Architecture as Context and Method for Designing and Implementing Information Security and Data Privacy Controls in Government Agencies

Scott Bernard
Carnegie Mellon University, USA

Shuyuan Mary Ho
Syracuse University, USA

ABSTRACT

Government agencies are committing an increasing amount of resources to information security and data privacy solutions in order to meet legal and mission requirements for protecting agency information in the face of increasingly sophisticated global threats. Enterprise Architecture (EA) provides an agency-wide context and method that includes a security sub-architecture which can be used to design and implement effective controls. EA is scalable, which promotes consistency and alignment in controls at the enterprise, program, and system levels. EA also can help government agencies improve existing security and data privacy programs by enabling them to move beyond a system-level perspective and begin to promote an enterprise-wide view of security and privacy, as well as improve the agility and effectiveness of lifecycle activities for the development, implementation, and operation of related security and privacy controls that will assure the confidentiality, integrity, and availability of the agency's data and information. This chapter presents the EA^3 "Cube" EA methodology and framework, including an integrated security architecture, that is suitable for use by government agencies for the development of risk-adjusted security and privacy controls that are designed into the agency's work processes, information flows, systems, applications, and network infrastructure.

INTRODUCTION

Designing and implementing effective controls for information security and data privacy in government agencies is optimized through integration with other areas of governance including: strategic planning, capital investment planning, enterprise architecture, program management, and workforce planning. This chapter focuses on the role that enterprise architecture (EA) plays in designing, implementing, and operating security and data privacy controls in complex organizations, including government agencies. Information security and data privacy are intertwined concepts that work like a thread that weaves through the strategic, business, and technology levels of an EA framework to produce risk-adjusted solutions that assure the confidentiality, integrity, and availability of the agency's data and information in the face of growing global threats to government functions and mission accomplishment.

The threats to the security of a government agency's business and technology operating environment come in many forms. This includes hackers, disgruntled employees, runaway technologies, poor system maintenance, natural disasters, terrorism, and unintentional mistakes. As the global use of information technology (IT) continues to accelerate, government agencies are increasingly exposed to daily threats to the confidentiality, integrity, and availability of their information. How seriously the agency addresses these threats is often related on how aware the agency is of its dependency on IT to support key government services, and the probability of a threat affecting the agency. Without an awareness of the full scope of global threats and/or industry best practices to counter those threats, government agencies may not invest in a sufficiently robust and scalable information security and data privacy program, nor will they incorporate best practices such as EA to promote program success.

One fundamental aspect of security and privacy is the realization that there isn't a 100% foolproof solution or set of solutions for any government agency. The reason for this is that program activities and controls are created by members of the agency, and even the people in the most trusted security or system administration positions can decide to disable, evade, or sabotage the security solutions. This type of insider threat is the "Achilles Heel" of all security and privacy programs, and creates what are referred to as "risk-adjusted" solutions. This means that a security or privacy solution is selected based on several considerations, including the cost, the level of protection needed, the effect on end-users and system administrators, and the effectiveness of available technologies.

An integrated set of security and privacy controls for the agency is best created by including these requirements in the planning of all EA segments, components, and systems; doing so in a top-down manner (beginning at the "strategic" level of the EA framework) so that security is an embedded part of all of the agency's strategic initiatives and business services. For information-centric enterprises, including security and privacy as a required design element of strategic initiatives can provide a strong and meaningful statement about the importance of protecting the business and technology operating environment.

Information security and data privacy requirements and solutions should be a consideration in business process reengineering and improvement activities throughout the agency, and should be part of the design of information flows, IT systems, applications, databases, knowledge warehouses, Websites, and network infrastructures. Information security and data privacy are also key checklist items when making acquisition decisions for IT hardware, software, and support services.

ENTERPRISE ARCHITECTURE GENERAL CONCEPTS

EA is a management practice and a documentation methodology that is devoted to improving the performance of organizations by enabling them to see themselves in terms of a holistic and integrated view of their strategic direction, business practices, information flows, and technology resources. By developing current and future versions of this integrated view, an organization can better manage the transition from current to future operating methods. This transition includes the identification of new goals, activities, and all types of capital and human resources (including information technology) that will improve bottom line financial and mission performance (Bernard, 2005).

The strategic use of resources is increasingly important to the success of public and private sector organizations as well as other types of enterprises such as consortia and extended enterprises involving parts of multiple internal and external participants (e.g., supply chains). How to get the most from business, technology, and human resources requires an organization to think in terms of enterprise-wide solutions, rather than individual system development projects. Doing this requires a new approach to planning and systems development, an approach that during the past twenty years has come to be known as Enterprise Architecture. The word 'enterprise' implies a high-level, strategic view of the entire organization, while the word 'architecture' implies a structured framework for the analysis, planning, and development of all types of resources.

With regard to resources, one of the greatest challenges that many enterprises continue to face is how to identify the business and technology components of strategic initiatives. A big part of this challenge is that IT in particular has historically not been viewed as a strategic asset. As such, planning activities often have focused on the development of individual technology solutions to meet particular organizational requirements. The following equation is the 'sound bite' version of what EA is all about, and is intended to show the difference between EA and technology planning (T) that it is driven by strategic goals (S) and business requirements (B): $EA = S + B + T$ (Bernard, 2005).

EA as a Management Program

EA is a management program that provides a strategic, integrated approach to resource planning. An EA program is part of an overall governance process that determines resource alignment, develops standardized policy, enhances decision support, and oversees resource development activities. EA can help to identify gaps in the performance of line of business activities and the capabilities of supporting IT services, systems, and networks. As a management program, EA provides:

- **Resource Alignment:** Resource planning and standards determination
- **Standardized Policy:** Resource governance and implementation
- **Decision Support:** Financial control and configuration management
- **Resource Oversight:** Lifecycle approach to development/management

Resource Alignment

EA supports strategic planning and other operational resource planning processes by providing macro and micro views of how resources are to be leveraged in accomplishing the goals of the organization. This helps to maximize the efficiency and effectiveness of these resources, which in turn will help to promote the organization's competitive capabilities. IT resources and associated development projects within the organization should be reviewed to determine if they support (and conform to) one or more strategic goals. If a resource and/or project is not aligned, then its value to the organization will remain in question.

Standardized Policy

EA supports the implementation of standardized management policy pertinent to the development and utilization of IT and other resources. By providing a holistic, hierarchical view of current and future resources, EA supports the establishment of policy for:

- Identifying strategic and operational requirements
- Determining the strategic alignment of activities and resources
- Developing enterprise-wide business and technology resources
- Prioritizing the funding of programs and projects
- Overseeing the management of programs and projects
- Identifying performance metrics for programs and projects
- Identifying and enforcing standards and configuration management

Policy documents include those which can be categorized as general guidance (e.g., high-level directives and memos); specific program guidance (e.g., plans, and manuals); and detailed process guidance (e.g., standard operating procedures). By using these hierarchical categories of documents, succinct and meaningful policy is established. It does so in a way that no single policy document is too long and therefore not too burdensome to read. It is also important to understand how the various areas of policy are inter-related so that program implementation across the enterprise is coordinated. EA policies must integrate with other policies in all governance areas, so as to create an effective overall resource management and oversight capability.

Decision Support

EA provides support for IT resource decision-making at the executive, management, and staff levels of the organization. At the executive level, EA provides visibility for large IT initiatives and supports the determination of strategic alignment. At the management level, EA supports design and configuration management decisions, as well as the alignment of IT initiatives with technical standards for voice, data, video, and security. At the staff level, EA supports decisions regarding operations, maintenance, and the development of IT resources and services.

Resource Development

EA supports standardized approaches for developing IT and other resources. Depending on the scope of the resources involved and the available timeframe for development, various system development lifecycle methods can be used to reduce the risk that cost, schedule, or performance parameters may not be met. EA further supports standardized, proven approaches to project management that promote the comprehensive and effective oversight of ongoing programs and new development projects. Finally, EA supports the use of a standardized process for selecting and evaluating investment in IT resources from a business and financial perspective.

EA as a Documentation Method

References to EA began to emerge in the late 1980's in various management and academic literatures, with an early focus on technical or systems architectures and schemas for organizing information (Zachman, 1987; Spewak 1992). The concept of 'enterprise' architecture documentation emerged in the early 1990's and has now evolved to include views of strategic goals, business services, information flows, systems and applications, networks, and the supporting infrastructure. Additionally, documentation includes 'threads' that pervade every level of the architecture. These threads include standards, security, and workforce planning.

As a documentation method, EA provides:

- EA Approach: A modeling framework and implementation methodology
- Current Views: Views of as-is strategies, processes, and resources
- Future Views: Views of to-be strategies, processes, and resources
- EA Management Plan: A plan to move from the current to the future EA

The approach to EA documentation is based on the adoption of (1) a documentation framework and (2) related implementation methodology. Documenting (3) the current and (4) future views of an EA helps the organization to identify and manage its current resources, select and implement future resources, and manage the EA transition in an effective, standardized manner. The (5) transition from current to future architectures and (6) security, standards, and workforce consider-

ations are an ongoing aspect of an EA program. Figure 1 shows the relationship of these six basic elements (Bernard, 2005).

EA Documentation Element 1: The Framework

The EA documentation framework identifies the scope of the architecture to be documented and establishes relationships between the architecture's areas. The framework's scope is reflected through its geometric design and the areas that are identified for documentation. The framework creates an abstracted set of "views" of an enterprise through the way that it collects and organizes architecture information. An example that will be used is the framework that is illustrated in Figure 2, which has a cubic shape with three dimensions that relate to different aspects of documenting the abstracted enterprise.

Known as the "EA³ Cube" (Bernard, 2005), the levels of this example framework are hierarchical so that the different sub-architectures (that describe distinct functional areas) can be logically related to each other. This is done by positioning

Figure 1. Elements of EA documentation

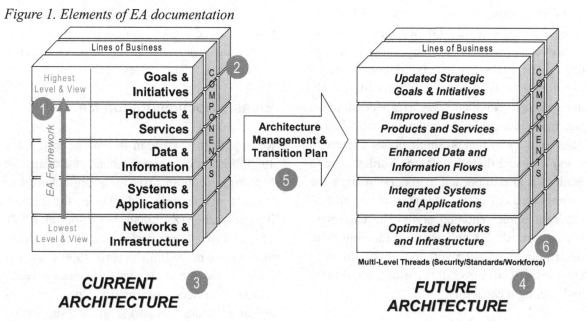

Figure 2. The EA³ cube documentation framework

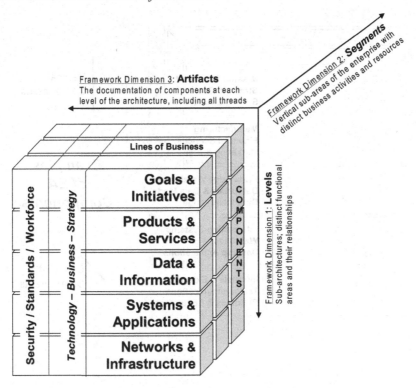

high-level strategic goals/initiatives at the top, business products/services and data/information flows in the middle, and supporting systems/applications and technology/infrastructure at the bottom. In this way alignment can be also be shown between strategy, information, and technology, which aids planning and decision-making.

To lower risk and promote efficient, phased implementation methods, the EA framework is divided into segments of distinct activity, also referred to as "Lines of Business" (LOBs). For example, each LOB has a complete sub-architecture that includes all five hierarchical levels of the EA³ Framework. The LOB therefore can in some ways stand alone architecturally within the enterprise except that duplication in data, application, and network functions would occur if each LOB were truly independent. An architecture

encompassing all five framework levels that is focused on one or more LOBs can be referred to as a segment of the overall EA.

EA Documentation Element 2: EA Components

EA "components" are the changeable processes and resources that may extend enterprise-wide or be contained within a specific line of business. Examples of EA components include strategic goals and initiatives; business products and services; information flows, knowledge warehouses, and data objects; information systems, software applications, enterprise resource programs, and Web sites; voice, data, and video networks; and supporting infrastructure including buildings, server rooms, wiring runs/closets, and capital

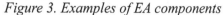

Figure 3. Examples of EA components

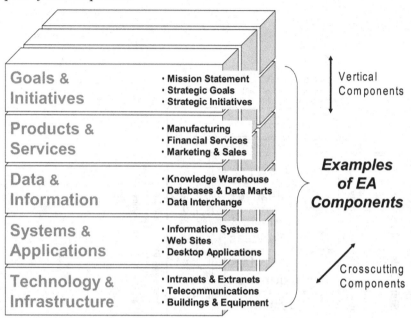

equipment. Figure 3 provides examples of vertical and crosscutting EA components at each level of the EA³ Framework.

EA Documentation Element 3: Current Architecture

The current architecture contains those EA components that currently exist within the enterprise at each level of the framework. This is sometimes referred to as the "as-is" view. The current view of the EA serves to create a 'baseline' inventory of current resources and activities that is documented in a consistent way with the future view of the EA so that analysts can see gaps in performance between future plans and the current capabilities. Having an accurate and comprehensive current view of EA components is an important reference for project planning, asset management, and investment decision-making. The current view of the EA is composed of 'artifacts' (documents, diagrams, data, spreadsheets, charts, etc.) at each

level of the framework, which are archived in an on-line EA repository to make them useable by various EA stakeholders.

EA Documentation Element 4: Future Architecture

The future architecture documents those new or modified EA components that are needed by the enterprise to close an existing performance gap or support a new strategic initiative, operational requirement, or technology solution.

As is shown in Figure 4, the future architecture is driven at both the strategic and tactical levels in three ways: new directions and goals; changing business priorities; and emerging technologies. The EA cannot reflect these changes in the future architecture unless the enterprise's leadership team provides the changes in strategic direction and goals; unless the line of business managers and program managers provide the changes in business processes and priorities that are needed

Figure 4. Enterprise architecture drivers of change

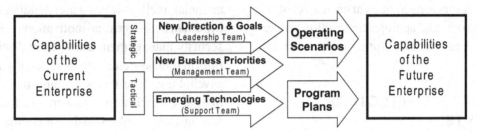

to accomplish the new goals; and unless the support/delivery staff identifies viable technology and staffing solutions to meet the new business requirements.

The future architecture should cover planned changes to EA components in the near term (tactical changes in the next 1-3 years), as well as changes to EA components that are a result of the implementation of long-term operating scenarios that look 4-10 years into the future. These scenarios incorporate different internal and external drivers and can help to identify needed changes in processes, resources, or technology that translate to future planning assumptions, which in turn drive the planning for new EA components.

EA Documentation Element 5: EA Management Plan

The EA Management Plan articulates the EA program and documentation approach. The EA Management Plan also provides descriptions of current and future views of the architecture, and a sequencing plan for managing the transition to the future business/technology operating environment. The EA Management Plan is a living document that is essential to realizing the benefits of the EA as a management program. How the enterprise is going to continually move from the current architecture to the future architecture is a significant planning and management challenge, especially if IT resources supporting key business functions are being replaced or upgraded. EA

Management Plans can also be called an "EA Transition Strategy" or an "EA Modernization Blueprint."

EA Documentation Element 6: Planning Threads

EA documentation includes 'threads' of common activity that are present in all levels of the framework. These threads include IT-related security, standards, and workforce considerations.

IT Security: Security is most effective when it is an integral part of the EA management program and documentation methodology. A comprehensive IT Security Program includes internal controls for systems security and data privacy, and within these areas has several focal areas including: information, personnel, operations, and facilities. To be effective, IT security must work at all levels of the EA framework and within all of the EA components.

IT Standards: One of the most important functions of the EA is that it provides technology-related standards at all levels of the EA framework. The EA should draw on accepted international, National, and industry standards in order to promote the use of non-proprietary solutions in EA components. This in turn enhances the integration of EA components, as well as better supporting the switch-out of components when needed.

IT Workforce: Perhaps the greatest resource that an enterprise has is people. It is therefore important to ensure that IT-related staffing, skill, and training requirements are identified for LOB and support service activities at each level of the EA framework, and appropriate solutions are reflected in the current and future architectures.

SECURITY ARCHITECTURE CONCEPTS

The term "Security Architecture" is used in this chapter to encompass IT security and data privacy requirements as well as solutions within the context of an over-arching enterprise architecture. The image of security architecture as part of an EA is that of a vertical thread that weaves its way through all levels of the EA framework. This image was chosen (as opposed to a separate dedicated level) because information security is most effective when it is integral to the enterprise's strategic initiatives, business services, information flows, systems/applications, and technology infrastructure.

The security architecture includes computing security, information content security and information security management. This scope forms an information security architecture that can be adopted as part of a larger security program. To explain, IT security and data privacy concepts are drawn from disciplines of computer science, information science and technology, engineering, and business management. The study of computing security emphasizes user-based approaches to modeling information systems with the goal of securing information and dataflow. Information *content* security draws from a variety of disciplines of information science as well as technology (such as classification, categorization, natural language processing, information retrieval, and information seeking and use, etc.), organizational science and psychology. The study of information content security also emphasizes user-based systematic approaches to information classification, information content filtering

processes within organizational structure, and artificial intelligence in understanding subtleties in human languages and motivation. Information security management draws from disciplines of information systems, organizational science and psychology. The levels of importance in information classification are perceived differently among individuals, which affects management decisions on the granularity of access control and system access privileges within an organization. Managing and discerning the obscurity of human behavior continues to challenge management decisions. While the security mechanism and infrastructure-building emphasizes information management, information is ultimately handled by humans.

CIA: Confidentiality, Integrity and Availability

Confidentiality refers to protecting and preserving private information, such as corporate data, social security numbers, and financial transactions, to the extent that it prevents improper disclosure from unauthorized entities. Entities here refer to both individuals and processes. The mechanism used to protect information is proper access control over information in storage, and the use of encryption when data is transmitted over untrusted or non-secured networks. Authentication through validation of credentials, identification and verification of both people and data, should be incorporated into the access control scheme. Proper authorization and granular access control should be adopted with the "Principle of Least Privileges," to allow applications to have sufficient rights.

Integrity of information means to ensure the accuracy and completeness of information in transit (or storage) from unauthorized modification. This includes protecting data from entry errors, malicious users, transmission errors, and application processing errors. It requires that all system actions are associated with an individual user who can be held responsible. It also requires that applications verify the origin of each message to ensure that a malicious individual (man-in-the-middle) is unable to insert data into the transaction stream. The concept of non-repudiation is enhanced here. Non-repudiation refers to the prevention of individuals to be able to deny receipt or transmission of a message; it also verifies the time of the electronic communications so that a transaction committed by two parties can not be repudiated. Furthermore, system auditing and monitoring should be reinforced to address the criticality of information integrity. These two concepts work hand-in-hand to provide chronological records of system activity and to track system usage. Auditing identifies incorrect system configurations, process or procedures while monitoring detects anomalies from a set of normalized system records.

Availability is a characteristic that applies to information assets. An asset should be appropriately resilient, available and accessible by an authorized entity on a timely basis. The assets can include property like information, information systems (both hardware and software), network infrastructure, facilities and resources.

Availability mainly refers to protecting information systems against Denial of Service attacks. It ensures system resiliency and timeliness. The best practice for availability is to over-build the infrastructure and avoid single points of failure within the architecture. Availability also refers to the utilization of incident response, disaster recovery and business continuity planning.

SECURITY ARCHITECTURE FRAMEWORK

The Security Architecture Framework (SAF) presented in this chapter is based on and works together with the EA[3] "Cube" Framework (Bernard, 2005). This eight-layered security architecture provides confidentiality, integrity and availability to assure risk-adjusted levels information security and data privacy throughout the enterprise. As is shown in Figure 6, the eight layers of the SAF are: (1) information security governance; (2) operations security; (3) personnel security; (4) information and data flow security; (5) systems security; (6) application development security; (7) infrastructure security; and (8) physical security.

Figure 6. Security architecture framework

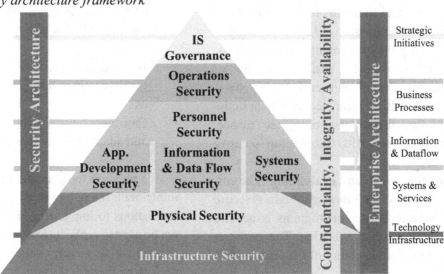

Table 1.

EA³ Framework Level	SAF/IS Governance Level Concepts & Goals
Strategic Initiatives	Helps facilitate the achievement of strategic initiatives.
Business Processes	Defines how the security policies and guidelines are used.
Information & Dataflow:	Defines which guidelines and policies will govern the flow of information and data in the enterprise.
Systems & Services	Defines which guidelines, policies and baseline will govern the systems, services, and applications.
Technology Infrastructure	Defines which guidelines and policies will govern the use and procurement of technology infrastructure on which systems, services and applications will reside.

Security Architecture Framework Layer 1: Information Security Governance

The purpose of the "IS Governance" layer of the SAF is to define security strategies, policies, standards and guidelines for the enterprise from an organizational viewpoint. Activities involved with, and documents produced in this layer include, but are not limited to, High Level Policy Statements, Access Definition Policies, Fair Information Practices, and Security Lifecycle Charts. The relationship of SAF/IS Governance concepts and goals to the EA³ Framework are as follows:

The IS Governance layer of the SAF also addresses policy and standards for IT security and data privacy as follows:

Policy: A policy statement defines a corporate general commitment, business direction, or intention. An information security policy statement reflects managements' commitment to the design, implementation, operations, maintenance, and improvement of its information security compliance.

Policy formation and evaluation: The corporate security policy is formed to address secure operations among different programs, issues and systems within an organization. The purpose, scope and the responsibility of the organization

need to be clearly stated. In addition, it's important to clarify to whom, what, where, when and how such policy applies. Security policy should state the principles to meet the compliance level. A separate document should describe the compliance requirements. Some questions can be asked to examine whether corporate security policies are good policies.

- Is the policy aligned with corporate mission statement? Is this policy accurate and interoperable with other policies that shape the organization's secure business operations?
- Does the policy function consistently throughout specified programs, issues, or system configurations? Are there any unintended "backdoor" loopholes in this policy?
- Is the development of the security policy overly costly in terms of time and resources?
- Can this policy be easily understood, learned and adapted to all lines of business?

If a policy is too general, it might be fuzzy to implement. If a policy is too specific, it might be too tedious to implement. In addition, it might not be easy to replicate to other lines of business. When making security policy, various concerns need to be thought through before roll-out.

Standards: A standard is a set of rules and regulations that control how information systems, materials, products, services, technologies, and management processes, etc. should be developed, managed and operated. For example, ISO IEC 27001 / ISO 17799 are sets of standards governing information systems security and secure management operations, which are developed and agreed among technical committees with broad support. In addition, standards such as FISMA, Sarbanes-Oxley, HIPAA, NIST, or Gramm-Leach-Biley Act have been made compliant, and implemented in private and public sectors.

Security Architecture Framework Layer 2: Operations Security

The purpose of the Operations Security Layer is to define the enterprise's intra-organizational and operational needs as they interact with and require access to the enterprise IT services, in order to identify and address security needs at the enterprises organizational level. Activities involved with, and documents produced in this layer include, but are not limited to, Risk Assessment, Authorization Models, Access Control User Requirements, Business Impact Analysis, and Disaster Recovery & Business Resumption Planning. The relationship of SAF/Operations Security concepts and goals to the EA[3] Framework are as follows:

The Operations Security layer of the SAF also addresses risk management and continuity of operations/disaster recovery planning for IT security and data privacy as follows:

Risk assessment: Risk assessment is a continuous and repeated process. Organizations need to identify critical components and resources. Then, assess risk exposure based on the asset values, probability of risks and threats, and the likely occurrence of those threats to the resources. It is important for organizations to recognize that the sources of threat can be both internal and external.

Vulnerability Assessment: Organizations can conduct self-assessments. General implementation phases include:

- **Discovery Phase:** This is a review-to-discover stage. Security analyzer reviews documentations about security policies, standards, guidelines, information classification schemes, access control plans, and applications/systems security requirements.
- **Manual Inspection Phase:** Compare existing systems with what was recorded in documentation.

Table 2.

EA[3] Framework Level	SAF/Operations Security Level Concepts & Goals
Strategic Initiatives	Creates security and assurance in the internal operations through the use of disaster recovery, etc. and based upon risk assessment analysis, etc.
Business Processes	Identifies specific needs of each LOB in the form of risk assessment, etc.
Information & Dataflow:	Defines levels of information classification and access control system to address enterprise specific problems. Plan the information flow during disaster recovery and the business continuity stage. Build Security Operations Center (SOC) for emergency response and incident handlings.
Systems & Services	Converts and documents logical information classification and access controls into system and service controls. Normalize system & service operations and emergency response centered by the SOC.
Technology Infrastructure	Meets standard operational requirements and procedures. Ensure the workability, testability and redundancy of component systems and devices. Assess financial liability and continuity of system operations.

- **Vulnerability Testing Phase:** It is also called penetration test. Penetration test is to systemically review configurations and identify security deficiencies.
- **Process Validation Phase:** Consideration of the human element is included in the self assessment. In this phase, how humans are alerted when security incidents happen needs to be reexamined. How process is executed at the management and operational levels -and how systems are controlled at the technical levels - should be assessed.

Contingency planning: Contingencies refer to incidents that may disrupt systems or business operations. Contingency planning means that business has immediate incident handling/response plan at both management as well as technical support level. This plan is documented in the Standard Operating Procedures (SOPs) to ensure that timely and effective action is taken by end-users and system administrators, when facing a security incident. This plan may include swappable choices and cost analysis during various disastrous scenarios.

Incident handling team: The mission for an incident handling team is to amend immediate, identifiable vulnerabilities on current information systems, to respond so as to quarantine malicious codes and viruses, to restore infected information systems, and to prevent future damages especially by advanced denial of services attack, unauthorized access, etc. An incident handling team can either be in-house, partially out-sourced, or fully out-sourced. Incident handling teams are linked with other groups of similar missions, and can form centralized communications with expertise in responding to computer incidents.

Disaster recovery planning (DRP): It is an assessment and recovery procedure that identifies critical information systems or operational sites needed to recover when a man-made or natural disaster occurs. Such a disaster, however, does not threaten the existence of the enterprise. This includes sabotage, theft or corruption of resources, successful large scale hacker/virus attacks, building damage, fire, flood, and electrical outages. Two time-related aspects of disaster recovery need to be periodically evaluated: (1) the method for recovery, and (2) the affect on mission accomplishment. Both of these may change as the amount of time increases from the moment the disaster occurred (e.g., data restore procedures and the affect on business services will probably be different for 2-minute, 2-hour, 2-day, and 2-week outages). In addition, priorities in this recovery procedure need to be sorted out. In this plan, it should specify the types of back-up mechanisms, alternative sites, equipment to be used, roles and responsibilities, and cost considerations.

Business Continuity Planning (BCP): This refers to procedures that are invoked if all or part of the enterprise are unexpectedly destroyed or forced to disband. This scenario, however, does mean that the enterprise is unable to conduct any business functions or information operations for a period of time. The recovery response is scripted in a Continuity of Operations Plans (COOP) that describes how organizations should operate in a contingency situation so that damages can be minimized. COOP also identifies where and when business and information infrastructure would be restored. If the contingencies are serious and it might take several months or longer period of time to recover, then corporations need to solidify business operations.

Security Operations Center (SOC): A SOC is a group, integrated with other operations in a center, which oversees all security issues within the organization. It designs and reinforces the implementation of security measures in the information systems infrastructure, monitors data and transactions, and provides incident handling and response capability during contingency situations. While security principles of defense are done in layers, details of implementation should be in physical and infrastructure security. SOC is the means to "centralized management."

Table 3.

EA³ Framework Level	SAF/Personnel Security Level Concepts & Goals
Strategic Initiatives	Defines and creates personnel security measure in the form of procedural and awareness training, (etc.) that are based upon the security needs of the organization and that are in alignment with security policies.
Business Processes	Identifies specific security needs for each LOB.
Information & Dataflow:	Assesses and documents the levels and mechanisms of personnel access control, authentication, authorization and accounting system according to their roles and responsibility throughout the enterprise.
Systems & Services	Defines and documents the personnel access policy based on their roles and responsibility on the systems and services.
Technology Infrastructure	Implements and reinforces the authentication, authorization and accounting over systems, devices and applications.

Security Architecture Framework Layer 3: Personnel Security

Personnel security is essential since employees are ultimately responsible for handling and controlling the dissemination of sensitive information. The purpose of the Personnel Security layer is to ensure that enterprise personnel are accessing and utilizing its information and technology services safely, securely, and in accordance with their predefined roles and responsibilities of their job functions, through proper access control plans and detection of employee anomalous behavior. Activities involved with, and documents produced in this layer include, but are not limited to, user authentication, role-based access control, awareness training, desktop security policies, procedural training. The relationship of SAF/Personnel Security concepts and goals to the EA³ Framework are as follows:

The Personnel Security layer of the SAF also addresses user-related threats and policies, due diligence practices, and training requirements for IT security and data privacy as follows:

Threats in personnel security: There are two different threat dimensions when discussing the personnel security issues. The first dimension is threat to personnel's physical safety especially the safety of the executives. This threat comes from terrorists who might assassinate or kidnap executives as hostages for either psychological or monetary reasons. Threats to personnel safety also include workplace violence, bombings or harassments. The second dimension is the threats caused by the alteration of personnel trustworthiness, commonly called the insider threats. Individuals who hold key position and have critical access to sensitive data or classified information in the organization could cause severe security breaches by illegally transporting or exchanging information for profits or psychological reasons. The real challenge here is to be able to detect the changes in a person's trust level after someone has obtained a high-level security clearance and trust.

Personnel security policy: Due to threats caused to and by personnel, it is essential to establish a crisis management plan and a crisis management team. Periodic threat analysis and evaluation would help to understand current organizational safety level in advance. Access control is an important concept that can be done at the physical level, personnel level, information systems level and information flows level. Information and critical infrastructural access should be restricted to individuals on a need-to-know basis. "Due diligence" is the ultimate rule of thumb when protecting personnel - as well as information systems - from unauthorized access.

"Due Diligence" practices: An organization's existence depends on the integrity of its employees. Without security processes in practice, an organization's reputation, assets and finances could be at risk. It is important to set up both criteria and checklists before hiring. Background checks and screening are common practices during hiring. Organizations should let employees know that they will be periodically monitored and audited in the workplace. Employers should also provide security awareness and best-practice training to avoid ignorance, mistakes and such. Personnel disciplinary actions should be announced explicitly. When employees are terminated, it is important to minimize potential violence or workplace disruption. All corporate tangible and intangible assets shall be returned. The procedure of examining the returned items should be done in an efficient and effective manner.

Security awareness training: Security awareness training should be provided to all end-users and system administrators. This should include the signing of security awareness agreements to acknowledge that the enterprise owns the associated resources and hosted information. This agreement should state explicitly that monitoring and auditing online and offline activity of both end-users and system administrators are to be expected. This security awareness training should be given periodically to reinforce employees' compliance to corporate security policy and security practices.

Security Architecture Framework Layer 4: Information & Dataflow Security

The purpose of the Information & Data Flow Security layer is to identify and classify information and data as it moves through the enterprise - in order to justify adequate security controls. The data needs to be valued from a quantitative and qualitative aspect, then classified into levels depending on the risk of data loss, repudiation, competition, and availability. Activities involved with, and documents produced in this layer include, but are not limited to, data design, dataflow assurance, information classification forms, logical access controls, associative access controls. The relationship of SAF/Information & Dataflow Security concepts and goals to the EA[3] Framework are as follows:

The Information & Dataflow Security layer of the SAF also addresses user-related threats and policies, due diligence practices, and training requirements for IT security and data privacy as follows:

Information classification: It is a set of guidelines and requirements that classify information according to its confidentiality and sensitivity level. Information classification scheme helps identify what information is vital to an organization, and which protection mechanism should be applied. Meeting requirements of information classification demonstrates an organization's com-

Table 3.

EA[3] Framework Level	SAF/Info-Data Security Level Concepts & Goals
Strategic Initiatives	Designs information flows and classifications of information.
Business Processes	Designs and defines information and data types shared between LOB's or internal business processes.
Information & Dataflow:	Classifies levels of data, information and knowledge. Converts associative access control system into logical access control system. Assess risks associated with the information classified system.
Systems & Services	Assesses risks quantitatively and qualitatively involves with systems and services during disaster, financial loss or reputation damage.
Technology Infrastructure	Ensures the accountability and availability of the systems, devices and infrastructure.

mitment to security best practices for regulatory, compliance or legal reasons. Information can be coarsely classified into four levels: public, internal, confidential and restricted. To an organization, public information is something that can be released to the press and made known to the public as well as competitors. Internal information is sensitive, such as physical layout of a workplace, and should remain within the organization. Confidential information should not be disclosed to the public without proper authorization. It could be customer or vendor contact information; it can include the source codes of a software product that is owned by the organization. Restricted information is something that is extremely sensitive, such as payroll, marketing/operations strategy, etc. Individuals would require need-to-know authorization before accessing restricted information.

Security models: Security models set principles of allowable paths of information flow in a secure system. These are used to define security requirements for systems to handle data at different sensitivity levels. Data and information must not be abused by execution of a process or by another sub-system. For example, the Bell La-Padula Security Model, ensuring confidentiality through access control rules, was developed by David Elliott Bell and Len LaPadula in 1973. It prevents write-down access within an information access matrix. Programs (or processes) with higher classification level cannot write to another programs (or processes) with lower classification level. Quickly after, the Biba Integrity Model assuring information integrity was developed by Kenneth J. Biba in 1977. This model prevents unauthorized users from making modifications. Subjects cannot read objects of lesser integrity; subjects cannot write to objects of higher integrity. The Clark-Wilson Integrity Model, developed by David D. Clark and David D. Wilson in 1987, addresses information integrity issues. It promotes the idea of performing steps in order. Additionally it initiates the concept of authenticating the indi-

viduals who perform the steps. It prevents not only unauthorized users from making modifications, but also authorized users from making improper modifications - by incorporating the principle of "separation of duty." Other models, such as the Multi-Level Security Model, emphasizes that not all personnel have approval or need-to-know authorization for all information on the system. The System High Security Model depicts that all users of a system may have clearance and approval to view systemic information, but not all personnel have need-to-know access for domain/application information.

Risk controls: Risk controls by nature are classified into three types: preventive controls, detective controls, and corrective controls. Preventive controls are steps designed to avoid potential nonconformities, make improvements, and thus mitigate risks. They attempt to prevent the occurrence of problems by removing their causes. Monitoring information access and the security models are examples of preventive controls. Detective controls are used to understand when something has happened that was meant to be prevented. With detective controls, the time required to identify and respond to triggers is critical. However, false alarms may happen from time to time. Eliminating false positives (falsely identifying occurrences) and false negatives (falsely ignoring occurrences) in the control mechanism are critical. Corrective controls are steps to address existing nonconformities and make improvements. This refers to fixing errant situations based on actual events that have already occurred. Effectiveness and cost are two important factors to consider when choosing a type of risk control. In addition, when circumstances or risks are changed, the associated controls might need to be reconfigured so that they are able to handle more sophisticated risks. In these situations, another rigorous development and testing cycle may need to be reconsidered. Regardless whether automated or manual controls are implemented, procedures for handling different types of controls and transactional logs need to be documented as risk assessment materials.

Risk management: Risk management is the ability and process of identifying, analyzing, controlling and minimizing losses associated with threats. Since it is not possible to eliminate risks completely, the goal of risk mitigation is to reduce risks to an acceptable and survivable level without making major adjustments to the strategy or mission. Risk management influences planning and decision-making processes dealing with both physical building safeties as well as information systems design. It helps an organization to understand the cost-to-value ratio of a security countermeasure.

Risk analysis: Risk analysis is the function of risk management. Risk analysis identifies actual threats, the possible consequences, the probable frequency of occurrences, and the probability that each identified threat might actually happen. In addition to analyzing the potential damage that a given threat would occur and the potential losses that a threat would cause an organization, risk analysis is performed to understand the cost and benefits of a protection mechanism. Risk analysis can be done quantitatively as well as qualitatively. The quantitative risk analysis quantifies the impact of potential threats, while qualitative risk analysis facilitates the delegation of management and responsibility down through organizational hierarchy.

Security Architecture Framework Layer 5: Application Development Security

The purpose of the Application Development Security layer is to design the authentication, authorization and accounting (AAA) components into the applications used in the enterprise; to enforce the application process flow throughout the enterprise; and to ingrain security in the SDLC. Activities involved with, and documents produced in this layer include, but are not limited to; design & development, application development security, application gateways, application security placement. The relationship of SAF/Application Development Security concepts and goals to the EA[3] Framework are as follows:

The Application Development Security layer of the SAF also addresses vulnerabilities, best practices, and lifecycle issues for IT security and data privacy as follows:

Common application vulnerabilities: The defense-in-depth concept starts at designing secure applications. Application developers need to understand the environment, and risks associated with it - so that applications can be developed and deployed securely. Developers also need to know about security implications when coding software so that the security infrastructure can be incorporated. One commonly programmed threat is a flawed access control policy that does not reflect the corporate policy. Other threats include buffer

Table 4.

EA[3] Framework Level	SAF/Application Security Level Concepts & Goals
Strategic Initiatives	Designs and models applications to support and process information flow.
Business Processes	Defines security measures needed to ensure LOB based on Information constraints.
Information & Dataflow:	Reinforces the personnel AAA in application systems during development life cycle and application logic process flow.
Systems & Services	AAA systems based on the personnel security policy should be designed, developed and documented into the process flow provided by the systems and services.
Technology Infrastructure	Ensures the integrity and maintainability of the newly updated application with existing infrastructure.

overflows, SQL injections, and script injection, etc. Lack of secure programming practices can have a cascading impact on application utilization.

Best practices: The application should specify and validate the types of the inputs coming from the network and make sure to call trusted external resources so that issues like buffer overflow, script injection, and SQL injection, etc. can be avoided. In addition, each application should be structured with good data flow and controls. The "principle of least privileges" should be followed whenever an application accesses database. For example, if the application only needs data located in certain cells in a row, the application should not be given full privileges to read or modify the table. When a process has failed, the full description of the failure should not be given to the end users. Instead, all error messages should be logged with exceptions for the system administrator to troubleshoot. Simply displaying that the application has failed is good enough, which avoids giving potential hackers too much configuration information.

Software Development Life Cycle (SDLC): In order to enhance security at the application development stage, it is critical to incorporate security into the software development life cycle. It starts first at the initial review with the customer, and includes technical requirements. An important lesson is that the application logical processes and procedures should be deployed so that the organizations can pursue business

continuity in contingent scenarios. Second, it's necessary to eliminate threatening factors, such as identifying entry, data flow, and exit points of the application, so that threats to each application can be mitigated at a minimum level. Third, a design review includes reviewing application documents and interviewing developers and business analysts - to not only make sure that all requirements are fulfilled, but also to make sure all logical processes and procedures have followed the "principles of least privileges." Fourth, a code review should be conducted to ensure that no "backdoor" or unnecessary process (modular calls) are executed. Fifth, before any application is rolled out to operations, it's critical to assess potential associative risks. This is the time to mitigate, transfer or eliminate risks. Furthermore, the application should be benchmarked with the industrial standards, such as ISO IEC 27001 / ISO IEC 17799, FISMA, Sarbanes-Oxley, HIPAA, NIST, or Gramm-Leach-Biley Act. Finally, security must be regularly maintained to avoid new exploits that cause the applications to become vulnerable.

Security Architecture Framework Layer 6: Systems Security

Systems here refer to the systems that support platform services for applications. The purpose

Table 5.

EA³ Framework Level	SAF/Systems Security Level Concepts & Goals
Strategic Initiatives	Designs and defines security measures and constraints for software systems.
Business Processes	Ensures each security requirement for the software system is implemented specifically for each LOB.
Information & Dataflow:	Prioritizes and controls information granular access during configuration, integration and implementation process.
Systems & Services	Hardens systems from kernel operating system throughout all system files and database repository. Tests and evaluates modular security components involved with systems and services. Compliance and consideration is given to public key infrastructure and cryptography modules that should be ingrained at all levels within systems.
Technology Infrastructure	Periodically updates versions and patches against known vulnerabilities.

of the Systems Security layer is to protect sensitive applications and provide granularity of access controls to sensitive resources. Activities involved with, and documents produced in this layer include, but are not limited to, user account management & privileges, certificate request management, password storage & management, remote access, authorization models, file system hardening procedures, patching, and security repositories. The relationship of SAF/Systems Security concepts and goals to the EA³ Framework are as follows:

The Systems Security layer of the SAF also addresses hardening, authentication, authorization, database, public key infrastructure, single sign-on, and intrusion detection issues for IT security and data privacy as follows:

Platform hardening: Most systems are manufactured and shipped with unnecessary features enabled. Platform hardening is a concept for analyzing vulnerability of operating kernels that run on a host. It also is a methodology of determining what unused ports and services should be closed out. For example, a server that is not functioning as an email server should disable its SMTP service. A database server should disable default user account access. A Web server should use HTTPS for viewing pages. In addition, a system should be regularly patched. Passwords and user permissions should be periodically checked and strengthened. In addition to functioning as a file server, a system also refers to a unit serving a communication purpose, such as a router or a switch. Therefore, hardening the platform refers to tightening up configurations and controls on all services and processes while preserving availability. The network layout should be designed and wired to fit the security requirements.

Authentication and authorization: Authentication is the verification of the claimed identity of a user. There are generally three types of authentication mechanisms: information (something you know, ex. Passwords, secret questions, etc.), biometrics (something you are, ex. Finger print,

retina scan, facial recognition, etc.), and possessions (something you have, ex. Smart card, ID card, etc.). User authentication is usually maintained in a directory service. Authorization is the process of giving user's access rights to computer resources based on their permissions and privileges. When the authentication mechanism is verified by the directory services, the access control system either allows or denies user's access.

Database security: Database security involves protecting the database from both internal and external threats. It includes issues of secure system administration, availability, recoverability, integrity, reliability and performance. It is important to recognize that each database has some built-in security features, but also has embedded vulnerabilities. One critical configuration issue involves setting up a database server based on whether it supplies information to a Web server. If it does, be sure to configure it in a way that it allows access only from that Web server. Then, disable all anonymous connection to database server. Avoid using default "sa" account (with system administrator privileges) and default values to access a database for every single connection. If your database server is providing information to dynamic applications, do not allow immediate unauthenticated updates to a database.

PKI-enabled applications: Public Key Infrastructure uses certificates as online digital identities. The authentication takes place when one user signs a message with a private key and a public key is contained in the certificate. The signature is signed on the message and sent over to a receiver (another user or a server). The receiver uses the public key to check the signature of the message. Web-based applications that can authenticate users through digital signatures look up the directory server for the user's attributes. Then, the applications check the CRL (Certificate Revocation List) issued by a CA (Certificate Authority) as to whether the user is currently active and trustworthy. Then, this Web-based application authenticates and interacts with the user through his/her certificate on a browser.

Single Sign-On (SSO): Single Sign-On is a mechanism where a single action of user authentication and authorization would permit a user to access all applications and systems where he/she has access permission. This user does not need to enter into multiple passwords. While Single Sign-On reduces human errors when accessing systems, it is costly and difficult to implement. It is recommended that you use combined authentication mechanism (such as smart card with a random password, or a certificate) instead of a simple password, since the chain effect is much greater once this authentication is broken into by a hacker.

Host-based Intrusion Detection System (HIDS): Intrusion detection is a process of monitoring incidents occurring in an information system or on a network, and analyzing them for signs of intrusion. HIDS monitors system files, logs, logon activity, and processing with the kernel and other resources. Since intrusion detection systems can be designed for different security purposes, its method is classified as anomaly detection, including signature-based detection, target monitoring, and stealth probes. Anomaly detection establishes baselines of normal usages of systems and then identifies any outliers or abnormal systemic usage. Signature-based detec-

tion uses known intrusion patterns to detect or predict subsequent similar attempts. This method of target monitoring looks for modification of specific system files. This is more of a corrective control, designed to uncover unauthorized actions performed on the system kernel files or Web pages. This type of monitoring is the easiest to implement, since it does not require constant monitoring. Integrity checksum hashes can be computed against the original files to determine if the files have been altered. If hackers probe for system vulnerability and open ports, the stealth probe can be used to detect this intrusion. Stealth probes can be combined with the anomaly detection and signature-based detection to uncover suspicious activity.

Security Architecture Framework Layer 7: Infrastructure Security

The purpose of the Infrastructure Security layer is to develop a secure infrastructure that meets all the security requirements of the enterprise and can safeguard against future attacks against the enterprise. This is a mixture of art and science. Activities involved with, and documents produced in this layer include, but are not limited to, network partitioning, VLAN's, firewalls, packet filtering, circuit level gateways, PKI architectures, VPN's,

Table 5.

EA³ Framework Level	SAF/Infrastructure Security Level Concepts & Goals
Strategic Initiatives	Defines security measures for the infrastructure that fits with the security policies and goals of the enterprise, and further strengthens the need of the software systems.
Business Processes	Defines how the infrastructure will be used by each LOB and what security concerns exist regarding those uses.
Information & Dataflow:	Defines how the information will flow between LOB and within the enterprise, and where infrastructure components need to be placed.
Systems & Services	Defines the appropriate countermeasures that will protect and regulate all Systems and Services, and ensure that devices are compliant with industrial security standards.
Technology Infrastructure	Installs the physical infrastructure components that will partition the network and implements safeguards to ensure the infrastructure is accessible by the authorized personnel. Implements confidentiality and integrity checks on the transmitted information.

SSL, and stateful inspections. The relationship of SAF/Infrastructure Security concepts and goals to the EA³ Framework are as follows:

The Infrastructure Security layer of the SAF also addresses network, testing, broadband, wireless, and telecommunications issues for IT security and data privacy as follows:

Network partitioning: Creating logical groups and users/systems which contain the flow of information to and from these components is an important concept in network partitioning. These virtual networks prevent sniffing activities because nodes are not allowed to see each other's ports without permission.

Firewall security: The firewall provides perimeter security. With packet filtering, the firewall examines the source address, destination address, and types of traffic for every packet, and makes decisions of "accept," "deny," or "discard" on each packet. With stateful inspection, firewall security oversees the state of communication sessions at packets level from source to destination. When a firewall is appliance-based, it provides high speed of filtering traffic. Very often, it is accompanied with a load balancer for high availability. When a firewall functions as an application proxy, it relays *point to process* and route requests between client and server. It can also incorporate more features such as user-based authentication, traffic filtering, content acceleration, and activity logging.

Network security testing: Security testing is necessary once a network is deployed. Security testing allows for the uncovering of network design and operational flaws that violate security policy. The degree of consistency between the system documentation and its implementation must be assessed. The goal of the network security testing is to maximize the benefits to the organization as a whole. Therefore, it normally requires participation and coordination among senior management, security officers, network administrators, and business managers, so that the security policy can be reinforced and applied at the systems level. The CIO (Corporate Information Officer) and CISO (Corporate Information Security Officer) should work together to prioritize the information flow and information process so as to ensure that the organizational perspective is considered.

Network-based Intrusion Detection System (NIDS): NIDS functions as a protocol analyzer or a network "sniffer." It is like a wire tap device that eavesdrops on the network. It works in stealth mode, like a single-purpose sensor, scanning and analyzing packets at various points on a network. NIDS detects probing, network configuration vulnerabilities, and monitors attacks to and from nodes while having little impact on network traffic. However, NIDS is very resource intensive because it logs massive quantities of network activity. It is not easy to analyze traffic in a complex network architecture unless one is an experienced security officer. NIDS could not analyze encrypted traffic, nor can it be applied to complex switched networks. If there is unusual traffic detected, NIDS cannot even tell if an attack was successful. It requires further investigation into that specific node or device, perhaps with the help of a HIDS. NIDS can detect known attacks with signatures or patterns - this is called misuse detection. NIDS can also create profiles of network usage over a long period of time in order to detect unusual activity - this is called anomaly detection. Anomaly detection establishes a baseline for normal traffic, then watches for outlier data points. But it requires extensive training to regulate the NIDS from frequent false positive alarms.

Broadband security: Since the broadband connection is always active, potential hackers can "arbitrarily" search for victims. A personal firewall is one of the solutions that consumers can install to protect their broadband connection. A personal firewall blocks unsafe incoming services and unauthorized outgoing services. If stealth mode is enabled, a personal firewall can monitor the connection. In addition, secure Web browsers using strong password and patch software are good tools for enhancing broadband security.

PKI associated risks: Public Key Infrastructure (PKI) has some associated risks. First, PKI binds the individual to the private/public key pair issued by a Certificate Authority, specifically by a Register Authority, using an identity proofing mechanism. Regardless of how the individual holds his own private key, there is no biometric element built in for digital signature. In a lawsuit, no physical or biometric characteristics (or evidence) can be found to link the person who signs a fraudulent claim with his digital signature key pair. Second, in addition to PKI, the electronic process depends on reliable software and hardware. If either software or hardware is not dependable, data integrity can be affected, which impedes forensic analysis. Third, the use of electronic process with public key technology itself might also have inherent risks. For example, if the PKI-enabled applications are not designed, coded or deployed properly, the systems might not function as planned.

PKI implementation issues: To implement PKI in a large scale, it involves many practical issues. The certificate policy and certification practices need to be specified. What directory services does your public key infrastructure intend to serve? How is your public key infrastructure interoperable with other public key infrastructures? What are the requirements for electronic commerce applications to be PKI-enabled? How do applications take in or send out the certificates and digitally-signed documents? What are the publication methods to revoke certificates? Whose responsibility is it to audit PKI certificate transactions? Liability is also a big issue in digital signature validation. Whose liability it is to provide long-term signature validation services? Should the organization which provides the PKI-enabled applications be responsible for the signature validation, or should the infrastructure be the ultimate provider for validating signatures automatically?

Virtual Private Networks (VPN): A VPN by definition is a private network on a public telecom infrastructure, with privacy afforded by reserved facilities (e.g., private circuits connected via shared switches), a tunneling protocol (e.g, IPsec), or encrypted transmission. A trusted VPN refers to circuits reserved exclusively by the service provider for one customer, to allow them private addressing & security policies, routed via shared switches. The customer trusts the VPN provider to maintain the integrity of circuits and prevent unauthorized access. A secure VPN encrypts traffic on entering the VPN provider's shared network, then decrypts on exiting. Information can't be read in transit. It will be rejected if changed. The VPN requires that all traffic must be encrypted and authenticated to address integrity and confidentiality issues. Some protocols allow either authentication or encryption. Although an encrypted network without authentication is a little more secure than a clear network, such a network is not technically a VPN because it lacks privacy. Administrators much agree on VPN's security properties for both ends of every tunnel. This peer authentication ensures that the data is sent from the expected host. It also eliminates the possibilities for an attacker to change the security properties of any part of a VPN, e.g., to either weaken encryption or change shared keys.

Concerns in wireless security: Assuring the physical security for mobile device access points that contain sensitive information is the first step in wireless security. Other security concerns include loss of confidentiality through passive eavesdropping, loss of availability through jammed wireless signals, and unauthorized access to network from terminals. Therefore, facilities that provide a wireless network need to also have physical access controls such as photo identification or biometrics to authenticate users. External boundary control with proper surveillance prevents unauthorized wanderers from eavesdropping on network communications by using a wireless device that picks up the RF emanations, or changing the settings on the access points. Proper control of the wireless coverage area by limiting signal dispersion

Table 6.

EA³ Framework Level	SAF/Physical Security Level Concepts & Goals
Strategic Initiatives	Identifies physical security methods to protect and regulate access enterprise infrastructure resources.
Business Processes	Defines how each LOB would need access to the physical infrastructure and what security measures need to be implemented to ensure each LOB appropriately
Information & Dataflow:	Ensures physical access facilities be properly controlled, safeguarded and governed. Controls and screens mobile devices or other available communication channels that have the capability to carry information and data.
Systems & Services	Server rooms, building security and cabling security should be planned, designed, built and safeguarded for protecting systems and services.
Technology Infrastructure	Implement and integrate data security devices with the physical security devices. Convergence Analysis enhances accountability and availability of wired and wireless infrastructure component devices. Meets industrial standards.

prevents the wireless signals from extending beyond the intended coverage area.

Security Architecture Framework Layer 8: Physical Security

The purpose of the Physical Security layer is to construct a secure perimeter physical defense system that safeguards the facility and physical resources for the enterprise. Activities involved with, and documents produced in this layer include, but are not limited to, Building & Facility Security, Physical Access Controls, Network Operation Centers (NOC) Server Rooms, Wiring Closets, and Cable Plants. The relationship of SAF/Physical Security concepts and goals to the EA³ Framework are as follows:

The Physical Security layer of the SAF also addresses access and assessment issues for IT security and data privacy as follows:

Physical security: Physical security is an essential part of information security architecture. Physical security refers to data protection against accidental destruction or modification by forces of nature or by people, against intentional destruction or modification by unauthorized people, and against accidental or intentional disclosure to unauthorized people. It encompasses not only the area of system hardware, but also loca-

tions of wiring used to connect systems and the provisioning of redundancy systems. Physical measures may be complemented by operations and personnel security measures, such as the "need-to-know" principle, which limits physical access to sensitive information only to appropriate personnel with clearance. In a governmental organization, the main physical defenses include security keys and containers to protect classified information, access control measures, as well as security alarm systems to detect unauthorized access, and physical barriers to deter, detect and delay unauthorized entry. By setting up security perimeters, organizations are able to physically, psychologically and legally deter intruders.

Physical security assessment: Physical security can be assessed by evaluating threat scenarios (x-axis) with business functional elements (y1-axis) and site subsystems (y2-axis). There are many different types of threat scenarios to be considered, such as accidents, contamination, natural disasters, cyber attack, power outages, system failure, etc. Threat scenarios must be considered in light of the different business functional areas. Business functional elements can include an assessment of facility criticality, e.g., mission critical area vs. vulnerable area. Once the business functional areas are identified, it's necessary to determine how to properly protect the site and building subsystems. There are various categories to be examined; including site/architectural design, structural elements, the building envelope, utility systems, mechanical systems, plumbing, electrical and gas systems, information and communication systems, etc. Subsystem examination also includes overall operations and maintenance assessment plans.

FUTURE TRENDS

Security Architecture Management

The security architecture and associated programs in a government agency should be managed by a specialist in this field. Increasingly, agencies are establishing positions for an Information Systems Security Manager (ISSM). The ISSM should have business and IT operating experience in addition to training in the various elements of information security. The ISSM should report to the Chief Information Officer (CIO) or Chief Technology Officer (CTO) and should work collaboratively with the Chief Enterprise Architect to ensure that EA component and artifact design, implementation, and operational activities have effective security as a requirement. The ISSM should also be responsible for the development, implementation, and maintenance of the enterprise's IT Security Plan. This plan should provide the security and privacy-related policies and procedures for the documentation, testing, certification, accreditation operation, and disposal of EA components and artifacts at all levels of the EA framework.

Emerging Threats

The evolution of information protection is very similar to a game of chess, where one move on the board can change all future strategies. Simply pulling information systems together, such as integrating active mechanism firewalls with passive mechanism "intrusion detection systems"

to defend corporate assets may not be sufficient. System administrators may still have to read thousand lines of logs everyday in order to understand what is going on within their information systems, as well as in the corporate networks. The real problem lies not only in the ineffective correlation analysis from multiple systems, but also the complex human social behavior. Whether organizations are able to protect information security while also protecting the individual's right to privacy through aggregating and analyzing problems in both a systems and social context is a real challenge today.

Lack of Theory-Based Defense Mechanisms to Address Information Integrity Issues

The phenomenon of the coordinated attack has led the information security industry to aggressively promote technology integration for coordinated defense. However, without a governing theory to explain existing threat phenomenon, simple information system integration cannot help organizations to effectively defend their information and intelligence resources. In other words, coordinated defense mechanisms cannot be built to defend from both outside and inside joint attacks. Instead of simply pulling information systems together, usability of the information systems managed by IT personnel should be emphasized to standardize the security components. Corporate defense theory and mechanisms should be researched and built so that the threat phenomenon can be traced and explained in a way that can prevent information and intelligence property from being cloned or modified. Only then can true information integrity be assured.

While mechanisms for aggregating system logs and human access logs are still being developed, the theories and methods built upon those analyses are not sufficient to explain or address the phenomenon of insider threats. It is important to develop a theory that addresses and explains insider threat phenomenon when human behavior and social activities threaten corporate security in loss of profit, intelligence property, or even corporate credibility.

Insufficient Balance between Information Availability and Access Control

Gathering identity-based or role-based information in order to monitor an individual's social activities requires a great deal of concern for legal and privacy issues. The Computer Matching and Privacy Protection Acts of 1988 (amending the Privacy Act of 1974) protect records that contain private information on individuals. It states; "no agency shall disclose any record which is contained in a system of records by any means of communication to any person, or to another agency, except pursuant to a written request by, or with the prior written consent of, the individual to whom the record pertains" (Privacy Act of 1974).

The dilemma of balancing information control with information availability is evident when human rights to privacy and freedom are considered. Although "social engineering" is used as a technique to get some level of confidential information or even used to penetrate a site, in-depth approaches that analyze insider threats through integrating activities of systems as well as humans are not yet fully available. The most sophisticated threats can occur when an individual's social power and freedom is exercised. While access control mechanisms are implemented to secure information access, authorized personnel will always have excessive privileges to copy or modify information. This creates the threat of excessive system privileges that can lead to a potential threat from a powerful user.

On the other hand, when information is classified and controlled, information becomes less available. When the types of Internet Websites are filtered by a proxy server that is constrained by security policy, then information becomes less available to employees. When information exists on different access-controlled database servers, it requires additional steps to gain access. This creates cumbersome administrative barriers to information availability. As a result, convenience of access and information availability cannot always go hand-in-hand with confidentiality and integrity.

Human Factors

Security industry emphasis has been on system-based, rather than behavior-based information confidentiality issues. Since ARPANET was invented in 1969, the government and military have always taken the lead on inventing information classification schemes and cryptographic algorithms. A system-based approach to information confidentiality is derived from a positivist approach. Security mechanisms are developed and implemented from the perspectives of system architect. But in a socially networked environment, it is not sufficient to use a single lens to view a complex issue as insider threats. As the "human factor" is the weakest linkage in the chain of security defense (Mitnick and Simon, 2002), a need to bolster this weak linkage becomes critical. Insider threats require not only system-based security analysis, but intensively behavioral-based security analysis.

Understanding and identifying human intention and motivation takes both social and cognitive psychological analysis. Traditional information systems architects and developers do not have the appropriate training to solve such complicated problems when the focus is insider threats. Protecting information has gone beyond what programmed, algorithmic analysis can achieve. Cryptography and security models are fundamental tools for information confidentiality, but a behavior-based approach to information security is the next step in building coordinated defense mechanisms.

The Concept of Information Assurance

Scientists and practitioners in the IT security and data privacy community of interest and inquiry share the goal of wishing to facilitate information assurance (IA). IA, as defined by the Alliance for Telecommunications Industry Solutions, means *"the information operations that protect and defend information and information systems (IS) by ensuring their availability, integrity, authentication, confidentiality and non-repudiation. This definition includes practitioners' perspectives of providing for restoration of information systems by incorporating protection, detection and reaction capabilities"* (ATIS Telecom Glossary 2000). Information assurance pertains to a set of processes or activities meant to ensure the service availability of information systems and system infrastructure, protect information content integrity, confidentiality and non-repudiation, and establish security-centric information management.

Information Systems Security

The scope of information systems security (ISS) is defined in the disciplines in which ISS resides. Its identity is drawn from information systems, information science, organizational science, psychology, and criminology (Figure 1). In the information systems discipline, ISS adopts a user-based approach of modeling information systems that provide security features and architecture. In the information science and technology discipline, ISS adopts approaches of analyzing information content through information architecture, classification, and categorization. How to perceive information behavior and human behavior so better prediction can be attained is the central theme for information content security. In the organizational/management science disciplines, ISS adopts views of information security policy and secure management practices. Creating

a security culture that becomes the norm in organizations is the focus of social psychology studying organizational behavior. In psychology, ISS especially focuses on issues that are related to motivation and thought processes. Along this same vein, when thinking of the security-related behavior of malicious individuals, the perspectives of criminology also influence ISS research.

SUMMARY

In this chapter the EA[3] "Cube" Framework and integrated security architecture were presented as examples of how the emerging management practice of enterprise architecture (EA) can provide the context and method for developing effective information security and data privacy controls in government agencies. The EA[3] Framework establishes the overall scope and relationship of the organization's strategic, business, and technology architecture. The security framework is a sub-architecture that pervades all five levels of the EA[3] Framework and includes eight layers that contain information security and data privacy requirements and resources at the enterprise, segment, and system levels of the government agency. The eight layers encompass information security governance; operations security; personnel security; information/data flow security; systems security; application development security; infrastructure security; and physical security.

The chapter covered an integral set of risk-adjusted information security and data privacy solutions that derive from an agency's mission requirements within and across the security architecture's eight layers. The idea of risk-adjusted solutions highlighted the fact that totally foolproof information security and data privacy controls do not exist because EA components (processes and systems) and security solutions are often designed and managed by members of the organization or contracted agents, and "insider" access is the ultimate threat which cannot completely be overcome due to inherent trust relationships and access privileges.

The chapter concluded with a discussion of future trends in EA and security architecture. Only by using EA, can an agency fully address insider threats and information security/data privacy requirements and solutions at the enterprise, segment, and system levels so that the best possible levels of confidentiality, integrity, and availability are provided for the agency's data and information.

REFERENCES

Ankolekar, V. (2003). Application Development Technology & Tools: Vulnerabilities & Threat Management with Secure Programming Practices, a defense in-depth approach. GIAC Security Essentials Certification (GSEC) Practical Assignment, Version 1.4b, Option 1. 10 November 2003.

Babb, J. (2006). Signification and Information Systems Security Policies: a Semiotic Analysis and Case Study. Virginia Commonwealth University School of Business, Department of Information Systems.

Bace, R., Mell, P. (?). NIST-SP800-31 Intrusion Detection Systems. NIST Special Publication on Intrusion Detection Systems.

Barker, W. (June 2004). NIST Special Publication 800-60 Volume 1: Guide for Mapping Types of Information and Information Systems to Security Categories. National Institute of Standards and Technology. Computer Security Division.

Bernard, S. (2001). Evaluating Clinger-Cohen Compliance in Federal Agency Chief Information Officer Positions. Doctoral Dissertation, Virginia Polytechnic Institute and State University, Blacksburg, VA.

Bernard, S. (2005).. An Introduction to Enterprise Architecture: Second Edition. AuthorHouse, Bloomington, IL. ISBN: 1-4208-8050-0. 2005

Center for Information Technology, National Institutes of Health Canadian Trusted Computer Product Evaluation Criteria (CTCPEC). Accessed from http://www.alw.nih.gov/Security/FIRST/papers/criteria/ctcpecl.ps.

CommonCriteria.org (2005) Common Criteria for Information Technology Security Evaluation (CCITSE). Accessed from http://www.commoncriteriaportal.org/public/consumer/index.php?menu=2.

CSIRT Services. Carnegie Mellon University. (2002). Software Engineering Institute. CERT Coordination Center. Stelvio bv, The Netherlands; PRESECURE Consulting GmbH, Germany. Accessed July 2002 from http://www.cert.org/csirts/services.html.

Department of Defense Directive 5200.28-STD (December 1985) Trusted Computer System Evaluation Criteria (TCSEC). Accessed from http://www.boran.com/security/tcsec.html.

Donnelly, M. (April 2000). An Introduction to LDAP. Obtained from http://www.ldapman.org/articles/intro_to_ldap.html.

Federal Information Processing Standards Publication 199. (February 2004).Standards for Security Categorization of Federal Information and Information Systems. National Institute for Standards and Technology, Computer Security Division.

Federal Trade Commission. (June 1998). Privacy Online: A Report to Congress. Chapter 3: Fair Information Practice Principals. Accessed July 2006, from http://www3.ftc.gov/reports/privacy3/priv-23a.pdf.

Federal Trade Commission. (May 2000). Privacy Online: Fair Information Practices in the Electronic Marketplace: A Report to Congress.

Accessed July 2006, from http://www.ftc.gov/reports/privacy2000/privacy2000.pdf.

FISMA Implementation Project. (2003). National Institute for Standards and Technology, Computer Security Division. Accessed July 2006, from http://csrc.nist.gov/sec-cert/ca-proj-phases.html.

Frankel, S., Kent, K., Lewkowski, R., Orebaugh, A., Ritchey, R., & Sharma, S. (December 2005). NIST-SP800-77 Guide to IPsec VPNs - Recommendations of the National Institute of Standards and Technology. Computer Security Division - Information Technology Laboratory - National Institute of Standards and Technology.

Grance, T. et. al. (October 2003). NIST Special Publication 800-64: Security Considerations in the Information System Development Life Cycle: Recommendations of the National Institute of Standards and Technology.

Grance, T. et. al. (January 2004). NIST Special Publication 800-61: Computer Security Incident Handling Guide: Recommendations of the National Institute of Standards and Technology.

Harris, S. (2003). CISSP All-In-One Exam Guide, Third Edition. McGraw-Hill/Osborne, Emeryville, CA. ISBN: 0-07-222966-7.

Hash, J. et. al. (March 2005). NIST Special Publication 800-66: An Introductory Resource Guide for Implementing the Health Insurance Portability and Accountability Act (HIPAA) Security Rule. National Institute of Standards and Technology.

Ho, S M. (2006). Conceptualizing Security Architecture based on Enterprise Architecture. End-of-Coursework Statement. School of Information Studies, Syracuse University. Obtained from http:// Web.syr.edu/~smho/research.htm.

Ho, S M. (2008). Towards A Deeper Understanding of Personnel Anomaly Detection. Encyclopedia of Cyber Warfare and Cyber Terrorism. IDEA Publications.

Ho, S M. (2006). The Mechanism Discovery of Personnel Anomaly Detection. ISOneWorld 2006 Doctoral Symposium, Las Vegas, Nevada, 19-21 April 2006.

Ho, S M. & Caldera, C. (2005). Eight Challenges Faced By a Defense Contractor: An Interview with a Security Chief. (ISC)2 Newsletter May-June 2005. Obtained from https://www.isc2.org/cgi-bin/content.cgi?page=766 on July 18, 2006.

Innella, P. (December 2001). An Introduction to IDS. SecurityFocus.com. Obtained from http://www.securityfocus.com/infocus/1520.

Jansen, W. & Karygiannis, T. NIST Special Publication 800-19: Mobile Agent Security. National Institute of Standards and Technology.

Karygiannis, T. & Owens, L. (November 2002). NIST SP-800-48 Wireless Network Security - 802.11, Bluetooth and Handheld Devices. Recommendations of the National Institute of Standards and Technology. Computer Security Division - Information Technology Laboratory - National Institute of Standards and Technology.

King, C., Dalton, C., and Osmanoglu, T. Security Architecture: Design, Deployment & Operations. Osborne/McGraw-Hill, Berkeley, CA. ISBN: 0-07-213385-6. 2001.

Kuhn, D. Richard, et. al. (August 2002). NIST Special Publication 800-46: Security for Telecommuting and Broadband Communications: Recommendations of the National Institute of Standards and Technology.

Kuhn, D. Richard, et. al. (January 2005). NIST Special Publication 800-58: Security Considerations for Voice Over IP Systems: Recommendations of the National Institute of Standards and Technology.

Kramer, J. (2003). The CISA Prep Guide: Mastering the Certified Information Systems Auditor Exam. Wiley Publishing, Indianapolis, Indiana. ISBN: 0-471-25032-5.

Lyons-Burke, Kathy. (October 2000). NIST Special Publication 800-25: Federal Agency Use of Public Key Technology for Digital Signatures and Authentication. Federal Public Key Infrastructure Steering Committee.

Mason, M. (2005). Obtained from www.asisonline.org/certification/ppt/CPPPersonnelSecurity-Training8-2-01.ppt, July 1, 2006. Lyondell/Equistar Chemical Companies.

Maynard & Ruighaver (2006). What Makes a Good Information Security Policy: A Preliminary Framework For Evaluating Security Policy Quality. Proceedings of the 5th International Security Conference, Las Vegas.

Nassar, M., et. al. (June 2006). Intrusion Detection Methods for VoIP Applications. The Third Annual VoIP Security Workshop. Accessed June 2006 from http://www.iptel.org/voipsecurity/

New Zealand, Security in the Government Sector (2002). Obtained from http://www.security.govt.nz/sigs/html/chapter7.html, June 29, 2006.

National Institute of Science and Technology. Federal Information Processing Standard Publication 199: Standards for Security Categorization of Federal Information and Information Systems.

National Institute of Science and Technology. Special Publication 800-37: Guide for the Security Certification and Accreditation of Information Systems.

National Institute of Science and Technology. Special Publication 800-12. An Introduction to Computer Security: The NIST Handbook. National Institute of Standards and Technology, Technology Administration. Published by U.S. Department of Commerce.

National Institute of Science and Technology. Special Publication 800-53 (Guide for the Selection and Specification of Security Controls for Federal Information Systems),

National Institute of Science and Technology. Special Publication 53A: Techniques and Procedures for Verifying the Effectiveness of Security Controls in Information Systems.

National Institute of Science and Technology. Special Publication 800-60 (Guide for Mapping Types of Information and Information Systems to Security Categorization Levels),

Office of Management and Budget, Federal EA Program Management Office. Federal Enterprise Architecture Security and Privacy Profile (version 1.1). June 2006.

Park, J. S. & Ho, S M. (2004). Composite Role-based Monitoring (CRBM) for Countering Insider Threats. Second Symposium on Intelligence and Security Informatics (ISI), Tucson, Arizona, June 2004.

Pattinson, M. & Anderson, G. (). Information Risk Management: Some Social-psychological Issues.

Qurashi, R. (2005). Eight Steps for Integrating Security Into Application Development. MCI NetSec. Published by ComputerWorld, December 6, 2005. Obtained from http://www.computerworld.com/securitytopics/security/story/0,10801,106805,00.html.

Rodriquez, E. (2005). Physical Network Security. Obtained from http://www.skullbox.net/physical-networksecurity.php, June 29, 2006.

Ross, R.. et. al. (May 2002). NIST Special Publication 800-37: Guide for the Security Certification and Accreditation of Federal Information Systems. National Institute of Standards and Technology, Computer Security Division.

Ross, R. et. al. (February 2005). NIST Special Publication 800-53: Recommended Security Controls for Federal Information Systems. National Institute of Standards and Technology, Computer Security Division.

Siegel, Lloyd H. (2006). Lessons Learned, Dept of Veterans Affairs, Physical Security Assessment Program. Federal Facility Council. Physical Security & Hazard Mitigation Committee, March 14th, 2006. Obtained from www.va.gov/facmgt, June 29, 2006.

Sinha, Rajiv. (March 2001) A Security Checklist for Oracle 9i. Oracle White Papers. Accessed June 2006 from http://www.oracle.com/technology/deploy/security/oracle9i/pdf/9i_checklist.pdf.

Snouffer, R., et. al. (June 2001). NIST Special Publication 800-29: A Comparison of the Security Requirements for Cryptographic Modules in FIPS 140-1 AND FIPS 140-2.

Spears, J. (2006). Defining Information Security. The Pennsylvania State University, Smeal College of Business. 5th Security Conference 2006. Las Vegas, Nevada.

Spewak, S. and Hill, S. (1992). Enterprise Architecture Planning. Developing a Blueprint for Data, Applications and Technology. John Wiley and Sons, Inc. New York. ISBN: 0-471-599859.

State of Arkansas (2004). Personnel Security. Office of Information Technology. Document Number SS-70-007. February 2004.

Stoneburner, G., et. al. (July 2002). NIST Special Publication 800-30: Risk Management Guide for Information Technology Systems: Recommendations of the National Institute of Standards and Technology.

Swanson, M. (November 2001). NIST Special Publication 800-26: Security Self-Assessment Guide for Information Technology Systems. National Institute of Standards and Technology, Computer Security Division.

Swanson, M. et. al. (June 2002). NIST Special Publication 800-34: Contingency Planning Guide for Information Technology Systems: Recommendations of the National Institute of Standards and Technology.

The Open Group. (1995-2005). Single Sign-On. Obtained from http://www.opengroup.org/security/sso/.

Tracy, M. et. al. (September 2002). NIST Special Publication 800-44: Guidelines on Securing Public Web Servers: Recommendations of the National Institute of Standards and Technology.

Tracy, M. et. al. (September 2002). NIST Special Publication 800-45: Guidelines on Electronic Mail Security: Recommendations of the National Institute of Standards and Technology.

United Kingdom, Department of Trade and Industry (June 1991) Information Technology System Evaluation Criteria (IITSEC). Accessed from http://nsi.org/Library/Compsec/eurooran.txt.

United States Congress (1996) Public Law 191-104 Health Information Portability and Accountability Act of 1996. Accessed from http://fr Webgate.access.gpo.gov/cgi-bin/getdoc.cgi?dbname=104_cong_public_laws&docid=f:publ191.104.

United States Congress (2002) Public Law 204-107 Sarbanes-Oxley Act of 2002. Accessed from Accessed from http://fr Webgate.access.gpo.gov/cgi-bin/getdoc.cgi?dbname=107_cong_public_laws&docid=f:publ204.107.

United States Congress (2002) Public Law 347-107 Federal Information Security Management Act of 2002. http://fr Webgate.access.gpo.gov/cgi-bin/getdoc.cgi?dbname=107_cong_public_laws&docid=f:publ347.107.

United States Department of Justice System Development Life Cycle Guidance Document. (2003). The Department of Justice Information Resource Management, January 2003. Obtained from http://www.usdoj.gov/jmd/irm/lifecycle/table.htm.

United States House of Representatives Government Reform Committee (February 2005) Federal Computer Security Report Card for 2003 – 2004.

Accessed from http://reform.house.gov/Upload-edFiles/Computer%20Security%20Report%20c ard%202%20years.pdf.

Wack, J., et. al. (January 2002). NIST Special Publication 800-41: Guidelines on Firewalls and Firewall Policy: Recommendations of the National Institute of Standards and Technology.

Wack, J., et. al. (October 2003). NIST Special Publication 800-42: Guideline on Network Security Testing: Recommendations of the National Institute of Standards and Technology.

Wiedman, B. (2005). Database Security (Common-Sense Principles.) GovernmentSecurity. org Network Security Resources. Obtained from http://www.governmentsecurity.org/articles/DatabaseSecurityCommon-sensePrinciples.php.

Wilson, M., Zafra, D., Pitcher, S., Tressler, J., Ippolito, J. (1998). NIST Special Publication 800-16: Information Technology Security Training Requirements: A Role- and Performance- Based Model. National Institute of Standards and Technology, Computer Security Division.

Zachman, J. (1989). "A Framework for Information Systems Architecture." IBM Systems Journal. Volume 26, Number 3.

Chapter XVI
Architecture Based Engineering of Enterprises with Government Involvement

RMIT University, Australia

Laszlo Nemes
Nemes Consulting, Australia

ABSTRACT

With a plethora of architectures, modelling techniques and methodologies on offer, it is difficult to decide how to begin building an enterprise and achieving seamless integration. This difficulty is most noticeable in consortia that need to deal with government participation. Various government projects have different objectives and agenda. In addition, changes in business environment (or) as well as government policies impose extra conditions onto the project. Failure to comply with the project requirement can lead to loss of business and sometimes unexpected penalty. We use three case studies to show various ways of government involvements in our projects. Based on the experiences of these cases, we discuss how enterprise engineering can help creating and managing the enterprise that can engage government services successfully

INTRODUCTION

Today's working environments are supported with a large number of technologies that serve wide va-

riety of purposes such as training (Shankararaman and Lee, 1994), support (Mo and Menzel, 1998), design (Jiang and Mo, 2001), project management (Hall, 2000), data analysis (Gabbar *et al*, 2002), and many others related to the management of the business. They are, arguably, advantages to all stakeholders, irrespective of whether they are the customers, staff, suppliers, managers or other roles related to the company.

In this environment, human organisations can become volatile. This is particularly noticeable in government activities because they are principally people-oriented services to the public. Government processes are changing to e-Government environment but there is still difficulty in capturing the concept of citizen engagement, which is a measure of success of government policies (Jones *et al*, 2007). Government services have a wide variety of forms and purposes. When people look at government services, they only realise the public face of the services, that is, the interactive portal of government departments. However, there are many other services that a government has to provide and the enterprise engineering processes in those services must be handled carefully to ensure the best outcome. Orange *et al* (2007) investigated the innovation value in government and recognized the importance of a clear vision for the future. Government funded programmes for enterprise development are difficult to manage. Some governments adopting a "private sector" model for delivering "public good" services faced with considerable challenges of understanding organizational dynamics, for which government agencies were not competent enough to handle effectively (Massey, 2003).

Enterprise architecture adoption in government businesses is important but there are many patterns (Hjort-Madsen, 2007). It is difficult to decide which one to adopt since they are emergent, evolving, embedded, fragmented, provisional. Wu (2007) proposed layering method in the direction of strategy, business, process, service and information for developing enterprise integration in e-government. Gregor *et al* (2007) used enterprise architecture for enabling alignment of IS/IT in government. Enterprise architecture should enable these services to be delivered to the

desired outcomes. The concept of the government operating as an enterprise is to include not only the systems that support government services, but also to understand the management processes that may affect the effectiveness of the execution of government policies.

The term enterprise refers to an identifiable group of people who have a common vision and mission. An enterprise concerns all aspects of tasks, activities, events related to this group. Integration of the enterprise activities requires modelling and analysis of the business processes, process data and knowledge within the enterprise (Shen *et al*, 2004). A holistic, customer oriented approach in enterprise integration helps companies to cater for different requirements and more importantly, provides a way to implement a good solution for integration (Oritz *et al*, 1999).

This chapter serves as a guide to the design and implementation of government supported enterprises. We discuss the importance of enterprise engineering in the design and execution of enterprise models to cope with changes. Three case studies are used to illustrate the different forms of government services and the impact different enterprise engineering approaches on the outcomes. By comparing these cases, we develop the view of a new dimension in modelling to cater for change.

BACKGROUND

Williams *et al* (1994) summarised architectures of enterprises as a result of evolution from years of experimentation and observation. The ultimate goal of enterprise integration is to develop a cohesive environment that can perform business activities in a seamless fashion and to be responsive to the external world in a timely way. However, the operating conditions of enterprises and more significantly, government environment, are now characterised by frequent changes. The challenge to management is to establish a structure that can cope with the changing operating conditions. Success for achieving the goal therefore demands well-coordinated agility in all internal and external relationships of the enterprise.

While it is clear that an enterprise exists to fulfil a mission, the owners of an enterprise still have to define their own objectives and establish rules and operating parameters that are leading to achieving the mission. Two desires are becoming more important in modern enterprise design and development:

- The customer's desire to get products and services to the exact specifications and to receive them in a timely manner.
- The enterprise's desire to produce goods and services only for orders, rather than for distribution networks to identified customers by maximizing operation flexibility.

Many different studies have been trying to develop a concrete body of knowledge that address these issues. Business process re-engineering has been popular in commercial businesses where changes of existing business environment are crucial to the survival of the company in highly competitive market. Wortman *et al* (2000) embedded enterprise software into extended enterprise models to adapt the business to changing operating conditions. Enabling agility in enterprise can be done through the introduction of reconfigurable systems and components to the operation (Weston, 1999). Depending on the problem at hand, human and organisational issues are often addressed as a secondary function and are developed separately on the basis of new information systems being put in place to extract efficiency out of the existing environment.

In practice, an enterprise will need an architecture that defines, not only to the knowledge of the owners but also to many others who are working on matters related to the enterprise. An enterprise architecture is the anatomy of the system defining the protocols, rules, processes and activities that the enterprise should run, and at the same time, enables a smooth business process environment for inter-company operations (Patankar and Sadiga, 1995). It is crucial that an enterprise involving government activities requires more public accountability than private organisations, should be supported by a systematic design methodology that adequately describes the logistics in the enterprise and helps the management to develop well defined policy and process across organisational boundaries.

Enterprise Engineering

Enterprise Engineering is a discipline that has taken an overarching view of all aspects of enterprise knowledge areas including:

- Integration of information, operation and services
- Business process modelling and analysis
- Total product life cycle development that includes concurrent engineering
- Globally networked organization taking supply chain management to a global view
- Resources planning that covers finance as well as human and organizational issues

Today very few companies offer their products and services from their own in house resources alone (Nemes and Mo, 2004). In fact most agile enterprises cooperate with large number of suppliers and sub-contractors. Similarly, government services must focus on the fundamental processes that are required to provide and encompass - as critical parts of - the entire chain of value adding activities in the society. Enterprise activities may change quickly and so the respective business process should follow them closely. The dynamism of the enterprise throughout the whole life-cycle of the enterprise is critical and should be assessed in the early stage of design (Van den Berg and Tolle, 2000).

To indicate the complexity of the issues, it is worth pointing out that integration of enterprise subsystems started in the seventies. The initial approaches had failed to deliver the complex integration of large system as they used different methods for linking various applications. Companies, university, research consortium in Japan, Europe and the US started addressing the problem of system integration applying different concepts and using special definitions. The International Federation of Information Processing (IFIP) and the International Federation of Automatic Control (IFAC) established a joint Task Force in early 1990s to investigate whether it was possible to find common grounds among different schools of thoughts on enterprise architectures so that enterprise designers have a common language to communicate and to cooperate. The IFIP-IFAC Task Force (1999) invited leading enterprise engineering researchers working together to develop a unified view of what enterprise engineering should be.

The work of the Task Force was based on several enterprise architectures existed at that time. The CIMOSA project funded by the European ESPRIT research program was the most significant effort to define an enterprise architecture that had four major views: functions, resources, human and finance (Kosanke *et al*, 1999). CIMOSA was particularly useful for discrete manufacturing systems where workflow and processes are highly versatile. PERA, on the other hand, originated from the study of computer integrated manufacturing in the process industries, handled the management of the enterprise using a phased development view (Williams, 1994). Through the top down approach and the visualisation of interconnectivity of phased functions and activities, the enterprise architecture could be laid out in advance of the project development stage (Li and Williams, 1997 and 2000). GRAI methodology took a different approach to segregate the enterprise as decision centres that were linked by an enterprise wide information system (Chen

et al, 1997). Execution of the decisions would be performed by the physical system at the operational level (Doumeingts *et al*, 2000).

Several immediate issues are almost unavoidable:

*   There are too many technologies. It is almost impossible for an individual enterprise to evaluate every technology and decide which one best suits the application.
*   There are different methods for mapping architectures one on another.
*   Modelling toolbox is large and it is full with variety of products
*   The enterprise engineer should familiarize oneself with the nature of the business before it starts working on its integration.

There are risks in enterprise engineering. Enterprises are complex entities that can fail easily if they are not designed properly, that is, the rules and processes are not established to handle changing circumstances. Malladi and Min (2005) used risk models to assist in the selection of information technology infrastructures for rural communities. The essence of enterprise engineering is to treat the enterprise as a complex product with a set of principles. Enterprise risks can be minimised by applying the science of enterprise engineering to design and make changes to the enterprise.

Enterprise Architecture Standards: Path to Solution

Government enterprise processes are inherently more complicated due to their nature of business. Mednikarov and Dereliev (2004) attempted to define naval tasks in structured description to assist in the development of enterprise architecture. Bruce (2006) described information linkages for multiple government agencies in New Zealand. Burk (2006) described the long term vision of the enterprise architecture managing US budget. Elliman *et al* (2007) were working on an exploratory project investigating enterprise architecture for government. There is no universally acceptable concept of enterprise architecture in government.

An enterprise involves people, assets and information. There are also processes that govern the interaction of these elements. The totality of these systems and subsystems forms the anatomy of an enterprise. Different industries have different practices that are usually evolved from experience. Past practices are useful references but they are not necessarily correct in a new environment. Design of an enterprise requires understanding the necessary elements in the anatomy of enterprises and their inter-relationships or constraints. An enterprise architecture provides the basic building blocks.

Experience has shown that if an enterprise is below a certain level of technology and management culture, integration by technologies is not feasible. On the other hand, if the enterprise is operating reasonably well, and there is already some form of process management and automated information capturing, then integration architectures and methods can dramatically improve the operation of the company (Sulin *et al*, 1997). The minimum criterion for readiness to integration is a management culture for willingness of thinking strategically and acting accordingly. Financial consideration is another major issue and the best way is to justify it with the returns from the integration process (in a way, self-financing).

The existence of many enterprise modelling methodologies makes it hard for general business practitioners to select the best for their modelling requirements (Vernadat, 2002). The method to design an enterprise that will perform as expected at the start depends on the expertise of the enterprise engineer in:

- Understanding the anatomy of the enterprise;
- Modelling system behaviours in sufficient details;

- Improving operations on a continuous, predictable fashion.

Once the architecture is defined, the details are captured using suitable modelling tools. System behaviours such as rules, procedures, decision criteria, quality controls and so on need to be described and understood. These enterprise behaviours are sometimes described as bureaucracy if not enough flexibility built into the system to adjust for unforeseeable situations.

HOW TO ENGINEER AN ENTERPRISE

To achieve the goal of designing an enterprise that is fit for the mission, we need to:

- Design the system architecture;
- Develop proven methods to eliminate errors in the system;
- Develop tools that assist in the design, validation, preparation and implementation phases.

Adoption of an enterprise architecture is an important starting point of enterprise engineering project. The Generalised Enterprise Reference Architecture and Methodology (GERAM) describes a set of principles that can be used for the design, management, continuous improvement and operation of enterprises (Figure 1). GERAM defines a complete methodology that captures the engineering and integration requirements for any organisation to develop a fit-for-purpose enterprise model supporting its business. GERAM encompasses essential enterprise concepts of life cycles, life history, partial models and generated views (Noran, 2005). It distinguishes the functions of modelling framework, modelling languages and modelling tools in the process of design, implementation and operation of enterprise architectures. Following the recommendations of

GERAM, an enterprise designer will be able to make informed, less risky decisions on which enterprise architecture should be used for his/her enterprise.

We now have a framework to work on. The next question is how this can be done step by step? What are the tasks that should go first and how? It is usual that the start of this activity can be seen easily but the rest of the project is not that visible when people are loaded with other simultaneous work.

Enterprise engineering processes prepare more thorough understanding of the project by three major steps:

- Build the AS-IS structure of the enterprise. This requires detailed analysis of the operation of functions, relationships in the

Figure 1. GERAM (Bernus & Nemes, 1996)

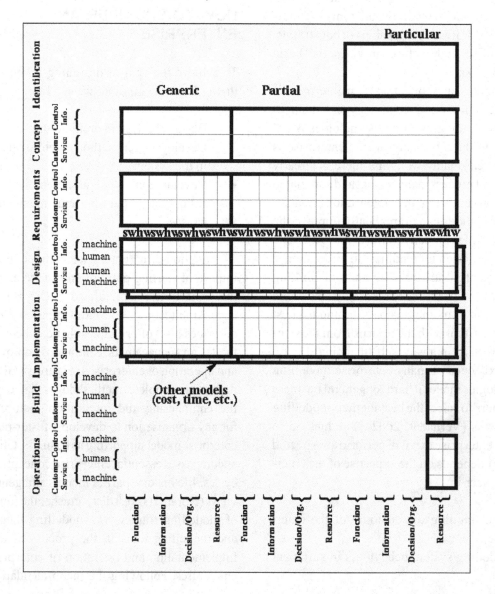

organisational structures, and the available information management systems. To do that the enterprise engineer organises focus groups addressing each of the areas, but making it sure that the groups will cooperate with each other. That sort of joint work has to be documented with the kind of systems description methods familiar with the people involved. The range of the tools varies depending on the technical background of the members of the teams. It can be drawings with simple labels on the components, or sophisticated modelling language (which usually requires technical training for the participants). This step requires a bottom up approach, analysis detailed solution and working upwards to create the bird eye views which is needed in later stages.

- The next major activity is to define the TO-BE state. This is a design phase where the enterprise engineers together with the management develop the model how the enterprise will operate in the future re-engineered state. The teams here work in a top down manner creating the overall views first and putting detailed information in the description as the model progresses.

- After that comes the Migration phase. When designing these activities one needs not only consider the logical steps in the change process. As most of the time we modify existing operations therefore the integration system must not bring the enterprise to halt, or compromise safety and security when making changes. The modification of the processes should be implemented in a proper time sequence making sure that the adjustments in the processes make use of the operation of all the other components.

To assist in understanding the development and implementation of an enterprise architecture, we use three case studies to illustrate the process and methods and their implications to engineering of

government related enterprises. These examples include: a defence service enterprise, a research enterprise and an industry enterprise.

Case Study: Product Life Time Service Enterprise

The ANZAC Ship Alliance (ASA) is an organization formed as a virtual enterprise agreement between Tenix Defence, Saab Systems and the Australian Government with the aim to provide design and implementation of changes to the ANZAC class frigates in service over the life time of the product. It is an attempt of all parties involved in the creation of the ANZAC fleet to provide a stable support environment ensuring that the ships are always combat ready, fit for purpose at any given time with the best value outcome. The Alliance is not a legal company (entity). It is indeed a Virtual Enterprise (VE) as activities span across the three main participants. It draws the most suitable resources such as staff and asset from the member organizations as required for a particular project.

The ASA case illustrates a defence related enterprise architecture design and development project in which the Government is a key component of the enterprise. It shows that when collaborating with the private sector for support of its asset, the Government needs to participate actively in the definition of the enterprise.

To engineer the enterprise, we developed the AS-IS structure using the PERA model and solicited information through an initial briefing session with the key executives of the ANZAC Ship Alliance (ASA). The AS-IS model served as an important guiding tool for formulating questions and focusing the effort of investigation during subsequent meetings and process examination. From this investigation, it was found that due to the requirements of the defence materiel acquisition process, there were a number of government processes that had to be satisfied before a final decision could be made. These processes formed a series of cascaded life cycles which were interconnected as shown in Figure 2.

The concept of a new organisation was evolved from a number of meetings with the Defence, both formally and informally, to identify the mission of this enterprise and define its structure. This was followed by signing of agreement and development of management plan for the alliance. The ASA was officially launched with the establishment of ANZAC Ship Alliance Management Office (ASAMO) in Perth. These series of actions were modelled as the left hand cycle in Figure 2.

When the ASAMO was in operation, it started to develop projects that were initiated by the customer, that is, the Royal Australian Navy. Each project would go through four initial stages of planning and two stages of completion (middle cycle).

For each of the step in the Projects cycle, depending on the expertise and responsibility, the task can be taken up by any of the partners in the ASA. The partners will have their own project cycle as shown in the spawned off projects in the right hand cycle.

Based on the life cycle model in Figure 2, the enterprise engineering team developed an ASA enterprise model using PERA. To populate the ASA model, we used two major instruments: questionnaires and interviews. On the basis of the PERA model, the questionnaire was structured in 22 parts. Each part examined different aspects of the virtual enterprise including the specific objectives of the virtual enterprise in a particular area, the actions that were taken to achieve the objectives and the performance indicators that the enterprise adopted. The questionnaire was distributed to all levels of personnel in the ASA. In conjunction with the questionnaire, a series of in-depth interviews was conducted with selected personnel and work groups. The objectives of the interviews were to clarify answers and verify the coherence of opinions between different parts of the enterprise. The ASA had many participants from different backgrounds and personal aspirations. In the process of soliciting commonality, there were contradicting views and deviations from normal practices. The purpose was not to suppress but rather find a way to deal with these non-common issues. The best method was to isolate these views and practices so that the enterprise could work out solutions for them.

Figure 2. Life cycle model in the ANZAC ship alliance

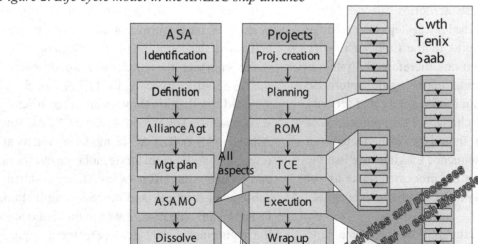

Note: ROM = Rough Order of Magnitude; TCE = Target Cost Estimate

Figure 3 – Effect of different performance indicators on organisational objective

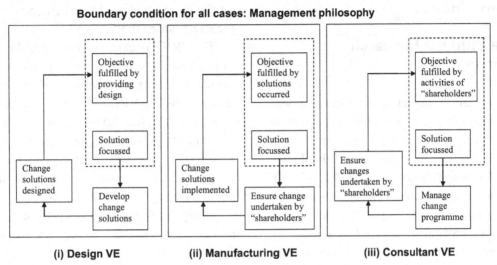

Boundary condition for all cases: Management philosophy

(i) Design VE **(ii) Manufacturing VE** **(iii) Consultant VE**

The focus was on how the decision centres operated within the boundary condition specified in that part of the interview, including their objectives (What do you want to achieve?), action (What do you do in order to achieve the objective?), performance indicator (How do you know you have achieved the objective?).

Next, we analysed the AS-IS enterprise model and developed the TO-BE model. The outcome of the model analysis was crucial to the study of the TO-BE enterprise architecture. Activity plans, information system design, processes and many other aspects of the enterprise were determined by the organisational objective. Three potential TO-BE enterprises were identified through this process. In Figure 3(i), the focus was to develop change solutions and the success for this action was measured by the solution successfully designed. The Alliance had the responsibility to provide design of the changes and hence the nature of the VE was a Design VE. In Figure 3(ii), the focus is to ensure that the industry partners (i.e. members of the Alliance) to undertake change for the ANZAC ships. The measure of success in this case is the occurrence of the solution. The Alliance has the responsibility of making the change and hence it

is a Manufacturing VE by nature. In the last case shown in Figure 3(iii), the focus is on managing the change programme. The VE has no obligation to effect change if the shareholders refuse to make changes. It is an arm's length situation and hence the VE is a Consultant VE.

It is important that the members of the ASA understand what goals they are working towards. Immediately after this part of the study, the ASA held a series of workshops involving all levels of personnel to define exactly what the organisational objective should be. The result was a clear statement that confirmed the ASA should be developed as a Consultant VE.

The migration phase was a long process. To begin with, the ASA searched for an information infrastructure system that could potentially be used throughout the lifecycle of the enterprise as well as its projects. There were some lessons learned, for example, in defining the expectation between different parts of the consortium. It was eventually decided to develop a Web-based project management system that provided the communication and coordination hub among all participants (Mo *et al*, 2006). This was proved to be vital as a first step towards implementing a

Consultant VE with different software platforms used by the partners.

A Case Study: A Research Enterprise

The Globeman21 project was an international research project under the Intelligent Manufacturing Systems Program investigating the application of information and communications technologies in the 21st century (Larsen and Vesterager, 1999). Although it was completed eight years ago and many aspects of it have been published but it is important that we point out some lessons relevant to this topic. The project was funded by several Governments including Japan (through Ministry of International Trade and Industry or MITI), European Commission (through Framework Program V or FP5), Australia (through Industrial Research Alliance Program or IRAP).

The Globeman21 project was a large scale international project and the results were disseminated through 15 industry demonstrators. The VRIDGE Demonstrator was initiated by Toyo Engineering (one of Japanese partners) and had involvement of partners from Australia, Finland, Denmark, Norway and UK. The objective of VRIDGE demonstrator project was to study how manufacturing systems, integrated with ICT, could change both the business and life styles of engineers. By applying the proper information access and control, the communication in extended enterprises was more secure than in ordinary companies.

The VRIDGE Demonstrator hypothesised the pervasive use of information and communication technologies in the future in such a way that was unimaginable at the time of the project. It was assumed that all business activities would be supported by the innovation of ICT through more efficient office processing which would carry out most of the manual works humans had to do at the time. IT would strongly support the collaboration through information and knowledge sharing on the network and staff could concentrate on the intellectual works, which could produce the value-added functions.

The VRIDGE example illustrated the application of enterprise engineering methodologies to the design and experimentation of new or future enterprises. The VRIDGE enterprise did not exist at the time when the project was done but the outcome of this work laid the foundation for Toyo Engineering to establish enterprise integration capabilities that eventually span off as an independent enterprise system developing company.

Using the three step enterprise engineering process, the VRIDGE project team developed the AS-IS enterprise model of the existing project enterprise using PERA architecture.

A formal definition was needed to identify the requirements for the enterprise model of the "VRIDGE Inc". In order to develop the necessary models, several commercial tools were evaluated. It was concluded that no single modelling tool satisfied all our requirements at this moment, and hence we used a combination of these tools for different modelling objectives.

The KBSI AI0Win, an IDEF0 based modelling tool, had been used for business process analysis and model presentation. The FirstSTEP, a user-friendly enterprise modelling tool from Interface Technologies, was selected for interactive enterprise modelling and simulation. The FirstSTEP had also been used to identify the cross company boundary information access and control requirements by using its "swimming lane" presentation. We also selected METIS, from NCR, as a core modelling tool and model repository because of its flexibility. The ontology based model mapping facility was developed in METIS environment.

According to the PERA methodology, we needed the Enterprise Business Entities (EBE) which was fundamental for achieving a shared understanding of the virtual enterprise. However, we found that there were quite different views on what would be the business for the VRIDGE Inc. In order to get a common understanding we categorised the business entities according to their lifecycles. We identified three lifecycles closely related to the VRIDGE Inc., as shown in Figure 4. They were:

- The lifecycle of the VRIDGE Inc. (i.e. producer of the XFU Plant),
- The lifecycle of the XFU Plant (i.e. product of the VRIDGE Inc.),
- The lifecycle of Xylene as a product (i.e. product of the XFU Plant).

The identification of these three lifecycles helped us to achieve a common understanding of the business process of the VRIDGE Inc. where the product lifecycle was embedded. It was in this business process (enterprise lifecycle) where we identified the product related activities (product lifecycle), and further identified the information access and control requirements of the product lifecycle. The AS-IS model showed a lot of constraints by the technology at the time, particularly on the availability of Internet, bandwidth, data

exchange standards, communication technologies and application integration platforms.

The authors held a series of training session on how to design enterprises using architectures and conducted workshops with the partners of the project as well as including other Globeman21 participants to determine the future vision and mission of the hypothetical company in the mid of 21st century. The TO-BE enterprise architecture that would overcome the constraints was developed and new business processes that could connect clients, employees and organisations flexibly on the network were defined (Shinonome *et al*, 1998). Part of this work was the definition for enterprise policies:

- Information policies:
  - o Secure, authenticated information exchange
  - o Use of minimal distributed database
  - o Use of open communication network (Internet, ISDN/telephone)
- Operation policies (plant engineering project):

Figure 4. Lifecycles related to the VRIDGE Inc.

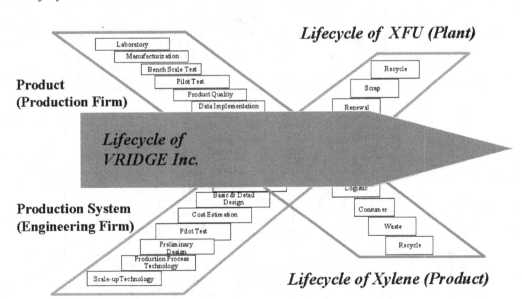

- o Client can enter at multiple points of the plant design / construction life-cycle
- o Distributed operation
- o Collaborative work demonstration
- • VRIDGE design policies:
  - o Use of object oriented technologies
  - o Use of version control
  - o Maintain dependence information
- • VRIDGE technology policies:
  - o Use of STEP
  - o Use of STEP tools
  - o Use of commercial CSCW tools
- • Security policies:
  - o Use of firewalls

Since the VRIDGE enterprise was a research enterprise, the partners decided to test the new architecture by executing it within Globeman21 project environment. To achieve this goal, the project team developed the VRIDGE Workbench, which provided an interface for visualizing and controlling the working environment. VRIDGE Workbench comprised three service layers (Figure 5).

1. Coordinator
   Tools for the VRIDGE Inc project initiation execution, and dismissal:
   - o The modeling/design tools for the VRIDGE Inc.
   - o The operation management tool (member profiles, contacts, capabilities, etc.)
   - o Negotiate/Specify the protocols
   - o Daily supervise/monitor/support
2. Collaborator
   Tools for VRIDGE Inc collaboration (mainly through information access and control):
   - o Manage the distribution/ exchange of product information
   - o Manage the review and release of product information
   - o Manage the access right
   - o Product information change management

Figure 5. VRIDGE workbench layers

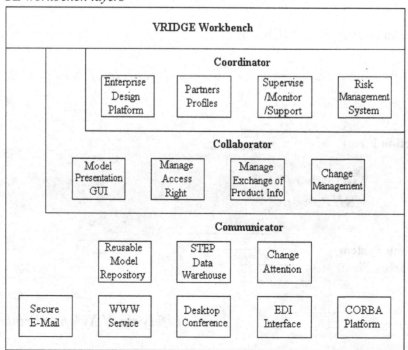

3. Communicator
    Tools for support the VRIDGE Inc Communication:
    o   Basic IT Infrastructure
    o   Enable/facilitate the exchange/sharing of product information
    o   Enable/facilitate the communication among the members of the VRIDGE Inc
    o   Provide a central information repository

The VRIDGE Workbench was implemented as a Web-based portal as shown in Figure 6.

The VRIDGE Inc. was a virtual enterprise which carried out the design, procurement, construction, and manufacturing of a chemical plant (Shinonome *et al*, 1998). The VRIDGE Inc. facilitated the understanding of global manufacturing business processes and the investigation of the requirements for global product information access and control. A group of 20 staff from the partners participated in the testing of the functionality of the system (Figure 7).

The success in this work was the development of the conceptual framework for understanding the formation, operations and information control of the extended enterprise. Substantial challenges were encountered at the starting stage of the project when the background of participants had prevented people to think more cohesively.

The VRIDGE case illustrates a research related Enterprise Architecture in which government provides funding to the industry on research work only. From the government's point of view, it is important that the companies in the project could research and improve their competitiveness in the global market. This was demonstrated using a short success story approach and simulated within the modelling tools used in this demonstrator (Figure 8).

Government enterprise design shares many similar aspects as VRIDGE. For example, existing government processes do not normally exist

Figure 6. Realised VRIDGE workbench

Figure 7. Roles to test VRIDGE Inc. concept

Region	Organization	Name	E-Mail	Role
Japan	TEC	Masashi Shinonome	shin@ims.toyo-eng.co.jp	Administrator
		Hidehisa Hashimoto	hashimoto@ims.toyo-eng.co.jp	Design Engineer/IT Engineer
		Atsuyoshi Fuse	afuse@ims.toyo-eng.co.jp	IT Engineer
	Takenaka	Tetsuya Miyagawa	miyagawa.tetsuya@takenaka.co.jp	Enterprise Engineer/Design Engineer
		Kazuyoshi Watanabe	watanabe.kazuyoshi@takenaka.co.jp	IT Engineer
	Omron	Norio Yoshikawa	ysk@fox.ybp.omron.co.jp	Enterprise Engineer/Design Engineer
		Ken-ichiro Mori	mori@rza.mac.omron.co.jp	IT Engineer
	MES	Yoshinori Naruko	ynaruko@mes.co.jp	Design Engineer/IT Engineer
	ETL	Michiharu Tukamoto	tukamoto@etl.go.jp	Consultant of Distributed OO Environment
Australia	CSIRO	Laszlo Nemes	lnm@mlb.dmt.csiro.au	Consultant of Enterprise Modelling
		Mingwei Zhou	mwz@mlb.dmt.csiro.au	Enterprise Engineer/Process Engineer
		John Mo	jmo@mlb.dmt.csiro.au	IT Engineer
		Yong Tie	yong@syd.dmt.csiro.au	IT Engineer
	Griffith U.	Peter Bernus	bernus@cit.gu.edu.au	Consultant of Enterprise Modelling
		Greg Uppington	greg@cit.gu.edu.au	Enterprise Engineer
	HDH	Doug McPherson	mcpherson.doug@hdh.com.au	Design Engineer
		Robert Alexandar	alexander.robert@hdh.com.au	Design Engineer
		John Politis	john_politis_at_hdh__bankstown@c ww.hdh.com.au	Design Engineer
Europe	NCR	Frank Lillehagen	fli@metis.no	Enterprise Engineer
		Sobah Abbas Petersen	sap@metis.no	Enterprise Engineer

Figure 8. Screens of the short success story

due to changes in government or its policies. The development is often one off and does not repeat in other governments (e.g. local government). The migration from manual paper based process to latest ICT based enterprise is clear. Hence, enterprise engineering approach, especially referencing to the use of specific enterprise architectures, is particularly relevant. The moral of the example is that visionary research will show the way for development, thus reduces the cost for not making too many mistakes. The final result is that technical and financial risks will be minimized.

An Example: Virtual Enterprise of SMEs

The Australian government strongly encouraged SMEs to be competitive on the world market

Figure 9. The RELINK VERA lifecycles

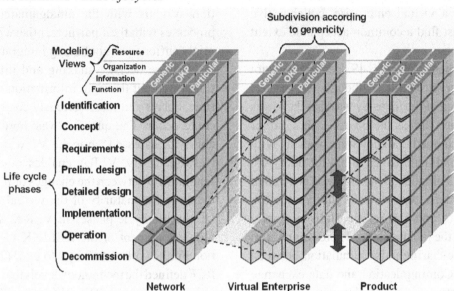

without being protected by tariffs. There was an important demonstrator project to show that small toolmakers, which usually compete for orders, could successfully cooperate when the job is too big, or when the deadline is too short for any one participant. Government involvement in this case has been predominantly an industry support role in which the work will be continued after the project. Intermediate reporting is essential on a quarterly basis.

The RELINK initiative demonstrated the methodologies and systems that would enable small firms in the tooling and automotive industry to participate with medium and large firms in turnkey projects as part of a broader supply chain. Globalisation has forced companies to work together in a new arrangement known as virtual enterprise. The characteristics of virtual enterprises are flexible, dynamic with minimal or sometimes no contractual agreements among the partners. A virtual enterprise can be created and disbanded in very short time frames. Interaction at organizational, technical, social and commercial levels give rise to emergent properties that have specific technical, communications and infra-

structural issues. The design of the enterprise is a crucial step towards successful operation. The enterprise engineering design of RELINK is based on the Virtual Enterprise Reference Architecture (VERA) (Zwegers *et al*, 2003), which defines three entities, the network entity, the VE entity and the product entity (Figure 9).

Each of these three entities is represented by a life cycle describing possible phases. An entity can be operating from identification to decommission. The important characteristic of VERA is the changes of architecture requirements in different phases of the virtual enterprise. Conceptually, there are 3 architectures: Information Systems, Manufacturing Equipment and Human and Organisational architectures. Information systems and manufacturing equipment architectures represent automation of information and materials flows. Human and organisational architecture sits between the two architectures and serves as the operating centre of the virtual enterprise. It is essential that a balance is required to ensure all three architectures are running in supporting each other rather than one moving too far ahead (or behind). Individual companies may vary the balancing point (known as extent of automation) but in a virtual enterprise, collaborative partners must find a common acceptable extent of automation.

Development of the AS-IS scenario was not a straight-forward task. Although the general understanding of the industry was that there was no cooperation across the board, several larger companies claimed that they were working with groups of small companies to bid for new jobs. After a series of industry visits, it was concluded that these groups were basically sub-contracting arrangements and the relationships normally ended when the job was done. There was no sign of knowledge sharing and accumulation, between the parties. Communication and data exchange between partners in these circumstances were largely through meetings and paper transfer. This situation was primarily classified as the Network entity.

VERA provided a clear migration path for this tooling industry virtual enterprise. The TO-BE scenario would logically be the Virtual Enterprise entity. For a virtual enterprise to succeed:

- All partners in the virtual enterprise, irrespective of its size, must communicate with the same protocol at the enterprise level;
- A unified (or standard) information and physical architecture must be agreed by all partners in the virtual enterprise;
- Irrespective of the level of ICT employed by individual toolmakers, the intermediate layer of functions must be fulfilled by alternative technologies;
- The information and physical architectures must be in place in all entities (network, VE and product) and in all phases of the virtual entities. The architectures will vary in content.

The migration from AS-IS to TO-BE scenario in RELINK required the ability of the companies to quickly align their objectives and information systems with the amalgamated business processes with their partners, otherwise, the VE might suffer from not having integrated support of effective decision-making and informed actions. Without the right information at the right time, delays and more seriously costly mistakes could occur. The question was: how could this ability be assessed while the VE was still in the Network entity. VERA enables modelling the relationship between the changes of ICT requirements to the maturity of the virtual enterprise, i.e. the life cycle phases in VERA. This led to the development of the RELINK Communication Framework (RCF) by Mo *et al* (2005). The RCF defined the technology levels that guided the industry partners in RELINK to quickly establish ICT alignment by identifying the technologies and possibly commercial products that could be acquired immediately.

The RELINK case study illustrated an important aspect for government enterprise architecture designer. SMEs do not have tremendous ICT resources. If there is a need for SMEs to work with the government enterprise in a new system, the ability of the SMEs to cope with the new technology level is vital to the success of the new project. The costs involved, irrespective of who is going to pay, must be taken into account.

The RELINK case illustrates an industry virtual enterprise in which government plays a monitoring role (with progress report and participation requirements). The Enterprise Architecture has to be both incentive to small business as well as return to government – in terms of SME engagement rate. We demonstrated that enterprise engineering could facilitate a simultaneous harmony of competition and cooperation of networked enterprises which the government had visibility on its formation, requirements, tasks and processes.

DYNAMICS OF CHANGE: FUTURE RESEARCH ISSUES

There are several messages from the three case studies. The involvement of government in enterprise formation is complex and often requires significant changes and innovative approaches to satisfy what is needed to achieve the goals. An important observation of these cases is the fact that they are all designed and executed in a virtual enterprise environment. Clarity of mission is critical to defining a pathway and adoption of appropriate enterprise architecture for the virtual enterprise. This point of view is supported by the findings by Sackett *et al* (2003). Once an enterprise architecture is adopted, enterprise engineering is the key to enable the project to proceed.

The global market is changing in an ever increasing speed. There are new entrants to compete or cooperate with, existing partners are changing their business profiles and leave the network together with old, established companies who simply go out of businesses. In this kaleidoscope dynamics of the business world it

Figure 10. Time dimension in enterprise engineering

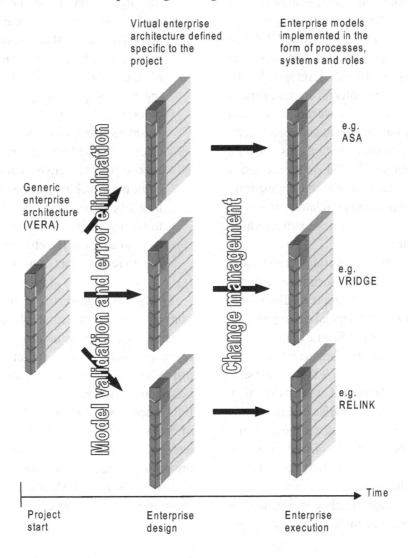

is vital that enterprises operating in such agile business environments can adapt to new, unforeseeable circumstances quickly. The use of integration methodologies alone is not enough as they require time consuming modelling done by iterations. By the time the models are ready the environment has changed, so the original mission goals which were the starting points of our re-engineering activities should be changed before we have finished designs. Hence, we need a new dimension in enterprise engineering to be ready for managing these changes.

Virtual enterprises are commonly project oriented collaborations from a network of people or organizations that have worked together in the past, and have some common, generally tacit understandings of what work is to be done, and how they can do it together. The use of VERA in the RELINK case study illustrated an important point: VERA was specifically developed for the application of virtual enterprise. Enterprises that involve interaction between government and SMEs are by nature virtual enterprises with ambiguous goals. Starting with a close enough enterprise architecture would make the job a lot easier. In a generic sense, the engineering of any specific government related enterprise architecture can be done in a stepwise fashion as shown in Figure 10.

At the start, when the consortium receives government participation, the consortium will use the generic enterprise architecture specified by VERA as a basis to form a default virtual enterprise. The enterprise design engineers from all partners will work together to assess what the current system is and design the virtual enterprise that is most suitable for supporting the project at hand (TO-BE). The design of specific enterprise architecture is iterative but with the help of modelling tools and mutually agreed processes, the virtual enterprise will be able to move to the TO-BE state by careful management of the changes.

The following factors must be considered when developing a new, dynamic enterprise architec-ture, irrespective of whether the new enterprise is evolved from an existing system or from a completely new venture:

- Increased complexity requires collaboration between a large numbers of participants. Increase of cooperating partners is a quantitative issue until certain size. There is a point when the partners are just too many to handle in the established ways as complexity demands different methods.
- Ever shortening delivery time requires optimisation across entire network. Companies have to realise, that their best performance (local optimum) does not necessarily deliver the biggest profit for the venture. (This poses a question when managers are paid according to the share price of their local operation.) There is a need for holistic view of the networked business. People say changing technology is easy; changing human perception is difficult.
- Business imperatives mutate the networks often and quickly. There are cases when not the company objectives change the priorities in the network but in the contrary: the global business environment forces the network to change its priorities and companies just have to adapt to the changes if they would like to remain part of the network.

Enterprise engineering will help organisations to overcome these problems by a number of ways. An enterprise model is a computational representation of the structure, activities, processes, information, resources, people, behaviour, goals and constraints of an enterprise. It is necessary that shareable representation of knowledge be available that minimizes ambiguity and maximizes understanding and precision in communication. The creation of such a representation should eliminate much of the programming required.

CONCLUSION

This chapter examines the issues of *creating* and *managing* the enterprises that have certain levels and characteristics of government involvement using enterprise engineering. The essence of enterprise engineering is the total life cycle approach that can be adopted across complex business, engineering and supply networks. The three case studies demonstrated the foundations of three different virtual enterprises with varying roles and degrees of government participation.

Most virtual enterprises will be working on projects of significant value and resource commitment; otherwise, it would not be cost effective to form a partnership. Under these circumstances, it is important to establish a framework of processes and systems to assist the operation of the virtual enterprise for the reason of extracting efficiency, even at a small percentage of savings. Enterprise engineering is therefore an important step in achieving the ultimate goal of the extended enterprise's mission. Government is itself a large enterprise and hence its interaction with the public varies from time to time. Starting with VERA, which fits well with the preamble of inter-organisational interaction, the virtual enterprise can be designed and implemented to fulfill the mission of the government sponsored project readily.

REFERENCES

Bernus, P., & Nemes, L. (1996). A framework to define a generic enterprise reference architecture and methodology. *Computer Integrated Manufacturing Systems, 9*(3), 179-191.

Bruce, E. (2005, 21-22 February). *Linking Enterprise Architectures between Multiple Government Agencies – The NZ Experience.* Paper presented at the Conference in Enterprise Architecture for Government, Canberra, Australia.

Burk, R.R. (2006, 21-22 February). *Enterprise Governance: Defining the Long Term Vision.* Paper presented at the Conference in Enterprise Architecture for Government, Canberra, Australia.

Chen, D., Vallespir, B., & Doumeingts, G. (1997). GRAI integrated methodology and its mapping onto generic enterprise reference architecture and methodology. *Computers in Industry, 33,* 387-394.

Doumeingts G., Ducq Y., Vallespir B., & Kleinhans S., (2000). Production management and enterprise modelling. *Computers in Industry, 42,* 245-263.

Elliman, T., Irani, Z., & Jackson, P. (2007). Establishing a framework for eGovernment research: project VIEGO. *Transforming Government: People, Process and Policy, 1*(4), 364-376.

Gabbar, H.A., Shimada Y., & Suzuki K., (2002). Computer-aided plant enterprise modelling environment (CAPE-ModE) – design initiatives. *Computers in Industry, 47,* 25-37.

Gregor, S., Hart, D., & Martin, N. (2007). Enterprise architectures: enables of business strategy and IS/IT alignment in government. *Information Technology & People, 20*(2), 96-120.

Hall, W.P. (2000). Managing Technical Documentation for Large Defence Projects: Engineering Corporate Knowledge. In J.P.T. Mo & L. Nemes (Eds.) *Global Engineering, Manufacturing and Enterprise Networks* (pp.370-378). Boston: Kluwer Academic Publishers.

Hjort-Madsen, K. (2007). Institutional patterns of enterprise architecture adoption in government. *Transforming Government: People, Process and Policy, 1*(4), 333-349.

IFIP–IFAC Task Force on Architectures for Enterprise Integration, (1999). *GERAM: Generalised Enterprise Reference Architecture and Methodology Version 1.6.3, Annex to ISO*

WD15704, Requirements for enterprise-reference architectures and methodologies. March, pub: IFIP and IFAC.

Jiang, H.C., & Mo, J.P.T. (2001). Internet Based Design System for Globally Distributed Concurrent Engineering. *Journal of Cybernetics and Systems, 32*(7), 737 754.

Jones, S., Hackney, R., & Irani, Z. (2007). Towards e-government transformation: conceptualising citizen engagement: A research note. *Transforming Government: People, Process and Policy, 1*(2), 145-152.

Kosanke, K., Vernadat, F., & Zelm, M. (1999). CIMOSA: enterprise engineering and integration, *Computers in Industry, 40*, 83-97.

Larsen, L.B., & Vesterager, J. (1999, 15-17 March). *Framework and methodology for creating virtual enterprises - Initial results from the Globeman21 project.* Paper presented at the 5th International conference on Concurrent Enterprising: The Concurrent Enterprise in Operation. The Hague, the Netherlands.

Li, H., & Williams, T.J., (1997). Some extensions to the Purdue Enterprise Reference Architecture (PERA) - I. Explaining the Purdue architecture and the Purdue methodology using the axioms of engineering design. *Computers in Industry, 34*, 247-259.

Li, H., & Williams, T.J., (2000). The interconnected chain of enterprises as presented by the Purdue Enterprise Reference Architecture. *Computers in Industry, 42*, 265-274.

Malladi, S., & Min, K.J., (2005). Decision support models for the selection of Internet access technologies in rural communities. *Telematics and Informatics, 22*, 201–219.

Massey, C. (2003). Enterprise assistance: responses from the public and private sectors. *Journal of Small Business and Enterprise Development, 10*(2), 128-135.

Mednikarov, B.K., & Dereliev, P.H. (2004). Structured description of naval tasks. *Information and Security, 13*, 25-34.

Mo, J.P.T., Beckett, R., Nemes, L. (2005, 26-28 September). *Technology Infrastructure for Virtual Organisation of Tooling.* Paper presented at Sixth IFIP Working Conference on Virtual Enterprises (PRO-VE'05). Valencia, Spain.

Mo, J.P.T., & Menzel, C. (1998). An integrated process model driven knowledge based system for remote customer support. *Computers in Industry, 37*, 171-183.

Mo, J.P.T., Zhou, M., Anticev, J., Nemes, L., Jones, M., Hall, W. (2006). A study on the logistics and performance of a real 'virtual enterprise'. *International Journal of Business Performance Management, 8*(2-3), 152-169.

Nemes, L., & Mo, J.P.T., (2004). Collaborative Networks in Australia – Challenges and Recommendations. In L.M. Camarinha-Matos, H. Afsarmanesh (Eds.). *Collaborative Networked Organizations* (pp.97-102). Boston: Kluwer Academic Publishers.

Noran, O. (2005). A systematic evaluation of the C4ISR AF using ISO15704 Annex A (GERAM). *Computers in Industry, 56*, 407-427.

Orange, G., Elliman, T., Kor, A.L., & Tassabehji, R. (2007). Local government and social or innovation value. *Transforming Government: People, Process and Policy, 1*(3), 242-254.

Ortiz, A., Lario, F., & Ros, L., (1999). Enterprise Integration – Business Processes Integrated Management: a proposal for a methodology to develop Enterprise Integration Programs. *Computers in Industry, 40*, 155–171.

Patankar, A.K., & Sadiga, S., (1995). Enterprise integration modelling: a review of theory and practice. *Computer Integrated Manufacturing Systems, 8*(1), 21-34.

Sackett, P., Rose, T., & Adamson, V. (2003). The importance of business process clarification within the virtual enterprise. *Journal of Small Business and Enterprise Development, 10*(3), 298-305.

Shankararaman, V., & Lee, B.S. (1994). Knowledge-Based Safety Training System (KBSTS) - A Prototype Implementation. *Computers in Industry, 25*, 145-157.

Shen, H., Wall, B., Zaremba, M., Chen, Y., & Browne, J. (2004). Integration of business modelling methods for enterprise information system analysis and user requirements gathering. *Computers in Industry, 54*, 307-323.

Shinonome, M., Hashimoto, H., Fuse, A., & Mo, J.P.T. (1998). Development of an information technology infrastructure for extended enterprise. In J. Mills & F. Kimura (Eds.). *Information Infrastructure Systems for Manufacturing* (pp.353-364). Boston: Kluwer Academic Publishers.

Sulin, B.A., Lang, K.R., & Whinston. A.B. (1997). Enterprise decision support using Intranet technology. *Decision Support Systems, 20*, 99-134.

Van den Berg, R.J., & Tolle, M. (2000). Assessing Ability to Execute in Virtual Enterprises. In J.P.T. Mo & L. Nemes (Eds.) *Global Engineering, Manufacturing and Enterprise Networks* (pp.370-378). Boston: Kluwer Academic Publishers.

Vernadat, F.B. (2002). Enterprise Modelling and Integration (EMI): Current Status and Research Perspectives. *Annual Reviews in Control, 26*, 15-25.

Weston, R.H. (1999). Reconfigurable, component-based systems and the role of enterprise engineering concepts, *Computers in Industry, 40*, 321-343.

Williams, T.J. (1994). The Purdue Enterprise Reference Architecture, *Computers in Industry, 24*(2-3), 141-158.

Williams, T.J., Bernus, P., Brosvic, J., Chen, D., Doumeingts, G., Nemes, L., Nevins, J.L., Vallespir, B., Vlietstra, J., & Zoetekouw, D. (1994). Architectures for integrating manufacturing activities and enterprises. *Computers in Industry, 24*, 111-139.

Wortmann, J.C., Hegge, H.M.H., & Rolefes, S. (2000). Embedding enterprise software in extended enterprise models. *Computers in Industry, 42*, 231-243.

Wu, R.C.Y. (2007). Enterprise integration in e-government. *Transforming Government: People, Process and Policy, 1*(1), 89-99.

Zwegers, A., Tolle, M., & Vesterager, J., (2003). VERAM: Virtual Enterprise Reference Architecture and Methodology. In I. Karvonen, R. Van den Berg, P. Bernus, Y. Fukuda, M. Hannus, I. Hartel, J. Vesterager (Eds.). *VTT Symposium 224* (pp.17-38), Helsinki, Finland.

Chapter XVII
Collaborative Enterprise Architecture for Municipal Environments

Leonidas G. Anthopoulos
Hellenic Ministry of Foreign Affairs, Greece

ABSTRACT

E-government evolves according to strategic plans with the coordination of central Governments. This top-down procedure succeeds in slow but sufficient transformation of public services into e-Government ones. However, public agencies adapt to e-Government with difficulty, requiring holistic guidance and a detailed legal framework provided by the Government. The setting up of common Enterprise Architecture for all public agencies requires careful analysis. Moreover, common Enterprise Architecture could fail to cover the special needs of small or municipal agencies. The chapter uses data from various major e-Government strategies, together with their enterprise architectures, in order to introduce a development model of municipal Enterprise Architecture. The model is based on the experience collected from the Digital City of Trikala, central Greece, and results in "Collaborative Enterprise Architecture".

INTRODUCTION

Governments worldwide are investing heavily in e-Government, according to ambitious strategic plans aimed at friendlier and more effective public Administrations. The strategic plans define the political targets for e-Government, such as "time and cost savings for citizens and public Agencies" (Cap Gemini Ernst & Young, 2003) and "the development of a citizen-centered, results-oriented and market-based public Administration" (Federal Enterprise Architecture, 2002). Moreover, strategic plans set the technological standards that will be followed during e-Government evolution, such as "openness, usability, customization and transparency for public portals" (Gant and Gant, 2002) and "interoperability between e-Government systems" (UK Cabinet Office, Office of the e-Envoy, 2002).

Strategic plans are being implemented according to the "top-down procedure" (Anthopoulos, Siozos and Tsoukalas, 2007), meaning that Governments define the primary targets and assign their implementation to central authorities, while e-Government target groups (citizens, enterprises, civil servants) are not involved in the design procedure. Top-down strategic planning defines policies and targets, but not methods and principles for e-Government. Information and Communication Technology (ICT) vendors have provided solutions for e-Government and for digital service execution that are mainly eCommerce-based applications, transformed and parameterized to public Administration methodologies (Lawry, Albrecht, Nunamaker and Lee, 2002).

The application of the strategic plan on the public Administration is a difficult procedure, since various Authorities did not participate in the "top-down" strategic planning, they do not know planning extensions and they are not aware of the upcoming changes. Distributed and local authorities require the existence of controlling procedures and of specific legal frameworks in order to adopt changes. Central Agencies defined by Governments are assigned strategic planning implementation, change management and the application of common technical standards in separate e-Government projects.

However, central supervision lacks functions (Peristeras and Tarabanis, 2004) that could establish common standards for interoperable, usable and accessible e-Government projects. The Enterprise Architecture (EA) is a "tool" that can establish standardization in e-Government

projects. EA is the "bridge" that joins strategic plans and their implementation (Federal Enterprise Architecture (FEA Group), 2005). Moreover, according to (Adigun and Biyela, 2003), the EA documents the elements that make up e-Government in a form that can be understood by its stakeholders (for example politicians, political parties, councils, heads of departments etc.). EA can assist central e-Government supervisors in understanding and combining technical standards and political aspects.

Each strategic plan is now accompanied by a centrally defined EA that can supply all e-Government projects with common standards and operation principles. However, central EA has to deal with problems similar to the ones that central strategic planning faces (Anthopoulos et. al., 2007): "smooth transition" of the public Agencies from traditional procedures to e-Government, change acceptance by all target groups, and the treatment of individual, local and peripheral needs.

The purpose of this chapter is the introduction of the "Collaborative Enterprise Architecture (CEA)" that can be applied in local, state or peripheral governments and Agencies. CEA is the result of: a) the experiences of the strategic plans that are being implemented by central Governments, such as those of the US, the UK, Canada, Germany and the European Union. All have followed the "top-down" planning procedure for e-Government and they have resulted in specific EAs for the public sector. b) The experiences extracted by the implementation of the metropolitan e-Government environment in the Digital City of Trikala, central Greece (Anthopoulos and Tsoukalas, 2005), where the "bottom-up" planning procedure (Anthopoulos et. al., 2007) was followed. Municipal area environments and individual Agencies can follow the "bottom-up" planning procedure for e-Government, and their implementation model can be common. The resulting "Collaborative Enterprise Architecture" combines the "bottom-up" planning method, major EAs and groupware tools.

In section 2 of this chapter, the background of the proposed CEA is given. In section 3 the contribution of this chapter is analyzed. The main thrust of this chapter is the proposal of the CEA. The notion begins with the key findings from existing e-Government strategies and Enterprise Architectures. All strategies culminate in Enterprise Architectures that have common features. Then, the implementation model that can be followed when a local Administration wishes to enter the e-Government era is analyzed. In the form of a step-by-step guide, the perspectives that public Agencies need to consider are analyzed. Major e-Government case studies and their experiences have to be combined with local needs. The implementation procedure is extracted by the case study performed in the Digital City of Trikala, Central Greece (e-Trikala), where the local Administration decided to move towards the Information Society: e-Government methods and local social needs were analyzed and combined. The result of this initial procedure was the development of an Enterprise Architecture that can extend national EA and is called the Collaborative Enterprise Architecture (CEA).

BACKGROUND

There are many definitions of e-Government. Some (Devadoss, Pan, Huang, 2002) refer to the installation and use of IT systems in Public Administration for offering digital public services. Others (Wimmer, Traunmuller, 2000) refer to the transformation of Public Administration, which is based on the re-designing and digitization of public transactions. Moreover, e-Government is related to social participation in policy making (Pavlichev, Garson, 2004) and in the improvement of all public transactions, such as procuring and auctioning methods (Schubert, Hausler, 2001). Furthermore, according to the Organization of Economic Co-operation and Development (OECD) (OECD, 2001) e-Government has to

do more with "Government" than with the "e", meaning that e-Government technologies exist, but their application requires the simplification of public services and the modernization of administrative structure and "culture".

The primary target of e-Government is the development of an efficient and citizen-centered Public Administration that will operate according to business methods and profit both citizens and the Public Sector. E-Government projects aim at cost- and time-minimization of public transactions, at the simplification and the elimination of paper production during public services and at the treatment of corruption in Public Administration.

The evolution of e-Government is currently based in the centralized design and implementation supervision of Strategic Plans, supported by huge investments in ICT infrastructures. Governments appear satisfied, since they have succeeded in cost and time savings. Moreover, Governments consider that the "pressure" they apply for the transformation of Public Administration will in the end achieve the primary targets of e-Government. *Enterprise Architecture* is a "tool" that supports the central implementation of a Strategic Plan, by setting targets, principles and methods that can be followed by all public Agencies. According to (Chief Information Officers (CIO), 2001) *"Enterprise Architecture (EA) is a strategic information asset base, which defines the mission, the information necessary to perform the mission and the technologies necessary to perform the mission, and the transitional processes for implementing new technologies in response to the changing mission needs. EA includes a baseline architecture, target architecture and a sequence plan".* EA is accompanied with a specific framework (CIO, 1999) containing the proper procedures that each public Agency has to follow in order to implement the EA. The EAs that were investigated for the purposes of this chapter have many similarities regarding their development procedures, while their missions have common primary targets.

The development of e-Government strategic plans is a "top-down" procedure (Anthopoulos et. al., 2007), meaning that central Governments supervise the design and execution of national e-Government initiatives. The "top-down" procedure is defined in detail by means of educational methods, where an instructor presents the general concept of a system and proceeds to its subsystems. In e-Government initiatives, the instructor is the Government – usually with the support and knowledge of special consultants invited from the private sector – which plans and monitors multiple projects. "Top-down" developed e-Government plans contain policies and targets, but not methods and principles. Information and Telecommunication Technology (ICT) vendors have provided solutions for e-Government and for digital service execution that are mainly eCommerce-based applications, transformed and parameterized to Public Administration methodologies.

On the other hand, current centralized design has specified neither citizen nor civil servant needs. Surveys carried out in the US (Accenture, 2005) (ACSI, 2005) show that citizens evaluate digital public services and seem to prefer traditional transactions. Citizens expect more from digital services (Accenture, 2005), while they are not confident regarding security and privacy aspects of e-Government transactions. Furthermore, surveys carried out in the Digital City of Trikala,

Central Greece (Anthopoulos, 2005), show that citizens prefer the involvement of public servants in digital transactions, while civil servants appear reluctant to support the diffusion of e-Government. Different points of views show that neither citizens nor civil servants trust e-Government.

The Digital City notion is used for the purposes of this chapter. Digital City is defined as *"the global municipal area information environment, focusing on the needs of a city area". The environment contains Information and Communication Technology (ICT) solutions, but is not designed to offer only digital public services or to create digital communities. The primary targets of the Digital City are: a) to offer digital means for supporting social needs in all daily transactions; b) to acclimate the local community to the notion of the Information Society; and c) to collect official and unofficial information from the local community in order to support sustainable growth of small societies* (Anthopoulos and Tsoukalas, 2005). The definition extends previous ones by (Sairamesh, Lee & Anania, 2004), (Sproull & Patterson, 2004), (Widmayer, 1999) and (Ishida, 2002).

In the Digital City of Trikala, [on behalf of the local Administration] e-Government issues were investigated (Anthopoulos, Tsoukalas, 2005), and the "bottom-up" planning method was applied. The "bottom-up" design, too, is defined in detail by means of educational methods (Anthopoulos

Table 1. Comparing "top-down" and "bottom-up" methods

	"Top-down" method	"Bottom-up" method
Instructor	Government with the support of experts from the private sector.	Participants from multiple target groups (end-users, public officials, politicians).
Process	Government sets the political targets and experts design projects to achieve them.	Participants extract target groups' needs and collaborate to find solutions for them.
Targets	E-Government political targets.	Treatment of end-users' needs, extracted by the collaboration.

et. al., 2007), where participants consider e-Government as a hierarchical system consisting of multiple elements (sub-systems) that need to be identified, combined and analyzed – from multiple perspectives – in order for the whole system to be realized. Participants (end-users, public officials, politicians) share knowledge, and support Administration modernization. A comparison of the "bottom-up" and "top-down" design methods is presented in (Table 1).

They start by setting out their expectations with regard to e-Government systems, digital public services and their simplification, and the smooth transition from traditional to ICT-based procedures. The "bottom-up" strategic planning was successful for the e-Trikala case, since in a mid-sized Greek town with a development index under national average values, the investment of more than €4 million for a metropolitan e-Government environment (Anthopoulos and Manos, 2005) was achieved in less than 3 years, and the closing of the digital divide with the contribution of all social groups was performed. E-Trikala can be a case study for similar cases, where local Agencies, municipal or state Governments wish to enter the e-Government era.

MAIN THRUST OF THIS CHAPTER

The main purpose of this chapter is to introduce the *Collaborative Enterprise Architecture (CEA)*: a model that can support local Agencies and municipal or state Governments in their e-Government projects. The CEA was extracted in the e-Trikala case study, where e-Government Strategies were analyzed and combined with individual needs. The summarized process and the data that were used in the e-Trikala case are contained in this section. Initially, the key findings of some major e-Government strategies are presented. This investigation culminates in a common central e-Government Information System and a common procedure for public service execution. This

data is useful for the introduction of CEA, as it was used in the e-Trikala case. CEA contains a mission statement and an implementation model, which follows a number of perspectives and steps that can be common for similar cases. CEA also contains a logical architecture and some technological principles that can be followed by local agencies.

Key Findings from Existing E-Government Strategies

A formal definition of public services suggests that "independent public services are legally grounded business of public organizations in an economical sense". They represent the development and delivery of products and services of an organized unit to the public. A *public service* is referenced to a *life event* or *business situation* and is analyzed in multiple *steps* that are executed according to relevant legal restrictions.

The US Federal Government's e-Government action plan (US Federal Government, 2002) aims at the transformation of public administration into a citizen-centered, results-oriented and market-based e-Government. Extensive investment, exceeding $52 billion by the end of 2003, is being made in e-Government projects. About 40,000 Web pages from State Governments and local authorities are accessible from a one-stop e-Government portal called FirstGov (www.firstgov.gov), while the e-Authentication (US Federal Government, 2003) platform provides secure services and preserves privacy during public transactions.

The US strategic plan is supported by the Federal Enterprise Architecture (FEA) (CIO, 2001), which was inspired by Zachman's model (Zachman, 1987), (Sowa, 2000). FEA adopted the National Institute of Standards and Technology (NIST) model (CIO, 1999), containing the following layers: *business, information, information systems, and data and delivery systems architectures.*

In Europe, member countries have signed the *eEurope Action Plans*, describing ways of building a favorable environment for all European citizens to participate in the *Information Society*. These plans have the power of contract between the member countries, presenting targets for IT projects. According to the previous eEurope 2005 plan (European Commission, 2002) – for instance – public authorities in all member countries should offer digital services by the end of 2005. Recently, the European Council adopted the i2010 Strategic Plan (Reding, 2005), where "innovation" and "inclusion" have become the main priorities for an "open information space" in Europe. European central Agencies did not suggest a specific EA for e-Government in member countries. However, e-Europe strategic plans (http://ec.europa.eu/information_society/eEurope) set out targets as defined by the Information Society Directorate General (http://ec.europa.eu/information_society) and approved by the European Council. European Directives support the implementation of e-Europe strategic plans, which are coordinated and supervised by the Information Society Directorate General. European member-state national strategies had to adapt to eEurope plans and to their targets. The UK's Modernizing Government plan (UK Crown, 2000) is one of the major European e-Government projects that matches the eEurope's targets, while German (http://www.bund.de), French (www.service-public.fr) and Italian (http://www.italia.gov.it) plans follow. European one-stop e-Government portals provide similar procedures to those of FirstGov for the execution of public services.

The UK's strategic plan runs under the management of the Office of the e-Envoy. Two ambitious programs, UK Online and UK Gateway, rooted in the highest level of government. UK Online developed the current *DirectGov portal* (http://www.direct.gov.uk), from where public services are offered centrally, while the Government Gateway (http://www.gateway.gov.uk) is a centrally financed infrastructure solution that connects existing systems with different data structures and establishes user authentication for all public agencies and civil servants. The e-GIF (e-Government Interoperability Framework) contains a range of standards for technical data exchange formats and protocols, in order to establish interoperability between different systems in British public Administration. By complying with the technical standards, all public Agencies access central solutions and principles. British Government approved its EA – called the "cross-Government Enterprise Architecture (xGEA)" – in 2005 (UK CIO, 2005), describing the common "business-led vision" and procedures for British Administration.

Germany has designed and followed the BundOnline 2005 strategic plan (German Federal Government, 2003) for its Information Society framework program, which contained specific targets for e-government. The Bund portal (www.bund.de) is the main point of access, where more than 100 agencies are interconnected and endeavour to offer more than 450 different services. The German Federal Government wants to make the Bund portal the main information platform for its public Administration, and a customer-centered and open environment. The German EA is called SAGA Framework (KBSt Publication Series, 2003) and contains centrally selected, common solutions and standards for ICT projects in German Administration. Furthermore, the framework presents different perspectives that the ICT architecture designers in public Administration must follow for e-Government projects.

The Federal Government of Canada designed its "Government on-Line (GOL)" e-Government Strategic plan in 1999 (Treasury Board Secretariat, Government of Canada, 2001), aiming at the availability of all digital public services by 2004. The Canadian strategic plan also aimed at a) spreading Internet use and b) public information offering via citizen-centered methods. In January 2001 both targets were initially achieved and the central e-Government portal was online (www.canada.gc.ca) (Treasury Board Secretariat, Government of Canada, 2001), where more than 450 unique public Websites are interconnected. Government on-Line targets include "the improvement of public transactions (accessibility, quality and response), social participation, transparency in public transactions, improvement of internal public procedures and efficiency in public Administration." The Government on-Line strategy has evolved the Service Oriented Architecture (SOA) Strategy (Treasury Board Secretariat, Government of Canada, 2006). Service orientation is defined as "*the planning and delivery of all services by formally componentizing each of the services and their subordinate services such that the overall collection of services work as a whole and supports a high level master-plan.*" The Canadian SOA can be regarded as its EA since it contains the vision, the rules and the methods for e-Government to be complied with by all public agencies.

A Common Architecture for E-Government Models

The e-Government strategic plans presented previously culminate in central information systems and one-stop portals to offer digital public services. Central systems and portals are based on multi-tier e-Government solutions, which contain the following entities (*Figure 1*):

a.   An RDBMS operating as a repository for digital public service descriptions. It can store XML documents (Wesley, Addison, 2003) describing the execution procedure of all available digital public services.

b.   An optional RDBMS for the legislative rules applied in public services contains the legal framework in LegalXML or LexML format and is available to all software modules of the system.

c.   Databases with public information (digital records and documents), uploaded or produced during public transactions. They transact with legacy systems already installed in the Public Administration via Web service architecture.

d.   Authentication systems and security options, which provide security and privacy during transactions, and offer different levels of authentication.

e.   Interoperability framework based on XML descriptions, are followed for the Web service transactions between the central information system and legacy systems.

f.   Content Management Systems that administer public information and software engines that execute different steps of the public services. The engines transact with multiple modules of the central Information System and with legacy systems via Web services.

g.   A government portal operates as the access point and the interface between citizens and public authorities. It uses multiple communication channels such as the Internet, 3rd generation mobile networks and voice communication.

The common procedure of a service execution consists of the following steps (*Figure 2*):

i.   Citizen visits a one-stop e-Government portal and selects among the public services offered online, presented in a UDDI catalogue.

ii.   Citizen is redirected to an authentication environment where he is authenticated according to simple logon methods or Public Key Infrastructure (PKI) credentials.

iii.   When the citizen is authenticated, he is directed to the back-office where the public service can be executed.

iv.   An on-line application form that the citizen must fill in is presented, and he either downloads it and follows traditional methods for public transactions or submits it to the back-office.

Table 2. Major key-findings from investigated case studies

Strategic Plan	Supervisor	Portal	Primary targets	Achievements	EA
"Expanding e-Government" Initiative (US)	e-Government Task Force	FirstGov	1. Citizen-centred, results-oriented, market-based Public Administration. 2. Federal and State Agencies interconnected in a one-stop portal. 3. Guidelines and standards for all unique initiatives, performed by state or local Agencies.	1. FirstGov portal. 2. G2C, G2B, G2G transactions 3. IEE: efficiency in Public Administration 4. e-Authentication environment. 5. Life-event driven public services. 6. Download-able digital forms for most of the public services. 7. Digitally executed simple public services.	FEA: mission, procedures
"Modernizing Government" (UK)	Office of the e-Envoy	UK-Online	1. Knowledge economy revolution. 2. Transformation of Business, Government, People. 3. Citizen-focused Government. 4. Better services for citizens and businesses. 5. Application of e-business methods in public sector. 6. All key services available online by 2008	1. UK-online portal. 2. Government Secure Intranet (GSI). 3. e-GIF interoperability Framework. 4. Gateway: portal for authenticated services. 5. Life-event driven public services. 6. Download-able digital forms for most of the public services. 7. Digitally executed simple public services.	xGEA mission, standards and procedures
"eEurope" and i2010 (European Commitee)	Information Society Directorate General	Europa.eu.int	1. Citizen-centerd Public Administration. 2. Encourage participation (inclusion). 3. Twenty five 25 primary digital public services for all European member countries. 4. Multilingual one-stop shop (inclusion). 5. Telecommunication's costs reduction and ICT investments ("open space" and investment) 6. Encourage Innovation	1. Europa multi-lingual portal containing documents and information from the European Committee 2. Most European countries have under implementation relevant strategic plans directed at primary targets. 3. Many e-Government projects have been funded by the IST program, while major directions have been set under the IDA program.	Not specified Primary targets, Available funding, technical principles, Directives
"Government on-Line" (Canada)	Federal Government of Canada	www.canada.gc.ca	1. Social participation 2. Cost savings 3. Transparency in public transactions 4) Simplification and modernization of internal public procedures 5. Efficiency with high-skilled staff.	1. canada.gc.ca government portal 2.Three tier e-Government architecture 3. Selected digital public services 4. Public service grouping in "electronic clusters"	GC SOA Mission, principles and technical standards
"BundOnline 2005" (Germany)	Federal Ministry of the Interior	Bund.de	1. Define and deliver online Federal Public services. 2. Client-orientation services. 3. Transparency and faster processing for federal services. 4. Quality and security of public services.	1. Bund.de one-stop portal. 2. Life-event driven public services. 3. Download-able digital forms for most of the public services. 4. Digitally executed simple public services.	SAGA Mission, perspectives

Figure 1. A logical view of a common central e-Government system. Arrows show possible paths chosen by citizens to access public information or services. Workflow systems in the back-office offer content management and service execution options

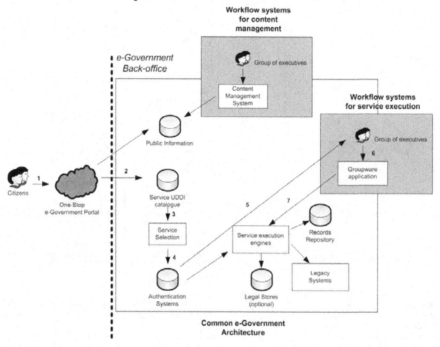

v. The application is directed to the proper Agency, where a workflow system, matched to the Weberian hierarchical architecture (Tat-Kei Ho, 2002), is installed. The workflow system receives the application form and public executives handle the occasion.

vi. Software modules – such as those presented previously – verify submitted data to records in the existing back-office databases or in legacy systems distributed in the public Administration, and execute different steps of the service.

The major problems and social issues that the implementation and installation of such an e-Government system faces are presented below:

a. The definition of XML schemas to describe public services and data produced and exchanged.

b. The re-designation and simplification of many public services so that they "fit" into specific workflow schemas and can be transformed into fully automated digital services. In Europe it is estimated that only 45% of the total public services (Cap Gemini, Ernst & Young, 2003) can become fully digital, due to the fact that most public services are *composite* and *customized*.

c. The legislation of the proper framework covering digital transactions.

d. The re-organization and transformation of public Agencies to transact with the back-office environment.

e. The training of both citizens and public executives in basic IT skills.

f. The minimization of telecommunication costs for citizens and enterprises. In Europe, broadband services are still very expensive for single users and thus hinder the diffusion of e-Government.

Figure 2. The common procedure of service execution

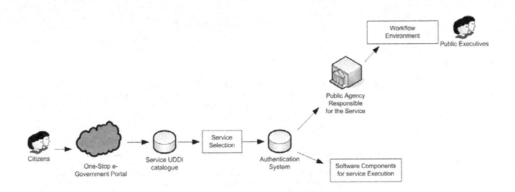

Public Agencies can select between workflow or service execution environments to cover their needs. On the other hand, they have to deal with all e-Government aspects in order to develop the proper digital environment.

The Collaborative Enterprise Architecture

The "bottom-up" strategic planning, where representatives of e-Government target groups participate in the design and implementation procedures, suggests *the Collaborative Enterprise Architecture (CEA) notion. The Collaboration Enterprise Architecture (CEA) is an information plan whereby the strategic e-Government mission and the information needed for the mission's performance are defined with the contribution of representatives of all the target groups and they meet end-users' needs. The enterprise lifecycle is executed with the collaboration of the working group, the involved social parties and experts invited from the private and academic sectors. The evaluation of the architecture's progress is based on end-user satisfaction and acceptance.* The implementation methodology is described in the following subsection and suggests the Enterprise Lifecycle of the CEA. CEA was inspired by the US Federal Enterprise Architecture (FEA)

(CIO, 1999) and by (Sowa) and consists of the following architecture layers placed in the columns of (Table 3):

a. The *organization* architecture, dealing with the organization's physiognomy and vision, and national EA.

b. The *collaborating* architecture that refers to the cooperating schema of the involved participants in the strategic planning and implementation phases. The cooperating schema contains descriptions about the collaborating procedure in different stages (UML rules, connections and data flow), together with groupware systems that establish the participation.

c. The *technical* architecture, which contains the technical standards for the development and interoperability of the architecture's subsystems.

d. The *data* architecture describing physical storages and repositories, file and records structure, semantics for information exchange, copyright and securing options.

e. The *accessibility* architecture that describes the efficiency of the architecture, since its vision and implementation are being evaluated by members of their target groups.

Table 3. The collaborative enterprise architecture

Architecture / Perspectives	Organization	Collaborating	Technical	Data	Accessibility
Authority	Structure	Roles for its representatives	Smooth migration from legacy to future systems	Existing file and records structure	End user definition
Business	Framework, procedures	Participating processes, decision making	Process simplification	Re-usability and migration where possible	Public service definition
Financial	Budget, operational costs	Cost savings from participant knowledge contribution	Time and cost savings from investments	Storage optimization. Statistical analysis methods over data	Operational costs from transactions
Political	Organization vision	Democratic planning tools and methods	Compliance with national interoperability standards and legal framework	Compliance with data accessibility initiatives	Improve user satisfaction and Agency's responses
Implementation	Representatives definition	Task assignment for investigation	Maximize potential from existing national initiatives: Innovating where possible	Common Semantic model for data description	Case studies about usability and accessibility
Technical	Existing systems	Groupware tools	Compliance with international standards.	Physical data models	Web and voice accessibility
Project Manager	Change management	Role assignment. Cooperation with other groups	Management and tools	Collect data during implementation procedures	Evaluate accessibility during implementation procedures
Administrative	Testing period definition, levels of access	Evaluation procedures.	Monitoring tools	Methods for statistical analysis and data monitoring.	Evaluation and improvement

Applying CEA in Local Administrations Cases

The significance of the Collaborative Enterprise Architecture (CEA) can be extracted from cases where a local Administration or an individual public Authority wishes to enter e-Government Era. In such cases the local Administration or public Authority must address certain critical issues that accompany its transformation: a) it must conform to the national EA and b) it must investigate local or individual needs. This section is a common implementation model for individual or local Authorities and is a conclusion drawn from the case study of the Digital City of Trikala, where the municipality decided to approach the Information Society. The implementation model is presented in the form of a guide and it is extracted from the "bottom up" procedure (Anthopoulos et. al, 2007). The implementation model consists of some primary perspectives, which are placed in the rows of (Table 3) and which were considered in the e-Trikala case. These perspectives are not strict and can be differentiated according to custom conditions.

A. Authority's Perspective: Setting up the Working Group

The heads of Agencies or the Municipal Council are the leaders of the Authority that wishes to enter the e-Government era. Agency heads and politicians are probably not aware of ICT in detail, but they can understand local and individual needs, they can diffuse their decisions to the local environments, and they must keep a "leading role" in the initiative. Heads of agencies need to invite highly-skilled ICT seniors (academics or staff from the private sector) to cooperate with representatives from the Agency or from the local society's organized groups. All participants will comprise the "working group" for e-Government transformation. The group will work on political targets, exchange ideas, extract local needs, find e-Government solutions for them conforming to EA architecture, implement these solutions and "close the digital divide" in the local environment. The whole process will deliver a business plan for e-Government. *In the case of e-Trikala, the working group was structured with representatives from the Municipality, Academics, people from the private sector and representatives from the organized social groups of the city of Trikala: educational society (students, teachers and parents), teams working on cultural aspects (cultural organizations and local museums), media (local newspapers and radio stations), teams of elderly citizens and citizens with disabilities and from the local market (local chamber of trade, groups of enterprises involved in local tourism and local production).*

B. Business Perspective: Discover the Individual Background

The first thing the working group must do is to define its resources (ICT, human resources who will use e-Government tools), its individual environment (the geographical field of action and the target-groups) and local needs. *In the case of e-Trikala, the resources deal with ICT infrastructures in the town hall and municipal agencies, and ICT-skilled municipal executives, public buildings, telecommunication vendors and connections over the city.*

Local needs arise from procedures occurring in the Agency or in the City, together with local conditions (social, economic and demographic characteristics, geographical and urban parameters, cultural and educational networks, transportation and telecommunication infrastructures, etc.). Local needs set the priorities for digital public services and e-Government. Their investigation is based on the contribution of the group members, while social participation may be requested via open dialogue. *In e-Trikala the investigation of local needs defined the axes of precedence for e-Government: a) Economy and employment, b) Improvement of everyday life, c) Education, professional training, life-long learning, and d) Tourism and culture. All public services that were implemented according to the above axes of precedence exceed Administrating activities and municipal authorities. However, the digital city is a global e-Government environment where multiple digital environments are combined for the improvement of the local community's life.*

C. Financial Perspective: Secure Funding, Re-Use Infrastructures, Encourage Private Investments and Minimize Maintenance Expenses

E-Government planning demands funding for the implementation and maintenance of information systems, software and digital service development, diffusion and training activities, and for telecommunication services. The financial perspective requires the examination of all existing ICT infrastructures and the necessary interoperability or updating costs. *In the case of e-Trikala funding was secured by the national Information Society Framework Program, from European Framework Programs and from national resources. The working group also encouraged ICT companies to offer volunteer support with pilot projects, testing their technologies and products in Trikala city. Interoperability between new, legacy and third-party infrastructures was built to comply with the national interoperability framework. The maintenance of the Digital City infrastructures and services will be based on payment policies over operators and digital public services.*

D. Political Perspective: Comply with National EA

EA is a tool that can succeed in e-Government initiatives with common standards and interoperable features. However national EA contains priorities that are formulated according to a political and economic background. All unique projects designed for e-Government must comply with the national EA mission and principles, and must comprise an architecture that will also follow EA's technological standards. Local administrators can define their primary targets, but they have to formulate them in a manner compatible with the national mission. *In the e-Trikala case, local needs were defined and assigned to axes of precedence that comply with the Greek strategy. The Greek Information Society strategy conforms to the European strategy and to the principles that are set by the European Council and by the European Information Society Framework Programme. Moreover, the Greek strategy has succeeded in the development of the broadband Network Syzefxis (www.syzefxis.gov.gr), which connects all public agencies; the Greek strategy has also legalized the Citizen Service Offices Information System (www.kep.gov.gr), with which all e-Government initiatives must conform and interoperate. E-Trikala Digital City EA contains interfaces that interoperate with both of the above public infrastructures.*

F. Implementation Perspective: Make Use of Experience from International Case Studies

"Excellence" is the key to encouraging progress. The European Commission identifies both best and worst practices from all over Europe using Eurostat (http://epp.eurostat.ec.europa.eu) and Eurobarometer (http://ec.europa.eu/public_opinion) services, in order to strengthen competitiveness and prevent further failures in Europe. Individual and municipal Agencies can make use of the results extracted from e-Government case studies: they can learn from both success and failure, via understanding the conditions and the factors that influenced results. *In the e-Trikala project, the experiences from the major strategic plans presented above were combined with digital city cases. National strategic plans contributed with their visions and their Enterprise Architectures. Digital city case studies were used for the evaluation of their different technological models and for their different physiognomies. The result extracted by this combination is a novel Digital City model, which is a metropolitan e-Government environment, where non-profit, social and administrative public services are offered to citizens* (Anthopoulos and Manos, 2005).

G. Technical Perspective: Use Common E-government Architectures and Standards to Cover Individual Needs

The implementation of the local e-Government environment requires common ICT infrastructures for the information system, the content management system and the service execution modules. Common tools and procedures were described previously. The local Agency has to opt for the optimal software, hardware and service solutions, according to common national and international standards. The local e-Government environment will interoperate with legacy and external environments, in order to transact data and forward service requests. *In e-Trikala the Digital City is based on an n-tier architecture, whose levels are compatible with national and international e-Government standards. The whole architecture is modular* (Anthopoulos and Tsoukalas, 2005) *and consists of sub-systems, which also follow the same architecture.*

I. Project Manager's Perspective: Project Life-Cycle (Design and Implement Projects, Evaluate and Improve the Resulting System)

Unique projects must be designed to cover special needs. All projects must comply with the global Architecture and with national EA. The implementation procedure must be administered by groups of experts with specialized knowledge of the projects' physiognomies. Implementation procedures can be based on common standards (such as PRINCE method), and assign tools for supervision, risk management and evaluation criteria. Specific deliverables must be expected in different phases of the projects, and must be evaluated and redesigned by demand. *In e-Trikala, a number of unique projects aimed to cover local needs: a) e-Government information system designed to offer services to citizens all over the province. b) smart transportation system designed to support and improve local mass transport means. c) e-voting and decision-making tools were designed to encourage social participation. d) tele-care system designed to support the elderly and citizens with disabilities. e) wireless hotspots and metro-wifi free for use by the citizens were designed and installed to "close" the digital divide. e) All above sub-systems were installed in public buildings, centrally operated and interconnected via a broadband fiber-optic network and mesh networks. The logical architectures of all sub-systems shared the same logical layers, which were also those of the Digital City's logical architecture. Their implementation was administered by specialists invited from the private and academic sectors who evaluated the quality of project deliverables by measuring end-user satisfaction and acceptance.*

K. Administrative Perspective: Define the Operational Procedures and Rules; Diffuse the Results in the Target Groups

Local Authority has to define the operational plan and the terms of use of the e-Government environment. The operational plan deals with the organizational structure that will administer the e-Government system: the layers of access, the roles and the rules of involvement for different kinds of users, administrative procedures, crisis management models, disaster recovery plans, etc. Moreover, the operational plan sets the limits, defines criminal activities in the e-Government environment and presents methods of reaction against different kinds of violation. Finally, different scenarios for communicating the e-Government environment to the target groups are contained. *In the e-Trikala case, although the Digital City's system is central, its sub-systems are distributed and they operate under the responsible municipal Authorities. The technical administration and the monitoring of the whole system are assigned to a specific municipal Agency. This Agency holds different plans for managing, monitoring, securing, recovering and extending the system. The legal framework of the Digital City environment complies with the Greek and the European frameworks, and is applied by national and municipal authorities. The diffusion of the Digital City principles and benefits was supported by the "bottom-up strategic planning" because social representatives participated in the implementation progress and they delivered their feedback to their groups of citizens. Furthermore, technical events and schools have been organized by the Municipal authorities in order to spread technical knowledge to young members of the local community.*

CONCLUSION

In this chapter we introduced the notion of the *Collaborative Enterprise Architecture (CEA)* as an EA that can support individual Agencies and municipal or state Governments who wish to enter the e-Government Era. The CEA was applied in the case of the Digital City of Trikala and it is modeled to support similar cases. The CEA resulted from the investigation of some major e-Government strategies, it considers common information system architecture and service processes, it incorporates participating methods and groupware tools, and it is accompanied by a step-by-step implementation model for e-Government initiatives. Moreover, the CEA suggests some primary principles that are common for all small-area e-Government projects that were verified in the e-Trikala case study. The CEA will also be tested in a Digital Geography case study in central Greece through 2013, where various Digital Cities will comprise a common e-Government environment.

REFERENCES

Accenture (2005) Leadership in Customer Service: New Expectations, New Experiences". The Government Executive Series, Accenture, April 2005. Retrieved May 25th, 2006, from http://www.accenture.com/NR/rdonlyres/F45CE4C8-9330-4450-BB4A-AF4E265C88D4/0/leadership_cust.pdf) .

Adigun M. O., & Biyela D. P. (2003) *Modelling and Enterprise for re-Engineering: A Case Study. In the 2003 annual research conference of the South African institute of computer scientists and information technologists on Enablement through technology (SAICSIT 2003)*, ACM.

American Customer Satisfaction Index (ACSI), e-Government Satisfaction Index (2005) "*Number of e-GOV sites measuring satisfaction surges, satisfaction growth stalls*". March 15, 2005. Retrieved May 25th, 2006, from

http://www.customerservice.gov/historical_commentaries/e-gov_comm_0305.pdf.

Anthopoulos L., Siozos P., & Tsoukalas I. A. (2007) Applying Participatory Design and Collaboration in Digital Public Services for discovering and re-designing e-Government services. *Government Information Quarterly*, Volume 24, Issue 2, April 2007, Pages 353-376, ElSevier.

Anthopoulos, L., & Tsoukalas, I.A. (2005) The implementation model of a Digital City. The case study of the first Digital City in Greece: e-Trikala. *Journal of e-Government, Vol.2, Issue 2, 2005*. Haworth Press, Inc., University of Southern California, Center for Digital Government.

Anthopoulos, L., & Manos A. (2005) e-Government beyond e-administration. The evolution of municipal area environments could establish a digital framework of confidence for citizens. *In the 5th European Conference on e-Government, (ECEG 2005) University of Antwerp*, Belgium, 16-17 June 2005.

Cap Gemini Ernst & Young (2003) Online availability of public services. How is Europe progressing? Information Society DG, 2003.

Chief Information Officer (CIO) Council (1999) Federal Enterprise Architecture Framework. Retrieved May 25th, 2006, from http://www.cio.gov/Documents/fedarch1.pdf

Chief Information Officer (CIO) Council (2001) A Practical Guide to Federal Enterprise Architecture, version 1.0, February 2001. Retrieved May 25th, 2006, from http://www.gao.gov/bestpractices/bpeaguide.pdf

Devadoss, P., Pan, S., & Huang, J. (2002) Structurational analysis of e-Government initiatives: a case study of SCO. *Decision Support Systems*, vol. 34, p. 253-269, ElSevier.

DG The Information Society (2004) User Satisfaction and Usage Survey of eGovernment services. Retrieved August 15th, 2007, from

http://europa.eu.int/information_society/activities/egovernment_research/doc/top_of_the_Web_report_2004.pdf)

eGov Consortium (2002) IST Project 2000 – 28471. An Integrated Platform for Realising One-Stop Government. D121–Services and process models functional specifications, 2002. Retrieved August 15th, 2007, from http://www.egov-project.org/egovsite/eGOV_D121.zip.

European Commission (2002) eEurope 2005: An information society for all. *European Commission - COM 263*, 2002. Retrieved August 15th, 2007, from http://europa.eu.int/eeurope

Federal Enterprise Architecture (FEA) Working Group (2002) E-Gov Enterprise Architecture Guidance Common Reference model. (July 25, 2002). Retrieved August 15th, 2007, from http://www.feapmo.gov/resources/E-Gov_Guidance_Final_Draft_v2.0.pdf

Federal Enterprise Architecture (FEA) Working Group (2005) Enabling Citizen-Centered Electronic Government. 2005-2006 FEA-PMO Action Plan. Retrieved August 15th, 2007, from www.whitehouse.gov/omb/egov/documents/2005_FEA_PMO_Action_Plan_FINAL.pdf

Gant, J., & Gant, D. (2002) Web portal functionality and State Government E-service. *In the proceedings of the 35th Hawaii international conference on system sciences* (IEEE 2002).

German Federal Government (2003). BundOnline 2005. 2003 Implementation Plan. Retrieved May 25th, 2005, from http://www.bunde.de

Godart, C. Saliou H., & Bignon, J.C. (2001) *"Asynchronous Coordination of Virtual Teams in Creative Applications (co-design or co-engineering): Requirements and Design Criteria"*. IEEE.

Ishida, T. (2002). Digital City Kyoto. *Communications of the ACM,* July 2002, vol.45, No.7.

KBSt Publication Series (2003) *"SAGA: Standards and Architectures for e-government Applications, Version 2.0"*. Retrieved August 15th, 2007, from http://egovstandards.gov.in/egs/eswg5/ enterprise-architecture-working-group-folder/standards-and-architectures-v2.pdf/ download

Lawry, P., Albrecht, C., Nunamaker, J., & Lee, J. (2002) Evolutionary development and research on Internet-based collaborative writing tools and processes to enhance eWriting in an eGovernment setting. *Decision Support Systems*, vol. 34, (2002), 229-252, ElSevier.

Organisation for Economic Co-operation and Development (OECD) (2001) *"The Hidden Threat to E-Government: Avoiding large government IT failures (Policy brief)"*. Retrieved August 15th, 2007, from http://www.oecd.org/dataoecd/19/12/1901677.pdf

Pavlichev, A., & Garson, G. D. (2004) *Digital Government Principles and Best Practices, Chapter 1 ("The promise of Digital Government")*, page 2, IDEA Group Publishing.

Peristeras V., & Tarabanis K. (2004). Governance Enterprise Architecture (GEA): Domain models for e-Governance. *In the 6th international conference on Electronic commerce* (ICEC), ACM.

Powel, A., & Picolli, G. (2004) Virtual Teams: A Review of Current Literature and Directions for Future Research. *The DATA BASE for advances in Information Systems-Winter 2004, vol 35, No.1*. ACM.

Reding, V. (2005) i2010: The European Commission's new programme to boost competitiveness in the ICT sector. *European Committee's press releases*. Retrieved August 15th, 2007, from http://europa.eu.int/rapid/pressReleasesAction.do?reference=SPEECH/05/format=HTML&aged=0&language=EN&guiLanguage=en)

Sairamesh, J., Lee, A., & Anania, L. (2004). Information Cities. *Communications of the ACM* February 2004, vol. 47, No.2.

Schubert, P., & Hausler, U. (2001) e-Government meets e-Business: A Portal Site for Startup Companies in Switzerland. *In the 34th International Conference on System Sciences* (IEEE 2001)

Sowa, F. J. (2000) Levels of Representation. *Knowledge Representation. Logical, philosophical and computational foundations* (pp. 188-189). Brooks/Cole Thomson Learning.

Sproull, L. & Patterson, J., (2004). Making Information Cities Livable. *Communications of the ACM* February 2004, vol. 49, No.2.

Tat-Kei Ho, A. (2002). Reinventing Local Governments and e-Government Initiative. *Public Administration Review,* July/August 2002, Vol. 62, No. 4., Blackwell Synergy.

Treasury Board Secretariat, Government of Canada (2001). Canada's Report on Portals, August 10, 2001.

Treasury Board Secretariat, Government of Canada (2006). Service Oriented Architecture Strategy. Retrieved May 25th, 2006, from http://www.tbs-sct.gc.ca/cio-dpi/Webapps/architecture/sd-eo/sd-eo_e.pdf)

UK Cabinet Office (2000). e-Government, a strategic framework for public services in the information age. Retrieved May 25th, 2006, from

http://archive.cabinetoffice.gov.uk/e-envoy/resources-pdfs/$file/Strategy.pdf

UK Cabinet Office, Office of the e-Envoy (2002) e-Government Interoperability Framework (e-GIF).

Part two: Technical Policies and Specifications. Retrieved August 15th, 2007, from http://www.govtalk.gov.uk/documents/e-GIF4Pt2_2002-04-25.pdf

UK Chief Information Officers Council (UK CIO) (2005) Enterprise Architecture for UK Government. An overview of the process and deliverables for Release 1. Retrieved August 15th, 2007, from http://www.cio.gov.uk/documents/cto/pdf/enterprise_architecture_uk.pdf

US Federal Government (2002) e-Government Strategy: Simplified Delivery of Services to Citizens. *Executive Office of the President, Office of Management and Budget, US Federal Government – February 2002.* Retrieved May 25th, 2006, from http://www.firstgov.gov/Topics/Includes/Reference/egov_strategy.pdf

Wesley, Addison (2003). *XML Data Management. Native XML and XML-enabled Database Systems. Pearson Education Inc.,* Boston,U.S.A.

Widmayer, P. (1999). "Building Digital Metropolis: Chicago's Future Networks". *IT Professional* Volume 1, Issue 4, July-Aug. 1999, p. 40 – 46. IEEE.

Wimmer, M., & Traunmuller, R. (2000) Trends in Electronic Government: Managing Distributed Knowledge. *In the 11th International Workshop on Database and Expert Systems Applications* (IEEE, DEXA'00)

Zachman, J. A. (1987) A Framework for Information Systems Architecture. *IBM Systems Journal,* vol. 26, No. 3, 1987 (available at http://www.research.ibm.com/journal/sj/263/ibmsj2603E.pdf)

Chapter XVIII
Government Enterprise Architectures:
Enabling the Alignment of Business Processes and Information Systems

Nigel Martin
The Australian National University, Australia

Shirley Gregor
The Australian National University, Australia

Dennis Hart
The Australian National University, Australia

ABSTRACT

This chapter describes the development and use of government enterprise architectures for the framing and alignment of the core business processes and enabling information systems at the Australian Bureau of Statistics (ABS) and the Centrelink Social Services agency. The chapter focuses on the construction and ongoing maintenance of public enterprise architectures that enable the alignment condition. An established research model has been used to guide the analysis and explication of the government business processes, enabling systems and architectures, and the resulting agency alignment. While the discussion acknowledges the existence of other formal and informal enablers of alignment (such as strategic planning or management support), this chapter concentrates on the enterprise architecture enabler. The functionally integrated government business processes and information systems that are established within the instantiated enterprise architecture are examined. The agencies' performance data reflects two public organizations that are closely aligned and have achieved upper benchmarked outcomes and recognition awards. The agencies' business processes and architectural practices conform to established theoretical frameworks.

INTRODUCTION

Since 1985 the Australian federal government has been directing public agencies to ensure that the business processes associated with service delivery are closely aligned and integrated with the enabling information systems and infrastructure. The introduction of Program Management and Budgeting (PMB) called for federal government organizations to align resource inputs, systems and processes with output results and performance in a framework designed to drive accountability, efficiency and effectiveness (Commonwealth of Australia, 1997). The PMB initiative represents the government's first attempt to draw together underlying government business processes with the supporting information systems in a coherent and performance enhancing fashion.

In 1997 the Australian government further developed these accountability and efficiency driven arrangements, and installed a new Outcomes-Outputs framework in 1999-2000 (Commonwealth of Australia, 2007b). The framework was intended to bring a sharper focus to the use of government resources, and the associated output of products and services. Importantly, public agencies were requested to identify the assets and resources under their control, and the specific service and product outputs that they would produce. This requirement formed part of the organizational regime that supported the linkage between agency resources and performance, management of growing complexities, and the movement of vast information and data stores.

These public efficiency initiatives had a profound impact on agencies, such as the Australian Bureau of Statistics (ABS) and Centrelink, which provide core government outputs of public services and products. The ABS is Australia's official statistical organization that provides over 600 different information products and services that assist and promote informed decision-making, research and discussion. Centrelink is Australia's primary social services agency, serving over 6.5 million customers, processing over 5 billion electronic transactions each year, and operating with an annual budget that exceeds A\$63 billion (Commonwealth of Australia, 2006b; Martin & Gregor, 2006). Given the inherent portfolio resource constraints, both agencies are focused on delivering their products and services in the most efficient and effective manner. The PMB and Outcomes-Outputs frameworks has forced the two agencies to examine the resources at their disposal, and how best to align and integrate those resources to meet their performance outcomes.

The aim of this chapter is to examine and analyze the agencies' enterprise architecture activities in order to develop an understanding of how the architecture can enable the alignment of the business processes and information systems. The ABS and Centrelink case organizations were selected for their exemplary public sector architectural practices, and continuing record of business and technical systems integration in the pursuit of quality public products and services delivery. Both organizations use a highly centralized architectural approach that supports the creation of integrated business and technically oriented artifacts (eg, business processes, technical systems infrastructure, and applications architectures). However, as a point of difference, the two agencies use different architectural frameworks and methods for the development of their respective enterprise architectures (ie, an internally developed ABS architecture method and the Zachman architecture framework for Centrelink). The research presented in this chapter adopts the internationally accepted definition of architecture as a description (model) of the basic arrangement and connectivity of parts of a system (either a physical or a conceptual object or entity) (International Standards Organization, 2000).

The agencies' data and experiences presented in this chapter were gathered as part of a larger doctoral study on the use of enterprise architectures in government organizations (Martin, 2005). The study used a qualitative research method which included discovery and analysis of architectural documents and designs, semi-structured and unstructured interviews with agencies executives and staff, studies of organizational public announcements and executive presentations, and participation in agencies' system and technology demonstrations. The research data includes the agencies enterprise architecture structures and components, and the business process and information systems alignment analysis.

While this first section has provided a brief introduction, the balance of the chapter is organized as follows. In the second section, the theoretical foundations for the chapter in the areas of strategic alignment, enterprise architecture, and government business processes are established. In the third section, a model of business process and information systems alignment is introduced and discussed in some detail. In the fourth section, the agencies enterprise architecture data and collection methods is presented. In the fifth section, the two agency case sites are discussed, including the enterprise architecture implementations (eg, frameworks, methods, governance arrangements, and resultant architectures). In the sixth section, the analysis of the alignment of government business processes and information systems is presented, including critical examples from the two cases. In the final section, the chapter concludes with a summary of the agency enterprise architectures and their capacity for enabling business process and information systems alignment, including the value of the architecture in the alignment dynamic and the importance of establishing foundation business processes.

BACKGROUND

The theoretical foundations of this chapter draw together several important concepts. The theory related to strategic alignment, enterprise architecture, and government business processes provides the underlying background for the chapter. These

critical alignment, architecture, and business process concepts are the subject of detailed discussions in the following sections.

Strategic Alignment

The organizational alignment construct has its roots in strategic management literature dating back to the mid 1950s (Drucker, 1954, 1980; Porter, 1980, 1981, 1991). In his seminal work in the management discipline, Porter (1980, 1981) termed the condition of internal and external compatibility as 'strategic fit' (sometimes also known as 'organizational fit'). Porter (1991) also identified an important condition for business success and leading corporate performance stating that *"an organization's internally consistent set of goals and policies aligns the firm's strengths and weaknesses with the external opportunities and threats"* (p. 99). Accordingly, Porter's concept of strategic fit was an early and important component of the alignment construct.

Following the work of management strategists, such as Drucker and Porter, Earl (1989) applied some of these strategic management principles to the information technology function, establishing a theory concept that links and integrates the organization's information technology strategy and infrastructure with business objectives. Importantly, this alignment and integration was considered to be enabled by formal organizational processes and mechanisms and more social people-based interactions, consistent with other established strategic planning principles (Horovitz, 1984). As a further advance in the alignment theory set, Henderson and Venkatraman (1993) developed a Strategic Alignment Model (SAM) that aligned and integrated business strategy, organizational infrastructure, information systems strategy, and information systems infrastructure (see Figure 1).

The SAM aligns the externally and internally focused components of the enterprise (termed strategic fit), while also integrating the business

Figure 1. Strategic alignment model (Source: Henderson & Venkatraman, 1993)

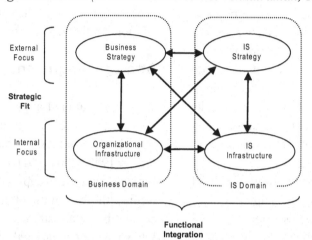

and information systems domains (termed functional integration). The model also represents four view points of alignment where the business strategy shapes the organizational and information system infrastructures design (strategy execution view); the business strategy shapes the information systems strategy and infrastructure design (technology transformation view); the information systems strategy shapes the business strategy and organizational infrastructure design (competitive potential view); and, the information systems strategy shapes the information system and organizational infrastructures design (service level view). Each of the four views depicts how a selected SAM component can be used as an anchor for shaping the alignment and integration conditions of the complete organization.

In this chapter, we will be primarily concerned with the functional integration dimension of alignment, where the business process segment of the organizational infrastructure is aligned with the information systems infrastructure. The selection of the SAM for use in the scoping of this chapter is based on its high level of theoretical utility, and its extensive use in other information systems and technology research studies (Chan, 2002; Chan, Huff, Copeland & Barclay, 1997; Croteau,

Solomon, Raymond & Bergeron, 2001; Reich & Benbasat, 1996, 2000; Sabherwal & Chan, 2001). Various studies have investigated the strategic fit and functional integration aspects of alignment with a view to determining whether improved alignment conditions can ultimately lead to increases in corporate and business performance (Chan, Huff, Copeland & Barclay, 1997; Croteau, Solomon, Raymond & Bergeron, 2001). In general, the findings of alignment research suggest that closer alignment and integration results in stronger organizational business performance, a seemingly desirable outcome for any public or private organization (Chan, Huff, Copeland & Barclay, 1997; Croteau, Solomon, Raymond & Bergeron, 2001; Sabherwal & Chan, 2001). These research outcomes, and the expansion of our understanding of the alignment construct, serve as a firm basis for the examination of business process and information systems alignment as a means of improving public agency efficiency and performance.

Enterprise Architecture

Some of the earliest literature in the Enterprise Architecture discipline was published during

Figure 1. Zachman enterprise architecture framework (Source: Sowa & Zachman, 1992)

Layer	What (Data)	How (Function)	Where (Network)	Who (People)	When (Time)	Why (Motivation)
Scope Context Boundary *(Planner)*	List of things important to the business	List of processes the business performs	List of locations in which the business operates	List of organizations important to the business	List of events significant to the business	List of business goals/ strategies
Business Model Concepts *(Owner)*	e.g., Semantic or Entity-Relationship Model	e.g., Business Process Model	e.g., Business Logistics System	e.g., Work Flow Model	e.g., Master Schedule	e.g., Business Plan
System Model Logic *(Designer)*	e.g., Logical Data Model	e.g., Application Architecture	e.g., Distributed System Architecture	e.g., Human Interface Architecture	e.g., Processing Structure	e.g., Business Rule Model
Technology Model Physics *(Builder)*	e.g., Physical Data Model	e.g., System Design	e.g., Technology Architecture	e.g., Presentation Architecture	e.g., Control Structure	e.g., Rule Design
Component Configuration *(Implementer)*	e.g., Data Definition	e.g., Program	e.g., Network Architecture	e.g., Security Architecture	e.g., Timing Definition	e.g., Rule Specification
Functioning Enterprise Instances *(Worker)*	e.g., Data	e.g., Function	e.g., Network	e.g., Organization	e.g., Schedule	e.g., Strategy

the late 1980s and early 1990s, when information systems specialists commenced developing systematic taxonomies for categorizing real world objects, computers, and other information systems entities (Sowa & Zachman, 1992; Zachman, 1987). The original Zachman (1987) information systems architecture framework developed three domain views (ie, data, function, and network) across five different perspectives (ie, scope, enterprise model, system model, technology model, and components). The framework columns depict different ways of representing real world entities (eg, in the network domain, an enterprise model might take the form of a sales network – retail stores linked by telephones). Importantly, the extended framework (see Figure 2) introduced additional formalisms, including people (ie, organizational structure or people-to-people relationships), time (ie, schedule or event-to-event relationships), and motivation (business motivation or ends-means-ends relationships) domains or columns, thereby providing a

greater level of non-technical content for artifact construction (Sowa & Zachman, 1992).

Over time, other technical architecture specialists and commercial information technology organizations and vendors have contributed to our understanding of enterprise architectures, concentrating their efforts in the areas of controlled planning of technical architectures and systems, technical systems analysis, business and technology architectures, and technology policy development (Gibson, 1994; Lloyd & Galambos, 1999; McDavid, 1999; Spewak & Hill, 1993; Targowski, 1990; The Open Group, 2006). This seemingly technology-focused approach to architecture, while wholly consistent with its technical origins, highlights an opportunity to consider and examine architecture as a more holistic and integrated business and technical systems artifact. If viewed in this way, architecture offers organizations a useful and valuable mechanism for combining, closely aligning, and functionally integrating their operating business and technology domains.

Indeed, further contemporary research in the area of organizational architectures shows a growing interest in the use of enterprise architectures for combining business and technology domains (Feurer, Chaharbaghi, Weber & Wargin, 2000; Gordon & Gordon, 2000; Murray & Trefts, 2000). For example, Gordon and Gordon (2000) examined the alignment and integration of strategic business and information technology units in eight large private organizations, and determined that internal and external business factors can impact the information technology unit structures. This research also showed that the information technology architecture directly influences the whole technology domain and the connective relationships with the business units. In a similar case study of the Hewlett Packard (HP) organization, researchers examined how the company developed and implemented a business alignment framework that incorporated business processes, information, applications, data and technology layers with a set of social organizational dimensions including culture, values and teams (Feurer, Chaharbaghi, Weber & Wargin, 2000). The researchers found that the HP business alignment framework was created for aligning the business and information technology strategies through mapping the core business processes and information technology solutions so as to facilitate and enable visible company changes.

Other studies have examined the theoretical engagement of business and information technology in true corporate partnerships. Murray and Trefts (2000) developed a new managerial process that combined the business and information technology architectures for the delivery of technology projects, while aligning the organization's business strategy and information technology infrastructure. The study also asserted the importance of ensuring that new business processes and information systems are coordinated and harmonized through the use of the combined whole-of-enterprise architecture.

What we can conclude from this evolving base of literature is that the use of enterprise architectures for enabling business-technology alignment and integration has taken on a growing importance in private and public organizational settings. It should be highlighted that while the business strategies, goals and processes portion of company enterprise architectures may not necessarily be comparable to government architectures (ie, profit motivated strategies and processes versus public service driven processes), the respective information technology and systems architecture components (such as the software, hardware, and IT infrastructure) may be similar in scope and scale (Martin, 2005).

Accordingly, architecture practitioners and researchers in private and public sector organizations are providing a greater level of focus on the alignment dimension, while establishing the blueprints and theoretical frameworks for combining the business and information systems domains. This chapter is directed at building further knowledge and understanding of government enterprise architecture implementations, and how these architectures might be used to align and integrate business processes and information systems in public organizations.

Government Business Processes

In the early 1990s, organizational business processes emerged as a major issue of concern for executive and technical managers within private and public organizations (Davenport & Short, 1990; Hammer, 1990; Hammer & Champy, 1993; Harrington, 1991). These concerns were based on the assertion that some business processes and intrinsic corporate activities were unplanned or under-designed in nature. Hammer (1990) typified some of these concerns when he posited *"Why did we design inefficient processes? In a way, we didn't. Many of our procedures were not designed at all; they just happened ... The hodgepodge of special cases and quick fixes was passed from one generation of workers to the next"* (p.107). The widely adopted definition of business processes as a set of logically related tasks that use the resources of an organization to achieve a defined business outcome further highlights the importance of task integration and resource planning (Davenport & Short, 1990). As a consequence, some organizations, such as the Ford Motor Company and Xerox, engaged in large scale business process re-engineering efforts (Davenport & Short, 1990; Hammer, 1990). Hence, the Business Process Re-engineering (BPR) discipline arose from the need to make work processes more efficient and organizationally integrated.

What this earlier business process work suggests for public sector agencies is a continual drive towards greater process and system alignment and integration for the delivery of larger volume and higher quality products and services. In support of this government direction, the Kettinger and Grover (1995) business process change model provides a comprehensive environmental schema that functionally aligns and integrates business processes, information technology, people and interpersonal aspects, management aspects, and the organizational structure for the delivery of products, services and corporate performance. Under this model, the alignment of core information systems (and the associated technologies) with business processes was considered to have a profound and lasting impact on the organization's ability to deliver public products and services in a dynamic and more efficient manner. Interestingly, the inclusion of the people and interpersonal aspects of process change underlines the importance of the interactions between the processes, systems, and socially based alignment mechanisms (Martin, Gregor & Hart, 2005).

In relation to government business operations there are possibly two further points that should be made. First, the implementation of new and more efficient business processes will likely involve the synergistic use of information systems and technologies (Alavi & Yoo, 1995; Johnson, 1993; Leith, 1994; Smith, 1994). Extant literature in the area of organizational business processes asserts that information systems combine with processes and associated tasks in the enabling of performance improvements (Gadd & Oakland, 1995; Hammer & Champy, 1993). In a further supporting study, McAdam and Donaghy (1999) found that the use of information systems and technologies is one of the critical success factors related to organizational process and performance improvement. Second, more efficient government business processes should target performance improvement from the customer's perspective (Chang, 1994). Some researchers have suggested that Deming's philosophy of continuous improvement can be readily applied to client services delivery in the public and private sectors (Deming, 1986; Parasuraman, Zeithaml & Berry, 1985). The assertion is that enhanced process management practices should ultimately lead to customer-focused business process improvements and elevated corporate performance. Some studies support this assertion and have found that the functional integration of information systems with organizational business processes positively impact knowledge and data sharing, expand corporate learning, and build transparency and trust with clients (Grover, Teng & Fiedler, 1993; Johnston & Carrico, 1988). In summary, government business processes readily combine with the organization's information systems and technology resources in delivering public products and services. The use of these types of customer-facing business processes, which are closely aligned with synergistic information systems, forms part of the larger machinery of government that delivers these products and services. Accordingly, these processes are worthy of some further investigation and improved understanding, especially in the context of process-system integration.

A MODEL OF BUSINESS PROCESS AND INFORMATION SYSTEMS ALIGNMENT

The study of government enterprise architectures, and their use as enablers of agency business processes and information systems alignment, required the combination of the key concepts into a suitably detailed research and analytical model. The model was constructed to provide a foundation for the critical analysis of the case organizations, enterprise architectures, and other high level alignment mechanisms, and was adapted from the work of Reich and Benbasat (1996, 2000) (see Figure 3) (Gregor,, Hart & Martin, 2007; Martin, 2005; Martin, Gregor & Hart, 2005; Reich & Benbasat, 1996, 2000).

The illustrated model is a dynamic process representation of alignment that flows from top to bottom, and includes interaction layers and feedback channels between the components. The enterprise conditions (eg, organizational structure,

dependence on technical systems, corporate history) interact and shape the context of the agency environment and its process-system alignment. The organizational alignment process is characterized by the dynamic interaction of social (eg, managerial support, communications) and formal (eg, enterprise architecture, governance processes) alignment mechanisms that result in an interactive and continuous state of alignment, represented by the alignment outcomes segment of the model.

In this form, the process model allows us to present four major research themes and associated questions for this chapter (Gregor, Hart & Martin, 2007; Martin, Gregor & Hart, 2005). First, Does an enterprise architecture framework, either internally developed or sourced commercially, influence the enabling of alignment? In the ABS case, the agency enterprise architecture method was developed internally, while in the Centrelink case, the agency used the Zachman framework. Second, Does the structure of an enterprise

Figure 3. Alignment research and analysis model (Source: Martin, 2005)

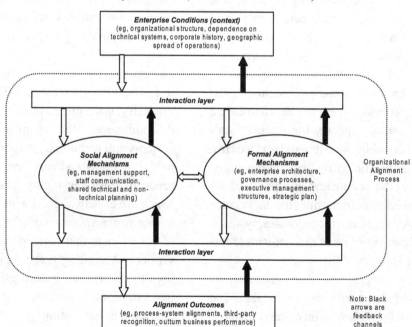

architecture influence the degree of alignment achieved? In this segment of the analysis we will present the structures, components and characteristics of the ABS and Centrelink architectures and their relative influence on the alignment state. Third, Does the use of an enterprise architecture combine with social mechanisms of alignment in processes that enable alignment outcomes? In this segment of the analysis we will examine and present the combination of the agencies' management support, business planning styles, and business plan communications with the enterprise architecture mechanisms in processes enabling alignment. Finally, Does the use of an enterprise architecture combine with other formal alignment mechanisms in processes that enable alignment? This segment of our analysis will briefly examine and present some of the combined relationships and interactive processes of the formal alignment mechanisms. In a holistic sense, the four research themes provide an aggregated view of government agency alignment and the relative contribution of the enterprise architecture as a formal alignment mechanism. Later in the chapter, we will present a process-system alignment analysis, further supported by resultant business performance data and third-party recognition of information system enabled business delivery, to illustrate the potential alignment outcomes.

The research and analysis model is consistent and complementary with the Henderson and Venkatraman (1993) SAM outlined earlier in the chapter. Strategic alignment is considered to be a dynamic and ubiquitous organizational state (ie, alignment, change, re-alignment), where the various segments of the model can be collectively and interactively influenced (Henderson & Venkatraman, 1993). The dynamism of agency alignment is represented by the feedback channels and posits that a change in any part of the model may impact the alignment state, and the model as a whole. As an example, a change in the agency enterprise architecture or strategic plan (formal alignment mechanisms) can stimulate changes in the agency structure (enterprise conditions or context), with structural changes having the potential to modify levels of management support or social communication (social alignment mechanisms). This is just one example of how dynamic change can impact the overall alignment outcome (ie, less or more alignment).

In studying government enterprise architectures, we acknowledge that some level of alignment would likely exist prior to an architectural implementation. Specifically, other research and analytical studies support our analytical approach, and have found that different types of social and formal alignment mechanisms, such as executive management support, collective planning styles, governance processes and strategic plans, can work to enable an organization's alignment condition (Henderson & Sifonis, 1988; Pyburn, 1983; Raghunathan & Raghunathan, 1989; Venkatraman, Henderson & Oldach, 1993). In the balance of this chapter, we will practically demonstrate how public organization's enterprise architectures can combine with other alignment mechanisms to functionally integrate and align business processes and information systems.

ENTERPRISE ARCHITECTURE DATA AND COLLECTION METHODS

The case data presented in this chapter was extracted from a larger doctoral study that investigated the use of enterprise architectures in four Australian government agencies, including the ABS and the Centrelink social services agency (Gregor, Hart & Martin, 2007; Martin, 2005; Martin, Gregor & Hart, 2005) (The agency corporate data has been updated to take account of the 2005-2006 financial year performance). The study's case organizations were selected from the Commonwealth Architecture Forum and the Queensland Government Forum for Enterprise Architecture Collaboration special interest groups that were established to further architecture goals

417

and initiatives at the federal and state government levels. The decision to present the ABS and Centrelink case material in this chapter was based on the highly detailed agency enterprise architecture implementations, high visibility of social and formal alignment mechanisms, and the capacity to examine the alignment of government business processes with corporate information systems.

Proven multiple qualitative research methods were adopted for case data collection (Burgelman, 1983, 1994). This approach allowed research data and information to be triangulated across multiple sources. The two agencies provided archival and publicly available documents (ie, audited parliamentary and agency papers) in the areas of governance, information systems, agency performance, enterprise architecture and business plans. Architectural documents and drawings were analyzed by comparing the agencies' architectural state with the requirements (ie, architecture coverage, concepts, components,

representation and glossary) contained in the ISO 15704 standard (Industrial Automation Systems – Requirements for Enterprise-Reference Architecture and Methodologies) that was modified to suit government agencies (Gregor, Hart & Martin, 2007; International Standards Organization, 2000; Martin, 2005; Martin, Gregor & Hart, 2005). The analysis for both agencies will be presented later in the chapter.

Also, seven executives and thirteen managers from both agencies offered comments and views during eighteen semi-structured interviews and fifteen follow-up discussions of up to one and a half hours in duration (Martin, 2005; Martin & Gregor, 2005, 2006; Martin, Gregor & Hart, 2005). The theme based questions are attached at Appendix A to the chapter. In accordance with the Miles and Huberman (1994) data processing principles, the interview comments were recorded, two pass coded, and stored on a purpose built database management system for use in the case

Table 2. Example case analysis codes (Source: Martin, 2005)

Code	Code Definition
T1-CM-ZA	Theme 1 – Commercial Architecture Method – Zachman architecture framework
T1-IM-AM	Theme 1 – Internally Developed Architecture Method – ABS architecture framework
T2-CO-AC	Theme 2 – Architecture Completeness – Architecture components
T2-CO-AP	Theme 2 – Architecture Completeness – Applicability and Coverage of Enterprise Entity
T2-CO-EC	types
T2-CO-GL	Theme 2 – Architecture Completeness – Enterprise concepts
T2-CO-RP	Theme 2 – Architecture Completeness – Architectural glossary
T2-CU-BF*	Theme 2 – Architecture Completeness – Architectural representation (depiction)
T2-CU-CM*	Theme 2 – Current characteristic – Business focused (driven) architecture
T2-CU-DD*	Theme 2 – Current characteristic – Capability management enabling architecture
T2-CU-GM*	Theme 2 – Current characteristic – Document management deficiencies in architecture
T2-CU-IS*	Theme 2 – Current characteristic – Governance mechanism in architecture
T2-CU-RA*	Theme 2 – Current characteristic – Information structuring architecture
T2-CU-TC*	Theme 2 – Current characteristic – Reusable (component) architecture
	Theme 2 – Current characteristic – Technology control architecture
T3-MS-HI	Theme 3 – Management Support – High
T3-MS-MO	Theme 3 – Management Support – Moderate
T3-MS-LO	Theme 3 – Management Support – Low
T3-PS-NO	Theme 3 – Business Planning Style – NO - Not present
T3-PS-YS	Theme 3 – Business Planning Style – YES - Present
T4-AL-SP	Theme 4 – Existence of Organizational Alignment – Supported
T4-AL-NU	Theme 4 – Existence of Organizational Alignment – Neutral (No valence in either direction)
T4-AL-NS	Theme 4 – Existence of Organizational Alignment – Not Supported

Note: Codes were replicated for non-current, or emerging, characteristics that were in development

analysis (Martin, 2005; Miles & Huberman, 1997). The codes were designed to classify, present and publish commentaries by research theme and summary notations within each theme (see code examples in Table 1) (Gregor, Hart & Martin, 2007; Martin, 2005; Martin, Gregor & Hart, 2005; Miles & Huberman, 1997).

In addition, executive presentations and corporate announcements by the ABS and Centrelink were collected and integrated into the written case evidence. In order to gain experience with agency information systems, the ABS and Centrelink also provided researchers with system demonstrations of data warehouse facilities, automatic workflow applications, corporate database environments, and legislative interpretation applications. This facilitated improved understanding of some of the underlying internal business processes and the enabling technical systems.

The aggregation of the collected and analyzed case data has culminated in a rich body of critically evaluated evidence that supports the augmentation of the research and analysis model. Staff members and executives at the agencies were not averse to providing critical comments on architectural practice, the social mechanisms of organizational alignment, or the potential limitations of using an Enterprise Architecture or other formal alignment mechanisms (Martin, 2005; Martin, Gregor & Hart, 2005).

GOVERNMENT AGENCY CASE STUDIES

In this section of the chapter, we will introduce the case agencies and develop a detailed discussion of the two enterprise architecture implementations. The opportunity will be taken to contrast the different architecture approaches adopted by the agencies, while highlighting the important consistencies with commercial architecture standards and frameworks.

The Australian Bureau of Statistics

The ABS is a federal government agency headquartered in Canberra, Australia that employs approximately 3,000 staff and has origins dating back to the early 1900s, when the Census and Statistics Act (1905) was passed and the Commonwealth Bureau of Census and Statistics (CBCS) established. The CBCS was abolished in 1974 and the ABS installed in its place. In its capacity as Australia's official statistical organization, the ABS has a mission to assist and encourage informed decision-making, research and discussion through the delivery of high quality and objective national statistics (Commonwealth of Australia, 2005b, 2005c, 2006a). The ABS manages a recurrent budget of approximately A$338 million (in 2006 dollars) (Commonwealth of Australia, 2006a).

The ABS is characterized as a quality information organisation that collects, processes and disseminates accurate and timely economic data and community information. The ABS offers statistical publications in the two major areas of economic statistics (eg, trade, business, national accounts, manufacturing, agriculture) and population statistics (eg, census, demography, labour, social conditions, crime), supported by three functional service groups (statistical methodology; information management and census; and technology and corporate services) (Commonwealth of Australia, 2005c, 2005d, 2006a).

The ABS has been recognised as a world leader in the statistics delivery business since the early 1990s (The Economist, 1991, 1993), while consistently rating well above average against international government and non-government organizations in Gartner Group information technology benchmarking studies, particularly in the areas of software and systems development (Commonwealth of Australia, 2000, 2001). The enterprise architecture mechanism is an integral part of the agency infrastructure, and has assisted with the understanding of future business directions and processes, while aiding the identification and management of the information systems and technologies required to support that future state (ie, maintain alignment) (Palmer, 2003).

The Centrelink Social Services Agency

The Centrelink agency operates as the government's social service delivery arm and is responsible for delivering services and payments, such as job seeker assessments and referrals, parenting payments, youth allowances, and social work services on behalf of eighteen (18) government agencies and departments at the state and federal levels (Commonwealth of Australia, 2006c). Centrelink was legislated as a federal agency in 1997, following the merger of the Department of Social Security and the Commonwealth Employment Service. The organization is headquartered in Canberra, Australia, employs approximately 25,000 staff at over 1,000 service delivery points, and supports over 6.5 million customers (representing approximately one-third of the population of Australia) (Commonwealth of Australia, 2006b, 2007a, 2007c). Centrelink manages a recurrent budget of approximately A\$2.3 billion (in 2006 dollars) (Commonwealth of Australia, 2006b).

In order to understand the scale of the Centrelink operations, it should be noted that on an annual basis the agency delivers more than 140 different products and services, pays over 10 million individual entitlements valued at over A\$63 billion, records 5.2 billion electronic customer transactions, and receives more than 30.77 million telephone calls and over 47 million online page views (Commonwealth of Australia, 2007a, 2007c). Centrelink has also won several national awards for business delivery and technology driven productivity in the area of electronic business and customer relationship management (Commonwealth of Australia, 2005a, 2006b; Martin & Gregor, 2006). As an example, the suite of five major e-Business projects secured an Australian government technology gold award in 2003. The enterprise architecture mechanism is a critical tool of the agency that has enabled the building of connections with customers and important information systems and technologies capabilities (Treadwell, 2003).

The Enterprise Architecture Frameworks and Methods

The creation of an enterprise architecture can take many development paths and, as we have seen earlier in the theory section of the chapter, can also involve the use of proven architectural frameworks and methods (Sowa & Zachman, 1992; The Open Group, 2006; Zachman, 1987). In the first case organization, four staff members from the ABS commenced the architecture development and documentation process in 1999 with a completed version 1.0 in September 2001, and an updated version 2.0 in March 2003. The internal architecture development method formed part of the information resource management process, and was based on the identification of business and technical systems capability gaps (see Figure 4) (Gregor, Hart & Martin, 2007; Martin, 2005; Martin & Gregor, 2006; Palmer, 2003).

The ABS enterprise architecture documentation was reviewed and updated periodically (every 6 to 12 months) by the Chief Information Officer (CIO) and technical services division, to reflect changing alignment, systems, environments, and business capability gaps. The architecture update process was typically triggered by shifts in business products and processes, changes in service delivery patterns, and associated investment activities. The business drivers (eg, new products, services, client needs, financial constraints) that stimulated the development of new and enhanced information systems for product and service delivery were a primary input to the architecture change process and method.

The primary mechanism for evolving the physical ABS enterprise architecture was the

Figure 4. ABS enterprise architecture method (Source: Palmer, 2003)

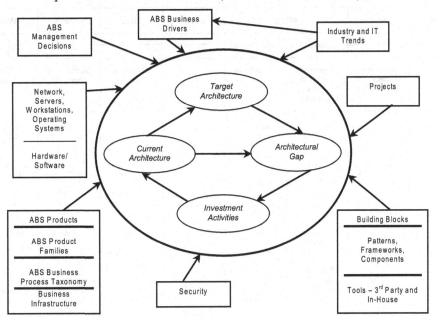

identification of an architectural gap (ie, difference between current and target architectures based on business drivers and changes) and the enunciation of the investment activities required to bridge the gap. A good example of architectural evolution was the development of the ABS Input Data Warehouse (IDW) (2001-2004) (Gregor, Hart & Martin, 2007; Martin & Gregor, 2005). In 2001, the ABS identified a gap in business capability (ie, statistics provider processes and workloads were high and inefficient due to multiple database entry tasks), coupled with the need for a single database structure and integration tool in the architecture (ie, SAS database software). The investment activities required to deliver the new system included the construction and documentation of a 'production pilot' warehouse, operating 'pilot' warehouse, and 'full production' warehouse, training of business operations staff, and the development of applications interfaces and associated systems. The full production warehouse holds over 400 million records and was commissioned into operation in mid-2004.

In our second case, the Centrelink agency adopted the Zachman Enterprise Architecture Framework for developing and documenting their architecture (Sowa & Zachman, 1992; Treadwell, 2003; Zachman, 1987). While Centrelink (as the former Department of Social Security) had been developing its technical architectures since the late 1980s, it made a conscious decision to adopt the Zachman framework as a more formal development method in late 2002, some four years after its physical establishment as a government agency. The framework had been divided into Zachman's Interrogatives (ie, Why, Who, What When, How and Where) and populated using the Centrelink business constructs and technical systems artifacts (see Figure 5) (Martin, 2005; Treadwell, 2003).

It should be noted that Centrelink did not augment the horizontal layers of the Zachman framework, instead choosing to identify the major clients, products, services, processes, systems, business drivers and delivery locations.

Importantly, the major business processes are encapsulated in the vertical programs and

Figure 5. Centrelink augmentation of the Zachman framework (Source: Treadwell, 2003)

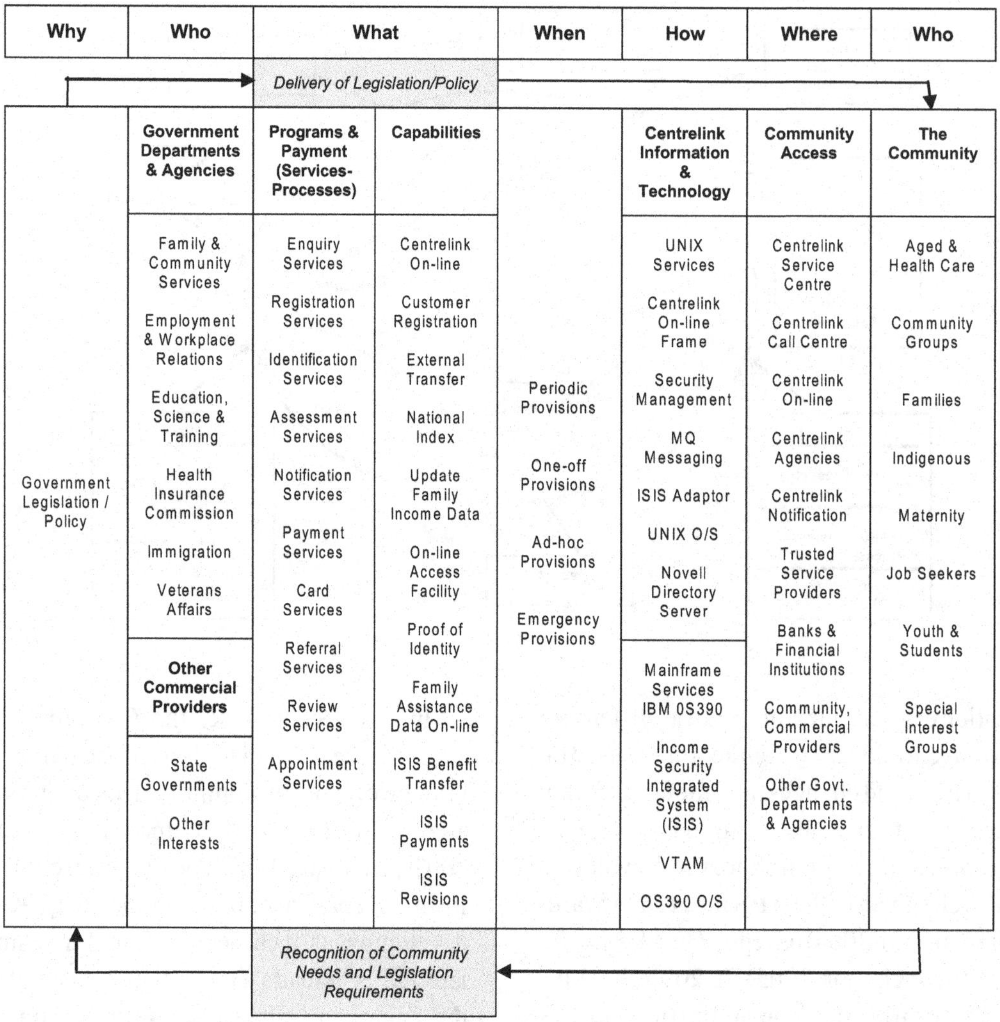

Why	Who	What		When	How	Where	Who
		Delivery of Legislation/Policy					
	Government Departments & Agencies	Programs & Payment (Services-Processes)	Capabilities		Centrelink Information & Technology	Community Access	The Community
Government Legislation / Policy	Family & Community Services	Enquiry Services	Centrelink On-line	Periodic Provisions	UNIX Services	Centrelink Service Centre	Aged & Health Care
	Employment & Workplace Relations	Registration Services	Customer Registration		Centrelink On-line Frame	Centrelink Call Centre	Community Groups
	Education, Science & Training	Identification Services	External Transfer		Security Management	Centrelink On-line	Families
	Health Insurance Commission	Assessment Services	National Index	One-off Provisions	MQ Messaging	Centrelink Agencies	Indigenous
	Immigration	Notification Services	Update Family Income Data		ISIS Adaptor	Centrelink Notification	Maternity
	Veterans Affairs	Payment Services	On-line Access Facility	Ad-hoc Provisions	UNIX O/S	Trusted Service Providers	Job Seekers
		Card Services	Proof of Identity	Emergency Provisions	Novell Directory Server	Banks & Financial Institutions	Youth & Students
	Other Commercial Providers	Referral Services	Family Assistance Data On-line		Mainframe Services IBM OS390	Community, Commercial Providers	Special Interest Groups
	State Governments	Review Services	ISIS Benefit Transfer		Income Security Integrated System (ISIS)	Other Govt. Departments & Agencies	
	Other Interests	Appointment Services	ISIS Payments		VTAM		
			ISIS Revisions		OS390 O/S		
		Recognition of Community Needs and Legislation Requirements					

payment layer of the augmented framework and are aligned with Centrelink's information and technology systems and community access layers (see process-system mappings later in the chapter). The architecture framework formed part of the larger agency management and governance arrangements, and was driven by changes in business posture and structures (including the underlying legislation). A typical example of architecture driven development was the Online Claims and Services system (Commonwealth of Australia, 2006d). Online claims and services systems were redeveloped in 2005-06 to provide more reliable health and welfare payments and streamline and better align internal agency business processes. Since mid-2005, payments such as the Youth Allowance, Austudy Student Payments, Maternity Payment and Family Tax Benefit have been available through online channels, forming a significant portion of the 250,000 online transactions processed each week. Centrelink's architectural practice has enabled the nationally recognized, continuous improvement of online services and payments, and the associated transformative business processes (Commonwealth of Australia, 2006b, 2006d). As a further example, the Student Notification of Employment Income Initiative supported the development and replication of e-Business services and processes in multiple customer groups, while reducing annual physical mail-outs by over 2 million notification letters (Commonwealth of Australia, 2005d).

A critical point in the comparison of the two architecture frameworks or methods is the parity of the two development artifacts in their capacity to describe the organization, and develop the matched business and technical system components. The two cases show that it is possible to establish and maintain a whole-of-enterprise architecture using internally developed or commercially available frameworks or methods. While several established architecture frameworks and methods exist (eg, The Open Group Architecture Framework, Federal Enterprise Architecture Framework), the creation of an architecting method that closely reflects the needs and scope of the agency should not be undervalued (Commonwealth of Australia, 2006d). The ABS method serves as an example of an architecture that is tailored to reflect the business environment and dynamics that characterize the work of the agency.

The Architecture Governance

The governance of the physical architecture is an important management dimension for the establishment and maintenance of process-system alignment (Information Technology Governance Institute, 2003). In this section of the chapter we will present the different lines of process-systems governance for each agency, and highlight the key structures for architecture management.

The two case agencies use a combination of information systems and technologies resource committees for the ongoing governance and management of the business and technical architecture artifacts (Martin & Gregor, 2006). The ABS used a dual committee structure supported by business and technology panels and working groups in managing the enterprise architecture (Gregor, Hart &

Martin, 2007; Martin, 2005; Martin & Gregor, 2006; Palmer, 2003). The ABS tabled larger project (such as the data warehouse mentioned earlier) business cases and documentation with the Information Resource Management Committee (IRMC) that was chaired by the Deputy Chief Executive Officer, with smaller projects (such as desktop operating system upgrades) passed to the CIO-chaired Investment Review Board (IRB) for consideration and guidance. Centrelink used a similar dual committee structure that included a Business Investment Committee (BIC) for large business directed projects, and a separate e-Business governance group for those key business process and online systems developments (Commonwealth of Australia, 2002, 2003a). Both agencies also used working level project boards and joint business-technical architecture panels for the provision of guidance and support (Martin, 2005; Martin & Gregor, 2006; Palmer, 2003).

Importantly, the two agencies used formal executive management structures to ensure that the architecture was corporately governed and managed, particularly in the areas of business process and technical systems implementation and alignment. The two agencies' practices were found to be wholly consistent with the Information Technology Governance Institute (ITGI) guidelines for corporate boards and executive management teams (Information Technology Governance Institute, 2003). We would stress that architectural governance is considered to be a prime responsibility of the government agency's leadership. However, ultimately this responsibility flows down to all operational members of staff, particularly those charged with process-systems implementations.

The Enterprise Architecture Structures

While the adoption of an enterprise architecture framework or method provides the instantiation tool for government architectures, the ultimate outcome is an agency architecture that accurately reflects the shape of the organization's business and its largely technical systems. In the following sections, we will discuss the resultant agency architectures and their consistency with international architecture standards.

In the ABS case, the architecting method yielded a highly structured business and technical systems architecture (see Figure 6) (Commonwealth of Australia, 2003b; Gregor, Hart & Martin, 2007; Martin, 2005; Palmer, 2003).

The ABS architecture was segmented into three major structural components. In the general component, the architecture included a set of principles and objectives that were used in the architectural construction. Importantly, the two driving objectives of the architecture were to ensure that the IT environment is aligned with the ABS business imperatives (its mission, outputs and outcomes, and processes) and, to help the ABS build an IT environment that can be easily changed and extended, so as to retain its alignment with changing business imperatives.

These objectives reinforced the ongoing connection between the architecture and the process-system alignment condition. In the business component (shaded in grey), the ABS first developed sub-structures that described how the architecture, technologies and online environment would be developed and maintained, and a comprehensive taxonomy and management arrangements for the pivotal corporate business processes (ie, Business survey, Household survey, Index survey, Administrative By-Product collection, and Derivation collection process classes). Importantly, the business process taxonomy component of the architecture integrated the primary corporate business processes with the enabling information systems and technologies (see process-system mappings later in the chapter).

In the technical component, the ABS defined and described its key domain architectures (ie, applications, security, data management); commercial systems, tools and technology standards (eg, XML); software components, objects and interface designs (eg, object oriented designs, application programming interfaces); and the hardware and software infrastructure required for business delivery (ie, mid range computing systems, DeveloperWorks technology demon-

Figure 6. ABS enterprise architecture (Source: Palmer, 2003)

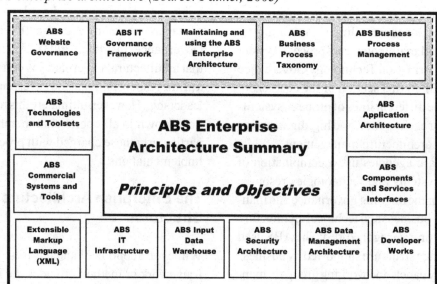

stration sandbox, data warehouses, desktop and mobile networks). The scope of the ABS technical systems is extensive and, when combined with the business component, shows a good measure of consistency with international architecture standards (see Table 2).

A comparative analysis shows that, in terms of the key requirements for instantiating the architecture (ie, architecture coverage, concepts, components, representation, and glossary), the ABS enterprise architecture is largely consistent with the ISO 15704 reference architecture standard (International Standards Organization, 2000). The table outlines a combination of business and technical system artefacts that are essential for enterprise operations and overall business delivery. Important examples include the description and explication of managerial governance, work activities, and business processes that are critical for corporate performance outcomes; and the technical system development methods, technologies, toolsets, and operating entities that directly support business delivery. The ABS architecture has benefited from the adoption and implementation of the internally developed architecture method that constructs and binds the business and technical parts of the organization.

In the Centrelink case, the Zachman framework offered the agency an opportunity to segment the architecture into five business and technical systems components and allocate these to senior executive managers (organizational architects) (see Figure 7).

In formally enunciating its architecture, Centrelink established a detailed list of architecture development principles. The principles that supported the process-system alignment condition included each (technical) architecture cluster having a unity of purpose which binds its unique business processes and data together and, each architecture cluster being owned by a technical systems team and having a business process sponsor.

The agency business architect held responsibility for business models, processes, capabilities, and governance frameworks (shaded in grey). Centrelink developed sub-architectures that modelled the organization's primary business behaviours and client relationships, a description of the high level business processes (ie, service delivery management, governance, relationship management, change management, information management and staff capability) and operating processes (ie, client registration, assessment,

Figure 7. Centrelink enterprise architecture (Source: Treadwell, 2003)

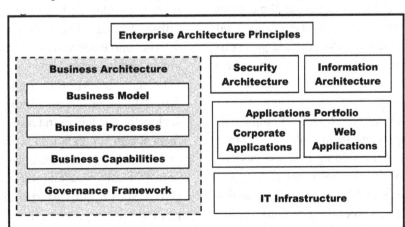

425

planning, referral, payments, and review) using benefits realisation techniques and process maps, a register of significant internal and external business capabilities (eg, project management, financial management, customer service, service providers, telephone call centres) that are critical to customer delivery, and the governance framework that guide and direct the business and supporting technical systems (see process-system mappings later in the chapter).

The technical segments of the architecture reflect Centrelink's critical business delivery systems. The information architecture includes a vast data warehouse, and data/information holdings in excess of 215 Terabytes at any point in time (Martin, 2005). The security architecture covers the mainframe processing and e-Business platforms with standards-based security access monitoring and intrusion systems (Martin, 2005). The IT infrastructure draws together the mainframe and on-line production and assurance activities for batch services, mail-outs, and systems upgrades; and the network services that are related to enterprise server and desktop design, management and support in local and wide areas. The applications portfolio is segmented into the larger corporate applications for mainframe, production, transaction processing and customer servicing, and the critical Web applications required for e-Business delivery in the Intranet and Internet service channels. Again, in the case of Centrelink, the combination of the business and technical architecture components is largely consistent with the ISO 15704 reference architecture standard (International Standards Organization, 2000) (see Table 2).

Some of the more relevant examples of compliant components include the description and explication of the guiding business models, corporate governance arrangements, and agency business processes; and the secure e-Business delivery and backroom processing systems that are underpinned by network systems infrastructure for business enablement. The Centrelink archi-

tecture reflects an augmentation of the Zachman framework that has enabled the creation and integration of the business and technical parts of the organization (Sowa & Zachman, 1992).

In both agencies, the architectures were found to have promoted early and continued concentration on the business aspects of the enterprise including the constituent items (eg, processes, models, capabilities), information systems and technology governance arrangements, integration of the business delivery units with the supporting corporate information, and reuse of architecture components for improved business efficiency and generic systems design (Gregor, Hart & Martin, 2007; Martin, 2005). These architecture characteristics further assisted the development and maintenance of the business and technical systems nexus and the agency alignment condition.

Other Alignment Mechanisms

Earlier in the chapter, we mentioned the capacity of other social and formal alignment mechanisms to promote and sustain alignment. During the course of our work, we were able to examine and detail executive mangement support, business planning styles, and business planning communications in the social alignment context (Martin, 2005; Martin, Gregor & Hart, 2005). The research showed that a strong executive management support regime, a collegiate business planning style that utilises business and technical staff, and open internal and external communications channels are compelling social mechanisms of alignment (Martin, 2005; Martin, Gregor & Hart, 2005). Similarly, other formal alignment mechanisms, such as the agencies' strategic plan, line management structures, balanced score cards, and audit and review actions, were uncovered and formed part of the ubiquitous alignment dynamic (Gregor, Hart & Martin, 2007; Martin, 2005). These cases illustrate the important point that the enterprise architecture is one of many alignment mechanisms present within organizations. In most cases, these

Table 2. Enterprise architecture requirements analysis (Adapted from ISO15704) (source: Commonwealth of Australia, 2003b; Gregor, Hart & Martin, 2007; International Standards Organization, 2000; Martin, 2005; Palmer, 2003; Treadwell, 2003)

Requirement	Sub-Requirement	Architecture Content	ABS	Centrelink	Examples of Architecture Content
Applicability and Coverage of Enterprise Entity Types	Enterprise Design	Activities required to design, build, maintain and manage enterprise entities.	•	•	The ABS design activities for surveys and information processing – business analysis, re-engineering, prototyping, synthesis. Centrelink design activities – value chain analysis, simulation, business redesign, and website design.
	Enterprise Operation	Work activities required in enterprise entities operations.	•	•	The ABS work activities – data collections, publishing operations, clearing house work. Centrelink work activities – customer service, call centre operations, transaction processing, notification, and client access.
Enterprise Concepts	Human Orientation	Human roles, responsibilities, authorizations, and relations to the enterprise	•	•	The ABS architecture – corporate directory and plans details the roles and responsibilities of the executive management team and staff. Centrelink architecture (governance section) – details roles and responsibilities of the board of management directors, executive management team and staff.
	Process Orientation	Business processes, process functionality, and operational behaviours	•	•	The ABS architecture – high level business processes (eg, Census, Business surveys, Household surveys), and operational behaviours (eg, data extraction, transformation, and loading). Centrelink architecture (business processes section) – eg, service delivery, relationship, and change management, staff capability, registration, assessment, referral.
	Technology Orientation	Technologies employed in enterprise operations and processes	•	•	The ABS architecture – ABS technologies and IS toolsets (eg, XML, Common Object Modelling, SQL, Java Tools, MS.net). The Centrelink architecture – technologies and IS toolsets (eg, Cobol, DB2, OS390, SQL, Java Tools, SAS, MS.net).
	Mission Performance	Processes or activities involved in the performance of the stated enterprise mission	•	•	The ABS architecture – critical business activities and processes for mission performance (eg, Client groups surveys/information dissemination, publication production processes, systems governance). The Centrelink architecture – critical business activities and processes for mission performance (eg, Client registration, customer service, payments/transactions, governance, social and welfare support).
	Life Cycle	Life cycle representations of the enterprise entities and constructs	•	•	The ABS architecture – systems/technology lifecycle phases and history (eg, 1980s mainframe computer retired in 2005, midrange systems implemented in 2000s). The Centrelink architecture – systems/technology lifecycle phases and history (eg, 1980s STRATPLAN M204 DB implementation, IT Refresh Program in 2003).
	Sub-architectures	Sub-architecture representations to the user	•	•	The ABS architecture – applications, security, data management and IT infrastructure sub-architectures. The Centrelink architecture – business, applications, security, information and IT infrastructure sub-architectures.
Architectural Components	Information Systems Development Methodologies, ISDM	Identification of ISDMs for systems development	•	•	The ABS architecture – ISDM, project management framework, and software development methodology. The Centrelink architecture – ISDM (Agile based), project management framework, joint applications development, and rapid applications development.
	Modelling Languages or Descriptive Constructs	Enterprise operations modeling languages or descriptive constructs	•	•	The ABS architecture – UML (for some software applications), XML and Lotus Workflow Architect to model and describe agency outputs, operations and processes. The Centrelink architecture – UML (for some software applications), XML, Forte Tools and MS Visio to model and describe agency outputs, operations and processes.
	Enterprise Tools	Computer-enabled tools that support integration projects and initiatives	•	•	The ABS mandated toolsets for integration projects – XML, Simple Object Access Protocol, UML, IBM Websphere, and MS.Net. The Centrelink toolsets for integration projects – XML, Internet Inter-Orb Protocol, UML, IBM Websphere-MQ Series, CORBA Tools, and MS.Net.
	Enterprise Modules	Enterprise module, building block or product family representations	•	•	The ABS architecture – software components, service interfaces, application families, and product line architectures. The Centrelink architecture – systems clusters (common business, benefit specific, support, development), mid range server, online, mobile hardware and associated software.
	Operational System Descriptions	Description of operational hardware and software systems	•	•	The ABS architecture – desktop, mid range server, online, mobile hardware and associated software. The Centrelink architecture – desktop, mid range server, mainframe, online, mobiles, call centres, and vendor and agency developed software.
Architectural	Graphical Depictions	High level graphical depictions of architecture structures	•	•	The ABS architecture – rich graphical depictions of the concepts/schemas (eg, IT Infrastructure depicted as a 'rain forest ecosystem'). The Centrelink architecture – graphical depictions (eg, clusters, architecture framework segments).
Architectural Glossary	Glossary of Terms	Reference all major terms used in the architecting approach	•	•	The ABS architecture – corporate glossary of terms. The Centrelink architecture – e-Reference suite, Data Dictionary, Thesaurus, and other reference tools (eg, EDGE Decision support systems).

Table 3. ABS process-systems analysis (Source: Gregor, Hart & Martin, 2007; Martin, 2005; Palmer, 2005)

Major Business Process	Business Sub-Process	Information Systems/Information Technology
Business Survey Class	• Provider Management	Lotus Notes DB, Survey Facility, Interim Despatch and Collection Control system (IDACC), SAS DB, Input Processing Systems (IPS), INSPECT process and report software, Optical Character Reader (OCR), Imputed Marker Reader (IMR), Optical Marker Reader (OMR), BLAISE computer assisted interview software
	• Input Quality Assurance	IPS, SAS DB, Lotus Notes DB
	• Derivation	SAS DB, Lotus Notes DB
	• Imputation, estimation, aggregation	Generalized survey imputation processor (GENIMP), Generalized survey estimation facility (GENEST), SAS
	• Macro-edit, analysis	SAS OLAP tool, SAS Assist tool, Generalized survey winsorisation component (GENWINS)
Administrative By-Product Collection Class	• Data Capture	Natural software system, PL1 system, SAS DB, EAI XML, Centura SQL Windows development tool (CENTURA), Computer assisted coding system (CAC)
	• Input Quality Assurance	Natural software system, PL1 system, SAS DB, CENTURA, Clipper DB
	• Derivation	SAS DB, Lotus Notes DB
	• Aggregation	Generalized survey imputation processor (GENIMP), Generalized survey estimation facility (GENEST), SAS DB
	• Macro-edit, analysis	SAS OLAP tool, SAS Assist tool
Derivation Collection Class	• Data Collect, Capture, Load	Lotus 123, MS Excel, Lotus Notes DB, Forecasting-Analysis-Modeling Environment (FAME)
	• Estimates compilation	Forecasting-Analysis-Modeling Environment (FAME), MODIS Online Visualisation and Analysis System (MOVAS)
	• Macro-edit	Forecasting-Analysis-Modeling Environment (FAME), Lotus 123, MS Excel
Index Survey Class	• Data Capture	CENTURA, XML, Lotus Notes DB, Constellar Hub collection system, Laptop computers
	• Input Quality Assurance	CENTURA, Lotus Notes DB
	• Input Index compilation	CENTURA
	• Index-edit, analysis	CENTURA, SQL OLAP
Household Survey Class	• Data Capture	OMR scanner, BLAISE, HS Office Management system
	• Input Quality Assurance	IPS, BLAISE, Procedural Language for Edit, Amend and Tabulation system (PLEAT), SAS DB
	• Derivation	IPS, PLEAT, SAS DB
	• Weighting and Tabulation	HS Facility
	• Edit, analysis	SAS DB

mechanisms are non-synchronized and tend to work in different time frames and cycles, transiting between alignment, change and re-alignment, as business circumstances evolve (Gregor, Hart & Martin, 2007; Martin, 2005; Venkatraman, Henderson & Oldach, 1993).

ALIGNING BUSINESS PROCESSES AND INFORMATION SYSTEMS USING ARCHITECTURE

The purpose of this chapter was to illustrate how the development and deployment of enterprise architectures can enable the alignment of core agency business processes with corporate information systems. In earlier sections of the chapter, the cases identified the presence of these two primary and integrated architectural components within the agencies. Architectural drawings and descriptive documents from both agencies allowed the analysis and construction of the process-system maps that show the linkages and points of integration (see Tables 3 and 4).

The process-system mappings represented in the tables show that the agencies have taken the opportunity to develop accurate depictions of the process and systems relationships that are

Table 4. Centrelink process-systems analysis (Source: Commonwealth of Australia, 2003b, 2007d; Martin, 2005; Treadwell, 2003)

Major Business Processes	Business Sub-Processes	Information Systems/Information Technology
• Service Delivery Management • Relationship Management • Change Management • Information Management	• Client Registration • Client Identification • Client Notification • Client Referral • Review (Clients) • Review (Information)	IBM OS/390 Mainframe, OS/390 MQ, ISIS M204, DB2, SAS, Teradata, SQL, Data Warehouse, Novell Directories, Security Management Security Access Management System/Access Control Facility 2 (SAMS/ACF2), EDGE Legislative Decision Support Software, Centrelink On-Line (COL) Java and MS.Net e-Business systems. Customer Service Centre, Call Centre, User Assurance Facility.
• Service Delivery Management • Information Management	• Payments (Clients) • Planning (Information)	
• Service Delivery Management • Relationship Management • Change Management • Information Management	• Client Assessment • Client Enquiry • Planning (Clients)	Unix Sun Solaris Services, Unix MQ, ISIS Adaptor Forte services, Novell Directories, Security Management SAMS/ACF2, EDGE Legislative Decision Support Software, COL e-Business systems. Customer Service Centre, Call Centre, User Assurance Facility.
• Governance	• Planning • Review (incl. Audit) • Payments (and Procurement)	SAP Infolink, SAS, Brio tools, Superstar systems, Cognos systems. Customer Service Centre, Call Centre.
• Staff Capability	• Planning (Staff)	SAP Infolink, SAS, Brio tools, Superstar systems, Cognos systems, UML. Customer Service Centre, Call Centre.
	• Payments (and Remuneration)	SAP Infolink, Data Warehouse
	• Review (Organization and Staffing)	SAP Infolink, SAS, Brio tools, Superstar systems, Cognos systems. Customer Service Centre, Call Centre.

directed at delivering government outputs and outcomes. Earlier in the chapter, it was highlighted that the Business Process Taxonomy (ABS) and augmented Zachman framework (Centrelink) were primary artifacts for the enablement of process-system alignment. Notably, these artifacts reflected several critical process-system relationships in both organizations, as illustrated in the aforementioned tables.

Examples of these relationships drawn from the ABS architecture shows that the Business survey process was integrated with a Generalized Survey Imputation Processor (GENIMP) system in order to create and maintain a complete client data set for forward statistics processing. Similarly, the ABS integrated the BLAISE computer assisted interview software systems into the Business and Household survey processes so as to improve data provider management and input quality for forward processing and statistical products publication. Within the Centrelink architecture, the agency's Income Security Integrated System (ISIS) enabled the client pension and benefits payment processes, resulting in over 10 million payments each year; while in a further example, the Centrelink On-Line (COL) e-Business system

enabled critical client registration processes in support of over 6.5 million agency customers.

The important outcome from this alignment analysis is the close coupling of the working processes and systems within the agency architecture and formative frameworks. The cases demonstrate that the integration of business processes and information systems under the architectural umbrella allows the agencies to collect and process data, publish information, and deliver critical government social services. These public sector organizations illustrate how the development and maintenance of the architecture can enable the fusion of the business and technical parts of the agency. The result is the functional integration of the business processes and information systems within the architecture frame (see Figure 8).

FUTURE RESEARCH OPPORTUNITIES

Future research opportunities to investigate and examine enterprise architecture enabled alignment include studies of private sector architecture users, the alignment of other business and tech-

Figure 8. Functional integration of business processes and information systems

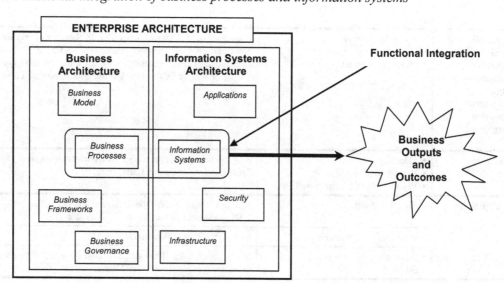

nology artifacts, the measurement, quantification and maturity of business process and technology systems alignment and integration, other social alignment enablers, and the physical architecting and design processes.

CONCLUSION

In concluding this chapter, we would stress that alignment is very much more than a theoretical concept. Alignment is a dynamic and ubiquitous construct that drives organizational performance, particularly with respect to the public sector outcomes and outputs required of government. While the government agency's enterprise architecture is not a panacea for all the corporate alignment ills, it does deliver intrinsic value in the creation, binding and ongoing relationships support of the business and its technical systems. It could also be argued that an architecture provides a consolidated depiction of public organizations that supports the early and deliberate concentration on important business issues and performance, enunciates the information systems and technology governance arrangements, unifies and shares corporate information and data with the operating business units, and allows the measured reuse and efficient replication of business and technical systems artifacts. Each of these attributes serves to combine and align the public agencies' business and technical systems.

The cases presented in this chapter provide a number of important lessons for enterprise architects. First, the origins of an architecting framework are not necessarily as important as implementing a structured architecture method and set of procedures. Whether an organization uses an internally developed or commercially available architecture framework is generally less critical than the institution of an architecting method that suits the workings of the public agency. Second, architectures that are reflective of the business and information systems components of the organiza-

tion provide opportunities to create and maintain close alignment conditions. It is important to make an early determination of what business processes are critical for achieving the agency mission. If parts of the business and/or information systems components and their relationships are missing, ongoing business process-systems alignment is less likely to be achieved. Third, architects should recognize that the social enablers of alignment are very important. Close business and information systems communications, planning, and management support provide the interpersonal facilitation mechanisms of the alignment condition. Finally, while the architecture provides a formal and highly visible means of linking and integrating business and information systems within public organizations, it remains one of many corporate alignment mechanisms. Architects should not underestimate the importance of other alignment mechanisms, such as audit and executive review, balanced score cards, and administrative governance measures, in drawing together the business processes and supporting information systems.

In closing, we would contend that establishing and maintaining a public sector enterprise architecture is a long and winding journey with no final destination. The constant evolution of business and information systems drives organizational and technological change, particularly in those government agencies that directly serve the community. However, the architecture journey is a necessary one if organizations are to successfully integrate and align all of their functions, and deliver the desired outcomes and outputs of government.

REFERENCES

Alavi, M., & Yoo, Y. (1995). Productivity gains of BPR: Achieving success where others have failed. *Information Systems Management*, 4, 43-47.

Burgelman, R.A. (1983). A Process Model of Internal Corporate Venturing in the Diversified

Major Firm. *Administrative Science Quarterly*, 28, 223-244.

Burgelman, R.A. (1994). Fading Memories: A Process Theory of Strategic Business Exit in Dynamic Environments. *Administrative Science Quarterly*, 39, 24-56.

Chan, Y.E. (2002). Why haven't we mastered Alignment? The importance of the Informal Organization structure, *MIS Quarterly Executive*, *1* (2), 97-112.

Chan, Y.E., Huff, S.L., Copeland, D.G., & Barclay, D.W. (1997) Business Strategy, Information Systems Strategy, and Strategic Alignment. *Information Systems Research, 8* (2), 125-150.

Chang, RY. (1994). Improve processes, reengineer them, or both? *Training and Development*, *48* (3), 54-58.

Commonwealth of Australia. (1997). *The Format of Portfolio Budget Statements.* Canberra, Australia: Australian Government Publishing Service.

Commonwealth of Australia. (2000). *Annual Report 1999-2000, Technology Services Division Benchmarking* (pp. 52). Canberra, Australia: Australian Bureau of Statistics Publishing. Retrieved February 12, 2004, from http://www.ausstats.abs.gov.au/ausstats/free.nsf/0/4ECE004BACFCECABCA256C0E007F3C1F/$File/10010_1999-00.pdf

Commonwealth of Australia. (2001). *Annual Report 2000-2001, Performance Information, Cost Effective Inputs* (pp. 80). Canberra, Australia: Australian Bureau of Statistics Publishing. Retrieved April 20, 2004, from http://www.ausstats.abs.gov.au/ausstats/free.nsf/0/D9E50335A060BDDDCA256C540006B320/$File/10010_2000-01.pdf

Commonwealth of Australia. (2002). *Annual Report 2001-2002* (pp. 22-33). Canberra, Australia: Centrelink Publishing.

Commonwealth of Australia. (2003a). *Annual Report 2002-2003* (pp. 195). Canberra, Australia: Centrelink Publishing.

Commonwealth of Australia. (2003b). *Transforming Government: Achievements in e-Government* (pp. 22-24, 54-56). Canberra, Australia: The National Office for the Information Economy.

Commonwealth of Australia. (2005a). *Annual Report 2004-2005* (pp. 102, 129, 153-155). Canberra, Australia: Centrelink Publishing.

Commonwealth of Australia. (2005b). *Corporate Plan* (pp. 1-18). Canberra, Australia: Australian Bureau of Statistics Publishing. Retrieved August 7, 2006, from http://www.abs.gov.au/Websitedbs/D3310114.nsf/51c9a3d36edfd0dfca256acb00118404/b1042c4ee5af9c71ca256a46008278d9!OpenDocument

Commonwealth of Australia. (2005c). *Forward Work Program 2005-2006 to 2007-2008* (pp. 1-17). Canberra, Australia: Australian Bureau of Statistics Publishing. Retrieved October 25, 2006, from http://www.ausstats.abs.gov.au/ausstats/free.nsf/0/B0812C31E3C00733CA257013000B5019/$File/10060_2005%20-%2006%20to%202007%20-08.pdf

Commonwealth of Australia. (2005d). *Transforming Government: Enhancing Productivity Volume 2* (pp. 7-12, 41-45). Canberra, Australia: The Australian Government Information Management Office.

Commonwealth of Australia. (2006a). *Annual Report 2005-2006* (pp. 166-220). Canberra, Australia: Australian Bureau of Statistics Publishing. Retrieved February 15, 2007, from http://www.ausstats.abs.gov.au/ausstats/subscriber.nsf/0/0407DA584588E138CA25720300182FBA/$File/10010_2005-06.pdf

Commonwealth of Australia. (2006b). *Annual Report 2005-2006* (pp. 9-10, 110-112, 199). Canberra, Australia: Centrelink Publishing.

Commonwealth of Australia. (2006c). *Business Plan 2006-2007* (pp. 23). Canberra, Australia: Centrelink Publishing. Retrieved February 15, 2007, from http://www.centrelink.gov.au/Internet/Internet.nsf/filestores/co055_0607/$file/co055_0607en.pdf

Commonwealth of Australia. (2006d). *Excellence in e-Government Awards 2006* (pp. 22-25). Canberra, Australia: The Australian Government Information Management Office.

Commonwealth of Australia. (2007a). *A Guide to Australian Government Payments September 2007.* Canberra, Australia: Centrelink Publishing. Retrieved April 20, 2007, from http://www.centrelink.gov.au/Internet/Internet.nsf/filestores/co029_0707/$file/co029_0707en.pdf

Commonwealth of Australia. (2007b). *Application of the Outputs and Outcomes Framework*, The Auditor-General Audit Report No.23, 2007. Canberra, Australia: The Australian National Audit Office.

Commonwealth of Australia. (2007c). *Centrelink Facts and Figures 2007.* Retrieved April 20, 2007, from http://www.centrelink.gov.au/Internet/Internet.nsf/about_us/facts.htm

Commonwealth of Australia (2007d), *Core Business Processes*, Centrelink. Retrieved April 20, 2007, from http://www.centrelink.gov.au/Internet/Internet.nsf/about_us/strategic_directions.htm

Croteau, A-M., Solomon, S., Raymond, L., & Bergeron, F. (2001). Organizational and Technological Infrastructures Alignment. *Proceedings of the Thirty-Fourth Annual Hawaii International Conference on System Sciences, 3-6 January* (pp. 234-242). New York: IEEE Press.

Davenport, T.H., & Short, J.E. (1990). The new industrial engineering: Information technology and business process redesign. *Sloan Management Review 31* (4), 11-27.

Deming, W. (Ed.) (1986) *Out of the Crisis.* Cambridge, MA: MIT Press.

Drucker, P.F. (Ed.) (1954). *The Practice of Management.* New York: Harper and Row Editors.

Drucker, P.F. (Ed.) (1980). *Managing in Turbulent Times First Edition.* New York: Harper and Row Editors.

Earl, M.J. (Ed.) (1989). *Management Strategies for Information Technology,* New York: Prentice Hall.

Feurer. R., Chaharbaghi, K., Weber, M., & Wargin, J. (2000) Aligning Strategies, Processes, and IT: A Case Study. *Information Systems Management 17* (1), 23-34.

Gadd, K.W., & Oakland, J.S. (1995). Discontinuous change in a total quality environment. D2D Lt.: A case study. *Business Process Reengineering and Management Journal 1* (2), 7-27.

Gibson, R. (1994). Global information technology architectures. *Journal of Global Information Management 2* (1), 28-38.

Gordon, J.R., & Gordon, S.R. (2000). Structuring the Interaction between IT and Business Units. *Information Systems Management 17* (1), 7-16.

Gregor, S.D., Hart, D.N., & Martin, N.J. (2007). Enterprise Architectures: Enablers of Business Strategy and IS/IT Alignment in Government. *Information Technology and People 20* (2), 96-120.

Grover, V., Teng, J.T.C., & Fiedler, K. (1993). Business process re-design: an integrated planning framework. *OMEGA: The International Journal of Management Science 21*, 4, 433-447.

Hammer, M. (1990). Reengineering work: Don't automate, obliterate. *Harvard Business Review July/August,* 104-112.

Hammer, M., & Champy, J. (1993). *Reengineering the Corporation: A Manifesto for Business Revolution.* New York: Harper Business.

Harrington, H.J. (1991). *Business Process Improvement.* New York: McGraw Hill.

Henderson, J., & Sifonis, J. (1988). Understanding the Value of IS Planning: Understanding Consistency, Validity and IS Markets, *MIS Quarterly 12* (2), 187-200.

Henderson, J.C., & Venkatraman, N. (1993). Strategic Alignment: Leveraging Information Technology for transforming organizations. *IBM Systems Journal 32* (1), 4-16.

Horovitz, J. (1984). New Perspectives on Strategic Management. *Journal of Business Strategy,* Winter, 19-33.

Information Technology Governance Institute. (2003). *Board Briefing on IT Governance, Second Edition,* Rolling Meadows, IL: ITGI Press.

International Standards Organization. (2000). *ISO 15704 Industrial Automation Systems – Requirements for Enterprise Reference Architectures and Methodologies.* Vienna, Austria: ISO.

Johnson, S.J. (1993). Re-engineering: what works, what doesn't? *Retail Business Review 61* (5), 28-30.

Johnston, H.R., & Carrico, SR. (1988). Developing capabilities to use information strategically. *MIS Quarterly 12* (1), 37-50.

Kettinger, W.J., & Grover, V. (1995). Toward a theory of Business Process Change Management. *Journal of Management Information Systems 12* (1), 9-30.

Leith, SA. (1994). Critical success factors for re-engineering business processes. *National Productivity Review 13* (4), 559-568.

Lloyd, P.T., & Galambos, G.M. (1999). Technical Reference Architectures. *IBM Systems Journal 38* (1), 51-75.

Martin, N.J. (2005). *Business Strategy and IS/IT Alignment: A study of Enterprise Architectures in Australian Government.* Unpublished doctoral dissertation, The Australian National University.

Martin, N.J., & Gregor, S.D. (2005). Requirements Engineering: A case of developing and managing quality software systems in the public sector. In C. Wohlin, and A. Aybuke, (Ed.), *Engineering and Managing Software Requirements* (pp. 353-372). Springer-Verlag, Berlin.

Martin, N.J., & Gregor, S.D. (2006). ICT Governance: Frameworks for managing Australian E-Government. *Journal of E-Government 2* (3), 19-49.

Martin, N.J., Gregor, S.D., & Hart, D.N. (2005). The Social Dimension of IS/IT Alignment: Six Case Studies of Public Sector Organizations. *Australian Accounting Review 15* (3), 28-38.

McAdam, R., & Donaghy, J. (1999). Business Process re-engineering in the public sector: A study of staff perceptions and critical success factors. *Business Process Management Journal 5* (1), 33-49.

McDavid, D.W. (1999). A Standard for Business Architecture Description. *IBM Systems Journal 38* (1), 12-31.

Miles, M.B., & Huberman, A.M. (1997). *Qualitative Data Analysis – An Expanded Case Book 2nd Edition,* Thousand Oaks: Sage Publications.

Murray, R.J., & Trefts, D.E. (2000). The IT Imperative in Business Transformation. *Information Systems Management 17* (1), 17-22.

Palmer, J. (2003, March). *IT Enterprise Architecture at the ABS.* Paper presented at the Australian Government Information Management Office (AGIMO) Seminar, Enterprise Architecture: Integrating Business and Technology Across the Australian Public Service, Canberra, Australia. Retrieved February 12, 2004, from http://www.agimo.gov.au/practice/delivery/events/2003/ent_arch

Parasuraman, A., Zeithaml, V.A., & Berry, L.L. (1985). A conceptual model of service quality and its implications for future research. *Journal of Marketing 49* (4), 41-50.

Porter, M.E. (1980). *Competitive Strategy: Techniques for analyzing Industry and Competitors.* New York: Free Press.

Porter, M.E. (1981). The Contributions of Industrial Organization to Strategic Management. *The Academy of Management Review 6* (4), 609-620.

Porter, M.E. (1991). Towards a Dynamic Theory of Strategy. *Strategic Management Journal 12*, 95-117.

Pyburn, P. (1983). Linking the MIS Plan with Corporate Strategy: An Exploratory Study. *MIS Quarterly 7* (2), 1-14.

Raghunathan, B., & Raghunathan, T.S. (1989). MIS Steering Committees: Their Effect on Information Systems Planning. *Journal of Information Systems*, Spring, 104-116.

Reich, B.H, & Benbasat, I. (1996). Measuring linkages between Business and IT Objectives. *MIS Quarterly 20* (1), 55-81.

Reich, B.H, & Benbasat, I. (2000). Factors that influence the Social Dimension of Alignment between Business and Information Technology Objectives. *MIS Quarterly 24* (1), 81-113.

Sabherwal, R., & Chan, Y.E. (2001). Alignment between Business and Information Systems Strategies: A Study of Prospectors, Analyzers, and Defenders. *Information Systems Research 12* (1), 11-33.

Smith, B. (1994). Business Process Re-engineering: more than a buzzword, *Human Resources Focus 7* (1), 17-18.

Sowa, J.F., & Zachman J.A. (1992). Extending and formalizing the framework for Information Systems Architecture. *IBM Systems Journal 31*, 590-616.

Spewak, S.H., & Hill, S.C. (1993). *Enterprise Architecture Planning: Developing a Blueprint for Data, Applications and Technology*, New York: John Wiley and Sons.

Targowski, A. (1990). *The Architecture and Planning of Enterprise-Wide Information Management Systems*, Harrisburg, PA: Idea Group Publishing.

The Economist. (Ed.). (1991). *The Good Statistics Guide*, July 320 (7723), 88.

The Economist. (Ed.). (1993). *The Good Statistics Guide*, November 328 (7828), 65.

The Open Group. (2006). *The Open Group Architecture Framework Version 8.1.1.* Boston, MA: The Open Group.

Treadwell, J. (2003, March). *Centrelink, Capabilities, and Connections.* Paper presented at the Australian Government Information Management Office (AGIMO) Seminar, Enterprise Architecture: Integrating Business and Technology Across the Australian Public Service, Canberra, Australia. Retrieved February 12, 2004, from http://www.agimo.gov.au/practice/delivery/events/2003/ent_arch

Venkatraman, N., Henderson, J.C., & Oldach. S. (1993). Continuous Strategic Alignment: Exploiting Information Technology Capabilities for Competitive Success. *European Management Journal 11* (2), 139-149.

Zachman, J.A. (1987). A framework for Information Systems Architecture. *IBM Systems Journal 26*, 276-292.

APPENDIX A ENTERPRISE ARCHITECTURE STUDY QUESTIONS GUIDE

Indicative questions that were used in the semi-structured and unstructured case interviews are outlined as follows:

Section 1. Enterprise Architecture Frameworks and Methods

Do you use Enterprise Architecture in your organization? If so, can you outline the framework or method used to build the architecture? What resources are used to implement the Enterprise Architecture?

What structures (eg, business, applications, infrastructure) are inherent in the architecture?

Can you please describe the artifacts (eg, systems, specific models, processes, plans, services) that comprise the architecture?

In your experience, what parts of the architecture work well and what parts work not so well? Why?

Section 2. Architecture Structure and Components

Please describe your IS/IT/IM environment and the various components (eg, staffing, governance, hardware, software, capabilities, technologies, toolsets, languages, modeling languages).

Can you describe some of the development/design activities, business processes and procedures used to develop your organization and guide its operations?

Do you use any specific systems development and/or project management methods for developing information systems or executing projects?

Does the systems development method consider the lifecycle aspects of the system?

Are data dictionaries or electronic glossaries available for use within your organization?

Is it possible to describe or graphically depict the organizational structure?

Section 3. Social Dimensions of Alignment

Does the management team support you and the work you do?

What type of management support do you get for the business strategy execution, information systems infrastructure proposals and Enterprise Architecture?

What management support mechanisms are in place?

Does your organization have a strategic plan? If so, how is the plan compiled ?

Does your organization have a corporate business plan? If so, how is the plan compiled ?

Are you aware of your organization's business/corporate/enterprise strategies and objectives?

How would you characterize the business planning style (eg, top-down, bottom-up, collegiate, decentralized) in your organization?

What business planning communications are in place for business strategy and information systems planning activities within the agency? Do you communicate with external stakeholders or parties? If so, how?

Section 4. Alignment Methods and Alignment

How do you achieve alignment? Do things like strategic planning, business modeling, and non-executive/executive reviews help alignment? How?

What other organizational mechanisms help alignment?

Do you think Enterprise Architecture helps alignment? How?

Would you consider that your organizational information systems help you deliver your business strategies? If yes, to what extent do they assist you?

Would you consider that your organizational information systems help you address external business drivers? If yes, to what extent do they assist you?

Do you meet your annual outputs, in terms of performance, reliability and service level agreement targets, using the organizational information systems?

Would you say that the business outputs would be negatively impacted if there was less (or a poorer) fit between information systems infrastructure and business strategy? Please provide reasons for your answer?

438

Compilation of References

Abramson, M.A., Breul, J.D., & Kamensky, J.M. (2006). Six Trends Transforming Government. *IBM Center for The Business of Government Report*. Retrieved September 7, 2007, from http://www.businessofgovernment.org/pdfs/SixTrends.pdf.

Accenture (2005) Leadership in Customer Service: New Expectations, New Experiences". The Government Executive Series, Accenture, April 2005. Retrieved May 25th, 2006, from http://www.accenture.com/NR/rdonlyres/F45CE4C8-9330-4450-BB4A-AF4E265C88D4/0/leadership_cust.pdf) .

Adams, Jonathan; Koushik, Srinivas; Vasudeva, Guru; and Galambos George. (2001). Patterns for E-Business: A Strategy for Reuse. Mc Pr Llc, ISBN: 1931182027.

Adigun M. O., & Biyela D. P. (2003) *Modelling and Enterprise for re-Engineering: A Case Study. In the 2003 annual research conference of the South African institute of computer scientists and information technologists on Enablement through technology (SAICSIT 2003)*, ACM.

Agha, Gul, A. (2002) . Adaptive Middleware. *Communications of the ACM, 45*(6).

Agranoff, R. and McGuire, M. (2001). Big questions in public network management research. *Journal of Public Administration Theory and Research 11*(3), 295–326.

Alexander, C; Ishikawa, S., Silverstein, M., Jacobson, M., Fiksdahl-King, I., and Angel, S. (1977). *A pattern Language*. Oxford University Press.

Alfred Tat-Hei. (July/August 2002). Reinventing Local Government and the E-government initiative. *Public Administration Review, 62*(4): 434-444.

Allan, K. (1994). Speech act classification and definition. In R. Asher (Ed.), *Encyclopedia of Language and Linguistics* (Vol. 8, pp. 4124- 4127): Oxford: Pergamon Press.

Allega, P.J. (2005); *Architecture framework debates are irrelevant*; Gartner report G00127331, 07 Jun 2005.

Allega, P.J. (2005); *Enterprise Architecture will never realize a return on investment*; Gartner report G00128285, 24 Jun 2005.

Alting van Geusau-Ghosh, S., Zeef, P, Toorn, H. van, & Visch, E. (2006). *Globaal Ontwerp Persoonlijke Internet Pagina*, version 1.2. The Hague, The Netherlands: Stichting ICTU. Retrieved July 17, 2007, from http://www.e-overheid.nl/data/files/PIP/Globaal_Ontwerp_versie_1[1].2.pdf.pdf

Ambite, José Luis; Giuliano, Genevieve; Gordon, Peter; Decker, Stefan; Harth, Andreas; Jassar, Karanbir; Pan, Qisheng; and Wang, LanLan. (2005). *Argos: An Ontology and Web Service Composition Infrastructure for Goods Movement Analysis*, Information Sciences Institute School of Policy, Planning, and Development, Digital Gov. Website.

Ambler, S. W. (2002). *Agile Modeling: Effective Practices for Extreme Programming and the Unified Process*. New York, New York: John Wiley & Sons.

American Customer Satisfaction Index (ACSI), e-Government Satisfaction Index (2005) *"Number of e-GOV sites measuring satisfaction surges, satisfaction growth stalls"*. March 15, 2005. Retrieved May 25th, 2006, from

Anderson, Ross (2001). *Security Engineering: A Guide to Building Dependable Distributed Systems.* New York: Wiley.

Ankolekar, V. (2003). Application Development Technology & Tools: Vulnerabilities & Threat Management with Secure Programming Practices, a defense in-depth approach. GIAC Security Essentials Certification (GSEC) Practical Assignment, Version 1.4b, Option 1. 10 November 2003.

Anthopoulos L., Siozos P., & Tsoukalas I. A. (2007) Applying Participatory Design and Collaboration in Digital Public Services for discovering and re-designing e-Government services. *Government Information Quarterly,* Volume 24, Issue 2, April 2007, Pages 353-376, ElSevier.

Anthopoulos, L., & Manos A. (2005) e-Government beyond e-administration. The evolution of municipal area environments could establish a digital framework of confidence for citizens. *In the 5th European Conference on e-Government, (ECEG 2005) University of Antwerp*, Belgium, 16-17 June 2005.

Anthopoulos, L., & Tsoukalas, I.A. (2005) The implementation model of a Digital City. The case study of the first Digital City in Greece: e-Trikala. *Journal of e-Government, Vol.2, Issue 2, 2005.* Haworth Press, Inc., University of Southern California, Center for Digital Government.

Arens, Yigal; and Rosenbloom, Paul. (2002). *Responding to the Unexpected*, USC/Information Sciences Institute, NSF Workshop.

Armour Dr. F., Kaisler Dr. S., Getter J., & Pippin D. (2003); *A UML-driven Enterprise Architecture case study*; Proceedings of the 36th Hawaii International Conference on System Sciences (HICSS) 2003.

Armour, F. J., Emery, C., Houk, J., Kaisler, S. H., & Kirk, J.S. (2007). The Integrated Enterprise Lifecycle: Enterprise Architecture, Investment Management and System Development. In Saha, P. (Ed.). *Handbook of Enterprise Systems Architecture in Practice.* Hershey, PA: IGI Global Information Science Reference.

Arora, A., Ramnath, R., Ertin, E., Sinha, P. (2005). ExScal: Elements of an Extreme Scale Wireless Sensor Network," 11th IEEE International Conference on Embedded and Real-Time Computing Systems and Applications, Hong Kong, China.

ATHENA Project. (2005). *D.A6.1, Specification of a Basic Architecture Reference Model.*

Austin, J. L. (1962). *How to do things with Words.* Cambridge, MA: Harvard University Press.

Austria (2006). *Administration on the Net – An ABC Guide to E-Government in Austria.* Vienna, Austria: Oesterreichische Computer Gesellschaft. Retrieved July 17, 2007, from http://www.cio.gv.at/egovernment/umbrella/Administration_on_the_Net.zip.

Babb, J. (2006). Signification and Information Systems Security Policies: a Semiotic Analysis and Case Study. Virginia Commonwealth University School of Business, Department of Information Systems.

Bace, R., Mell, P. (?). NIST-SP800-31 Intrusion Detection Systems. NIST Special Publication on Intrusion Detection Systems.

Bach, K., & Harnish, R. M. (1979). *Linguistic Communication and Speech Acts.* Cambridge MA: MIT Press.

Barker, W. (June 2004). NIST Special Publication 800-60 Volume 1: Guide for Mapping Types of Information and Information Systems to Security Categories. National Institute of Standards and Technology. Computer Security Division.

Barnett W., Presley A., Johnson M., & Loles D.H. (1994); *An Architecture for the Virtual Enterprise*; 1994 IEEE International Conference on Systems, Man, and Cybernetics, 1 (pp. 506-511)

Battle, S., Bernstein, A., Boley, H., Grosof, B., Gruninger, M., Hull, R., et al. (2005). *Semantic Web Services Framework (SWSF).*

Bauer, Johannes M. (2004). Harnessing the Swarm: Communications Policy in an Era of Ubiquitous Networks and Disruptive Technologies. *Communications & Strategies, 54*, 2nd quarter.

Baum, C., & Di Maio, A. (2000). Gartner's Four Phases of E-Government Model. *Gartner Group Research Note.* Retrieved June 15, 2007, from http://aln.hha.dk/IFI/Hdi/2001/ITstrat/Download/Gartner_eGovernment.pdf.

Bayens, G.I.H.M. (2006). E-Government in The Netherlands: An Architectural Approach, *Via Nova Architectura*, October 9, 2006. Retrieved July 17, 2007, from http://www.via-nova-architectura.org.

Bayens, G.I.H.M., et al. (2007). *Nederlandse Overheid Referentie Architectuur (NORA) v. 2.0.* The Hague, The Netherlands: Stichting ICTU. Retrieved July 17, 2007, from http://www.e-overheid.nl/atlas/referentiearchitectuur/

B-dossier (2007). *B-dossier project Website.* Enschede, The Netherlands: Telematica Instituut. Retrieved July 17, 2007, from http://www.b-dossier.nl.

Beck, K. (1999). *Extreme Programming Explained: Embrace Change.* Boston: Addison-Wesley Professional.

Bernard, S, A. (2005). *An Introduction To Enterprise Architecture: Second Edition.* Bloomington, Indiana: AuthorHouse.

Bernard, S. (2001). Evaluating Clinger-Cohen Compliance in Federal Agency Chief Information Officer Positions. Doctoral Dissertation, Virginia Polytechnic Institute and State University, Blacksburg, VA.

Bernard, S. A. (2004). *An introduction to enterprise architecture.* Bloomington, IN: AuthorHouse.

Bernard, S. A. (2004). *Enterprise Architecture Management Maturity (EAMM) – Enterprise Architecture Development, Documentation and Measurement.* Lecture notes for the enterprise architecture course sponsored by Korea IT Industry Promotion Agency, Seoul, Korea.

Berners-Lee, T., Hendler, J., & Lassila, O. (2001). The Semantic Web. *SCIENTIFIC AMERICAN, May 2001.*

Bernus, P., & Nemes, L. (1996). A framework to define a generic enterprise reference architecture and methodology. *Computer Integrated Manufacturing Systems, 9*(3), 179-191.

Bernus, P., Nemes, L., & Schmidt, G, (Eds.). (2003). *Handbook on Enterprise Architecture.* Berlin : Springer.

Betz, C. T. (2006). *Architecture and Patterns for IT Service Management, Resource Planning, and Governance: Making Shoes for the Cobbler's Children.* San Francisco, CA: Morgan Kaufmann.

Bevir, M., & Rhodes, R. A. W. (2001). *A Decentered Theory of Governance* (Working Paper 2001-10). Berkeley: Institute of Governmental Studies, University of California.

Bittler, R.S., & Kreizman, G. (2005). Gartner Enterprise Architecture Process: Evolution 2005. *Gartner Group Research Note,* G00130849. Retrieved July 27, 2007, from http://www.gartner.com/research/spotlight/asset_50080.jsp.

Booch, G., Rumbaugh, J., and Jacobson I. (1999). *The Unified Modeling Language User Guide.* New York, NY: Addison-Wesley Object Technology Series.

Borins, Sandford. (2006). *The Challenge of Innovating in Government* (2nd ed.). Retrieved 5 June 2007 from IBM Center for the Business of Government Web site: http://www.businessofgovernment.org/pdfs/BorinsReprint.pdf

Bos, H. (2005). *De ICT-strategie van de Gemeente The Hague (2001-2007).* Utrecht, The Netherlands: Informatiehuis. Retrieved July 17, 2007, from http://www.egem.nl/projecten/voorhoedegemeenten/kennisconferentie2006/documenten/Evaluatie%20Haagse%20aanpak%20door%20Informatiehuis.pdf?searchterm=None

Bovens, M.; and Zouridis, S. (2002). From Street-Level to System-Level Bureaucracies. *Public Administration Review 62*(2): 174-184.

Bozeman, B., and Straussman, J.D. (1990). *Public management strategies: Guidelines for managerial effectiveness.* San Francisco, CA: Jossey-Bass, Inc.

BPMI. *Business Process Management Initiative,* www.BPMI.org.

Brahim Medjahed, Abdelmounaam Rezgui, Athman Bouguettaya, & Ouzzani, M. (2003). Infrastructure for E-Government Web Services. *IEEE Internet Computing, 7*(1), 58-65.

Breul, J.D. (2006). What is Transformation?. In M.A. Abramson, J.D. Breul, & J.M. Kamensky (Eds.), *Six Trends Transforming Government* (p. 7). Retrieved 16 April 2007 from IBM Center for the Business of Government Web site: http://www.businessofgovernment.org/pdfs/SixTrends.pdf

Breul, J.D., & Morales, A. (2007, June). 2007-2008 Research Announcement: Providing Cutting Edge Knowledge to Government Leaders. Retrieved 16 July 2007 from IBM Center for Business of Government Web site: http://www.businessofgovernment.org/pdfs/Research_Announcement_07.pdf

Browne, A., & Wildavsky, A. (1984). *Should Evolution become Implementation*: Pressman and Wildavsky.

Bruce, E. (2005, 21-22 February). *Linking Enterprise Architectures between Multiple Government Agencies – The NZ Experience*. Paper presented at the Conference in Enterprise Architecture for Government, Canberra, Australia.

BSI DISC. (1998). *The TickIT Guide – A Guide to Software Quality Management System, Consturction and Certification to ISO 9001*.

Burger@Overheid (2005). *BurgerServiceCode, versie 2.1*. The Hague, The Netherlands: Burger@Overheid.nl. Retrieved July 17, 2007, from http://www.burger.overheid.nl/files/burgerservicecode_nl.pdf

Burger@Overheid (2006). *Evaluatieonderzoek 2006*. The Hague, The Netherlands: Burger@Overheid.nl. Retrieved July 17, 2007, from http://www.burger.overheid.nl/files/b@o_evaluatieonderzoek_bop_2006.pdf

Burk, R.R. (2006, 21-22 February). *Enterprise Governance: Defining the Long Term Vision*. Paper presented at the Conference in Enterprise Architecture for Government, Canberra, Australia.

BuyIT Best Practice Network & Shared Services Advisory Group. (2006). "Shared Services in the Public Sector: Vision." Retrieved 27 April 2007 from BuyIT Best Practice Network Web site: http://www.buyitnet.org/Best_Practice_Guidelines/SharedServicesPubSect/docs/Gl%20Vision.pdf

C4ISR Architecture Framework (Version 2.0) (1997); C4ISR Architectures Working Group (USA); Department of Defense (USA)

Cabinet Office (2005), Transformational Government, Enabled by IT. Retrieved 31st July 2007 from http://www.cio.gov.uk/documents/pdf/transgov/transgov-strategy.pdf

Cabinet Office (2007), Chief Technology Officer Council. Retrieved 31st July 2007 from http://www.cio.gov.uk/chief_technology_officer/index.asp

Cap Gemini Ernst & Young (2003) Online availability of public services. How is Europe progressing? Information Society DG, 2003.

CCA. (1996). *Clinger-Cohen Act of 1996: Information Technology Management Reform*, Public Law 104-106, Fiscal Year 1996 Defense Authorization Act.

Center for Information Technology, National Institutes of Health Canadian Trusted Computer Product Evaluation Criteria (CTCPEC). Accessed from http://www.alw.nih.gov/Security/FIRST/papers/criteria/ctcpec1.ps.

Checkland, P. (1981). *Systems Thinking, Systems Practice*. Chichester: Wiley.

Chen, D., Vallespir, B., & Doumeingts, G. (1997). GRAI integrated methodology and its mapping onto generic enterprise reference architecture and methodology. *Computers in Industry, 33*, 387-394.

Chief Information Officer (CIO) Council (2001) A Practical Guide to Federal Enterprise Architecture, version 1.0, February 2001. Retrieved May 25th, 2006, from http://www.gao.gov/bestpractices/bpeaguide.pdf

Child, J. (1972). Organizations, Structure, Environment, and Performance: *The Role of Strategic Choice*. *Sociology, 6* 1-22.

Chrissis, B. M., Konrad, M., & Shrum, S. (2007). *CMMI – Guidelines for Process Integration and Product Improvement*. 2nd Ed. Addison-Wesley.

CIO Council. (1999). Federal Enterprise Architecture Framework, Version 1.1. Retrieved February 20, 2008 from http://www.whitehouse.gov/omb/egov/a-1-fea.html

Claudio Masolo, Stefano Borgo, Aldo Gangemi, Nicola Guarino, & Oltramari, A. (2003). *WonderWeb: Deliverable D1.8, Ontology Library (IST Project 2001-33052).*

Clements, P. et. al. (2003). Software Architecture in Practice, (2nd ed.) New York, NY: Addison Wesley.

CMG. Capacity Management Group

Collison C., & Parcell G. (2005); *KM Self-Assessment*; Retrieved 01/04/2007 from "Learning to Fly" Website (http://www.chriscollison.com/l2f/whatiskm.html#assessment)

Commission on Federal Paperwork. (1977). *Information resources management: A report of the commission on federal paperwork.* Washington, D.C.: Government Printing Office.

CommonCriteria.org (2005) Common Criteria for Information Technology Security Evaluation (CCITSE). Accessed from http://www.commoncriteriaportal.org/public/consumer/index.php?menu=2.

Computer Systems Laboratory of the National Institute of Standards and Technology. (1993). FIPS Publication 183.

COPS 03-1. http://www.cops.usdoj.gov/txt/fact_sheets/e01060007.txt

Cross, Cross, S. et al. (2002). *SEI Independent Research and Development Projects,* TECHNICAL REPORT CMU/SEI-2002-TR-023 ESC-TR-2002-023.

CSIRT Services. Carnegie Mellon University. (2002). Software Engineering Institute. CERT Coordination Center. Stelvio bv, The Netherlands; PRESECURE Consulting GmbH, Germany. Accessed July 2002 from http://www.cert.org/csirts/services.html.

D. Apostolou, L. Stojanovic, T. Pariente Lobo, & Thoenssen, B. (2005). Towards a Semantically-Driven Software Engineering Environment for eGovernment. In (Vol. 3416, pp. 157 –168): LNAI.

DAML. www.daml.org. The DARPA Agent Markup Language (DAML).

Davenport, T. H. (1992). *Process innovation: Reengineering work through information technology.* Boston, MA: Harvard Business School Press.

Defence Architecture Framework – Resources (CD) (Version 1.0) (2005); Australian Government, Department of Defence (Chief Information Officer Group)

Deloitte and Touché (2001). The Citizen as Customer. *CMA Management,* 74(10), 58.

Demchenko, Y., Gommans, L., De Laat, C., Oudenaarde, B., Tokmakoff, A., Snijders, M., et al. (2005). *Security Architecture for Open Collaborative Environment.* Paper presented at the European Grid Conference - EGC 2005, Amsterdam, The Netherlands.

Deming W. E. (1982). *Out of the Crisis,* Cambridge, MA: MIT Press.

Denmark (2006). *Architecture for e-Government in Denmark.* Offentlig Information Online. Retrieved July 17, 2007, from http://www.oio.dk/arkitektur/eng.

Department of Defense Directive 5200.28-STD (December 1985) Trusted Computer System Evaluation Criteria (TCSEC). Accessed from http://www.boran.com/security/tcsec.html.

Department of Defense. (2007). *The Department of Defense Architecture Framework Version 1.0.* The Department of Defense. Retrieved February 20, 2008 from http://www.defenselink.mil/cio-nii/docs/DoDAF_Volume_I.pdf DoDAF 1.5

Derks, W.L.A., & Lankhorst, M.M. (2006). *Definitie en conceptualisatie van het B-dossier.* Technical Report TI/RS/2006/013. Enschede, The Netherlands: Telematica Instituut. Retrieved July 17, 2007, from https://doc.telin.nl/dscgi/ds.py/Get/File-61820

Desai, Anand. (2005). Special Issue: Adaptive Complex Systems. *CACM 49*(5).

Devadoss, P., Pan, S., & Huang, J. (2002) Structurational analysis of e-Government initiatives: a case study of SCO. *Decision Support Systems,* vol. 34, p. 253-269, ElSevier.

DGI. (2003). *Deutscher Corporate Governance Kodex.* Retrieved May 21, 2003 from http://www.corporate-governance-code.de/ger/kodex/index.html.

Dietz, J. L. G., & Mulder, J. B. F. (1998). *Organisational transformation requires constructional knowledge of business systems*. Paper presented at the 31st Annual HICCS.

Digtalgovernment. Government agencies affiliated with dg.o, are known as the "Digital Government Consortium." Member agencies often partner with NSF research performers and the private sector to leverage information technology research and identify financial resources to help build the Digital Government of the 21st Century. www.digitalgovernment.org

DIP Project. (2004). *D9.3 e-Government ontology*.

DoD. (2006). *Department of Defense Chief Information Officer Desk Reference. Vol.1 Foundation Documents*. United States Department of Defense,

Donaldson, L. (1999). *The Normal Science of Structural Contingency Theory, in S.R.*

Donnelly, M. (April 2000). An Introduction to LDAP. Obtained from http://www.ldapman.org/articles/intro_to_ldap.html.

Dool, F. van den, Keller, W.J., Wagenaar, R. & Hinfelaar, J.A.F. (2002) *Architectuur elektronische overheid. Samenhang en Samenwerking*. Zoetermeer, The Netherlands: Verdonck Klooster & Associates. Retrieved July 17, 2007, from http://www.e-overheid.nl/data/files/architectuur/architectuurelektronische-overheid.pdf.

Doumeingts G., Ducq Y., Vallespir B., & Kleinhans S., (2000). Production management and enterprise modelling. *Computers in Industry, 42*, 245-263.

Drazin, Robert; and Van de Van, Andrew H. (1985). Alternative Forms of Fit in Contingency Theory. *Administrative Science Quarterly, 30*, 514-539.

Duttaroy A. (2005); *Five Ms of Meta Data*; DM Review (http://www.dmreview.com) April 2005.

EA Shared Interest Group. (2005). *Advancing Enterprise Architecture Maturity, version 2.0*. American Council for Technology/Industry Advisory Council.

EFQM. (2006). *The EFQM Excellence Award, Information Brochure for 2006, Version 2*. European Foundation for Quality Management.

eGov Consortium (2002) IST Project 2000 – 28471. An Integrated Platform for Realising One-Stop Government. D121–Services and process models functional specifications, 2002. Retrieved August 15th, 2007, from http://www.egov-project.org/egov-site/eGOV_D121.zip.

Elliman, T., Irani, Z., & Jackson, P. (2007). Establishing a framework for eGovernment research: project VIEGO. *Transforming Government: People, Process and Policy, 1*(4), 364-376.

Emery, G.R. (2003, July 21). It ain't easy getting to green: Most agencies making progress but management goals yet to be achieved. Washington Technology. Retrieved Oct 25, 2007 from http://www.washington-technology.com/print/18_8/21225-1.html

EquaTerra & International Public Management Association for Human Resources [IPMA-HR]. (2006, June). *Human Resources Transformation in Public Sector Organizations*. Retrieved 2 May 2007 from the IPMA-HR Web site: http://www.ipma-hr.org/pdf/TransformationWhitePaper.pdf

Eriksson, H; and Penker, M. (2000). Business Modeling with UML: Business Patterns at Work. New York, NY: John Wiley.

European Commission (2002) eEurope 2005: An information society for all. *European Commission - COM 263*, 2002. Retrieved August 15th, 2007, from http://europa.eu.int/eeurope

European Commission (2004). *European Interoperability Framework for Pan-European e-Government Services*, version 1.0. Retrieved July 17, 2007, from http://ec.europa.eu/idabc/servlets/Doc?id=19529.

Fayyad, Usama; and Uthurusamy, Ramasamy. (2002). Into Evolving Data Mining Solutions for Insights. *CACM, 45*,(8).

Federal Enterprise Architecture (FEA) Working Group (2002) E-Gov Enterprise Architecture Guidance Common Reference model. (July 25, 2002). Retrieved August 15th, 2007, from http://www.feapmo.gov/resources/E-Gov_Guidance_Final_Draft_v2.0.pdf

Federal Enterprise Architecture (FEA) Working Group (2005) Enabling Citizen-Centered Electronic Government. 2005-2006 FEA-PMO Action Plan. Retrieved August 15th, 2007, from www.whitehouse.

gov/omb/egov/documents/2005_FEA_PMO_Action_Plan_FINAL.pdf

Federal Information Processing Standards Publication 199. (February 2004).Standards for Security Categorization of Federal Information and Information Systems. National Institute for Standards and Technology, Computer Security Division.

Federal Trade Commission. (June 1998). Privacy Online: A Report to Congress. Chapter 3: Fair Information Practice Principals. Accessed July 2006, from http://www3.ftc.gov/reports/privacy3/priv-23a.pdf.

Federal Trade Commission. (May 2000). Privacy Online: Fair Information Practices in the Electronic Marketplace: A Report to Congress. Accessed July 2006, from http://www.ftc.gov/reports/privacy2000/privacy2000.pdf.

Fensel D., C. Bussler, & Maedche, A. (2002). *Semantic Web Enabled Web Services*. Paper presented at the ISWC 2002.

Firstgov. To facilitate efforts to transform the Federal Government to one that is citizen-centered, results-oriented, and market-based, the Office of Management and Budget (OMB) is developing the Federal Enterprise Architecture (FEA), a business-based framework for Government-wide improvement. www.firstgov.gov.

FISMA Implementation Project. (2003). National Institute for Standards and Technology, Computer Security Division. Accessed July 2006, from http://csrc.nist.gov/sec-cert/ca-proj-phases.html.

Flinders, M. (2005). The Politics of Public-Private Partnerships. *The British Journal of Politics and International Relations (BJPIR), 7*, 215-239.

Fountain, J.E. (2001). *Building the Virtual State – Information Technology and Institutional Change*. Washington, DC: Brookings Institution Press.

Fowler, M. (1997). *Analysis Patterns*: Addison-Wesley. New Performance Framework Measures Public Value of IT, Research Note, 8 July 2003 2003).

Frankel, S., Kent, K., Lewkowski, R., Orebaugh, A., Ritchey, R., & Sharma, S. (December 2005). NIST-SP800-77 Guide to IPsec VPNs - Recommendations of the National Institute of Standards and Technology.

Computer Security Division - Information Technology Laboratory - National Institute of Standards and Technology.

Friedman, T.L. (2005). *The world is flat: A brief history of the twenty-first century*. New York, NY: Farrar, Straus and Giroux

Furlong G. (2001); *Knowledge management and the competitive edge*; University of Greenwich Business School; 2001, revised May 2003.

Gabbar, H.A., Shimada Y., & Suzuki K., (2002). Computer-aided plant enterprise modelling environment (CAPE-ModE) – design initiatives. *Computers in Industry, 47*, 25-37.

Gamma, E., R.; Helm, R. Johnson; Vlissides, J. (1995). Design Patterns, Elements of Reuseable Object Oriented Software. New York, NY: Addison Wesley.

Gant, J., & Gant, D. (2002) Web portal functionality and State Government E-service. *In the proceedings of the 35th Hawaii international conference on system sciences* (IEEE 2002).

GAO. (2003). *A Framework for Assessing and Improving Enterprise Architecture Management, version 1.1*. United States General Accounting Office.

German Federal Government (2003). BundOnline 2005. 2003 Implementation Plan. Retrieved May 25th, 2005, from http://www.bunde.de

Germany (2007). *Standards und Architekturen für E-Government-Anwendungen (SAGA 3.0)*. Berlin: Koordinierungs- und Beratungsstelle der Bundesregierung für Informationstechnik in der Bundesverwaltung. Retrieved July 17, 2007, from http://www.kbst.bund.de/saga.

Ghosh, S. (2006). *PIP Architectuur white paper*, version 0.3. Stichting ICTU, The Hague, The Netherlands. Retrieved July 17, 2007, from http://www.e-overheid.nl/data/files/PIP/PIP%20architectuur%20whitepaper%20v0.3%20concept.pdf

Gil-Garcia, J.R., & Pardo, T.A. (2005). E-Government success factors: mapping practical tools to theoretical foundations. *Government Information Quarterly, 22*(2), 187-216.

Godart, C. Saliou H., & Bignon, J.C. (2001) *"Asynchronous Coordination of Virtual Teams in Creative Applications (co-design or co-engineering): Requirements and Design Criteria"*. IEEE.

Goldkuhl, G. (1996). *Generic business frameworks and action modeling*. Paper presented at the 1st International Workshop on Communications Modeling - The Language/Action Perspective.

Goldstein, H (2005) *Who Killed the Virtual Case File?*, IEEE Spectrum September 2005, http://www.spectrum.ieee.org/print/1455

Good, J (2004) *Defining an Architecture Roadmap that talks to the Enterprise Culture*, EA Conference Europe 2004, London, IRM UK Ltd

Good, J and Fairhead, N (2007) *Getting started in Enterprise Architecture* EA Conference Europe 2007, London, IRM UK Ltd (copyright Serco Consulting, used with permission)

Gore, A. (1993). *Creating a government that works better and costs less: The report of the national performance review*. New York, NY: Penguin Books.

Gortmaker, J. (2008). Designing a Reference Architecture for the Accountable & Adaptive Orchestration of Public Service Networks. Unpublished doctoral dissertation (forthcoming). Delft University of Technology.

Gortmaker, J., & Janssen, M. (2004). Business Process Orchestration in e-Government: A Gap Analysis. *International Resources Management Association (IRMA)*.

Gortmaker, J., & Janssen, M. (2007). Automating Governmental Cross-Agency Processes Using Web Service Orchestration: A Gap Analysis. In L. Al-Hakim (Ed.), *Global E-Government: Theory, Applications and Benchmarking*. Hershey: Idea Group Publishing.

Gortmaker, J., Janssen, M., & Wagenaar, R. W. (2005). Accountability of Electronic Cross-Agency Service-Delivery Processes. *EGOV2005, 4th International Conference on Electronic Government*, 49-56.

Gortmaker, Jeffrey; Janssen, Marijn; and Wagenaar, René W. (2004). *The Advantages of Web Service Orchestration in Perspective*. ICEC'04, Sixth International Conference on Electronic Commerce Edited by: Marijn Janssen, Henk G. Sol, and René W. Wagenaar. Copyright ACM 1-58113-930-6/04/10.

Governance and Performance: New Perspectives Washington, DC: Georgetown University Press pp. 263-291.

Government of British Columbia (2004). e-Government Plan. Office of the Chief Information Officer, Ministry of Management Services. Retrieved June 18, 2007, from www.cio.gov.bc.ca/ebc/egovplan20041215.pdf.

Government of Ontario, Office of the Premier (2006). Description of the role of the Treasury Board / Management Board of Cabinet. Retrieved 30th July 2007, from http://www.premier.gov.on.ca/team/Committee.asp?Team=2

Government of Western Australia (2004). e-Government Strategy for the Western Australian Public Sector. Office of e-Government, Department of the Premier and Cabinet. Retrieved June 18, 2007, from http://www.egov.dpc.wa.gov.au/documents/e-government_strategy.doc.

Grance, T. et. al. (January 2004). NIST Special Publication 800-61: Computer Security Incident Handling Guide: Recommendations of the National Institute of Standards and Technology.

Grance, T. et. al. (October 2003). NIST Special Publication 800-64: Security Considerations in the Information System Development Life Cycle: Recommendations of the National Institute of Standards and Technology.

Gregor, S., Hart, D., & Martin, N. (2007). Enterprise architectures: enables of business strategy and IS/IT alignment in government. *Information Technology & People, 20*(2), 96-120.

Gresov, C. (1989). Exploring Fit and Misfit with Multiple Contingencies. *Administrative Science Quarterly 34*, 431-453.

Groenlund, A. (1997). Public Computer Systems – A New Focus for Information Systems Research. *Information Infrastructure and Policy, 6*, 47-65.

Gronlund, A. (2005). *What's In a Field – Exploring the eGoverment Domain*. Paper presented at the 38th Hawaii International Conference on System Sciences.

H. Koontz, Donnell, C. O., & Weihreich, H. (1980). *Management* (7th Edition ed.): McGraw Hill.

Hall, M. (2005). *Building and Enterprise Architecture Website and Repository*. Lecture notes for the enterprise architecture course sponsored by Korea IT Industry Promotion Agency, Seoul, Korea.

Hall, W.P. (2000). Managing Technical Documentation for Large Defence Projects: Engineering Corporate Knowledge. In J.P.T. Mo & L. Nemes (Eds.) *Global Engineering, Manufacturing and Enterprise Networks* (pp.370-378). Boston: Kluwer Academic Publishers.

Hammer, M.; and J. Champy. (1993). *Reengineering the Corporation: A Manifesto for Business Revolution*. New York, NY: Harper.

Harris, S. (2003). CISSP All-In-One Exam Guide, Third Edition. McGraw-Hill/Osborne, Emeryville, CA. ISBN: 0-07-222966-7.

Harvard Policy Group on Network Enabled Services and Government (2000). *Eight Imperatives for Leaders in a Networked World: Guidelines for the 2000 Election and Beyond*, John F. Kennedy School of Government, Cambridge, MA. Retrieved June 18, 2007, from www.ksg.harvard.edu/stratcom/hpg/index.htm.

Hash, J. et. al. (March 2005). NIST Special Publication 800-66: An Introductory Resource Guide for Implementing the Health Insurance Portability and Accountability Act (HIPAA) Security Rule. National Institute of Standards and Technology.

Hay, D. (1996). *Data Models Patterns*. NY: Dorste House Publishing.

Hepp, M., Leymann, F., Domingue, J., Wahler, A., & Fensel, D. (2005, October 18-20). *Semantic Business Process Management: A Vision Towards Using Semantic Web Services for Business Process Management*. Paper presented at the IEEE ICEBE 2005, Beijing, China.

Hiller, J. & Belanger, F. (2001). *Privacy Strategies for Electronic Government*. E-Government Series.

Arlington, VA: PricewaterhouseCoopers Endowment for the Business of Government.

Hjort-Madsen, K. (2007). Institutional patterns of enterprise architecture adoption in government. *Transforming Government: People, Process and Policy, 1*(4), 333-349.

Ho, S M. & Caldera, C. (2005). Eight Challenges Faced By a Defense Contractor: An Interview with a Security Chief. (ISC)2 Newsletter May-June 2005. Obtained from https://www.isc2.org/cgi-bin/content.cgi?page=766 on July 18, 2006.

Ho, S M. (2006). Conceptualizing Security Architecture based on Enterprise Architecture. End-of-Coursework Statement. School of Information Studies, Syracuse University. Obtained from http:// Web.syr.edu/~smho/research.htm.

Ho, S M. (2006). The Mechanism Discovery of Personnel Anomaly Detection. ISOneWorld 2006 Doctoral Symposium, Las Vegas, Nevada, 19-21 April 2006.

Ho, S M. (2008). Towards A Deeper Understanding of Personnel Anomaly Detection. Encyclopedia of Cyber Warfare and Cyber Terrorism. IDEA Publications.

Hogwood, B. W., & Gunn, L. A. (1984). *Policy Analysis for the Real World*. Oxford: Oxford University Press.

Holmes, A. (2007). *Gov. Perdue knows IT*. Government Executive. Retrieved August 8, 2007, from http://blogs.govexec.com/techinsider/archives/2007/08/gov_aligns_it_with_government.php

Holowczak, Richard D.; Soon, Ae Chun; Artigas, Francisco J.; and Atlurit, Vijayalakshmi. (2003). "Customized Geospatial Workflows for E-Government Services," *Proceedings of the IEEE/WIC International Conference on Web Intelligence, IEEE*.

Hong Kong (2007). *The HKSARG Interoperability Framework. Version: 5.1*. Hong Kong: Government of the Hong Kong Special Administrative Region, Office of the Government Chief Information Officer. Retrieved July 17, 2007, from http://www.ogcio.gov.hk/eng/infra/download/s18.pdf

Horn, R. E. (1998). *Visual language: Global communication for the 21st century.* Bainbridge Island, WA: MacroVu.

Hoven, J. van den, Wagenaar, R., Daskapan, S., Manders, N. Kenny, S. & Eldin, A.A. (2005), *Managing Identity, Privacy & Profiles.* Technical Report TI/RS/2005/101, Enschede, The Netherlands: Telematica Instituut. Retrieved July 17, 2007, from https://doc.telin.nl/dscgi/ds.py/Get/File-52040/TUD_sotas.pdf

Hughes, & Owen E. (1994). *Public Management and Administration: an introduction.* New York: St. Martin's Press.

ICTU. (2007). Flyer NORA v2. Retrieved June, 15, 2007, from http://www.e-overheid.nl/data/files/architectuur/flyer-nora-v2.pdf

IFIP–IFAC Task Force on Architectures for Enterprise Integration, (1999). *GERAM: Generalised Enterprise Reference Architecture and Methodology Version 1.6.3, Annex to ISO WD15704, Requirements for enterprise-reference architectures and methodologies.* March, pub: IFIP and IFAC.

Iftikhar Z., Eriksson I.V., & Dickson G.W. (2003); *Developing an Instrument for Knowledge Management Project Evaluation*; Electronic Journal of Knowledge Management, Vol1, Issue 1, 2003, pp55-62

Infocomm Development Authority of Singapore (2005). Singapore E-Government 2005. *2005 Report on Singapore E-Government.* Retrieved November 13, 2007, from www.igov.gov.sg/NR/rdonlyres/C586E52F-176A-44B6-B21E-2DB7E4FA45D1/11228/2005ReportonSporeeGov.pdf.

Innella, P. (December 2001). An Introduction to IDS. SecurityFocus.com. Obtained from http://www.securityfocus.com/infocus/1520.

Inter-Agency Benchmarking & Best Practices Council. (1996). Government Process Classification Scheme. Retrieved Dec. 2001, from http://www.va.gov/fedsbest/index.htm

Ishida, T. (2002). Digital City Kyoto. *Communications of the ACM,* July 2002, vol.45, No.7.

IT Governance Institute. (2000): *Management Guidelines for COBIT.* Retreived June 29, 2004 from http://www.isaca.org

ITU (1995), Open Distributed Processing - Reference Model - Part 3: Architecture, ITU Recommendation X.903 | ISO/IEC 10746-3. Geneva, Switzerland: International Telecommunication Union.

Iyer B., Shankaranarayanan G., & Wyner G. (2006); *Process Coordination Requirements: Implications for the design of Knowledge Management Systems*; The Journal of Computer Information Systems; Volume 46, Issue 5; 2006

J Ramanathan and R. Ramnath. (2006). *Co-engineering Business, Information Use, and Operations Systems for IT-enabled Adaptation.* Book chapter in "Adaptive Technologies and Business Integration: Social, Managerial and organizational Dimensions", Publisher IDEAS.

Jain, Sanjay; and McLean, Chuck; (2003). *Modeling and Simulation for Emergency Response,* NISY Technical Report, NISTIR 7071.

Jansen, W. & Karygiannis, T. NIST Special Publication 800-19: Mobile Agent Security. National Institute of Standards and Technology.

Janssen, M., & Hjort-Madsen, K. (2007). *Analyzing Enterprise Architecture in National Governments: The cases of Denmark and the Netherlands.* Paper presented at the Hawaii International Conference on System Sciences (HICSS), Hawaii, Big Island.

Janssen, M., Gortmaker, J., & Wagenaar, R. (2006). Web Service Orchestration in Public Administration: Challenges, Roles, and Growth Stages. *Information Systems Management,* Spring 2006, pp. 44–55.

Janssen, M., Gortmaker, J., & Wagenaar, R. W. (2006). Web Service Orchestration in Public Administration: Challenges, Roles, and Growth Stages. *Information Systems Management*(Spring 2006), 44-55.

Janssen, M., Kuk, G., & Wagenaar, R. W. (2008). A Survey of Web-based Business Models for e-Government in the Netherlands. *Government Information Quarterly, 25*(2) (forthcoming).

Japan Quality Award Committee. (2000). Japan Quality Award – Award Criteria: Innovation and Creation for Competitiveness – 2000 Ed. Japan Quality Award Committee. Tokyo.

Jiang, H.C., & Mo, J.P.T. (2001). Internet Based Design System for Globally Distributed Concurrent Engineering. *Journal of Cybernetics and Systems, 32*(7), 737 754.

Johannesson, P. (2001). A Language/Action based Approach to Information Modeling. In Rossi M. & Siau K. (Eds.), *Information Modeling in the new Millenium*: IDEA Publishing.

Johannesson, P., & Wohed, P. (1998). *Deontic Specification Patterns - Generalisation and Classification.* Paper presented at the International Conference on Formal Ontologies in Information Systems, Trento, Italy.

Jones, S., Hackney, R., & Irani, Z. (2007). Towards e-government transformation: conceptualising citizen engagement: A research note. *Transforming Government: People, Process and Policy, 1*(2), 145-152.

Jonkers H., van Buuren R., Arbab F., de Boer F., Bonsangue M., Bosma H., ter Doest H., Groenewegen L., Scholten J.G., Hoppenbrouwers S., Iacob M., Janssen W., Lankhorst M., van Leeuwen D., Proper E., Stam A., van der Torre L., & van Zanten G.V. (2003); *Towards an Language for Coherent Enterprise Architecture Descriptions*; Proceedings of the Seventh IEEE International Enterprise Distributed Object Computing Conference (EDOC) 2003.

Kankanhalli A., & Tan B.C.Y, (2004); *A review of Metrics for Knowledge Management Systems and Knowledge Management Initiatives*; Proceedings of the 37th Hawaii International Conference on System Sciences – 2004.

Kaplan, R. S.; and D. P. Norton. (1996). *The Balanced Scorecard*. Boston MA: Harvard.

Karygiannis, T. & Owens, L. (November 2002). NIST SP-800-48 Wireless Network Security - 802.11, Bluetooth and Handheld Devices. Recommendations of the National Institute of Standards and Technology. Computer Security Division - Information Technology Laboratory - National Institute of Standards and Technology.

KBSt Publication Series (2003) *"SAGA: Standards and Architectures for e-government Applications, Version 2.0"*. Retrieved August 15th, 2007, from http://egovstandards.gov.in/egs/eswg5/ enterprise-architecture-working-group-folder/standards-and-architectures-v2.pdf/ download

Kelly, S.; and Allison. M. A. (1998). *The Complexity Advantage*. New York, NY: McGraw Hill.

Kenniscentrum. (2007). *NORA 2.0 (Nederlandse Overheid Referentie Architectuur)*: Stichting ICTU.

Kettl, D. (2000). *The global public management revolution: A report on the transformation of governance.* Washington, D.C.: Brookings Institution Press.

Kettl, D. (2002). *The transformation of governance.* Baltimore, MD: The Johns Hopkins University Press.

King, C., Dalton, C., and Osmanoglu, T. Security Architecture: Design, Deployment & Operations. Osborne/McGraw-Hill, Berkeley, CA. ISBN: 0-07-213385-6. 2001.

Klein J; *ECM best practices for the Enlightened Enterprise*, KM World; Vol 14, Issue5, May 2005

Klijn, Erik-Hans. (1996). Analyzing and Managing Policy Processes in Complex Networks. *Administration and Society, 28*(1), 90-119.

Kling, R. et al. (2001). *Transforming Coordination: The Promise and Problems of Information Technology in Coordination.* In G. Olson, T. Malone, J.B. Smith. The Interdisciplinary Study of Coordination. Mahwah, NJ: Lawrence Erlbaum Associates.

Klischewski, R. (2004). Semantic Web for e-Government - a Research Agenda. *AIS SIG SEMIS Newsletter Volume 1, Issue 1.*

Klischewski, R., & Jeenicke, M. (2004). *Semantic Web Technologies for Information Management within e-Government Services.* Paper presented at the 37th Hawaii International Conference on System Sciences.

Kosanke, K., Vernadat, F., & Zelm, M. (1999). CIMOSA: enterprise engineering and integration, *Computers in Industry, 40*, 83-97.

Kramer, J. (2003). The CISA Prep Guide: Mastering the Certified Information Systems Auditor Exam.

Wiley Publishing, Indianapolis, Indiana. ISBN: 0-471-25032-5.

Kreizman, G., Baum, C., & Fraga, E. (2003). Gartner Enterprise Architecture: A Home for E-Government. *Gartner Group Research Note*, TU-20-1831. Retrieved June 15, 2007, from http://www.gartner.com/research/spotlight/asset_50080.jsp.

Kuhn, D. Richard, et. al. (August 2002). NIST Special Publication 800-46: Security for Telecommuting and Broadband Communications: Recommendations of the National Institute of Standards and Technology.

Kuhn, D. Richard, et. al. (January 2005). NIST Special Publication 800-58: Security Considerations for Voice Over IP Systems: Recommendations of the National Institute of Standards and Technology.

Ladley J. (2002); *Beyond the Data Warehouse: Information Management Maturity*; DM Review (http://www.dmreview.com) August 2002.

Lakoff, G.; and Johnson, M. (1980). *Metaphors we live by*. Chicago, IL: University of Chicago Press.

Landsbergen, D. and Wolken, G. (2001). *Realizing the Promise: Government Information Systems and the Fourth Generation of Information Technology*, Public Administration Review.

Lane, J.-E. (1995). *The Public Sector: Concepts, Models and Approaches* (2nd ed. ed.): Sage Publications.

Lankhorst, M. M., & Derks, W. L. A. (2007). *Towards a Service-Oriented Architecture for Demand-Driven e-Government*. Paper presented at the 11th IEEE International EDOC Conference (EDOC 2007).

Lankhorst, M. M., Derks, W. L. A., Fennema, P., Iacob, M. E., & Joosten, S. (2006). *B-dossier architectuur*. Enschede: Telematica Instituut.

Lankhorst, M.M. & Derks, W.L.A. (2006). *B-dossier architectuur*. Technical Report TI/RS/2006/014, Enschede, The Netherlands: Telematica Instituut. Retrieved July 17, 2007, from https://doc.telin.nl/dscgi/ds.py/Get/File-61826

Lankhorst, M.M. & Derks, W.L.A. (2007). Towards a Service-Oriented Architecture for Demand-Driven e-Government. *11th IEEE International EDOC Conference (EDOC 2007)*. Los Alamitos, CA: IEEE Computer Society.

Lankhorst, M.M., et al. (2005). *Enterprise Architecture at Work – Modelling, Communication, and Analysis*. Berlin: Springer-Verlag.

Lapkin A. (2004); *A users guide to architectural patterns*; Gartner Report G00124049, 22 October 2004

Lapkin A. (2004); *Architecture Frameworks: How to Choose*; Gartner Report G00124230, 19 November 2004

Larsen, L.B., & Vesterager, J. (1999, 15-17 March). *Framework and methodology for creating virtual enterprises - Initial results from the Globeman21 project*. Paper presented at the 5th International conference on Concurrent Enterprising: The Concurrent Enterprise in Operation. The Hague, the Netherlands.

Laurence, P.R. and J.W. Lorsch. (1967). *Organization and Environment (Boston: Division of Research*, Graduate School of Business Administration, Harvard University.

Lawrence, T. B., Dyck, B., Maitlis, S., & Mauws, M. K. (2006). The underlying structure of continuous change. *MIT Sloan Management Review*, (2006, Summer), 59-66.

Lawry, P., Albrecht, C., Nunamaker, J., & Lee, J. (2002) Evolutionary development and research on Internet-based collaborative writing tools and processes to enhance eWriting in an eGovernment setting. *Decision Support Systems*, vol. 34, (2002), 229-252, ElSevier.

Layne, K., & Lee, J. (2001). Developing fully functional e-government: a four stage model. *Government Information Quarterly*, 18(2), 122-136.

Li, H., & Williams, T.J., (1997). Some extensions to the Purdue Enterprise Reference Architecture (PERA) - I. Explaining the Purdue architecture and the Purdue methodology using the axioms of engineering design. *Computers in Industry, 34*, 247-259.

Li, H., & Williams, T.J., (2000). The interconnected chain of enterprises as presented by the Purdue Enterprise Reference Architecture. *Computers in Industry, 42*, 265-274.

Light, Paul C (1999). *The Changing Shape of Government* The Brookings Institute, Policy Brief # 45

Lind M., & Goldkuhl, G. (2001). *Generic Layered Patterns for Business Modeling*. Paper presented at the 6th International Workshop on the Language-Action Perspective on Communication Modeling, Montreal, Canada.

Linder, S. H. (1999). Coming to Terms With the Public-Private Partnership: A Grammar of Multiple Meanings. *American Behavioral Scientist, 43*(1), 35-51.

Lohr, Steve and Markoff, John (in press) Windows Is So Slow, but Why? *New York Times; March 27, 2006*

Longstaff, P.H. (2005). *Security, Resilience, and Communication In Unpredictable Environments Such as Terrorism, Natural Disasters and Complex Technology Program for Information Resources Policy*, Harvard University.

Lopez, J. (2002); *Return on Enterprise Architecture: Measure it in Asset Productivity*; Gartner Report: RPT-0702-0119, 19 July 2002

Lowi, T. J. (1979). *The End of Liberalism: The Second Republic of the United States*. New York: W.W. Norton.

Lyons-Burke, Kathy. (October 2000). NIST Special Publication 800-25: Federal Agency Use of Public Key Technology for Digital Signatures and Authentication. Federal Public Key Infrastructure Steering Committee.

MacKenzie, C.M., Laskey, K., McCabe, F., Brown, P. F., & Metz, R. (2006). *Reference Model for Service Oriented Architecture 1.0*, OASIS Committee Specification. OASIS Open 2005-2006.

Mackenzie, D. (2002). The Science of Surprise - Can complexity theory help us understand the real consequences of a convoluted event like September. *DISCOVER, 23*(2).

Maes, R. (1999). *A Generic Framework for Information Management*, PrimaVera Working Paper 99-03, Amsterdam, The Netherlands: University of Amsterdam, Department of Accountancy & Information Management.

Maier, M.W. Emery, D. and Hilliard, R. (2001). Software Architecture: Introducing IEEE Standard 1471, *IEEE Computer*. April 2001, Vol. 34-4, 107-109.

Malladi, S., & Min, K.J., (2005). Decision support models for the selection of Internet access technologies in rural communities. *Telematics and Informatics, 22*, 201–219.

Malone, T.; and K. Crowston. (2001). The Interdisciplinary Study of Coordination. In Coordination Theory and Collaboration Technology, Gary M. Olson, Thomas W.

Mandelbrot, B. B. (1982). *Fractal Geometry of Nature*. New York, NY: W H Freeman.

Mandler, Niemann, von Henning (2007). Serviceorientierte Architekturen: Governance, Compliance und Security. Duesseldorf, Euroforum.

Marco D. (2002); *Meta Data & Knowledge Management: Capability Maturity Model*; DM Review (http://www.dmreview.com) August/September/October/November 2002.

Martin P. (2006); *Measuring KM-Based improvements in decision-making*; personal communication through the ACTKM forum (http://www.actKM.org) March 2006.

Mason, M. (2005). Obtained from www.asisonline.org/certification/ ppt/CPPPersonnelSecurityTraining8-2-01.ppt, July 1, 2006. Lyondell/Equistar Chemical Companies.

Massey, C. (2003). Enterprise assistance: responses from the public and private sectors. *Journal of Small Business and Enterprise Development, 10*(2), 128-135.

Matthes, F., Wittenburg, A. (2004). *Softwarekarten zur Visualisierung von Anwendungslandschaften und ihren Aspekten – Eine Bestandsaufnahme*. Retrieved December 19, 2004, from http://wwwmatthes.in.tum.de/de/main.htm.

Maynard & Ruighaver (2006). What Makes a Good Information Security Policy: A Preliminary Framework For Evaluating Security Policy Quality. Proceedings of the 5th International Security Conference, Las Vegas.

McDavid, D.W. (1999). A standard for business architecture description. IBM Systems Journal, 38 (1), 12-31. Retrieved 20 April 2007 from IBM Systems Journal Web site: http://www.research.ibm.com/journal/sj/381/mcdavid.html

Medjahed, B., Benatallah, B., Bouguettaya, A., Ngu, A. H. H., & Elmagarmid, A. K. (2003). Business-to-business interactions: issues and enabling technologies. *The VLDB Journal The International Journal on Very Large Data Bases, 12*(1), 59-85.

Mednikarov, B.K., & Dereliev, P.H. (2004). Structured description of naval tasks. *Information and Security, 13,* 25-34.

Mendonca, D., Jefferson, T., Harrald, J. (March, 2007). Collaborative Adhocracies and Mix-and-Match Technologies in Emergency Management. *Communications of the ACM.*

Metainnovation (2004); *KM Concepts Module 8: Metrics*; Retrieved May 2006 from Metainnovation KM Concepts course (www.metainnovation.com)

Mettau, P. (2005). *mijnoverheid.nl – Publieke Dienstverlening in de toekomst.* The Hague: Het Expertise Centrum.

Mintzberg, H. (1996). Managing Government, Governing Management. *Harvard Business Review* (May-June 1996).

MIPT. (2004). *Responder Knowledge base, National Technology Emergency Plan for Emergency Response to Catastrophic Terrorism, MIPT* (National Memorial Institute for the Prevention of Terrorism), April, www.rkb.mipt.org. .

Missikoff, M. (2002). Harmonise – an ontology-based approach for semantic interoperability. *ERCIM News, 51,* 33-34.

Mo, J.P.T., & Menzel, C. (1998). An integrated process model driven knowledge based system for remote customer support. *Computers in Industry, 37,* 171-183.

Mo, J.P.T., Beckett, R., Nemes, L. (2005, 26-28 September). *Technology Infrastructure for Virtual Organisation of Tooling.* Paper presented at Sixth IFIP Working Conference on Virtual Enterprises (PRO-VE'05). Valencia, Spain.

Mo, J.P.T., Zhou, M., Anticev, J., Nemes, L., Jones, M., Hall, W. (2006). A study on the logistics and performance of a real 'virtual enterprise'. *International Journal of Business Performance Management, 8*(2-3), 152-169.

Mohanty S., & Chand M. (2005); *5iKM3 Knowledge Management Maturity Model*; TATA Consultancy Services 2005.

Monmonier, M., 2ed. (1996). *How to lie with maps.* Chicago, IL: University of Chicago Press.

Moon, M. Jae. (2002). *The Evolution of E-government among municipalities, Rhetoric or Reality* Public Administration Review (July / August), 62:4: 424-433.

Moon, M.J. (2002). The evolution of e-government among municipalities: rhetoric or reality?. *Public Administration Review, 62*(4), 424-433.

Moore A. (2005); *What makes government different?*; KM World Vol 14 Issue 6; Jun 2005

Morçöl, G. (2002). *A New Mind for Policy Analysis* Westport CT: Praeger.

Morgan, Gareth (1997) *Images of Organisation*, 2nd Edition, London. Sage Publications

Motta, E., Domingue, J., Cabral, L., & Gaspari, M. (2003). *IRS II: A Framework and Infrastructure for Semantic Web Services.* Paper presented at the 2nd International Semantic Web Conference.

Musgrave, R. A. (1959). *The Theory of Public Finance.* New York: McGraw-Hill.

NASCIO. (2003). *NASCIO Enterprise Architecture Maturity Model, Version 1.3.* National Association of State Chief Information Officers.

Nassar, M., et. al. (June 2006). Intrusion Detection Methods for VoIP Applications. The Third Annual VoIP Security Workshop. Accessed June 2006 from http://www.iptel.org/voipsecurity/

National Institute of Science and Technology. Federal Information Processing Standard Publication 1999: Standards for Security Categorization of Federal Information and Information Systems.

National Institute of Science and Technology. Special Publication 800-37: Guide for the Security Certification and Accreditation of Information Systems.

National Institute of Science and Technology. Special Publication 800-12. An Introduction to Computer Security: The NIST Handbook. National Institute of Standards and Technology, Technology Administration. Published by U.S. Department of Commerce.

National Institute of Science and Technology. Special Publication 800-53 (Guide for the Selection and Specification of Security Controls for Federal Information Systems),

National Institute of Science and Technology. Special Publication 53A: Techniques and Procedures for Verifying the Effectiveness of Security Controls in Information Systems.

National Institute of Science and Technology. Special Publication 800-60 (Guide for Mapping Types of Information and Information Systems to Security Categorization Levels),

National Research Council (2004). McGroddy, James C., and Lin, Herbert S., Editors, *A Review of the FBI's Trilogy Information Technology*, Committee on the FBI's Trilogy Information Technology Modernization Program, Computer Science and Telecommunications Board, Division on Engineering and Physical Sciences, National Research Council of the National Academies, . ISBN:0-309-09224-8. Retrieved on August 6 2007 from http://www.nap.edu/catalog/10991.html

Nemes, L., & Mo, J.P.T., (2004). Collaborative Networks in Australia – Challenges and Recommendations. In L.M. Camarinha-Matos, H. Afsarmanesh (Eds.). *Collaborative Networked Organizations* (pp.97-102). Boston: Kluwer Academic Publishers.

New Zealand, Security in the Government Sector (2002). Obtained from http://www.security.govt.nz/sigs/html/chapter7.html, June 29, 2006.

NIA. (2006). *Government Information Technology Architecture-Maturity Model, Version 1.0 (Draft)*. National Information Society Agency. Korea.

Niemann, K. (2005). IT Governance and Enterprise Architecture - Impact of IT cost reduction on innova-

tion power. *The Journal of Enterprise Architecture*, 1 (1), 31-40.

Niemann, K. (2006). *From Enterprise Architecture to IT-Governance*. Wiesbaden: Vieweg.

Niles, I., & Pease, A. (2001, October 17-19). *Towards a Standard Upper Ontology*. Paper presented at the 2nd International Conference on Formal Ontology in Information Systems (FOIS-2001), Ogunquit, Maine.

NIMS. *National Incident Management System*, www.fema.gov.

NIST. (2007). *Baldrige National Quality Program. NIST. Technology Administration*. Department of Commerce.

Nohria, N. (1992). *Is a Network Perspective a Useful Way of Studying organizations?* In N. Nohria and R. G. Eccles (eds.), Networks and organizations: Structure, Form and Fit (Boston: Harvard Business School Press).

Noran O. (2003); *A systematic evaluation of the C4ISR AF using ISO1504 Annex A (GERAM)*; Computers in Industry vol 56 (2005) pp 407-427.

Noran O. (2005); *An analysis of the Zachman framework of enterprise architecture from the GERAM perspective*; Annual Reviews in Control Vol 27 (2003) pp 163-183.

Noran, O. (2005). A systematic evaluation of the C4ISR AF using ISO15704 Annex A (GERAM). *Computers in Industry, 56*, 407-427.

O'Toole, Laurence and Meier, Kenneth. (2000). Networks, Hierarchies, and Management: Modeling the nonlinearities, in Heinrich, C. and L. Lynn (eds.).

OAG. Open applications group. *Uses XML for every where to every where integration*.

OASIS: www.oasis-open.org, OASIS (Organization for the Advancement of Structured Information Standards) is a not-for-profit, international consortium that drives the development, convergence, and adoption of e-business standards

Office of e-Envoy UK. (2002). e-Services Development Framework Primer v1.0b. Retrieved Noe 2002, from http://www.govtalk.gov.uk/documents/eSDF-primerV1b.pdf

Office of Government Commerce (2005). *Managing Successful Projects with PRINCE2 Manual 2005*, 4th Ed. TSO (The Stationery Office).

Office of Management and Budget, Federal EA Program Management Office. Federal Enterprise Architecture Security and Privacy Profile (version 1.1). June 2006.

Office of Management and Budget. (2001, July 18). Citizen-centered e-government: Developing the action plan. (OMB Memorandum 01-28). Retrieved June 10, 2007, from http://www.whitehouse.gov/omb/memoranda/m01-28.html

Office of Management and Budget. (2002, February 27). E-government strategy. Retrieved June 10, 2007, from http://www.whitehouse.gov/omb/inforeg/egov-strategy.pdf

Office of Management and Budget. (2007a, July). FEA consolidated reference model document version 2.2. Retrieved June 10, 2007, from http://www.whitehouse.gov/omb/egov/documents/FEA_CRM_v22_Final_July_2007.pdf

Office of Management and Budget. (2007b, July). FEA reference model mapping quick guide (FY09 budget preparation). Retrieved June 10, 2007 from http://www.whitehouse.gov/omb/egov/documents/FY09_Ref_Model_Mapping_QuickGuide_July_2007.pdf

OGC: The Open Geospatial Consortium, Inc. (OGC) is a non-profit, international, voluntary consensus standards organization that is leading the development of standards for geospatial and location based services. www.opengeospatial.org.

Oltramari A., Gangemi A., Guarino N., & Masolo C. (2002, October 2002). *Sweeting ontologies with DOLCE. Ontologies and the Semantic Web.* Paper presented at the 13th International Conference, EKAW 2002, Siguenza, Spain.

OMG: http://www.omg.org.

Orange, G., Elliman, T., Kor, A.L., & Tassabehji, R. (2007). Local government and social or innovation value. *Transforming Government: People, Process and Policy, 1*(3), 242-254.

Organisation for Economic Co-operation and Development (OECD) (2001) *"The Hidden Threat to E-Government: Avoiding large government IT failures (Policy brief)"*. Retrieved August 15th, 2007, from http://www.oecd.org/dataoecd/19/12/1901677.pdf

Ortiz, A., Lario, F., & Ros, L., (1999). Enterprise Integration – Business Processes Integrated Management: a proposal for a methodology to develop Enterprise Integration Programs. *Computers in Industry, 40,* 155–171.

OSI. The Open Source Initiative (OSI), a non-profit corporation responsible for the management and promotion of the Open Source Definition (OSD). www.opensource.org.

OWL Services Coalition. (2004). OWL-S: Semantic Markup for Web Services. Retrieved March 2005, from http://www.daml.org/services/owl-s/1.1/

Page, S. (2003). Entrepreneurial Strategies for Managing Interagency Collaboration. *Journal of Public Administration Research and Theory, 13*(3), 311-340.

Pande, P., & Holpp L. (2006) *What is Six Sigma?*, New York, NY: McGraw-Hill.

Park, J. S. & Ho, S M. (2004). Composite Role-based Monitoring (CRBM) for Countering Insider Threats. Second Symposium on Intelligence and Security Informatics (ISI), Tucson, Arizona, June 2004.

Patankar, A.K., & Sadiga, S., (1995). Enterprise integration modelling: a review of theory and practice. *Computer Integrated Manufacturing Systems, 8*(1), 21-34.

Pattinson, M. & Anderson, G. (). Information Risk Management: Some Social-psychological Issues.

Paulzen O., & Perc P. (2002); *A maturity model for quality improvement in knowledge management*; Proceedings of the 13th Australasian Conference on Information Systems (ACIS 2002).

Pavlichev, A., & Garson, G. D. (2004) *Digital Government Principles and Best Practices, Chapter 1 ("The promise of Digital Government")*, page 2, IDEA Group Publishing.

Peitgen, H.; Jurgens, H.; and Saupe, D. (1992). Chaos and Fractals: New Frontiers of Science. Berlin: Springer Verlag.

Peristeras V., & Tarabanis K. (2004). Governance Enterprise Architecture (GEA): Domain models for e-Governance. *In the 6th international conference on Electronic commerce* (ICEC), ACM.

Peristeras V., & Tarabanis K. (2004a). Advancing the Government Enterprise Architecture - GEA: The Service Execution Object Model. In R. Traunmuller (Ed.), *Electronic Government, DEXA, 3rd International Conference EGOV 2004, Zaragoza, Lecture Notes in Computer Science 3183* (pp. 476-482): Springer.

Peristeras V., & Tarabanis K. (2004b). The Governance Enterprise Architecture (GEA) Object Model. In M. A. Wimmer (Ed.), *Knowledge Management in Electronic Government, Lecture Notes in Computer Science 3035, (5th IFIP International Working Conference, KMGov 2004, Krems, Austria, May 27-29)* (pp. 101-110): Springer.

Peristeras V., & Tarabanis K. (2005, 22-24 April 2005). *The GEA Generic Process Model for Public Administration Service Execution.* Paper presented at the 8th International Conference for Business Information Systems (8th BIS 2005), Poznan, Poland.

Peristeras V., & Tarabanis K. (2006, Mar. 27-29). *Reengineering the public administration modus operandi through the use of reference domain models and Semantic Web Service technologies.* Paper presented at the 2006 AAAI Spring Symposium, The Semantic Web meets eGovernment (SWEG), Stanford University, California, USA.

Peristeras V., Goudos S., Vitvar T., Mocan A., & Tarabanis K. (2006). *Towards Semantic Web Services for Public Administration based on the Web Service Modeling Ontology (WSMO) and the Governance Enterprise Architecture (GEA).* Paper presented at the 5th EGOV International Conference, DEXA Krakow, Poland.

Peristeras, V., & Tarabanis, K. (2000). Towards an Enterprise Architecture for Public Administration: A Top Down Approach. *European Journal of Information Systems, 9*(Dec. 2000), 252-260.

Peristeras, V., Tsekos, T., & Tarabanis, K. (2003, 31 Jul.-2 Aug.). *Building Domain Models for the (e-) Governance System.* Paper presented at the International Conference on Politics and Information Systems: Technologies and Applications (PISTA '03), Orlando, Florida, USA.

Platt, M. (2007). *CIO Definitions – Enterprise Architecture.* Retrieved August 13, 2007, from http://searchcio.techtarget.com/sDefinition/0,,sid19_gci1081274,00.html

Pólya, G. (1971). *How to Solve it: A New Aspect of Mathematical Method.* Princeton, NJ: Princeton University Press.

Pongsiri, N. (2003). Public-Private Partnerships in Thailand: A Case Study of the Electric Utility Industry. *Public Policy and Administration, 18*(3), 69.

Porter, M. (1985). *Competitive Advantage: Creating and Sustaining Superior Performance.* New York, NY: The Free Press.

Porter, M. E. (1998). Competitive Strategy: Techniques For Analyzing Industries And Competitors. New York, NY: Free Press.

Powel, A., & Picolli, G. (2004) Virtual Teams: A Review of Current Literature and Directions for Future Research. *The DATA BASE for advances in Information Systems-Winter 2004, vol 35,* No.1. ACM.

Prabandham, S.M. (2007, June). *A Case Study in Service Component Reusability and Interoperability: HR LOB Technical Reference Model.* Unpublished manuscript.

Prime Minister's Strategy Unit (2004). Strategy Survival Guide v2.1. Retrieved 31st July 2007 from http://www.cabinetoffice.gov.uk/strategy/downloads/survivalguide/skills/s_pestle.htm

Provan, K. G., & Milward, H. B. (2001). Do Networks Really Work? A Framework for Evaluating Public-Sector Organizational Networks. *Public Administration Review, 61*(4), 414-423.

Punia, Devendra K.; and Saxena, K. B. C. (March 2004). E-government services and policy track: Managing inter-organizational workflows in eGovernment services, *Proceedings of the 6th international conference on Electronic commerce.*

Qurashi, R. (2005). Eight Steps for Integrating Security Into Application Development. MCI NetSec. Published by ComputerWorld, December 6, 2005. Obtained from http://www.computerworld.com/securitytopics/security/story/0,10801,106805,00.html.

R.E. Asher (ed.). (1994). *The Encyclopedia of Language and Linguistics*. Oxford: Pergamon.

Ramanathan, J. (1999). *Enterprise Integration with NIIIP Protocols, SME, ASME* Autofact Proceedings.

Ramanathan, J. (2005). *Fractal Architecture for the Adaptive Complex Enterprise*, Communications of the ACM, May.

Ramanathan, J. and Ramnath, Rajiv. (2004) *IT Architecture and the Case for Lean eBusiness Process Management,* Knowledge Supply and Information Logistics in Enterprises and Networked organizations, Fraunhofer-Institute for Software and Systems Engineering ISST.

Ramanathan, J.; and Beswick, R. (2000). *Imperative: Why Process-based Architecture is Essential for Successful Supply-Chain Participation. EAI Journal.*

Ramnath, R. and Desai, A. (2007). *City of Columbus, 311 Impact Evaluation, Final Report.*

Ramnath, R., Landsbergen, D. (May, 2005) IT-enabled sense-and-respond strategies in complex public organizations. *Communications of the ACM, 48*(5).

Reding, V. (2005) i2010: The European Commission's new programme to boost competitiveness in the ICT sector. *European Committee's press releases.* Retrieved August 15th, 2007, from http://europa.eu.int/rapid/pressReleasesAction.do?reference=SPEECH/05/format=HTML&aged=0&language=EN&guiLanguage=en)

Rhodes, R. A. W. (1997). *Understanding Governance*: Open University Press.

Richardson, L., Jackson, B. M., & Dickson, G. (1990). A Principle-Based Enterprise Architecture: Lessons From Texaco and Star Enterprise. *MIS Quarterly, 14*(4), 385-403.

Riggins, F. J., & Mukhopadhyay, T. (1994). Interdependent benefits from interorganizational systems: opportunities for business partner reengineering. *Journal of Management Information Systems, 11*(2), 37-57.

Riley, B. T. (2003). *e-Government vs. e-Governance* (International Tracking Survey Report, No 4). Ottawa: Commonwealth Centre for E-Governance.

Robertson J. (2003); *Metrics for knowledge management and content management*; Step Two Designs (www.steptwo.com.au) February 2003, accessed May 2006.

Rodriquez, E. (2005). Physical Network Security. Obtained from http://www.skullbox.net/physicalnetworksecurity.php, June 29, 2006.

Rosati, L., Lai, M. E., & Gnoli, C. (2004, 10th December). *Faceted Classification for Public Administration.* Paper presented at the Semantic Web Applications and Perspectives (SWAP) - 1st Italian Semantic Web Workshop, Ancona, Italy.

Rosenau, P. V. (1999). Introduction. The Strengths and Weaknesses of Public-Private Policy Partnerships. *American Behavioral Scientist, 43*(1), 10-34.

Rosetta Net. http://www.rosettanet.org/.

Ross, J. (2003). Creating a strategic IT architecture competency: Learning in stage. *MISQ Quarterly Executive, 2*(1), 31-43.

Ross, J.W. (2006). Design Priorities for the IT Unit of the Future. *MIT Sloan CISR Research Briefings*, 4(3D). Retrieved September 7, 2007, from http://mitsloan.mit.edu/cisr/papers.php.

Ross, J.W., Weill, P., & Robertson, D.C. (2006). *Enterprise Architecture as Strategy*. Boston, MA: Harvard Business School Press.

Ross, R. et. al. (February 2005). NIST Special Publication 800-53: Recommended Security Controls for Federal Information Systems. National Institute of Standards and Technology, Computer Security Division.

Ross, R.. et. al. (May 2002). NIST Special Publication 800-37: Guide for the Security Certification and Accreditation of Federal Information Systems. National Institute of Standards and Technology, Computer Security Division.

Rosser B. (2002); *Architectural styles and Enterprise Architecture*; Gartner report AV-17-4384, 13 August 2002.

Sackett, P., Rose, T., & Adamson, V. (2003). The importance of business process clarification within the virtual enterprise. *Journal of Small Business and Enterprise Development, 10*(3), 298-305.

Saha, P. (2004); *A real options perspective to Enterprise Architecture as an investment activity*; (accessed 24 Aug 05 through The Open Group Architecture Forum http://www.opengroup.org/architecture).

Saha, P. (2006). A Real Options Perspective to Enterprise Architecture as an Investment Activity. *Journal of Enterprise Architecture*, 2(3), 32-52.

Saha, P. (2007a). A Synergistic Assessment of the Federal Enterprise Architecture Framework against GERAM (ISO 15704:2000). In Saha, P. (Ed.). *Handbook of Enterprise Systems Architecture in Practice*. Hershey, PA: IGI Global Information Science Reference.

Saha, P. (Ed.). (2007b). *Handbook of Enterprise Systems Architecture in Practice*. Hershey, PA: IGI Global Information Science Reference.

Sairamesh, J., Lee, A., & Anania, L. (2004). Information Cities. *Communications of the ACM* February 2004, vol. 47, No.2.

Salmela, H.; and Spil, T.A.M. (2002). Dynamic and emergent information systems strategy formulation and implementation. *International Journal of Information Management, 22*, 441-460.

SAP. (2000). R/3 System SAP Solution Map. Retrieved Dec. 2000, from www.sap.com

Schekkerman J. (2004); *Enterprise Architecture Validation*; Institute for Enterprise Architecture Developments, August 2004.

Schekkerman J. (2004); *Trends in Enterprise Architecture: How are organizations progressing?*; Institute for Enterprise Architecture Developments, 2004.

Schekkerman J. (2006); *How to survive in the jungle of Enterprise Architecture Frameworks: Creating or choosing an Enterprise Architecture Framework*; Trafford Publishing; 3rd Edition 2006 (First published 2004).

Schekkerman, J. (2005). *Trends in Enterprise Architecture 2005: How are Organizations Progressing? 1st Ed.* Institute for Enterprise Architecture Developments (IFEAD).

Scholl, H.J. (2003). E-government: A special case of IT-enabled Business Process Change, *Chapter presented at the 36th Hawaiian Conference of Systems Sciences*, Hawaii.

Schubert, P., & Hausler, U. (2001) e-Government meets e-Business: A Portal Site for Startup Companies in Switzerland. *In the 34th International Conference on System Sciences* (IEEE 2001)

Schulman J. (2004); *Architecture Frameworks provide system road maps*; Gartner Report G00125007, 29 November 2004.

Schwartz, Peter. (2003). *Inevitable Surprises: Thinking Ahead in a Time of Turbulence.* New York: Gotham Books.

SCOR. http://wwwsupply-chain.org.

Searle, J. R. (1969). *Speech Acts. An Essay in the Philosophy of Language.* London: Cambridge University Press.

Searle, J. R. (1975). A taxonomy of illocutionary acts. In Gunderson K. (Ed.), *Language, Mind and Knowledge.* Minneapolis: University of Minesota.

Semantic Interoperability Community of Practice (SICoP). (2005). *Introducing Semantic Technologies and the Vision of the Semantic Web, White Paper Series Module 1.*

Semy, S. K., Pulvermacher, M. K., & Obrst, L. J. (2004). *Toward the Use of an Upper Ontology for U.S. Government and U.S. Military Domains: An Evaluation* (No. 04B0000063): The MITRE Corporation.

Shankararaman, V., & Lee, B.S. (1994). Knowledge-Based Safety Training System (KBSTS) - A Prototype Implementation. *Computers in Industry, 25*, 145-157.

Shen, H., Wall, B., Zaremba, M., Chen, Y., & Browne, J. (2004). Integration of business modelling methods for enterprise information system analysis and user requirements gathering. *Computers in Industry, 54*, 307-323.

Shinonome, M., Hashimoto, H., Fuse, A., & Mo, J.P.T. (1998). Development of an information technology infrastructure for extended enterprise. In J. Mills & F. Kimura (Eds.). *Information Infrastructure Systems for Manufacturing* (pp.353-364). Boston: Kluwer Academic Publishers.

Siegel, Lloyd H. (2006). Lessons Learned, Dept of Veterans Affairs, Physical Security Assessment Program. Federal Facility Council. Physical Security & Hazard Mitigation Committee, March 14th, 2006. Obtained from www.va.gov/facmgt, June 29, 2006.

Simsion, G. (2006). *Conceptual, Logical, Physical: Clearing the Confusion.* The Data Administration Newsletter, No. 36. Robert S. Seiner.

Sinha, Rajiv. (March 2001) A Security Checklist for Oracle 9i. Oracle White Papers. Accessed June 2006 from http://www.oracle.com/technology/deploy/security/oracle9i/pdf/9i_checklist.pdf.

Snouffer, R., et. al. (June 2001). NIST Special Publication 800-29: A Comparison of the Security Requirements for Cryptographic Modules in FIPS 140-1 AND FIPS 140-2.

Snyman S., & Kruger CJ; *The interdependency between strategic management and strategic knowledge management*; Journal of Knowledge Management; Vol 8, Issue 1, 2004).

Sowa J.F., & Zachman J.A.(1992); *Extending and formalizing the framework for information systems architecture*; IBM Systems Journal, Vol 31, No 3, 1992.

Sowa, F. J. (2000) Levels of Representation. *Knowledge Representation. Logical, philosophical and computational foundations* (pp. 188-189).Brooks/Cole Thomson Learning.

Spears, J. (2006). Defining Information Security. The Pennsylvania State University, Smeal College of Business. 5th Security Conference 2006. Las Vegas, Nevada.

Spewak, S. H. (1992). *Enterprise architecture planning: Developing a blueprint for data, applications, and technology.* New York, NY: Wiley.

Springer, L.M. (n.d.). Retirement Systems Modernization. Retrieved 1 August 2007 from the OPM Web site: http://www.opm.gov/rsm/index.asp

Sproull, L. & Patterson, J., (2004). Making Information Cities Livable. *Communications of the ACM* February 2004, vol. 49, No.2.

Standards Australia (2005); *Australian Standard 5037-2005: Knowledge management – a guide*; Standards Australia, September 2005.

State of Arkansas (2004). Personnel Security. Office of Information Technology. Document Number SS-70-007. February 2004.

Steen M.W.A., Akehurst D.H., ter Doest H.W.L., & Lankhorst M.M.(2004); *Supporting Viewpoint-Oriented Enterprise Architecture*; Proceedings of the 8th IEEE International Enterprise Distributed Object Computing Conference (EDOC) 2004.

Steen, M.W.A., Lankhorst, M.M., Doest, H. ter, Strating, P., & Iacob, M.-E. (2005). Service-Oriented Enterprise Architecture". In Z. Stojanovic and A. Dahanayake (Eds.), *Service-Oriented Software System Engineering: Challenges and Practices*, Hershey, PA: IDEA Group.

Stevenson, D.A. (1996, April). Positioning Enterprise Architecture. In D.A. Stevenson, *Component Based Enterprise Architecture.* Dissertation presented to the Department of Information Systems, University of Cape Town, South Africa. Retrieved 10 August 2007 from the IS World Net Web site: http://users.iafrica.com/o/om/omisditd/denniss/text/eapositn.html

Stoneburner, G., et. al. (July 2002). NIST Special Publication 800-30: Risk Management Guide for Information Technology Systems: Recommendations of the National Institute of Standards and Technology.

Sulin, B.A., Lang, K.R., & Whinston. A.B. (1997). Enterprise decision support using Intranet technology. *Decision Support Systems, 20*, 99-134.

Swanson, M. (November 2001). NIST Special Publication 800-26: Security Self-Assessment Guide for Information Technology Systems. National Institute of Standards and Technology, Computer Security Division.

Swanson, M. et. al. (June 2002). NIST Special Publication 800-34: Contingency Planning Guide for Information Technology Systems: Recommendations of the National Institute of Standards and Technology.

Tambouris, E. (2001). *An Integrated Platform for Realising One-Stop Government: The eGOV project.* Paper presented at the E-Government Workshop within DEXA01.

Tambouris, E., Kavadias, G., & Spanos, E. (2004). The Governmental Markup Language (GovML). *Journal of E-Government, vol. 1 (2).*

Tan, E.P., & Gan, W.B. (2007). Enterprise Architecture in Singapore Government. In Saha, P. (Ed.). *Handbook of Enterprise Systems Architecture in Practice.* Hershey, PA: IGI Global Information Science Reference.

Tapscott, D., & Caston, A. (1994). *Paradigm Shift : The New Promise of Information Technology.*

Tarabanis, K., Peristeras, V., & Fragidis, G. (2001, June 2001). *Building an Enterprise Architecture for Public Administration: A High Level Data Model for Strategic Planning.* Paper presented at the 9th European Conference on Information Systems, Bled, Slovenia.

Tat-Kei Ho, A. (2002). Reinventing Local Governments and e-Government Initiative. *Public Administration Review,* July/August 2002, Vol. 62, No. 4., Blackwell Synergy.

Teisman, G. and E.H. Klijn. (2002). Partnership Arrangements: Governmental Rhetoric or Governance Scheme? *Public Administration Review, 62*(2), 197-205.

The Open Group (2006). *The Open Group Architectural Framework (TOGAF) Version 8.1.1 'Enterprise Edi-*

tion'. Reading, UK: The Open Group. Retrieved July 17, 2007, from http://www.opengroup.org/togaf/.

The Open Group. (1995-2005). Single Sign-On. Obtained from http://www.opengroup.org/security/sso/.

The Open Group. (2006). *The Open Group Architecture Framework Enterprise Edition Version 8.1.1.* The Open Group Architecture Forum. Retrieved February 20, 2008 from http://www.theopengroup.org/

The World Bank (2003). Retrieved June 18, 2007, from http://Web.worldbank.org/WBSITE/EXTERNAL/TOPICS/EXTINFORMATIONANDCOMMUNI-CATIONANDTECHNOLOGIES/EXTEGOVERN-MENT/contentMDK:20507153~menuPK:702592~pagePK:148956~piPK:216618~theSitePK:702586,00.html.

The World Bank. (1992). *Governance and Development.* Washington: World Bank.

Thiétart, R.A. and B. Forgues. (1995). *Chaos Theory and Organization Science,* 6(1):19-31.

Toavs, D. (2004). *Pixelating policy: Issue transformation in real and virtual worlds.* (Doctoral dissertation, Virginia Polytechnic Institute and State University, 2004). Retrieved June 10, 2007, from http://scholar.lib.vt.edu/theses/available/etd-12222004-094635/

TopQuadrant. (2005a). FEA Reference Models Ontologies v.1.1. Retrieved 16 Mar., 2006, from http://www.topquadrant.com/documents/TQFEARMO.pdf

Tracy, M. et. al. (September 2002). NIST Special Publication 800-44: Guidelines on Securing Public Web Servers: Recommendations of the National Institute of Standards and Technology.

Tracy, M. et. al. (September 2002). NIST Special Publication 800-45: Guidelines on Electronic Mail Security: Recommendations of the National Institute of Standards and Technology.

Treasury Board Secretariat, Government of Canada (2001). Canada's Report on Portals, August 10, 2001.

Treasury Board Secretariat, Government of Canada (2006). Service Oriented Architecture Strategy. Retrieved May 25th, 2006, from http://www.tbs-sct.gc.ca/cio-dpi/Webapps/architecture/sd-eo/sd-eo_e.pdf)

Tsichritzis, D., & Klug, A. (Eds.). (1978). *The ANSI/ XWSPARC DBMS framework report of the study group on database management systems.* Information Systems, 3(3), 173-191.

U.S. General Accounting Office (2003). *Information Technology: A Framework for Assessing and Improving Enterprise Architecture Management (Version 1.1),* GAO-03-584G, April 1, 2003. Retrieved 3rd August 2007 from http://www.gao.gov/new.items/d03584g. pdf

U.S. General Accounting Office. (2002). *Homeland security: Proposal for cabinet agency has merit, but implementation will be pivotal to success.* (GAO Publication No. GAO-02-886T). Washington, D.C. Retrieved June 9, 2007, from http://www.gao.gov/new. items/d02886t.pdf

UK (2005). *e-Government Interoperability Framework Version 6.1.* London: Cabinet Office. Retrieved July 17, 2007, from http://www.govtalk.gov.uk/schemasstandards/egif_document.asp?docnum=949

UK Cabinet Office (2000). e-Government, a strategic framework for public services in the information age. Retrieved May 25th, 2006, from

UK Cabinet Office, Office of the e-Envoy (2002) e-Government Interoperability Framework (e-GIF). Part two: Technical Policies and Specifications. Retrieved August 15th, 2007, from http://www.govtalk.gov.uk/ documents/e-GIF4Pt2_2002-04-25.pdf

UK Chief Information Officers Council (UK CIO) (2005) Enterprise Architecture for UK Government. An overview of the process and deliverables for Release 1. Retrieved August 15th, 2007, from http://www. cio.gov.uk/documents/cto/pdf/enterprise_architecture_uk.pdf

United Kingdom, Department of Trade and Industry (June 1991) Information Technology System Evaluation Criteria (IITSEC). Accessed from http://nsi. org/Library/Compsec/eurooran.txt.

United Nations and American Society for Public Administration (2001). Global Survey of E-Government, Retrieved June 15, 2007, from http://www.unpan. org/egovernment2.asp.

United States Congress (1996) Public Law 191-104 Health Information Portability and Accountability Act of 1996. Accessed from http://fr Webgate.access. gpo.gov/cgi-bin/getdoc.cgi?dbname=104_cong_public_laws&docid=f:publ191.104.

United States Congress (2002) Public Law 204-107 Sarbanes-Oxley Act of 2002. Accessed from Accessed from http://fr Webgate.access.gpo.gov/cgi-bin/getdoc.cgi?dbname=107_cong_public_laws&docid=f: publ204.107.

United States Congress (2002) Public Law 347-107 Federal Information Security Management Act of 2002. http://fr Webgate.access.gpo.gov/cgi-bin/getdoc.cgi?dbname=107_cong_public_laws&docid=f: publ347.107.

United States Department of Justice System Development Life Cycle Guidance Document. (2003). The Department of Justice Information Resource Management, January 2003. Obtained from http://www.usdoj. gov/jmd/irm/lifecycle/table.htm.

United States Federal Enterprise Architecture Programme Management Office (2006). FEA Consolidated Reference Model, Version 2.0. Retrieved June 18, 2007, from http://www.whitehouse.gov/omb/egov/ a-1-fea.html.

United States House of Representatives Government Reform Committee (February 2005) Federal Computer Security Report Card for 2003 – 2004. Accessed from http://reform.house.gov/UploadedFiles/Computer%20 Security%20Report%20card%202%20years.pdf.

United States. Executive Office of the President. Office of Management and Budget [OMB]. (2005, November). *The Data Reference Model Version 2.0.* Retrieved 10 August 2007 from the OMB E-Gov Web site: http://www.whitehouse.gov/omb/egov/documents/DRM_2_0_Final.pdf

United States. Executive Office of the President. Office of Management and Budget [OMB]. Federal Enterprise Architecture Program Management Office [FEAPMO]. (2006, December). *FEA Practice Guidance.* Retrieved 22 October 2007 from the OMB E-Gov Web site: http://www.whitehouse.gov/omb/egov/documents/FEA_Practice_Guidance.pdf

United States. Executive Office of the President. Office of Management and Budget [OMB]. (2006, December). *Expanding E-Government: Making a Difference for the American People Using Information Technology.* Retrieved 30 April 2007 from the OMB E-Gov Web site: http://www.whitehouse.gov/omb/egov/documents/expanding_egov_2006.pdf

United States. Executive Office of the President. Office of Management and Budget [OMB]. (2007, February). *Report to Congress on the Benefits of the E-Government Initiatives.* Retrieved 16 May 2007 from the OMB E-Gov Web site: http://www.whitehouse.gov/omb/egov/documents/FY07_Benefits_Report.pdf

United States. Executive Office of the President. Office of Management and Budget [OMB]. (2007, July). *FEA Consolidated Reference Model Document Version 2.2.* Retrieved 16 July 2007 from the OMB E-Gov Web site: http://www.whitehouse.gov/omb/egov/documents/FEA_CRM_v22_Final_July_2007.pdf

United States. Executive Office of the President. Office of Management and Budget [OMB]. (n.d.a). E-Gov Background. Retrieved 8 May 2007 from the OMB E-Gov Web site: http://www.whitehouse.gov/omb/egov/g-1-background.html

United States. Executive Office of the President. Office of Management and Budget [OMB]. (n.d.b) Federal Enterprise Architecture. Retrieved 22 May 2007 from the OMB E-Gov Web site: http://www.whitehouse.gov/omb/egov/a-1-fea.html

United States. General Accounting Office [GAO]. (2003, November). *Information Technology: Leadership Remains Key to Agencies Making Progress on Enterprise Architecture Efforts.* Retrieved 10 October 2007 from the GAO Web site: http://www.gao.gov/new.items/d0440.pdf

United States. Office of Personnel Management [OPM]. (n.d.). Human Capital Assessment and Accountability Framework [HCAAF]. Retrieved 18 May 2007 from the OPM Web site: http://www.opm.gov/hcaaf_resource_center/2-2.asp

United States. Office of Personnel Management [OPM]. GoLearn. (n.d.) The Office of Personnel Management's GoLearn Program. Retrieved 24 October 2007 from the

GoLearn Web site: http://www.golearn.gov/MaestroC/index.cfm?room=welcome&roomaction=about

United States. Office of Personnel Management [OPM]. Human Resources Line of Business [HR LOB]. (2006, January). *HR LOB Business Reference Model version 2.* Retrieved 23 April 2007 from the OPM HR LOB Web site: http://www.opm.gov/egov/documents/architecture/BRM_Report_V2.pdf

United States. Office of Personnel Management [OPM]. Human Resources Line of Business [HR LOB]. (2006, February). *HR LOB Data Model version 1.* Retrieved 23 April 2007 from the OPM HR LOB Web site: http://www.opm.gov/egov/documents/architecture/HRLOB_DM.pdf

United States. Office of Personnel Management [OPM]. Human Resources Line of Business [HR LOB]. (2006, June). *HR LOB Performance Model version 1.* Retrieved 23 April 2007 from the OPM HR LOB Web site: http://www.opm.gov/egov/documents/architecture/HRLOB_PM_6.30.06.pdf

United States. Office of Personnel Management [OPM]. Human Resources Line of Business [HR LOB]. (2006, September). *HR LOB Target Requirements for Shared Service Centers version 2.0.* Retrieved 23 April 2007 from the OPM HR LOB Web site: http://www.opm.gov/egov/documents/requirements/Reqv2.pdf

United States. Office of Personnel Management [OPM]. Human Resources Line of Business [HR LOB]. (2006, September). *HR LOB Service Component Model version 1.* Retrieved 23 April 2007 from the OPM HR LOB Web site: http://www.opm.gov/egov/documents/architecture/HRLOBSCMv1.pdf

United States. Office of Personnel Management [OPM]. Human Resources Line of Business [HR LOB]. (2007, September). *HR LOB Service Component Model version 2.* Retrieved 15 November 2007 from the OPM HR LOB Web site: http://www.opm.gov/egov/documents/architecture/HRLOBSCMv2.pdf

United States. Office of Personnel Management [OPM]. Human Resources Line of Business [HR LOB]. (n.d.). HR LOB Benefits and Accomplishments. Retrieved 30 May 2007 from the OPM HR LOB Web site: http://www.opm.gov/egov/HR_LOB/benefits/

US (2007). *Federal Enterprise Architecture*. Washington, DC: Office of Management and Budget. Retrieved July 17, 2007, from http://www.whitehouse.gov/omb/egov/a-1-fea.html.

US Federal Government (2002) e-Government Strategy: Simplified Delivery of Services to Citizens. *Executive Office of the President, Office of Management and Budget, US Federal Government – February 2002*. Retrieved May 25th, 2006, from http://www.firstgov.gov/Topics/Includes/Reference/egov_strategy.pdf

Van den Berg, R.J., & Tolle, M. (2000). Assessing Ability to Execute in Virtual Enterprises. In J.P.T. Mo & L. Nemes (Eds.) *Global Engineering, Manufacturing and Enterprise Networks* (pp.370-378). Boston: Kluwer Academic Publishers.

Vandegriff L.J. (2006); *Unified approach to agile knowledge-based enterprise decision support*; VINE Vol 36, Issue 2; 2006)

Vendler, Z. (1972). *Res Cogitans*: Ithaca: Cornell University Press.

Vernadat, F.B. (2002). Enterprise Modelling and Integration (EMI): Current Status and Research Perspectives. *Annual Reviews in Control, 26*, 15-25.

Vitvar T., Kerrigan M., Overeem v. A., V., P., & K., T. (2006, Mar. 27-29). *Infrastructure for the Semantic Pan-European E-government Services*. Paper presented at the AAAI Spring Symposium, The Semantic Web meets eGovernment (SWEG), Stanford University, California, USA.

Vu, J. (2004). *Process Improvement Journey*. Lecture notes for the CMMI course sponsored by Korea IT Industry Promotion Agency, Seoul, Korea.

W3C. www.w3c.org. (August 2003). *WSA, Web Services Architecture*. W3C working Draft 8.

Wack, J., et. al. (January 2002). NIST Special Publication 800-41: Guidelines on Firewalls and Firewall Policy: Recommendations of the National Institute of Standards and Technology.

Wack, J., et. al. (October 2003). NIST Special Publication 800-42: Guideline on Network Security Testing: Recommendations of the National Institute of Standards and Technology.

Warmer, Kleppe A, J.; and Bast, W. (2003). *MDA Explained: The Model Driven Architecture--Practice and Promise*. New York, NY: Addison-Wesley.

Weerdmeester R., Pocterra C., & Hefke M. (2003); *Thematic Network/Roadmap: Knowledge Management Maturity Model*; Information Societies Technology Programme, June 2003.

Weill, P. (2004). Don't Just Lead, Govern: How Top-Performing Firms Govern IT. *MIS Quarterly Executive, 3*(1), 1-17.

Weill, P., & Ross, J. (2004). *IT Governance: How Top Performers Manage IT Decision Rights for Superior Results*. Boston, Massachusetts: Harvard Business School Press.

Weill, P., & Ross, J. (2005). A Matrixed Approach to Designing IT Governance. *MIT Sloan Management Review, 46*(2), 26-34.

Wesley, Addison (2003). *XML Data Management. Native XML and XML-enabled Database Systems*. Pearson Education Inc., Boston,U.S.A.

Weston, R.H. (1999). Reconfigurable, component-based systems and the role of enterprise engineering concepts, *Computers in Industry, 40*, 321-343.

WfMC. www.wfmc.org.

Widmayer, P. (1999). "Building Digital Metropolis: Chicago's Future Networks". *IT Professional* Volume 1, Issue 4, July-Aug. 1999, p. 40 – 46. IEEE.

Wiedman, B. (2005). Database Security (Common-Sense Principles.) GovernmentSecurity.org Network Security Resources. Obtained from http://www.governmentsecurity.org/articles/DatabaseSecurityCommon-sensePrinciples.php.

Wieringa, R., & Meyer, J. (1993). *Applications of Deontic Logic in Computer Science: A Concise Overview*: Wiley.

Williams, T.J. (1994). The Purdue Enterprise Reference Architecture, *Computers in Industry, 24*(2-3), 141-158.

Williams, T.J., Bernus, P., Brosvic, J., Chen, D., Doumeingts, G., Nemes, L., Nevins, J.L., Vallespir, B., Vlietstra, J., & Zoetekouw, D. (1994). Architectures for integrating manufacturing activities and enterprises. *Computers in Industry, 24*, 111-139.

Williamson, O. E. (1975). *Markets and Hierarchies.* New York: The Free Press.

Wilson, M., Zafra, D., Pitcher, S., Tressler, J., Ippolito, J. (1998). NIST Special Publication 800-16: Information Technology Security Training Requirements: A Role- and Performance- Based Model. National Institute of Standards and Technology, Computer Security Division.

Wimmer, M., & Traunmuller, R. (2000) Trends in Electronic Government: Managing Distributed Knowledge. *In the 11ʰ International Workshop on Database and Expert Systems Applications* (IEEE, DEXA'00)

Wimmer, M.A. (2002). Integrated Service Modelling for One-Stop Government. *Electronic Markets, special issue on e-Government,* 12(3):1–8.

Winograd, T. and Flores F. (1987). *Understanding Computers and Cognition - A New Foundation for Design.* Reading: Addison Wesley.

Wortmann, J.C., Hegge, H.M.H., & Rolefes, S. (2000). Embedding enterprise software in extended enterprise models. *Computers in Industry, 42*, 231-243.

Wu, R.C.Y. (2007). Enterprise integration in e-government. *Transforming Government: People, Process and Policy, 1*(1), 89-99.

Xia Wang, Goudos S., Peristeras V., Vitvar T., Mocan A., & Tarabanis K. (2007, 4-10 Jan.). *WSMO-PA: Formal Specification of Public Administration Service Model on Semantic Web Service Ontology.* Paper presented at the 40th HICSS, Hawaii.

Yergin, D., & Stanislaw, J. (1998). *The Commanding Heights: The Battle Between Government and the Marketplace That is Remaking the Modern World.* New York: Simon & Schuster.

Zachman J.; *The Physics of Knowledge Management;* undated, retrieved 29 Apr 2007 from http://www.zifa.com

Zachman J.A. (1996); *Enterprise Architecture and legacy systems. Getting beyond the legacy;* accessed from Information Engineering Services Pty Ltd via http://members.ozemail.com.au/~visible/papers/zachman1.htm on 25/07/2005

Zachman J.A. (1997); *Concepts of the framework for enterprise architecture. Background, description and utility;* accessed from Information Engineering Services Pty Ltd via http://members.ozemail.com.au/~visible/papers/zachman3.htm on 25/07/2005

Zachman J.A. (1997); *The challenge is change: a management paper;* accessed from Information Engineering Services Pty Ltd via http://members.ozemail.com.au/~visible/papers/zachman2.htm on 25/07/2005

Zachman, J. A. (1987), *A Framework for Information Systems Architecture.* IBM Systems Journal, 26(3), 276-292.

Zachman, J. A. (2005). *The Zachman Framework for Enterprise Architecture: A Primer for Enterprise Engineering and Manufacturing.* Zachman International, www.ZachmanInternational.com.

Zachman, J. A., & Sowa, J. F. (1992). Extending and formalizing the framework for information systems architecture. *IBM Systems Journal, 31*(3).

Zwegers, A., Tolle, M., & Vesterager, J., (2003). VE-RAM: Virtual Enterprise Reference Architecture and Methodology. In I. Karvonen, R. Van den Berg, P. Bernus, Y. Fukuda, M. Hannus, I. Hartel, J. Vesterager. *VTT Symposium 224* (pp.17-38), Helsinki, Finland.

About the Contributors

Pallab Saha is currently a member of the faculty with the National University of Singapore (NUS). His current research and consulting interests include Enterprise Architecture, IT Governance, and Business Process Management. He has published several research papers in these areas. Pallab is an active researcher in the area of Enterprise Architecture and has published his first book titled "Handbook of Enterprise Systems Architecture in Practice" in March 2007. Dr. Saha also leads the Information Systems Management research group within NUS–Institute of Systems Science. Dr. Saha teaches courses in Enterprise Architecture, IT Governance and Business Process Management at the post-graduate and senior executive levels (including CIOs). His current consulting engagements are in Enterprise Architecture for Singapore Government agencies. He has provided consulting and advisory services to Infocomm Development Authority of Singapore, Intellectual Property Office of Singapore, CPF Board, and Great Eastern Life Assurance among others. Dr. Saha is the primary author of the Enterprise Architecture Methodology and Toolkit for the Government of Singapore. He is also a contributing author of the Enterprise Architecture Management Guide being developed by the International Association of Enterprise Architects (a|EA) and is a frequently invited speaker at international and local conferences on Enterprise architecture and IT governance (including keynote sessions). Prior to academia, he was instrumental in managing Baxter's environmental health and safety offshore development centre in Bangalore as Head of Projects and Development. He has worked on engagements in several Fortune 100 organizations in various capacities. Pallab received his Ph.D in 1999 from the Indian Institute of Science, Bangalore. His Ph.D dissertation was awarded the best thesis in the department. His Ph.D. proposal was selected as one of the top five in India and received a special research grant for the same. Earlier he completed an M.B.A in Information Systems and prior to that gained a B.Sc. in Electronic Sciences from Bangalore University. He can be contacted at pallab@nus.edu.sg.

* * *

Chris Aitken holds a PhD in psychophysiology and has worked with a variety of government agencies over the last 15 years in both clinical and IM & ICT roles. During the last 6 years he has held a number of IM & ICT related positions and is currently Manager Enterprise Architecture and Information Management in Queensland Health in Australia. Chris' clinical applied research background means that he brings a combination of a strong human service delivery perspective and a keen logical rigour to his approach to enterprise architecture and IM & ICT implementation. Chris' current interests include topics as varied as; the development of an abstract enterprise meta-model, IM & ICT policy and standards development, and the integration of IM & ICT strategic planning with enterprise architecture.

Leonidas G. Anthopoulos was born in Trikala, Greece in 1974. He graduated (1996) and he got his PHD in the e-Government area (2005) from the Department of Informatics of the Aristotle University of Thessaloniki (AUTh). He is an Expert Counselor in e-Government and e-Diplomacy of the Hellenic Ministry of Foreign Affairs, while he has worked for many organizations such as the Greek Ministry of Education, the Research Committee (AUTh), the Information Society S.A. (Ministry of Interior of Greece) etc. He has published several works for international journals, magazines and conferences and his research interests concern e-Government, Information Society aspects and social networks.

Guido Bayens, MSc, MBA is a principal consultant at Novius Business & Information Management. He is also the head of the architecture team at ICTU and responsible for the Dutch government reference architecture. Guido studied sociology in Utrecht and attained a Master of Business Administration degree at Henley. From 2001 – 2005 he was responsible for the business and ICT architecture of UWV, the national Dutch Social Security agency. His vision on the possibilities of business architecture is based on almost 20 years of management experience in environments where fundamental changes of strategic policy were to be made.

Scott Bernard has over twenty years of experience in information technology management including work in the academic, federal, military, and private sectors. He is currently the Deputy CIO and Chief Enterprise Architect. at the Federal Railroad Administration in Washington DC. He also serves on the faculty of the School of Information Studies at Syracuse University and is a lecturer at the School of Computer Science at Carnegie Mellon University. Dr. Bernard wrote a textbook on Enterprise Architecture in 2004 and is the Chief Editor of the Journal of Enterprise Architecture.

Amit Bhagwat has worked on Enterprise-wide IT transformation programs through two decades. Amit has served as strategist, leader, mentor, manager and auditor for Enterprise Architecture and Systems Engineering practices in enterprises leading in the world / Europe in their sector. He serves on the British Computer Society Elite (Effective Leadership in Information Technology) group. Among the very small number of IBM-Rational accredited instructors to educate IBM and premier-partner staff consultants, Amit is also TOGAF-8 accredited and contributes to Ethics Workgroup of AOGEA. Amit has written widely on Requirement-Project-Process Management, Analysis, Design, Visual Modeling Concepts and Estimation Techniques, with 17 publications, including an oft-quoted cover feature for The Rational Edge, to his credit. In 2007, Amit led Enterprise Architecture Maturity Appraisal for one of the largest British government departments and advised CTOs of two multinational institutions, both leaders in their field in the UK.

Timothy Biggert has led the Human Resources Line of Business enterprise architecture team since June 2004. In that role, he has guided his team in the development of the HR LOB EA artifacts and target requirements. He is now working with HR LOB Program stakeholders to benchmark existing practices and help define the Federal HR enterprise of the future. Tim is an IBM-certified Senior Managing Consultant with IBM's Global Business Services (GBS) Public Sector Human Capital Management consulting practice. Over the course of his 19 years working for the world's largest consulting firm, Tim has led teams in many different project areas including human capital strategy, enterprise architecture, business transformation, organization change, project management, education development and delivery, methodology creation and implementation, and application development. He has worked on a broad range of business environments including federal, state, and local government, education, aerospace, retail, manufacturing, distribution and logistics, financial services, banking, life sciences, pharmaceutical, agriculture, utility and telecommunications. He has a Masters Degree in Business Administration from the University of Minnesota.

William S. Boddie serves as the Professor of Systems Management at the U.S. National Defense University (NDU) Information Resources Management (IRM) College. Dr. Boddie has nearly 30 years experience leading and managing information technology (IT) environments for public, private, and non-profit-sector organizations. Dr. Boddie specializes in organizational leadership, enterprise performance effectiveness, enterprise architecture, and program and project management and is the *NDU IRM College Professor of the Year for 2006 – 2007.* Further, Dr. Boddie developed and delivered the *Business Information Technology Leadership Certificate Program*, a continuing education program, to various Washington DC colleges since 1999.

Anand Desai is Professor in the John Glenn School of Public Affairs at the Ohio State University. His research interests include performance measurement and evaluation in the public sector and the use of policy modeling to support public sector decision-making.

Wijnand Derks (1973) is scientific researcher at Telematica Instituut since 2005. Previously, he worked at the research department of the largest Dutch telecom company KPN Telecom (1997-2001) and the faculty of computer science at University of Twente (2001-2005). In the past ten years he worked on several fundamental and applied research projects in national and international context in the domains of scaleable database- and transaction technology, enterprise architecture and cross-enterprise workflow management. His prime interests involve the development and application of fundamentally new ICT solutions in the industry. Within Telematica Institute he develops new application concepts for demand-driven and integral electronic service provisioning in the context of public-private partnerships. In addition, he is involved in the research program Software for Service where ICT-users, ICT-suppliers and research parties jointly to develop novel business models and ICT-based applications.

Alan Dyer has many years experience with organisational decision-making, from a variety of perspectives (including as a "consumer", "provider" and "developer"); the majority of these experiences were gained through the Australian Defence Forces. Alan has been directly involved in information and knowledge management – in the form of technology, projects or abstract application of principles – for the last 17 years. Alan's current studies include post-graduate research in Enterprise Architecture, building upon a B.Sc. (Maths and CompSci) and an M.Sc.(IT). Alan is currently employed by EWA-Australia (http://www.ewa-australia.com).

Neil Fairhead, in a 30 year career in information technology has worked as an enterprise architect and technology strategist with a number of major organizations including the Canada Post, the Canadian Imperial Bank of Commerce, the British Home Office and a major British bank. He also brings service management experience to bear following several years at Microsoft where he helped to introduce ITIL. His IT experience includes systems engineering at IBM, office and distributed systems at Digital (DEC), information engineering at James Martin Associates and he is currently focused on structured managed service offerings at Fujitsu Services. He has studied at Cambridge, Manchester Business School and, post-experience, at Harvard Business School. He is a certified management consultant and a Fellow of the Institute of Service Management as well as being TOGAF certified.

John Good is currently a Director at Serco Consulting where he leads the Enterprise Architecture capability group. He focuses on helping organisations establish Enterprise Architecture teams and specializes in data and information architecture and the use of enterprise architecture in enabling major business transformation. His career spans 20 years in information and media technology as a solutions and enterprise architect, principal technologist and technology strategist. A graduate of Edinburgh University in Computer and Management Sciences, and a TOGAF certified practitioner, he trained in information systems with Price Waterhouse before a career with DHL, the BBC and his current consulting role.

Shirley Gregor heads the National Centre for Information Systems Research in the College of Business and Economics at the Australian National University. Professor Gregor has led several large projects in the e-commerce area funded by the private sector and government. Professor Gregor was inaugural President of the Australasian Association of Information Systems and is Vice-President of the Australian Council of Professors and Heads of Information Systems. Professor Gregor was made an Officer of the Order of Australia in the Queen's Birthday Honour's list in June 2005 for services as an educator and researcher in the field of information systems and in the development of applications for electronic commerce in the agribusiness sector.

Dennis Hart is a Senior Lecturer in the College of Business and Economics at the Australian National University and has research interests in the areas of ownership issues in information systems development and information management; Semiotics and information systems. Dr Hart was a former senior officer in the Royal Australian Navy before commencing a career as an academic. In addition to his academic activities, Dr Hart also manages and runs a 20 acre vineyard with his partner on a property near Yass in the state of New South Wales.

Shuyuan Mary Ho is a PhD Candidate at School of Information Studies, Syracuse University. Her research interests focus on information systems security, which includes information content security, information security management and computing security. Her dissertation is in the interdisciplinary area of behavioral anomaly detection for online community. This research is aimed to discover the mechanism for detecting changes in trustworthiness for countering insider threats. Shuyuan is a CISSP certified by (ISC)2 and a CISM certified by ISACA. She has acquired a Master in Philosophy in Information Science and Technology, a Master in Business Administration, and a Bachelor in Computer Science.

Marijn Janssen is director of education of the Systems Engineering, Policy Analysis & Management Master at the Faculty of Technology, Policy and Management of Delft University of Technology. He is elected as secretary of the IFIP WP 8.5 working group on Information Systems in Public Administration. He also teaches courses on middleware architecture, web-information systems and management, and designing large-scale ICT-infrastructure and services. He conducted several research projects in the field of e-government, enterprise architecture and orchestration in interorganizational networks. He is an associate editor of the International Journal of E-Government Research (IJEGR) and International Journal of E-business Research (IJEBR) and co-chair of the E-government Architecture, Infrastructure and Interoperability minitrack at the HICSS conference. He serves on several international program committees and is a program chair of the Annual Conference on Digital Government (dg.o2008). He published over 100 refereed publications.

Hong Sik Kim is Adjunct Professor of Korea Polytechnic University, Computer Engineering Department and Secretary of KIITA (Korea Institute of Information Technology Architecture). He had been involved in the a|EA standardization project (EAMG: Enterprise Architecture Management Guide) for 2 years as a vice president of a|EA Korean Chapter. He suggested a more practical and sustainable development strategy to the EA community world wide, especially for area of the quality and maturity model of EIA in stead of EA. He had experiences to consolidate 21 MIS departments of Hyundai Group into one mega center as a foundation member of Hyundai Information Technology. And He introduced company wide QMS (Quality Management System), TickIT scheme (British standard version of ISO 9000-3) and institutionalized the QMS for 6 years. He also had introduced customer satisfaction system company-wide and executed pilot project of MBNQA (Malcolm Baldridge National Quality Award).

Bram Klievink is research assistant and Ph.D. researcher at Delft University of Technology at the faculty of Technology, Policy and Management. Bram holds a degree in political science from the University of Nijmegen (M.Sc, 2006) and a degree in business information systems (2004). His research focus is on coordination mechanisms for public-private cooperation in electronic government service-delivery. For this research he participates in two major research projects. One is on creating demand-driven integrated electronic service-delivery by government and private partners, which aims at exploring future directions for public services. The other project is on the coordination of multiple channels operated by government, private parties may be part of these channels.

Marc M. Lankhorst is a senior member of scientific staff at Telematica Instituut where he heads the institute's expertise group on Service Architectures. His research interests range from enterprise architecture and business process management to service orientation and model-driven software development. In the past, he has managed several multi-party research projects with partners from government, industry and academia. At the moment, he is responsible for a major project on integrated, demand-driven e-government services. Furthermore, he teaches several courses on architecture at universities and other institutes. Marc holds an MSc in Computer Science from the University of Twente and a PhD from the University of Groningen in the Netherlands.

Ryan Kobb has provided business performance management and program management leadership to the IBM team supporting the OPM Office of the Human Resources Line of Business since March 2005. In that role, he helps lead the management of the HR LOB governance structure and provides support in the areas of enterprise architecture, change management, and communications and outreach. He is now working to complete the migration planning guidance that agencies will leverage to select and migrate to a shared service center as well developing a transformation toolkit for agencies as they prepare for their selection and migration to a shared service center. Ryan is a Senior Consultant in IBM's Global Business Services (GBS) Public Sector Financial Management Practice. He is IBM-certified in Earned Value Management and recently has been recognized by *Consulting Magazine* as one of the "Top 30 Consultants Under the Age of 30".

Nigel Martin is a Lecturer in the College of Business and Economics at the Australian National University, and has principal research interests in the areas of Enterprise Architecture, Requirements Engineering, IT Governance, ICT Strategy, Systems Design and Electronic Government. Dr Martin was a former oil industry manager, and government executive working primarily in the areas of defence, national security, and law enforcement.

John Mo is a Professor and Discipline Head for Manufacturing and Materials Engineering at the RMIT University, Melbourne, Australia. Prior to this, John was the Team Leader of the Manufacturing Systems and Infrastructure Networks research group in the Division of Manufacturing and Infrastructure Technology of Commonwealth Scientific and Industrial Research Organisation (CSIRO). John led several large scale international projects involving multi-disciplinary teams in the development of advanced project collaboration systems for designing one-off facilities such as chemical plants and high value computer controlled assets. His team of 15 professionals had completed projects on developing methodologies for risks analysis, critical infrastructure protection modelling, electricity market simulation, wireless communication, fault detection and production scheduling. He also led the National EPC Network Demonstrator Project and its extension, which were the first EPC implementation conforming to EPC Global standard. He obtained his PhD from Loughborough University, UK. John is a Fellow of the Institution of Engineers, Australia.

Sungwook Moon is working as a software consultant at ComponentBasis, Co., Ltd., Korea. He has experienced dozens of software development projects, and mainly played a role for component-based development discipline mentoring and software quality assurance. In addition, he has much interest in software process improvement and software architecture. Since 2003, he has presented his researches at several conferences such as the European Software Process Improvement and the Korea Society of Management Information Systems. Recently, he joined in MIS department of University of Seoul as a PhD candidate to research into service-oriented architecture and enterprise architecture. He obtained his MS degree in Chemical Engineering from Korea Advanced Institute of Science and Technology in 1998 and his BS degree in Chemical Engineering from Yonsei University in 1996.

Laszlo Nemes was Chief Research Scientist and Science Director in the Division of Manufacturing and Infrastructure Technology of Commonwealth Scientific and Industrial Research Organisation (CSIRO) Australia. He led a research program with more than 50 staff working on enterprise integration, machine vision, autonomous robotics, signal diagnostics and process control. In addition, he also led complex international research teams to complete large, industry related R&D projects in the area of computer aided design and manufacturing, within the international Intelligent Manufacturing Systems program. His achievements are hallmarked with six industry related patents; over 100 papers published internationally, six books/monographs. His major achievement, the development of the Generic Enterprise Reference Architecture was developed in a team of international experts and was endorsed as the Annex to ISO enterprise engineering standard. Dr Nemes is a Fellow of the Australian Academy of Technological Sciences and Engineering, Fellow of the Institution of Engineers, Australia.

Klaus Niemann has more than 25 years experience with the design of complex IT-architectures in the telecommunication and financial sector. He worked as system designer, software architect, consultant, project manager and enterprise architect in several positions and for a wide range of clients. Klaus holds a diploma in computer science from the Technical University of Berlin. In the 80s his main focus was on distributed systems, telecommunication and banking networks in Europe as well as in the Far East. In the 90s he worked on the introduction of object orientation to large organizations and then focused on client/server architectures. He frequently gave professional training sessions, published several articles and books, and also became a frequent speaker to conferences. He founded ACT! Consulting in 1998 with special emphasis on enterprise architecture management. He developed the enterprise architecture framework t-eam (toolbox for enterprise architecture management). Klaus is a member of the OpenGroup's Architecture Forum and works with the International Committee on EA Standards (Association of Enterprise Architects).

Vassilios Peristeras is a Research Fellow and Adjunct Lecturer at the National University of Ireland, Galway, Digital Enterprise Research Institute (DERI). He has studied Political Science and holds M.Sc and PhD in Information Systems. For the last 12 years, he has worked for the Greek National Center for Public Administration and Decentralization, the United Nations, the Center for Research and Technology Hellas (CERTH), the University of Macedonia and as consultant for many governments and private companies. His main research areas are eGovernment, enterprise architecture and semantic technologies. He has published more than 40 papers in international conferences and scientific journals.

Jay Ramanathan is the Director of Research at the Collaborative for Enterprise Transformation and Innovation (or CETI). She is currently engaged in developing programs of industry-focused research, practice, and education. Particular areas of interest are Adaptive Complex Enterprise Architectures for Business-IT alignment and management; and business-driven IT innovation.

Rajiv Ramnath is Director of Practice at the Collaborative for Enterprise Transformation and Innovation (CETI) at OSU. His expertise ranges from wireless sensor networking and pervasive computing to business-IT alignment, enterprise architecture, software engineering, e-Government, collaborative environments and work-management systems.

Kunal Suryavanshi has led the IBM team supporting the OPM Office of the Human Resources Line of Business since April 2003. In that role, he provides thought leadership and strategic advice to the OPM HR LOB leadership team. He was influential in building the coalition of 24 Federal agencies that crafted the vision, goals, and concept of operations of the HR LOB program and that subsequently developed the HR LOB target enterprise architecture and requirements for shared service centers. Kunal is an Associate Partner and IBM-certified strategy consultant in IBM's Global Business Services (GBS) Federal Strategy and Change Practice. He has led teams in many different project areas including electronic government strategy, enterprise architecture, business transformation, organization change, project management, and business case development for Federal IT projects. Kunal has an undergraduate degree in Civil Engineering from University of Bombay and an MBA from Carnegie Mellon University.

Konstantinos Tarabanis is a Professor at the Department of Business Administration of the University of Macedonia, Greece and the Director of the Information Systems Laboratory at the same university. He received an Engineering Diploma in Mechanical Engineering from the National Technical University of Athens (1983), an M.S. degree in both Mechanical Engineering and Computer Science (1984 and 1988 respectively), and a Ph.D. degree in Computer Science (1991), at Columbia University, New York, NY.

He was a research staff member at the IBM T.J. Watson Research Center 1991-1994 and was employed by the IBM Corporation as a whole during 1984-1994. In recognition of his research, he was the recipient of the Anton Philips Best Paper Award at the 1991 IEEE International Conference on Robotics and Automation. His current research interests include e-government and e-business. In recognition of his work in the field of e-government, he was the recipient of the Best Paper Award in the e-government track at the European Conference on Information Systems in 2000. Also in recognition of his work in the field of e-Business he received the Outstanding Research Paper Award in the 7th Annual Conference of the International Academy of e-Business in 2007.

Dwight Toavs, PhD, is a Professor of Systems Management at the National Defense University's Information Resources Management College in Washington, D.C. His academic, teaching, and research interests lie at the intersection of public policy, governance, and information technology in public organizations. In particular, he is interested in visual techniques and technologies as a means to understand and explain policy topics. He is the creator of PolicyWorld, the first virtual reality depiction of a contemporary public policy topic, a 3D collaborative virtual environment for exploring information resources management policies in the US Federal government. His interest in information visualization, cognitive mapping, and virtual environments results from the expressive and communicative potential of these approaches to aid in understanding complex policy and governance issues. He can be contacted at toavs@ndu.edu.

John A. Zachman is the originator of the "Framework for Enterprise Architecture" which has received broad acceptance around the world as an integrative framework, or "periodic table" of descriptive representations for Enterprises. John is not only known for this work on Enterprise Architecture, but is also known for his early contributions to IBM's Information Strategy methodology (Business Systems Planning) as well as to their Executive team planning techniques (Intensive Planning). He retired from IBM in 1990, having served them for 26 years. He presently is Chairman of the Board of Zachman Framework Associates, a worldwide consortium managing conformance to the Zachman Framework principles. He is Chief Executive Officer of the Zachman Institute for Framework Advancement (ZIFA), an organization dedicated to advancing the conceptual and implementation states of the art in Enterprise Architecture. He also operates his own education and consulting business, Zachman International (www. ZachmanInternational.com). John serves on the Executive Council for Information Management and Technology (ECIMT) of the United States Government Accountability Office (GAO). He is a Fellow for the College of Business Administration of the University of North Texas. He serves on the Advisory Board for the Data Resource Management Program at the University of Washington and on the Advisory Board of the Data Administration Management Association International (DAMA-I) from whom he was awarded the 2002 Lifetime Achievement Award. He was awarded the 2004 Oakland University, Applied Technology in Business (ATIB), Award for IS Excellence and Innovation. John has been focusing on Enterprise Architecture since 1970 and has written extensively on the subject. He is the author of the book, "The Zachman Framework for Enterprise Architecture: A Primer on Enterprise Engineering and Manufacturing." He has facilitated innumerable executive team planning sessions. He travels nationally and internationally, teaching and consulting, and is a popular conference speaker, known for his motivating messages on Enterprise Architecture issues. He has spoken to many thousands of enterprise managers and information professionals on every continent. In addition to his professional activities, John Zachman serves on the Elder Council of the Church on the Way (First Foursquare Church of Van

Nuys, California), the Board of Directors of Living Way Ministries, a radio and television ministry of the Church on the Way, the President's Cabinet of the King's College and Seminary, the Board of Directors of the Los Angeles Citywide Children's Christian Choir and on the Board of Directors of Native Hope International, a Los Angeles-based ministry to the Native American people. Prior to joining IBM, John served as a line officer in the United States Navy and is a retired Commander in the U. S. Naval Reserve. He chaired a panel on "Planning, Development and Maintenance Tools and Methods Integration" for the U.S. National Institute of Standards and Technology. He holds a degree in Chemistry from Northwestern University, has taught at Tufts University, has served on the Board of Councilors for the School of Library and Information Management at the University of Southern California, as a Special Advisor to the School of Library and Information Management at Emporia State University, and on the Advisory Council to the School of Library and Information Management at Dominican University.

Index

Symbols

311 system 160

A

ACE framework 153
ANZAC Ship Alliance (ASA) 377
ArchiMate 40
architecture maturity model 9
Australian Bureau of Statistics 409, 419

B

Beacon Architecture 56–81

C

capability maturity profile (CMP) 110
Centrelink Social Services Agency 409, 420
collaborative enterprise architecture, for municipal
     environments 392–408
Columbus, Ohio 157
communication 138
confidentiality 348
cooperation, public-private 269
corporate governance 211

D

Department of Homeland Security (DHS) 193
design integrity 174
design integrity, implementing 179
design integrity framework 176, 181
design integrity framework, and enterprise architec-
     ture governance 173–190
Digital City 395
Dutch e-government 34
Dutch government 30–55, 263

E

e-government 392
e-government, in Singapore 10
e-government, overview of 3
e-government, stages of 4
E-Government Act of 2002 309
E-Gov Travel 310
E-Payroll initiative 310
e-Training initiative 310
EA³ cube 345
EIA maturity model 90
enterprise architecture, and government 194
enterprise architecture, and information security
     340–370
enterprise architecture, as documentation method
     343

enterprise architecture, aspects of 58
enterprise architecture, challenges to public sector 66
enterprise architecture, definition of 84
enterprise architecture, linked to KM 114
enterprise architecture, measuring benefits of 106–129
enterprise architecture, patterns for 152
enterprise architecture, people-led 285–306
enterprise architecture, transforming of 60
enterprise architecture, U.S. government 132
enterprise architecture adoption, in government businesses 372
enterprise architecture management, and IT governance 208–228
enterprise architecture standards 374
enterprise engineering 373
enterprise information architecture, definition of 89
European interoperability framework (EIF) 35

G

GovBenefits.gov 310
governance enterprise architecture (GEA) 229–262
governance enterprise architecture (GEA), framework 234
government, and enterprise architecture 194
government, and IT challenges 151
government business processes 414
government enterprise architecture 409–437
government enterprise architecture (GEA) 2
government transformation, and MAGENTA 22
Grants.gov 310

H

HR LOB performance model 317

I

information security 340–370
integrated service delivery 270
integrity 348
investment planning 208, 214
IRS Free File 310
ITA/EA area 82
IT governance 211

K

knowledge management 111
knowledge management, linked to enterprise architecture 114

knowledge management, measuring 112
knowledge management maturity model framework 116

L

leadership 135

M

MAGENTA 1
maturity model 113

O

operational agility 173

P

PA Service Model 250
people-led enterprise architecture 285
policy map, and relationships 200
policy map, why create a 197
policy mapping 191–207
policy mapping, challenges 204
public institutions, and hierarchies 149

R

Recruitment One-Stop 311
resource alignment 342

S

SAFECOM 310
security architecture 348
security architecture framework (SAF) 349
service-oriented computing (SOC) 36
service-oriented reference architecture, and Dutch government 30–55
service delivery, using enterprise architecture 307–339
service oriented architecture (SOA) 264
shared service providers 335
Singapore, e-government programme 10
speech act theory (SAT) 239
stakeholders 289
stakeholders, builder 289
stakeholders, customer 289
stakeholders, user 290

T

total quality management (TQM) 86
transformational leaders 135

transformational leadership 130–148
transformational leadership model 136

U

U.S. Government Accountability Office 130
U.S. Government enterprise architecture 132
U.S. Office of Management and Budget 130, 309
U.S. Office of Personnel Management 311

V

VICIE model 136
virtual private networks (VPN) 361

W

wireless security 361